S0-ESR-311

AutoCAD® 14
RELEASE

User's Guide

00114-000000-5010   March 29, 1997

Copyright © 1997 Autodesk, Inc.
All Rights Reserved

This publication, or parts thereof, may not be reproduced in any form, by any method, for any purpose.

AUTODESK, INC. MAKES NO WARRANTY, EITHER EXPRESSED OR IMPLIED, INCLUDING BUT NOT LIMITED TO ANY IMPLIED WARRANTIES OF MERCHANTABILITY OR FITNESS FOR A PARTICULAR PURPOSE, REGARDING THESE MATERIALS AND MAKES SUCH MATERIALS AVAILABLE SOLELY ON AN "AS-IS" BASIS.

IN NO EVENT SHALL AUTODESK, INC. BE LIABLE TO ANYONE FOR SPECIAL, COLLATERAL, INCIDENTAL, OR CONSEQUENTIAL DAMAGES IN CONNECTION WITH OR ARISING OUT OF PURCHASE OR USE OF THESE MATERIALS. THE SOLE AND EXCLUSIVE LIABILITY TO AUTODESK, INC., REGARDLESS OF THE FORM OF ACTION, SHALL NOT EXCEED THE PURCHASE PRICE OF THE MATERIALS DESCRIBED HEREIN.

Autodesk, Inc. reserves the right to revise and improve its products as it sees fit. This publication describes the state of this product at the time of its publication, and may not reflect the product at all times in the future.

Autodesk Trademarks

The following are registered trademarks of Autodesk, Inc., in the USA and/or other countries: 3D Plan, 3D Studio, ADE, ADI, Advanced Modeling Extension, AME, Animator Pro, ATC, AutoCAD, AutoCAD Data Extension, AutoCAD Development System, Autodesk, Autodesk Animator, Autodesk LT, the Autodesk logo, Autodesk University, AutoLISP, AutoShade, AutoSketch, AutoSolid, AutoSurf, AutoVision, Design Companion, Education by Design, Generic, Generic CADD, Generic Software, Generic 3D Drafting, Geodyssey, HOOPS, MaterialSpec, Multimedia Explorer, NAAUG, Office Series, Opus, Solution 3000, PartSpec, Regis, TinkerTech, Texture Universe, Woodbourne, WorkCenter, and World-Creating Toolkit.

The following are trademarks of Autodesk, Inc., in the USA and/or other countries: 3D Props, 3D Studio MAX, 3DSurfer, ACAD, Advanced User Interface, AME Link, Animation Partner, Animation Player, Animation Pro Player, A Studio in Every Computer, ATLAST, AUGI, AutoCAD Simulator, AutoCAD SQL Extension, AutoCAD SQL Interface, AutoCAD Map, AutoCDM, Autodesk Animator Clips, Autodesk Animator Theatre, Autodesk Device Interface, Autodesk MapGuide, Autodesk PhotoEdit, Autodesk Software Developer's Kit, Autodesk WalkThrough, Autodesk World, AutoEDM, AutoFlix, AutoLathe, AutoSnap, BIPED, Bringing Information Down to Earth, Carpe Datum, Character Studio, Concept Studio, Content Explorer, DesignBlocks, DESIGNX, DesignScape, Design Your World, DXF, DWG Unplugged, Exegis, FLI, FLIC, GenCADD, Generic 3D, Heidi, Home Series, HyperWire, Inside Track, Kinetix, MAX DWG, Mechanical Desktop, Multiped, NetHead, ObjectARX, Octoped, PeopleTracker, Physique, Picture This Home, PlantSpec, Power and Light, Powered with Autodesk Technology, Quadruped, SketchTools, Smoke and Mirrors, Suddenly Everything Clicks, Supportdesk, Topper, Transforms Ideas Into Reality, and *WHIP!*.

Third Party Trademarks

All other brand names, product names or trademarks belong to their respective holders.

Third Party Software Program Credits

ACIS ® Copyright © 1994, 1997 Spatial Technology, Inc., Three-Space Ltd., and Applied Geometry Corp. All rights reserved.

Copyright © 1997 Microsoft Corporation. All rights reserved.

International CorrectSpell™ Spelling Correction System © 1995 by INSO Corporation. All rights reserved. Reproduction or disassembly of embodied algorithms or database prohibited.

InstallShield™ 3.0. Copyright © 1997 InstallShield Software Corporation. All rights reserved.

Portions Copyright © 1991-1996 Arthur D. Applegate. All rights reserved.

Portions of this software are based on the work of the Independent JPEG Group.

Typefaces from the Bitstream ® typeface library copyright 1992.

Typefaces from Payne Loving Trust © 1996. All rights reserved.

The license management portion of this product is based on Élan License Manager ©1989, 1990 Élan Computer Group, Inc. All rights reserved.

GOVERNMENT USE

Use, duplication, or disclosure by the U. S. Government is subject to restrictions as set forth in FAR 12.212 (Commercial Computer Software-Restricted Rights) and DFAR 267.7202 (Rights in Technical Data and Computer Software), as applicable.

5 6 7 8 9 10 CO

Contents

Image Gallery 1

About AutoCAD Documentation 33

The AutoCAD Documentation Suite 34
    Online Documentation 34
    Learning Tools 35
    Printed Guides 35
Where to Start 35
Additional Help Resources 36
Using This Guide 37

Introduction to AutoCAD 39

The AutoCAD Interface 40
    AutoCAD's Main Window 40
    How to Access Commands 41
    Getting Help 41
Starting a Drawing 42
Drawing Objects 43
    Undoing Mistakes 45
    Drawing Accurately 46
    Object Properties 48
    Creating Standard Symbols 49
Viewing and Editing 50
    Viewing Your Drawing 50
    Editing Your Drawing 52
    Looking Up Drawing Data 54
Preparing Your Drawing for Plotting 54
    Setting Up a Drawing Environment 54
    Printing or Plotting Your Drawing 55
Advanced Features 55
    3D Modeling 55
    Raster Images 56
    Database Support 56
    Internet Features 56

iii

Customizing and Programming   56
    Customizing   56
    Programming   57

Chapter 1   Getting Started   59

Checking System Requirements   60
Installing AutoCAD   60
Starting AutoCAD   62
Accessing Information from the Help Menu   63
    Online Documentation   64
Pointing Devices   64
    Using the Mouse   64
    Using the Tablet   65
Understanding the AutoCAD Interface   66
    Toolbars   67
    Menus   68
    Cursor Menu   68
    The Command Window   69
    The Text Window   70
Accessing Commands   72
    Using a Toolbar   72
    Using a Menu   73
    Using the Command Line   73
    Using Commands Transparently   76
    Using Long File Names   77
    Switching from Dialog Box to Command Line   78
    Using Scripts to Run Commands   78
    Editing Command or Text Window Text   79
Using System Variables   79
Correcting Mistakes   80
Refreshing the Screen Display   81
Modifying the AutoCAD Environment   81
    Controlling Warnings   82
    Saving Your Drawing Automatically   83
    Selecting Colors for the AutoCAD Window   83
    Selecting Fonts for AutoCAD   84
    Specifying Support Directories and Menu Files   84
    Setting the System of Measurement   86
    Specifying the Location of Temporary Files   86
Opening Existing Drawings   87
    Using the Drawing Browser   88
Saving Drawings   90
Exiting AutoCAD   90

Chapter 2	**Organizing Your Project** 91
	Conforming to Standards 92
	Setting Up New Drawings 93
	Using the Quick Setup Wizard 94
	Using the Advanced Setup Wizard 94
	Using Setup Wizard System Variables 96
	Using Other Setup Methods 97
	Setting Units Style 97
	Determining the Scale Factor 99
	Setting Grid Limits 100
	Setting the Grid 101
	Setting Snap Spacing 102
	Adding Borders and Title Blocks 103
	Customizing Title Blocks for the Advanced Setup Wizard 104
	Organizing Information on Layers 106
	Planning Layers 106
	Creating and Naming Layers 106
	Using Linetypes 108
	Loading Linetypes 108
	Using Templates 110
	Using an Existing Template 110
	Creating a Template 110
	Recovering the Default Template 111
Chapter 3	**Using Coordinate Systems** 113
	Using a Coordinate System to Specify Points 114
	Using Cartesian and Polar Coordinate Systems 114
	Specifying Cartesian and Polar Coordinates 115
	Using Direct Distance Entry 118
	Shifting and Rotating the Coordinate System 119
	Shifting the *XY* Plane 120
	Locating a New UCS Origin 120
	Restoring the UCS to WCS 121
	Displaying the UCS Icon 121
	Saving and Reusing a UCS 123
Chapter 4	**Creating Objects** 125
	Drawing Lines 126
	Drawing Line Objects 126
	Drawing Polylines 126
	Drawing Multilines 128
	Drawing Polygons 132
	Sketching Freehand 133

Drawing Curved Objects 135
    Drawing Spline Curves 135
    Drawing Circles 137
    Drawing Arcs 139
    Drawing Ellipses 141
    Drawing Donuts 143
Creating Point Objects 144
Changing the Drawing Order of Objects 145
    Regenerating the Drawing Order 146
    Setting the SORTENTS System Variable 146
Creating Solid-Filled Areas 147
Creating Regions 148
    Creating Composite Regions 149
Hatching Areas 150
    Creating an Associative Hatch 151
    Defining Hatch Boundaries 152
    Using Hatch Styles 155
    Using Hatch Patterns 156
Custom Objects and Proxies 157

Chapter 5   **Drawing with Precision 159**

Adjusting Snap and Grid Alignment 160
    Changing the Snap Angle and Base Point 160
    Using Isometric Snap and Grid 162
Using Ortho Mode 163
Snapping to Geometric Points on Objects 164
    Object Snaps 164
    Using Object Snap for a Single Point 172
    Setting Running Object Snaps 173
    Using AutoSnap 174
    Using Osnap to Offset Temporary Reference Points 176
Using Point Filters 177
Using Tracking 178
Specifying Measurements and Divisions 180
    Specifying Measured Intervals on Objects 181
    Dividing Objects into Segments 182
Drawing Construction Lines 184
    Creating Construction Xlines 184
    Creating Rays 187
Calculating Points and Values 188
    Evaluating Expressions 188
    Calculating Points 189
Calculating Areas 190
    Calculating a Defined Area 190

    Calculating the Area Enclosed by an Object 191
    Calculating Combined Areas 192
    Subtracting Areas from Combined Areas 192
 Calculating Distance and Angle 194
 Displaying Coordinates and Locating Points 195
 Inquiry Methods 196
    Listing Database Information for Objects 196
    Displaying the Drawing Status 197
    Tracking Drawing Time 198

Chapter 6 **Controlling the Drawing Display 199**

 Using Zoom and Pan 200
    Zooming and Panning with Realtime 200
    Defining a Zoom Window 202
    Displaying the Previous View 203
    Using Dynamic Zooming 203
    Scaling a View 205
    Centering 207
    Displaying Drawing Limits and Extents 208
    Using Fast Zoom 209
 Using Aerial View 210
    Opening and Closing the Aerial View Window 211
    Zooming with Aerial View 211
    Panning with Aerial View 212
    Changing the Size of the Aerial View Image 213
    Changing the Aerial View Update 214
 Using Named Views 214
    Saving Views 214
    Restoring Named Views 216
    Deleting Named Views 216
 Using Tiled Viewports 216
    Displaying Multiple Tiled Viewports 217
    Changing the Tiling Configuration 218
    Working in Tiled Viewports 220
    Reusing Viewport Configurations 221
 Turning Visual Elements On and Off 224
    Turning Fill On and Off 224
    Turning Text On and Off 224
    Turning Blips On and Off 225
    Turning Selection Highlighting On and Off 226

Chapter 7   **Editing Methods**   227

    Working with Named Objects   228
        Purging Named Objects   228
        Renaming Objects   229
        Renaming Groups of Objects   229
    Selecting Objects   230
        Choosing the Command First   231
        Removing Objects from a Selection Set   236
        Selecting Objects First   237
        Editing with Grips   239
        Using Groups   240
    Editing Objects Using the Object Properties Toolbar   244
        Selecting an Object in PICKFIRST Mode   245
        Editing Layers   245
        Editing Colors   247
        Editing Linetypes   249
    Matching Properties of Other Objects   250
    Copying Objects   253
        Copying within a Drawing   253
        Multiple Copying Using Grips   254
        Copying with the Clipboard   255
        Copying Views   256
        Offsetting Objects   258
        Mirroring Objects   259
        Arraying Objects   261
    Moving Objects   263
        Rotating Objects   264
        Aligning Objects   266
    Erasing Objects   267
    Resizing Objects   268
        Stretching Objects   268
        Scaling Objects   270
        Extending Objects   273
        Changing the Length of Objects   274
        Trimming Objects   275
    Inserting Breaks in Objects   278
    Exploding Objects   278
    Editing Polylines   279
    Editing Multilines   281
        Adding and Deleting Multiline Vertices   281
        Editing Multiline Intersections   282
        Editing Multiline Styles   282

Editing Splines   283
Chamfering Objects   285
    Chamfering by Specifying Distances   285
    Trimming Chamfered Objects   286
    Chamfering by Specifying Length and Angle   287
    Chamfering Polyline Segments   288
    Chamfering an Entire Polyline   288
Filleting Objects   289
    Setting the Fillet Radius   289
    Trimming Filleted Objects   290
    Filleting Circles and Arcs   290
    Filleting Line and Polyline Combinations   291
    Filleting an Entire Polyline   291
    Filleting Parallel Lines   292
Editing Hatches   293
    Removing Hatch Associativity   293
    Editing Hatch Boundaries and Patterns   293

Chapter 8   **Using Layers, Colors, and Linetypes   297**
Working with Layers   298
    Sorting Layers and Linetypes   298
    Creating and Naming Layers   298
    Making a Layer Current   300
    Making an Object's Layer Current   300
    Controlling Layer Visibility   300
    Controlling Visibility in Floating Viewports   304
    Locking and Unlocking Layers   304
    Assigning Color to a Layer   305
    Assigning a Linetype to a Layer   306
    Filtering Layers   306
    Renaming Layers   308
    Deleting Layers   308
    Retaining Changes to Xref-Dependent Layers   309
Working with Colors   309
    Specifying Colors   310
    Setting the Current Color   310
Working with Linetypes   311
    Making a Linetype Current   313
    Renaming Linetypes   313
    Deleting Linetypes   314
    Changing Linetype Descriptions   314
    Filtering Linetypes   315
    Specifying Linetype Scale   315

Assigning Layers, Colors, and Linetypes to Objects 317
    Changing an Object's Layer 317
    Changing an Object's Color 318
    Changing an Object's Linetype 319
    Displaying Polyline Linetypes 320

Chapter 9   Adding Text to Drawings 323

Working with Text Styles 324
    Creating and Modifying Text Styles 324
    Using Styles with Previous Releases 333
Using Line Text 333
    Creating Line Text 334
    Formatting Line Text 334
    Changing Line Text 336
Using Multiline Text 338
    Creating Multiline Text 339
    Using External Text Files 341
    Formatting Multiline Text 342
    Changing Multiline Text 348
Substituting Fonts 352
    Specifying an Alternative Default Font 353
Checking Spelling 354
    Switching Dictionaries 355
    Creating and Editing Custom Dictionaries 356
Using Text Editors for Multiline Text 357
    Specifying a Multiline Text Editor 357
    Creating Multiline Text in a Text Editor 358
    Formatting Multiline Text in a Text Editor 359
    Changing Text with an ASCII Text Editor 363

Chapter 10   Dimensioning and Tolerancing 365

Dimensioning Concepts 366
    Parts of a Dimension 366
    Dimensioning System Variables 367
    Dimension Text 367
    Leader Lines 368
    Associative Dimensions 368
Creating Dimensions 369
    Linear Dimensions 370
    Radial Dimensions 374
    Angular Dimensions 375
    Ordinate Dimensions 376
    Leaders and Annotation 377
Adding Dimensions 381

Editing Dimensions   381
    Stretching Dimensions   383
    Trimming and Extending Dimensions   384
    Making Dimensions Oblique   385
    Editing Dimension Text   386
Creating Dimension Styles   388
    Controlling Dimension Geometry   389
    Controlling Dimension Format   398
    Controlling Dimension Text   406
Using Style Families   416
Using Style Overrides   418
Working with Dimension Styles   420
    Applying Styles to Existing Dimensions   420
    Comparing Dimension Styles   421
    Listing Dimension Styles and Variables   421
    Using Externally Referenced Dimension Styles   423
Adding Geometric Tolerances   424
    Material Conditions   426
    Datum Reference Frames   426
    Projected Tolerance Zones   427
    Composite Tolerances   427
Creating and Modifying Arrowheads   429

Chapter 11   Using Blocks, Attributes, and Xrefs   433

Working with Blocks   434
    Working with Layers, Colors, and Linetypes   435
    Nesting Blocks   435
    Creating Unnamed Blocks   437
    Defining Blocks   437
    Inserting Blocks   438
    Exploding a Block   440
    Redefining a Block   441
Working with Attributes   441
    Creating Attributes   442
    Editing Attribute Definitions   443
    Attaching Attributes to Blocks   443
    Editing Attributes Attached to Blocks   444
    Extracting Attribute Information   444
Using External References   448
    Updating Xrefs   448
    Using the External Reference Dialog Box   449
    Demand Loading and Maximizing Xref Performance   453
    Attaching Xrefs   457
    Overlaying Xrefs   459

Deciding Whether to Attach or to Overlay an Xref   460
Detaching Xrefs   461
Reloading Xrefs   462
Unloading Xrefs   462
Binding Xrefs to Drawings   462
Clipping Blocks and Xrefs   464
Controlling Dependent Symbols   467
Changing Xref Paths   467
Changing Nested Xref Paths   468
Defining Alternate Xref Search Paths   469
Handling Xref Errors   472
Using the Xref Log File   473

Chapter 12   Layout and Plotting   475
Using Paper Space and Model Space   476
Switching to Paper Space   477
Switching to Model Space   478
Preparing a Layout   480
Adding a Title Block and Border   480
Creating Floating Viewports   481
Rearranging and Removing Floating Viewports   484
Controlling Visibility in Floating Viewports   484
Changing Viewport Views and Content   487
Using Named Views in Paper Space   493
Plotting Your Drawing   494
Preparing Your Plotter   495
Performing Basic Plotting   495
Setting Up a Plotter Configuration   498
Reusing a Plot Configuration   508
Using BATCHPLT for Batch Plotting   512
Plotting to a File   514
Printing More Quickly   515
Optimizing Pen Motion   515
Calibrating the Plotter   516
Multipen Plotting with a Single-Pen Plotter   517

Chapter 13   Working in Three-Dimensional Space   519
Specifying 3D Coordinates   520
The Right-Hand Rule   520
Entering *X,Y,Z* Coordinates   521
Using *XYZ* Point Filters   521
Entering Cylindrical Coordinates   522
Entering Spherical Coordinates   524
Defining a User Coordinate System   524

Defining a UCS in 3D Space   526
Selecting a Preset UCS   526
The UCS Icon   527
Viewing in 3D   527
Setting a Viewing Direction   528
Displaying a Plan View   530
Setting a View with the Compass and Axis Tripod   530
Defining a Parallel Projection or a Perspective View   531
Setting View Clipping Planes   533
Removing Hidden Lines   534
Creating 3D Objects   535
Creating Wireframes   536
Creating Meshes   537
Creating Solids   548
Editing in 3D   556
Rotating in 3D   556
Arraying in 3D   556
Mirroring in 3D   558
Trimming and Extending in 3D   558
Filleting in 3D   560
Editing 3D Solids   561
Chamfering Solids   561
Filleting Solids   562
Sectioning Solids   562
Slicing Solids   563

Chapter 14   Creating Three-Dimensional Images   565

Using 3D Image Types   566
Drawing 3D Models   567
Surfaces   567
Abutting and Intersecting Objects   568
Creating Hidden-Line Images   570
Hiding Lines of All Objects   570
Hiding Lines of Selected Objects   571
Hiding Solid Objects   571
Creating Shaded Images   571
Shading Models   572
Setting a Shading Method   573
Setting Diffuse Reflection   573
Creating Rendered Images   574
Preparing Models for Rendering   575
Configuring Render for Different Displays   580
Using Render   582
Loading, Unloading, and Stopping   582

Setting Rendering Conditions   582
Accessing the Render Window   585
Merging a Rendering with a Background   586
Changing Color Depth for Rendering   588
Using Lights in Rendering   588
Using Shadows in Rendering   592
Understanding Lighting Principles   594
Adding Lights   600
Deleting and Modifying Lights   601
Using Materials in Rendering   604
Defining Materials   606
Modifying Materials   609
Attaching Materials   610
Using Materials, Blocks, and Layers   611
Mapping   611
Importing and Exporting Materials   617
Using Scenes in Rendering   618
Saving and Redisplaying Renderings   620
Printing Rendered Images   624
Updating Existing Drawings   628
Using Render with Related Applications   628
3D Studio   628
AME   629
AutoSurf and AutoCAD Designer   629

Chapter 15   Using Raster Images   631

Raster Images in Drawings   632
Attaching and Scaling Raster Images   633
Managing Raster Images   636
Viewing Image Information   636
Changing Image File Paths   640
Naming Images   641
Unloading and Reloading Images   642
Detaching Images   642
Modifying Images and Image Boundaries   643
Showing and Hiding Image Boundaries   644
Changing Image Layer, Boundary Color, and Linetype   644
Changing Image Location   645
Changing Image Scale, Rotation, Width, and Height   645
Modifying Bitonal Image Color and Transparency   646
Adjusting Image Brightness, Contrast, and Fade   647
Changing Quality and Speed of Image Display   648
Clipping Images   649
Changing the Clipping Boundary   650

Showing and Hiding the Clipping Boundary   651
Deleting a Clipping Boundary   651

Chapter 16   Creating Compound Documents with OLE   653

Understanding OLE Terminology   654
Linking and Embedding   654
Using AutoCAD Information in Other Applications   656
   Linking AutoCAD Views to Other Documents   656
   Editing Linked Views   657
   Embedding AutoCAD Objects in Other Documents   657
Using Information from Other Applications in AutoCAD   658
   Dragging Objects into AutoCAD   659
   Linking Information to AutoCAD Drawings   659
   Embedding Objects in AutoCAD Drawings   662
   Working with OLE Objects   664

Chapter 17   Accessing External Databases   667

Connecting to Existing Databases   668
Accessing Databases from AutoCAD   669
   Viewing External Data   670
   Viewing and Accessing New Databases Dynamically   672
   Modifying External Data   673
Associating Database Rows with AutoCAD Objects   676
   Defining Key Columns   676
   Setting Link Paths   677
   Choosing Isolation Levels   682
   Linking Objects to the Database   683
   Referencing Link Path Names in Blocks and Xrefs   684
   Creating Links to Xrefs   686
   Creating Links to Blocks   686
   Editing Links   687
   Accessing Links in Xrefs and Blocks   689
   Editing Rows Linked to Objects   691
Creating Text Objects from Database Rows   691
Selecting Objects Using Nongraphic Search Criteria   694
Exporting Associated Data   697
Accessing External Data with SQL   699
Checking Data Integrity   701
   Opening Files Containing Links   702

Appendix A   Using Unicode Fonts   705

Unicode Fonts   706
   Code Page Independent Format (CIF)   706
   The Multibyte Interchange Format (MIF)   708
   Code Page Information   709

Appendix B   Customizing Toolbars   711

Creating and Modifying Toolbars   712
    Creating a New Toolbar   712
    Displaying Toolbar Properties   713
    Adding, Deleting, Moving, and Copying Tools   714
    Displaying Toolbars   716
    Positioning a Toolbar   717
    Modifying a Toolbar   718
Creating and Editing Tools   719
    Creating a Tool   719
    Changing the Command Assigned to a Tool   720
    Creating a Flyout   721
    Editing Tool Icons   722

Appendix C   Using Other File Formats   725

Working with Slides   726
    Creating Slides   726
    Viewing Slides   727
    Viewing Slide Libraries   728
Creating Other File Formats   729
    Creating a DWF File   729
    Creating a DXF File   730
    Creating an ACIS File   731
    Creating a 3DS File   731
    Creating a Windows WMF File   732
    Creating a BMP File   733
    Creating a PostScript File   733
    Writing a Solid in Stereolithograph Format   735
Using Files Created in Other Formats   736
    Using DXF Files   736
    Using DXB Files   737
    Using ACIS SAT Files   737
    Using 3D Studio Files   737
    Using Windows WMF Files   738
    Using PostScript Files   739

Glossary   743

Index   755

Image Gallery

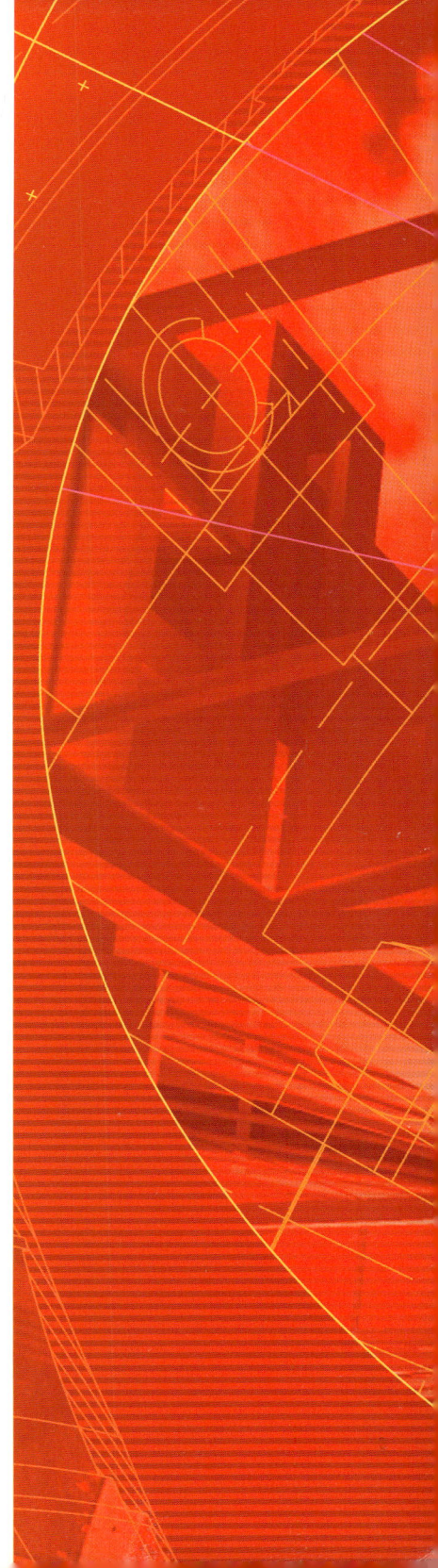

Design professionals use AutoCAD to create myriad images for every drafting and design application, such as architecture, engineering, and mechanical. To exemplify the capabilities of this full-featured drafting and design software, the following images showcase the work of AutoCAD users from around the world. Many of these drawing files can be found in the *Sample* directory of your AutoCAD Release 14 installation.

Sports Complex

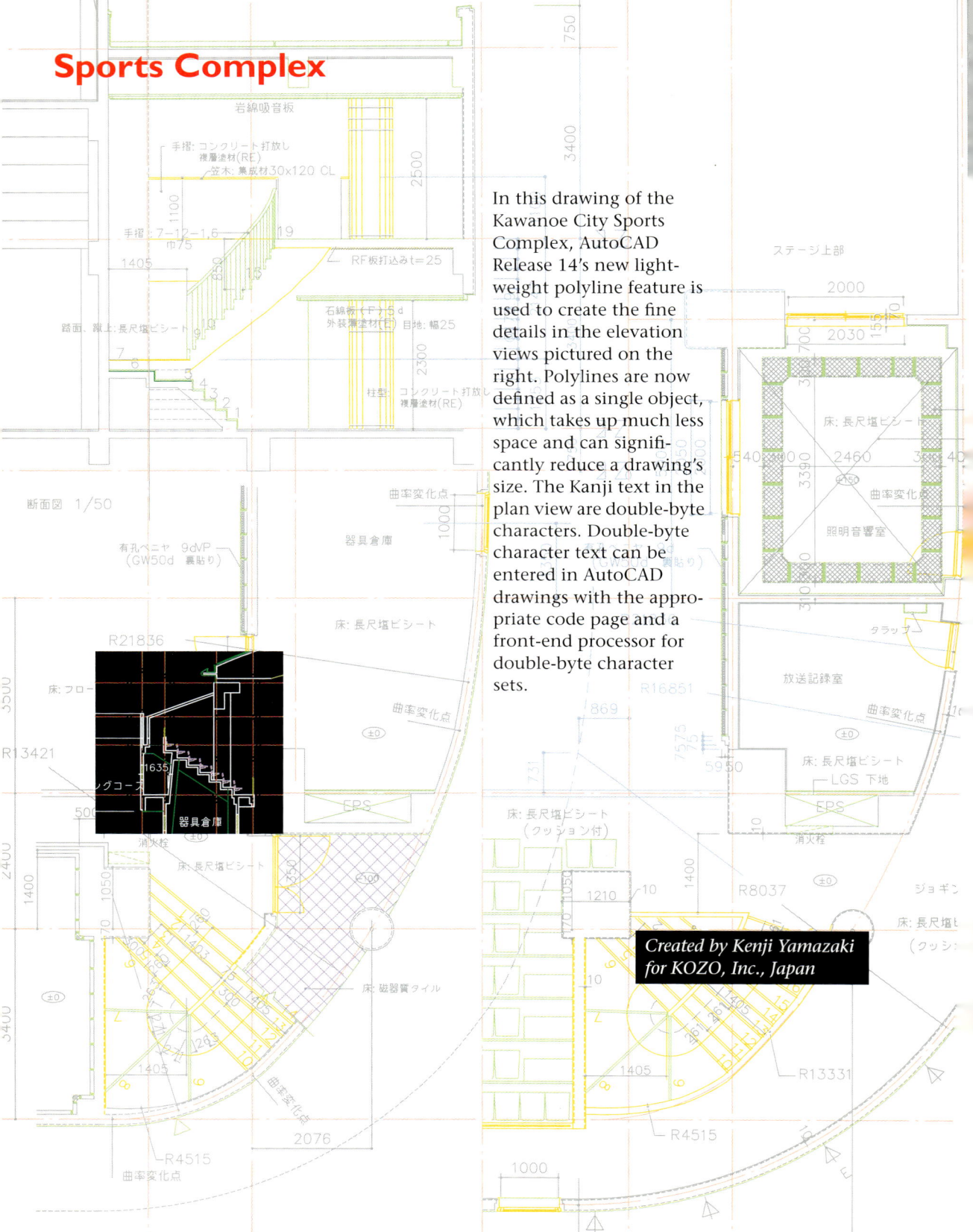

In this drawing of the Kawanoe City Sports Complex, AutoCAD Release 14's new lightweight polyline feature is used to create the fine details in the elevation views pictured on the right. Polylines are now defined as a single object, which takes up much less space and can significantly reduce a drawing's size. The Kanji text in the plan view are double-byte characters. Double-byte character text can be entered in AutoCAD drawings with the appropriate code page and a front-end processor for double-byte character sets.

Created by Kenji Yamazaki for KOZO, Inc., Japan

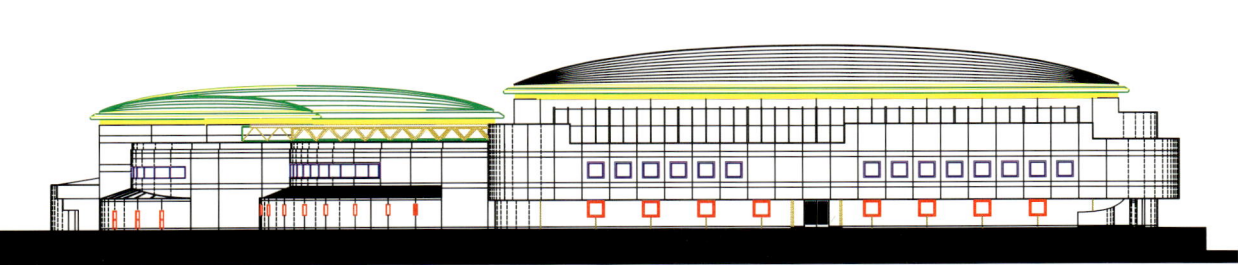

東側立面図　1/150

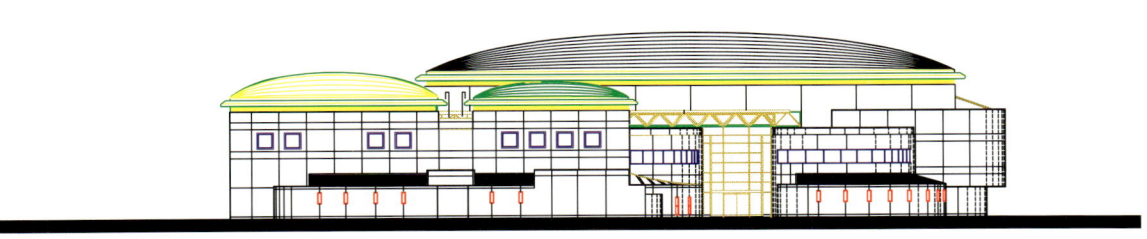

南側立面図　1/150

Image Gallery

Wristwatch

AutoCAD's Solid, Union, Interference, and Subtract commands were used to create this 3D model of a wristwatch. To achieve irregular 3D solid shapes around the edge of the watch's face, Boolean operations were applied. Two-dimensional regions were used in the watch face to facilitate the rendering of the model. Multiple background bitmaps, combined with multiple light sources, were used to create complex reflections on the metallic surfaces.

Image Gallery

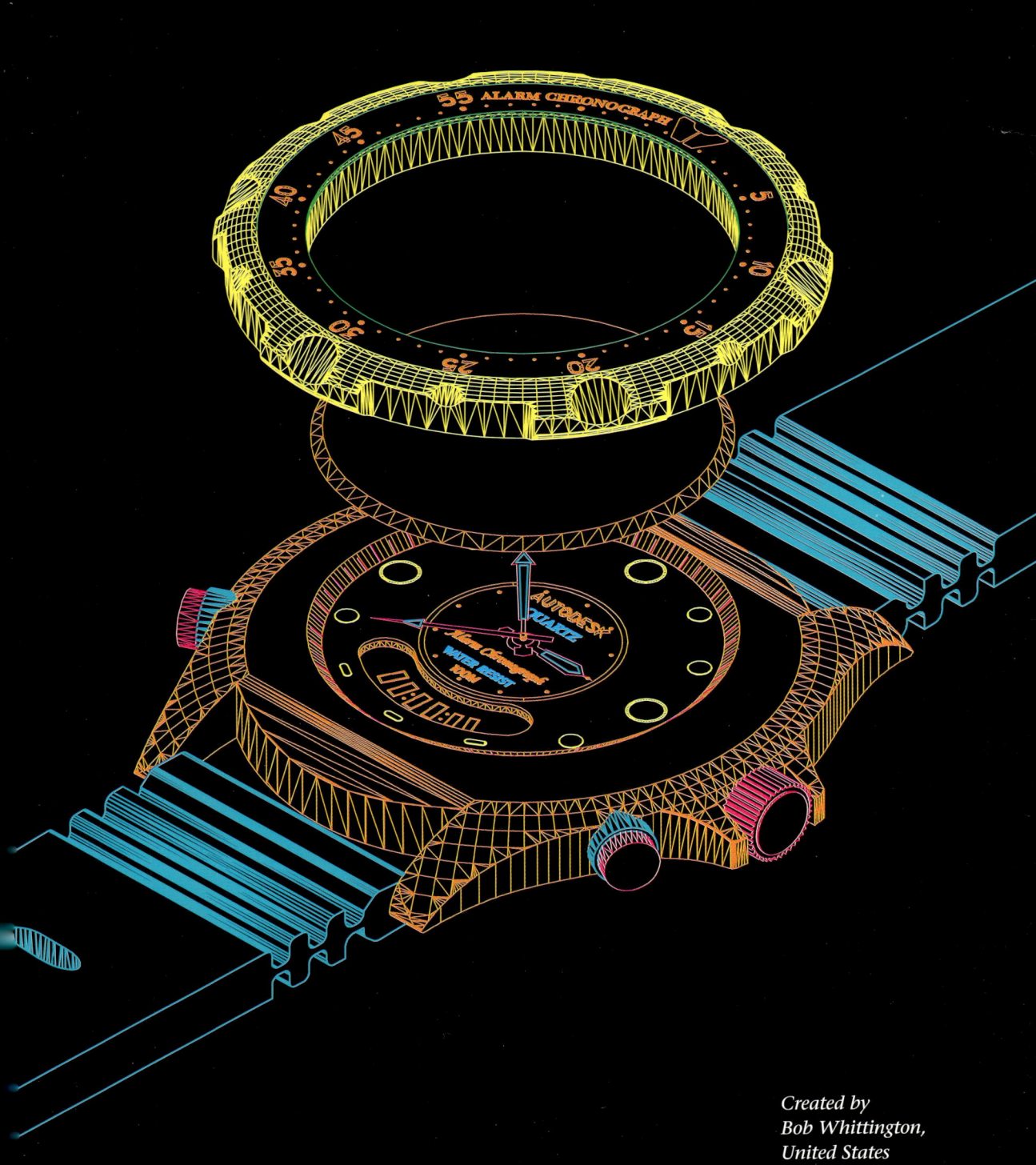

Created by
Bob Whittington,
United States

Office Tower

Created by Neil Bourne, Hong Kong

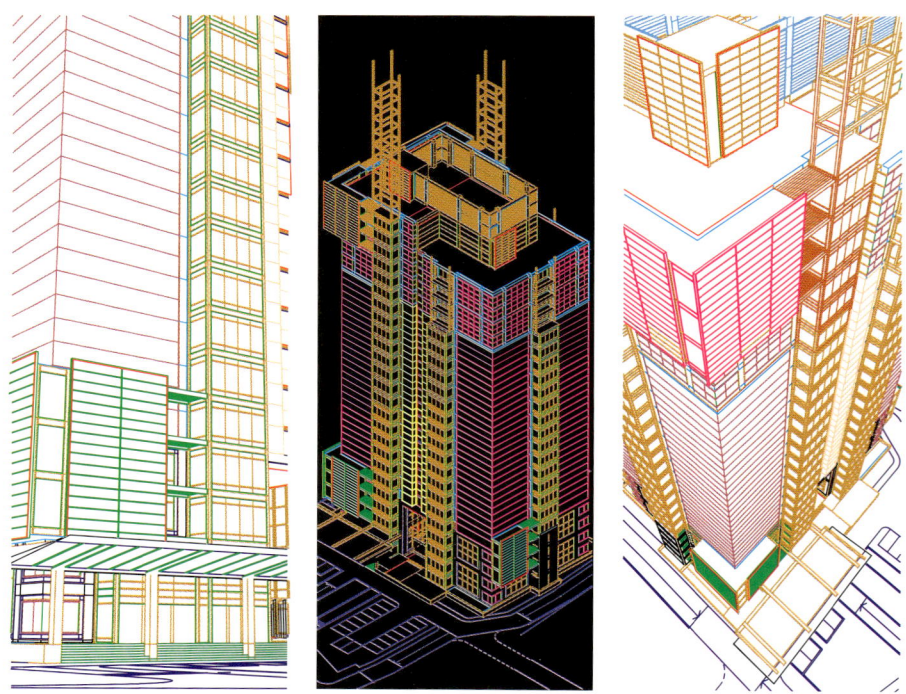

Fifty different views of this Hong Kong office tower are stored in the original AutoCAD drawing. In AutoCAD drawings, you can name, save, and store any desired view, as well as name and store the viewing position and its scale settings. Various settings, including those for Grid, Snap, and the UCS icon, can also be stored with the view. Views can be stored in either model space or paper space. By saving views, specific perspectives and all relevant data can be retrieved from your drawing at any time.

Image Gallery

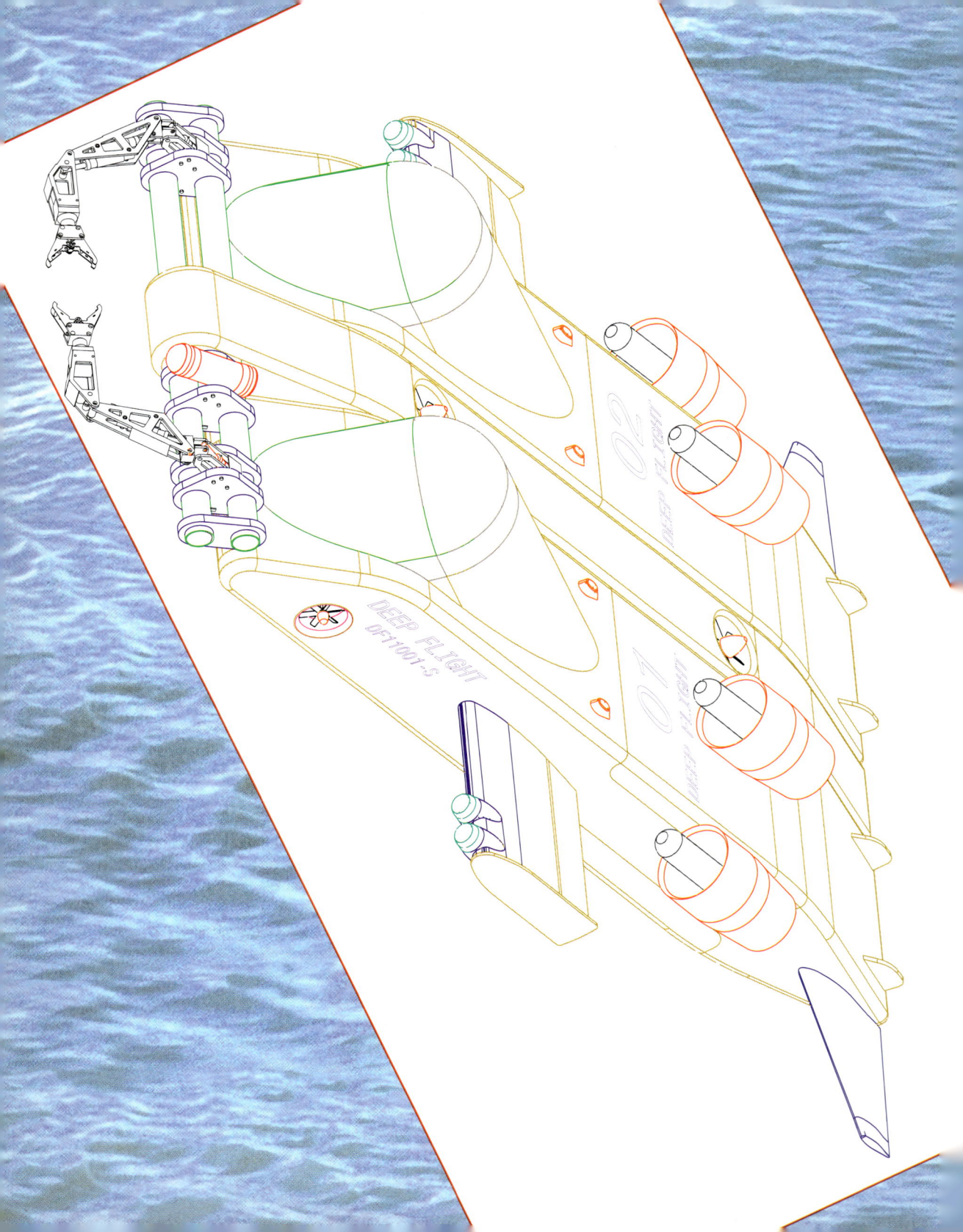

Underwater Exploration Vessel

*Created by Eric Hobson
for Hawkes Ocean Technologies, United States*

This 3D solid model of Deep Flight II, an underwater exploration vessel, was created from 2D machine parts. For example, the external rear thrusters are modified versions of 2D parts from the original Deep Flight I design. To convert the parts from 2D to 3D, the Intersect, Subtract, Extrude, and Revolve commands were used. The complex tapered wing profiles were created with Autodesk Mechanical Desktop. With Mechanical Desktop, advanced NURBS-based surface models can be integrated with feature-based parametric solids. After the modeling was completed, the image was rendered using 3D Studio MAX.

Residential Plan and Elevations

Text styles are used extensively in this drawing of the Williams residence, which includes a floor plan and interior elevations. In AutoCAD, you can use or modify the default Standard text style, load another style, or create a new one. Custom linetypes were also used to create this drawing. Linetypes are useful to convey specific visual information. In addition, specific data, such as dimensions, can be retrieved by snapping on any line in the drawing.

Created by William Harkins for Harkins and Associates, United States

12
6
2'-0"
LIGHTING
SOFFIT
SOFFIT
W4230
W4230
DW
SPACE
CB36
LAZY
SUSAN
CB36
LAZY
SUSAN
B36
BD18
B9
13'-6"
10"
1'-0"
2'-6"
1'-8"
9'-0"
3'-0"

6"
6"
+ 0
- 1.5"
ART RECESS
- 3"
+ 8"
3'-6"
8"
+ 6"
4"
36"
SEE THRU
FIREPLACE
TO
GRAND ROOM
3'-6"
4'-6"
4'-2 1/2"
4'-2 1/2"
8'-5"
7

1x3 FACING
ON SHELVES
1'-4"
1'-4"
1'-0"
3" FILLER
2'-6"
30"
LAP DWR
5'-3"

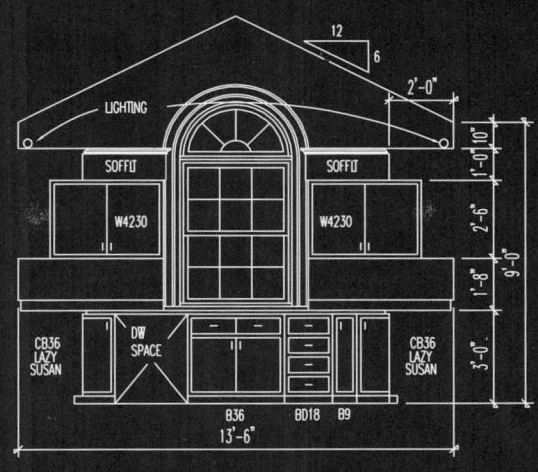

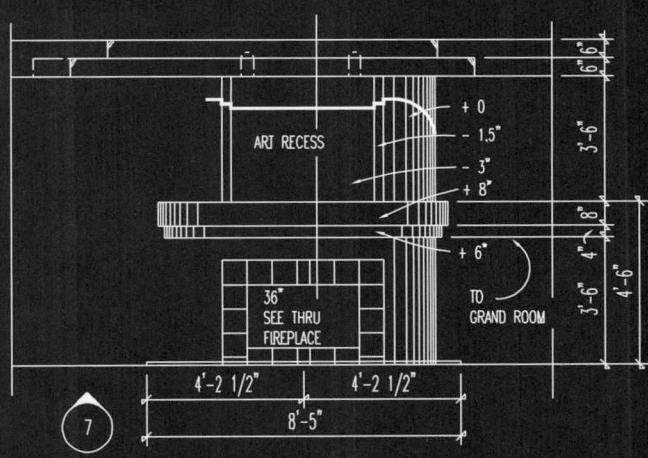

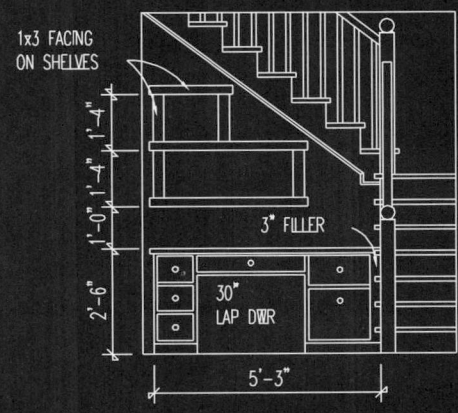

Rotating Universal Joint Assembly

The parts in this drawing of a rotating universal joint assembly were imported from more than 100 individual detail drawings. The hatch patterns, sections, and other drawing data were imported, using separate blocks, and are externally referenced. By manipulating the image in both model space and paper space, it's possible to view the smallest details. The solid filled hatched areas of the compression spring insert were created with AutoCAD Release 14's new solid fill feature.

Created by David Cross
United States

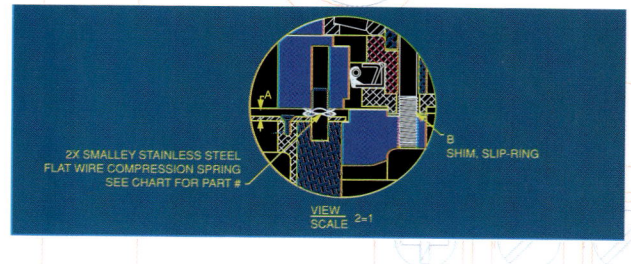

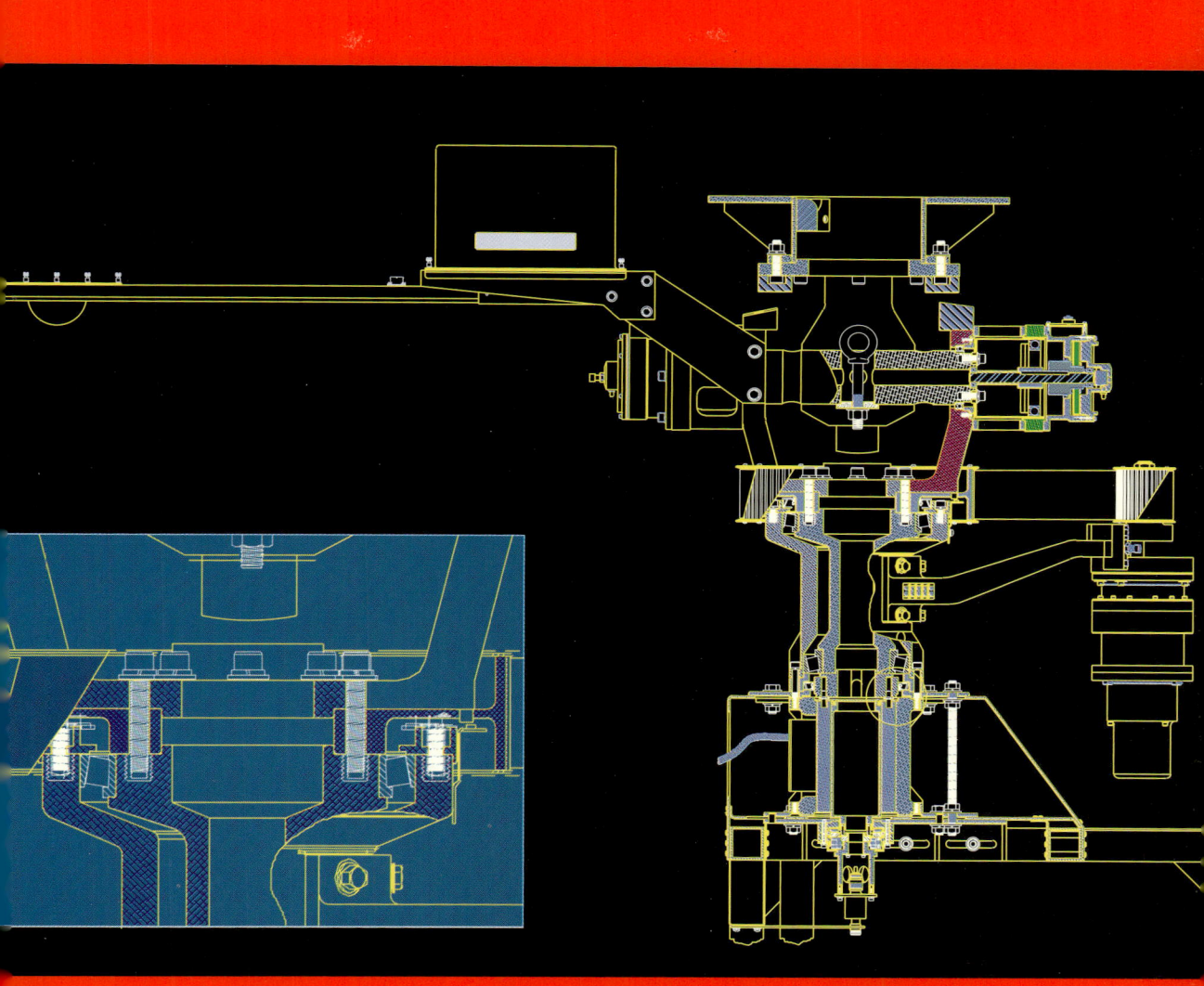

Image Gallery

Japanese Temple

In this drawing of a traditional-style Japanese castle, combinations of lines, curves, and arc segments make up the kin no shachihoko ("style of fish") in the roof section. Lightweight polylines and circles create the fine detail and symmetry of the other roof areas. Lightweight polylines are created as single objects in AutoCAD, thereby reducing the drawing's size.

*Created by Kenji Yamazaki
for KOZO, Inc., Japan*

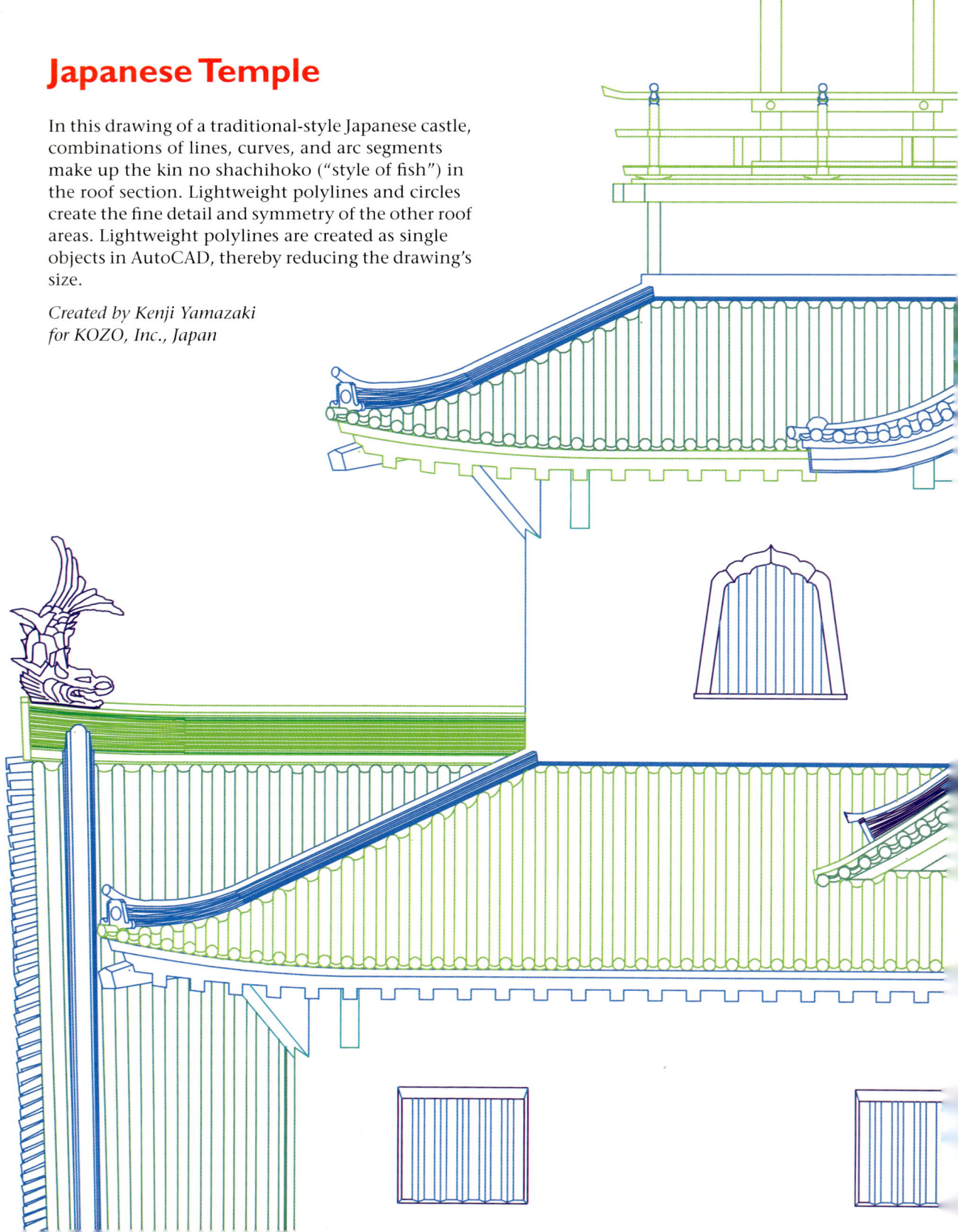

Universal Pneumatic Clamp Cylinder

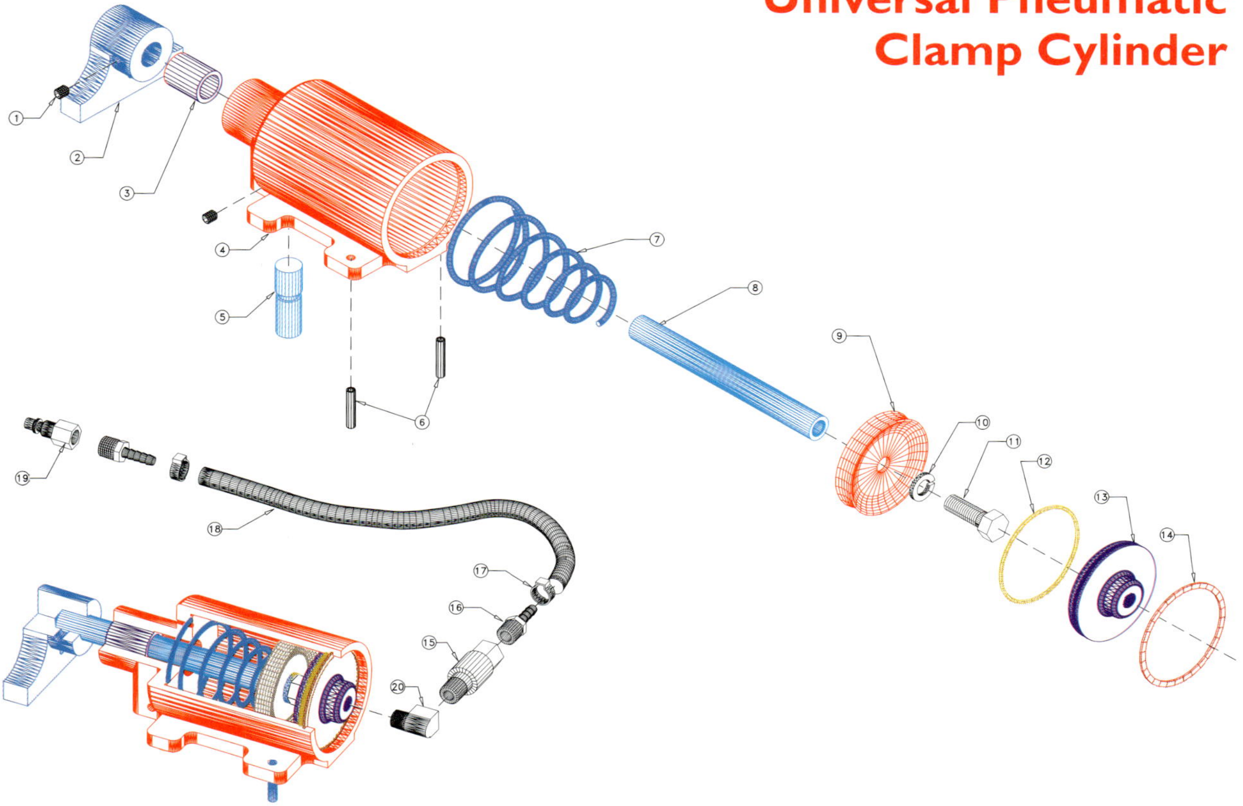

Both model space and paper space are used to create this drawing of a universal pneumatic clamp cylinder assembly. In model space, the basic 3D model was created by using tiled viewports. In paper space, floating viewports are treated as objects that can be moved or resized to create suitable layouts for viewing the model. The full assembly is shown here in a single paper space viewport. Invisible attributes for each part are exported to a file that is used to generate a parts list.

Created by Bob Whittington, United States

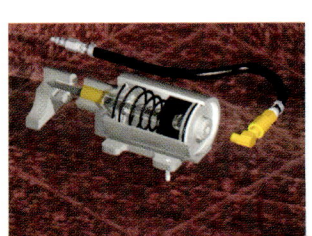

Image Gallery

15

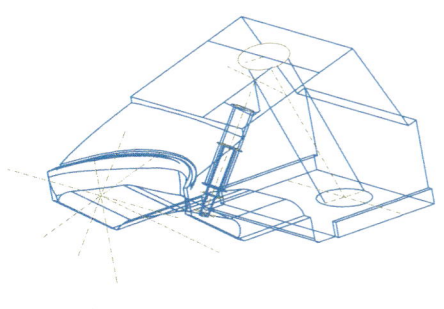

Mold Design

The 2D cross-section view shown in the lower-left was created from a 3D model of a mold design. To derive precise 2D profiles, accurate ACIS solids were finely tuned with AutoCAD's Isoline and Solprof commands, creating a mesh representation. Associative hatches were used to model most of the mold plate's cross section. As the design changed, the hatching in the plates conformed automatically to the new boundaries. Now, the interior of the model can be easily visualized, and the 2D cross section is also in a format that's useful to a machinist for manufacturing the part.

Created by ZPK Mold, Germany

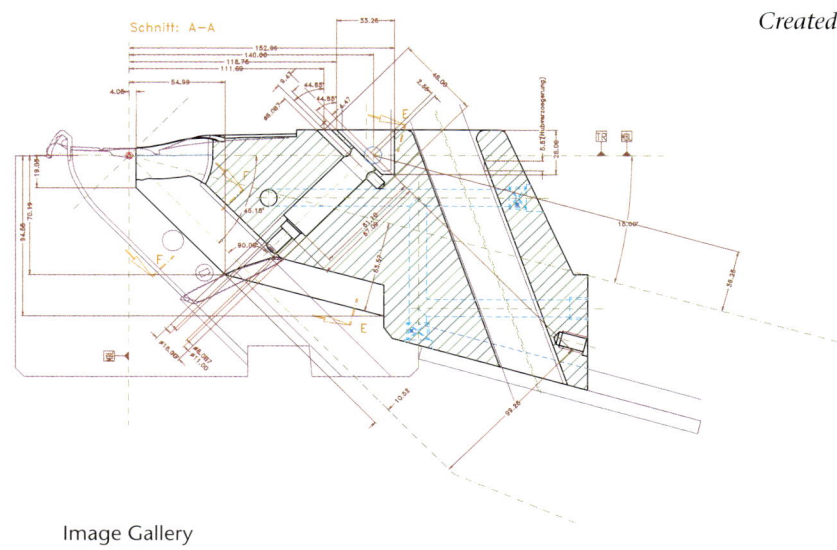

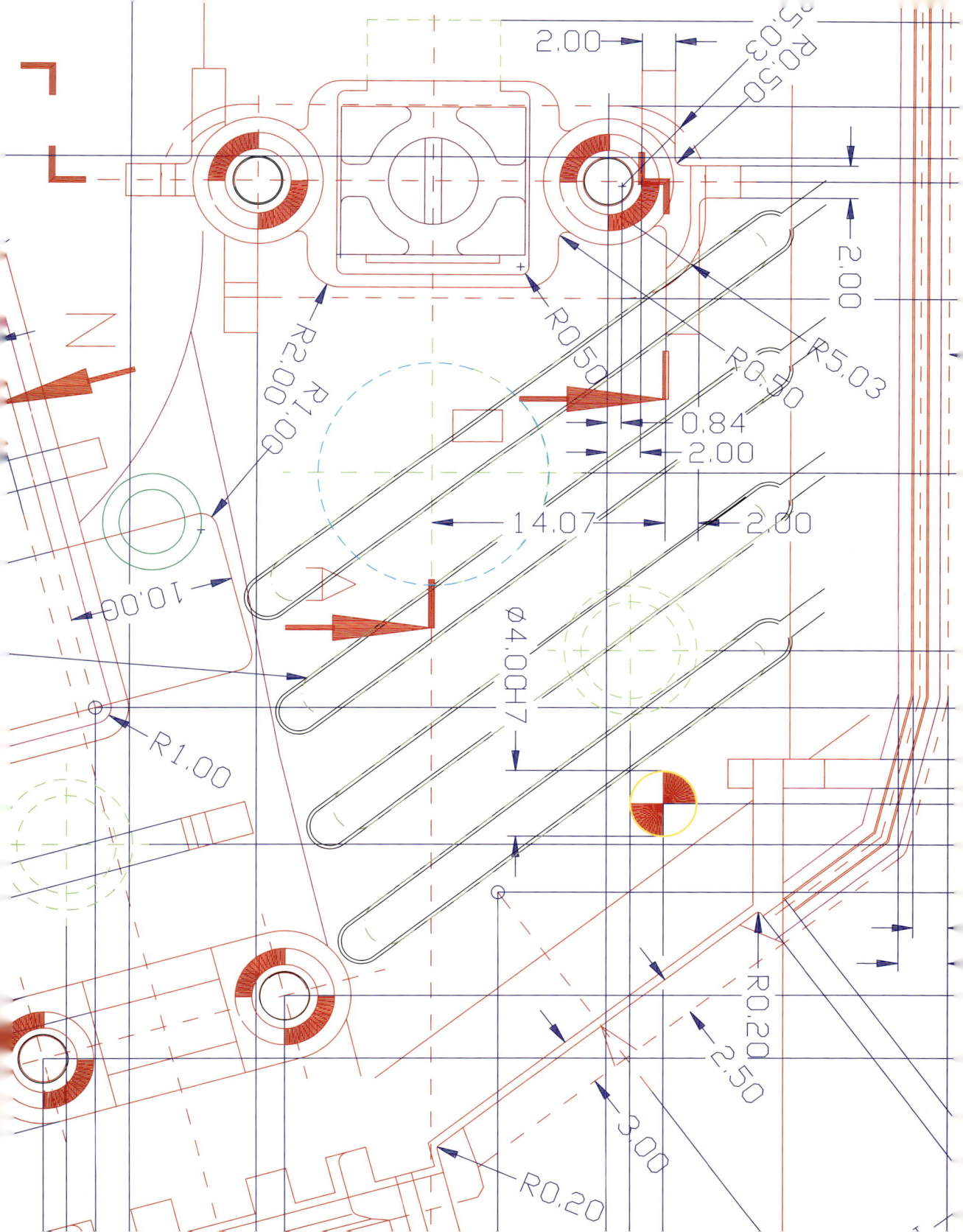

Residential Exterior

The design for an addition to this house was created by the architect as a line drawing. The large dormer doors were added to the original drawing, as shown in the rendered image. Using layers extensively, the architect modified the drawing to prepare it for rendering. All visible details of the line drawing were modified to be fully 3D. The raster image pictured on the right represents the final rendering created in 3D Studio MAX.

Created by John Schmidt, United States

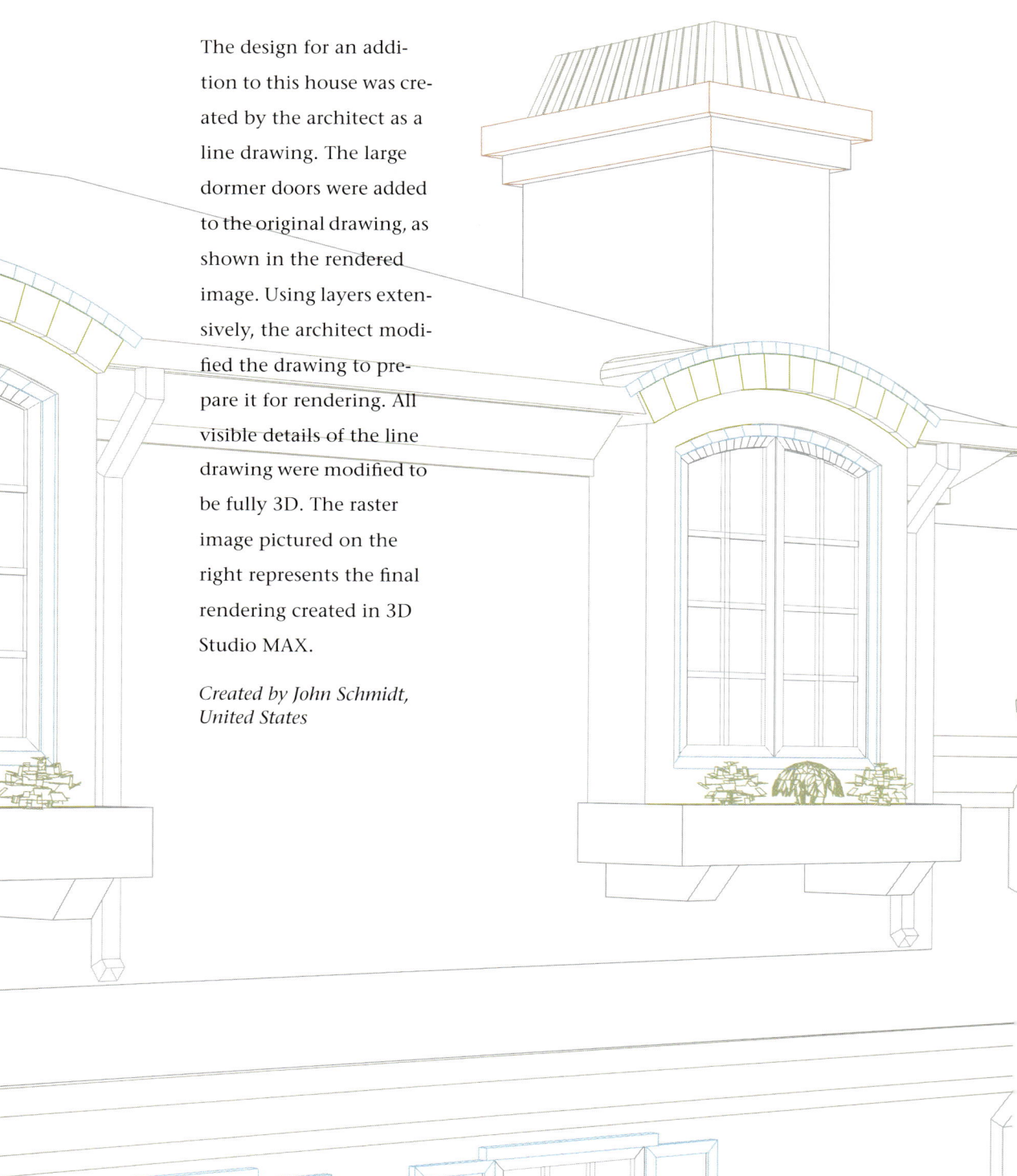

Image Gallery
19

Maps of Milan and Paris

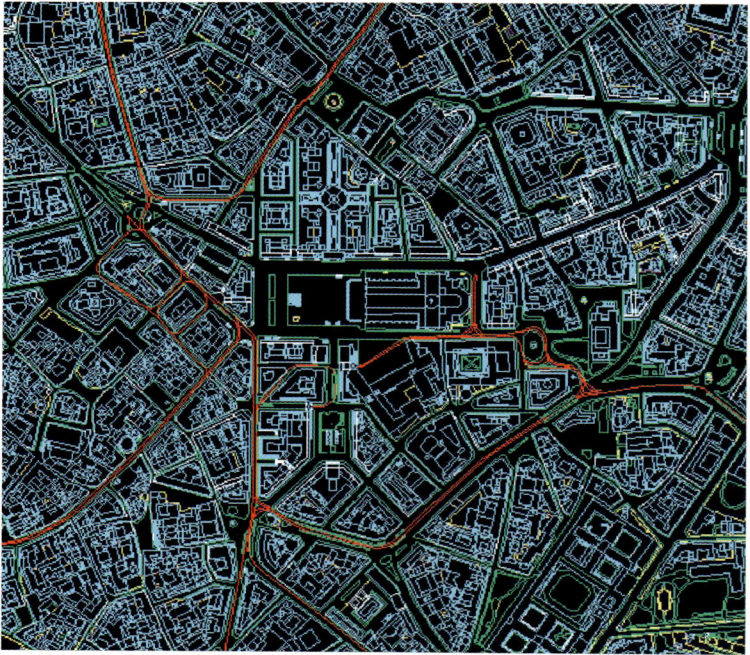

Created by Moleri Giacom for AEM Milano, Italy

AutoCAD was used to create and edit the base geometry of these maps of Paris and Milan. The map of Milan was saved as a TIF file, a raster file format. Because AutoCAD Release 14 has the ability to import most raster image formats, you can trace vectors over raster data, known as heads-up digitizing. The AutoCAD Map product, based on AutoCAD, adds powerful new data management features, advanced mapping tools, and essential GIS analysis functionality.

Image Gallery

20

Created by Vuattoux for PC Vision, France

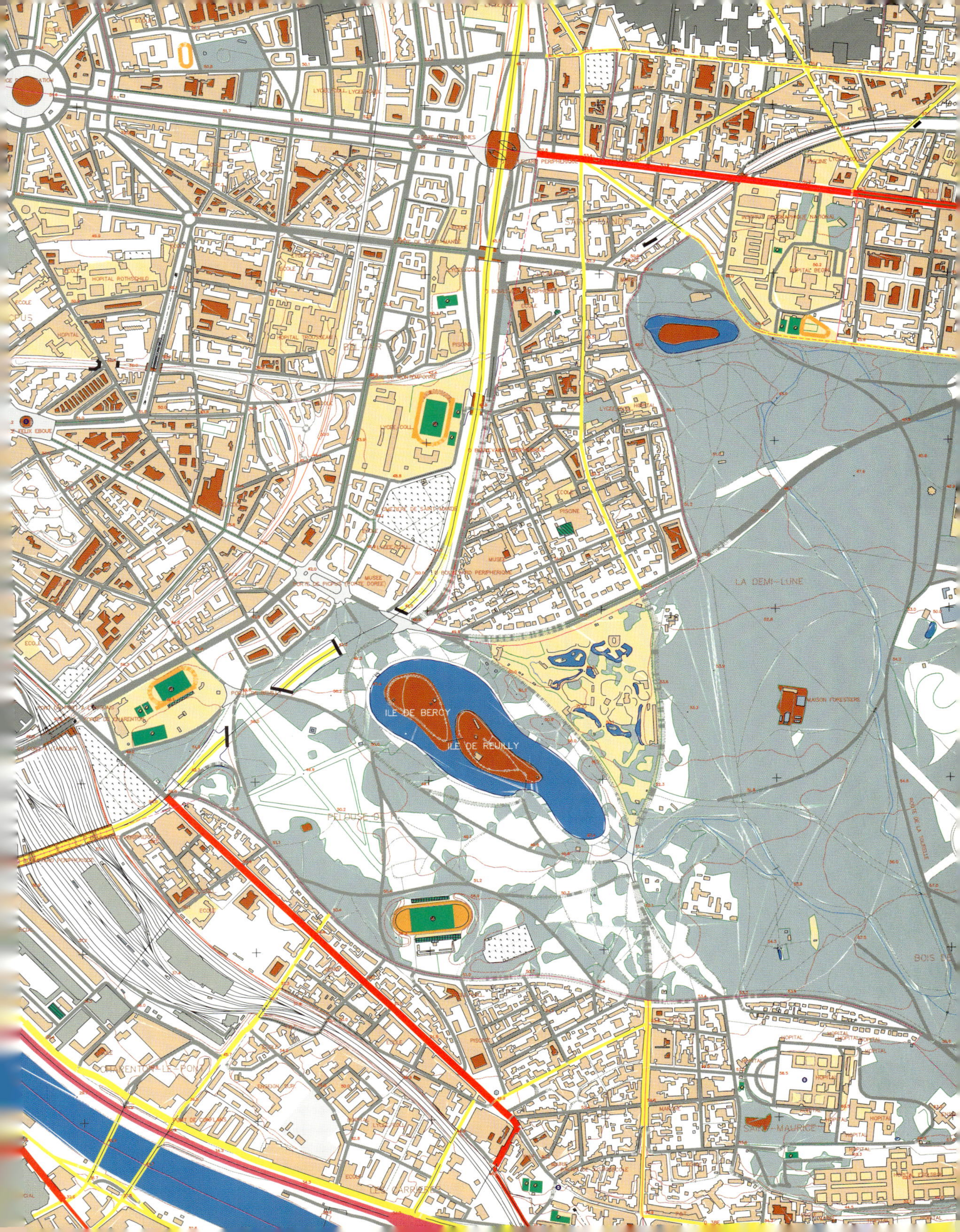

Electric Guitar

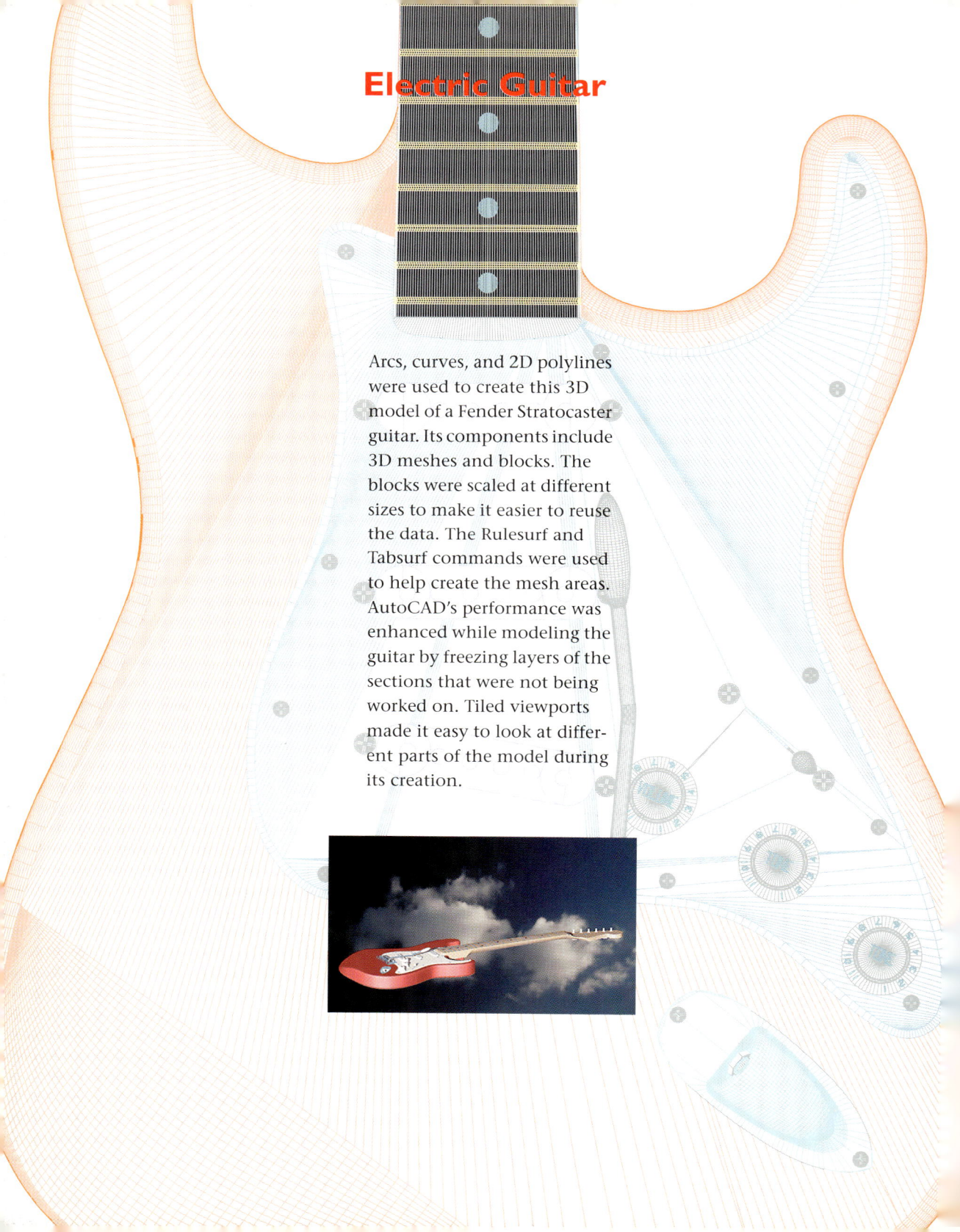

Arcs, curves, and 2D polylines were used to create this 3D model of a Fender Stratocaster guitar. Its components include 3D meshes and blocks. The blocks were scaled at different sizes to make it easier to reuse the data. The Rulesurf and Tabsurf commands were used to help create the mesh areas. AutoCAD's performance was enhanced while modeling the guitar by freezing layers of the sections that were not being worked on. Tiled viewports made it easy to look at different parts of the model during its creation.

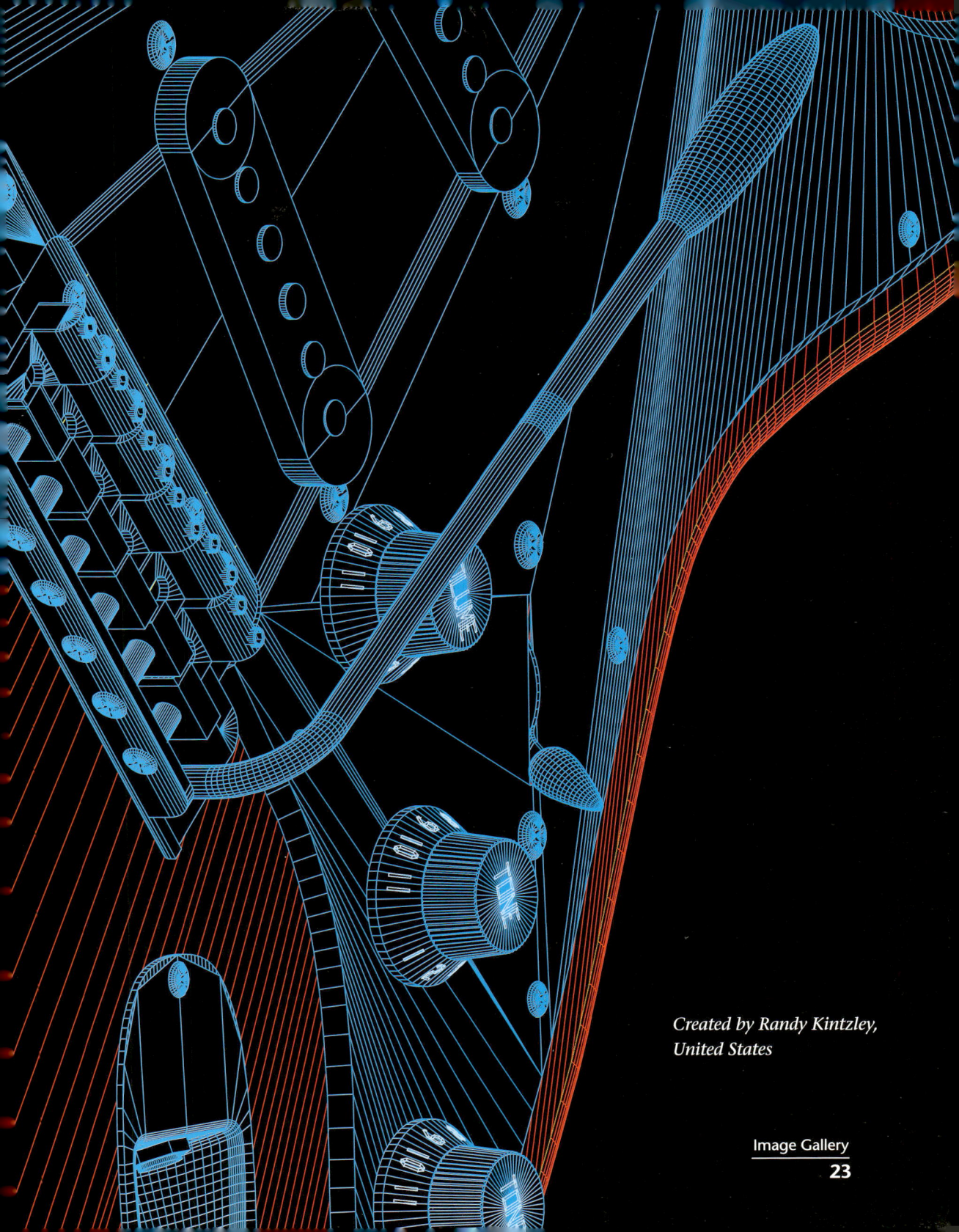

Created by Randy Kintzley, United States

Water Treatment Plant

Created by CADAGUA, Spain

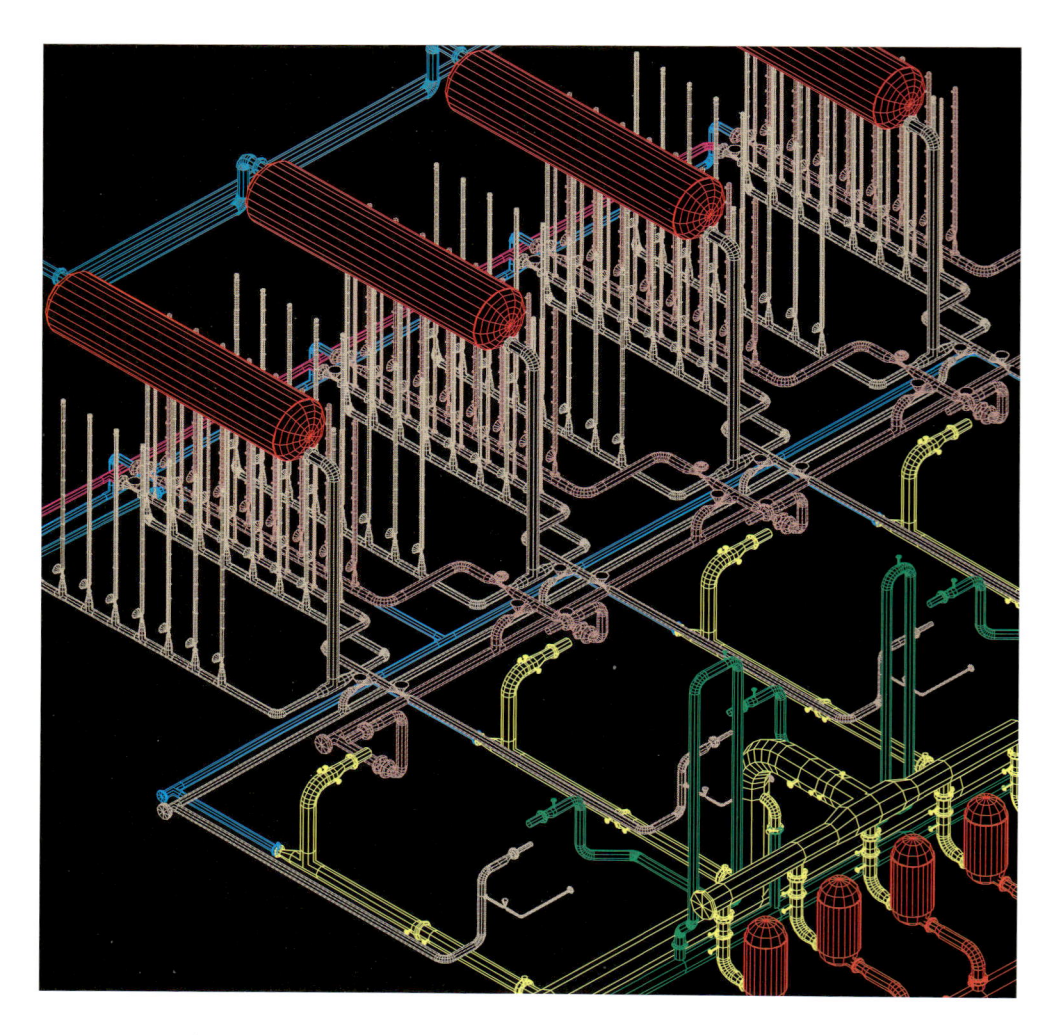

This standard isometric view shows the details of a water treatment plant in Cyprus. The Block command was used extensively to reuse the drawing's data and produce symmetrical objects. More than 100 named blocks are in this drawing. The blocks for the different sized cylinders, pipes, and their fittings were all positioned in the drawing with the Insert command. With the Insert command's options, you can preset the scale and rotation of the blocks before specifying their position.

College Campus

These perspective views of St. Mary's College in Moraga, California, depict current structures, as well as future expansion. The drawing was created to help the designer envision how all the buildings would fit together on the campus site. AutoCAD's user coordinate system and coordinate filters were used extensively to construct 3D views. With coordinate filters, the designer can project and extract new coordinate values from existing geometric objects. By using *X,Y,Z* Cartesian coordinates in this manner, the drafter specified an unknown point based on a known point to create new and accurate perspectives. The different views in this drawing were then saved with the AutoCAD drawing. This allowed the designer to quickly display any view for modification.

Created by Ed Thorp, United States

Image Gallery

Space Flight Operations Center

This drawing of a simulated space flight center was created to demonstrate the size and scope of the company's projects to customers. Architectural floor plans were created in AutoCAD and then converted to a 3D wireframe model. The various elements in this drawing are textures and materials that were duplicated from customer-supplied samples for mapping in 3D Studio MAX and inserted into the design. AutoCAD was used to render the image with the Shade command before the drawing was exported to 3D Studio MAX for final rendering.

Created by Barrie Loberg for Evans Consoles, Canada

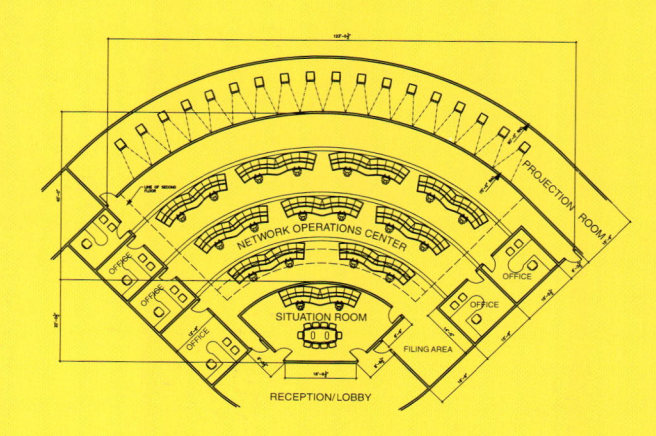

Image Gallery

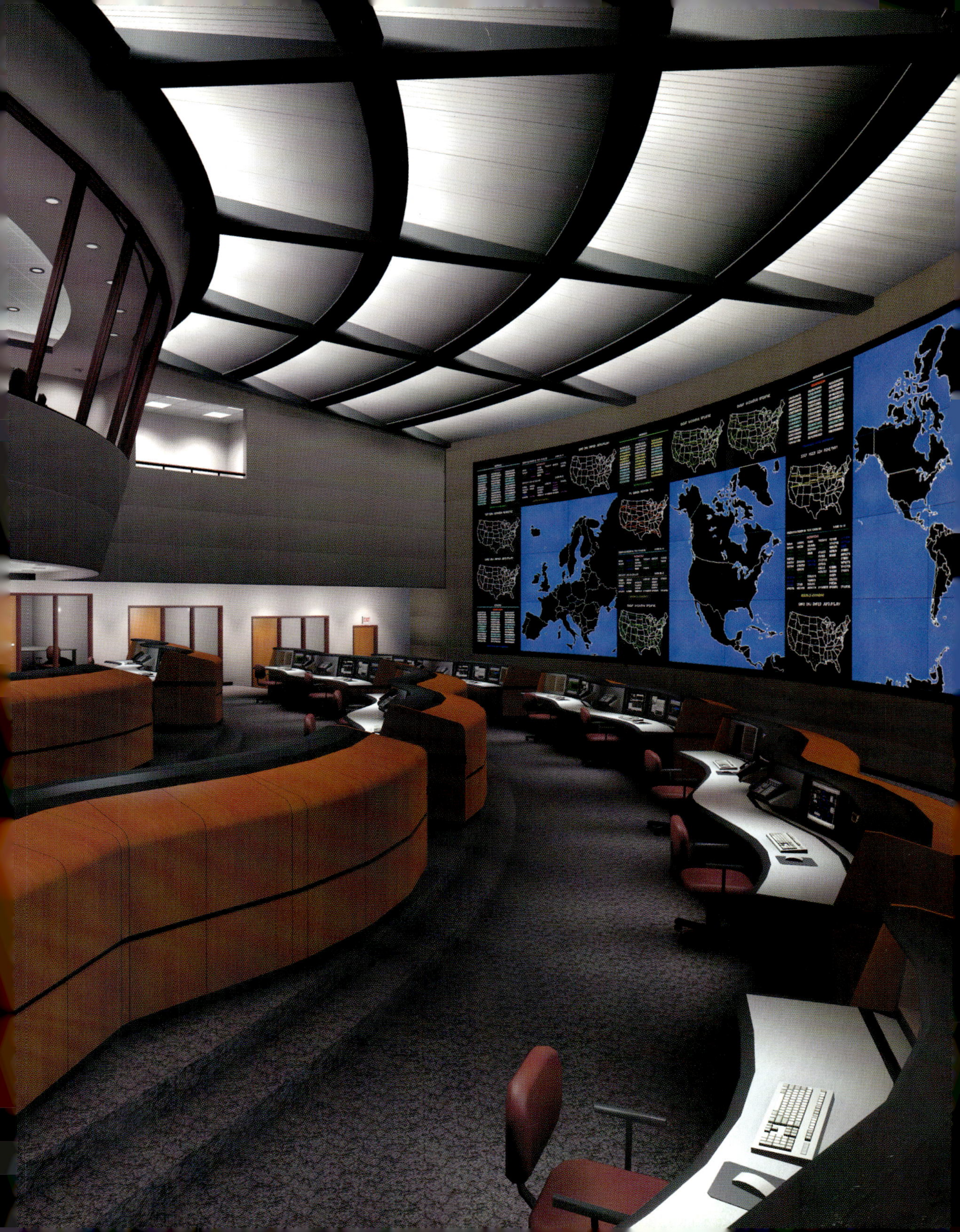

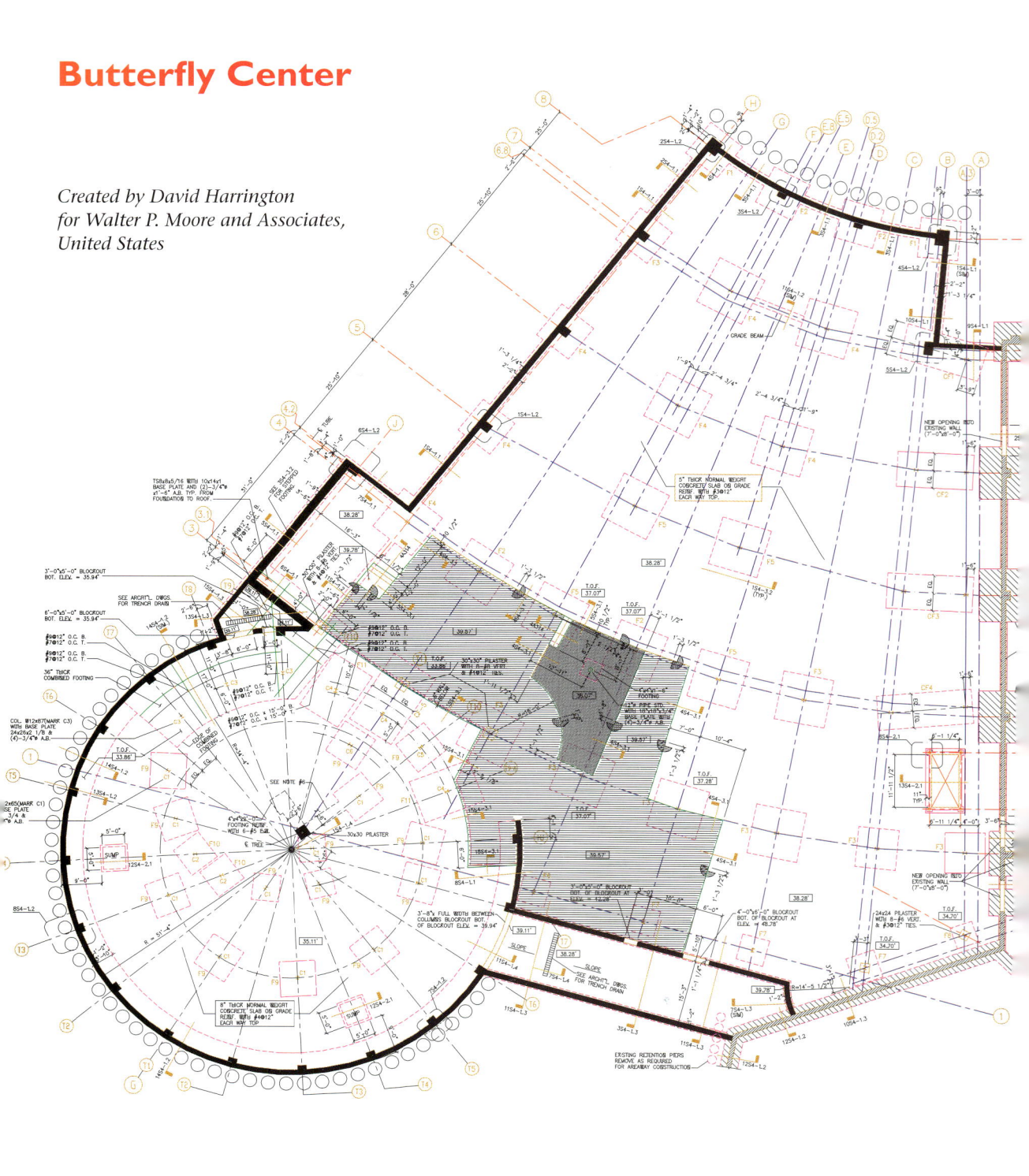

Butterfly Center

*Created by David Harrington
for Walter P. Moore and Associates,
United States*

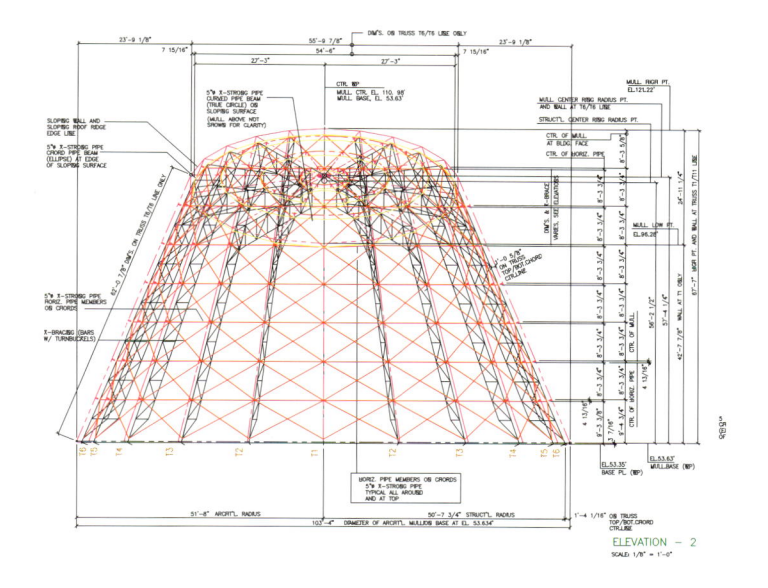

This design for a butterfly center incorporates a series of vertical trusses that are arranged radially around the perimeter of a glass enclosure. The trusses were created in different user coordinate systems with the Line command. AutoCAD stores the dimensions of this unique structure in the drawing. Thousands of independent dimensions can be extracted from the drawing by simply snapping on any part. This is vital to engineers, who need the details of every discrete part of the building when listing its specifications.

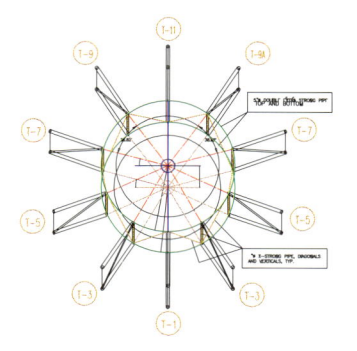

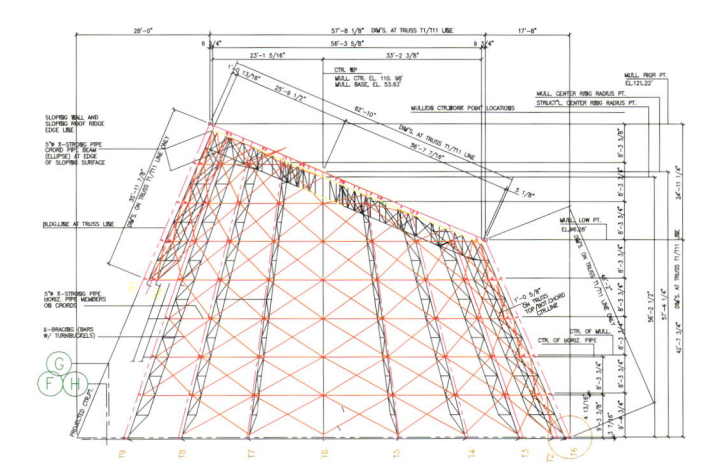

Image Gallery

29

Suspension Bridge

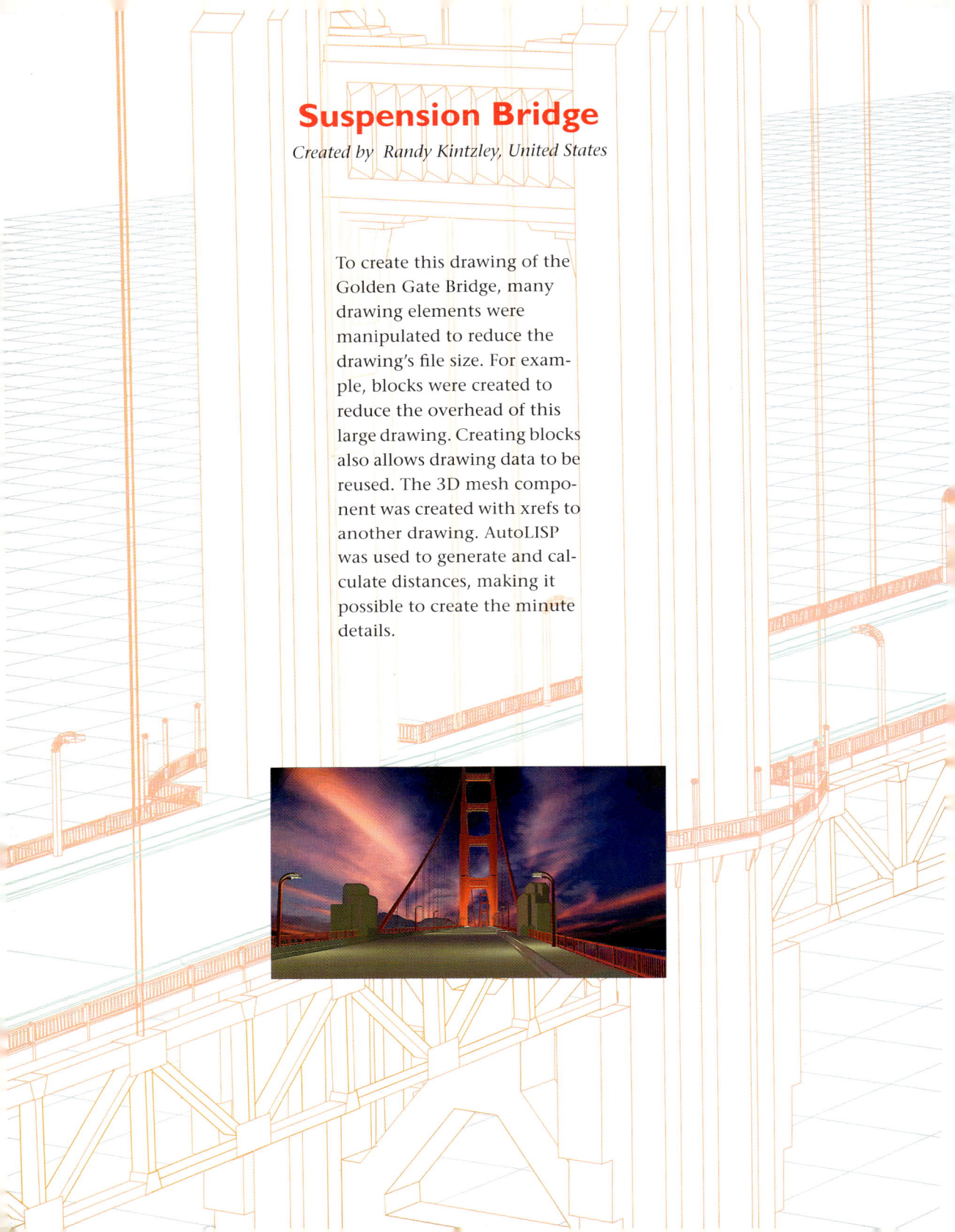

Created by Randy Kintzley, United States

To create this drawing of the Golden Gate Bridge, many drawing elements were manipulated to reduce the drawing's file size. For example, blocks were created to reduce the overhead of this large drawing. Creating blocks also allows drawing data to be reused. The 3D mesh component was created with xrefs to another drawing. AutoLISP was used to generate and calculate distances, making it possible to create the minute details.

Image Gallery

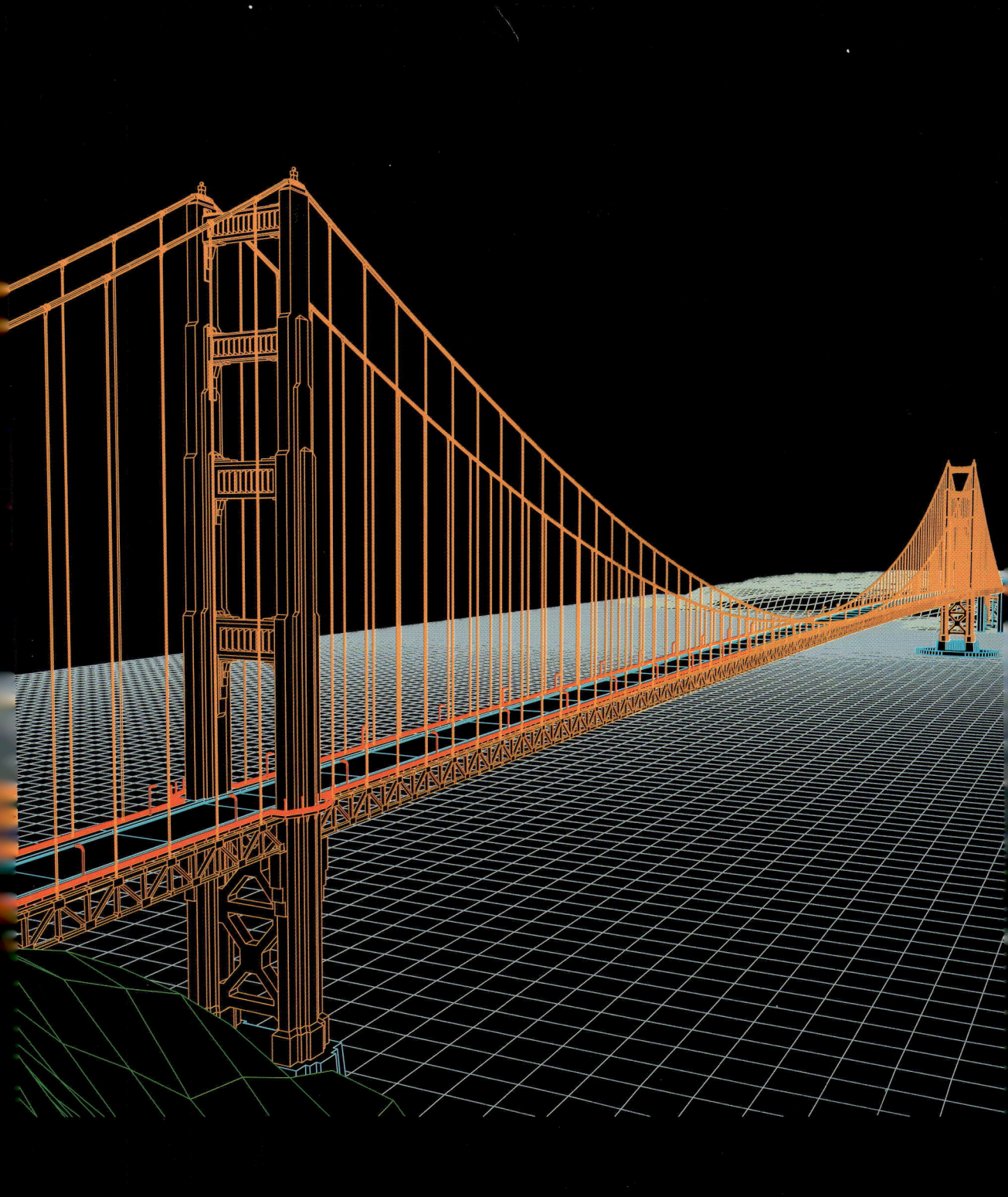

Vacation Resort

This drawing of a resort home in Aspen, Colorado, is shown as a high-resolution raster image. The trusses, roof, and logs are modeled with extruded lines and 3D faces in AutoCAD. AutoCAD's compatibility with adjacent products makes it possible to import AutoCAD models into other applications. 3D Studio MAX was used to add images of the people, clouds, and background, as well as the texture of the lake and its reflections. During the course of the project, the designer was able to use AutoCAD's Shade command to show changes to his client before the final rendering in 3D Studio MAX.

Created by James Biebl
for Graviota Graphics, United States

About AutoCAD® Documentation

AutoCAD Release 14 contains an extensive documentation suite that comprises online documentation, multimedia learning tools, and printed manuals. Understanding their organization and content will help you find the information you need to use AutoCAD more productively.

In this chapter

- Detailed descriptions of the documentation
- Learning strategies for new and upgrade users
- Getting additional help
- Conventions used in this guide

The AutoCAD Documentation Suite

The AutoCAD Release 14 documentation suite includes the following online documentation, learning tools, and printed manuals.

Online Documentation

You access the online documentation by selecting AutoCAD Help Topics (defined in the following list) from the AutoCAD Help menu. Additional methods for getting help are described in "Accessing Information from the Help Menu" on page 63.

- *Using Help*   For all users. Explains how to use the online documentation system to find the information you need.
- *AutoCAD Tutorial*   For new users. An online tutorial containing several lessons that provide hands-on experience using AutoCAD's basic set of drafting tools.
- *How to...*   For all users. Step-by-step procedures for using AutoCAD to complete a wide variety of drafting tasks.
- *Command Reference*   For intermediate to experienced users. An alphabetical listing of all AutoCAD commands and system variables.
- *User's Guide*   For beginning to intermediate users. Combines the concepts and step-by-step procedures previously mentioned into a single manual, which also includes basic installation instructions, examples, cross-references to the *Command Reference*, and a glossary of AutoCAD terms.
- *Installation Guide*   For users installing AutoCAD on a network or configuring of peripheral devices such as plotters and tablets. If you are using only a standard Microsoft Windows-system pointing device and printer, you can follow the basic installation instructions in the *User's Guide*.
- *Customization Guide*   For experienced users. A guide to customizing AutoCAD, organized into three parts: "Customization," "AutoLISP," and "Programmable Dialog Boxes." DXF file format and group code information is also included.
- *ActiveX Automation*   For experienced users. Provides information about developing Automation applications for use with AutoCAD.

NOTE For last minute changes or additions to AutoCAD, see the *Readme* file located in your AutoCAD Release 14 program group.

Learning Tools

You access the learning tools from the AutoCAD Help menu.

- **Quick Tour**   For new users. An online overview of basic AutoCAD concepts and functions.
- **What's New**   For users upgrading from AutoCAD Release 13. An online presentation highlighting the significant new features of AutoCAD Release 14.
- **Learning Assistance**   For intermediate to experienced users. A multimedia learning tool with three projects that focus on working in AutoCAD for Windows®, understanding difficult concepts and underutilized AutoCAD features, and collaborating with other AutoCAD professionals.

Printed Guides

A reference card and two printed manuals are provided with AutoCAD:

- **Quick Reference Card**   For all users. This printed card, located at the back of the *User's Guide*, provides an at-a-glance reference to toolbars, object selection methods, keyboard shortcuts, and coordinate entry methods. Not available online.
- **Installation Guide**   The same content as the online *Installation Guide* except in printed format.
- **User's Guide**   The same content as the online *User's Guide*, except in printed format.

As an option, you can order the printed *Command Reference* and *Customization Guide* as a set by ordering the AutoCAD Release 14 Documentation Pack through your Authorized Autodesk® Dealer or Reseller.

Where to Start

As a user of AutoCAD Release 14, you have one of two experience backgrounds: you are new to AutoCAD (even though you may have used other CAD programs) or you are upgrading from a previous release of AutoCAD. Based on your experience background, the following will help you determine the documentation and learning components that best meet your needs.

New User

If you are new to AutoCAD, start by viewing the online presentation *Quick Tour* on the AutoCAD Help menu. This is a good overview of AutoCAD's capabilities and the concepts of computerized drafting.

If you'd like to try some of the things you saw in the *Quick Tour*, practice the exercises in the *AutoCAD Tutorial* (see AutoCAD Help Topics on the Help menu) for a hands-on AutoCAD experience.

Next, move to the *User's Guide*, which explains concepts and provides step-by-step procedures for completing common drafting tasks. The glossary will help familiarize you with AutoCAD terminology.

As you gain experience, you can learn more about specific commands and options by referring to the *Command Reference*. The *Quick Reference Card* can serve as a handy reminder to common selection and input methods.

Once you have gained some proficiency with AutoCAD, you can use the *Customization Guide* to learn how to customize AutoCAD and develop specialized capabilities.

Upgrade User

If you are upgrading from a previous version of AutoCAD, select *What's New* from the AutoCAD Help menu. This online presentation highlights the significant changes and improvements made in AutoCAD Release 14. More detail about the features described in *What's New* can be found in the *User's Guide* and in the *Command Reference*.

To increase your knowledge and productivity, use *Learning Assistance* on the AutoCAD Help menu. These tutorials will help you work more efficiently in the AutoCAD and Windows interfaces, teach you about difficult and underutilized AutoCAD features, and show you how to collaborate with others by sharing designs across the Internet.

Additional Help Resources

The following resources help you get information on Autodesk products and assistance with your AutoCAD questions.

- Autodesk Web site: *http://www.autodesk.com*
- AutoCAD Release 14 Web site: *http//www.autodesk.com/autocad*
- AutoCAD Forum on Compuserve (GO ADESK)
- Autodesk Fax Information System: (415) 507-5595
- AutoCAD documentation suggestions, errors, or questions: send email to *acad_docs@autodesk.com*
- Autodesk Official Training Courseware (AOTC): contact an Autodesk Authorized Training Center or Dealer to inquire about AutoCAD Release 14 training using AOTC, the Autodesk-endorsed courseware for instructor-led training.

Using This Guide

The following conventions are used in this manual.

Setting Grid Limits

When you open a new drawing and use the Quick Setup or Advanced Setup wizard, you set grid limits in model space. The following procedure describes how to set limits once the drawing is open.

To set grid limits

1   From the Format menu, choose Drawing Limits.

2   Specify the lower-left corner of the limits, which corresponds to the lower-left corner of your drawing area. Press ENTER to use the default (0,0).

3   Specify the upper-right corner of the limits, which corresponds to the upper-right corner of your drawing area.

    For example, enter **30,10** to specify a limits area that is 30 wide and 10 high (assuming the lower-left corner is at 0,0 as specified in step 2).

4   From the View menu, choose Zoom ➤ All.

Command line LIMITS

Related The LIMMAX system variable stores the upper-right drawing limit for the current space. LIMMIN stores the lower-left drawing limit.

Setting Snap Spacing

Snap spacing does not have to match grid spacing. For example, you might set a wide grid spacing to be used as a reference but maintain a closer snap spacing for accuracy in specifying points. You also can set the grid spacing to be smaller than the snap spacing.

For more information, see SNAP in the *Command Reference*.

To turn on Snap mode and set snap spacing

1   From the Format menu, choose Drawing Aids.

2   In the Drawing Aids dialog box under Snap, select On.

3   Enter the horizontal snap X spacing in units.

4   To specify the same vertical snap spacing, press ENTER. Otherwise, enter a new distance under Y Spacing.

5   Choose OK.

Command line DDRMODES

Related To turn Snap mode on and off, double-click the Snap button on the status bar, enter the SNAP command, press CTRL+B, or press F9.

Chapter 2 Organizing Your Project
68

Callouts:
- keys you press on the keyboard are uppercase
- text you enter is bold
- submenus follow a right arrow
- commands, system variables, and named objects are uppercase
- filenames and manual names are italicized
- step-by-step procedure
- command used for a procedure
- other commands related to a procedure

Introduction to AutoCAD

This introduction describes the concepts of electronic drafting and the capabilities of AutoCAD. Also included is an introduction to AutoCAD terminology and documentation.

The *Quick Tour* on the Help menu provides a self-paced presentation of AutoCAD concepts and capabilities. For a description of the features that have been added or changed since AutoCAD Release 13, see *What's New*, also on the Help menu.

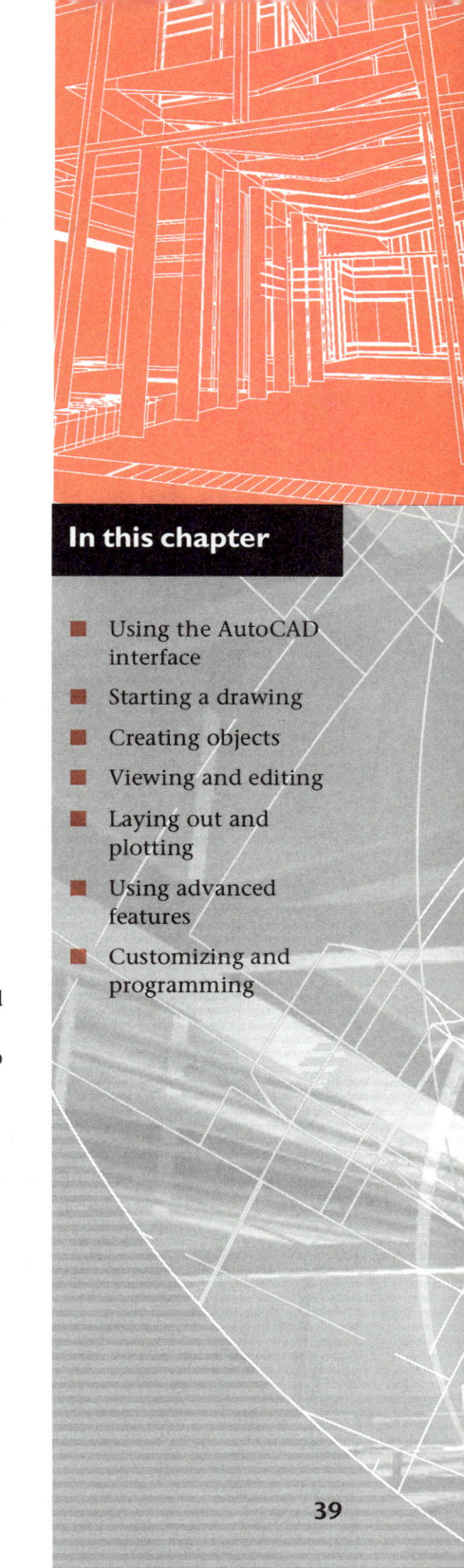

In this chapter

- Using the AutoCAD interface
- Starting a drawing
- Creating objects
- Viewing and editing
- Laying out and plotting
- Using advanced features
- Customizing and programming

The AutoCAD Interface

This section describes the main components of the AutoCAD interface, and explains how to enter commands, and how to find help.

AutoCAD's Main Window

AutoCAD's main window comprises the components shown in the following figure.

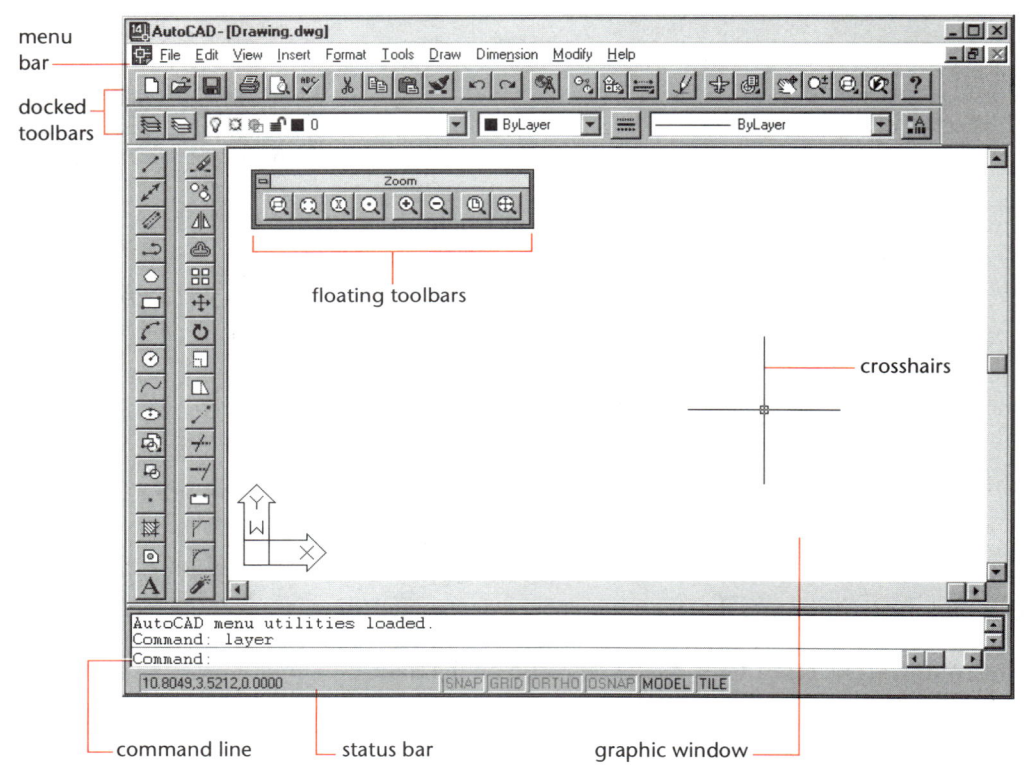

The *graphics window* is where AutoCAD displays your drawing and where you work on your drawing. The *text window* displays a history of the commands and options you have entered.

Introduction to AutoCAD

The *crosshairs* are controlled by your *pointing device* (usually a mouse) and are used to locate *points* and select *objects* in your drawing. The *status bar* displays the *coordinate location* of your crosshairs and the current settings of grid, snap, and other drawing aids.

How to Access Commands

You use AutoCAD by running commands using one of these methods:

- Choosing a menu item
- Clicking a tool on toolbar
- Entering a command

Most commands that can be entered on the command line can be found on a menu or a toolbar, and most commands have additional choices, or *options*. Some commands display these options on the command line, while others display them in a *dialog box*. You enter command line options by typing at least the capitalized portion of the option name and then pressing ENTER. You set command options in a dialog box by clicking the option with the *pointing device* and then choosing OK.

By placing an apostrophe (') before some commands, these commands can be entered "transparently," that is, while another command is active. For example, while using the LINE command, you can enter **'zoom** to change your drawing display without exiting the LINE command. When you exit the 'ZOOM command, the LINE command remains active.

The last-used settings of most command options are "remembered" in *system variables*, which are stored in the drawing file. System variables determine the behavior and *default values* for a command the next time you run it.

At the Command prompt, you can invoke the last-used command by pressing ENTER. You can exit any command by pressing ESC.

Getting Help

All of AutoCAD's documentation is online for quick access. You can get help about a command or procedure by selecting AutoCAD Help Topics from the Help menu.

You can also get help about the current command, menu item, or tool by using one of these context-sensitive methods.

- For a command, enter '**help** or press F1 while a command is active.
- For a dialog box, choose the dialog box Help button or press F1.
- For a menu, highlight the menu item and then press F1.

Starting a Drawing

When you start AutoCAD, it creates a new unnamed drawing for you. You can either start drawing objects in this blank drawing or open an existing drawing.

If you open an existing drawing, all of the command and system variable settings last used on that drawing are restored because this information is saved in the drawing file.

When you start a new drawing, there are a few settings you will want to establish to assist you during the drawing process. The Setup Wizard will assist you automatically; however, you can change these basic settings at any time.

- *Units* determines the measuring units you will use to draw objects: feet and inches, millimeters, miles, furlongs, and so on.
- *Scale* determines the size of a unit when plotted on paper. In AutoCAD, you draw everything full scale in the units you set up, so you don't have to worry about scale until you're ready to plot your drawing.
- To help you visualize units, you can display an array of dots, called a *grid*, on your screen. The grid helps you visualize the size of units on your screen if you increase or decrease the magnification (zoom in or out) of your drawing.
- *Limits* indicate to AutoCAD where in the drawing area's infinite space you intend to draw. AutoCAD displays the grid only within these limits. Limits also control some viewing options.
- *Snap* enables you to locate and position points exactly on the grid or some subdivision of it. For example, you could display a grid with intervals of 4 millimeters but have points snap to exactly 1 millimeter, thus making it easier and faster to draw objects accurately.

Once you have established these basic settings, you may want to use them for subsequent new drawings. You can do this by saving the drawing as a *template drawing*. A template drawing is typically a blank drawing with preset settings that you use to start a new drawing.

Drawing Objects

To help you draw a variety of geometric shapes, AutoCAD has commands that create many different types of *objects*. The following illustration portrays some of the objects you can create and the name of the command that creates them.

lines

multilines

sketch

circles

donuts

arcs

splines

points

ellipses

rectangles

polygons

In addition to these simple geometric shapes, AutoCAD provides the following capabilities for creating more complex objects.

Drawing Objects

43

Polylines are complex multisegment lines that can contain both lines and arcs. You can control the width of individual segments in a polyline.

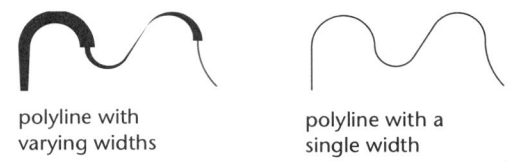

polyline with varying widths

polyline with a single width

Hatching fills an irregular area or object with a line pattern. The hatch can be associated with the object, so if you modify the object later, the hatching automatically adjusts. You can control the style, spacing, and angle of the hatch pattern.

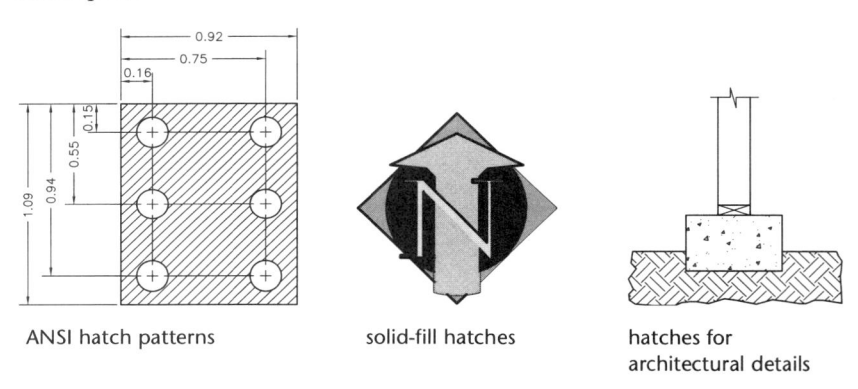

ANSI hatch patterns

solid-fill hatches

hatches for architectural details

Fills are similar to hatching except that the area is filled completely. A *region* is a unique object type with which you can create enclosed areas by adding, subtracting, or finding the difference between several objects. Regions provide an easy method to create complex enclosed areas for filling or hatching.

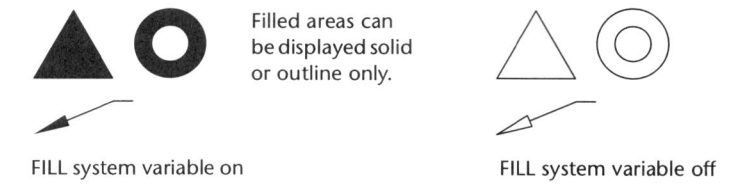

Filled areas can be displayed solid or outline only.

FILL system variable on

FILL system variable off

Introduction to AutoCAD

AutoCAD has several *text* creation and editing commands. Text can be created as a single line or as a paragraph. You can control the text style, font, size, angle, and properties. You can attach invisible (or visible) text to objects that describes the object. Such text is known as an *attribute* and can later be extracted into a list or report.

Different text styles in AutoCAD — romans
Different text styles in AutoCAD — script
Different text styles in AutoCAD — romand
Different text styles in AutoCAD — complex
𝔇ifferent text styles in AutoCAD — gothics

AutoCAD has extensive *dimensioning*, *leader*, and *tolerancing* capabilities. You can control every aspect of a dimension's appearance and behavior. Once you have created a custom dimension you can save it as a named dimension style. Like hatching, a dimension can also be associated with the object it is measuring. If the object changes, the dimension is automatically updated. Following are some examples of standard AutoCAD dimension types.

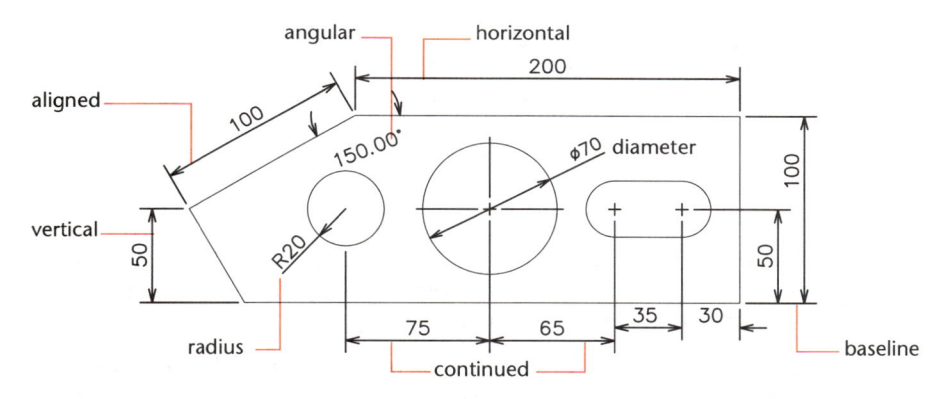

Undoing Mistakes

If you make a mistake while creating, editing, or viewing objects, you can almost always undo what you have done. You can undo only the last operation or undo several previous operations. And, if you undo too much, you can even undo the undo operation itself.

Drawing Accurately

In addition to grid and snap, AutoCAD has many tools that you can use to locate points and create objects accurately.

One method is to specify *coordinates*. All drawings are superimposed on an invisible grid, or *coordinate system*, with a horizontal X axis and a vertical Y axis. A single unit in the coordinate system represents the unit that you chose to use for drawing (an inch, millimeter, kilometer, and so on). You can establish grid and snap settings that match the units of the coordinate system or are some multiple or fraction of it.

As you draw, you can enter a coordinate to locate a point. For example, you can draw a line by starting it at the 0,0 location in the coordinate system and end it at the –4,2 location, as shown in the following figure.

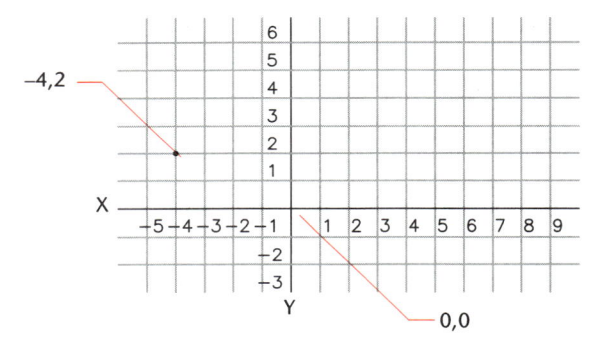

Point –4,2 is 4 units left on the X (horizontal) axis and 2 units up on the Y (vertical) axis.

Other types of coordinate entry are also available. A *relative coordinate* is entered as the X and Y distance from the last point you located, and a *polar coordinate* is entered as a distance and angle from the last point.

AutoCAD has a fixed coordinate system called the *World Coordinate System (WCS)* and a movable coordinate system known as the *user coordinate system (UCS)*. When you enter coordinates, you can specify which coordinate system you want to use.

To help you visualize the current location and orientation of the movable UCS, you can display the symbol known as the *UCS icon*. UCS icons in various orientations are shown in the following illustration.

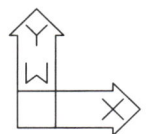

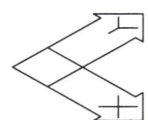

Introduction to AutoCAD

The other precision drawing tools you can use are *direct distance entry* and *tracking*. To use direct distance entry, you move your pointing device to indicate a direction, and then you enter a distance. With tracking, you locate a point relative to previous points instead of specifying its absolute position in the graphics area.

To gain accuracy without entering coordinates, you can set a snap interval, which will force the crosshair to jump, or "snap," to the interval you set. If you set the interval to 2, the crosshair snaps to points that are two units apart. Displaying a grid that matches, or is some multiple of, the snap value helps you see where the snap points are in your drawing.

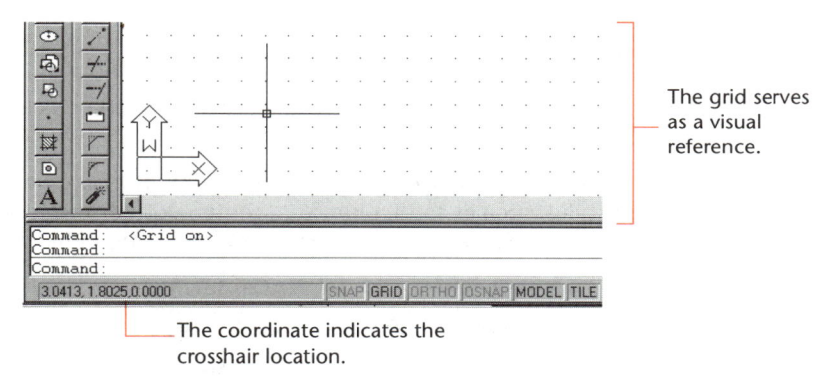

The grid serves as a visual reference.

The coordinate indicates the crosshair location.

You can also specify precise points by snapping to specific points on an existing object. For example, you can snap to the center point of a circle, the midpoint of a line, the intersection of two lines, and many other *object snap* options.

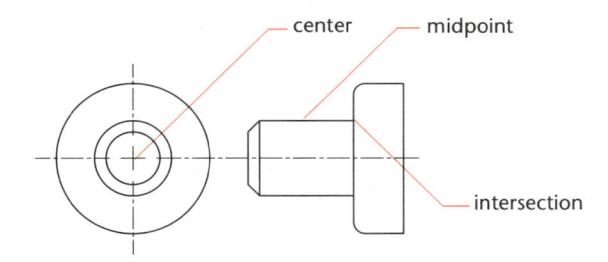

When you need to constrain lines to the horizontal and vertical axes, you can use the *Ortho* (orthogonal) tool.

Drawing Objects

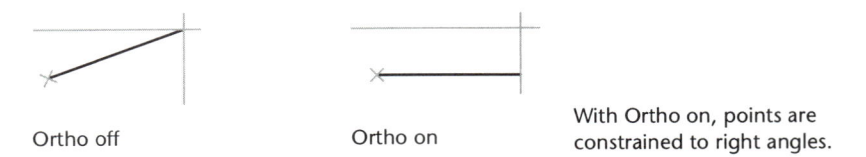

Ortho off   Ortho on   With Ortho on, points are constrained to right angles.

Another AutoCAD feature that can help you draw with precision is construction lines. Construction lines are not printed, so you never have to remove them from your drawing if you don't want to. A construction line passes through a point that you specify and is infinite in either one direction (called a *ray*) or both directions (called an *xline*).

Object Properties

There are certain properties that are associated with all objects that you create in AutoCAD.

The style of line, or *linetype*, that an object is drawn in can be set to many different styles, such as solid, phantom, center, dotted, and hidden. You can create your own dashed lines or more complex linetypes like the following.

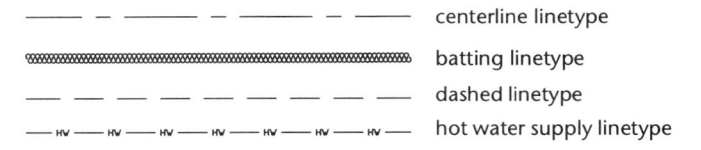

centerline linetype
batting linetype
dashed linetype
hot water supply linetype

You can set the *color* of objects you create to help you visually distinguish them. When you print or plot your drawing, you can map a color to a specific pen or line weight on the plotter. By standardizing a specific color scheme, you will know that objects displayed in a given color will have a heavier line weight when output to paper.

Layers in AutoCAD are equivalent to overlays in manual drafting. Layers provide an efficient way to organize drawing elements into logical groupings. You can name each layer and assign a color and linetype to it as dictated by industry, job, or company standards.

In addition to helping you organize your drawing, layers also give you greater control over the graphic display. You can turn off one or more layers to remove details as you work and then turn them on again when you plot.

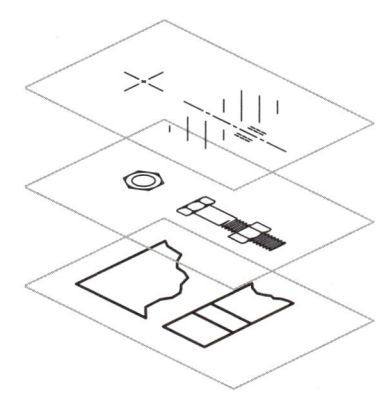

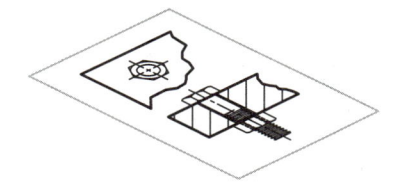

Turned-off layers hide details as you work.

All layers can be displayed when you need them.

Creating Standard Symbols

Most engineering and architectural drawings contain repetitive symbols. In AutoCAD, you create such symbols by combining several objects together into a single object called a *block*. The block can then be inserted into your drawing many times as a standard symbol. If you change the master *block definition*, all instances of the block, or *block references*, are automatically updated (unless you have modified a block reference in some way).

A block definition can be saved either with the current drawing or as a separate drawing file. If you want to insert the block into other drawings, you need to save the block as a separate drawing.

After you insert a block into your drawing, you can disassemble it to its individual components again by *exploding* it.

All or part of another drawing can be inserted or overlaid on your drawing by creating an *external reference*, or *xref*, to another drawing. An xref creates a pointer to another drawing but does not add that drawing's data to your drawing. Consequently, it does not significantly increase the size of your drawing file. The main advantage of using xrefs is that a single master drawing can be referenced by many drawings. When you modify the master, all the drawings that reference it are automatically updated.

Drawing Objects

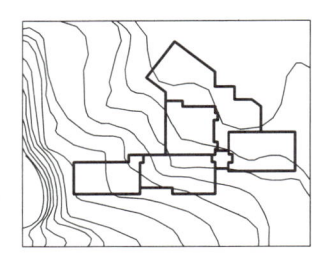

externally referenced drawing
inserted on topological view

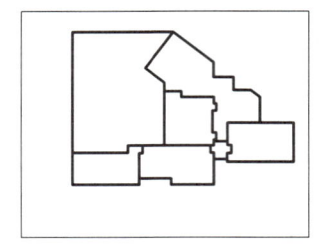

master drawing changed

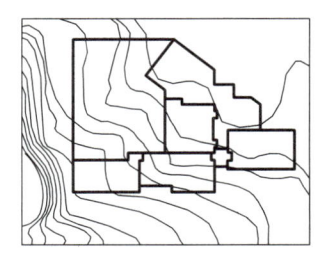

drawing with xref updated
automatically

Similar updating capabilities are available when you use Windows' object linking and embedding (OLE) to link a file from another application to your AutoCAD drawing. The inverse is also possible; you can insert all or part of an AutoCAD drawing into a file created by another application. For example, you might illustrate a document created by a word processor by embedding an AutoCAD drawing as an OLE object.

Viewing and Editing

Once you have created objects in your drawing, you can use AutoCAD's editing and viewing tools to modify objects and display your drawing in various ways.

Viewing Your Drawing

With AutoCAD you can change the magnification of the drawing on your screen. You can increase magnification (zoom in) for close-up work or decrease magnification (zoom out) to view the entire drawing.

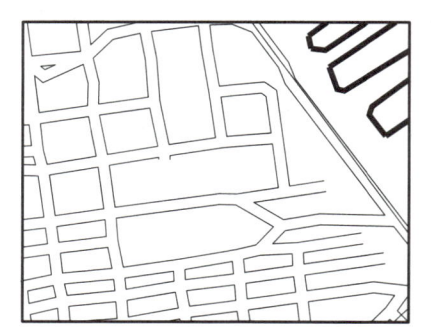

Zoom in for a close-up view . . .

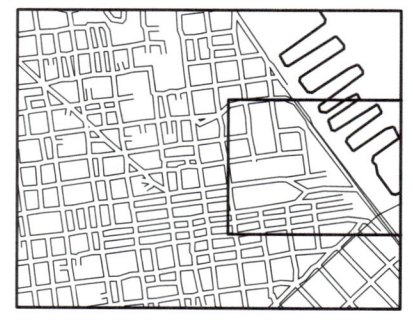

. . . or zoom out for an overview.

Introduction to AutoCAD

To view another section of your drawing, you can *pan* the drawing, which shifts the display without changing magnification. You can pan with the PAN command or with the scroll bars.

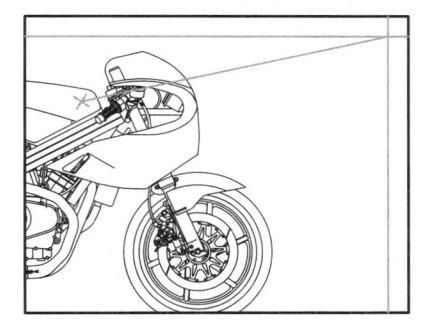

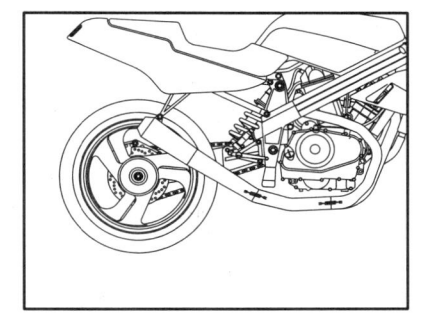

Indicate the direction and distance . . .   . . . to shift, or pan, the image.

You might have several views showing different areas of your drawing that you want to switch between. AutoCAD can "remember" a view by name so that you can recall it later.

You can view different parts of the drawing simultaneously by splitting the screen into stationary windows known as *tiled viewports*. You can control the drawing display in each tiled viewport independently by panning, zooming, or changing the viewing angle.

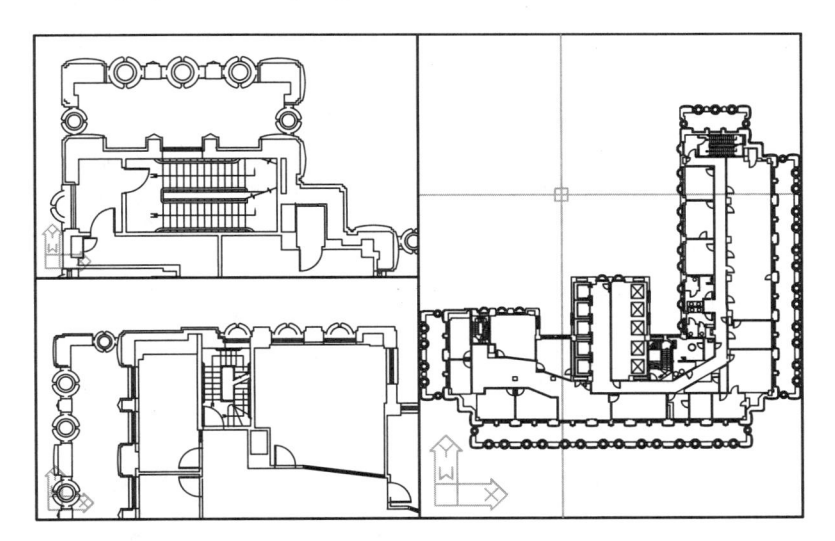

Different areas of the drawing can be at different scales in tiled viewports.

Viewing and Editing

Editing Your Drawing

After you create objects in your drawing, you will usually need to modify them in some way. AutoCAD provides a variety of editing tools that minimize the time it takes to make corrections.

Often, you may need to move an object to another location, align it with other objects, or change its rotation. The MOVE, ALIGN, and ROTATE commands provide this capability.

If you need to duplicate objects in your drawing, there are several ways to accomplish this. You can duplicate an object and place copies at multiple locations in your drawing. You can create a block and insert it multiple times. If you need a reverse copy of an object, you can create a mirror image. You can also create an array, which copies an object into an orthogonal or circular grid pattern.

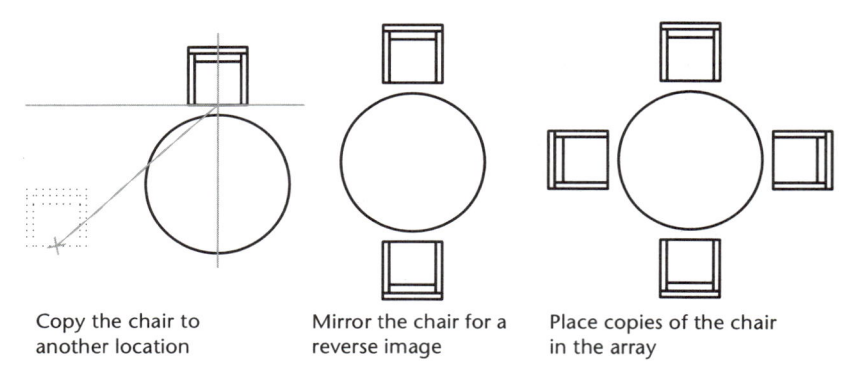

Copy the chair to another location

Mirror the chair for a reverse image

Place copies of the chair in the array

A capability similar to copying is the ability to offset an object. An offset is a copy of an object in which all of the line segments are copied a given distance from the original object.

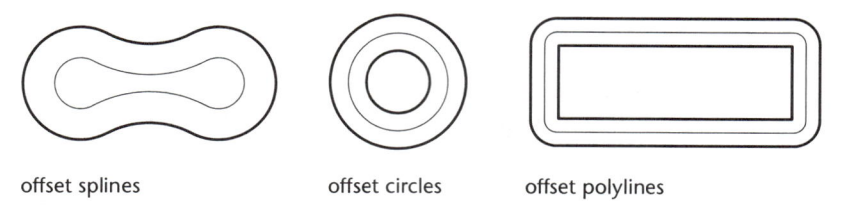

offset splines

offset circles

offset polylines

If you decide an object must be longer in one direction, you can *stretch* it. Another form of stretching can be performed on lines: you can *trim* or *extend* them to a specific length or until they intersect another object.

Introduction to AutoCAD

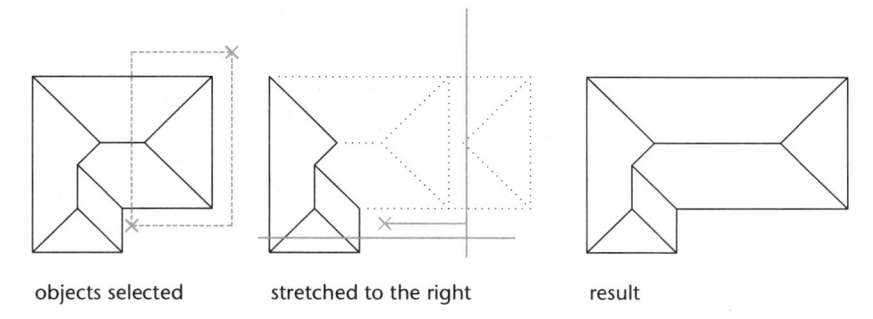

objects selected   stretched to the right   result

You can also move, copy, mirror, stretch, and rotate objects in a single operation using *grips*. This is done by selecting an object first (before entering a command) and then using the grips displayed and grip options to modify the object.

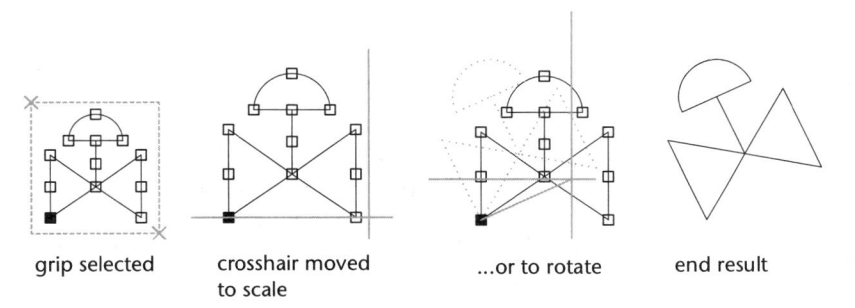

grip selected   crosshair moved to scale   ...or to rotate   end result

Another way you can edit objects is to *chamfer* (bevel) or *fillet* (round) the intersection of lines and arcs.

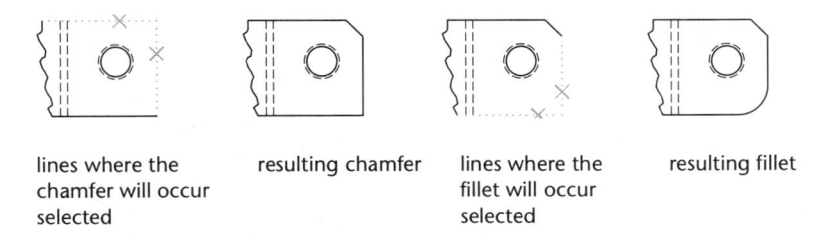

lines where the chamfer will occur selected   resulting chamfer   lines where the fillet will occur selected   resulting fillet

You can remove objects from your drawing at any time by *erasing* them.

Viewing and Editing

Looking Up Drawing Data

Your AutoCAD drawing contains many types of data that you can look up. You can *list* the properties of an existing object, like its color, layer, or linetype, and you can copy those properties and apply them to another object using the Match Properties command. You can calculate an area that you define or that is enclosed by an object. The distance and angle of a line or points can be also be calculated.

Preparing Your Drawing for Plotting

The last step in completing a drawing is printing or plotting it on paper. Before printing or plotting you may want to lay out several views of your drawing that will appear on the final plot.

Setting Up a Drawing Environment

AutoCAD provides two drawing environments for creating and laying out your drawing: *model space* and *paper space*. You usually create your drawing, called a model, at full scale in an area known as model space without regard to the final layout or size when you plot it on paper. When you're ready to print, you can arrange the elements of your drawing on your "sheet of paper" in paper space. Conceptually, paper space represents the paper on which you plot.

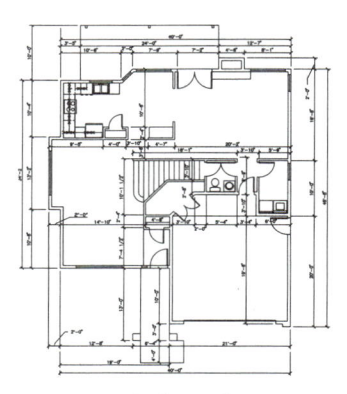

You create the basic drawing, or model, in a drawing area known as model space.

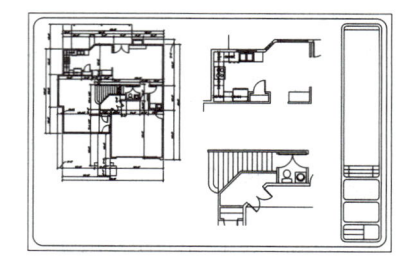

When you're ready to print, you can arrange different views and details of the model in paper space.

In model space and paper space, you can configure the graphics area of your screen into one or more viewing areas known as *floating viewports*. A viewport can display a view of your drawing at any scale and from any vantage point. In paper space, you can move these viewports to create the layout you want for plotting.

Printing or Plotting Your Drawing

You can output your drawing to either a printer or a plotter. If you are using a Windows system printer you generally don't need to do any preparation to print. When you use a plotter, however, you need to configure several things: the plotter driver, output ports, pen configuration, and so forth.

When you print or plot, you can control the area of the drawing that you are plotting and its scale, rotation, and location on the paper. You can also control the pens that are used to plot objects drawn in each color and the weight of the line. Linetypes can also be substituted at the time of plotting.

Advanced Features

As you gain experience, you can take advantage of AutoCAD's many advanced features to further enhance your designs.

3D Modeling

Most of the functions described earlier in this chapter apply to creating two-dimensional (2D) drawings. But AutoCAD is also a three-dimensional (3D) modeling tool.

3D coordinates can be specified by entering their *X, Y,* and *Z* components. Spherical and cylindrical coordinate systems can be used in addition to the relative and polar coordinates mentioned earlier. The UCS can be positioned anywhere in 3D space.

AutoCAD's 3D objects include wireframes, meshes, solids, and 3D polylines. AutoCAD's 2D objects (such as circles, rectangles, and so on) can be drawn on a plane that can be positioned anywhere in 3D space.

Most of AutoCAD's editing tools also work in 3D. For example, you can move, copy, mirror, trim, extend, and create 3D arrays.

Three-dimensional models can be rendered in AutoCAD to create shaded or hidden line images. You can apply materials to your rendered models and define light sources to obtain the shading you want.

Raster Images

You can import raster files into your AutoCAD drawing as unique object types. Raster images can be copied, moved, rotated, resized, and clipped. You can also adjust the image color, contrast, brightness, transparency, and more.

Database Support

AutoCAD supports Structured Query Language (SQL) so you can link objects in your drawing to information in an external database created with applications such as dBase III, Informix, ORACLE, or Paradox. With AutoCAD SQL Environment (ASE) commands, you can link data to objects, execute database queries, create new database files, and generate reports.

Internet Features

Using the DWFOUT command, AutoCAD lets you share your designs over the World Wide Web by saving them in AutoCAD's Drawing Web Format (DWF). Using a Web browser and the *WHIP!* plug-in, you can view DWF files directly or while they are embedded in a Web (HTML) page. The new BROWSER command lets you launch Netscape Navigator or Microsoft Internet Explorer from within AutoCAD.

The AutoCAD Internet Utilities let you open, insert, and save drawings from anywhere on the Web. You can also embed URLs (Universal Resource Locators) into your AutoCAD drawings to provide hyperlinks to other Web pages. For more information, see *Internet Utilities* in the *Command Reference* (online only).

Customizing and Programming

One of AutoCAD's strengths is its open architecture. You can customize virtually any aspect of AutoCAD. In addition, AutoCAD supports several programming languages, which you can use to add additional functionality for your specific application.

Customizing

You can add, remove, or modify the menus and toolbars that are provided with AutoCAD. You can also alter or add to AutoCAD's fonts, shapes, linetypes, and hatch patterns.

Programming

AutoCAD supports several programming languages, from simple scripts to a C++ interface.

A script is a series of AutoCAD commands in a text file that you run to carry out a repetitive task. With DIESEL (Direct Interpretively Evaluated String Expression Language), you can alter the AutoCAD status line. It can also be used in menus as a macro language.

AutoLISP is a full-featured interpretive programming language from which you can call AutoCAD commands, system variables, and dialog boxes. AutoLISP is the programming language of choice for users who are doing simple programming or just starting to program AutoCAD because it doesn't require a compiler. You can use AutoLISP in conjunction with the DCL (Dialog Control Language) to create your own dialog boxes.

AutoCAD's C++ language interface is called ARX (AutoCAD Runtime Extension). Information on ARX is distributed as part of the Autodesk Developer Network (ADN) and is not included in this documentation set.

Getting Started

This chapter describes the fundamentals that you need to know to use AutoCAD. It explains how to set up the drawing environment and work effectively in that environment.

In this chapter

- Installing and starting AutoCAD
- Accessing information on the Help menu
- Understanding the AutoCAD interface
- Using commands and system variables
- Modifying the drawing environment
- Opening, saving, and exiting drawings

Checking System Requirements

To run AutoCAD on Windows NT or Windows 95, the following minimum software and hardware are required:

- Windows NT 3.51/4.0 or Windows 95
  It is recommended that you install and run your copy of AutoCAD on an operating system in the same language as your AutoCAD software or on an English version of one of the supported operating systems.
- Intel 486 or Pentium processor or compatible
- 32 MB of RAM — Windows 95
- 32 MB of RAM — Windows NT
- 50 MB of hard disk space
- 64 MB of disk swap space
- 10 MB of additional RAM for each concurrent session
- 2.5 MB of free disk space during installation only (this space is used for temporary files that are removed when installation is complete)
- Windows NT 3.51 *only*: Service Pack 4 or 5 if you install Internet Utilities with the custom or full installation method

NOTE An additional 8 MB to 15 MB of space may be required for files installed in the system folder. This doesn't need to be on the same drive as the program folder where you load AutoCAD.

- CD-ROM drive
- 640 × 480 VGA video display (1024 × 768 recommended)
- Windows-supported display adapter
- Mouse or other pointing device
- For international single-users and student locked versions *only*: IBM-compatible parallel port and hardware lock

For a more detailed listing of system requirements, see the *Installation Guide*.

Installing AutoCAD

When you install AutoCAD, a setup program guides you through the process. The program transfers files from the CD to a folder that it creates on your hard disk. The following procedure describes a typical single-user installation. As you install the program, AutoCAD automatically configures your system to use the Windows system pointing device and the WHIP display driver. To reconfigure your system, select Preferences from the Tools menu and select the tabs that apply to your changes. For a more detailed installation and configuration procedure, see the *Installation Guide*.

To install AutoCAD as a single user

1 Insert the CD into the CD-ROM drive.

   If you are running Windows NT 4.0 or Windows 95, Autorun begins the installation process as soon as you insert the CD unless you hold down the SHIFT key while you insert the CD.

2 If you are running Windows NT 3.51 or you have turned off Autorun, choose one of the following to run the setup program.

Windows NT 3.51	From the File menu, choose Run, designate the CD-ROM drive, enter the path name, and then enter **setup**.
Windows 95 or NT 4.0	Click Start on the taskbar, choose Run, designate the CD-ROM drive, enter the path name, and then enter **setup**.

3 When the Welcome screen is displayed, choose Next.

4 The Software License Agreement dialog box presents information for you to review. If you accept the terms of the agreement, choose Yes.

   If you do not accept the terms of the agreement, choose No to cancel the installation program.

5 In the Serial Number dialog box, enter the serial number on your AutoCAD Release 14 CD. Then choose Next.

6 In the Personal Information dialog box, enter your name, your organization's name, and your dealer's name and telephone number. Then choose Next.

   The Personal Information dialog box is displayed with the information you entered. Choose Back to correct or change any of the information you entered. Choose Next to proceed.

7 In the Destination Location dialog box, specify a drive and directory for AutoCAD. Then choose Next.

   You can accept the default or choose Browse to specify a different location. If you specify a directory that doesn't exist, the install program creates it.

8   In the Setup Type dialog box, select Typical.

    The following files are installed:

    - Executables and support files
    - US dictionary
    - Fonts
    - Sample drawings and LISP routines
    - ASE files
    - Peripheral drivers
    - Learning tools
    - Online documentation

9   In the Folder Name dialog box, specify a folder for AutoCAD. Then choose Next.

    The Setup Confirmation dialog box prompts you to verify the setup type, destination directory, and program folder. Choose Next to start the installation.

    When the installation is complete, you are prompted to view the *Readme* file. This online help document provides information that was not available at the time of the printing of this guide. You can read the *Readme* file at any time by choosing it from the Help menu.

Starting AutoCAD

You can start AutoCAD by using the following procedures.

To start AutoCAD

1   Perform one of the following steps, depending upon which platform you are running:

    | Windows 95 and NT 4.0 | On the taskbar, click Start, and then choose Programs. Choose AutoCAD from the menu. |
    | Windows NT 3.1 | From the Windows NT Program Manager, double-click the AutoCAD icon. |

2   In the Create New Drawing dialog box, make one of the following choices to set up a new drawing:

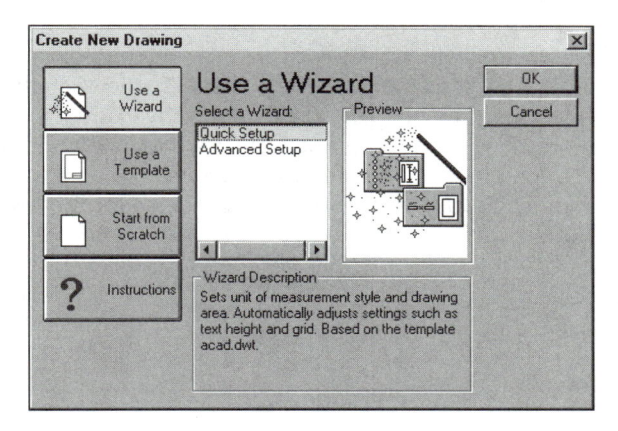

- Choose Use a Wizard. Under Select a Wizard, choose Quick Setup or Advanced Setup to use AutoCAD's automatic setup features.
- Choose Use a Template, and then choose a template to establish your drawing settings.
- Choose Start from Scratch and select one of the two measurement systems.

You can control whether the Create New Drawing dialog box is displayed. To suppress the display of all dialog boxes, set the FILEDIA system variable to 0.

Accessing Information from the Help Menu

At any time during an AutoCAD session, you can access online information from the Help menu. Use Help topics for assistance as you work. For more information about using about the AutoCAD documentation suite, see the following section, "Online Documentation."

To access Help topics

- From the Help menu, choose AutoCAD Help Topics.

Command line HELP

Related Press F1 or enter **?** on the command line.

Online Documentation

All of the AutoCAD manuals are available online. To view a manual from the Help menu, choose AutoCAD Help Topics. From the Contents tab, select the manual you want to view. Each manual contains a table of contents in which you can search for a specific section or topic. When you are in a particular section, you can click any underlined word to search for related documentation.

For more detailed information about using the online documentation, see "Using Help" in the online Help Topics.

Pointing Devices

You can control AutoCAD with a wide range of pointing devices. You can specify points either by clicking the pointing device or by entering coordinates from a keyboard. A pointing device, such as a mouse or a digitizing puck, may have a number of buttons. The first 10 buttons are automatically assigned by AutoCAD, but you can reassign all but the pick button by modifying the menu file.

Using the Mouse

You can choose menu options and tools by clicking them with a mouse. You also can use the mouse to draw or to select objects on the screen.

On a two-button mouse, the left button is the pick button, used to specify points on the screen. The right button is the return button. Pressing the return button is equivalent to pressing ENTER. If you hold down SHIFT and click the right mouse button, a cursor menu is displayed. (With a three-button mouse, you open the cursor menu by clicking the middle button.) In some situations, the right button has a special function. For example, you can customize the tools in the toolbar after clicking them with the right mouse button.

To practice using the mouse

1 Move your mouse and notice how the pointer on the screen changes from crosshairs while the pointer is in the graphics area, to an arrow when it's *not* in the graphics area, and to an I-beam when it's in the text window or on the command line.

2 As you continue to move the mouse, notice how the numbers change in the coordinate display on the status bar. These numbers indicate the exact loca-

tion, or coordinate, of the crosshairs on the screen.

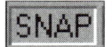

```
Command:
NEW
Command:
0.6935, 5.8754,0.0000        SNAP GRID ORTHO OSNAP MODEL TILE
```

SNAP   **3**   Find Snap on the status bar and double-click it with the pick button on your mouse (usually the left button). Notice that Snap darkens to indicate that Snap mode has been turned on.

Move the pointer around the screen and observe how it seems to adhere, or "snap," to points at predetermined and equivalent intervals on the screen. You can change these intervals.

4 Double-click Snap on the status bar again to turn Snap mode off.

5 Move the pointer over the Standard toolbar at the top of the graphics area. As you leave the cursor over a tool icon for a few moments, notice a pop-up label, called a tooltip, that identifies the tool.

6 Move the pointer over the panel at the top of the toolbar labeled Draw. Then, as you hold down the pick button, drag the toolbar around the screen.

Using the Tablet

You can use a digitizing tablet to select frequently used commands, to select objects on the screen, or to draw. The tablet's pointing device, which you use for selection, can be a *puck* or a *stylus*. The crosshairs on the screen follow the movement of the pointing device in the graphics area of the tablet.

You can also use a tablet to digitize drawings by tracing objects into the AutoCAD drawing database using coordinates that relate to the original drawing. For example, if you are working with a printed circuit design that was originally prepared by hand, you can now store and edit that drawing in AutoCAD.

To digitize a drawing, you *calibrate*, or align, the tablet with the paper drawing's coordinate system. If the paper drawing is too big to fit on the tablet, you can enter the drawing in pieces, making sure to align each piece. AutoCAD has a special input mode called Tablet mode. Tablet mode differs from digitizer mode in that the active area of your tablet coincides with the current display window. In the digitizer mode, an area of your tablet coincides with specific coordinates in your drawing; the portion of your drawing that you are currently viewing is irrelevant. The TABMODE system variable turns Tablet mode on and off. For more information about calibrating tablets, see chapter 6, "Configuring a Digitizer" in the *Installation Guide*.

Any command that requires you to select objects with the pointing device works in Tablet mode. For example, to erase an object, start the ERASE command and move the tablet pointing device until the pickbox is over the object. For more information about calibrating the tablet, see TABLET in the *Command Reference*.

Understanding the AutoCAD Interface

When you first start AutoCAD, the initial screen contains the menu bar at the top, the status bar at the bottom, the drawing window, the command window, and several toolbars. Toolbars contain icons that represent commands.

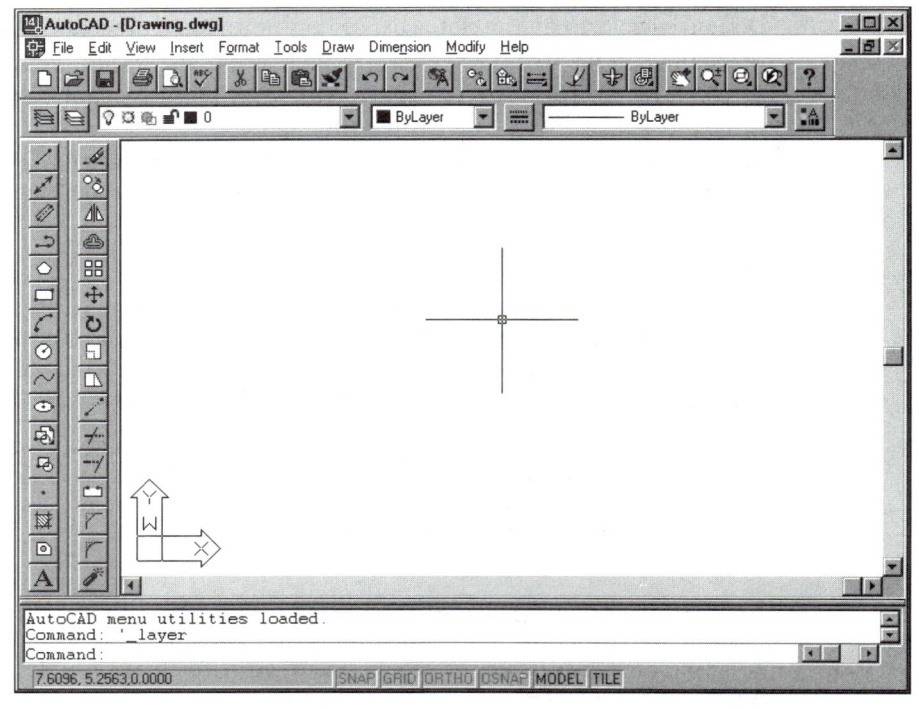

The menu bar contains the menus. The status bar displays the cursor coordinates and the status of modes such as Grid and Snap. Mode names are always visible in the status bar as selectable buttons. Double-click Snap, Grid, or Ortho to turn it on.

Toolbars

Toolbars contain tools, represented by icons, that start commands. When you move the pointing device over a tool, a tooltip displays the name of the tool. Tool icons with a small black triangle in the lower-right corner have fly-outs that contain related commands. With the cursor over the tool icon, hold the pick button down until the flyout is displayed.

The UCS flyout

The Standard toolbar at the top of the graphics area is visible by default. It contains frequently used AutoCAD tools such as Redraw, Undo, and Zoom, as well as Microsoft Office standard tools such as Open, Save, Print, and Spell Check. You can display multiple toolbars on screen at once, change their contents, and resize them.

To display a toolbar

1 From the View menu, choose Toolbars.

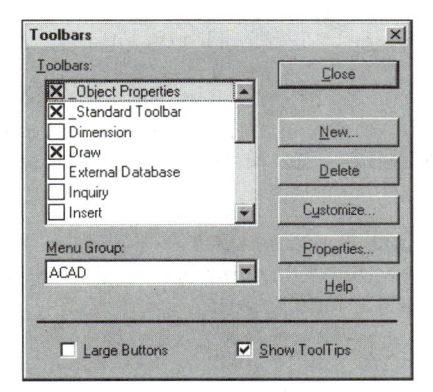

2 Click the box beside the name of the toolbar you want to display.

You can "dock" or "float" a toolbar. A docked toolbar attaches to any edge of the graphics area. You can drag a floating toolbar anywhere on your computer screen, and it can be resized. A docked toolbar cannot be resized and does not overlap the drawing window.

Understanding the AutoCAD Interface

67

To dock or undock a toolbar

1 To dock a toolbar, position the cursor on the background or name of the toolbar, and press the pick button on your pointing device.
2 Drag the toolbar to a dock location at the top, bottom, or either side of the drawing window.
3 When the outline of the toolbar appears in the docking area, release the pick button.
4 To undock a toolbar, drag and drop it outside the docking region.
5 To place a toolbar in a docking region without docking it, hold down CTRL as you drag.

To close a toolbar

1 If the toolbar is docked, drag it to an undocked location in the graphics area.
2 Click the Close button in the upper-left corner of the toolbar.

Menus

The menus are available from the menu bar at the top of the AutoCAD window. You can choose menu options in one of the following ways:

- After you click the menu name to display a list of options, click the option to choose it.
- Hold down ALT and then enter the underlined letter in the menu name. For example, to open a new drawing, hold down ALT while pressing F (ALT+F) to open the File menu. Then press ENTER to choose the highlighted New option.

The default menu file is *acad.mnu*. You can specify a different menu (for example, a menu you have customized) in the Preferences dialog box by using the PREFERENCES or MENU commands.

Cursor Menu

The cursor menu is displayed at your cursor location when you hold down SHIFT while pressing the return button on the pointing device. On a two-button mouse, the return button is usually the right button. On a three-button mouse, you can use the middle button to display the cursor menu.

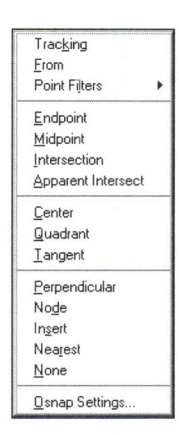

```
Tracking
From
Point Filters      ▶

Endpoint
Midpoint
Intersection
Apparent Intersect

Center
Quadrant
Tangent

Perpendicular
Node
Insert
Nearest
None

Osnap Settings...
```

The default cursor menu lists object snap modes and tracking. If you want to change the options, you can customize the cursor menu.

The Command Window

The command window is a dockable window in which you enter commands and AutoCAD displays prompts and messages. For most commands, a command line with two or three lines of previous prompts, called the command history, is sufficient. For commands with text output, such as LIST, you might need to make the command window larger. Press F2 to display the text screen so that you can view more of the command history. Once there is more than one line of command history, you can scroll through it with scroll bars.

By default, the command window is docked and is the width of the AutoCAD window. If text that is entered becomes longer than the width of the command line, the window pops up in front of the command line to show the full text of the line.

You can resize the window vertically using the splitter bar, which is located on the top edge of the window when the window is docked on the bottom and on the bottom edge when it's docked on the top. Resize by grabbing the splitter bar with your pointing device and dragging the window to the required height.

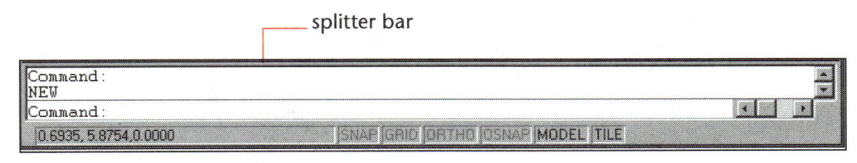

— splitter bar

```
Command:
NEW
Command:
0.6935, 5.8754,0.0000         SNAP GRID ORTHO OSNAP MODEL TILE
```

Docked command window

Understanding the AutoCAD Interface

69

To permanently resize the window so that more of the command history is showing, change the default value on the Display tab in the Preferences dialog box (see "Setting Text Window Preferences" on page 71).

Undock the command window by selecting any part of its border and dragging it away from the docking region. Drop the window to make it a floating window. When you undock the window, the floating window is the size it was the last time you undocked it. You can move the floating command window anywhere on the screen and resize its width and height with the pointing device.

Floating command window

Dock the command window by dragging it until it is over the top or bottom docking regions of the AutoCAD window.

The Text Window

The text window is similar to the command window in which you enter commands and view prompts and messages. Unlike the command window, the text window contains a complete command history for the current AutoCAD session. Use the text window to view lengthy output of commands such as LIST, which displays detailed information about objects you select.

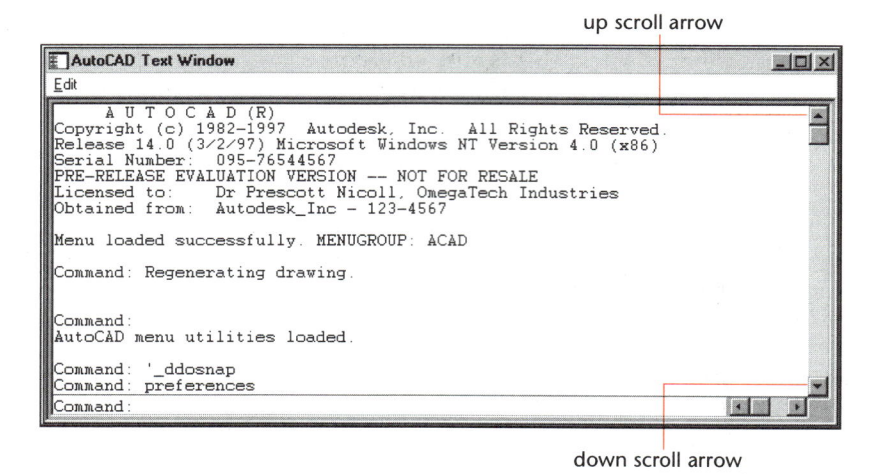

up scroll arrow

down scroll arrow

Chapter 1   Getting Started

To display the text window while you are in the graphics area, press F2. The text window is displayed in front of the graphics area. If you press F2 while in the text window, the graphics area is redisplayed. If either the graphics area or the text window has been minimized, press F2 to display it at its last configured size. The F2 key functions as a toggle only if both the graphics window and the text window are open.

Navigating in the Text Window

You can view previous command lines in the text window. Identical text input several times in succession is displayed only once. To view the window's contents, use the scrollbar or the keys in the following table.

Text window and command window navigation

Key	Action
LEFT ARROW	Moves cursor to the left
RIGHT ARROW	Moves cursor to the right
UP ARROW	Moves the cursor up one line
DOWN ARROW	Moves the cursor down one line
PAGE UP	Moves to the previous window
PAGE DOWN	Moves to the next window
HOME	Places cursor at the beginning of the line
END	Places cursor at the end of the line
CTRL+V	Pastes text from the Clipboard

Setting Text Window Preferences

You can change the size of the text window, toggle beeps to indicate errors, and set certain accelerator keys to conform to Microsoft Windows or AutoCAD conventions.

To set up the command line and text windows

1 From the Tools menu, choose Preferences.

2 To define the number of lines of text to display in the docked command line window, choose the Display tab and enter a value.

3   To reassign accelerator keys (such as CTRL+X, CTRL+V, and CTRL+C) to be compatible with Windows or with AutoCAD, choose the Compatibility tab and select the appropriate option.

4   To turn beeping on or off for text window navigation, choose the General tab and then select or clear Beep On Error in User Input.

Command line   PREFERENCES

Accessing Commands

You can access AutoCAD commands by selecting them from menus, toolbars, or the cursor menu or by entering commands on the command line. The following sections contain more detailed information on using these methods.

Using a Toolbar

You can start a command by choosing a tool from a toolbar and then choosing options in a dialog box or responding to the prompts displayed on the command line. In the following procedure, you draw a line by first choosing a tool.

To use a tool from a toolbar to draw a line

1   From the Draw toolbar, choose

Notice that the command line now displays a prompt:

From point:

The prompt directs you to the next step. In this case, AutoCAD is asking you to indicate where you want to start the line.

2   Click anywhere in the graphics area to specify a point location.

The prompt changes:

To point:

3   Move your pointing device and click anywhere else in the graphics area to indicate the endpoint of the line.

4   Create a second segment of the line by moving the pointing device and clicking once again.

5   Press the return button on your pointing device (usually the right button on a mouse) to end the command.

You have drawn two line segments.

Using a Menu

You can start many commands by choosing them from a menu. In the following steps, you draw a circle. In addition, you specify an object snap that places the center point of the circle at the endpoint of one of the lines you have drawn.

To use a command on a menu to draw a circle

1 To create a line, follow the steps in the preceding procedure.

2 Move the cursor to the menu bar and choose the Draw menu by clicking Draw.

A menu lists the Draw menu options.

3 Click Circle. When a second menu is displayed, choose Center, Radius to indicate which input preference to use.

The command line now lists several options. The option in angle brackets, Center Point, is the current choice.

4 To place the circle's center point exactly at the end of one of the lines you drew, press SHIFT while pressing the return button on the pointing device. From the cursor menu, select Endpoint.

The box that appears at the intersection of the crosshairs indicates that an object snap has been specified.

5 Click on either of the lines that you have drawn.

The center point of the circle snaps to the endpoint of the line nearest the point you specified.

6 As you move the cursor, notice that the circle expands and contracts. To complete the circle, either enter a value for the radius on the command line or click to specify another point.

Using the Command Line

When you enter commands on the command line, AutoCAD displays either a set of options or a dialog box. For example, when you enter **circle** at the Command prompt, the following prompt is displayed.

3P/2P/TTR/<Center point>:

The brackets around Center Point indicate that it is the current option. You can choose the Center Point option either by entering an *X,Y* coordinate or by selecting (clicking) a point on the screen.

Accessing Commands

73

To choose a different option, enter the capitalized letters of the option name. You can enter uppercase or lowercase letters. For example, to choose the three-point option (3P), enter **3p**.

> **NOTE** To execute commands, press SPACEBAR, ENTER, or the return button on your pointing device after entering command names or responses to prompts. This guide does not specifically instruct you to press ENTER after each entry you make on the command line.

You can run any command by entering its full name at the Command prompt. Some commands also have abbreviated names. Instead of entering **circle** to start the CIRCLE command, for example, you can enter **c**. Abbvreviated command names are called aliases, and are defined in the *acad.pgp* file.

Changing Command Line Text

You can delete text on the command line by using either BACKSPACE or DEL. You can paste text from the Clipboard, but you cannot select text to cut or copy to the Clipboard. Use the keys in the following table to navigate or change text on the command line.

Command line navigation

Key	Action
LEFT ARROW	Moves cursor back (to the left)
RIGHT ARROW	Moves cursor forward (to the right)
UP ARROW	Displays the previous line in the command history
DOWN ARROW	Displays the next line in the command history
HOME	Places cursor at the beginning of the line
END	Places cursor at the end of the line
INS	Turns insertion mode and off
DEL	Deletes the character to the right of the cursor
BACKSPACE	Deletes the character to the left of the cursor
ENTER	Moves cursor to the end of the line and terminates the command
CTRL+V	Pastes text from the Clipboard

Copying Text to the Command Line

You can enter text on the command line by copying it from the text window (or elsewhere). Select the text you want to use, choose Copy from the text window cursor menu or the Edit menu, and then paste it to the AutoCAD command line. Use the pointing device to select the text in the text window, or use the keys in the following table.

Text window or command window navigation	
Keys	Select text from...
SHIFT+RIGHT ARROW	First cursor position to the last cursor position
SHIFT+LEFT ARROW	First cursor position to the last cursor position
SHIFT+END	Cursor to the end of the line
SHIFT+HOME	Cursor to the beginning of the line
CTRL+SHIFT+END	Cursor to the end of the window
CTRL+SHIFT+HOME	Cursor to the beginning of the window
CTRL+SHIFT+PGUP	Cursor through the preceding screen of text
CTRL+SHIFT+PGDN	Cursor through the next screen of text

NOTE The contents of the text window are read-only and cannot be modified.

Repeating and Canceling Commands

If you want to repeat a command that you have just used, press ENTER, SPACEBAR, or the return button on your pointing device at the Command prompt. You also can repeat a command by entering **multiple** on the command line before the command name, separated by a space, as shown in the following example.

Command: **multiple circle**

The default method for canceling any command is to press ESC, but it can be changed to CTRL+C by changing settings in the Preferences dialog box. For information about undoing the previous action, see "Correcting Mistakes" on page 80.

If you want to reissue a command you used during the current AutoCAD session, you can access it in the command history above the command line.

Accessing Commands

Use the navigation keys as described in "Navigating in the Text Window" on page 71.

The command history displays user-input lines that contain spaces, such as AutoLISP expressions, or command options that accept text strings, such as GROUP descriptions or ATTDEF attribute values. AutoCAD interprets the first space on the command line as a line terminator unless it is part of an AutoLISP command (enclosed in parentheses) or part of a text string.

To prevent invalid commands contained in the text from generating error messages and causing subsequent dependent commands to fail, recalled history lines are not displayed at the Command prompt unless the text line is an AutoLISP expression, that is, begins with a parenthesis, or the text line begins with a double quotation mark ("). However, if you scroll up or down through the history list while a command is active, text lines with spaces are displayed. This allows repetitive input of text strings in commands that accept textual input.

To repeat any command used in the current session

1 Activate the text window by pressing F2 or by clicking above the command line (in the history area).
2 Locate the line containing the command you want to issue by pressing UP ARROW or DOWN ARROW.
3 After locating the command, press ENTER.

If you press the return button on the pointing device while the cursor is over the command window or the text window, the cursor menu is displayed.

The Preferences option is not available if a command is active.

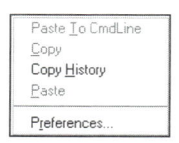

```
Paste To CmdLine
Copy
Copy History
Paste
Preferences...
```

Using Commands Transparently

Many commands can be used transparently, which means they can be entered on the command line while you are using another command. Transparent commands frequently are commands that change drawing settings or that turn on drawing aids such as SNAP, GRID, or ZOOM.

To use a command transparently, enter an apostrophe (') before choosing a tool or entering the command at any prompt. On the command line, double angle brackets (>>) precede prompts for transparent commands. After you complete the transparent command, the original command resumes. For example, to turn on the grid and set it to one-unit intervals while you are drawing a line, enter the following.

Command: **line**
From point: **'grid**
>>Grid spacing (X) or ON/OFF/Snap/Aspect <0.000>:   **1**
Resuming LINE command
From point: *Continue drawing the line*

Commands that do *not* select objects, create new objects, cause regenerations, or end the drawing session can be used transparently. Changes made in dialog boxes that have been opened transparently cannot take effect until the interrupted command has been executed. Similarly, if you reset a system variable transparently, the new value cannot take effect until you start the next command.

Some commands, such as DVIEW, cannot be used transparently.

Using Long File Names

Both Windows 95 and NT support long file names. These names can contain up to 255 characters and can contain embedded spaces and punctuation: for example, *summer home.dwg* and *test file*.

Because a block name cannot include spaces, when you insert or externally reference a drawing that uses a long file name, specify the block name using quotation marks, as follows:

blockname="filename"

You must use the double quotation marks (" "). For example, enter the following to assign *summer home.dwg* to the xref (external reference) *house:*

Xref to attach: **house="summer home.dwg"**

You *cannot* select the file from a file list in a dialog box, because the name of the block definition is taken from the file name and does not include the necessary quotation marks.

Switching from Dialog Box to Command Line

Some functions are available both on the command line and in a dialog box. In many cases, you can enter a hyphen before the command to suppress the dialog box and display prompts on the command line instead. For example, entering **layer** at the command line displays the Layer & Linetype dialog box, in which you can define layer and linetype properties. Entering **-layer** at the command line displays the equivalent command line options for defining layer and linetype properties.

> **NOTE** There may be slight differences between the options in the dialog box and those available on the command line.

The CMDDIA system variable controls the display of dialog boxes used for plotting. If CMDDIA is set to 1, dialog boxes are displayed when you use the PLOT command. If CMDDIA is set to 0, you use the command line.

The FILEDIA system variable controls the display of dialog boxes used with commands that read and write files. For example, if FILEDIA is set to 1, SAVEAS displays the Save Drawing As dialog box. If FILEDIA is set to 0, SAVEAS is displayed as prompts on the command line. The procedures in this guide assume that FILEDIA is set to 1 (dialog boxes). Even when FILEDIA is set to 0, you can display a file dialog box by entering a tilde (~) in response to the first prompt.

CMDDIA and FILEDIA are useful for turning off display of dialog boxes when you use scripts to run commands.

Using Scripts to Run Commands

A script is a series of AutoCAD commands in a text file that can be used to carry out a task. With scripts, you can run several commands in succession. For example, you can script a series of AutoCAD commands for overnight batch processing. You also can create a group of drawing display files known as slides and then write a script that displays them in a slide show. For slide shows, you can specify a delay in the running of the script, resume scripts that you have canceled, or stop a script and restart it at the beginning.

Editing Command or Text Window Text

You can copy text in the command history to the Windows Clipboard. You can also paste the contents of the Clipboard to the command line (see "Copying with the Clipboard" on page 255). If there are multiple lines of text on the Clipboard, only the first line is pasted. This prevents invalid commands contained in the text from generating error messages and causing subsequent dependent commands in the text to fail.

To copy text from the text window to the command line

1 From the command line, press F2 to display the text window, or click in the history window.
2 Highlight the text to be copied.
3 Position the cursor over the command window and right-click.
4 From the cursor menu, choose Paste to Command Line.

Text is copied to the Clipboard and pasted on the command line.

NOTE If there are multiple lines of text on the Clipboard, only the first line is pasted.

Related Use the COPYHIST command to copy all the text in the command history to the Clipboard.

Using System Variables

System variables are settings that control how certain commands work. They can turn on or off modes such as Snap, Grid, or Ortho. They can set default scales for hatch patterns. They can store information about the current drawing and AutoCAD's configuration. Sometimes you use a system variable to change a setting; sometimes you use a system variable to display the current status.

For example, the GRIDMODE system variable turns the dot grid display on and off. In this case, the GRIDMODE system variable is functionally equivalent to the GRID command. DATE is a read-only system variable that stores the current date. You can display this value, but you cannot change it.

You can examine or change a variable's setting transparently, that is, while using another command; however, new values may not take effect until the interrupted command ends. For a listing of system variables, see the *Command Reference*.

To change the setting of the GRIDMODE system variable

1 On the command line, enter **gridmode**.

   You can press ENTER to select the current value of the variable.

2 Enter **1** for on or **0** for off.

   Related   To see a complete list of system variables, enter **?** at the SETVAR Variable Name prompt, and press ENTER at the Variable(s) to List prompt.

Correcting Mistakes

With AutoCAD you can undo your most recent action or actions using any of several methods. The simplest is to use the U command to undo a single action.

To undo the most recent action

- From the Edit menu, choose Undo.

   Command line   U

   Related   Use OOPS to restore what you have just undone.

   With AutoCAD, you can backtrack your recent activities in several ways. For example, you can undo a specific number of actions.

To undo a specific number of actions

1 At the Command prompt, enter **undo**.

2 On the command line, enter the number of actions to undo.

   For example, to undo the last ten actions, enter **10**. AutoCAD displays the commands or system variable settings that were undone.

   Related   Use the Mark option of UNDO to mark an action as you work. You can then use the Back option of UNDO to undo all activities that occurred after the marked action. You also can use the Begin and End options of UNDO to undo actions you've defined as a group.

   To redo U or UNDO, you must use REDO immediately after using U or UNDO.

To redo an action

- From the Edit menu, choose Redo.

   Command line   REDO

Refreshing the Screen Display

You refresh the display to remove blips or temporary markers that indicate points you have specified. To refresh the drawing display, you can either redraw or regenerate. Because regeneration can take a long time in complex drawings, you will usually redraw. Redrawing cleans up only the display. Regenerating, however, not only cleans up the display, but also updates the drawing database with the screen coordinates for all objects in the drawing.

The database stores information about a drawing's objects as floating-point values. A floating-point format ensures a high level of precision, but it may make calculations time consuming. When AutoCAD regenerates an object, it converts the floating-point database values to the appropriate screen coordinates.

Some commands automatically regenerate the entire drawing and recompute the screen coordinates for all objects. When this happens, AutoCAD displays a message.

To redraw the screen

- From the View menu, choose Redraw.

Command line REDRAW

To regenerate a drawing

- From the View menu, choose Regen.

Command line REGEN

Modifying the AutoCAD Environment

You can change many of the settings that affect the AutoCAD interface and drawing environment in the Preferences dialog box. For example, you can establish how often AutoCAD automatically saves the drawing to a temporary file, and you can specify the support directories that contain the files that you use most often. Experiment with the settings in the Preferences dialog box until you find the best environment for your needs.

To change environment preferences

1 From the Tools menu, choose Preferences.

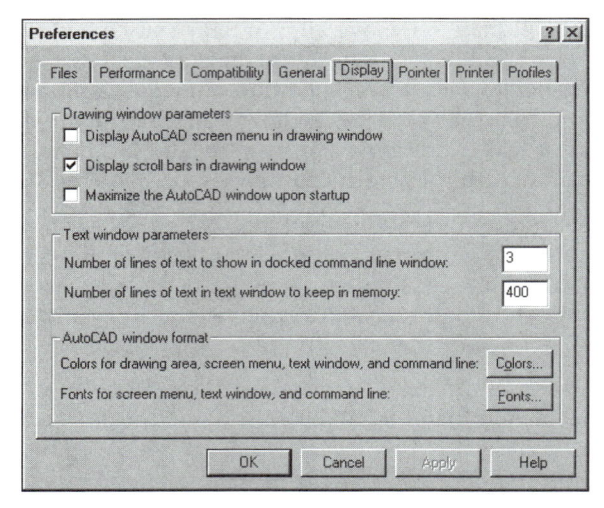

2 These are some of the settings you can change on the tabs in the Preferences dialog box:

- Screen colors, fonts, and text display
- Digitizer drivers and the input device type
- Location of temporary files
- Demand loading of external references
- Location of support and menu files

3 When you've finished setting preferences, choose OK.

Command line PREFERENCES

The following sections provide more information about the options in the Preferences dialog box.

Controlling Warnings

By using the Preferences dialog box, you can configure the user interface of AutoCAD. The Beep on Error in the User Input option controls whether AutoCAD issues a warning beep when you enter an unknown command or take an action that is not permitted.

Saving Your Drawing Automatically

If you turn on the automatic save option, AutoCAD saves your drawing at specified time intervals. To use this option, in the Preferences dialog box, choose the General tab and then select Automatic Save and enter the interval in minutes.

By default, files saved automatically are temporarily assigned the file name *acad.sv$*. If you want to use a different name, specify the name under Automatic Save File under Menu, Help, Log, and Miscellaneous File Names on the Files tab.

Selecting Colors for the AutoCAD Window

You can specify the colors used by the AutoCAD Window to suit your personal taste. You can change the color of the graphics area, the text window background, the text in the graphics area or text window, and the crosshairs.

To customize AutoCAD colors

1 From the Tools menu, choose Preferences.
2 In the Preferences dialog box, choose the Display tab.
3 On the Display tab, choose Colors.

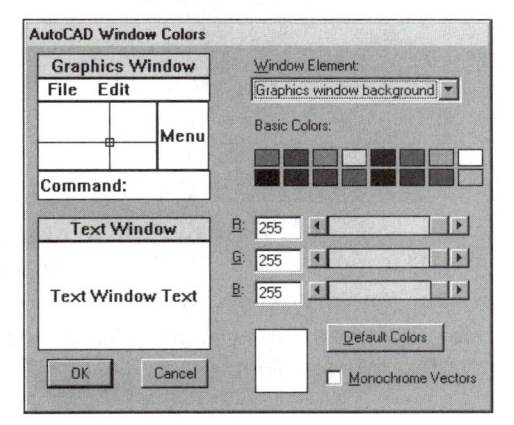

If you have a monochrome display, Monochrome Vectors already is selected.

4 Select the item you want to change from the Window Element list.
5 Under Basic Colors, select the color you want to use. To change the color using the RGB (red, green, blue) colors, drag the slider controls next to R, G, and B or enter a number from 0 through 255.

Modifying the AutoCAD Environment

83

6   If you want to revert to the colors specified by the Windows Control Panel, choose Default Colors.

7   Choose OK.

Selecting Fonts for AutoCAD

You can change the fonts used in the AutoCAD graphics window and in the text window. This setting does not affect the text in your drawings.

NOTE If you have a low-resolution monitor, changing the fonts in the AutoCAD graphics window is one method to create more space for displaying more buttons on the toolbar.

To change the font used by AutoCAD

1   From the Tools menu, choose Preferences.
2   In the Preferences dialog box, choose the Display tab.
3   On the Display tab, choose Fonts.

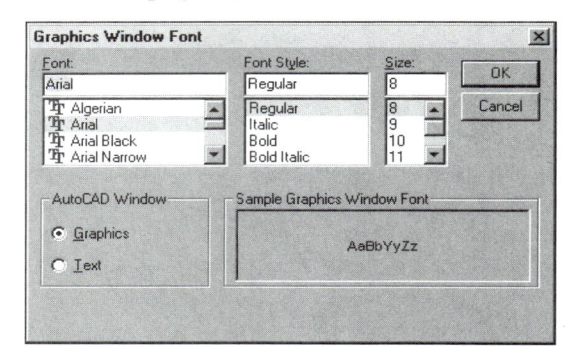

4   In the Fonts dialog box, to change the font of the text in the graphics area, choose Graphics. To change the fonts in the text window, choose Text.

5   Select the appropriate Font, Font Style, and Size.

    An example of the current choices is displayed under Sample Graphics Window Font or Sample Text Window Font.

6   Choose OK.

Specifying Support Directories and Menu Files

By specifying support directories in the Preferences dialog box, you set the search path AutoCAD uses to find support files such as text fonts, drawings, linetypes, and hatch patterns. This option helps improve performance when AutoCAD is loading these files.

Chapter 1   Getting Started

If you want to use a custom menu, you can specify it in the Menu File box. The default menu is *acad.mnu*.

To add support directories using Browse

1 From the Tools menu, choose Preferences.

2 In the Preferences dialog box, choose the Files tab.

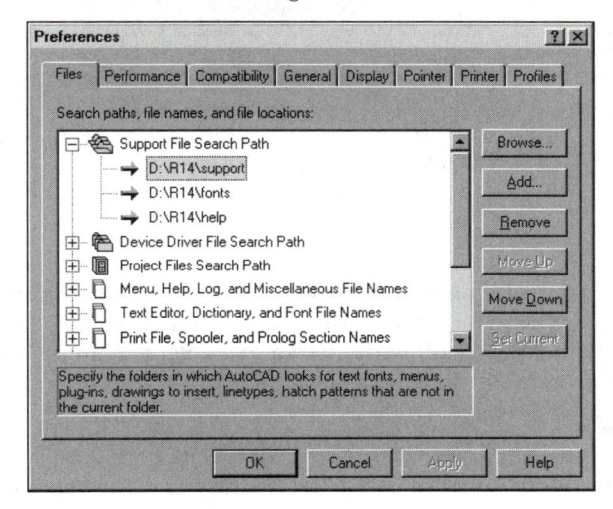

3 On the Files tab, click the plus sign (+) to the left of the title of the path you want to change.

4 Select the path you want to change.

5 Choose Browse. Then search drives and directories until you find the one you want to use.

6 Select the drive and directory you want to use. Then choose OK.

To change menus using Browse

1 From the Tools menu, choose Preferences.

2 In the Preferences dialog box, choose the Files tab.

3 On the Files tab, under Menu, Help, Log, and Miscellaneous File Names, select the Menus folder.

4 In the Menu File folder, select the default menu file, and then choose Browse.

5 Search drives or directories until you find the file you want to use. (You can identify menu files by their *.mnu* or *.mnx* extension.)

6 Select the file you want to use. Then choose OK.

Setting the System of Measurement

Whether you work with an English or a metric system of measurement affects the files AutoCAD uses for the template drawing, linetype, and hatch pattern.

File names for English and metric units		
File type	English	Metric
Template drawing	*acad.dwt*	*acadiso.dwt*
Hatch pattern	*acad.pat*	*acadiso.pat*
Linetype	*acad.lin*	*acadiso.lin*

If you start a drawing using one system of measurement and then want to switch to the other, you need to scale the drawing by a conversion factor in order to obtain accurate dimensions. For example, to convert inches to millimeters, you scale the drawing by a factor of 25.4. To convert from millimeters to inches, the scale factor is 1/25.4.

When you open a new drawing, AutoCAD uses the MEASUREMENT system variable settings to determine whether the new drawing will use English or metric. When you create a new drawing using a setup method chosen from the Create New Drawing dialog box, AutoCAD determines the measurement settings:

- *Use a Wizard* Uses either the *acad.dwt* (English) or the *acadiso.dwt* (metric) template drawing file depending upon the measurement settings in system registry.
- *Use a Template* Uses measurement settings saved in the template file to determine hatch and linetype files.
- *Start from Scratch* Uses measurement settings in the registry when the new drawing is created.

Specifying the Location of Temporary Files

AutoCAD creates temporary files on disk and then deletes them when you exit the program. AutoCAD sets the temporary directory to the location that Windows uses. If you plan to run AutoCAD from a write-protected directory (for example, if you are working on a network or are opening files on a CD), specify must *not* be write-protected. Be sure to specify a drive with plenty of free disk space.

To specify the location of temporary files

1 From the Tools menu, choose Preferences.
2 In the Preferences dialog box, choose the Files tab.
3 On the Files tab, select Temporary Drawing File Location.
4 Use Browse to enter a new directory path or enter the path in the box.
5 Choose OK.

Opening Existing Drawings

To open an existing AutoCAD drawing, you choose its name from a list. If you already have a drawing open, AutoCAD prompts you to save that drawing when you open another one.

To open a drawing

1 From the File menu, choose Open.

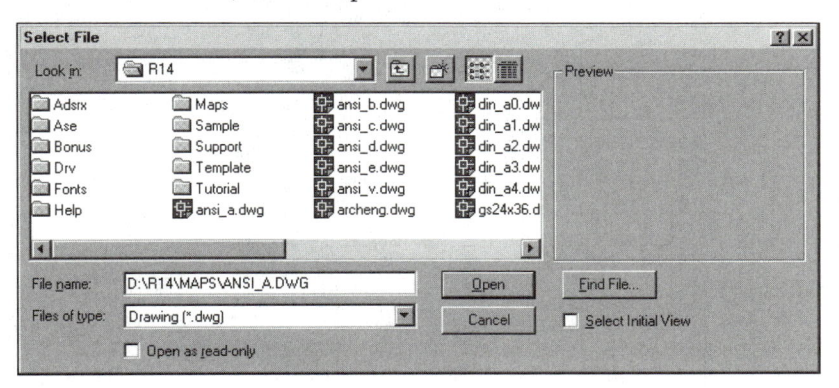

2 In the Select File dialog box, double-click the file name in the list of files. You can also open the drawing by entering the drawing name and choosing OK.

Command line OPEN

Related THE NEW command creates a new drawing file.

Opening Existing Drawings

87

Using the Drawing Browser

Use the drawing browser to view small images of drawings, to open drawings, and to search for files. You can use the browser to search for files across multiple directories on a single drive or on multiple drives.

Browsing Through Files

The Browse/Search dialog box displays small images of drawings in the directory you specify. You can sort the images by file type. Click an image to select it.

You can change the size of the images by choosing from the Size list on the Browse tab in the Browse/Search dialog box.

To open drawings using the drawing browser

1   From the File menu, choose Open.
2   In the Select File dialog box, choose Find File.
3   In the Browse/Search dialog box on the Browse tab, select the drive and directory containing the files you want to view.

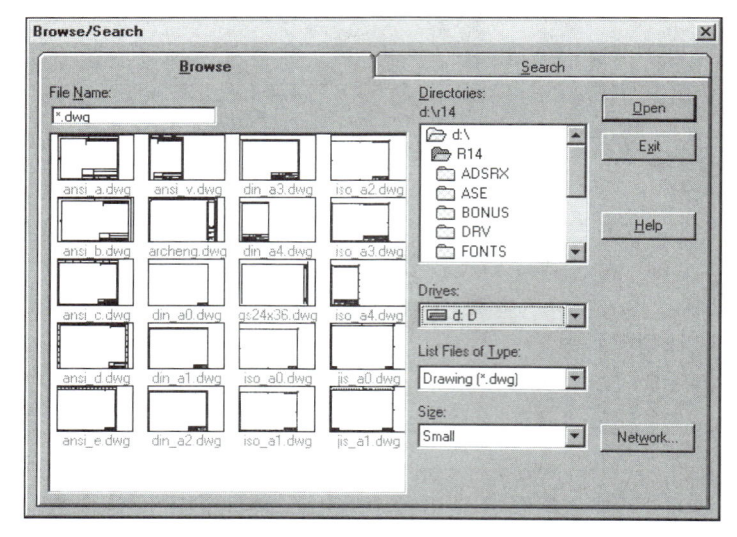

4   Under List Files of Type, select a file type to list.
5   To open a file, either double-click its image or select its image and choose Open.

Command line   OPEN

Chapter 1   Getting Started

88

Searching for Files

You can search for files by specifying a file type and referencing the date of creation. For example, you could search for *.lin* files that were created after 3:00 P.M. on a certain day.

To search for files

1 From the File menu, choose Open.

2 In the Select File dialog box, choose Find File.

3 In the Browse/Search dialog box, choose the Search tab.

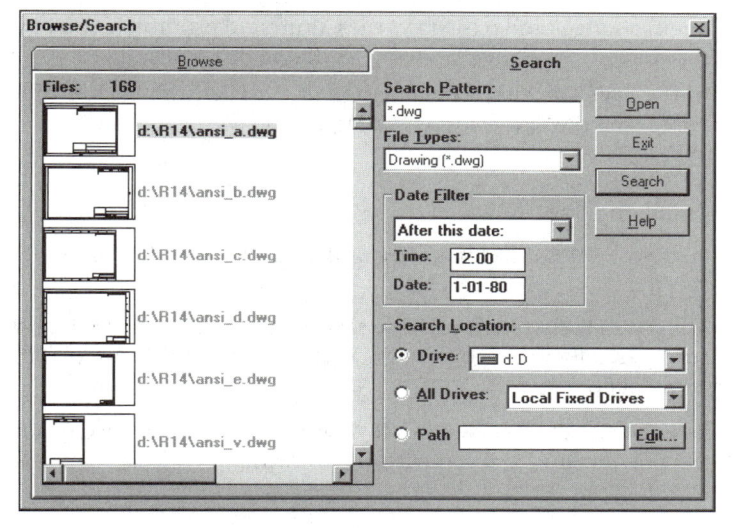

4 On the Search tab, enter a search pattern or select a file type to search for. You can use wild cards in search patterns.

5 Under Date Filter, select a reference, for example, Before This Date or After This Date, and enter the time and date to refer to.

6 Under Search Location, specify a drive and directory path. Choose Edit to change the search path in the Edit Path dialog box.

7 Choose Search.

This button changes to Stop Search. Press it to stop the search at any time.

8 When the search is completed, double-click the file you want to open in the Files list. To open this file, select the file name and choose Open.

9 Choose Exit.

Opening Existing Drawings

89

Saving Drawings

When you are working on a drawing, you should save it frequently. If you want to create a new version of a drawing without affecting the original drawing, you can save it under another name.

To save a drawing

1 From the File menu, choose Save.

If you previously saved and named the drawing, AutoCAD saves any subsequent changes and redisplays the Command prompt. If you have never saved the drawing, the Save Drawing As dialog box is displayed.

2 In the Save Drawing As dialog box under File Name, enter the new drawing name (the file extension is *not* required).

3 Choose OK.

Command line   SAVE

Related   SAVEAS saves a copy of the current drawing under the name you specify.

The SAVETIME system variable sets the time interval at which AutoCAD automatically saves your work. You also can set this interval in the Preferences dialog box.

You can use the RASTERPREVIEW system variable to specify a file format for the preview image saved with the drawing.

Exiting AutoCAD

If you have saved your most recent changes, you can exit AutoCAD without saving the drawing again. If you have not saved your changes, AutoCAD prompts you to save or discard the changes or cancel the command.

To exit a drawing

- From the File menu, choose Exit.

Command line   EXIT or QUIT or END

Chapter 1   Getting Started

Organizing Your Project

Organizing your drawing project begins by establishing layer, linetype, and lettering standards. After the drawing is complete, you can refine the layout and then plot to the scale you require. This chapter describes activities you should do before you start drawing.

In this chapter

- Units style settings
- Scale factor settings
- Drawing boundary settings
- Grid and snap settings
- How to create layers to organize your drawing
- How to use templates

Conforming to Standards

Drawing standards come from many sources. Perhaps you are following standards dictated by a client or by industry requirements, or maybe you are establishing your own standards. Whether you are handling all aspects of the project yourself or supervising it, the initial drawing setup is a key factor in producing a professional drawing.

For example, an architectural drawing might consist of several elements: a floor plan, piping, and heating and air conditioning. If you use different contractors to draft each of these elements, you want them to adhere to the same standards as they produce their parts of the drawing. You can do this by providing a template file containing the standard initial drawing setup. An initial drawing setup includes border, title block, units of measurement, layering, and linetypes.

Equally important are the styles used for text, hatching, and dimensions. By setting up styles for these in advance, you can ensure that everyone working on the drawing is conforming to your established standards.

You should also consider the scale. By choosing a scale factor—the size of what's being drawn versus the size of the plotted drawing—you can help ensure that the lettering for annotations and dimensions is appropriate for the final scale of your project.

Although you can delay laying out the final drawing until later in the project, proper planning will save you the time needed to edit the drawing to the established standard. This planning may involve using model space, where you create your drawing, and paper space, where you arrange the drawing layout. In paper space, you apply the appropriate scaling factors to ensure that the final plotted product is at the correct scale with respect to text, linetypes, dimensions, and drawn entities.

The work you put into setting up the drawing can be saved as a template and reused for similar drawings or altered to accommodate slightly different needs.

Setting Up New Drawings

When you create a new drawing, you can use a template that contains standard settings. This template can be one of the default templates supplied with AutoCAD, or it can be a template that has been customized to include the settings you need. You can use any existing drawing as a template drawing. When you use an existing drawing as a template, all information is passed on to the new drawing. You can also choose to start AutoCAD without a template.

AutoCAD also supplies two wizards. These wizards use the current template, but they modify certain scale settings based on information you provide. For example, both wizards automatically adjust scale factors for dimension settings and text height. The adjusted settings are based on the full-scale size of the objects you draw. For small-scale drawings, AutoCAD decreases the default text height so that it is legible on the screen. By making this automatic adjustment, AutoCAD ensures that text and other elements are visible when the entire drawing is displayed.

Any settings you change using the setup options can be changed again later.

To create a new drawing using Start from Scratch

1   From the File menu, choose New.
2   In the Create New Drawing dialog box, choose Start from Scratch.

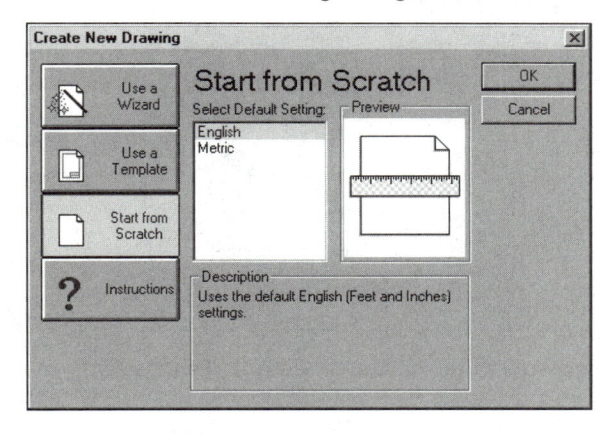

3   Under Select Default Setting, select English or Metric, and then choose OK. The drawing opens with the default AutoCAD settings.
4   From the File menu, choose Save As.

5   In the Save Drawing As dialog box under File Name, enter a name for the drawing and choose OK.

The drawing extension (*.dwg*) is automatically appended to the file name.

Command line   NEW

Using the Quick Setup Wizard

With the Quick Setup wizard, you establish basic settings that help define the units of measure and drawing area. These settings include the basic unit type (such as architectural, decimal, engineering, fractional, or scientific units) to be used for display and plotting. You also specify the width and length of the drawing area, and thereby establish the drawing's boundaries, called limits. The area within these limits defines the final plotted sheet size. After you accept the settings, the Quick Setup wizard starts your drawing session in the model space environment.

To set up a drawing using the Quick Setup wizard

If you are already working in a drawing, save it with SAVE or SAVEAS.

1   From the File menu, choose New.
2   In the Create New Drawing dialog box, choose Use a Wizard.

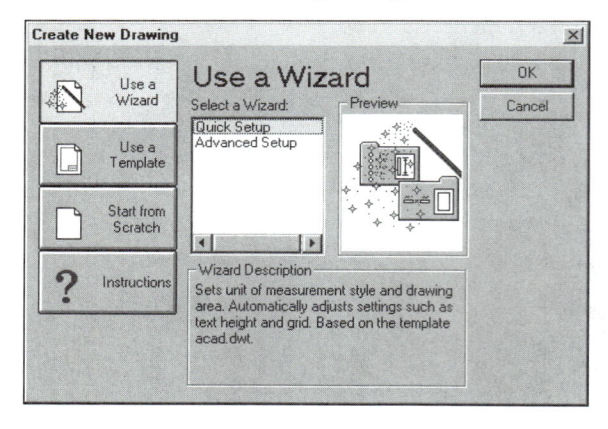

3   Under Select a Wizard, select Quick Setup and choose OK.

Using the Advanced Setup Wizard

With the Advanced Setup wizard, you can define unit of measurement, angle of measurement, and direction. In addition to these setup controls in model space, you can also designate angles and angle direction and insert an existing title block and border in paper space. The Quick Setup wizard affects only model space; the Advanced Setup wizard affects both model and paper space.

After you have used the Advanced Setup wizard to specify the drawing settings, a new drawing is opened with the title block and border displayed in paper space. A single model-space floating viewport is available for you to begin drawing.

To open a new drawing using the Advanced Setup wizard

1 From the File menu, choose New.
2 In the Create New Drawing dialog box, choose Use a Wizard.
3 Under Select a Wizard, select Advanced Setup. Then choose OK.

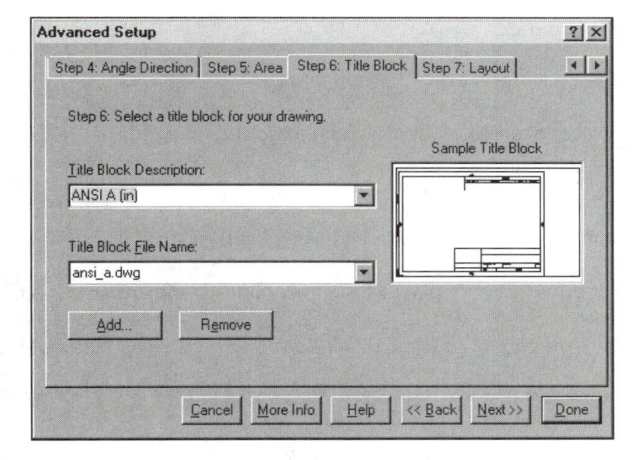

4 In the Advanced Setup wizard, choose any of the available steps to change settings. For example, to specify units, choose the Step 1: Units tab. To move on to the next tab, press the Next button or choose the tab directly.
5 When you have finished indicating the desired setup, choose Done.

AutoCAD opens the new drawing with a single floating viewport displayed in paper space on the VIEWPORT layer.

Command line NEW

Setting Up New Drawings

95

Using Setup Wizard System Variables

Whenever you change the default settings in the Quick Setup or the Advanced Setup wizard, AutoCAD automatically adjusts the system variables as shown in the following table.

NOTE If the DIMSCALE system variable is set to 1, the dimensioning variables are *not* adjusted.

System variables changed by Quick Setup and Advanced Setup wizards	
Setting changed	System variable
First chamfer distance	CHAMFERA
Second chamfer distance	CHAMFERB
Size of dimension line and leader line arrowheads	DIMASZ
Number of places of precision displayed for angular dimensions	DIMADEC
Angle format for angular dimensions	DIMAUNIT
Drawing of circle or arc center marks and centerlines	DIMCEN
Number of decimal places displayed for primary units of dimension	DIMDEC
Dimension line spacing for baseline dimensions	DIMDLI
Distance of the extension line beyond the dimension line	DIMEXE
Distance dimension lines are offset from origin points	DIMEXO
Distance around dimension text that breaks dimension lines	DIMGAP
Height of dimension text	DIMTXT
Units for all dimension style family members except angular	DIMUNIT
Default for the inside diameter of a donut	DONUTID
Default for the outside diameter of a donut	DONUTOD

System variables changed by Quick Setup and Advanced Setup wizards (*continued*)	
Setting changed	System variable
Hatch pattern scale factor	HPSCALE
Hatch pattern spacing for "U" user-defined simple patterns	HPSPACE
Global linetype scale factor	LTSCALE
Default height of new text drawn with the current text style	TEXTSIZE

Using Other Setup Methods

Once a drawing is open, you can change the values that were initially specified with the setup options. The following sections describe additional procedures for setting up your drawing and provide more information about some of the Quick Setup and Advanced Setup wizard features.

Setting Units Style

Every object you draw is measured in units. You determine the value of the units within AutoCAD before you draw. For example, in one drawing, a unit might equal one millimeter of the real-world object. In another drawing, a unit might equal an inch. You can set the unit type and precision in the Units Control dialog box. These settings control how AutoCAD interprets your coordinate and angle entries and how it displays coordinates and dimensions.

You can set the unit type in the Quick Setup or Advanced Setup wizard when you create a new drawing. You also can change the settings once the drawing is open, as described in the following procedure.

To set the units type and precision

1   From the Format menu, choose Units.

unit measurements — [Units section with: Scientific, Decimal, Engineering, Architectural, Fractional]

angle measurements — [Angles section with: Decimal Degrees, Deg/Min/Sec, Grads, Radians, Surveyor]

precision for units — 0.0000

precision for angles — 0

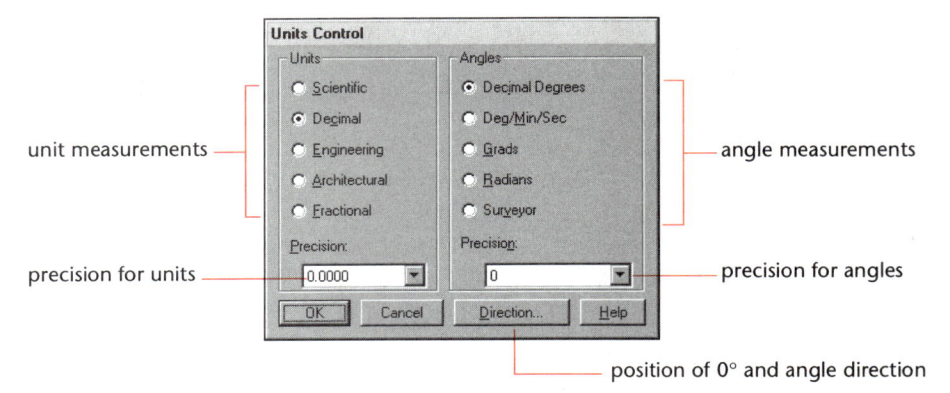

position of 0° and angle direction — Direction...

2 In the Units Control dialog box under Units, select a unit type and precision.

The Precision box shows an example of the unit type at the current precision.

3 Under Angles, select an angle type and precision.

The Precision box in the Angles area shows an example of the format at the current precision.

4 To specify an angle direction, choose Direction.

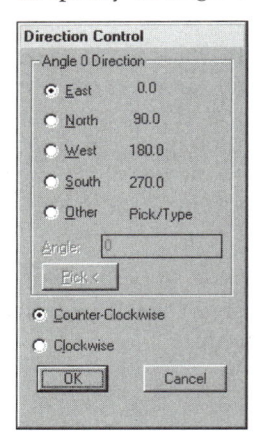

[Direction Control dialog: Angle 0 Direction — East 0.0, North 90.0, West 180.0, South 270.0, Other Pick/Type; Counter-Clockwise / Clockwise]

The angle direction controls the point from which AutoCAD measures angles and the direction in which they're measured. The default is 0 degrees on the right side of the figure and measured counterclockwise.

5 Select the options you want to use.

6 Choose OK to exit each dialog box.

Command line   DDUNITS

Related   UNITS sets coordinate and angle display formats and precision on the command line.

You can use the ANGBASE, ANGDIR, AUNITS, AUPREC, LUNITS, and LUPREC system variables to change individual unit and angle settings. For more detailed information about these system variables, see the *Command Reference*.

Determining the Scale Factor

Although you do not specify the scale of your drawing until you plot, you can specify the scale factor for elements such as dimensions, text height, and linetype scale in advance. Establishing a scale factor for text, dimensions, linetypes, and so on ensures that these elements are the appropriate size in the final drawing.

Within model space, if you use the Quick Setup or Advanced Setup wizard when you open a new drawing, AutoCAD adjusts many of the scale factors to be appropriate for the world size, or limits, you specify. However, you can also manually calculate the scale factor by converting the drawing scale to a ratio of 1:*n*. This ratio compares plotted units to drawing units. You can then multiply your sheet size by the scale factor to calculate the limits of your drawing.

For example, if you plot at a ratio of 1/4 inch = 1 foot, you would calculate the scale ratio 48 as follows:

1/4" = 12"
1 = 12 × 4
1 = 48

Using the same calculation, the scale ratio for 1/8 inch = 1 foot is 96, and the scale ratio for 1 inch = 20 feet is 240.

If you are working in metric units, you might have a sheet size of 210 × 297 mm (A4 size) and a scale ratio of 20. You calculate drawing limits as follows:

210 × 20 = 4,200 mm = 4.2 m
297 × 20 = 5,900 mm = 5.9 m

Using Other Setup Methods

Once you establish the scale factor, you can use it to set text and dimension sizes. The following table shows some standard architectural scale ratios and equivalent text sizes.

Using scale factors to derive text size

Scale		Scale factor	To plot text size at…	Set drawing text size to…
1/8"	= 1'-0"	96	1/8"	12"
3/16"	= 1'-0"	64	1/8"	8"
1/4"	= 1'-0"	48	1/8"	6"
3/8"	= 1'-0"	32	1/8"	4"
1/2"	= 1'-0"	24	1/8"	3"
3/4"	= 1'-0"	16	1/8"	2"
1"	= 1'-0"	12	1/8"	1.5"
1 1/2"	= 1'-0"	8	1/8"	1.0"

When the drawing is complete, you can plot it at any scale, or you can plot different views of your drawing at different scales. You can position and scale paper space views without affecting the scale of the objects in the drawing. For more information, see "Scaling Views Relative to Paper Space" on page 488.

Setting Grid Limits

You can set the rectangular boundary, or limits, of the drawing area covered by grid dots when the grid is turned on. The grid provides a visual representation of the limits. Setting the limits controls the extent of the display of the grid, and serves as

- A reference tool that marks the area in your drawing on which you're currently working
- A drawing tool that optionally prevents drawing outside the grid limits
- A plot option that defines an area to be printed

In model space, the limits should encompass the full-scale size of the model. For example, if the object is 100 × 200 mm, you might want to set your limits to represent a slightly larger area.

If you define limits in paper space, the limits boundary usually represents the final sheet size of the paper. Therefore, in paper space, the grid limits should be set to the proper size to contain the entire sheet of paper, including the drawing, dimensions, title blocks, and other information. For example, if you have a sheet of paper that is 210 × 297 mm, you could set decimal units and then specify 0,0 as the lower-left corner and 210,297 as the upper-right corner of the limits.

When you open a new drawing and use the Quick Setup or Advanced Setup wizard, you set grid limits in model space. The following procedure describes how to set limits once the drawing is open.

grid limits shown by range of grid

To set grid limits

1 From the Format menu, choose Drawing Limits.

2 Specify the lower-left corner of the limits, which corresponds to the lower-left corner of your drawing area. Press ENTER to use the default (0,0).

3 Specify the upper-right corner of the limits, which corresponds to the upper-right corner of your drawing area.

For example, if the lower-left corner is at 0,0 (as specified in step 2), you can specify a limits area that is 30 wide and 10 high by entering **30,10**.

4 On the status bar, double-click Grid. Then from the View menu, choose Zoom ➤ All.

The graphics screen changes to show the area defined by the limits.

Command line LIMITS

Related The LIMMAX system variable stores the upper-right drawing limit for the current space. LIMMIN stores the lower-left drawing limit.

Setting the Grid

The grid is a pattern of dots that extends over the area specified by the limits. Using the grid is similar to placing a sheet of grid paper under a drawing. The grid helps you align objects and visualize the distances between them. You can turn the grid on and off in the middle of another command. The grid does not appear in the plotted drawing.

Using Other Setup Methods

If you zoom in or out of your drawing, you might need to adjust grid spacing to be more appropriate for the new magnification.

To turn on the grid and set grid spacing

1 From the Tools menu, choose Drawing Aids.

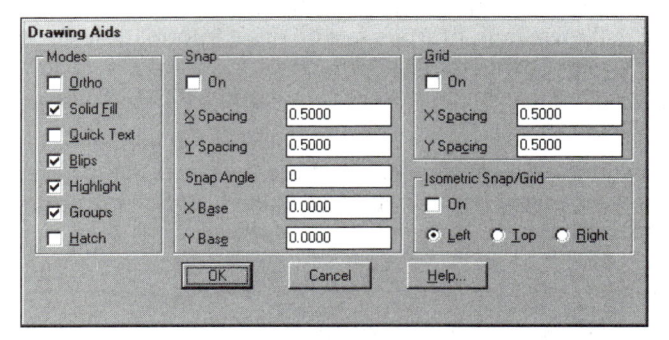

2 In the Drawing Aids dialog box under Grid, select On to display the grid.
3 Enter the value for grid X Spacing in units.
4 To use the same value for vertical grid spacing, press ENTER. Otherwise, enter a new value for Y Spacing.
5 Choose OK.

Command line   DDRMODES

Related   To turn the grid on or off, double-click Grid on the status bar, use the GRID command, press CTRL+G, or press F7.

Although the grid dots do not necessarily correspond to the current snap interval, they do reflect the current snap angle and Isometric Snap/Grid settings.

Setting Snap Spacing

Snap mode restricts the movement of the crosshairs to intervals that you have defined. When Snap is on, the cursor seems to adhere, or "snap," to an invisible grid. Snap is useful for specifying precise points with the keyboard or pointing device. You control snap precision by setting the X and Y spacing. Snap has a toggle control and can be turned on or off during another command.

Snap spacing does not have to match grid spacing. For example, you might set a wide grid spacing to be used as a reference but maintain a closer snap spacing for accuracy in specifying points. You also can set the grid spacing to be smaller than the snap spacing.

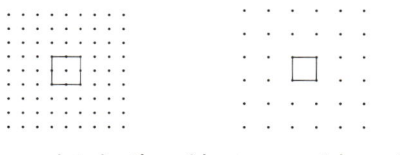

snap is twice the grid   snap matches grid

To turn on Snap mode and set snap spacing

1 From the Tools menu, choose Drawing Aids.
2 In the Drawing Aids dialog box under Snap, select On.
3 Enter the horizontal snap X Spacing in units.
4 To specify the same vertical snap spacing, press ENTER. Otherwise, enter a new distance under Y Spacing.
5 Choose OK.

Command line   DDRMODES

Related   To turn Snap mode on and off, double-click the Snap button on the status bar, enter the SNAP command, press CTRL+B, or press F9.

Adding Borders and Title Blocks

The border and title block can be customized to meet your company requirements and then used in several ways. As you open a new drawing, you can use the Advanced Setup wizard to insert a title block and border on their own layer in paper space.

The title block and border reside in a separate drawing that is inserted as a block—a single object created by grouping one or more objects. AutoCAD provides several standard title blocks to choose from. If you prefer, you can open a new drawing using a template that already contains a title block and border.

AutoCAD provides standard title blocks that you can use at any time. You can open and customize them with any standard information, or you can add the information after they're inserted in your drawing. You also can create and use your own title blocks and add them to the list that is displayed when you use the Advanced Setup wizard.

The following procedure describes how to insert a title block using the Advanced Setup wizard.

To insert a title block and border with the Advanced Setup wizard

1 From the File menu, choose New.
2 In the Create New Drawing dialog box, choose Use a Wizard and select Advanced Setup. Choose OK.
3 In the Advanced Setup wizard, choose Step 6: Title Block.

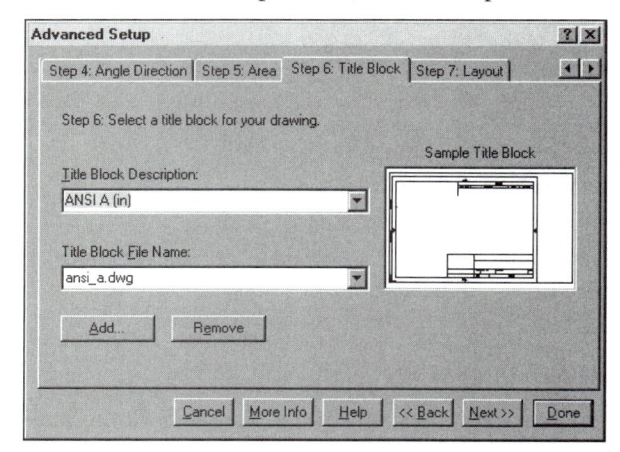

4 On the Step 6: Title Block tab under Title Block Description, select the file name of the title block and border you want to use. The file names generally correspond to paper sizes.
5 Choose Done.

Command line NEW

Related Use DDINSERT to insert a title block drawing as a block. Use XREF to attach a title block drawing as an external reference.

Customizing Title Blocks for the Advanced Setup Wizard

You can modify the list of drawings displayed on the Step 6: Title Block tab by adding or deleting drawings or by saving an existing title block under a new file name.

To modify the list of title block drawings in the Advanced Setup wizard

1 From the File menu, choose New.
2 In the Create New Drawing dialog box, select Use a Wizard and Advanced Setup. Choose OK.
3 In the Advanced Setup wizard, choose Step 6: Title Block.
4 Modify the title block list using *one* of the following methods:
   - To add a new title block drawing, choose Add. In the Select Title Block File dialog box, enter a name for the new title block under Description (in the title block panel file). Then specify a drawing file by choosing File and selecting a file name from the list. Choose OK twice to exit both dialog boxes.
   - To remove a title block drawing, select the title block description you want to delete and choose Remove.

Command line NEW

NOTE You can create your own title block drawings and add them to the title block list. They can then be accessed by the Advanced Setup wizard.

If you want the Advanced Setup wizard to automatically insert a viewport of a specific size, you must add four attribute definitions with the following tag names to the title block drawing. The attribute definitions should be invisible and constant.

- The MINX value equals the *X* value of the coordinate of the lower-left corner of the viewport.
- The MINY value equals the *Y* value of the coordinate of the lower-left corner of the viewport.
- The MAXX value equals the *X* value of the coordinate of the upper-right corner of the viewport.
- The MAXY value equals the *Y* value of the coordinate of the upper-right corner of the viewport.

When you use the Advanced Setup wizard to set up a drawing with these attributes, AutoCAD automatically creates a viewport of the size specified under Value in the Attribute Definition dialog box. Only one viewport per title block can be specified with this method.

Using Other Setup Methods

Organizing Information on Layers

Layers are the equivalent of the overlays used in paper-based drafting. They are the primary organizational tool in AutoCAD. Layers are used to group information by function and to enforce linetype, color, and other standards.

Planning Layers

You are always drawing on a layer. It may be the default layer (0) or a layer you create and name yourself. Each layer has an associated color and linetype. You can group drawing components by assigning similar objects to the same layer. The number of layers you can create in a drawing and the number of objects you can create per layer are virtually unlimited.

For example, you can create a layer for centerlines and assign the color blue and the CENTERLINE linetype to that layer. Then, whenever you draw centerlines, you switch to that layer and start drawing. Every object you draw on that layer will be blue and use the CENTERLINE linetype. Later, if you don't want to display or plot centerlines, you can turn off that layer.

With layers, you have great flexibility in the amount of detail you can display. You can display any combination of layers. You can hide construction lines or details. In paper space, you can make some layers visible only in certain viewports.

If you use a black-and-white plotter, layer colors can be used to control line width. When you plot, you assign each color to a certain pen. Your plotter then uses the pen (or pen width) associated with the layer color.

Creating and Naming Layers

AutoCAD sorts layers alphabetically by name. If you're organizing your own layer scheme, choose layer names carefully. By using common prefixes to name layers with related drawing components, you can use wild-card characters or filters when you need to find those layers quickly. For example, if you create a set of layers that start with PIPING, such as PIPING-FLOOR 1, PIPING-FLOOR 2, and so on, you can later sort for PIPING to display only those layers.

To create a new layer

1 From the Format menu, choose Layer.

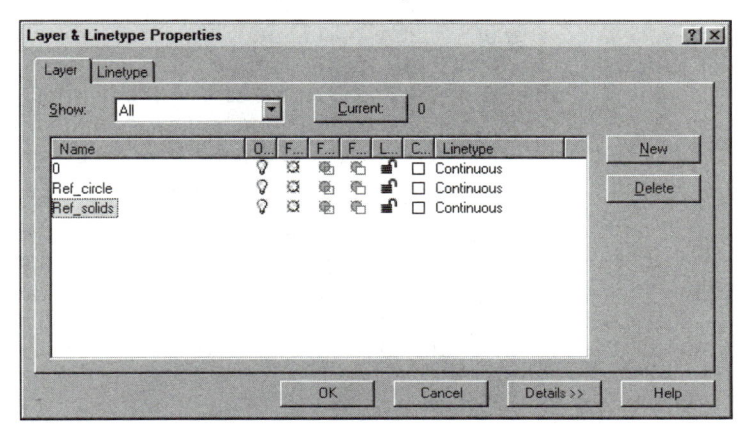

2 In the Layer & Linetype Properties dialog box, choose New.

   A layer called Layer1 is displayed.

3 Click Layer1 and enter a new layer name.

   The layer name can include up to 31 characters. Layer names can contain letters, digits, and the special characters dollar sign ($), hyphen (–), and underscore (_). Layer names cannot include blank spaces.

4 To change a layer's color, select the layer and click its Color icon. In the Select Color dialog box, select a color and choose OK.

5 To change a layer's linetype, select the layer and click its Linetype icon. In the Select Linetype dialog box, select a linetype.

6 Choose OK to exit each dialog box.

Command line   LAYER

Related   -LAYER creates layers on the command line.

For more detailed information about layers, see "Working with Layers" on page 298.

Organizing Information on Layers

107

Using Linetypes

A linetype is a repeating pattern of dashes, dots, and blank spaces. Linetypes provide another way to convey visual information. You can use them to distinguish the purpose of one line from another. Each linetype has a name and a definition. The definition describes the sequence of dashes, dots, and spaces; the relative lengths of dashes and blank spaces; and the characteristics of any included text or shapes. You can use any of the standard linetypes that AutoCAD provides, or you can create your own linetypes.

At the start of a project, you load the linetypes that are required for the project so that they are available when you need them. You can associate linetypes with all AutoCAD objects except text, points, viewports, xlines, rays, and blocks. If a line is too short to hold even one dash sequence, AutoCAD draws a continuous line between the endpoints.

Loading Linetypes

To use a linetype, you must first load it into your drawing. A linetype definition must exist in an LIN linetype library file before it can be loaded into a drawing.

To load a linetype

1   From the Format menu, choose Linetype.

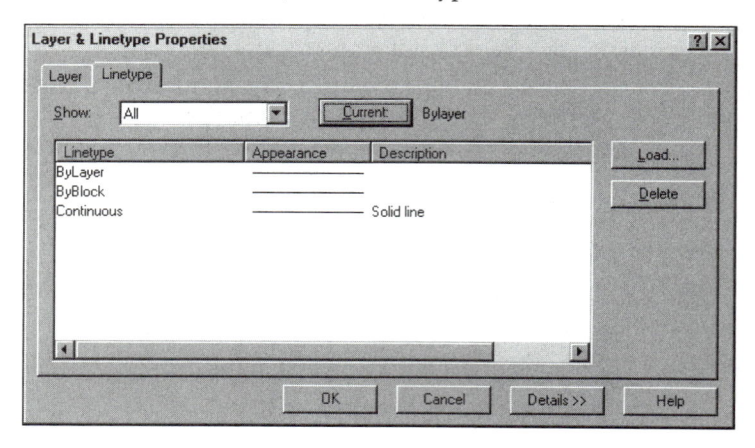

2   In the Layer & Linetype Properties dialog box, choose the Linetype tab, and then choose Load.

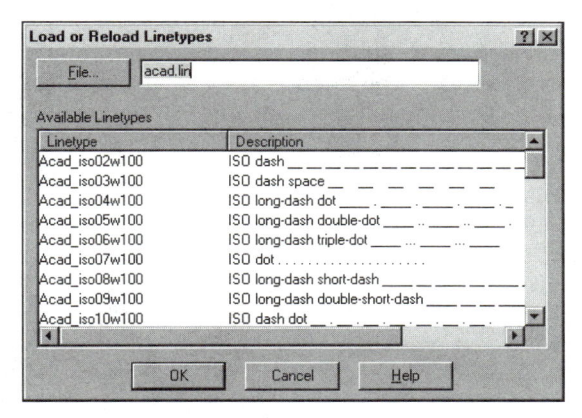

3   In the Load or Reload Linetypes dialog box, select a linetype from the Available Linetypes list. Then choose OK.

You can use the File option to load an alternate LIN file containing additional linetypes.

The linetype you selected is displayed in the linetype list.

4   Choose OK to exit the Layer & Linetype Properties dialog box.

NOTE   The ISO Pen Width option is available only if you've selected a linetype whose name begins with ACAD.ISO.

Command line   LINETYPE

Related   -LINETYPE loads linetypes from the command line. LTSCALE sets the linetype scale. CELTYPE sets the current linetype on the command line. For more detailed information about linetypes, see "Working with Linetypes" on page 311.

Organizing Information on Layers

Using Templates

AutoCAD uses templates for starting a new drawing. Although you can save any drawing as a template, you might want to prepare some standard templates that include settings and basic drawing elements consistent with your office standards:

- Unit type and precision
- Drawing limits
- Snap, Grid, and Ortho settings
- Layer organization
- Title blocks, borders, and logos
- Dimension and text styles
- Linetypes

template with border and title block

Using an Existing Template

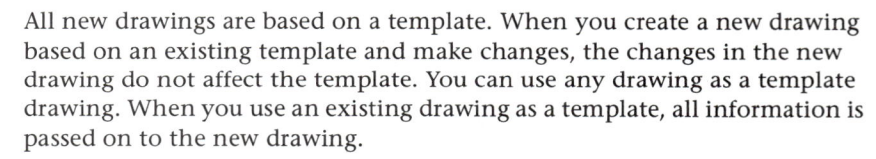

All new drawings are based on a template. When you create a new drawing based on an existing template and make changes, the changes in the new drawing do not affect the template. You can use any drawing as a template drawing. When you use an existing drawing as a template, all information is passed on to the new drawing.

Both the Quick Setup and the Advanced Setup wizards cause AutoCAD to adjust certain scale factors that are established in the template. To avoid changing those custom settings, use the following procedure to create a new drawing.

To use an existing template

1 From the File menu, choose New.
2 In the Create New Drawing dialog box, choose Use a Template.
3 Select a template file from the Select a Template list and choose OK.

AutoCAD opens the drawing as *drawing.dwg*.

Command line NEW

Creating a Template

When you need to create several drawings with similar requirements, you can save time by saving one of the drawings as a template.

To create a template

1. Open a drawing.
2. Change any drawing settings to match what you plan to use as defaults in your template.

   Add a border and title block if needed.
3. Erase all existing objects except the border and title block by starting ERASE and entering **all** at the Select Objects prompt. Then enter **r** (Remove) and select the border and title block.
4. From the File menu, choose Save As.
5. In the Save Drawing As dialog box under Save Files as Type, choose the Drawing Template file type.
6. Under File Name, enter a name for the template. Choose OK.
7. In the Template Description dialog box, enter a brief description of the template.

   This description is displayed whenever you select this template from the Create New Drawing dialog box.
8. Specify the measurement system (metric or English) to use for the template.
9. Choose OK.

   The new template is saved in the *template* folder.

Recovering the Default Template

If the settings in the AutoCAD template *acad.dwt* have been changed from the original defaults, you can reset them.

The following procedure describes how to restore template (*acad.dwt*) settings if you use English (as opposed to metric) measurements.

To recover the default template

1. From the File menu, choose New.
2. In the Create New Drawing dialog box, select Start from Scratch, then select English under Select Default Setting.
3. Choose OK.

   The drawing opens with the default AutoCAD settings.
4. From the File menu, choose Save As.
5. In the Save Drawing As dialog box, select the Drawing Template file type. Save the drawing with its original name (*acad.dwt*).

   Command line   NEW

Using Coordinate Systems

As you draw, you use some AutoCAD features repeatedly. One such feature is the coordinate system, which you will use to specify points in the drawing. You can locate your own movable user coordinate system (UCS) for working on angled, isometric, or three-dimensional (3D) views.

In this chapter

■ Working with polar and Cartesian coordinates

■ Specifying coordinates

■ Using direct distance entry

■ Moving and rotating a user coordinate system (UCS)

Using a Coordinate System to Specify Points

When a command prompts you for a point, you can use the pointing device to specify a point in the graphics area or you can enter coordinate values on the command line. This section describes how to enter coordinate values. Use Grid and Snap mode to specify evenly spaced points on the graphics area.

Using Cartesian and Polar Coordinate Systems

A Cartesian coordinate system has three axes, X, Y, and Z. When you enter coordinate values, you indicate a point's distance (in units) and its direction (+ or –) along the X, Y, and Z axes relative to the coordinate system origin (0,0,0). When you begin a new drawing in AutoCAD, you are automatically in the World Coordinate System (WCS): the X axis is horizontal, the Y axis is vertical, and the Z axis is perpendicular to the XY plane.

Polar coordinate systems use a distance and an angle to locate a point.

Locating Points

The following illustration demonstrates the location of points on the XY plane. The 8,5 coordinate indicates a point 8 units in the positive X direction and 5 units in the positive Y direction. The –4,2 coordinate represents a point 4 units in the negative X direction and 2 units in the positive Y direction.

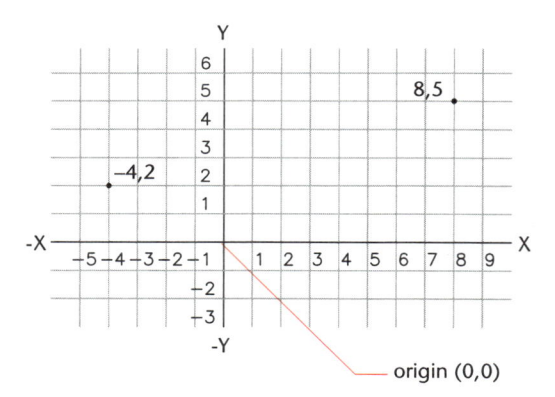

Two-dimensional coordinate system

In AutoCAD, you can enter coordinates in scientific, decimal, engineering, architectural, or fractional notation. You can enter angles in grads, radians, and surveyor's units or in degrees, minutes, and seconds. This guide uses decimal units and degrees.

If your work involves 3D modeling, you can add the Z axis to your coordinates so that a point is specified as X,Y,Z. The origin in a 3D coordinate system is the point where the values of X, Y, and Z are zero.

Displaying Coordinates

AutoCAD displays the current cursor location as a coordinate in the status bar at the bottom of the Windows screen.

```
1.5405,4.3774,0.0000
```
└─ current cursor location

There are three types of coordinate display available:

- Dynamic display is updated as you move the cursor.
- Static display updates only when you specify a point.
- Distance and angle *(distance<angle)* display is updated as you move the cursor. This option is available only when you draw lines or other objects that prompt for more than one point.

When you are editing objects, you can cycle through the three types of coordinate display by pressing F6 or CTRL+D. Another method is to set the COORDS system variable to 0 for static display, 1 for dynamic absolute display, or 2 for distance and angle display.

To find the coordinate of a given point on an existing object, use the LIST or the ID command. To ensure precision, use object snaps to select the point on the object.

Another method is to select the object using grips. Grips are small boxes that appear at strategic locations on objects, such as endpoints and midpoints. When the cursor snaps to a grip, the coordinate display shows its coordinate.

Specifying Cartesian and Polar Coordinates

In two-dimensional space, you specify points on the XY plane, also called the construction plane. The construction plane is similar to a flat sheet of grid paper. The X value of a Cartesian coordinate specifies horizontal distance, and the Y value specifies vertical distance. The origin point (0,0) indicates where the two axes intersect.

Using a Coordinate System to Specify Points

115

You can enter 2D coordinates as either Cartesian (X,Y) or polar coordinates. Polar coordinates use a distance and an angle to locate a point. You can use absolute or relative values with each method. Absolute coordinate values are based on the origin (0,0). Relative coordinate values are based on the last point entered. They are useful for finding a series of points that are a known distance apart.

Entering Absolute X,Y Coordinates

To enter an absolute X,Y coordinate, specify a point by entering its X and Y values in the format X,Y. Use absolute X,Y coordinates when you know the precise X and Y values of the location of the point.

For example, to draw a line beginning at an X value of –2 and a Y value of 1, make the following entries on the command line:

Command: *Enter* **line**
From point: *Enter* **–2,1**
To point: *Enter* **3,4**

AutoCAD locates the line as follows:

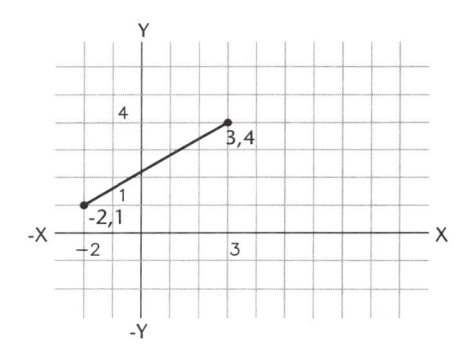

Entering Relative Coordinates

Use relative X,Y coordinates when you know the position of a point in relation to the previous point. For example, to locate a point relative to –2,1, precede the next coordinate with the @ symbol:

Command: *Enter* **line**
From point: *Enter* **–2,1**
To point: *Enter* **@5,3**

This draws the same line shown in the preceding illustration.

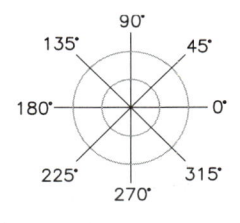

Entering Polar Coordinates

To enter a polar coordinate, enter a distance and an angle, separated by an angle bracket (<). For example, to specify a point that is at a distance of 1 unit from the previous point and at an angle of 45 degrees, enter **@1<45**.

By default, angles increase in the counterclockwise and decrease in the clockwise direction. To move clockwise, enter a negative value for the angle. For example, entering **1<315** is the same as entering **1<–45**. You can change the angle direction for the current drawing with the DDUNITS command or the ANGDIR system variable. Also, ANGBASE sets the direction of the Ø angle.

The following example shows a line drawn with polar coordinates.

Command: Enter **line**
From point: Enter **0,0**
To point: Enter **4<120**
To point: Enter **5<30**

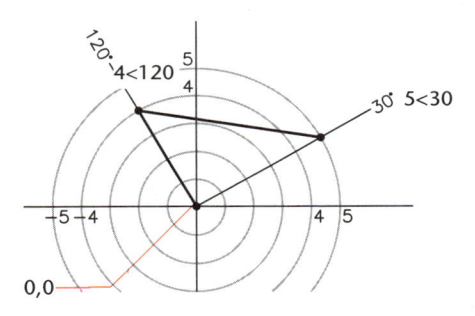

To point: Enter **@3<45**
To point: Enter **@5<285**
To point: Press ENTER

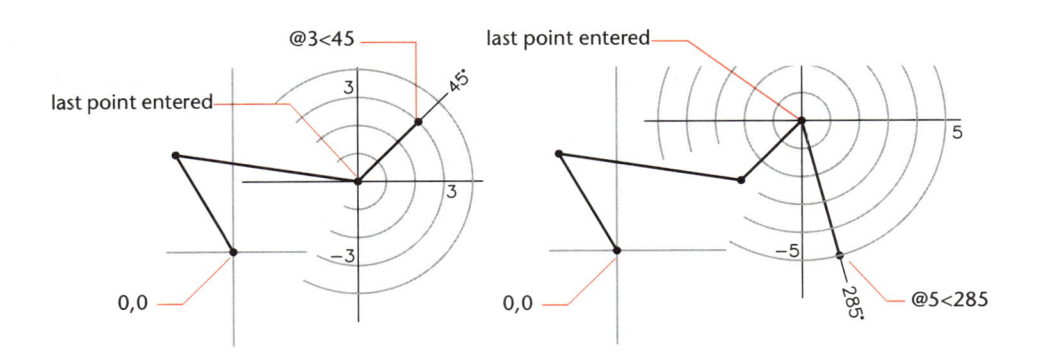

Using a Coordinate System to Specify Points

117

You also can use a feature called direct distance entry. With direct distance entry, you can specify a relative coordinate by moving the cursor to specify a direction and then entering a distance. For more information, see "Using Direct Distance Entry" on page 118.

Specifying Units and Angles

You can specify the unit type according to your drawing's requirements: architectural, decimal, scientific, engineering, or fractional. Depending on what you specify, you can enter coordinates in decimal form or in feet, inches, and degrees or in other notation. To enter architectural feet and inches, indicate feet using the prime symbol ('): for example, **72'3,34'4**. You don't need to enter the double prime symbol or quotation marks (") to specify inches.

If you use surveyor angles when specifying polar coordinates, indicate whether the surveyor angles are in the north, south, east, or west direction. For example, to enter a coordinate relative to the current coordinate for a property line that is 72 feet, 8 inches, long with a bearing of 45 degrees north, 20 feet, 6 inches, east, enter

@72'8"<n45d20'6"e

You can enter 3D coordinates in the same input formats as 2D coordinates: scientific, decimal, engineering, architectural, or fractional notation. Also, you can enter angles using grads, radians, or surveyor's units or using degrees, minutes, and seconds.

Using Direct Distance Entry

Instead of entering coordinate values with direct distance entry, you can specify a point by moving the cursor to indicate a direction and then entering the distance from the first point. This is a good way to specify a line length quickly.

You can use direct distance entry to specify points for all commands except those that prompt you to enter a single real value, such as ARRAY, MEASURE, and DIVIDE. When Ortho is on, this method is an efficient way to draw perpendicular lines. In the following example, you draw a line 25 units long using direct distance entry.

To draw a line using direct distance entry

1 From the Draw menu, choose Line.
2 Specify the first point (1).
3 Move the pointing device until the rubber-band line extends at the same angle as the line you want to draw. Do *not* press ENTER.
4 On the command line, enter **25** to specify a distance. Then press ENTER.

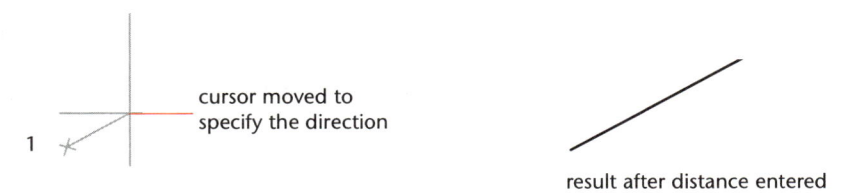

cursor moved to specify the direction

result after distance entered

The line is drawn at the length and angle you specified.

Related You can use polar coordinates to find a point by specifying a distance and angle.

Shifting and Rotating the Coordinate System

In AutoCAD, there are two coordinate systems: a fixed system called the World Coordinate System (WCS), and a movable system called the user coordinate system (UCS). In the WCS, the X axis is horizontal, the Y axis is vertical, and the Z axis is perpendicular to the XY plane. The origin is where the X and Y axes intersect (0,0) in the lower-left corner of the drawing. When you move the UCS, you define its new location in terms of the WCS. Virtually all coordinate entry is performed using the current UCS.

Moving the UCS can make it easier to work on particular sections of your drawing. Rotating the UCS helps you specify points in 3D or rotated views. Snap, Grid, and Ortho modes all rotate in line with the new UCS.

You can also set up a new angled baseline and draw lines relative to it. Snap, Grid, and Ortho rotate in line with the new UCS orientation.

With a customized UCS, you can rotate the X,Y plane and change the origin point of the coordinate system. This feature is particularly useful for working on sections where the baseline deviates from a horizontal or vertical orientation.

You can relocate the user coordinate system using several methods:

- Specify a new *XY* plane
- Specify a new origin
- Align the UCS with an existing object
- Align the UCS with the current viewing direction
- Rotate the current UCS around any of its axes
- Select a previously saved UCS

Two methods, specifying a new *XY* plane and specifying a new origin, are described in this chapter. The other methods are more appropriate for working with 3D viewpoints. You can save any number of UCSs for repeated use.

Shifting the XY Plane

One way to relocate a UCS is to specify a new UCS origin and the direction of its positive *X* and *Y* axes.

To shift the *XY* plane

1 From the Tools menu, choose UCS ➤ 3 Point.

2 Specify the new origin point (1).

For example, in a large drawing, you might specify an origin point near the area in which you want to work.

3 Specify a point to indicate the horizontal orientation of the new UCS. This point should be on the positive portion of the new *X* axis (2).

4 Specify a point to indicate the vertical orientation of the new UCS. This point should be on the positive portion of the new *Y* axis (3).

The UCS, including grid, shifts to represent the *X* and *Y* axes you have specified.

Command line   UCS

Related   The UCSXDIR and UCSYDIR system variables display the *X* and *Y* directions of the current UCS for the current space (model space or paper space).

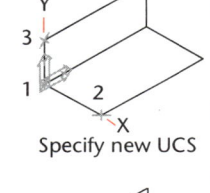

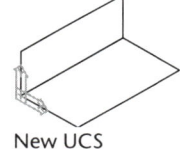

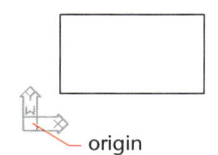

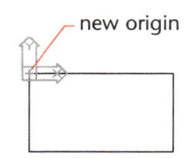

Locating a New UCS Origin

By locating a new origin, you can adjust coordinate entry to be relevant to a specific area or object in your drawing. For example, you might relocate the origin point to the corner of a building or to serve as a reference point on a map.

To use a new UCS origin

1. From the Tools menu, choose UCS ➤ Origin.
2. Specify a point for the new origin.

Command line   UCS

Restoring the UCS to WCS

If you have been working with a UCS, you can restore the UCS to be coincident with the WCS.

To restore the WCS

1. From the Tools menu, choose UCS ➤ Named UCS.

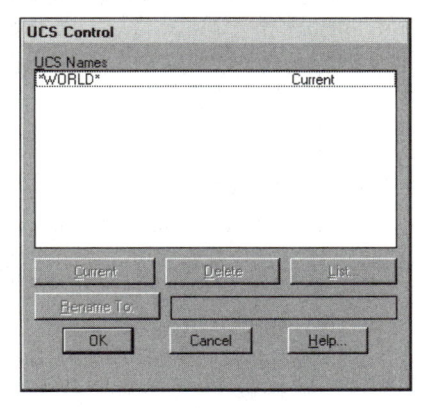

2. In the UCS Control dialog box, select *WORLD*.
3. Select Current.
4. Choose OK.

Command line   DDUCS

Related   UCS World

Displaying the UCS Icon

To indicate the location and orientation of the UCS, AutoCAD displays the UCS icon either at the UCS origin point or in the lower-left corner of the current viewport. If the icon is displayed at the origin of the current UCS, a cross (+) appears in the icon. If the icon is displayed in the lower-left corner of the viewport, no cross appears in the icon.

Shifting and Rotating the Coordinate System

121

AutoCAD displays the UCS icon in various ways to help you visualize the orientation of the drawing plane. The following figure shows some of the possible icon displays.

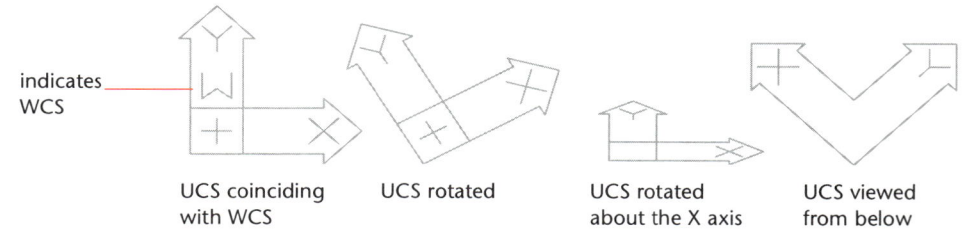

indicates WCS

| UCS coinciding with WCS | UCS rotated | UCS rotated about the X axis | UCS viewed from below |

Examples of UCS icon display

broken pencil icon

The broken pencil icon indicates that the edge of the *XY* plane is perpendicular to your viewing direction. Specifying coordinates with the pointing device while the broken pencil icon is current, results in pick points with nonzero Z values. Results may not be what you expect.

To turn the display of the UCS icon on and off

1 From the View menu, choose Display ➤ UCS Icon.

   A check mark beside the Icon option indicates that the icon is displayed.

2 Choose Display ➤ UCS Icon and select On or Off to turn the display of the UCS Icon on or off.

   Command line   UCSICON

   Related   Used with the SETVAR command, the UCSICON system variable can display (1) or hide (0) the UCS icon.

To display the UCS icon at the UCS origin

1 From the View menu, choose UCS ➤ Origin.

   A check mark beside the Origin option indicates that the icon is displayed.

   The UCS icon is displayed at the origin of the current coordinate system.

2 Choose Origin again to remove the check mark and turn this display off.

   Command line   UCSICON

   Related   The UCSORG system variable stores the origin point of the current coordinate system for the current space.

Saving and Reusing a UCS

Once you have defined a UCS, you can name it and then restore it when you need to use it again. If you no longer need a named UCS, you can delete it.

To save a UCS

1 From the Tools menu, choose UCS ➤ Save.
2 On the command line, enter a name.

You can use up to 31 characters, including letters, digits, and the special characters dollar sign ($), hyphen (–), and underscore(_). All UCS names are converted to uppercase.

Command line UCS

Related The UCSNAME system variable stores the name of the current coordinate system for the current space.

To restore a named UCS

1 From the Tools menu, choose UCS ➤ Named UCS.
2 In the UCS Control dialog box, you can view the origin and axis direction of a listed UCS by selecting the UCS name and choosing List.
3 In the UCS dialog box, you can view the origin, *X* axis, *Y* axis, and *Z* axis settings. After viewing, choose OK.
4 In the UCS Control dialog box, select the coordinate system you want to restore and select Current.
5 Choose OK.

Command line DDUCS

Related UCS Restore restores a named UCS on the command line.

To rename a UCS

1 From the Tools menu, choose UCS ➤ Named UCS.
2 In the UCS Control dialog box, select the coordinate system you want to rename.
3 At Rename To, enter a new name.
4 Choose OK.

Command line DDUCS

Related DDRENAME

To delete a UCS

1 From the Tools menu, choose UCS ➤ Named UCS.
2 In the UCS Control dialog box, select a UCS, then choose Delete.
3 Choose OK.

Related   UCS Del deletes a named UCS on the command line.

Creating Objects

4

With AutoCAD's drawing tools, you can create a range of objects, from simple lines and circles to spline curves, ellipses, and associative hatch areas. In general, you draw objects by specifying points with the pointing device or by entering coordinate values on the command line.

For information about drawing three-dimensional objects, see chapter 13, "Working in Three-Dimensional Space."

In this chapter

- Drawing line objects, polylines, multilines, and freehand sketches
- Drawing curved objects such as circles, arcs, ellipses, and spline curves
- Creating solid-filled areas, regions, and hatched areas

Drawing Lines

The line is the most basic object in AutoCAD. You can create a variety of lines—single lines, multiple line segments with and without arcs, multiple parallel lines, and freehand sketch lines. In general, you draw lines by specifying coordinate points, properties such as linetype or color, and measurements such as angles. For information on how to specify coordinates, see "Using a Coordinate System to Specify Points" on page 114. The default linetype is CONTINUOUS, an unbroken line, but various linetypes are available that use dots and dashes. For more information about linetypes, see "Working with Linetypes" on page 311.

Drawing Line Objects

A line can be one segment or a series of connected segments, but each segment is a separate line object. Use lines if you want to edit individual segments. If you need to draw a series of line segments as a single object, use a polyline. See the following section, "Drawing Polylines." You can close a sequence of lines so that the first and last segments join to form a closed loop.

To draw a line

1 From the Draw menu, choose Line.
2 Specify the start point (1).
3 Specify the endpoint (2).
4 Specify the endpoint of the next segments (3, 4, 5, 6).
5 Press ENTER to complete the line.

To undo the previous line segment during the LINE command, enter **u**. You can start a new line at the endpoint of the last line drawn by starting the LINE command again and pressing ENTER at the Start Point prompt.

Command line LINE

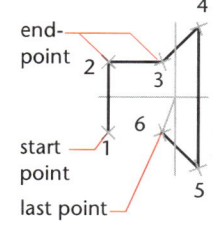

Related PLINE draws polyline line and arc segments that form a single object. MLINE draws multiple parallel lines. OFFSET creates copies of lines offset at a specified distance to one side or through a point. LINETYPE sets the current linetype.

Drawing Polylines

A polyline is a connected sequence of line or arc segments created as a single object. Use polylines if you want to edit all segments at once, although you can also edit them singly. You can set the width of individual segments, make segments taper, and close the polyline. When you draw arc segments, the first point of the arc is the endpoint of the previous segment. You can specify the angle, center point, direction, or radius of the arc. You can also complete the arc by specifying a second point and an endpoint.

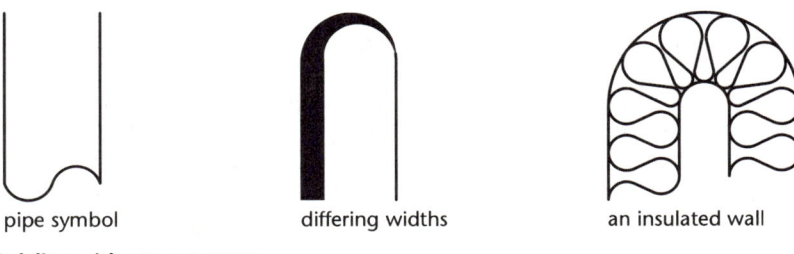

pipe symbol differing widths an insulated wall

Polyline with arc segments

To draw a polyline with straight segments

1 From the Draw menu, choose Polyline.
2 Specify the first point of the polyline.
3 Specify the endpoint of each polyline segment.
4 Press ENTER to end or to close the polyline.

Command line PLINE

Related LINE creates single or multiple line segments that are separate objects. MLINE creates multiple parallel lines.

In the next example, you draw a polyline line segment, continue with an arc segment, and then draw another line segment in a tangential direction.

To draw a line and arc combination polyline

First draw the line segment.

1 From the Draw menu, choose Polyline.
2 Specify the start point of the line segment (1).
3 Specify the endpoint of the line segment (2).
4 Enter **a** to switch to Arc mode.
5 Specify the endpoint of the arc (3).
6 Enter **l** to return to Line mode.
7 Enter the distance and angle of the line in relation to the endpoint of the arc. You can enter these relative values in the form *@distance<angle* (in this case, you would enter **@3<100**).

Drawing Lines

127

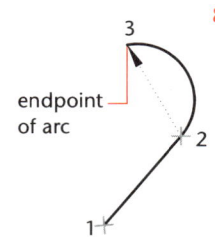

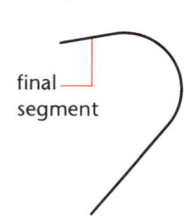

8   Press ENTER to end the polyline.

After you've created a polyline, you can edit it with PEDIT or use EXPLODE to convert it to individual line and arc segments. When you explode a wide polyline, the line width reverts to 0 and the resulting polyline is positioned along the center of what was the wide polyline.

endpoint of arc

final segment

Drawing Multilines

Multilines consist of between 1 and 16 parallel lines, called elements. You position the elements by specifying the desired offset of each element from the origin of the multiline. You can create and save multiline styles or use the default style, which has two elements. You can set the color and linetype of each element and display or hide the joints of the multiline. Joints are lines that appear at each vertex. There are several types of end caps you can give the multiline, for example, lines or arcs.

To draw a multiline

1   From the Draw menu, choose Multiline.
2   At the Command prompt, enter **st** to select a style.
3   To list available styles, enter the style name or enter **?**.
4   To justify the multiline, enter **j** and choose from top, zero, or bottom justification.
5   To change the scale of the multiline, enter **s** and enter a new scale.

Now draw the multiline.

6   Specify the starting point.
7   Specify the second point.
8   Specify the third point.
9   Specify the fourth point or enter **c** to close the multiline, or press ENTER.

Command line   MLINE

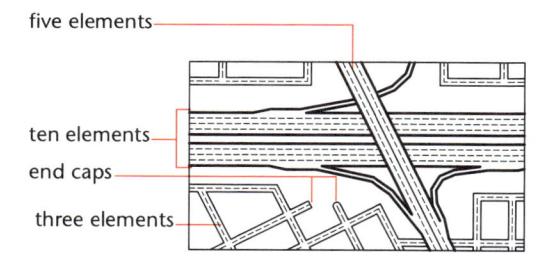

five elements

ten elements

end caps

three elements

Examples of multilines

Chapter 4   Creating Objects

128

Creating Multiline Styles

You can create named styles for multilines to control the number of elements and the properties of each element. The style also controls the background fill and the end cap. You can edit multilines to control intersections, corner joints, and the number of vertices. For more information, see "Editing Multilines" on page 281.

NOTE You cannot change the definitions of a STANDARD multiline style or of a multiline style that is being used in the current drawing.

To create a multiline style

1 From the Format menu, choose Multiline Style.

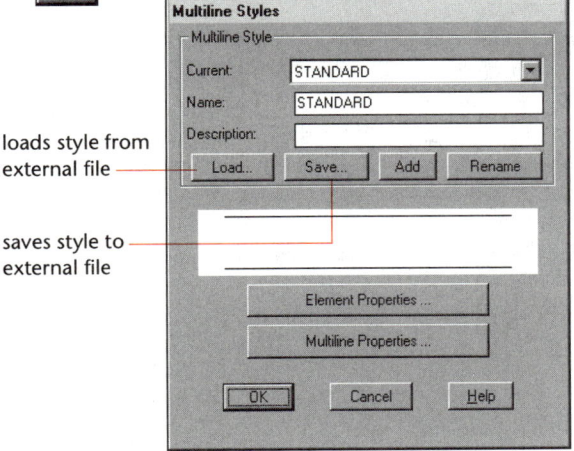

loads style from external file
saves style to external file

2 In the Multiline Styles dialog box at Name, enter a style name.
3 At Description, enter a description of the style (optional), which can have up to 255 characters, including spaces.
4 Choose Add to make the style current.
5 Choose Element Properties to add elements to the style or to modify existing elements.
6 In the Element Properties dialog box, select Offset, Color, or Linetype. Modify the element you have chosen, and then choose OK to return to the Element Properties dialog box.
7 To add an element, choose Add, and then make any necessary changes to Offset, Color, and Linetype. Choose OK.

The offset defines the 0,0 origin of the multiline relative to which other elements are drawn. There doesn't have to be an element drawn at the origin.

Drawing Lines

129

8 In the Multiline Styles dialog box, select Add to add the style to the drawing and to set this style as current.

9 Choose Save to save the style to an external multiline style file (the default is *acad.mln*).

You can add up to 16 elements to a multiline style. If you create or modify an element so that it has a negative offset, it appears below the origin in the image tile of the Multiline Style dialog box.

To specify the properties of the entire multiline

1 From the Format menu, choose Multiline Style.

2 In the Multiline Styles dialog box, choose Multiline Properties.

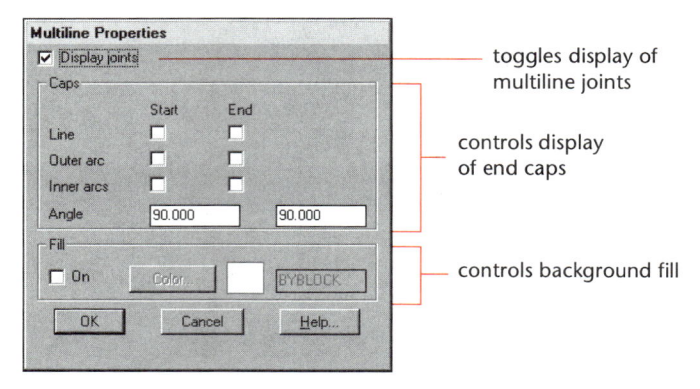

- toggles display of multiline joints
- controls display of end caps
- controls background fill

3 In the Multiline Properties dialog box, select Display Joints to display a line at the vertices of the multiline.

4 Under Caps, select a line or an arc for each end of the multiline, and enter an angle.

Lines cross the end of the whole multiline and outer arcs join the ends of the outermost elements. Inner arcs connect pairs of elements, leaving the centerline unconnected if there is an odd number of elements. For example, if there are six elements, inner arcs connect elements 2 and 5 and elements 3 and 4. If there are seven elements, inner arcs connect elements 2 and 6 and elements 3 and 5; element 4 is left unconnected.

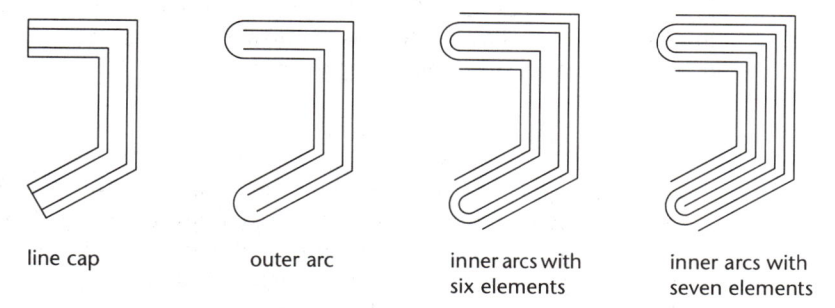

line cap   outer arc   inner arcs with   inner arcs with
                               six elements   seven elements

5 Under Fill, select On to display a background color. This color is not displayed in the image tile of the Multiline Styles dialog box.

6 Choose Color. In the Select Color dialog box, select the background fill color and choose OK.

7 In the Multiline Properties dialog box, choose OK to return to the Multiline Styles dialog box.

Next, save the Multiline style.

To save a multiline style name

1 In the Multiline Styles dialog box under Name, enter a style name.

2 Under Description, enter a description (optional), which may have up to 255 characters, including spaces.

3 Select Add to add the newly created mline style to the drawing and set this style as current.

4 Select Save to save the style to an external MLN file.

5 Choose OK.

Command line   MLSTYLE

Related   The CMLSTYLE system variable stores the name of the current multiline style. OFFSET creates new objects at a specified offset from a selected object or through a specified point.

Using Existing Multiline Styles

When you start drawing a multiline, you can use the default style, which has two elements, or specify a style you created previously. You can also change the justification and scale of the multiline before you draw it. Justification determines whether the multiline is drawn below or above the cursor, or with its origin centered on the cursor. The default is below (top justification). Scale controls the overall width of the multiline using the current units.

Multiline scale does not affect linetype scale. If you are changing the multiline scale, you might need to make equivalent changes to linetype scale to prevent dots or dashes from being disproportionately sized.

Drawing Polygons

Polygons are closed polylines with between 3 and 1,024 equal-length sides. You draw a polygon by inscribing it in, or circumscribing it about, an imaginary circle or by specifying the endpoints of one of the edges of the polygon. Because polygons always have equal-length sides, they provide a simple way to draw squares and equilateral triangles.

The following illustrations show polygons drawn using the three methods. In the first two illustrations, (1) is the center of the polygon and (2) defines the radius length, which is being specified with the pointing device.

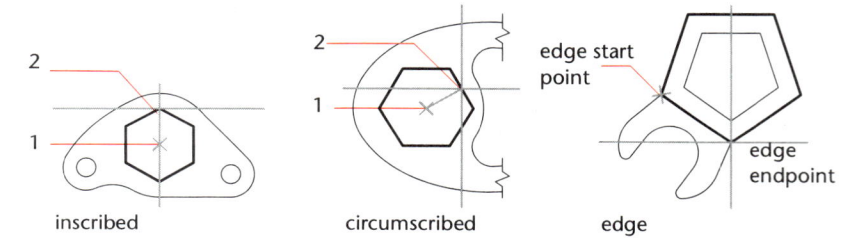

Three methods for drawing polygons

Drawing Inscribed Polygons

Use inscribed polygons when you want to specify the distance between the center of the polygon and each vertex. This distance is the radius of the circle within which the polygon is inscribed. In this example, you draw an inscribed square, the default polygon.

To draw an inscribed square

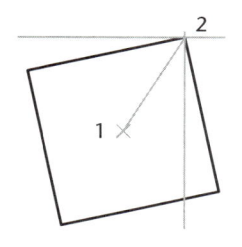

1 From the Draw menu, choose Polygon.
2 Enter **4** to specify four sides for the polygon.
3 Specify the center point for the polygon (1).
4 Enter **i** (Inscribed in Circle).
5 Specify the radius (2).

Command line POLYGON

Related RECTANG creates polyline rectangles.

Chapter 4   Creating Objects

Drawing Circumscribed Polygons

Use circumscribed polygons when you want to specify the distance between the center of the polygon and the midpoint of each side. This distance is the radius of the circle the polygon circumscribes.

To draw a circumscribed hexagon

1. From the Draw menu, choose Polygon.
2. Enter **6** for the number of sides.
3. Specify the center of the polygon (1).
4. Enter **c** (Circumscribed about Circle).
5. Specify the radius length (2).

After you've created a polygon, you can edit it with PEDIT or convert it to individual line segments with EXPLODE.

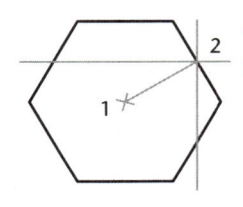

Sketching Freehand

Freehand sketches comprise many line segments. Each line segment can be a separate object or a polyline. You set the minimum length or increment of the segments. Sketching is useful for creating irregular boundaries or for tracing with a digitizer. Small line segments allow greater accuracy, but they can greatly increase the drawing file size. For this reason, use this tool sparingly.

To sketch, use the pointing device pick button like a pen, clicking to put the "pen" down on the screen to draw and clicking again to lift it up and stop drawing.

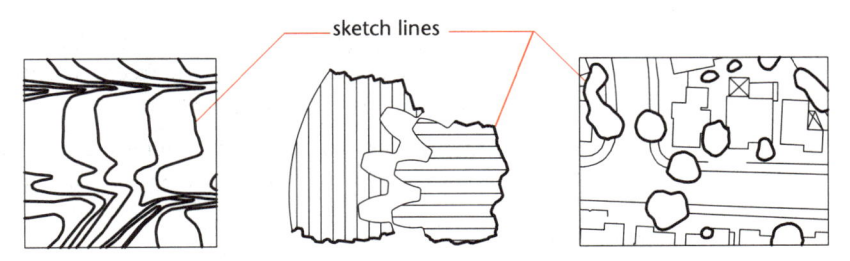

Freehand sketches

Before sketching, check the CELTYPE system variable to make sure the current linetype is CONTINUOUS. If you use a linetype with dots or dashes and set the sketch line segment shorter than the spaces or dashes, you won't see the spaces or dashes.

To prevent undesired results, it is best to turn off Ortho mode.

Drawing Lines

To sketch and record freehand lines

1. At the Command prompt, enter **sketch**.
2. At the Record Increment prompt, enter the minimum line segment length.
3. Click the pick button of your pointing device to put the "pen" down.

   When you move the pointing device, AutoCAD draws temporary freehand line segments of the length you specified. SKETCH doesn't accept coordinate input.

4. Click the pick button again to lift the "pen" up so that you can move the cursor around the screen without drawing. Click the button again to resume drawing from the new cursor position.
5. Enter **r** at any time to record (save) in the database the line you're drawing and those already drawn.

   If the pen is down, you can continue drawing after recording. If the pen is up, click the pick button to resume drawing. The freehand line starts from wherever the cursor is when you click.

6. Press ENTER to complete the sketch and record all unrecorded lines.

   If you want to use Snap or Ortho mode while sketching, you must use the keyboard toggles (F8 for Ortho, F9 for Snap). The status bar toggles have no effect. The Snap setting overrides the record increment if Snap is the larger setting. If Snap is smaller, the record increment takes precedence.

   Related Set the size of freehand line segments with the SKETCHINC system variable. To draw the freehand line as a polyline so that it is a single object, set the SKPOLY system variable to nonzero before drawing.

Erasing Freehand Lines

You erase freehand lines by using the Erase option of the SKETCH command. In Erase mode, wherever the cursor intersects the freehand line, everything from the intersection to the end of the line is erased.

Once you record freehand lines, you can't edit them or erase them with the Erase option of SKETCH. Use ERASE after you finish sketching.

To erase freehand lines

1. With the pen up or down, enter **e** (Erase).

   If the pen was down, it moves up.

2. Move the cursor to the end of the line you drew last and then move it back as far along the line as you want to erase.
3. To end the erasure and return to the SKETCH Command prompt, enter **p**. To undo the erasure, enter **e**.

If you want to change the current viewport while sketching, make sure the pen is up, all lines entered so far have been recorded, and Tablet mode is off.

Sketching in Tablet Mode

You use Tablet mode with a digitizer. Sketching in Tablet mode is useful for such things as tracing map outlines from paper directly into an AutoCAD drawing. You can't turn off Tablet mode while sketching.

When Tablet mode is on, you can configure AutoCAD to map the paper drawing's coordinate system directly into the AutoCAD World Coordinate System. Thus, there is a direct correlation between the coordinates where screen crosshairs appear, the coordinates on the tablet, and the coordinates in the original paper drawing. After configuring AutoCAD to match the coordinates of the paper drawing, you may find that the area shown on screen is not the area you need. To avoid this problem, use ZOOM to show your entire work area before you start to sketch.

With some digitizers you can't select the menus while Tablet mode is on. See your digitizer documentation for details.

Maintaining Sketching Accuracy

To ensure accuracy on a slow computer, set the record increment value to a negative value. SKETCH uses this value as if it were positive but tests every point received from the pointer against twice the record increment. If the point is more than two record increments away, your computer beeps as a warning that you should slow down to avoid losing accuracy. For example, if the record increment is –1, you should move the cursor in increments of no more than 2. Using this method does not slow down the tracing speed.

Drawing Curved Objects

You can create a variety of curved objects with AutoCAD, including spline curves, circles, arcs, ellipses, and donuts.

Drawing Spline Curves

A spline is a smooth curve passing through a given set of points. AutoCAD uses a particular type of spline known as a nonuniform rational B-spline (NURBS) curve. A NURBS curve produces a smooth curve between control points. Splines are useful for creating irregular-shaped curves, for example, drawing contour lines for geographic information system (GIS) applications or automobile design.

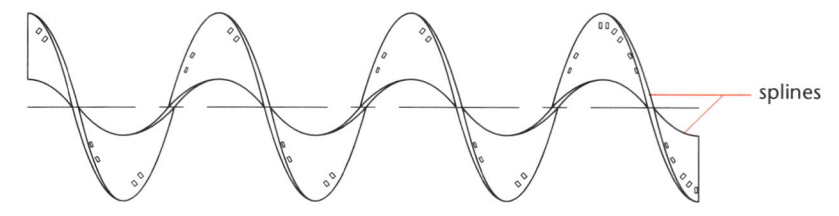

AutoCAD creates "true" splines, which are NURBS curves, with the SPLINE command. You can also create linear approximations of splines by smoothing polylines with the PEDIT command. You can convert 2D and 3D smoothed polylines to splines with the SPLINE command.

Creating true spline curves rather than editing polylines to approximate splines has three advantages:

- Spline curves can be created by interpolating the spline through a set of points that lie on the desired path of the curve. This method creates curved boundaries far more accurately than polylines for both 2D drafting and 3D modeling.
- Splines can be edited easily either with the SPLINEDIT command or with grips, and the spline definition is maintained. This definition is lost with PEDIT-smoothed polylines. See "Editing Splines" on page 283.
- A drawing containing splines uses less disk space and memory than a drawing with smoothed polylines.

You create splines by specifying coordinate points. You can close the spline so the start point and endpoint are coincident and tangent. You can also change the spline-fitting *tolerance* while drawing the spline so that you see the effect. Tolerance refers to how closely the spline fits the set of fit points you specify. The lower the tolerance, the more closely the spline fits the points. At zero tolerance, the spline passes through the points.

To create a spline by specifying points

1 From the Draw menu, choose Spline.
2 Specify the spline's start point (1).
3 Specify points (2–5) to create the spline and press ENTER.

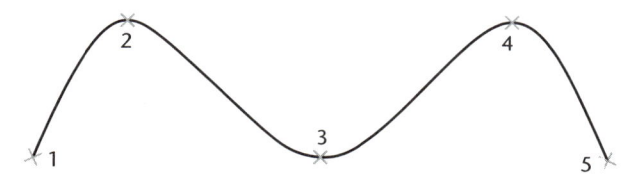

4 Specify the start and end tangents (6, 7).

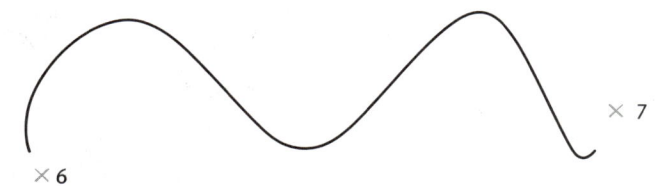

The following illustration shows the result when you use the same points but different start and end tangents.

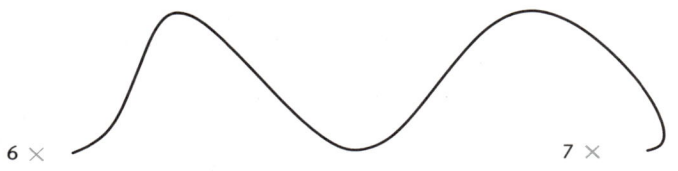

The following spline is drawn using the same points but a higher tolerance and different start and end tangents.

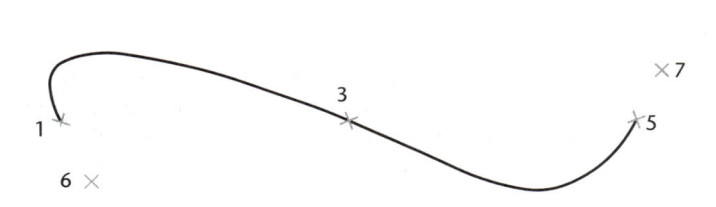

Command line   SPLINE

Related   SPLINEDIT edits a spline object. PLINE draws polyline line and arc segments that form a single object. PEDIT can modify a polyline into an approximation of a spline.

Drawing Circles

You can create circles in several ways. The default method is to specify the center and radius. You can also specify the center and diameter or define the diameter alone with two points. You can define the circle's circumference with three points. You can also create the circle tangent to three existing objects or create it tangent to two objects and specify a radius. In the following illustrations, the darker circles are the ones being drawn.

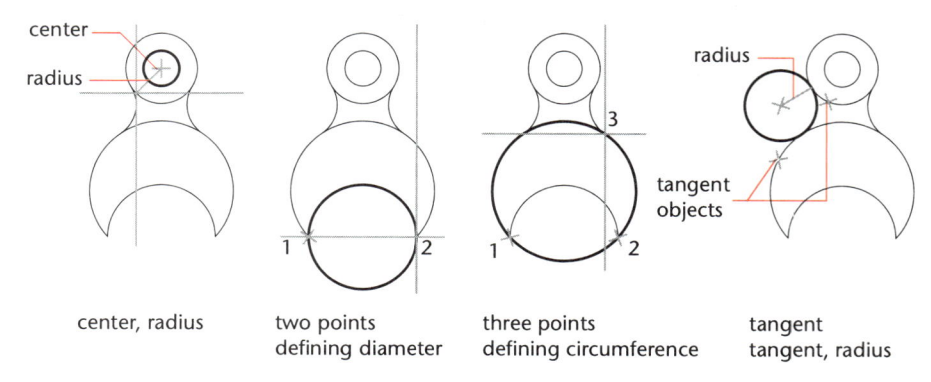

| center, radius | two points defining diameter | three points defining circumference | tangent tangent, radius |

Four methods of drawing circles

To draw a circle by specifying a center point and radius

1 From the Draw menu, choose Circle ➤ Center, Radius.
2 Specify the center point.
3 Specify the radius.

Command line CIRCLE

To create a circle that is tangent to two objects, specify a tangent point on each of the objects and the radius of the circle. The tangent point can be any point on the object. In the following illustration, the darker circle is the one being drawn, and the tangent points are points (1) and (2).

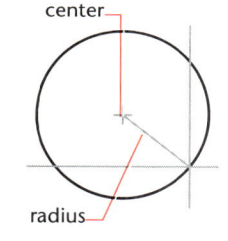

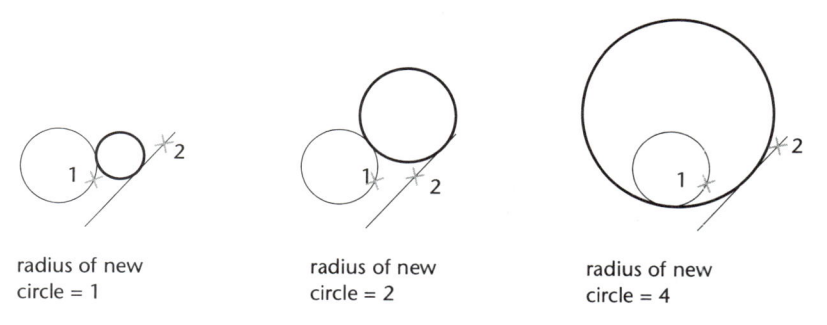

| radius of new circle = 1 | radius of new circle = 2 | radius of new circle = 4 |

Circles created tangent to two objects

To create a circle tangent to existing objects

1 From the Draw menu, choose Circle ➤ Tan, Tan, Radius.
   You are now in Tangent snap mode.
2 Select the first object to draw the circle tangent to.

Chapter 4   Creating Objects

3 Select the second object to draw the circle tangent to.

4 Specify the radius of the circle.

Related   To create a circle tangent at two or three points, set OSNAP to Tangent and use the two-point or three-point method to create the circle (see "Using Object Snap for a Single Point" on page 172).

Drawing Arcs

You can create arcs in many ways. The default method is to specify three points—a starting point, a second point on the arc, and an endpoint. You can also specify the included angle, radius, direction, and chord length of arcs. The chord of an arc is a straight line between the endpoints. By default, AutoCAD draws arcs counterclockwise.

In the following example, the start point of the arc snaps to the endpoint of a line. The second point of the arc snaps to the middle circle.

To draw an arc by specifying three points

1 From the Draw menu, choose Arc ➤ 3 Points.

2 Specify the start point (1) by entering **endp** and selecting the line.

The arc snaps to the endpoint of the line.

3 Specify the second point (2) by entering **qua** and selecting the quadrant of the middle circle to snap to.

4 Specify the endpoint of the arc (3).

Command line   ARC

Related   ELLIPSE creates elliptical arcs. PLINE creates arc segments within 2D polylines.

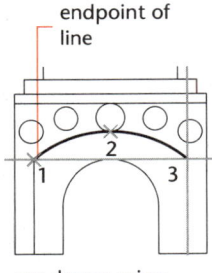

endpoint of line

arc drawn using default 3-point method

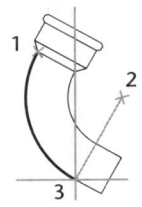

start (1), center (2), end (3)

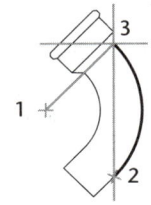

center (1), start (2), end (3)

In the following illustrations, the center of an existing circle is used as the center of the arc. Once you specify the center and start points of the arc, you complete the arc by specifying the chord length. The distances shown in these illustrations from one endpoint to the cursor are chord lengths.

Drawing Curved Objects

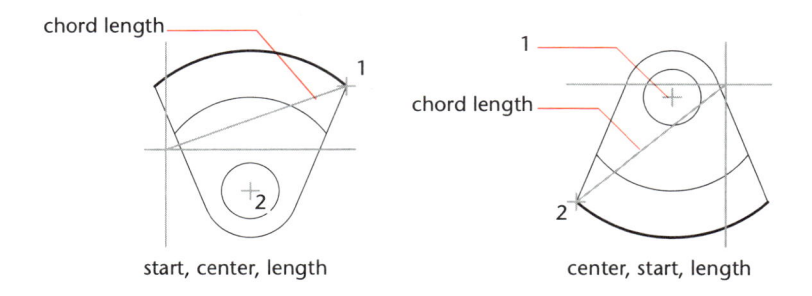

chord length

start, center, length

chord length

center, start, length

To draw an arc using a start point, a center point, and a chord length

1. From the Draw menu, choose Arc ➤ Start, Center, Length.
2. Specify a start point (1).
3. Specify the center point.
4. Specify the chord length.

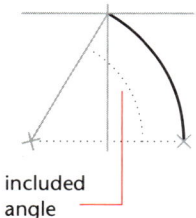

Use the Start, Center, Angle or Center, Start, Angle method when you have a start point and a center point you can snap to. The angle determines the endpoint of the arc. Use the Start, End, Angle method when you have both endpoints but no center point to snap to.

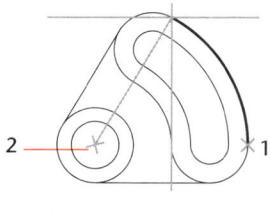

included angle

start, center, angle

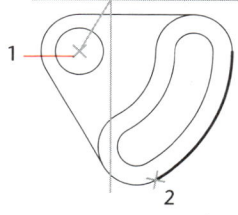

center, start, angle

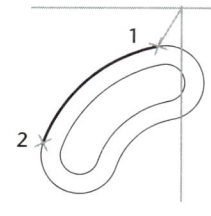

start, end, angle

The following illustration on the left shows an arc drawn by specifying a start point, endpoint, and radius. You can specify the radius by entering a length or by moving the cursor clockwise or counterclockwise and clicking to specify a distance.

start, end, radius

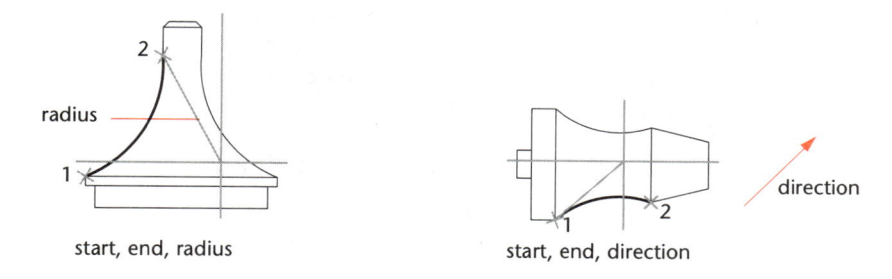

start, end, direction

The illustration on the right shows an arc drawn with the pointing device by specifying a start and endpoint and a direction of the tangent. Moving the cursor up from the start point and endpoint draws the arc concave to the object, as shown here. Moving the cursor down would draw the arc convex to the object.

You can start a line at the endpoint of the last drawn arc by starting LINE and pressing ENTER at the Start Point prompt. The arc's endpoint defines the starting point and the tangential direction of the new line. You need to specify the length.

Drawing Ellipses

You can create full ellipses and elliptical arcs, both of which are exact mathematical representations of ellipses. The default method of drawing an ellipse is to specify the endpoints of the first axis and the distance, which is half the length of the second axis. The longer axis of an ellipse is called the major axis, and the shorter one is the minor axis. The order in which you define the axes does not matter.

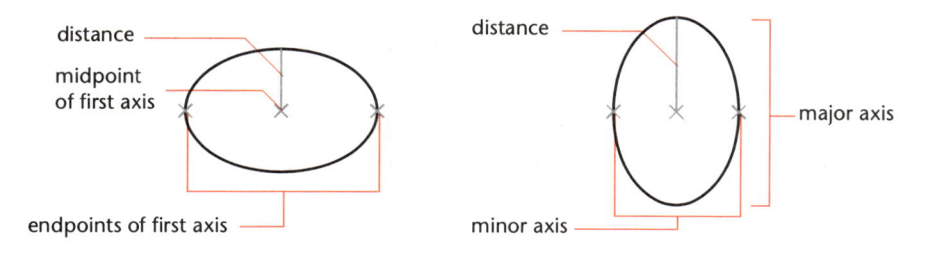

Drawing Curved Objects

In the following procedure, you draw an ellipse using the default method and the pointing device. Here, the first axis is the major axis, and the second is the minor. The distance increases as you drag the pointing device away from the midpoint.

To draw a true ellipse using endpoints and distance

1. From the Draw menu, choose Ellipse ➤ Axis, End.
2. Specify the first endpoint of the first axis (1).
3. Specify the second endpoint of the first axis (2).
4. Drag the pointing device away from the midpoint (3) of the first axis and click to specify the distance.

Command line   ELLIPSE

You can provide a rotation angle instead of a distance or draw the ellipse based on a center point, an endpoint of one axis, and half the length of the other axis.

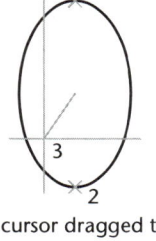

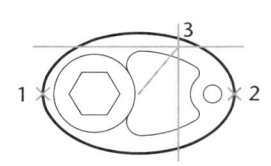

cursor dragged to specify distance

first axis as major axis

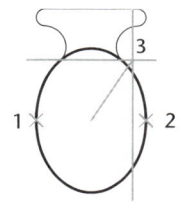

first axis as minor axis

Ellipses created by specifying axis endpoints and distance

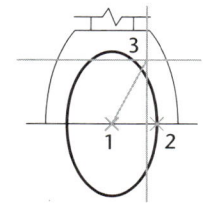

In the illustrations above, (1) and (2) are the endpoints of the first axis, and (3) defines the distance (half the length) of the second axis. The ellipse at the left is drawn by specifying the center (1) and two axes. The endpoint of the first axis is at (2), and (3) defines half the length of the second axis.

Related   Create a polyline representation of an ellipse by setting the PELLIPSE system variable to 1. PELLIPSE is set to 0 by default.

Drawing Elliptical Arcs

The default method of drawing elliptical arcs uses the first axis endpoints and the second axis distance, as for full ellipses. You then specify start and end angles. These angles are measured from the center of the ellipse and the direction of the major axis. This point is defined as Ø degrees. The start angle defines the start point of the elliptical arc. The end angle defines the endpoint, and the arc is drawn between these points in the direction set by the ANGDIR system variable. If ANGDIR is 0, the angles are measured in a counterclockwise direction. If ANGDIR is 1, they are measured in a clockwise direction.

If the start and end angles are the same, you create a full ellipse. You can also specify a start angle and an included angle. The included angle is measured relative to the start point instead of from Ø degrees.

In the following procedure, start and end angles are measured from (1), which is the first endpoint of the first axis. ANGDIR is set to 0, so the angles are measured counterclockwise from (1). The start angle (4) is 230 degrees and the end angle (5) is 50 degrees.

To draw an elliptical arc using start and end angles

1 From the Draw menu, choose Ellipse ➤ Arc.
2 Specify endpoints for the first axis (1, 2).
3 Specify the distance of the second axis (3).
4 Specify a start angle (4).
5 Specify an end angle (5).

Related   ARC creates arcs. PLINE creates arc segments within polylines.

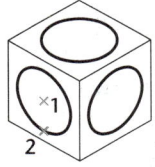

Drawing Isometric Circles

If you are drawing on isometric planes to simulate 3D, you can use ellipses to represent circles viewed from an oblique angle. First you need to turn on an isometric plane (see "Using Isometric Snap and Grid" on page 162).

isometric circles

To draw an isometric circle

1 Turn on the isometric Snap and Grid.
2 From the Draw menu, choose Ellipse ➤ Axis, End.
3 Enter **i** (Isocircle).
4 Specify the center of the circle (1).
5 Specify the radius or diameter of the circle (2).

Drawing Donuts

Drawing donuts is a quick way to create filled rings or solid-filled circles. Donuts are actually closed polylines having width. To create a donut, specify its inside and outside diameters and its center. You can continue creating multiple copies with the same diameter by specifying different centers until you press ENTER to complete the command. To create solid-filled circles, specify an inside diameter of 0.

Drawing Curved Objects

donuts

donut

filled rings

solid-filled circles

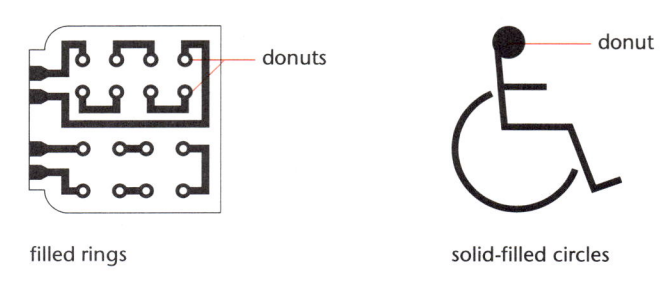

Donuts created as filled rings and solid-filled circles

To draw a donut

1. From the Draw menu, choose Donut.
2. Specify the inside diameter (1).
3. Specify the outside diameter (2).
4. Specify the center of the donut (3).
5. Specify the center point for another donut or press ENTER to complete the command.

Command line   DONUT

Related   The DONUTID system variable stores the inside diameter value of a donut, and DONUTOD stores the outside diameter value. The FILLMODE system variable controls the display of donuts and other wide polylines.

After you've created a donut, you can edit it with PEDIT or convert it to two arcs with EXPLODE. If you explode a donut, its line width reverts to 0.

Creating Point Objects

Point objects can be useful, for example, as node or reference points that you can snap to and offset objects from. You can set the style of the point and its size relative to the screen or in absolute units.

To set point style and size

1. From the Format menu, choose Point Style.

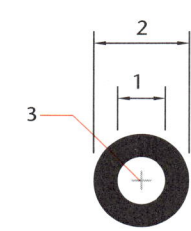

Chapter 4   Creating Objects

144

sets style

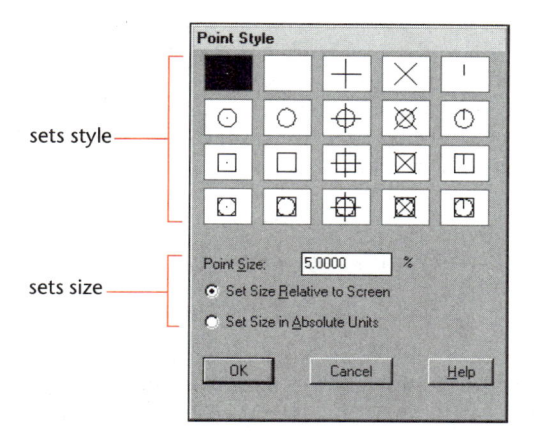

sets size

2 In the Point Style dialog box, select a point style.
3 Under Point Size, specify a size.
4 Choose OK.

Command line DDPTYPE

To create a point marker

1 From the Draw menu, choose Point ➤ Single Point.
2 Specify the point location.

Command line POINT draws a single point.

Related The PDMODE system variable sets different point styles. The PDSIZE system variable controls point size.

Changing the Drawing Order of Objects

By default, objects are drawn in the order they are created. DRAWORDER changes the display order of objects, moving one in front of another, for example.

Ordering ensures proper display and plotting output when two or more objects overlay one another. An example of when ordering may be necessary is when a raster image is drawn over existing objects, obscuring them from view.

Changing the Drawing Order of Objects

145

To change the drawing order of an object

1. From the Tools menu, choose Display Order.
2. Select Bring to Front or Send to Back to indicate the drawing order of the current objects. Or, select Bring Above Object or Send Under Object to select the object you want to move above or below.

Command line   DRAWORDER

For more information, see DRAWORDER in the *Command Reference*.

Regenerating the Drawing Order

When you open a drawing that was previously saved with drawing order specified, the display is regenerated based on the order in which the objects were originally created. To display objects in the drawing order you specified using the DRAWORDER command, you must issue a REGEN command.

The REGEN command regenerates the display in the current viewport, but because it also regenerates the entire drawing, the screen coordinates for all objects are also regenerated.

Using REDRAW refreshes the display in the current viewport but does not recalculate the coordinates for all objects. REDRAW takes much less time than REGEN.

If you specify drawing order in a Release 14 drawing and save that drawing as a Release 12 drawing, the drawing order you specified will not be maintained. In the Release 12 drawing, objects will be drawn in the order they were originally created.

Setting the SORTENTS System Variable

The initial SORTENTS value is 96, which means sorting is turned on only for plotting and PostScript output, and objects are drawn in the order they are created. By default, when you issue the DRAWORDER command, object sorting is turned on for all sorting operations, and SORTENTS is automatically set to 127, which is the sum of all the bit code values.

Changing the SORTENTS system variable may temporarily disable the display order of the objects you have just ordered. However, if you reissue the DRAWORDER command, the drawing order is restored.

In large drawings, regeneration and redrawing can be slower when SORTENTS is set. Setting SORTENTS to 0 turns off the sort order. For more information about the SORTENTS system variable and the code values, see the *Command Reference*.

Creating Solid-Filled Areas

You can create triangular and quadrilateral areas filled with a color. For quicker results, create these areas with the FILLMODE system variable off, and then turn on FILLMODE to fill the finished area. You don't see the area outline until it is complete.

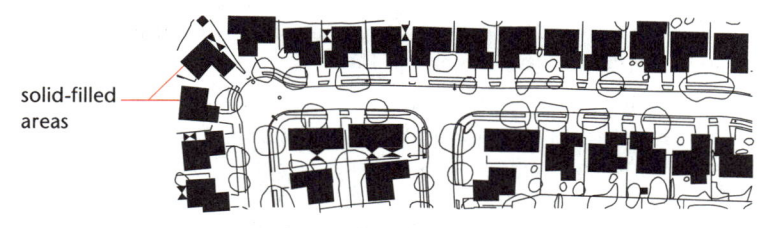

Solid-filled areas used to depict buildings

To create a triangular solid filled area

1 From the Draw menu, choose Surfaces ➤ 2D Solid.
2 Specify the first point (1).
3 Specify the second point (2).
4 Specify the third point (3). Then press ENTER.
5 Press ENTER again to exit the command.

When you create a quadrilateral solid-filled area, the sequence of the third and fourth points determines its shape. Compare the following illustrations:

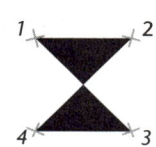

Command line   SOLID

Related   3DFACE creates a three-dimensional face.

Creating Solid-Filled Areas

147

Creating Regions

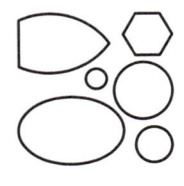

Regions are two-dimensional enclosed areas you create from closed shapes called loops. A loop is a curve or a sequence of connected curves that defines an area on a plane with a boundary that does not intersect itself. Loops can be combinations of lines, polylines, circles, arcs, ellipses, elliptical arcs, splines, 3D faces, traces, and solids. The objects that make up the loops must either be closed or form closed areas by sharing endpoints with other objects. They must also be coplanar (on the same plane).

basic shapes that can form regions

You can create regions out of multiple loops and out of open curves whose endpoints are connected and form loops. If the open curves intersect in their interior, they cannot form a region. Objects such as 3D polylines and face meshes can be converted to regions by being exploded. You cannot form regions from open objects that intersect to form a closed area: for example, intersecting arcs or self-intersecting curves.

You can apply hatching and shading to regions and you can analyze properties such as their area and moments of inertia. You can create shapes, as shown in the following illustration, then select objects to create regions using the following procedure.

To create regions

1 From the Draw menu, choose Region.
2 Select objects to create the region (must be closed loops).
3 Press ENTER.

A message on the command line indicates how many loops were detected and how many regions were created.

Command line   REGION

Related   BOUNDARY creates polyline boundaries that are composite regions from intersecting objects, whether they share endpoints or not. BHATCH creates an associative hatch boundary. BLOCK creates a compound object (a block definition) from a group of objects.

With the REGION command, you can create a region from objects that form a closed boundary. With the BOUNDARY command, you can create a region that is determined by the enclosed area of overlapping objects.

To create regions by using boundaries

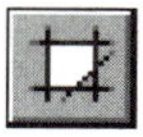

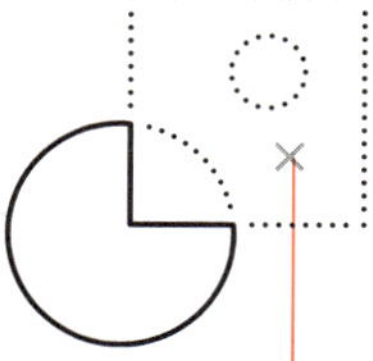

1 From the Draw menu, choose Boundary.
2 In the Boundary Creation dialog box at Object Type, select Region.
3 Choose Make New Boundary Set.
4 Select objects to create regions with their boundaries.
5 Select either From Everything on Screen or From Existing Boundary Set, and then choose Pick Points.
6 Specify a point in your drawing inside each area that you want defined as a region and press ENTER. This point is known as the internal point.

Command line   -BOUNDARY

Related   REGION creates a region object from a selection set of existing objects.

Creating Composite Regions

You create composite regions by subtracting, combining, or finding the intersection of regions. You can then extrude or revolve composite regions to create complex solids (see chapter 13, "Working in Three-Dimensional Space").

When you subtract one region from another, you first select the region from which you want to subtract. For example, to calculate how much carpeting is needed for a floor plan, select the outer boundary of the floor space and subtract all the uncarpeted areas, such as pillars and counters. Find the area of the resulting region with the AREA command.

To create a composite region by subtraction

1 From the Modify menu, choose Boolean ➤ Subtract.
2 Select the region from which to subtract (1) and press ENTER.
3 Select the region to subtract (2).

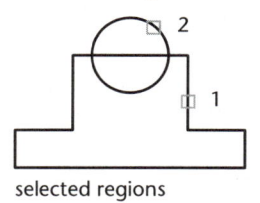

selected regions 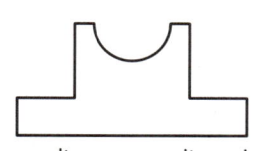   result—a composite region

Command line   SUBTRACT

Related   UNION and INTERSECT also create composite regions.

You can select regions in any order to unite them with the UNION command or to find their intersection with the INTERSECT command. AutoCAD ignores objects within the selection set that are not regions.

The following illustration shows the uniting of two regions.

selected regions   result

The following illustration shows the intersection of three regions, which you find using the INTERSECT command.

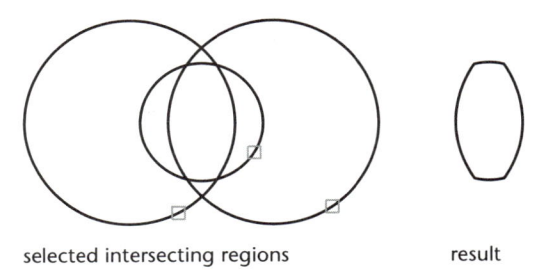

selected intersecting regions   result

You can select the regions whose intersection you want to find in any order. The resulting object is also a region.

Hatching Areas

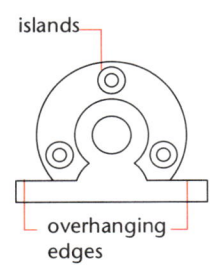

islands
overhanging edges

Hatching fills a specified area in a drawing with a pattern. You can hatch an enclosed area or a specified boundary using the BHATCH and HATCH commands.

BHATCH creates associative or nonassociative hatches. Associative hatches are linked to their boundaries and update when the boundaries are modified. Nonassociative hatches are independent of their boundaries. BHATCH defines boundaries automatically when you specify a point within the area to be hatched. Any whole or partial objects that are not part of the boundary are ignored and do not affect the hatch. The boundary can have overhanging edges and islands (enclosed areas within the hatch area) that you choose to hatch or leave unhatched. You can also define a boundary by selecting objects.

HATCH creates nonassociative hatches only. It is useful for hatching areas that do not have closed boundaries. See "Using Point Acquisition" on page 155. HATCH is available only at the command line.

Creating an Associative Hatch

Hatched areas created with BHATCH are associative by default. You can remove hatch associativity at any time or create a nonassociative hatch.

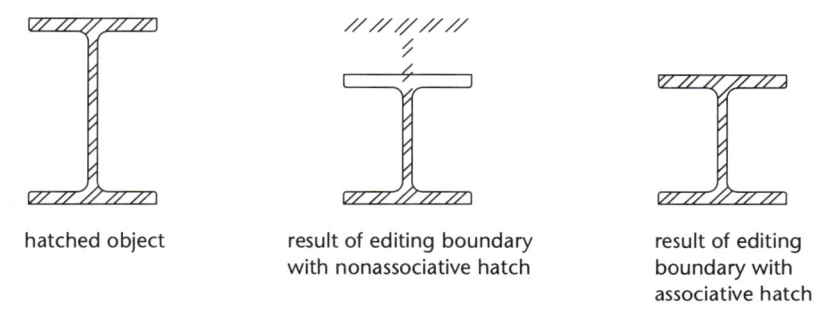

hatched object

result of editing boundary with nonassociative hatch

result of editing boundary with associative hatch

To hatch an enclosed area

1 From the Draw menu, choose Hatch.
2 In the Boundary Hatch dialog box under Boundary, choose Pick Points.
3 Specify a point in your drawing inside each area you want hatched.
4 Press ENTER.
5 In the Boundary Hatch dialog box, choose Apply to apply the hatch.

NOTE When using Pick Points to create an associative hatch, specify one internal point per hatch block placement. Specifying more than one internal point can produce unexpected results when you edit the hatch boundary.

To hatch selected objects

1 From the Draw menu, choose Hatch.
2 In the Boundary Hatch dialog box under Boundary, choose Select Objects.
3 Specify the object or objects you want to hatch. The objects need not form a closed boundary. You can also specify any islands that should remain unhatched.
4 Press ENTER.
5 In the Boundary Hatch dialog box, choose Apply to apply the hatch.

Command line   BHATCH

Related The Direct Hatch option of the HATCH command creates a boundary and fills it with a nonassociative hatch. The BOUNDARY command (-BOUNDARY at the command line) makes a polyline or region boundary of internal areas. -BHATCH changes boundary hatch settings from the command line.

> **NOTE** Due to the large number of combinations of geometry that can be hatched, editing hatched geometry can produce unexpected results. In this event, delete the hatch object and rehatch.

Defining Hatch Boundaries

Boundaries can be any combination of lines, arcs, circles, 2D polylines, ellipses, splines, blocks, and paper space viewports (see "Preparing a Layout" on page 480). Each boundary component must be at least partially within the current view. By default, AutoCAD defines the boundary by analyzing all the closed objects in the current view. If you hatch using the Normal style, islands remain unhatched and islands within islands are hatched, as in the mechanical part shown in the following illustrations.

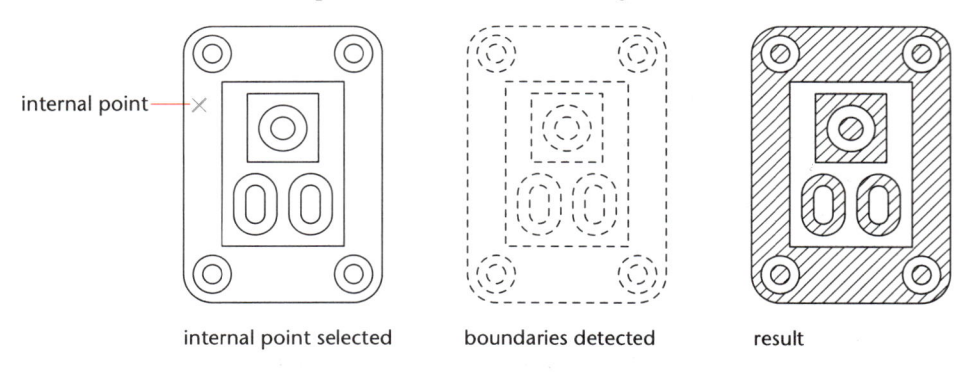

internal point

internal point selected   boundaries detected   result

Once all the islands have been detected, you can remove any islands from the hatch area. In the following procedure, you remove islands so that the part is hatched as illustrated.

internal point

boundaries detected

islands to remove
(solid boundaries)

result

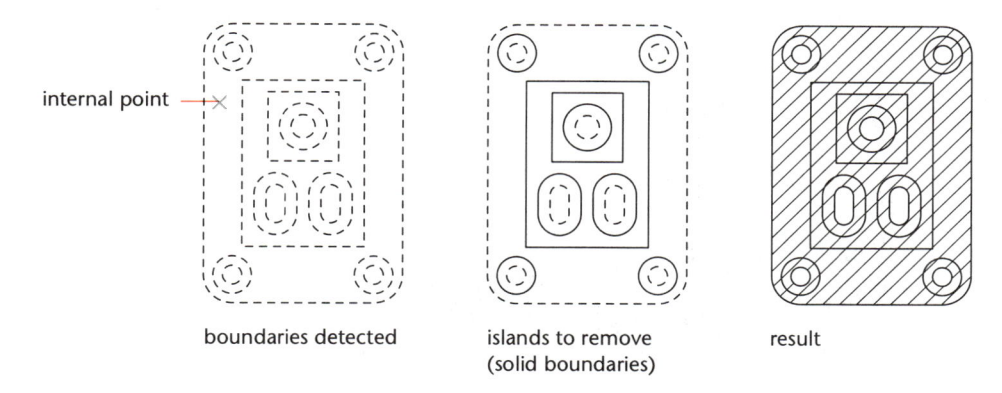

To remove islands from the hatch area

1. From the Draw menu, choose Hatch.
2. In the Boundary Hatch dialog box under Boundary, choose Pick Points.
3. Specify a point in your drawing inside the hatch area and press ENTER.
4. In the Boundary Hatch dialog box, choose Remove Islands.
5. Specify the islands for removal (see the solid boundaries in the middle illustration) and press ENTER.
6. In the Boundary Hatch dialog box, choose Apply to apply the hatch.

Related To detect only the external boundary of an area to hatch, turn off island detection in the BHATCH Advanced Options dialog box. AutoCAD hatches over the undetected objects within the defined boundary. You can select objects within the boundary that remain unhatched. To do this, use the Select Objects option in the Boundary Hatch dialog box.

Using Boundary Sets

Analysis of all objects fully or partially on screen as boundaries can be time-consuming in a complex drawing. To hatch a small area of a complex drawing, you can define a boundary set. A boundary set is a set of objects in the drawing. When you pick an internal point within the boundary set, AutoCAD does not analyze objects not included in the boundary set. Boundary sets are also useful for applying different hatch styles in different sections of a drawing.

You can define a boundary set within a map and hatch only part of the area. For clarity, first zoom into the area you want to hatch (see "Defining a Zoom Window" on page 202).

area for hatching

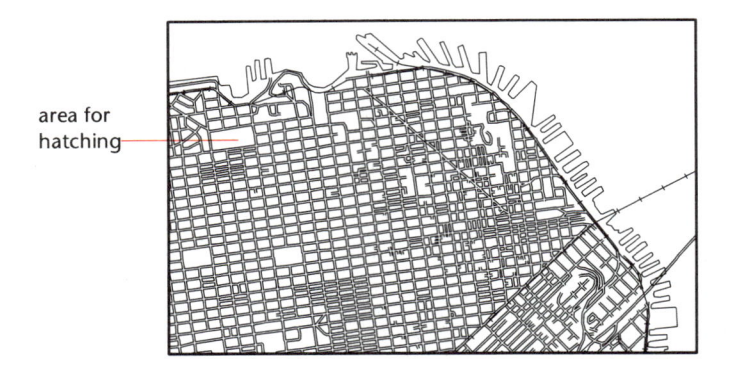

To define a boundary set in a complex drawing

1 From the Draw menu, choose Hatch.
2 In the Boundary Hatch dialog box under Boundary, choose Advanced.
3 In the Advanced Options dialog box, choose Make New Boundary Set.
4 At the Select Objects prompt, specify the corner points for the boundary set (1, 2) and press ENTER.

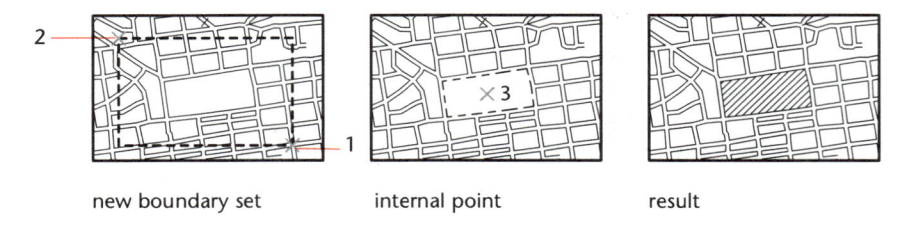

new boundary set   internal point   result

By drawing the selection box from right to left, you select all objects the box encloses or crosses.

5 In the Advanced Options dialog box, choose OK.
6 In the Boundary Hatch dialog box, choose Pick Points.
7 Specify the internal point (3) and press ENTER.
8 In the Boundary Hatch dialog box, choose Apply to apply the hatch.

Related The View Selections option in the Boundary Hatch dialog box highlights the objects in the drawing that define the boundary. Use the Inherit Properties option in the Boundary Hatch dialog box to set the current hatch pattern settings to be the same as an existing hatch pattern.

Using Point Acquisition

You can define a hatch boundary by specifying points directly. For example, you might want to illustrate that a whole area of a drawing is filled with a pattern by filling just a small section of that area, as shown in the following illustration.

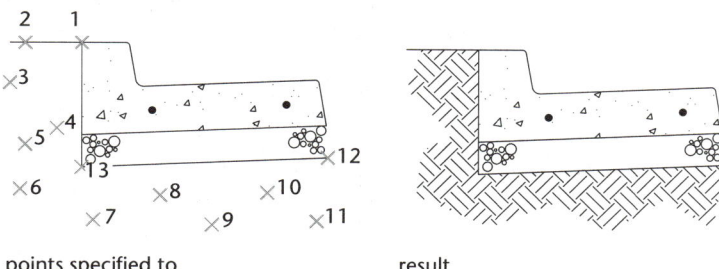

points specified to define hatch boundary

result

In this procedure, you define an area to be hatched by specifying points directly. The hatch pattern is Earth, and it is rotated 45 degrees. Once the hatch is created, the polyline is discarded.

To define a boundary by point acquisition

1 On the command line, enter **hatch**.
2 Enter **earth** to select the Earth pattern.
3 Specify the scale and angle (in this case 1.0 for scale and 45 degrees for angle) for the pattern.
4 At the Select Objects prompt, press ENTER.

   AutoCAD creates a boundary from the points you specify.

5 Enter **n** to discard the polyline boundary once it has been defined.
6 Specify the points that define the boundary (1–13). Then enter **c** and press ENTER.

Using Hatch Styles

You can further determine how islands are hatched using the three hatching styles: Normal, Outer, and Ignore. You can find these styles under Style in the Advanced Options dialog box (in the Boundary Hatch dialog box, choose Advanced).

The Normal style hatches inward from the outer boundary. If it encounters an internal intersection, it turns off hatching until it encounters another intersection. Thus, areas separated from the outside of the hatched area by an odd number of intersections are hatched, and areas separated by an even number are not. The Outer style hatches inward from the outer boundary and stops at the next boundary. The Ignore style hatches the entire enclosed area, ignoring internal boundaries.

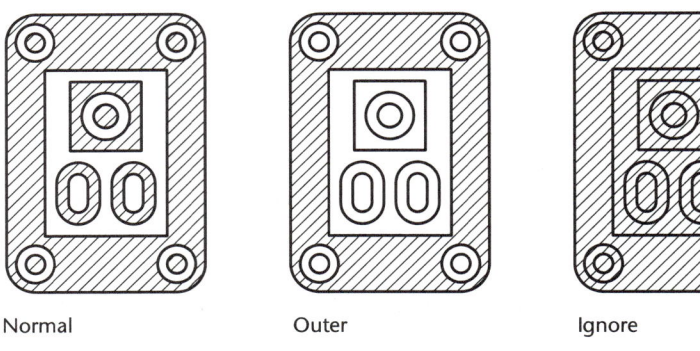

Normal   Outer   Ignore

Hatch styles

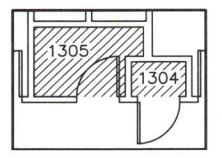

default hatching of text

If a hatch line encounters a text, attribute, shape, trace, or solid-fill object, and if the object is selected as part of the boundary set, AutoCAD does not hatch through the object. You can draw a pie slice, for example, label it with text, and hatch it, and the text will remain readable. If you want to hatch through such objects, use the Ignore style.

The interiors of traces and solids cannot be hatched, because their outlines are not accepted as boundaries.

Using Hatch Patterns

AutoCAD supplies a solid fill and more than 50 industry-standard hatch patterns. Hatch patterns highlight a particular feature or area of a drawing. For example, patterns can help differentiate the components of a 3D object or represent the materials that make up an object. AutoCAD supplies 14 hatch patterns that conform to the ISO (International Standardization Organization) standards. These patterns are listed at the end of the pattern list in the Boundary Hatch and Hatch Pattern Palette dialog boxes. When you select an ISO pattern, you can specify a pen width, which determines the line weight in the pattern.

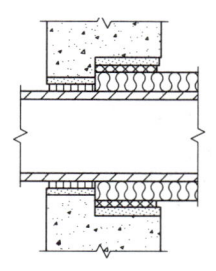

industry-standard hatch patterns

You can use a pattern supplied with AutoCAD or one from an external pattern library. For a table of the hatch patterns supplied with AutoCAD, see "Standard Libraries" in the *Command Reference*. These patterns are also listed by name and shown in the Hatch Pattern Palette dialog box. You can define a simple line pattern using the current linetype with the User-Defined Pattern option, or you can create more complex hatch patterns. For information about creating hatch patterns, see "Linetypes and Hatch Patterns" in the *Customization Guide*. To reduce file size, a hatch pattern is defined in the drawing database as a single graphic object.

In the following procedure, you create a simple line pattern, defining the spacing between the lines and creating a second set of lines at 90 degrees to the original lines.

To define a hatch pattern

1. From the Draw menu, choose Hatch.
2. In the Boundary Hatch dialog box under Pattern Type, select User-defined.
3. Under Spacing, enter the spacing between lines.
4. Select Double to add lines at 90 degrees to the original.
5. Select Pick Points and specify the internal point.
6. Choose Apply.

Command line BHATCH

Custom Objects and Proxies

AutoCAD provides application developers with the ability to create custom objects, both graphical or nongraphical. Because custom objects are created by ARX applications, those applications must be available to AutoCAD when the custom object is to be displayed or used. If the application that created a custom object is not available, AutoCAD temporarily replaces that object with a proxy object. When the application is made available to AutoCAD, the proxy object is replaced by the custom object.

There are two situations that force AutoCAD to replace a custom object with a proxy. The first, and most common, is when you open a drawing that contains custom objects, but the application that created these objects is not installed on your system. The second situation occurs when you unload the ARX application that defined a custom object in the current drawing. When this happens, AutoCAD displays the Proxy Information dialog box, which reports the number of proxy objects that exist in the drawing. The Proxy Information dialog box provides you with the name of the missing application, the total number of proxy objects (both graphical and nongraphical), and additional information about the type and display state of the proxy objects. With this dialog box, you can also control the display of proxy objects in the drawing.

Drawing with Precision

5

With AutoCAD you can create your drawings with precise geometry without performing tedious calculations. Often you can specify precise points without knowing the coordinates. Without leaving the drawing screen, you can perform calculations on your drawing and display various types of status information.

In this chapter

- Changing the grid and snap alignment
- Using Ortho mode to restrict point selection
- Snapping to geometric points on objects
- Using point filters and the tracking feature to enter coordinates
- Creating construction lines
- Calculating distances, angles, and areas
- Listing object information

Adjusting Snap and Grid Alignment

You can use the grid as a visual guideline and turn on Snap mode to restrict cursor movement. In addition to setting the spacing, you can adjust the snap and grid alignment. You can rotate the alignment, or you can set it for use with isometric drawings.

Changing the Snap Angle and Base Point

If you need to draw along a specific alignment or angle, you can rotate the snap angle. This rotation realigns the crosshairs and constrains the cursor to the new alignment when Snap or Ortho mode is on. In the following example, the snap angle is adjusted to match the angle of the anchor bracket. With this adjustment, you can use the grid to draw objects at a 30-degree angle.

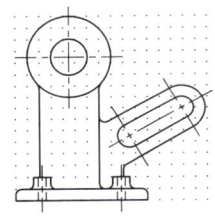

default snap angle 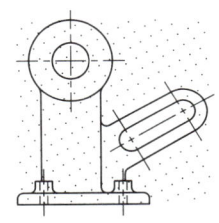   rotated snap angle

When you set the snap angle from the Drawing Aids dialog box, the grid angle also changes.

The center point of the snap angle rotation is the snap base point. If you need to align a hatch pattern, you can change this point, which is normally set to 0,0.

To rotate the snap angle and change its base point

1   From the Tools menu, choose Drawing Aids.

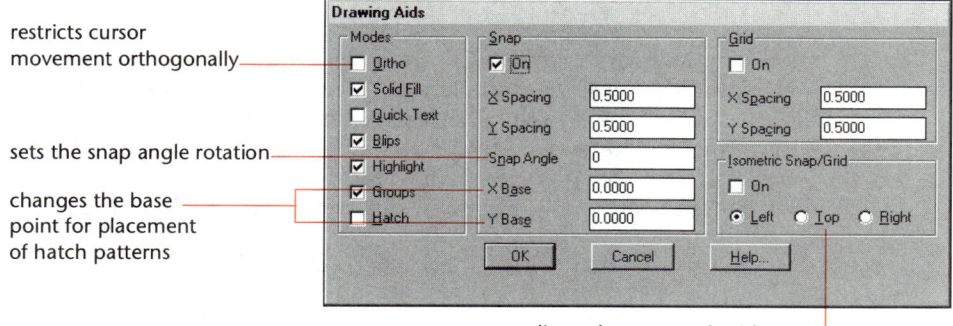

restricts cursor movement orthogonally

sets the snap angle rotation

changes the base point for placement of hatch patterns

adjusts the snap and grid settings along isometric axes

2 In the Drawing Aids dialog box under Snap, enter a snap angle rotation.

3 To set the base point in order to align snap locations, enter the *X* and *Y* coordinate values for X Base and Y Base.

4 Choose OK.

The SNAPANG system variable sets the snap rotation angle for the current viewport without changing the grid angle. The SNAPBASE system variable sets the snap base point for the current viewport. One advantage setting these system variables has over using the dialog box is that you can specify the base point or rotation angle by using the pointing device.

> **NOTE** When you turn on the Isometric Snap Grid, AutoCAD automatically adjusts the X value of the SNAPUNIT system variable to accommodate the isometric snap. To turn on isometric snap, you can set the SNAPSTYL system variable to 1 at the Command prompt.

Command line   DDRMODES

Related   You can also realign the grid by using the UCS command to redefine the current user coordinate system. Because you can establish a new planar orientation, UCS is especially useful for 3D drawings. Changing the base point establishes a snap angle rotation point; however, the UCS command can be used to define a new 0,0 origin for your drawing.

Using Isometric Snap and Grid

The Isometric Snap/Grid mode helps you create 2D drawings that represent 3D objects, such as cubes. Isometric drawings are not true 3D drawings, because they cannot be viewed in perspective or from another angle. However, they can simulate 3D by aligning along three major axes. If the snap angle is 0, the axes of the isometric planes are 30 degrees, 90 degrees, and 150 degrees. You can select from three planes, each with an associated pair of axes:

- *Left*-orients the snap and grid alignment along 90- and 150-degree axes.
- *Top*-orients the snap and grid alignment along 30- and 150-degree axes.
- *Right*-orients the snap and grid alignment along 90- and 30-degree axes.

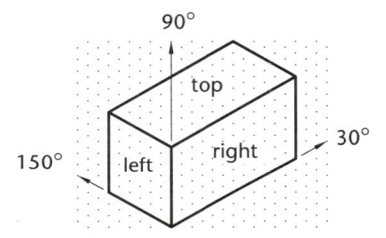

isometric drawing planes

Choosing an isometric plane causes the snap intervals, grid, and crosshairs to realign along the corresponding isometric axes. AutoCAD restricts certain point selections to two of three axes under certain conditions. For example, when Ortho mode is on, the points you select when drawing objects will align along the plane on which you are drawing. Therefore, you can draw the top plane of a model, switch to the left plane to draw another side, and switch to the right plane to complete the drawing. The cursor is similarly constrained when you use the arrow keys with Snap on.

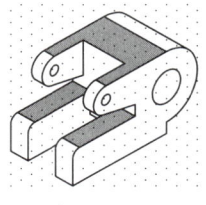

top plane 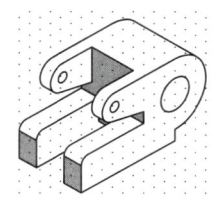   left plane 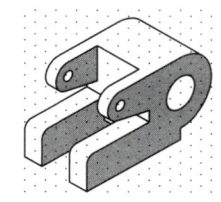   right plane

Planes of a model

To turn on an isometric plane

1. From the Tools menu, choose Drawing Aids.
2. In the Drawing Aids dialog box, under Isometric Snap/Grid, select On.
3. Under Isometric Snap/Grid, select Top, Left, or Right.
4. Choose OK.

Command line DDRMODES

Related Use ISOPLANE to specify the current isometric plane. You can cycle through the planes by pressing F5 or CTRL+E.

Using Ortho Mode

As you draw lines or move objects, you can use Ortho mode to restrict the cursor to the horizontal or vertical axis. (The orthogonal alignment depends on the current snap angle or UCS.) Ortho mode works with activities that require you to specify a second point. You can use Ortho not only to establish vertical or horizontal alignment but also to enforce parallelism or create regular offsets.

By allowing AutoCAD to impose orthogonal restraints, you can draw more quickly. For example, you can create a series of perpendicular lines by turning on Ortho mode before you start drawing. Because the lines are constrained to the horizontal and vertical axes, you can draw faster, knowing that the lines are perpendicular.

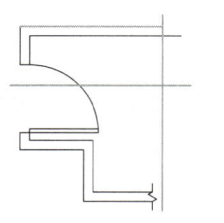

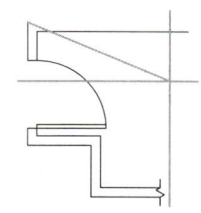

Ortho mode on   Ortho mode off

As you move the cursor, a rubber-band line that defines the displacement follows the horizontal or vertical axis, depending on which axis is nearest to the cursor. AutoCAD ignores Ortho mode in perspective views, or when you enter coordinates on the command line or specify an object snap.

To turn Ortho mode on or off

- On the status bar, double-click Ortho.

Command line ORTHO

Snapping to Geometric Points on Objects

Using object snaps is a quick way to locate an exact position on an object without having to know the coordinate or draw construction lines. For example, you can use an object snap to draw a line to the center of a circle, to the midpoint of a polyline segment, or to an imaginary intersection. Using object snaps is far more accurate than drawing points on paper.

You can specify an object snap whenever AutoCAD prompts for a point. Single object snaps affect only the next object you select. You also can turn on one or more running object snaps. Running object snaps stay active until you turn them off.

Object Snaps

Most of the object snaps that are described here affect only objects visible on the screen, including objects on locked layers, floating viewport boundaries, solids, and polyline segments. You *cannot* snap to objects on turned-off layers or to the blank portions of dashed lines.

You can use the From object snap to establish a temporary reference point for use with relative offsets. For more information, see "Using Osnap to Offset Temporary Reference Points" on page 176.

You choose object snaps in a variety of ways. See "Using Object Snap for a Single Point" on page 172 and "Setting Running Object Snaps" on page 173.

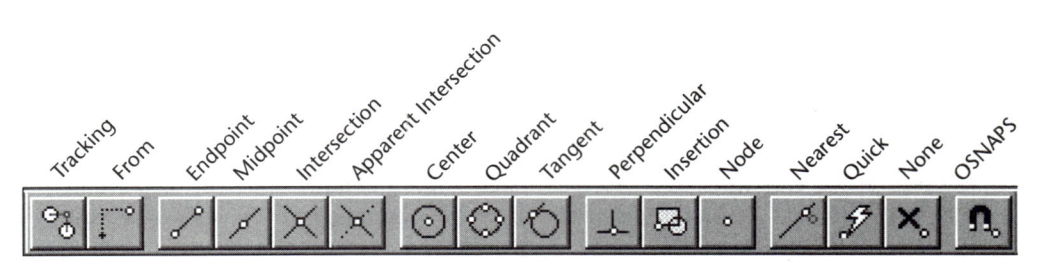

Object Snap flyout

Chapter 5   Drawing with Precision

Endpoint
Endpoint snaps to the closest endpoint of objects such as lines or arcs.

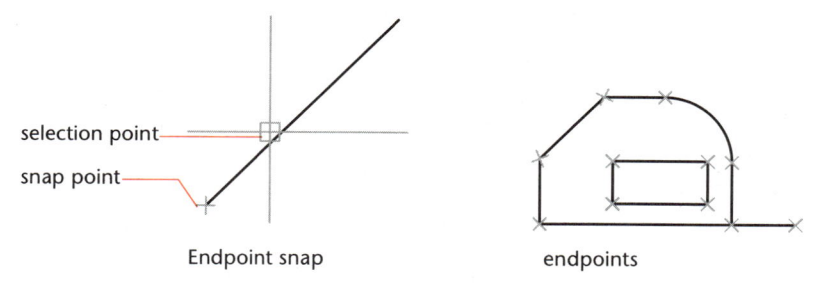

selection point

snap point

Endpoint snap   endpoints

If you have given an object thickness, you can snap to its edges. Endpoint also snaps to the edges of 3D solids, bodies, and regions. For example, you can snap to the endpoint (vertex) of a box.

Command line   ENDP

Midpoint
Midpoint snaps to the midpoint of objects such as lines or arcs.

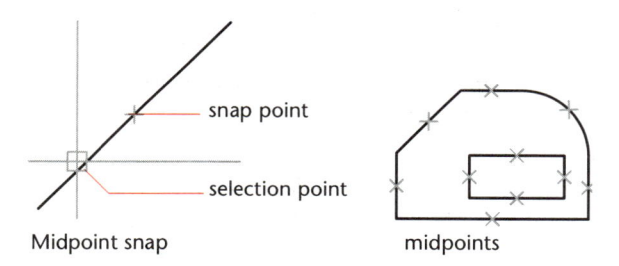

snap point

selection point

Midpoint snap   midpoints

On infinite lines, Midpoint snaps to the first point defined (the root). When you select a spline or an elliptical arc, Midpoint snaps to a point on the object that is halfway between the starting point and the endpoint.

If you have given a line or arc thickness, you also can snap to the midpoints of the edges. Midpoint also snaps to the edges of 3D solids, bodies, and regions.

Command line   MID

Snapping to Geometric Points on Objects

Intersection

Intersection snaps to the intersection of objects such as lines, circles, arcs, and splines.

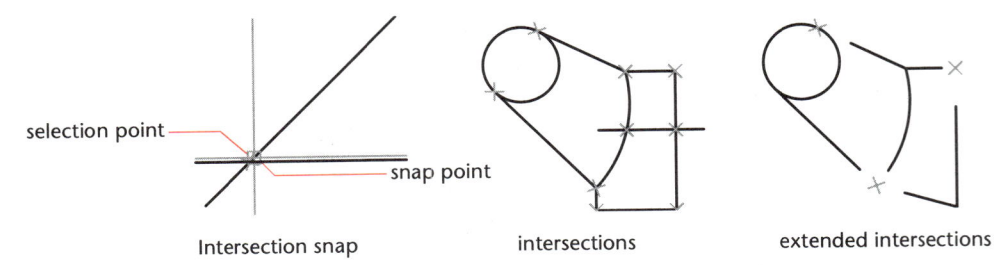

Intersection snap — *intersections* — *extended intersections*

You can also use Intersection to snap to the corners of objects that have been given thickness. If two thickened objects extend in the same direction and have intersecting bases, you can snap to the intersection of the edges. If the objects have different thicknesses, the lesser thickness defines the intersection point.

Intersections of arcs and circles that are part of a block (a group of objects that are treated as a single object) work only if the block has been uniformly scaled. Line intersections within blocks work normally.

Intersection works with the edges of regions and curves, but not with edges or corners of 3D solids.

Extended Intersection snaps to the imaginary intersection of two objects that would intersect if the objects were extended along their natural paths. If the aperture box covers only one object, AutoCAD prompts you to select a second object and then snaps to the imaginary intersection formed by extensions of those objects. Extended Intersection is automatically enabled when you select the Intersection object snap mode.

Command line INT

Apparent Intersection

Apparent Intersection includes two separate snap modes: Apparent Intersection and Extended Apparent Intersection. You can also locate Intersection and Extended Intersection snap points while running Apparent Intersection object snap mode.

Apparent and Extended Apparent Intersection work with edges of regions and curves, but not with edges or corners of 3D solids.

Apparent Intersection snaps to the intersection of two objects that do not intersect each other in 3D space but might appear to intersect on screen. When several apparent intersections are possible, AutoCAD snaps to the intersection closest to the second point you select. You can use AutoSnap with Apparent Intersection to visually locate the intersection of objects that don't intersect in 3D space. In this case, AutoCAD displays a marker and a Snaptip on the first object you select. If object snap sorting is on, AutoCAD displays the coordinates of the last object drawn.

Apparent Intersection snap

3D viewpoint of the objects' actual placement in 3D space

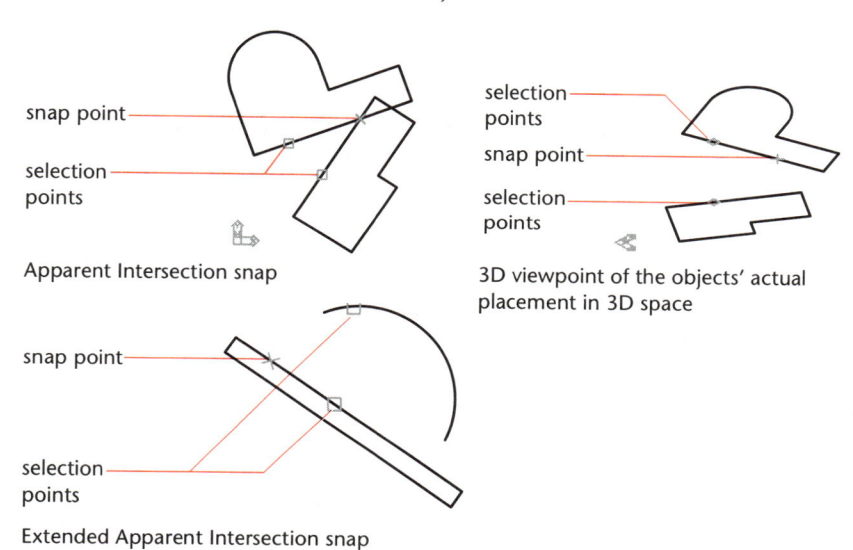

Extended Apparent Intersection snap

Extended and Apparent Intersection snap

Extended Apparent Intersection snaps to the imaginary intersection of two objects that would appear to intersect if the objects were extended along their natural paths. If the aperture box covers only one object, AutoCAD prompts you to select a second object and then snaps to the imaginary intersection formed if the objects were extended. Extended Apparent Intersection is automatically enabled when you select the Apparent Intersection object snap mode. Extended Apparent Intersection is active only if there is exactly one object within the aperture box and there are no other object snap modes active. Both Apparent and Extended Apparent Intersection snaps work as either a single-point override object snap mode or as a running osnap mode.

Command line   APPINT or APP

Center
Center snaps to the center of an arc, circle, or ellipse.

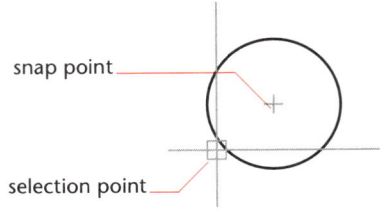

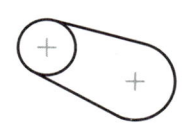

Center snap

centers

Center also snaps to the center of circles that are part of solids, bodies, or regions. When you snap to the center, select a visible part of the arc, circle, or ellipse.

Command line   CEN

Quadrant
Quadrant snaps to the closest quadrant of an arc, circle, or ellipse (the 0-, 90, 180-, and 270-degree points).

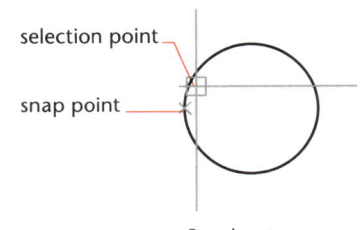

Quadrant snap

quadrants

The location of the quadrant points for circles and arcs is determined by the current orientation of the UCS. If the arc, circle, or ellipse is a member of a rotated block, the quadrant points rotate with the block.

Command line   QUA

Node
Node snaps to a point object drawn with the POINT command.

Node snap   nodes

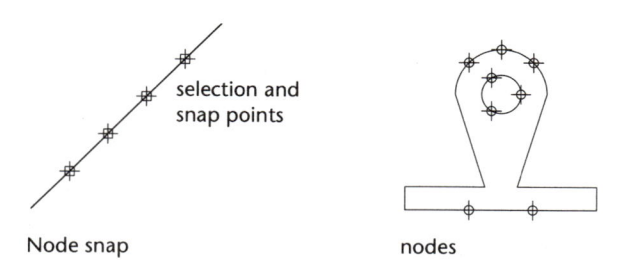

Points included in a block can function as convenient snap points for attachment locations.

Command line   NODE

Insertion
Insertion snaps to the insertion point of a block, shape, text, attribute (which contains information about a block), or attribute definition (which describes the characteristics of the attribute).

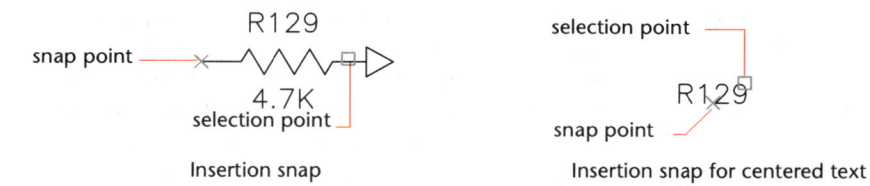

Insertion snap   Insertion snap for centered text

If you select an attribute within a block, AutoCAD snaps to the insertion point of the attribute, not the block. Therefore, if a block consists entirely of attributes, you can snap to its insertion point only if that point coincides with an attribute insertion point.

Command line   INS

Perpendicular
Perpendicular snaps to the point on an object that forms a normal, or perpendicular, alignment with another object or with an imaginary extension of that object. You can use the Perpendicular object snap with objects such as lines, circles, ellipses, splines, or arcs.

Snapping to Geometric Points on Objects

Perpendicular snaps

perpendiculars

selection point

snap point

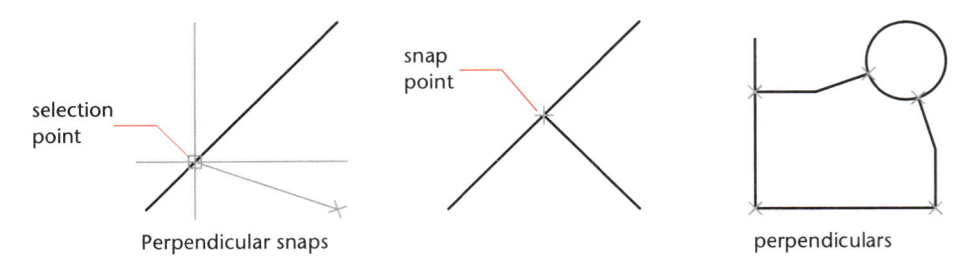

When you use the Perpendicular object snap to specify the first point of a line or circle, you construct a line or circle that is perpendicular to the object you select. When you use the Perpendicular object snap to specify the second point of a line or circle, AutoCAD snaps to a point that creates a normal from that object to the first point selected.

When you use Perpendicular object snap with spline curves, the object snap returns points on the spline where the normal vector passes through the specified point. The normal vector on any point on a spline is the vector perpendicular to the tangent at that point. If the specified point lies on the spline, then the perpendicular object snap returns that point as one of the object snap points. In some cases, when working with spline curves, it isn't obvious where the perpendicular object snap points are. There may be some instances where no perpendicular object snap points exist.

The Deferred Perpendicular snap mode is automatically enabled when you use a line, arc, circle, pline, ray, xline, mline, or 3D solid edge as the first snap point from which to draw a perpendicular line. If AutoSnap is enabled, a deferred perpendicular marker and Snaptip will be displayed when you select the first point, and you will be prompted to enter a second point. Deferred Perpendicular object snap does not work with ellipses or splines. If you draw a line that is perpendicular to an ellipse or spline, you will get the point on the ellipse or spline that is perpendicular to the last point chosen causing unpredictable results.

A Perpendicular snap to arcs and circles that belong to a block works only if the block has been uniformly scaled and the object's thickness direction is parallel to the current UCS. The normal created for 3D splines is relative to a plane defined by the tangent of the curve at the snap point.

Command line PER

Tangent

Tangent snaps to the point on a circle or arc that, when connected to the last point, forms a line tangent to that object.

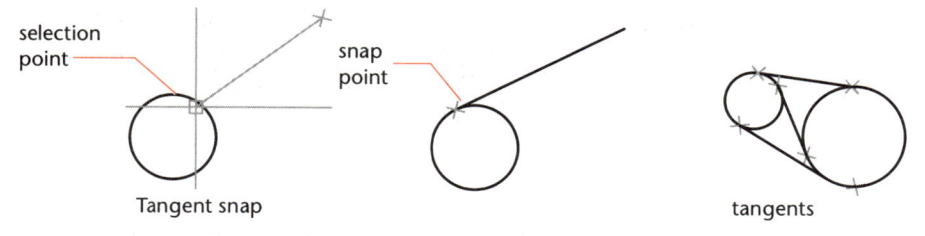

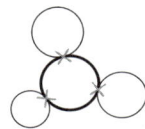

Tangent snap

tangents

When drawing a circle with the three-point method, for example, you can use the Tangent object snap to construct a circle tangent to three other circles.

The Deferred Tangent snap point is automatically enabled when you select an arc, pline arc, or circle as a starting point for a tangent line. If AutoSnap is enabled, you will see the deferred tangent Snaptip and marker appear when you select the first point, and you will be prompted to enter a second point. Deferred Tangent can also be used to create 2- or 3-point circles when the circle to be drawn is tangent to two or three other objects. Deferred tangent snap points do not work with ellipses or splines. If you draw a line that is tangent to an ellipse or spline, you will get the point on the ellipse or spline that is tanget to the last point picked causing unpredictable results.

Tangents with arcs and circles that are part of a block work only if the block has been uniformly scaled and the object's thickness direction is parallel to the current UCS. For both splines and ellipses, the other point you specify must be on the same plane as the snap point.

NOTE If you use the From option in conjunction with the Tangent object snap mode to draw objects other than lines from arcs or circles, the first point drawn is tangent to the arc or circle in relation to the last point selected in the drawing area.

Command line TAN

Nearest

Nearest snaps to a point object or to the location on another type of object that is closest to the specified point.

Command line NEA

Quick

Quick, when used with other object snaps, snaps to the first eligible point on the first object it finds. If Object Snap Sort is on, Quick finds the last object drawn. When Quick is off, AutoCAD snaps to the point nearest the center of the crosshairs. In complex drawings, the Quick object snap shortens time otherwise required to analyze which point is closest. When the Intersection object snap is on, AutoCAD ignores Quick and performs a full search of all the candidates within the aperture box.

Command line   QUI

None

None turns off both single and running object snaps. None can also be used to disable running object snaps for one point.

Command line   NONE

Using Object Snap for a Single Point

Specifying an object snap converts the cursor to an aperture box. When you select an object, AutoCAD snaps to the eligible snap point closest to the center of the aperture box.

If you have trouble snapping to the correct locations, you can zoom in to magnify the image, or you can use AutoSnap. For more information about AutoSnap, see "Setting Running Object Snaps" on page 173.

To snap to a geometric point on an object

1   After entering a drawing command, choose an object snap tool from the Object Snap flyout on the standard toolbar.
2   Move your cursor over the desired snap location.
3   If AutoSnap is enabled, your cursor automatically locks onto the snap location you selected, and a marker and tooltip are displayed describing the snap point. If AutoSnap is turned off, you will receive no visual cue that you are snapping to the point you have selected.

Command line   Each object snap has a unique abbreviation that you can enter on the command line. For information about individual modes, see "Object Snaps" on page 164. Use commas to separate multiple object snaps on the command line.

Related   To choose object snaps from the cursor menu, hold down SHIFT and press the return button on your pointing device. Then choose the object snap you want to use. To display the Osnap Settings dialog box, choose Osnap Settings.

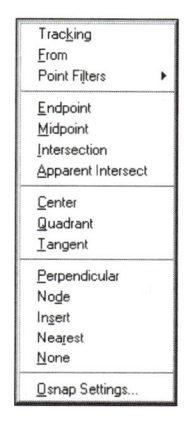

```
Tracking
From
Point Filters      ▶

Endpoint
Midpoint
Intersection
Apparent Intersect

Center
Quadrant
Tangent

Perpendicular
Node
Insert
Nearest
None

Osnap Settings...
```

Cursor menu

Setting Running Object Snaps

You can set single as well as multiple location types with running object snaps, such as endpoints and center points. As with single object snaps, an AutoSnap marker indicates that an object snap is on and identifies the selection area. You can change the size of the aperture box in the Osnap Settings dialog box, or by entering APERTURE at the command prompt.

When you select multiple object snaps, AutoCAD uses the one appropriate to the object you select. If two potential snap points fall within the selection area, AutoCAD snaps to the eligible point closest to the center of the aperture box.

NOTE   The From object snap *cannot* be set as a running object snap.

To set running object snaps

1 From the Tools menu, choose Object Snap Settings.

Snapping to Geometric Points on Objects

173

— sets running object snaps

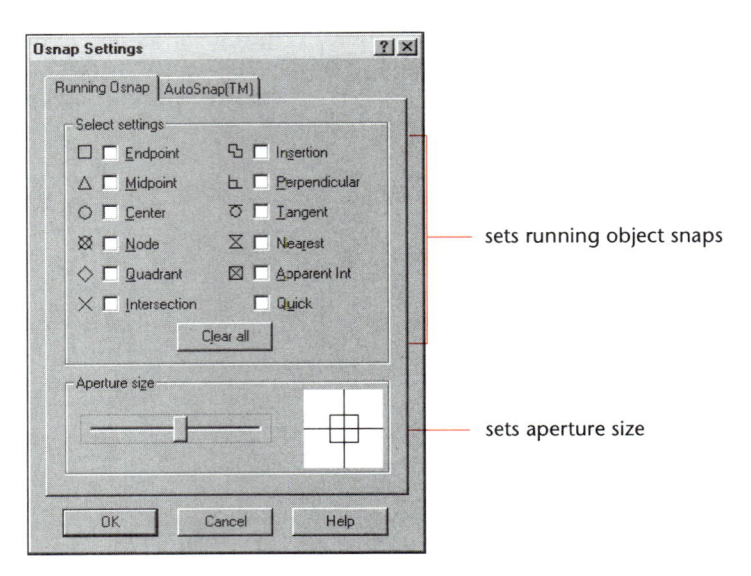

— sets aperture size

OSNAP 2 In the Osnap Settings dialog box, select the running object snaps you want to use.

3 To change the size of the aperture box, drag the slider bar under Aperture Size.

4 Choose OK.

You can quickly turn object snaps on and off without having to respecify your object snap settings by double-clicking Osnap on the status bar. You can also switch Running Object Snaps on and off by pressing CTRL+F or F3.

NOTE Double-clicking Osnap when no object snaps are set displays the Osnap Settings dialog box.

Command line OSNAP

Related -OSNAP sets running object snaps on the command line. The OSMODE system variable also sets running object snaps. The APERTURE system variable sets the size of the aperture box.

Using AutoSnap

When you use any of the object snap settings, AutoSnap displays a marker and a Snaptip when you move the cursor over a snap point. AutoSnap is automatically turned on when you enter an object snap on the command line or turn on object snaps in the Osnap Settings dialog box.

Chapter 5 Drawing with Precision

174

After entering a drawing command, AutoSnap indicates the snap points as you drag your pointing device over the object.

With the cycling feature, you can cycle through all the snap points available for a particular object by pressing TAB. For example, if you press TAB while the aperture box is on the circle in the following illustration, AutoSnap gives you the option to snap to quadrant, intersection, and center.

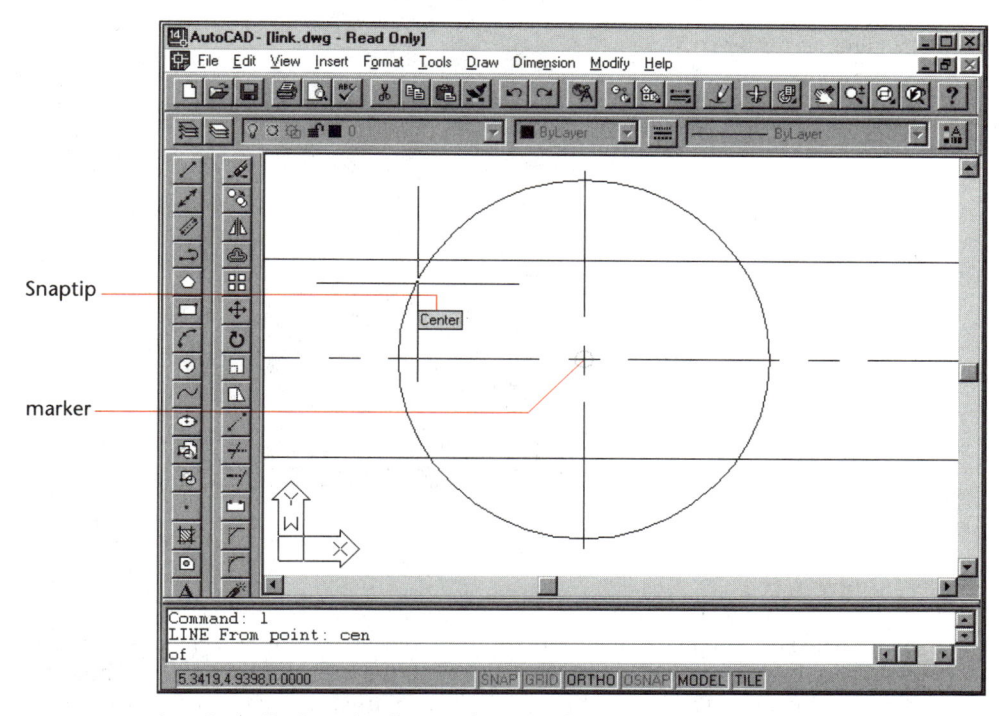

AutoSnap displays visual cues when you drag your aperture box over an object.

Marker	A geometric symbol that displays the object snap location when the cursor moves over snap points of an object.
Snaptip	A small flag that describes which part of the object you are snapping to.
Magnet	An automatic movement of the cursor that locks the cursor onto the snap point.
Aperture Box	A box that appears at the center of the cursor after you select one or more object snaps.

Snapping to Geometric Points on Objects

175

To change the AutoSnap settings

1 From the Tools menu, choose Object Snap Settings.
2 In the Osnap Settings dialog box, select the AutoSnap tab.
3 Change settings and choose OK.

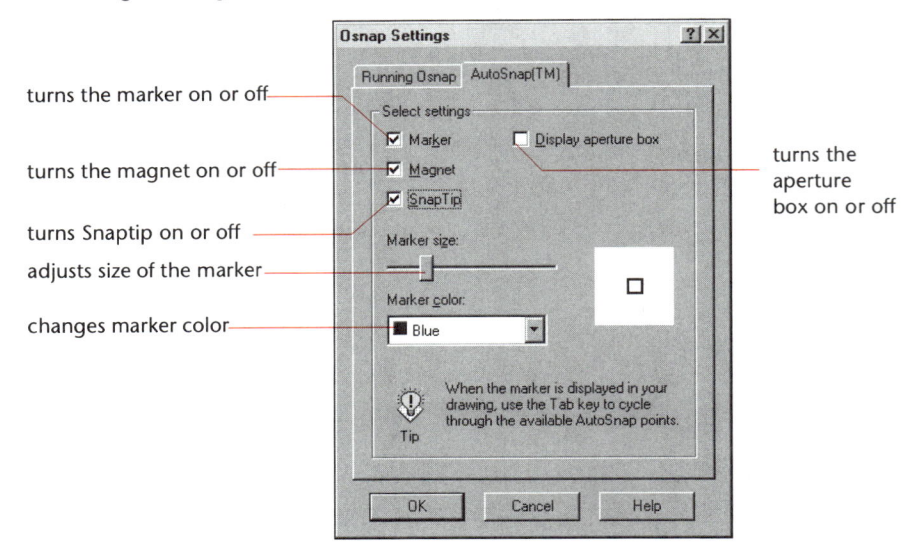

- turns the marker on or off
- turns the magnet on or off
- turns Snaptip on or off
- adjusts size of the marker
- changes marker color
- turns the aperture box on or off

Using Osnap to Offset Temporary Reference Points

The From object snap differs from the other types of object snaps because it establishes a temporary reference point as a basis for specifying subsequent points. The From object snap is normally used in combination with other object snaps and relative coordinates.

For example, at a prompt for a point when drawing a polyline, you can enter **from mid**, select a line, and then enter **@2,3** to locate a point two units to the right and three units up from the midpoint of the line.

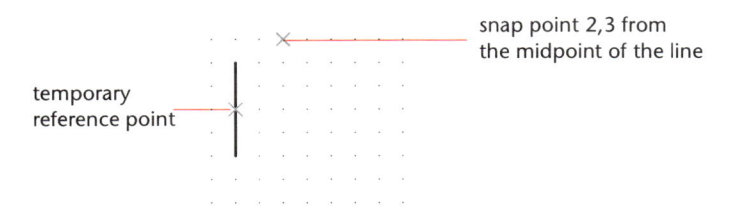

- snap point 2,3 from the midpoint of the line
- temporary reference point

Chapter 5   Drawing with Precision

Command: *Enter* **pline**
From point: *Enter* **from**
Base point: *Enter* **mid**
of: *Select the line*
of <Offset>: *Enter* **@2,3**

You can specify an absolute coordinate for use as a base point; however, specifying an absolute coordinate for the offset essentially cancels the From object snap and locates the point at the specified coordinate.

Command line   FROM

Using Point Filters

With point filters, you can specify one coordinate value at a time while temporarily ignoring the other coordinate values. Used with object snaps, point filters can extract coordinate values from an existing object so you can locate another point.

Specifying a point filter limits the next entry to a specific ordinate value, such as the *X* or the *Y* value, or an *X,Y* coordinate value. For 3D models, you also can specify *Z* values. After you specify the first value, AutoCAD prompts for the remaining values.

To use point filters to specify points

1 From the Draw menu, choose Point ➤ Single Point.
2 Specify a point or choose an object snap and select an object.
3 At the prompt for the next coordinate value(s), specify a point or choose an object snap and select an object.

If you specified an *X* value, the coordinate of the new point matches the *X* value of the first point and the *Y,Z* value of the second point.

Command line   POINT. At the prompt for a point, you can enter **.x** or **.y** to indicate which value you want to specify.

Related   To use point filters from the cursor menu, hold down SHIFT and press the return button on your pointing device. Then choose the filter you want to use.

Example

In the following illustration, the hole in the holding plate was centered in the rectangle by extracting the *X,Y* coordinates from the midpoints of the plate's horizontal and vertical line segments.

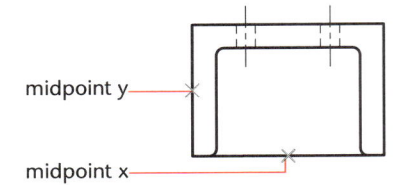

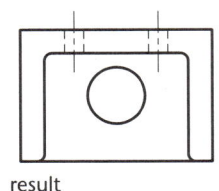

midpoint y

midpoint x

result

The following example shows how to use point filters to create the hole.

Command: *Enter* **circle**
3P/2P/TTR/<Center point>:   *Enter* **.x**
of: *Enter* **mid**
of: *Select the horizontal line on the lower edge of the holding plate*
of: (need YZ):   *Enter* **mid**
of: *Select the vertical line on the left side of the holding plate*
of: Diameter/<Radius> *Specify the radius of the hole*

Using Tracking

In addition to using point filters, you can use tracking to visually locate points relative to other points in your drawing. Tracking combines both *X* and *Y* point filters and allows you to use them on the fly.

You can use tracking whenever AutoCAD prompts you for a point. When you start tracking and then specify a point, AutoCAD turns Ortho on and constrains the next point selection to a path that extends vertically or horizontally from the first point. To change the orthogonal path, you return to your last tracking point and move in the desired vertical or horizontal direction.

The orthogonal path determines which of the old point's values (*X* or *Y*) is retained and which is replaced with the new point's *X* or *Y* value. If the rubber-band line is constrained horizontally, then the *X* value is replaced. If the rubber-band line is constrained vertically, then the *Y* value is replaced.

After you select a second point and press ENTER to end tracking, AutoCAD locates the new point at the intersection of the imaginary orthogonal line extending from the first two points.

Tracking is a quick way to find the center point of a rectangle. To start tracking, click the Tracking tool on the Standard toolbar or enter **tk**, and then specify the midpoints of the horizontal and vertical lines.

You can use tracking with direct distance entry to place text a specified distance from another object, to insert windows or doors in walls at a specified distance from a corner, or to break a wall, for example.

Once you start tracking, AutoCAD does not place the point until you turn off tracking by pressing ENTER. Therefore, you can track as many points as you need.

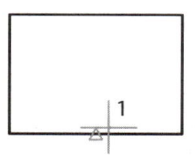

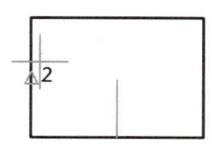

first midpoint specified

second midpoint specified with cursor moving up and to the left

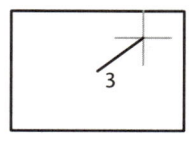

line starts at the orthogonal intersection

To use tracking to find the center of a rectangle

1 Start a drawing command such as LINE.

2 From the Object Snap cursor menu (hold down SHIFT and right-click the pointing device), choose Tracking.

3 When prompted for a tracking point, choose Midpoint from the Object Snap cursor menu.

4 Select the bottom line of the rectangle (1).

5 Move the cursor up, until you see the rubber-band line. The direction of your movement affects the tracking direction. Notice that if you move the cursor from left to right, you must then move it directly over the last point selected in order to move it up and down.

6 When prompted for the second midpoint, choose Midpoint from the cursor menu. Select the left side of the rectangle (2).

7 Press ENTER to end tracking.

The start point of the line (3) snaps to the imaginary intersection of vertical and horizontal paths extending from the points you specified. The position is determined by the direction in which you moved the cursor after specifying the first point.

Command line TRACKING, TRACK, or TK

In the following example, you create an opening in a rectangle using BREAK and tracking. By using tracking, you can specify the break points at a relative distance from points on one side of the rectangle.

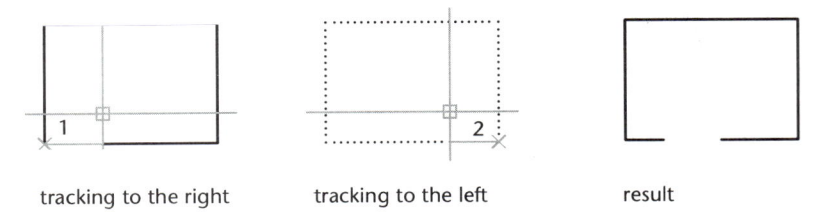

tracking to the right   tracking to the left   result

To use tracking to break a rectangle

1   From the Modify menu, choose Break.
2   Select object when prompted, then enter **f** (first point).
3   Hold down SHIFT and right-click the pointing device to display the cursor menu. From the cursor menu, choose Tracking. Again, from the cursor menu, choose Intersection, and then select the lower-left corner of the rectangle (1).
4   Move the cursor to the right to establish a tracking direction. Then enter **1** to indicate the distance. Press ENTER to accept the distance and end tracking.
5   At the prompt for the second point, choose Tracking from the cursor menu again. Again, from the cursor menu, choose Intersection, and select the lower-right corner of the rectangle (2).
6   Move the cursor to the left to establish tracking direction. Then enter **2**. Press ENTER to end tracking.

A break is inserted in the rectangle.

Command line   TRACKING, TRAK, or TK

Specifying Measurements and Divisions

Sometimes you need to create points or blocks at specific intervals on an object. For example, you may need to snap to points at half-unit intervals or insert markers on an object to identify five equal segments. You can use one of the following commands:

- To specify the length of each segment, use MEASURE.
- To specify the number of equal segments, use DIVIDE.

You can measure or divide lines, arcs, splines, circles, ellipses, and polylines. With both methods, you can identify the intervals by inserting either a point or a named set of objects known as a block.

By specifying points, you then can use the Node object snap to align other objects at even intervals on the measured or divided object. By specifying blocks, you can create precise geometric constructions or insert custom markers. You can rotate blocks at each insertion point.

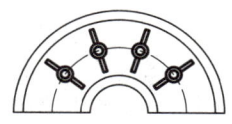

blocks aligned

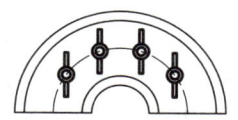

blocks not aligned

To be inserted, blocks must already be defined within the drawing. Any variable attributes within the block are excluded from the insertion. For more information about blocks, see "Working with Blocks" on page 434.

The starting point for measurements or divisions varies with the object type. For lines or polylines, segments start at the endpoint closest to the selection point. Segments in closed polylines begin at the polyline's starting point. Segments in circles start at the angle from the center point that is equivalent to the current snap angle. For example, if the snap angle is 0, the circle starts at the three o'clock position and continues in a counterclockwise direction.

Points or blocks drawn using MEASURE or DIVIDE are placed in the Previous selection set. Therefore, if you want to edit them immediately, you can select them by using the Previous option.

Specifying Measured Intervals on Objects

You use the MEASURE command to mark intervals on an object. You can mark the intervals with either points or blocks.

To insert points at measured intervals on an object

1 From the Draw menu, choose Point ➤ Measure.
2 Select a line, arc, spline, circle, ellipse, or polyline.
3 Enter an interval length or specify points on the screen to indicate a length. AutoCAD places points on the object at the specified intervals.

object selected

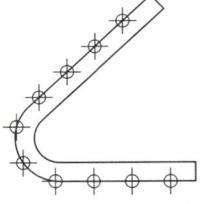

points at measured intervals

Command line MEASURE

Related PDPTYPE controls the size and style of print markers. Changes made with DDPTYPE are stored in the PDMODE and PDSIZE system variables.

To insert blocks at measured intervals on an object

1. If necessary, create the block you want to insert (see "Defining Blocks" on page 437).
2. From the Draw menu, choose Point ➤ Measure.
3. Select the object you want to measure.
4. Enter **b** (Block).
5. Enter the name of the block you want to insert.
6. Specify the block orientation. Enter **y** to rotate the block at its insertion point so that the horizontal alignment of each inserted block is tangent to the divided object. Enter **n** to use a rotation angle of 0 degrees.
7. Enter an interval length or specify points on the screen to indicate a length.

   AutoCAD inserts blocks on the object at the specified intervals.

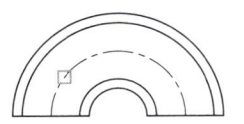

object selected

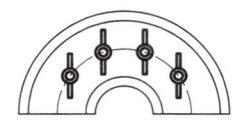

blocks at measured intervals, not rotated

Command line MEASURE

Dividing Objects into Segments

Use the DIVIDE command to create points or blocks on an object at a specific number of equal intervals. This command does not actually break the object into individual objects; it only identifies the location of the divisions so that you can use them as geometric reference points.

To insert points at a specified number of intervals on an object

1 From the Draw menu, choose Point ➤ Divide.
2 Select a line, arc, spline, circle, ellipse, or polyline.
3 Enter the number of intervals you want to represent.

AutoCAD places a point at each interval on the object.

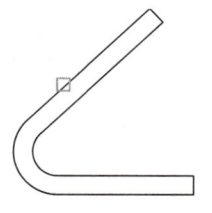

object selected 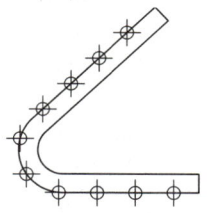   points indicating divisions

Command line   DIVIDE

Related   PDPTYPE controls the size and style of print markers. Changes made with DDPTYPE are stored in the PDMODE and PDSIZE system variables.

To insert blocks at a specified number of intervals on an object

1 If necessary, create the block you want to insert (see "Defining Blocks" on page 437). 
2 From the Draw menu, choose Point ➤ Divide.
3 Select a line, arc, spline, circle, ellipse, or polyline.
4 Enter **b** (Block).
5 Enter the name of the block you want to insert.
6 Specify the block orientation. Enter **y** to rotate the block at its insertion point so that the horizontal alignment of each inserted block is tangent to the divided object. Enter **n** to use a rotation angle of 0 degrees.
7 Enter the number of intervals you want to represent.

AutoCAD inserts a block at each interval on the object.

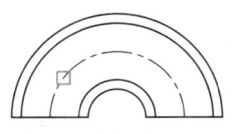

object selected 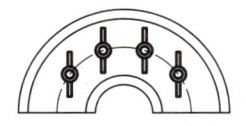   blocks indicating five divisions

Command line   DIVIDE

Specifying Measurements and Divisions

Drawing Construction Lines

You can create construction lines that extend to infinity in one or both directions. Construction lines that extend in one direction are known as rays. Construction lines that extend in both directions are known as xlines. These construction lines can be used as a reference for creating other objects. For example, you can use construction lines to find the center of a triangle, prepare multiple views of the same item, or create temporary intersections that you can use for object snaps.

Construction lines do not change the total area of the drawing; therefore, their infinite dimensions have no effect on zooming or viewpoints. You can move, rotate, and copy construction lines just as you move, rotate, and copy other objects. You may want to create construction lines on a construction line layer that can be frozen or turned off before plotting (see "Freezing and Thawing Layers" on page 301).

Creating Construction Xlines

A construction xline can be placed anywhere in 3D space and extends to infinity in both directions. You can specify its orientation in several ways. The default method for creating the line is the two-point method: you select two points to define the orientation. The first point, the root, is considered the midpoint of the construction line.

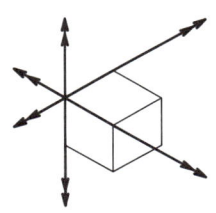

construction lines

Commands that display the drawing extents ignore construction lines.

To create a construction xline by specifying two points

1. From the Draw menu, choose Construction Line.
2. Specify a point to define the root of the construction line (1).

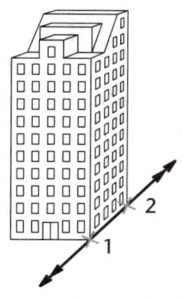

two-point method

3   Specify a second point through which the construction line should pass (2).
4   Continue to specify construction lines as needed.
5   Press ENTER to end the command.

Command line   XLINE

You can create construction lines in several other ways.

Horizontal and vertical

The horizontal and vertical methods create construction lines that pass through a point (1) you specify and are parallel to the *X* or *Y* axis of the current UCS.

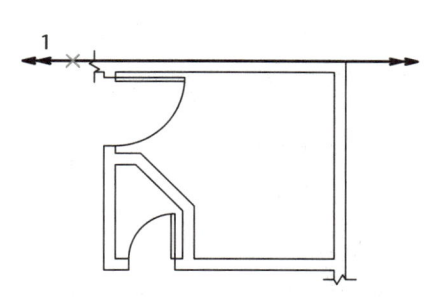

horizontal construction line

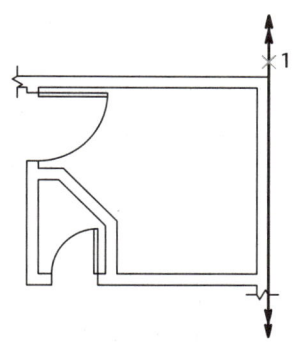

vertical construction line

Drawing Construction Lines

Angle

The angle method creates a construction line in one of two ways. You can select a reference line and then define the angle of the construction line from that line. To create a construction line at a specific angle to the horizontal axis, you specify an angle and then specify a point through which the construction line should pass (1). The construction line always is parallel to the current UCS.

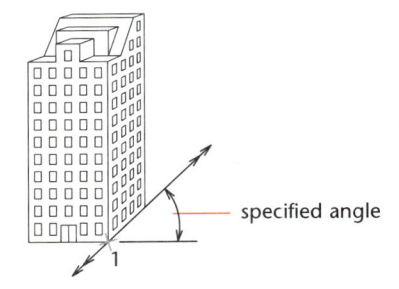

Bisector

The bisector method creates a construction line that bisects an angle you specify. You specify the vertex (1) and the lines that create the angle (2, 3).

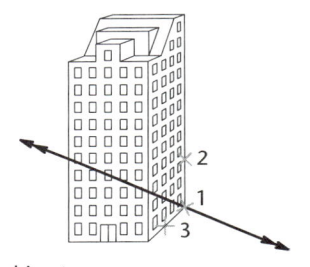

bisector

Offset

The offset method creates a construction line parallel to a baseline you specify. You specify the offset distance, select the baseline (1), and then indicate on which side of the baseline the construction line is located (2).

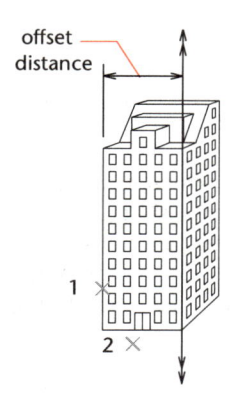

Creating Rays

A ray is a line in 3D space that starts at a point you specify and extends to infinity. Unlike xline construction lines, which extend in two directions, rays extend in only one direction. As a result, rays help reduce the visual clutter caused by numerous construction lines. Like construction lines, rays are ignored by commands that display the drawing extents.

To create a ray

1 From the Draw menu, choose Ray.
2 Specify a starting point for the ray (1).
3 Specify a point through which the ray should pass (2).
4 Continue to specify points to create additional rays as needed (3, 4).

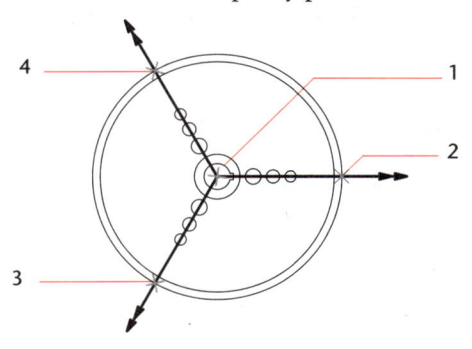

three rays

All subsequent rays pass through the first point specified.

5 Press ENTER to end the command.

Command line   RAY

Drawing Construction Lines

187

Calculating Points and Values

By entering a formula on the command line, you can quickly solve a mathematical problem or locate points on your drawing. The CAL command runs a 3D calculator utility—a geometry calculator, which evaluates vector expressions (combining points, vectors, and numbers) and real and integer expressions. In addition to the standard mathematical functions, a geometry calculator contains a set of specialized functions for performing operations on points, vectors, and AutoCAD geometry. With the CAL command, you can

- Calculate a vector from two points, the length of a vector, a normal vector (perpendicular to the *XY* plane), or a point on a line
- Calculate a distance, radius, or angle
- Specify a point with the pointing device
- Specify the last-specified point or an intersection
- Use object snaps as variables in an expression
- Convert points between a UCS and the WCS
- Filter the *X*, *Y*, and *Z* components of a vector
- Rotate a point about an axis

The following sections describe two ways to use CAL. For more information, see CAL in the *Command Reference*.

Evaluating Expressions

You can calculate values at the Command prompt just as you would with a handheld calculator. CAL evaluates expressions according to standard mathematical rules of precedence.

Mathematical operators in order of precedence	
Operator	Operation
( )	Groups expressions
^	Indicates numeric exponent
*, /	Multiplies and divides numbers
+, −	Adds and subtracts numbers

To evaluate an expression

1   From the Tools menu, choose Calculator.
2   Enter an expression, following the rules of precedence described in the table. For example, enter **(53*12)/2** to multiply 53 by 12 and then divide the result by 2.

    You can add spaces as needed without ending the command.
3   Press ENTER.

    AutoCAD displays the result of the calculation.

    Command line   CAL

Calculating Points

You can use CAL whenever you need to calculate a point or a number within an AutoCAD command.

To calculate a point

1   From the Tools menu, choose Inquiry ➤ ID Point.
2   When prompted for a point, enter '**cal**.
3   Using a combination of mathematical operators and object snaps, enter an expression to specify an object snap point.

    For example, you enter **(mid+cen)/2** to specify a point halfway between the midpoint of a line and the center of a circle.

    The following example uses CAL as a construction tool. It locates a center point for a new circle and then calculates one fifth of the radius of an existing circle.

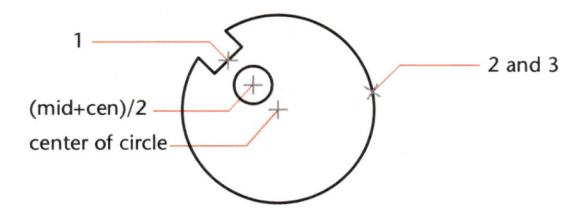

1
(mid+cen)/2
center of circle

2 and 3

Calculating Points and Values

189

```
Command:   Enter circle
3P/2P/TTR/<Center point>:   Enter 'cal
>> Expression:   Enter (mid+cen)/2
>> Select object for MID snap:   Select the notch line (1)
>> Select object for CEN snap:   Select the large circle (2)
Diameter/<Radius>:   Enter 'cal
>> Expression:   Enter 1/5*rad
>> Select circle, arc or polyline segment for RAD function:
              Select the large circle (3)
```

Calculating Areas

You can display the area and perimeter of several types of objects or of a sequence of points. If you need to calculate the combined area of more than one object, you can keep a running total as you add or subtract areas from the selection set.

Calculating a Defined Area

You can measure an arbitrary closed region defined by the 2D or 3D points you specify. The points must lie on a plane parallel to the *XY* plane of the current UCS.

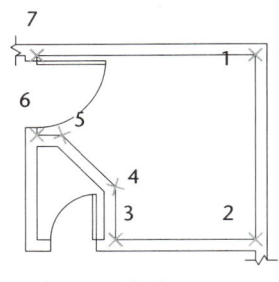

points specified   arbitrary closed region

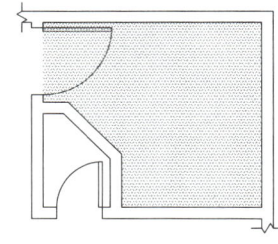

To calculate an area you define

1 From the Tools menu, choose Inquiry ➤ Area.
2 Select points in a sequence that defines the perimeter of the area to be measured. Then press ENTER.

   AutoCAD connects the first and last points to form a closed area and displays the area and perimeter measurements.

   Command line   AREA

Calculating the Area Enclosed by an Object

You can calculate the enclosed area and perimeter, or circumference, of circles, ellipses, polylines, polygons, splines, regions, and solids. The displayed information differs according to the type of object you select.

- ***Circles, ellipses, and planar closed spline curves***   The area and circumference or length are displayed.
- ***Closed polylines and polygons***   The area and perimeter are displayed. For wide polylines, this area is defined by the center of the width.
- ***Open objects, such as open spline curves and open polylines***   The area and perimeter are displayed. The area is computed as though a straight line connected the starting point and endpoint.
- ***Regions***   The combined area for objects in the region is displayed.
- ***Solids***   The surface area of the 3D solid model is displayed.

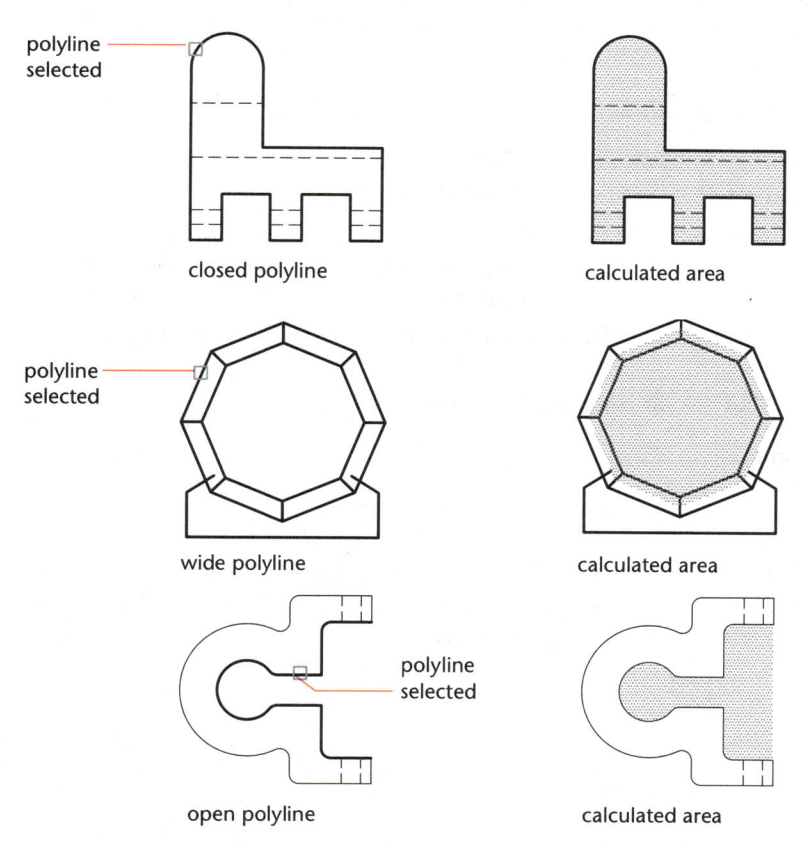

How areas are calculated for various types of objects

Calculating Areas

191

To calculate the area of an object

1 From the Tools menu, choose Inquiry ➤ Area.
2 Enter **o** (Object).
3 Select an object.

   AutoCAD displays the area and perimeter.

   Command line   AREA

   Related   You also can use DDMODIFY to display an object's area and other information. Use MASSPROP to display additional information about solids and regions.

Calculating Combined Areas

You can measure more than one area either by specifying points or by selecting objects. For example, you can measure the total area of rooms in a floor plan.

To add areas as you calculate

1 From the Tools menu, choose Inquiry ➤ Area.
2 To add an area to the calculation, enter **a** (Add).
3 Specify a point or enter **o** (Object).
4 Depending on which method you chose, specify points and press ENTER or select the objects you want to measure.

   AutoCAD displays the measurements of each new area and a running total of all areas.

5 Press ENTER twice to complete the command.

   Command line   AREA

Subtracting Areas from Combined Areas

You can also subtract one or more areas from a combined area that you have already calculated. In the following example, the area of the floor plan is first measured, and then a room is subtracted.

original calculated area

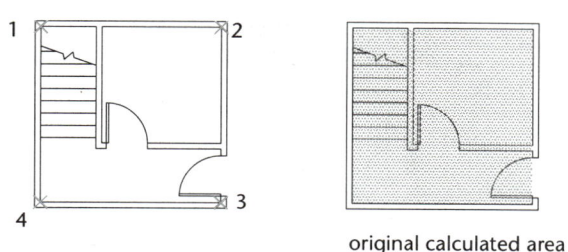

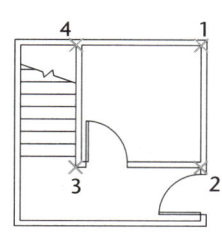

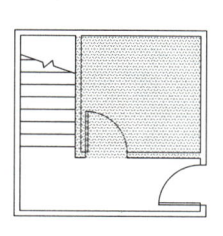

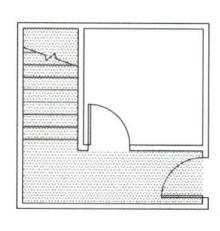

subtracted area

total remaining area

To subtract areas from a calculation

1. While the combined area is still displayed, enter **s** (Subtract).
2. Specify a point (1) or enter **o** (Object).
3. Specify points (2, 3, 4) or select objects to define the areas to be subtracted. AutoCAD updates the running total as you define new areas.
4. Press ENTER to complete the command.

   Command line   AREA

   Example

   Add   Adds areas to measure, either by point specification or by object. For example, you can get a total measurement of rooms in a floor plan, rather than entering the AREA command for each room. AutoCAD displays the area and perimeter of each area and a running total as you define new areas. The <First point>/Object/Subtract option repeats, and you can specify another area or press ENTER to complete the area definition.

   Subtract   Subtracts areas to measure from the AREA operation. As with Add, AutoCAD displays the area and perimeter of each area you subtract, and a running total as you subtract more areas.

Calculating Areas

193

In the following example, the closed polyline represents a metal plate with two large holes. You can calculate the area by measuring the polygon and then subtracting the holes.

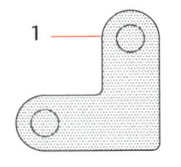

Command: *Enter* **area**
<First point>/Object/Add/Subtract: *Enter* **a**
<First point>/Object/Subtract: *Enter* **o**
(ADD mode) Select objects: *Select the polyline (1)*
Area = 0.34,   Perimeter = 2.71
Total area = 0.34
(ADD mode) Select objects: *Press* ENTER
<First point>/Object/Subtract: *Enter* **s**
<First point>/Object/Add: *Enter* **o**
(SUBTRACT mode) Select objects: *Select the lower circle (2)*
Area = 0.02,   Circumference = 0.46
Total area = 0.32
(SUBTRACT mode) Select objects: *Select the upper circle (3)*
Area = 0.02,   Circumference = 0.46
Total area = 0.30
(SUBTRACT mode) Select circle or polyline: *Press* ENTER
<First point>/Object/Add: *Press* ENTER

Related   You can use REGION to convert the plate to a region, then subtract the holes, and then use AREA to measure the plate.

Calculating Distance and Angle

You can quickly display the following information for two points you specify:

- The distance between them in drawing units
- The angle between the points in the *XY* plane
- The angle of the points from the *XY* plane
- The delta *X*, *Y*, and *Z* distance between the designated points

You can use this information to quickly determine the relationship between the two points.

To calculate a distance

1 From the Tools menu, choose Inquiry ➤ Distance.
2 Specify the first and second points of the distance you want to calculate.
AutoCAD displays a brief report.

Command line   DIST

Related   If you enter a single number or fraction at the First Point prompt, AutoCAD displays that number in the current unit of measurement. For example, if units are set to Decimal (four places) and you enter **1/2**, AutoCAD displays 0.5000.

Displaying Coordinates and Locating Points

You can display the coordinate of a designated point in a drawing or visually locate a point by specifying its coordinate. This ID command also sets the LASTPOINT system variable, which can be used to establish relative coordinates.

To display a coordinate

1 From the Tools menu, choose Inquiry ➤ ID Point.
2 Select the point you want to identify.

For 3D objects, use an object snap to display the Z coordinate value. Otherwise, the Z value reflects the current elevation.

To visually locate a point

1 From the Tools menu, choose Inquiry ➤ ID Point.
2 Enter the coordinate of the point you want to locate.

If the BLIPMODE system variable is on, a blip (a small cross) appears at the point location.

Command line   ID

Inquiry Methods

You can display a variety of information regarding your drawing and the objects it contains, including

- Database information for selected objects
- Drawing status
- Time spent working on the drawing

The information is displayed in the command history area of the command window. Press F2 to switch between a large and small text window as needed.

Listing Database Information for Objects

You can display database information for any objects in your drawing. The information varies according to the object. All listings display the following information:

- Object type
- *XYZ* position relative to the current UCS
- Layer
- Whether model space or paper space is current

The following information may also appear:

- Thickness, if greater than zero
- UCS coordinates if an object's extrusion direction differs from the *Z* axis (0,0,1) of the current UCS
- How color, linetype, and line weight are specified (if they are not specified by layer)

The following example shows the information typically listed for a circle.

```
Command: list
Select objects: 1 found
Select objects:
                CIRCLE    Layer: 0
                          Space: Model space
                Handle = 1E
        center point, X=   6.2174  Y=   4.9861  Z=    0.0000
              radius    1.7247
       circumference   10.8369
                area    9.3455
```

To list an object's database information

1 From the Tools menu, choose Inquiry ➤ List.
2 Select the objects for which you're seeking information.

The text window displays a report.

Command line   LIST

Related   DBLIST lists information on every object in the drawing.

Displaying the Drawing Status

You can display general information about the current drawing, including

- Current drawing extents
- Settings of various drawing modes and parameters
- Free physical memory and disk space

To display a drawing's status information

- From the Tools menu, choose Inquiry ➤ Status.

AutoCAD displays the report.

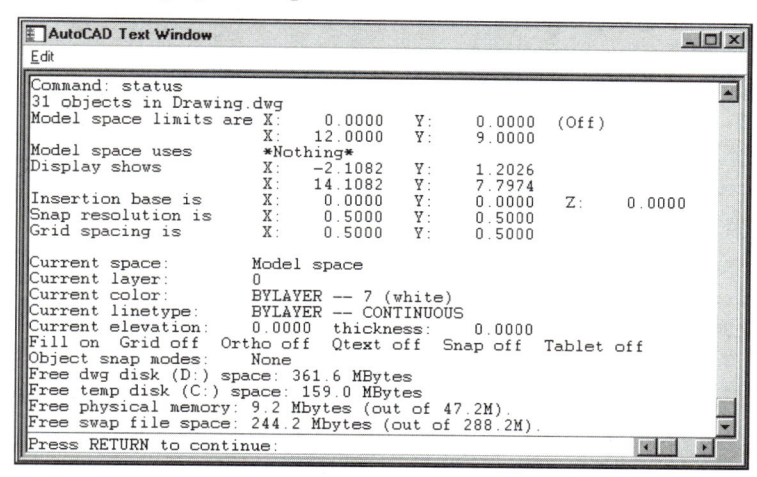

```
AutoCAD Text Window
Edit
Command: status
31 objects in Drawing.dwg
Model space limits are X:     0.0000    Y:    0.0000   (Off)
                       X:    12.0000    Y:    9.0000
Model space uses       *Nothing*
Display shows          X:    -2.1082    Y:    1.2026
                       X:    14.1082    Y:    7.7974
Insertion base is      X:     0.0000    Y:    0.0000   Z:   0.0000
Snap resolution is     X:     0.5000    Y:    0.5000
Grid spacing is        X:     0.5000    Y:    0.5000

Current space:         Model space
Current layer:         0
Current color:         BYLAYER -- 7 (white)
Current linetype:      BYLAYER -- CONTINUOUS
Current elevation:     0.0000   thickness:   0.0000
Fill on  Grid off  Ortho off  Qtext off  Snap off  Tablet off
Object snap modes:     None
Free dwg disk (D:) space: 361.6 MBytes
Free temp disk (C:) space: 159.0 MBytes
Free physical memory: 9.2 Mbytes (out of 47.2M).
Free swap file space: 244.2 Mbytes (out of 288.2M).
Press RETURN to continue:
```

Command line   STATUS

Inquiry Methods
197

Tracking Drawing Time

You can track the time you've spent on a drawing by displaying the time of creation and revision, total editing time, and elapsed time for the current drawing session. The screen also displays the current time and the time of the next automatic saving of the drawing file.

The timer feature is on by default. You can turn it off or reset it.

To display drawing time and set time variables

1 From the Tools menu, choose Inquiry ➤ Time.

   AutoCAD displays the report.

2 Enter **d** to redisplay the time status. You can also turn the timer off and on and reset it to zero.

   Command line TIME

Controlling the Drawing Display

AutoCAD provides many ways to display views of your drawing. As you edit your drawing, you can control the drawing display to move quickly to different areas of your drawing while you track the overall effect of your changes. You can zoom to change magnification or pan to reposition the view in the graphics area; save a view and then restore it when you need to plot or refer to specific details; or display several views at one time by splitting the screen into several tiled viewports.

In this chapter

- Using real-time panning and zooming to change the view area and magnification
- Using aerial views to zoom and pan the drawing
- Using named views
- Using tiled viewports
- Turning off visual elements to improve productivity

Using Zoom and Pan

A specific magnification, position, and orientation is known as a view. The most common way to change a view is to use one of AutoCAD's many zoom options, which increases or decreases the size of the image displayed in the graphics area.

Magnifying the image to view the details more closely is called zooming in. Shrinking the image to see a larger portion of the drawing is called zooming out.

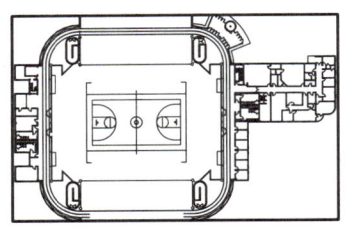

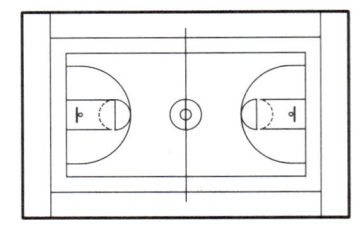

zoomed out

zoomed in

Zooming does not change the absolute size of the drawing. It changes the size of the view within the graphics area. AutoCAD offers several ways to change the view, including specifying a display window, zooming to a specific scale, and displaying the entire drawing.

Zooming and Panning with Realtime

Along with the ability to pan and zoom the image incrementally, AutoCAD provides the Realtime option for interactive zooming and panning. With ZOOM Realtime, you can zoom in or out of the drawing by moving the cursor vertically up or down.

Using PAN Realtime, you can pan the drawing image to a new location by clicking the image with the pointing device and moving the cursor.

When you are using the Realtime option of ZOOM or PAN, you can right-click the pointing device and use the cursor menu to move quickly between zooming and panning.

Using Real-Time Zooming

ZOOM Realtime provides interactive zooming capability. As you move the pointing device, the drawing image zooms in or out. To use real-time zooming, either click the Zoom icon on the Standard toolbar, choose Zoom ➤ Realtime from the View menu, or enter **zoom** on the command line.

The Realtime option is the default setting for ZOOM. Pressing ENTER after entering **zoom** on the command line automatically places you in Realtime mode.

In Realtime zoom mode, you can zoom in or out of the drawing by moving the cursor vertically up or down. Hold the pick button down at the midpoint of the drawing and move the cursor vertically to the top (positive direction) of the window to zoom in to 100% (2x magnification). Hold the pick button down at the midpoint of the drawing and move the cursor vertically to the bottom (negative direction) of the window to zoom out 100% (.5x magnification).

During Plot Preview, zoom-in is limited by the resolution of your plotter. Plot Preview stops your zoom-in at the point where one pixel on your display is equal to one pixel (or plotter step) on your plotter. You can only zoom in to the level of detail that your plotter or printer is capable of plotting.

When you have reached the zoom-in limit (the current view), the plus sign (+) is no longer displayed, indicating that you cannot zoom in any further. When you have zoomed out to the limit (the extents of the current view), the minus sign (-) is no longer displayed, indicating that you cannot zoom out any further. You cannot zoom out beyond the extents of the current view.

When you release the pick button, zooming stops. You can release the pick button, move the cursor to another location in the drawing, and then press the pick button again and continue zooming from that location.

Use the cursor menu to exit Realtime Zoom or Plot, or to enter Pan mode, Zoom Window, Zoom Previous, or Zoom Extents. To exit Realtime Zoom mode, press ENTER or ESC.

NOTE If you are using a Microsoft Intellimouse, you can zoom in by pushing the top of the wheel toward the front of the mouse. To zoom out, pull the top of the wheel backward.

To zoom in Realtime mode

1 From the View menu, choose Zoom ➤ Realtime.

2 To zoom in or out to different magnifications, press the pick button on your pointing device and move the cursor vertically.

Move the cursor above the midpoint of the drawing window to zoom in on the image. Move the cursor below the midpoint of the drawing window to zoom out from the image.

Command line ZOOM

Using Zoom and Pan

Using Real-Time Panning

PAN Realtime provides interactive panning capability. As you move the pointing device, the drawing image pans to a new location. To use real-time panning, click the Pan icon on the Standard toolbar, choose Pan from the View menu, or enter **pan** on the command line.

Realtime is the default setting for PAN. Pressing ENTER after entering **pan** on the command line automatically places you in Realtime Pan mode.

Hold down the pick button on the pointing device and move the hand cursor to pan the drawing. When you reach the edge of the drawing list regeneration, the cursor displays with an angle.

Use the cursor menu to exit Realtime Pan mode, or to enter Realtime Zoom mode. To exit Realtime Pan mode, press ENTER or ESC.

To pan in Realtime mode

1. From the View menu, choose Pan ➤ Realtime.
2. To pan interactively, hold down the pick button on the pointing device and move the drawing graphics to a new location.

Defining a Zoom Window

You can quickly zoom in on an area by specifying the corners that define it.

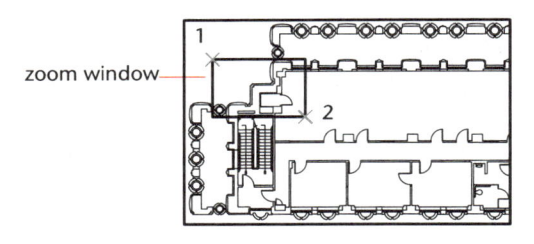

zoom window

original view

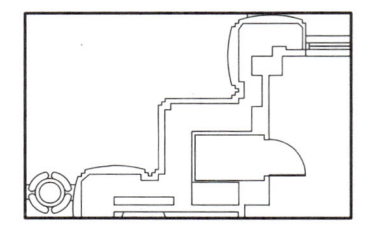

new view

The region specified by the corners you select is centered in the new display if it does not exactly match the aspect ratio of the viewport being zoomed. The shape of the zoom window you specify does not necessarily correspond to the new view, which fits the shape of the graphics area.

To zoom in on an area by specifying its boundaries

1 From the View menu, choose Zoom ➤ Window.
2 Specify one corner of the area you want to view (1).
3 Specify the opposite corner of the area you want to view (2).

Command line   ZOOM Window

Displaying the Previous View

When you work with close-up details in your drawing, you may need to zoom out frequently to see an overview of your work. Use ZOOM Previous to return quickly to the prior view. If you are using ZOOM Realtime, by right-clicking the pointing device and selecting Zoom Previous from the cursor menu, you can return to the last zoomed view that was displayed when you initially invoked ZOOM Realtime.

AutoCAD can restore up to 10 previous views in succession. These views include not only zoomed views, but also views that have been panned, restored, or set to perspective or plan view. ZOOM Previous restores only the view magnification and position, not the previous content of an edited drawing.

To restore the previous view

- From the View menu, choose Zoom ➤ Previous.
- From Realtime zoom mode, right-click the pointing device, and then choose Zoom Previous from the cursor menu.

Command line   ZOOM Previous

Using Dynamic Zooming

When Fast Zoom is turned on, you can use ZOOM Dynamic to change the view without regenerating the drawing. ZOOM Dynamic displays the generated portion of your drawing in a view box that represents the current viewport. By moving and resizing the view box, you can pan and zoom the drawing.

current view *view box*

drawing extents

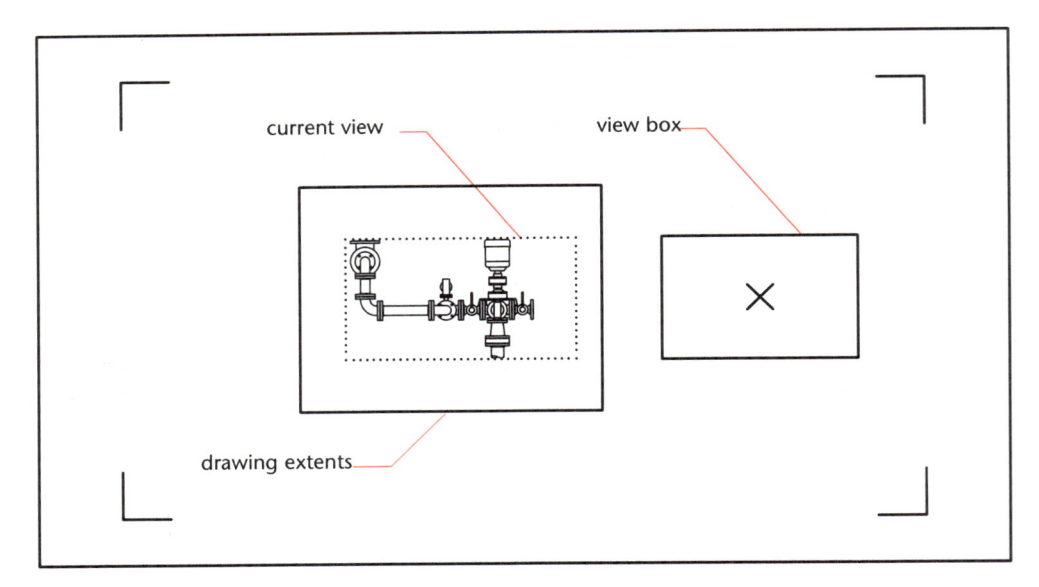

Depending on your display, the area occupied by the current view is outlined by a green dotted line. A dashed blue box indicates the drawing extents. These extents correspond to the drawing limits or the area actually occupied by your drawing, whichever is larger.

To zoom dynamically

1 From the View menu, choose Zoom ➤ Dynamic.

   A view of the drawing extents and limits appears.

2 When the view box contains an X, drag the view box around the screen to pan to a different area.

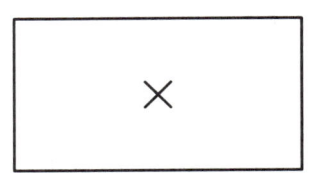

3 To zoom to a different magnification, press the pick button on your pointing device. The X in the view box changes to an arrow.

Resize the view box by dragging the border to the right or left. A larger box displays a smaller image. A smaller box displays a larger image.

You can press the pick button on your pointing device to switch between zooming and panning as needed.

4 When the view box defines the area you want to view, press ENTER.

The image enclosed by the view box becomes the current view.

Command line ZOOM Dynamic

Scaling a View

If you need to increase or decrease the magnification of the image by a precise scale, you can specify a zoom scale in three ways:

- Relative to the drawing limits
- Relative to the current view
- Relative to paper space units

To scale a view relative to the drawing limits, enter a simple scale value. For example, enter **1** to display the limits as large as possible in the graphics area, centered at the center point of the previous view. To zoom in or out, enter a higher or lower number. As shown in the following example, you can enter **2** to display the image at twice the full size or **.5** to display the image at half the full size. The limits are shown by the grid.

current view

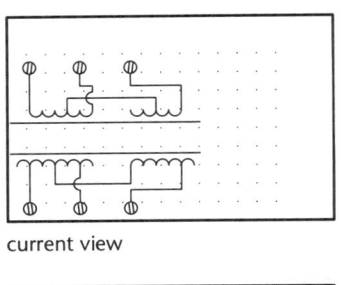

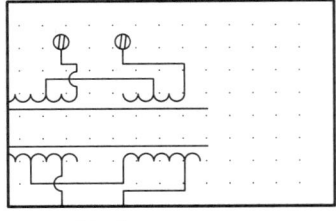

zoomed to 1

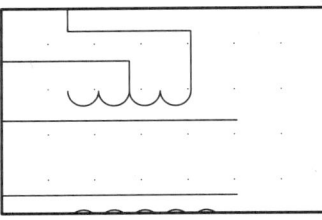

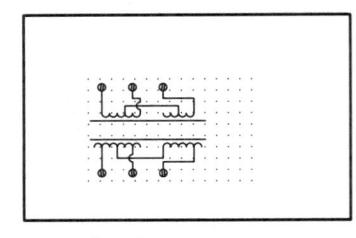

zoomed to 2

zoomed to .5

Scaling the view relative to the drawing limits

To scale a view relative to the current view, add **x** after the value you enter. As shown in the following example, you can enter **2x** to double the size of the current view or **.5x** to display a view half the size of the current view. Entering **1x** has no effect.

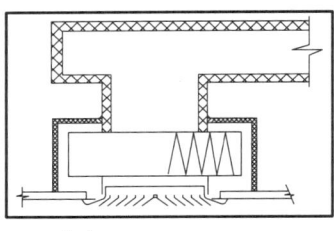

current view

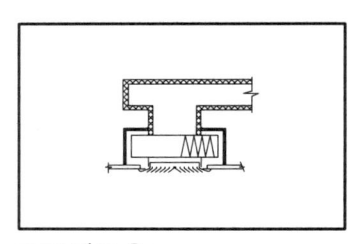

zoomed to .5x

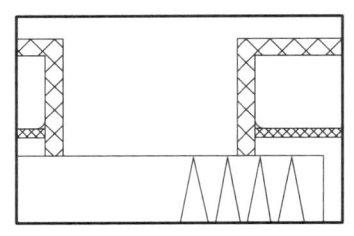

zoomed to 2x

Scaling the view relative to the current view

Chapter 6 Controlling the Drawing Display

To scale a view relative to paper space units, add **xp** after the value you enter. This specification increases or decreases the view relative to the current paper space scale and is used to scale the viewport before plotting (see "Scaling Views Relative to Paper Space" on page 488).

To zoom using a precise scale

1 From the View menu, choose Zoom ➤ Scale.

2 Enter the scale factor relative to the drawing limits, current view, or paper space view.

Command line   ZOOM Scale

Centering

You can move a specific point in your drawing to the center of the graphics area. ZOOM Center is useful for resizing an object and bringing it to the center of the viewport. The following example shows the effects of using ZOOM Center to display a view at the same size and at twice the size.

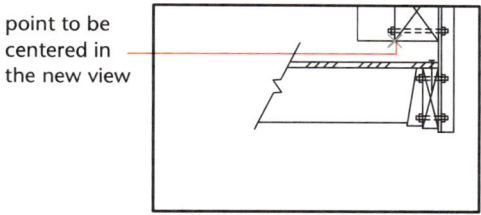

point to be centered in the new view

current view

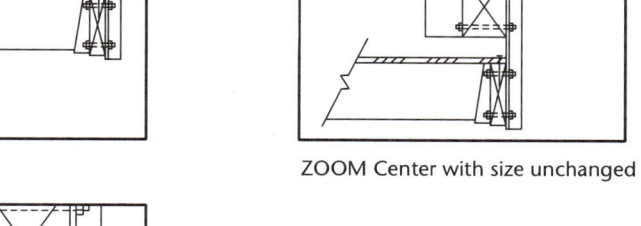

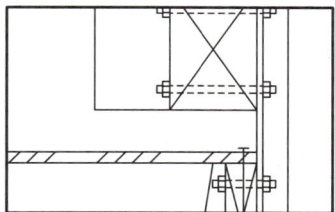

ZOOM Center with size unchanged

ZOOM Center using 2x scale

Centering a specific point

With ZOOM Center, you can specify size by entering either the number of vertical drawing units or a magnification relative to the current view.

Using Zoom and Pan

To center the drawing in the graphics area

1 From the View menu, choose Zoom ➤ Center.
2 Specify the point you want in the center of the drawing.
3 Enter a height in drawing units or enter a scale factor.

For example, to specify a height, enter **2** to display a view that is two drawing units high. Values smaller than the default value increase the size of the image. Larger values decrease the size of the image.

To specify relative magnification, enter a scale factor followed by **x**. For example, enter **2x** to display a view that is twice as large as the current view. If you are working with floating viewports, you can enter **xp** to scale the view relative to paper space (see "Scaling Views Relative to Paper Space" on page 488).

Command line   ZOOM Center

Displaying Drawing Limits and Extents

To display a view based on the drawing boundaries or the extents of the objects in the drawing, use ZOOM All or ZOOM Extents.

ZOOM All displays the entire drawing. If the objects extend beyond the limits, ZOOM All displays the extents of the objects. If the objects are drawn within the limits, ZOOM All displays the limits.

ZOOM Extents calculates zooms based on the extents of the active viewport, not the current view. Usually the active viewport is entirely visible, so the results are obvious and intuituve. However, when using the ZOOM command in model space while working in a paper space viewport, if you are zoomed in beyond the paper space viewport's borders, some of the area zoomed may not be visible.

ZOOM Extents changes the view to encompass the entity extents for the current drawing. In some cases (for both ZOOM All and Extents), this may cause a regeneration. If REGENAUTO is on, the regeneration occurs automatically. If REGENAUTO is off, you are prompted to approve the regeneration. Regeneration will not occur on layers that are frozen or off. If your drawing has no objects, ZOOM Extents displays the drawing limits.

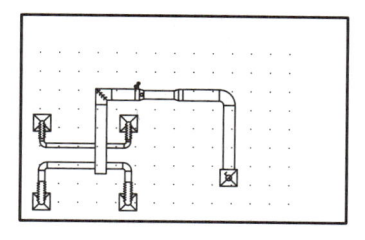

current view

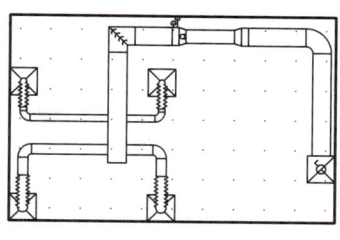

zoomed to extents

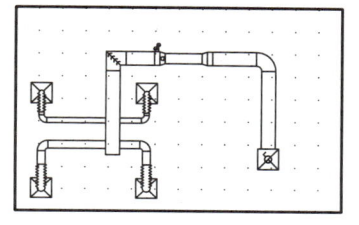

zoomed to show entire drawing (all)

Zoomed views with grid defining drawing limits

For 3D views, ZOOM All and ZOOM Extents have the same effect. Infinite construction lines (xlines) and rays do not affect either option.

To display the entire drawing or the extents

- From the View menu, choose Zoom ➤ All or Zoom ➤ Extents.

Command line   ZOOM All, ZOOM Extents

Using Fast Zoom

Fast Zoom mode turns on a large virtual screen. The virtual screen defines the area in which the screen is redrawn with display commands (ZOOM, PAN, VIEW). VIEWRES turns Fast Zoom mode on and off, and controls regeneration of the drawing display. By default, Fast Zoom mode is on.

If Fast Zoom is on, the maximum virtual screen shows as much of the drawing as possible without forcing complete regeneration of the screen. When Fast Zoom mode is off, the virtual screen is turned off. Also, when Fast Zoom is off, Realtime Pan and Zoom are turned off.

Using Zoom and Pan

209

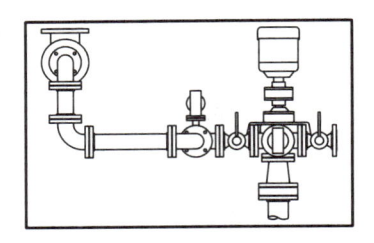

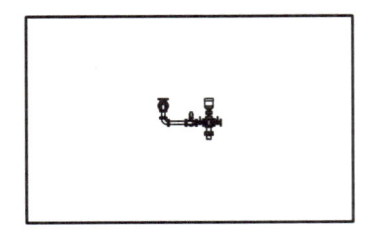

original view   virtual screen, Fast Zoom on

Fast Zoom operates in both model space and paper space and it can be set independently for each viewport. If Fast Zoom mode is on, display changes do not regenerate the drawing. If Fast Zoom mode is off, display changes always regenerate the drawing.

NOTE If Fast Zoom mode is off, Aerial View is not available.

To turn Fast Zoom on or off

1 At the Command prompt, enter **viewres**.
2 At the prompt, enter **y** to turn on Fast Zoom mode, or enter **n** to turn off Fast Zoom mode.
3 Press ENTER.

Using Aerial View

Aerial View is a navigation tool that displays a view of the drawing in a separate window so that you can quickly move to that area. If you keep the Aerial View window open as you work, you can zoom and pan without choosing a menu option or entering a command.

Each time AutoCAD regenerates the drawing, the virtual display space is recalculated, and the current contents of the screen are erased and redrawn. The Aerial View window provides you with a navigation tool to view the contents of the virtual display space. However, using the Aerial View window to zoom into and view a portion of the drawing does not force regeneration of the drawing.

Aerial View works in all model space views. Aerial View does not work when Fast Zoom mode is off. You can easily move the Aerial View window by dragging it to another location. Also, you can resize the window by dragging its border.

Opening and Closing the Aerial View Window

Once you open the Aerial View window, you can keep it visible as you work and then close it when you no longer need it. The Aerial View window provides real-time zooming and panning of the AutoCAD window. However, this real-time updating of the AutoCAD window is not available in paper space.

To open and close the Aerial View window

1 From the View menu, choose Aerial View.

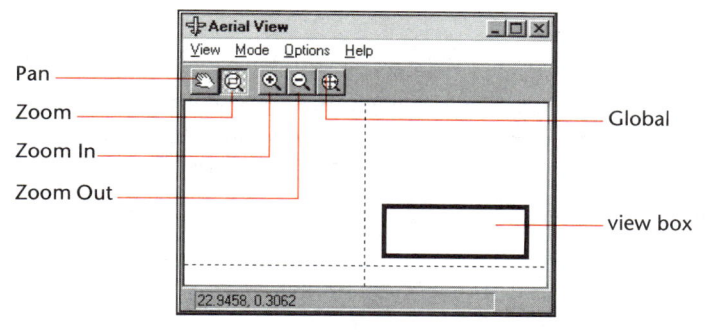

Pan
Zoom
Zoom In
Zoom Out
Global
view box

2 To close the Aerial View window, click the Close button in the upper-right corner of the Aerial View window.

Command line DSVIEWER

Zooming with Aerial View

You can change the view by creating a new view box in the Aerial View window. To zoom in to the drawing, make the view box smaller. To zoom out of the drawing, make the view box larger. As you zoom in or out of the drawing, a real-time view of the current zoom location is displayed in the graphics area. The following illustration shows how the view box works.

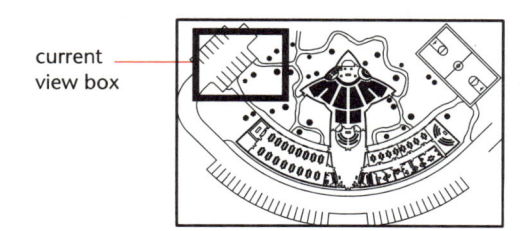

current view box

Aerial View window

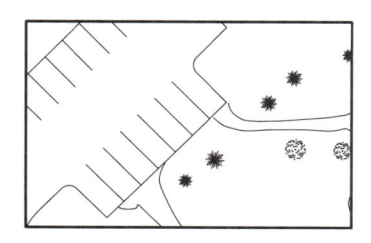

current view in graphics area

Using Aerial View

211

new view box

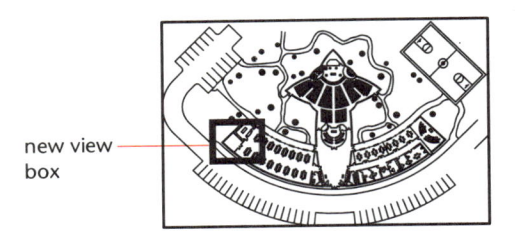

Aerial View window

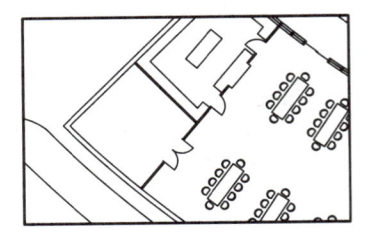

new view in graphics area

To zoom using Aerial View

1. From the View menu, choose Aerial View.
2. In the Aerial View window, from the Mode menu, choose Zoom.
3. Press the pick button on the pointing device for the first point. Then drag the rectangle to the desired zoom window size and release the pick button.

The graphics area zooms along with the Aerial View window to reflect the current zoom view.

Panning with Aerial View

You can pan the drawing by moving the view box without changing its size. As you zoom in or out of the drawing, a realtime view of the current pan location is displayed in the graphics area. This method changes the view without changing the magnification.

current view box

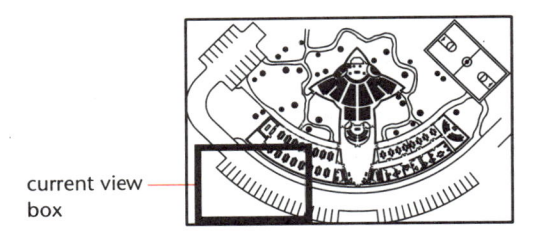

Aerial View window

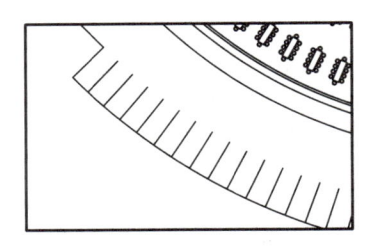

current view in graphics area

Chapter 6   Controlling the Drawing Display

212

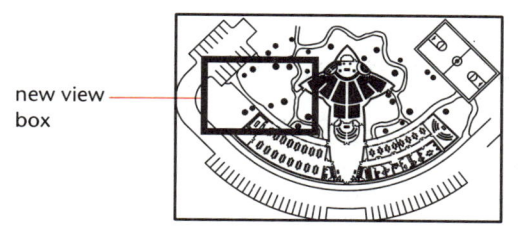

new view box

Aerial View window

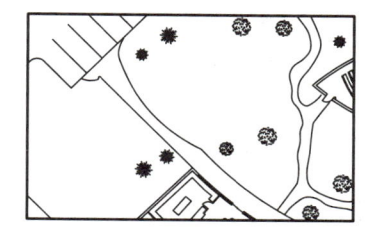

new view in graphics area

To pan using Aerial View

1 From the View menu, choose Aerial View.
2 In the Aerial View window, from the Mode menu, choose Pan.

The crosshairs change to a dashed-line pan box the same size as the current view box.

3 Use the pointing device to drag the pan box to a new position.

You can also interactively pan the drawing display by pressing and holding the pick button, then moving the current view box. This pans the drawing display in real-time.

4 Press the pick button on the pointing device.

The graphics area pans along with the Aerial View window to reflect the new position.

Changing the Size of the Aerial View Image

You can change the size of the image in the Aerial View window by displaying the entire drawing or by incrementally resizing the image. These changes do not affect the view in the graphics area.

When the entire drawing is displayed in the Aerial View, the Zoom Out menu item and button are grayed out and unavailable. When the current view nearly fills the Aerial View window, the Zoom In menu item and button item are grayed out and unavailable. It is possible for both of these conditions to exist at the same time, causing both to be grayed out, such as when the drawing extents are displayed.

To display the entire drawing in the Aerial View window

- In the Aerial View window, from the View menu, choose Global.

To increase or decrease the size of the Aerial View image

- In the Aerial View window, from the View menu, choose Zoom In or Zoom Out.

Changing the Aerial View Update

AutoCAD automatically updates the Aerial View window to reflect the changes you make in your drawing. When working on complex drawings, you may want to turn off this dynamic updating to improve program performance.

Similarly, if you work with multiple viewports, the Aerial View image changes as you select different viewports. You can turn off this feature so that AutoCAD updates the Aerial View window only when you activate it.

To turn dynamic updating on and off

- In the Aerial View window, from the Options menu, choose Dynamic Update. (A check mark indicates that the Aerial View window shows changes as they occur.)

To turn viewport updating on and off

- In the Aerial View window, from the Options menu, choose Auto Viewport. (A check mark indicates that Aerial View is displaying the current viewport.)

Using Named Views

You can name and save a view you want to reuse. When you no longer need the view, you can delete it.

Saving Views

When you save a view, the viewing position and scale are saved. When you begin a new drawing, you usually use a single viewport that fills the entire graphics area. If you are working with multiple viewports, the view in the current viewport is saved. If you are working in paper space, the paper space view is saved.

To save and name a view

1 From the View menu, choose Named Views.

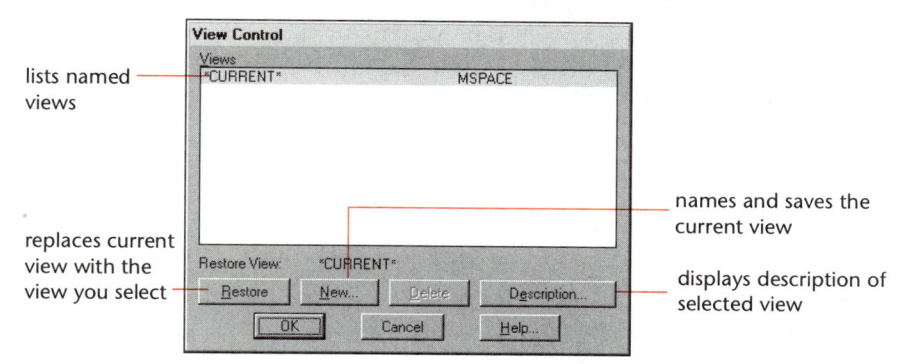

lists named views — (View Control dialog)

replaces current view with the view you select — Restore

names and saves the current view — New

displays description of selected view — Description

2 In the View Control dialog box, choose New.

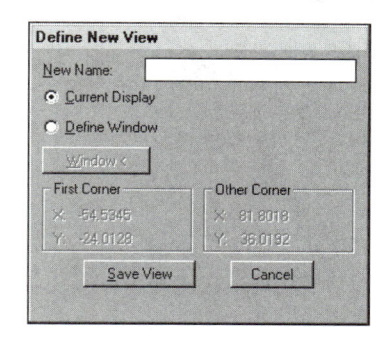

3 In the Define New View dialog box, enter a name for the view.

The name can be up to 31 characters long and contain letters, digits, and the special characters dollar sign ($), hyphen (–), and underscore (_).

4 If you want to save only part of the current view, select Define Window, and then choose Window. In the graphics area, specify opposite corners of the view.

5 Choose Save View.

6 In the View Control dialog box, choose OK.

Command line   DDVIEW

Related   VIEW saves views on the command line.

Using Named Views

215

Restoring Named Views

When you need to reuse a named view, you can restore it. If you are working with multiple viewports, the view is restored to the current viewport. You can use named views in a paper space layout or specify them when you plot (see "Using Tiled Viewports" on page 216 and "Using Named Views in Paper Space" on page 493).

To restore a named view

1. To make it current, click within the viewport that contains the view you want to replace.
2. From the View menu, choose Named Views.
3. In the View Control dialog box, select the view you want to restore.
4. Select Restore. Then choose OK.

Command line   DDVIEW

Deleting Named Views

When you no longer need a view, you can delete it.

To delete a named view

1. From the View menu, choose Named Views.
2. In the View Control dialog box, select the view you want to delete.
3. Select Delete. Then choose OK.

Command line   DDVIEW

Using Tiled Viewports

AutoCAD usually begins a new drawing using a single viewport that fills the entire graphics area. You can split the graphics area to display several viewports simultaneously. For example, if you keep both the full and the detail views visible, you can see the effects of your detail changes on the entire drawing. In each tiled viewport, you can

- Pan; zoom; set Snap, Grid, and UCS icon modes; and restore named views in individual viewports
- Draw from one viewport to another when executing a command
- Name a configuration of viewports so that you can reuse it

Chapter 6   Controlling the Drawing Display

The following illustration shows a drawing with three tiled viewports. The crosshairs cursor is in the current viewport. The viewports completely fill the graphics area and do not overlap.

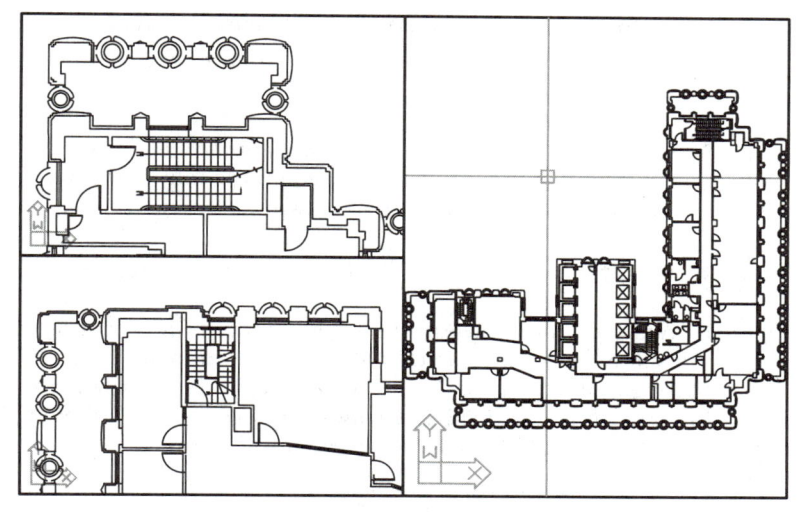

Tiled viewports

As you draw, changes made in one viewport are instantly reflected in the others. You can switch among these viewports at any time, including in the middle of a command.

Tiled viewports differ from the viewports arranged in paper space. Paper space viewports, also known as floating viewports, are used to establish a final layout for a drawing. They can overlap and be printed or plotted at the same time. For more information about paper space viewports, see "Preparing a Layout" on page 480.

Displaying Multiple Tiled Viewports

You can display tiled viewports in various configurations. How you display the viewports depends on the number and size of the views you need to see. If you're not familiar with the available configurations, you can select a display by choosing its picture. Use the following procedure to replace any existing configurations.

To display tiled viewports

1 On the status bar, make sure Tile is highlighted.

If Tile is not highlighted, double-click it.

2 From the View menu, choose Tiled Viewports ➤ Layout.
3 Select the picture or name of the configuration you want to use.
4 Choose OK.

Related MVIEW creates viewports in paper space. Use VPORTS to display tiled viewports. If multiple tiled viewports already exist, VPORTS inserts the new configuration in the current viewport.

Changing the Tiling Configuration

If you need more viewports than the standard configurations provide, you can subdivide a selected viewport. This procedure modifies the current viewport without replacing the entire display. To replace the entire display, use the procedure described in the previous section. The following illustrations show the default viewport configurations.

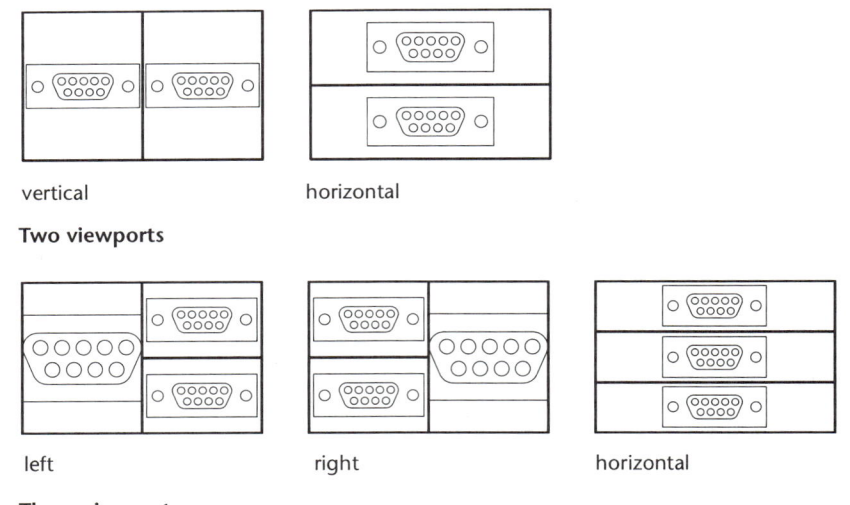

vertical   horizontal

Two viewports

left   right   horizontal

Three viewports

vertical   above   below

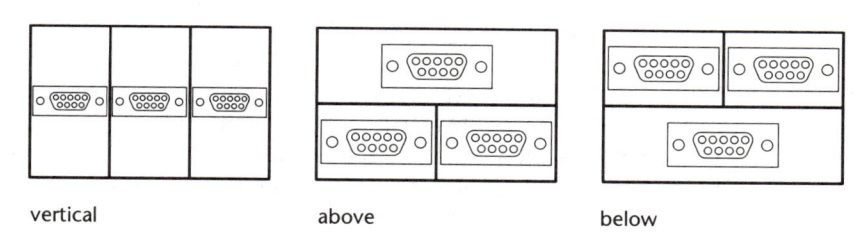

Three viewports

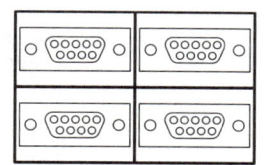

Four viewports

Also, you can join adjacent viewports if their common boundary is the same size. When you join viewports, the view is based on the first viewport you select.

To subdivide a viewport

1 Click inside the viewport you want to subdivide to make it current.
2 From the View menu, choose Tiled Viewports. Then choose 2 Viewports, 3 Viewports, or 4 Viewports to indicate how many viewports should be displayed.
3 At the prompt, specify the viewport orientations.

Command line VPORTS

To join two viewports

1 From the View menu, choose Tiled Viewports ➤ Join.
2 Click within the viewport containing the view you want to keep.
3 Click within an adjacent viewport to join it to the first viewport.

Command line VPORTS

Using Tiled Viewports

Working in Tiled Viewports

With multiple tiled viewports, you can see the overall effect of detail work or connect elements in one viewport to elements in another. For example, in a very large drawing, you can draw a line from a detail in one corner to a detail in a distant corner by displaying each section and then drawing the line from one viewport to the other.

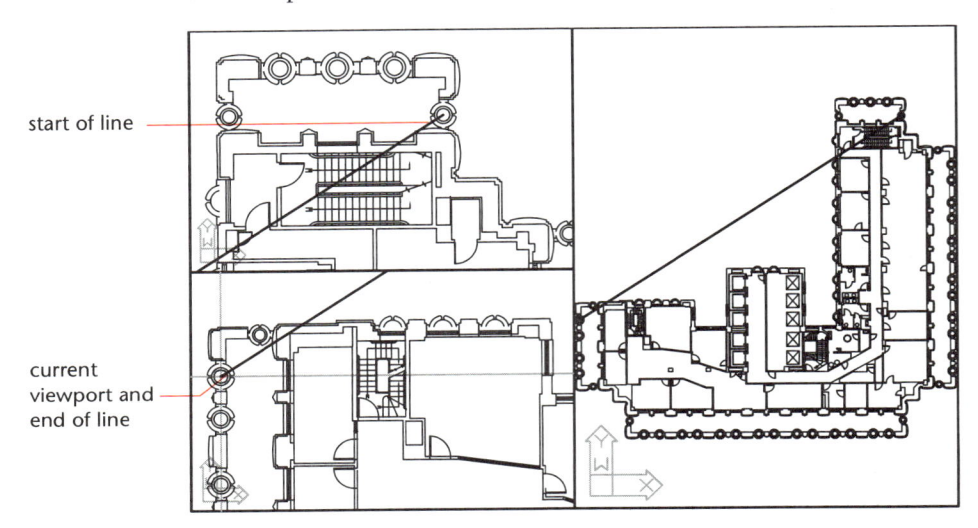

start of line

current viewport and end of line

Drawing a line between viewports

As you work, you can display different views of the drawing, such as a plan or a front or side elevation. The viewports can show the progress of your work from different views. Errors you might miss in one view may be apparent in other views. This feature is especially useful for 3D modeling.

Making Another Tiled Viewport Current

You enter points and select objects in the current viewport. When a viewport is current, the arrow cursor changes to crosshairs, and the borders are highlighted. You can move between viewports in the middle of a command.

For example, to draw a line using two viewports, you must start the line in the current viewport, make another viewport current by clicking within it, and then specify the endpoint of the line in the second viewport.

To make a viewport current

- Click within the viewport borders.

Selecting and Dragging Objects in Tiled Viewports

When you work with multiple viewports, the display of selection sets or dragged objects depends on which viewport is current. As you select objects in different viewports, the highlighting appears only in the viewport where you select each object, as shown in the following illustration.

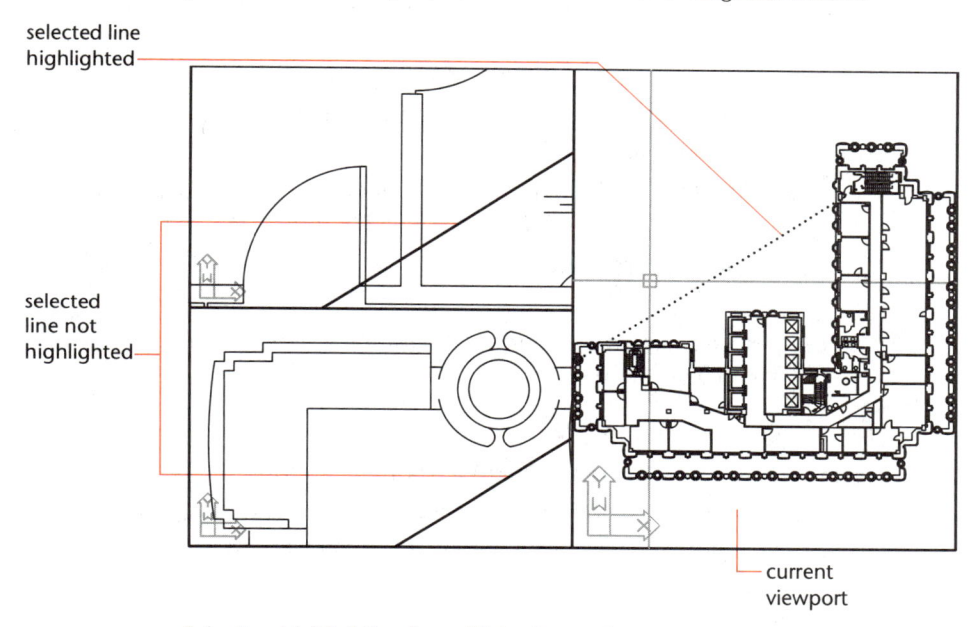

selected line highlighted

selected line not highlighted

current viewport

Selection highlighting in multiple viewports

When you start dragging the objects to their new locations, *all* selected objects become highlighted in the current viewport. The other viewports show highlighting only for objects selected in those viewports. When you complete the command, all of the objects' new positions are reflected in all viewports.

Reusing Viewport Configurations

You can set up and save tiled viewport configurations for reuse at any time so that you don't have to set up the viewports and views every time you need them.

Using Tiled Viewports

221

Saving Viewport Configurations

When you name and save a specific viewport configuration with the current drawing, the saved information includes the number of viewports, their positions on the screen, and the settings for each viewport. These settings are the same as the settings saved with individual views (see "Saving Views" on page 214).

To save and name a viewport configuration

1 From the View menu, choose Tiled Viewports ➤ Save.
2 Enter a configuration name.

   The name can be up to 31 characters long and contain letters, digits, and the special characters dollar sign ($), hyphen (–), and underscore (_).

   Command line   VPORTS Save

Restoring Viewport Configurations

You can restore a named viewport configuration any time you need to redisplay the views it contains.

To restore a named viewport configuration

1 From the View menu, choose Tiled Viewports ➤ Restore.
2 Enter ? and press ENTER twice if you want to see a list of configurations.
3 Enter the name of the viewport configuration you want to use.

   Command line   VPORTS Restore

Deleting Viewport Configurations

If you no longer need a configuration, you can delete it.

To delete a named viewport configuration

1 From the View menu, choose Tiled Viewports ➤ Delete.
2 Enter ? and press ENTER twice if you want to see a list of configurations.
3 Enter the name of the viewport configuration you want to delete.

   Command line   VPORTS Delete

Listing Viewport Configurations

You can display information about the current and saved configurations. A text screen describes the location of each viewport's lower-left and upper-right corners. These corners are described by values in which 0,0 represents the lower-left corner of the graphics area and 1,1 represents the upper-right corner.

id #3 viewport

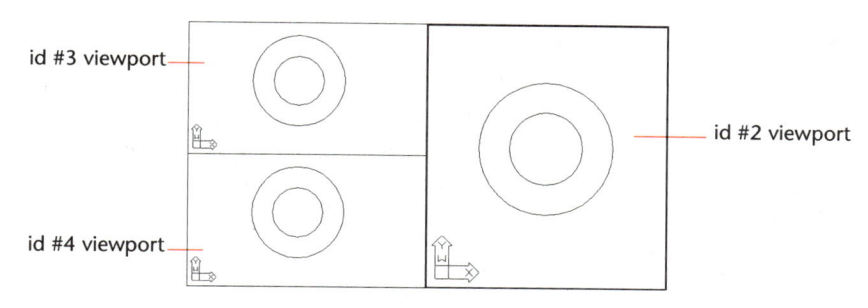

id #2 viewport

id #4 viewport

Three-viewport configuration

Current configuration:
id# 2
   corners: 0.5000,0.0000 1.0000,1.0000 ——— current viewport
id# 3
   corners: 0.0000,0.5000 0.5000,1.0000
id# 4
   corners: 0.0000,0.0000 0.5000,0.5000

Configuration PLANS: ——————————— named configuration with three viewports
  0.5000,0.5000 1.0000,1.0000
  0.5000,0.0000 1.0000,0.5000
  0.0000,0.0000 0.5000,1.0000

Configuration 3D_VIEWS: ——————————— named configuration with four viewports
  0.5000,0.0000 1.0000,0.5000
  0.0000,0.5000 0.5000,1.0000
  0.0000,0.0000 0.5000,0.5000
  0.5000,0.5000 1.0000,1.0000

Sample list of viewport configurations

The viewports in the current configuration have identification numbers. The current viewport is listed first.

To list the viewport configurations

1. At the Command prompt, enter **vports**.
2. Enter **?** and press ENTER twice to list all the viewport configurations in the drawing.

   Also, you can enter wild-card characters to filter the names. For example, enter **ar*** to list configuration names beginning with AR.

Using Tiled Viewports

Turning Visual Elements On and Off

The complexity of your drawing affects how fast AutoCAD refreshes the screen or processes commands. You can increase program performance by turning off the display of text, fill, or selection highlighting. You also can turn off blips.

Turning Fill On and Off

You can turn fill on or off for traces, wide polylines, and solid-filled polygons. Turning off fill can improve performance. When Solid Fill mode is off, the fill is not plotted.

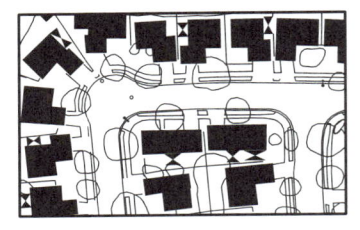

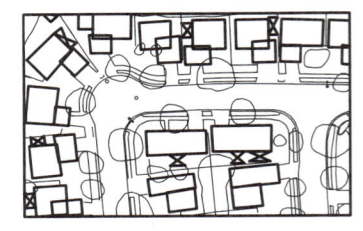

Fill mode on

Fill mode off

Whenever you change Solid Fill mode, use REGEN to see the effect on existing objects. New objects automatically reflect the new setting.

To turn fill on or off

1 At the Command prompt, enter **fill**.
2 Enter **1** to display fill or **0** to display only an outline.
3 Enter **regen** to display your changes.

Command line   FILLMODE

Related   The DDRMODES command opens the Drawing Aids dialog box, where you can select the Solid Fill Mode option to turn it on or off.

Turning Text On and Off

You can turn off the display of text by turning on Quick Text mode. When Quick Text mode is on, only a frame defining the text is displayed. As with Fill mode, turning off the text display can improve drawing performance. When Quick Text is on, the text frame, but not the text, is plotted.

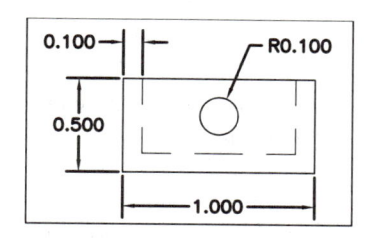

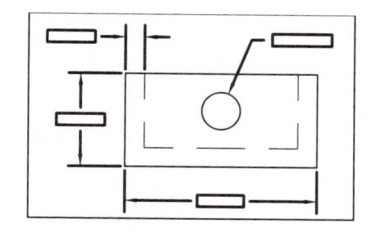

Quick Text mode off

Quick Text mode on

Whenever you change Quick Text mode, use REGEN to see the effect on existing text. New text automatically reflects the new setting.

To turn the display of text on or off

1. At the Command prompt, enter **qtext**.
2. Enter **regen** to display your changes.

Command line   QTEXTMODE

Related   The DDRMODES command opens the Drawing Aids dialog box, where you can select the Quick Text option to turn it on or off.

Turning Blips On and Off

Blips are temporary markers that appear in the graphics area when you select objects or locations. You can use them as references or remove them with REDRAW or REGEN. You also can prevent blips from appearing by turning off Blip mode. For example, if you copy a nut with Blip mode on, a blip appears at the selection and displacement points. When Blip mode is off, blips do not appear.

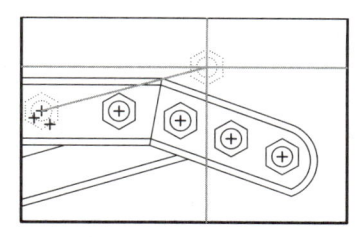

Blip mode on

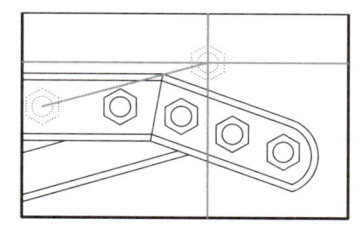

Blip mode off

Blips never appear on plotted drawings.

Turning Visual Elements On and Off

225

To turn the display of blips on or off

1 From the Tools menu, choose Drawing Aids.
2 In the Drawing Aids dialog box, select Blips. Then choose OK.
   A check mark indicates that Blip mode is on.

   Command line   DDRMODES

   Related   BLIPMODE turns blips on or off from the command line.

Turning Selection Highlighting On and Off

You can turn on or off the highlighting that identifies selected objects. Turning off highlighting can improve performance.

To turn selection highlighting on or off

1 From the Tools menu, choose Drawing Aids.
2 In the Drawing Aids dialog box, select Highlight.
3 Choose OK.
   A check mark indicates that Highlight mode is on.

   Command line   DDRMODES

   Related   HIGHLIGHT turns highlighting on or off from the command line.

Editing Methods

AutoCAD offers two approaches to editing: you can issue a command first and then select the objects to edit, or you can select the objects first and then edit them. This chapter describes how to select and edit two-dimensional (2D) objects.

In this chapter

- Selecting objects individually and in groups
- Editing objects using grips
- Editing object properties
- Copying, moving, erasing, and resizing objects
- Converting objects into their components
- Modifying polylines, multilines, and splines
- Chamfering and filleting objects
- Modifying hatch patterns and boundaries

Working with Named Objects

In addition to the graphic objects used by AutoCAD, there are several types of nongraphic objects that are stored in drawing files. These objects have descriptive designations associated with them, for example, blocks, layers, groups, and dimension styles. In most cases, you name objects as you create them, and you can later rename them. Names are stored in symbol tables. When you specify a named object on the command line or select one from a dialog box, you are referencing the name and associated data of the object in the symbol table.

Purging Named Objects

You can purge unused, unreferenced named objects from a drawing at any time during an editing session. Purging reduces drawing size. You cannot purge objects that are referenced by other objects. For example, a font file might be referenced by a text style. A layer is referenced by the objects on the layer.

You can purge individual objects, all objects of a specific type, or all named objects in a drawing. Purging removes only one level of reference. For example, if purging a layer removes the only reference to a linetype, the linetype is not purged until you purge again using the linetype option.

To purge unreferenced objects

1 From the File menu, choose Drawing Utilities ➤ Purge.
2 Choose an object type to purge, or All to purge all unreferenced objects.

   AutoCAD prompts you with the name of each unreferenced object of the specified type.

3 Enter the object names to be purged or an asterisk (*) for All.
4 Enter **y** or **n** to verify each object name to be purged.

   If you answer **y**, AutoCAD displays the symbol table reference and name of the purged object.

5 Enter **y** or **n** in response to each prompt.

   Command line   PURGE

Renaming Objects

You can rename any named object except those that AutoCAD names by default, for example, layer 0 or the CONTINUOUS linetype. Names cannot exceed 31 characters or contain 8-bit characters. Valid characters are letters, digits, and the special characters dollar sign ($), hyphen (-), and underscore (_). After you enter a name, AutoCAD converts the characters to uppercase.

As your drawings become more complex, you can rename objects to keep the names meaningful or to avoid conflicts with names in drawings you have inserted in the main drawings.

When you are naming objects with dependent symbols, the object and symbol table names are combined to form one name that contains up to 31 characters. When an object and symbol name are combined, AutoCAD removes the vertical symbol bar (|) from each dependent symbol name and replaces it with two dollar signs ($) separated by a number (usually zero), for example, STAIR0STEEL.

For more information about symbol table naming conventions, see "Binding Xrefs to Drawings" on page 462.

To rename objects

1 From the Format menu, choose Rename.
2 In the Rename dialog box under Named Objects, select the object type.
3 Select the named object from the Items list, or enter the name under Old Name.
4 Under Rename To, enter the new name, and then choose Rename To.
5 When you're finished renaming objects, choose OK.

Command line   DDRENAME

Related   RENAME

Renaming Groups of Objects

To rename groups of similarly named objects all at once, use wild-card symbols. For example, to rename the group of layers STAIR$LEVEL-1, STAIR$LEVEL-2, STAIR$LEVEL-3 to S_LEVEL-1, S_LEVEL-2, S_LEVEL-3, enter **stair$*** under Old Name and **s_*** under Rename To.

The table defines the wild-card characters you can use.

Valid wild-card characters

Character	Definition
# (Pound)	Matches any numeric digit
@ (At)	Matches any alphabetic character
. (Period)	Matches any nonalphanumeric character
* (Asterisk)	Matches any string and can be used anywhere in the search string
? (Question mark)	Matches any single character, for example, ?BC matches ABC, 3BC, and so on
~ (Tilde)	Matches anything but the pattern, for example, ~*AB* matches all strings that don't contain AB
[...]	Matches any one of the characters enclosed, for example, [AB]C matches AC and BC
[~...]	Matches any character not enclosed, for example, [~AB]C matches XC but not AC
- (Hyphen)	Inside brackets, specifies a range for a single character, for example [A-G]C matches AC, BC, and so on to GC, but not HC
' (Reverse quote)	Reads next character literally, for example, '*AB matches *AB

NOTE In addition to using the wild-cards specified in this table, you can also use the RENAME command for renaming objects.

Selecting Objects

Before you can edit objects, you need to create a selection set of the objects. A selection set can consist of a single object, or it can be a more complex grouping: for example, the set of objects of a certain color on a certain layer. You can create the selection set either before or after you choose the editing command. If the HIGHLIGHT system variable is on, AutoCAD highlights selected objects. You can make several changes to the same selection set. Use one of the following methods to create selection sets.

- Choose an editing command. Then select the objects and press ENTER.
- Enter **select**. Then select the objects and press ENTER. (For more information, see SELECT in the *Command Reference*.)
- Select the objects with the pointing device.
- Define groups.

NOTE To select objects before choosing an edit command, the PICKFIRST system variable must be on.

Choosing the Command First

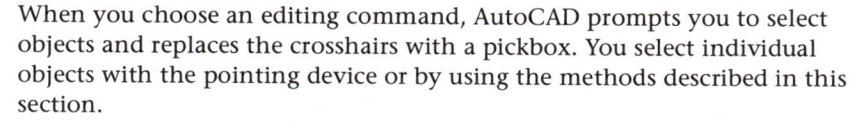

When you choose an editing command, AutoCAD prompts you to select objects and replaces the crosshairs with a pickbox. You select individual objects with the pointing device or by using the methods described in this section.

crosshairs   pickbox

You can respond to the Select Objects prompt in various ways. You can select the most recently created object, the previous selection set, or all objects in the drawing. You can add objects to and remove objects from a selection set. You can also use more than one selection method to make a selection. For example, to select most of the objects in the graphics area, select all objects and then remove the objects you don't want selected.

Using Selection Windows

You can select objects by enclosing them in a selection window. A selection window is a rectangular area that you define in the graphics area by specifying two corner points at the Select Objects prompt. The order in which you specify the points makes a difference. Dragging from left to right (*window* selection) selects only objects entirely within the selection area. Dragging from right to left (*crossing* selection) selects objects within and crossing the selection area. Objects must be at least partially visible to be selected.

NOTE When selecting objects with the window option, usually the entire object must be contained in the window. However, if the object extends off screen, but all the visible vectors (noncontinuous linetypes) can be enclosed within the window, the entire object is selected.

Selecting Objects

231

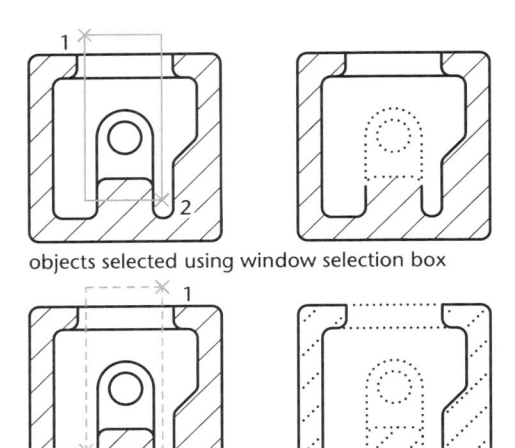

objects selected using window selection box

objects selected using crossing selection box

Related If the PICKDRAG system variable is on, you can hold down the pick button while you create the window. If PICKDRAG is off, specify the window corners individually. PICKDRAG is off by default.

To select objects within an irregularly shaped area, enclose them in a polygon selection window. Create the window by specifying points to enclose the area. The order in which you specify points defines a window or a crossing polygon. A window polygon selects only objects it encloses entirely, and a crossing polygon selects objects it encloses or crosses.

In the following example, you use a window polygon to select all the bricks entirely within an irregularly shaped area.

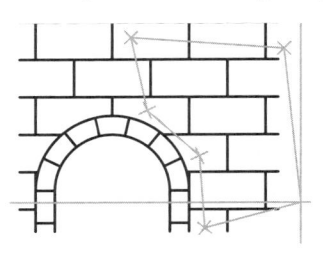

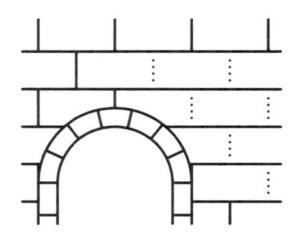

window polygon   result

To select objects within an irregularly shaped area

1 At the Select Objects prompt, enter **cp** for Crossing Polygon.
2 Specify points from left to right to define an area that entirely encloses the lines you want to select.
3 Press ENTER to close the polygon and complete the selection.

The following illustration shows the result of specifying the same selection area as a crossing polygon.

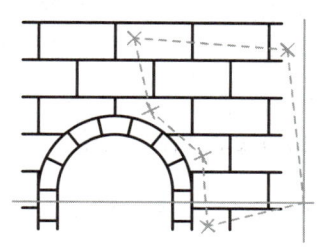

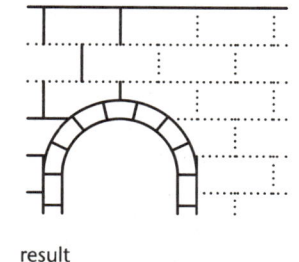

crossing polygon   result

Using Selection Fences

You can select nonadjacent objects in a complex drawing most easily with a selection fence. A fence is a line that selects all the objects it passes through. This circuit board illustration shows a fence selecting several components.

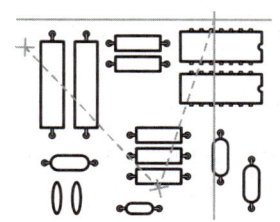

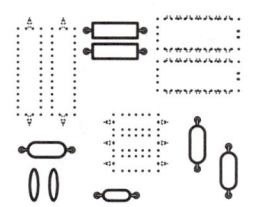

fence selection   selected objects highlighted

To select nonadjacent objects with a fence

1 At the Select Objects prompt, enter **f** (Fence).
2 Specify the fence points.
3 Press ENTER to complete the selection.

Selecting Objects Close Together

It is difficult to select objects that are close together or lie directly on top of one another. You can use the pick button to cycle through these objects, one after the other, until you reach the one you want.

In the following example, two lines and a circle all lie within the scope of the selection pickbox.

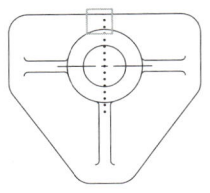

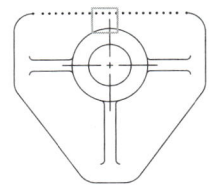

first selected object   second selected object   third selected object

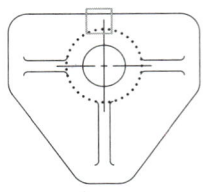

To cycle through objects for selection

1   At the Select Objects prompt, hold down CTRL and select a point as near as possible to the object you want.

2   Press the pick button on your pointing device repeatedly until the object you want is highlighted.

3   Press ENTER to select the object.

Customizing Object Selection

You can control how objects are selected by choosing the selection mode, pickbox size, and object sorting method.

To use the object selection settings

1   From the Tools menu, choose Selection.

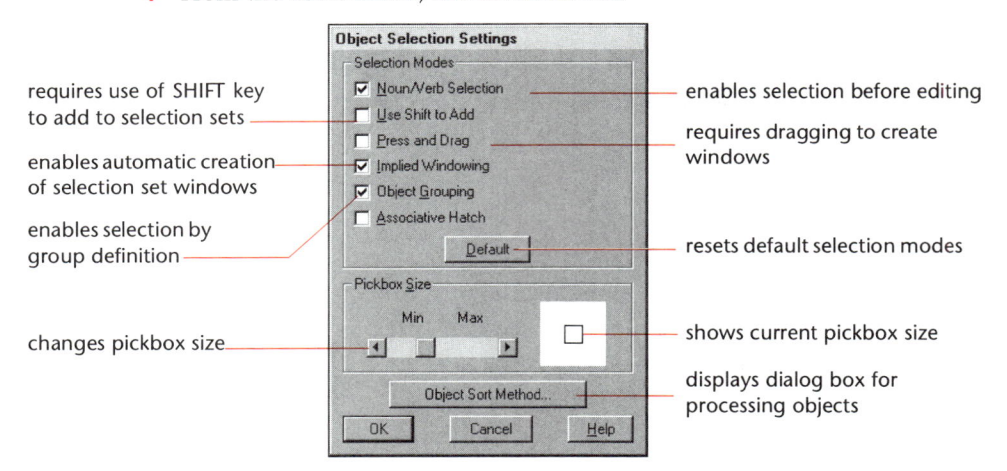

requires use of SHIFT key to add to selection sets

enables automatic creation of selection set windows

enables selection by group definition

changes pickbox size

enables selection before editing

requires dragging to create windows

resets default selection modes

shows current pickbox size

displays dialog box for processing objects

2   In the Object Selection Settings dialog box, specify any selection modes and the pickbox size.

Chapter 7   Editing Methods

3 To modify the object sorting method, choose Object Sort Method.

For more information about these methods, see DDSELECT in the *Command Reference*.

4 Choose OK.

Command line   DDSELECT

Filtering Selection Sets

You can limit selection sets by property, such as color, or by object type by using filter lists. For example, you can copy only the red objects in a circuit board drawing or only objects on a certain layer. You create a filter list after you have started an editing command.

You can name filter lists and save them in a file so that you can use them repeatedly. Filtering recognizes only colors or linetypes that have been explicitly assigned to objects, not those that are inherited by layer. For information about assigning properties by layers, see "Working with Layers" on page 298.

In the following example, you move all the line objects in a drawing. After starting the MOVE command, you create the filter list. Then you select objects. AutoCAD applies the filter list, selecting only line objects for the move.

To create a filter list based on object type

1 From the Modify menu, choose Move.

2 Select objects.

3 On the Command line, enter **'filter**.

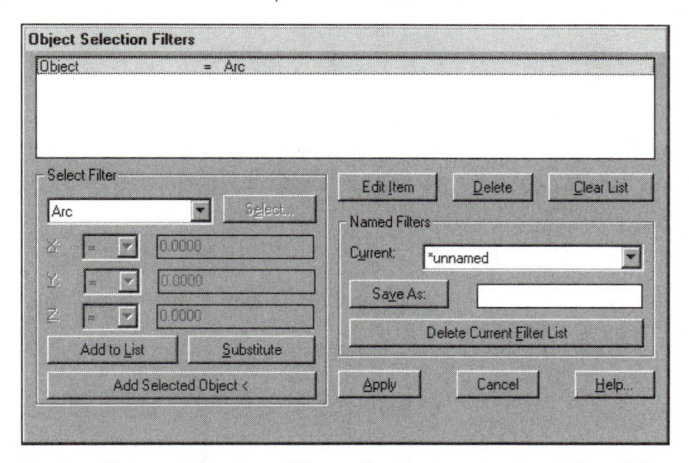

4 In the Object Selection Filters dialog box under Select Filter, select Line.

Selecting Objects

235

5 Select Add to List.
6 Choose Apply. AutoCAD applies the filter list to whatever you now select.

With the MOVE command still active, you can select objects with a window, and AutoCAD applies the filter list to all objects in the window.

To select objects using a filter set

1 At the Select Objects prompt, use a window to select objects.

   AutoCAD states how many objects were found and how many were filtered out.

2 Press ENTER to exit the selection filter.

   The line objects are now selected.

3 At the Select Objects prompt, press ENTER to continue the MOVE command.
4 Specify a base point.
5 Specify a point of displacement.

   AutoCAD moves only the line objects in the drawing.

   Command line 'FILTER

Removing Objects from a Selection Set

After you create a selection set, you can choose to remove individual objects from that set. For example, you can select an entire group of densely grouped objects and then remove specific objects within the group, leaving only the objects you want to be in the set. You can choose to remove objects only while object selection is already in progress or when objects in a selection set are highlighted and have grips.

To remove objects while creating a selection set

1 Select some objects.
2 At the Select Objects prompt, enter **remove**.
3 At the Remove Objects prompt, select the objects you want to remove from the selection set.
4 To return to adding objects to the selection set, enter **add**.

   NOTE You can also remove an object from a selection set by pressing the SHIFT key as you select the object.

Selecting Objects First

There are several ways you can select objects before you choose a method of editing them. You can use the SELECT command, which provides all the options you can use at the Select Objects prompt. You can turn on Noun/Verb Selection in the Object Selection Settings dialog box. This is equivalent to setting the PICKFIRST system variable to 1.

You can also select objects with the pointing device so that they are marked with grips, if grips are turned on. Grips mark control locations on a selected object, as shown in the illustration.

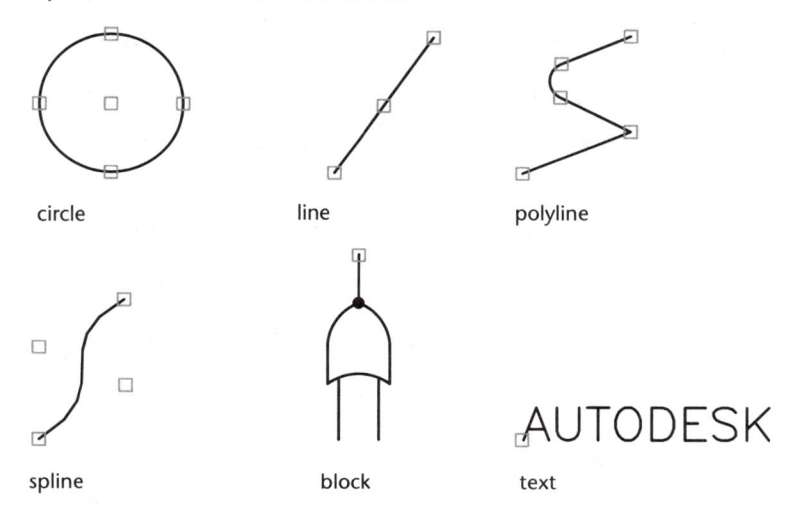

circle   line   polyline

spline   block   text

Examples of grip locations

Selecting a block turns on a grip at its insertion point. A selected group doesn't have a location that can be associated with it like the insertion point of a block. When you select a group, each member of the group is marked with its own grips (see "Multiple Grips as Base Grips" on page 240).

With grips you can use the pointing device to combine command and object selection and therefore edit more quickly. When grips are turned on, you select the objects you want *before* editing. With the grips, you can manipulate the objects with the graphics cursor or keywords. By using grips, you can reduce your use of menus.

The graphics cursor snaps to any grip over which it is moved. Objects removed from a grip selection set are no longer highlighted, but their grips remain active. Remove grips from the selection set by pressing ESC. To remove a specific object from the gripped selection set, hold down the SHIFT key as you select the object.

To turn on grips

1 From the Tools menu, choose Grips.

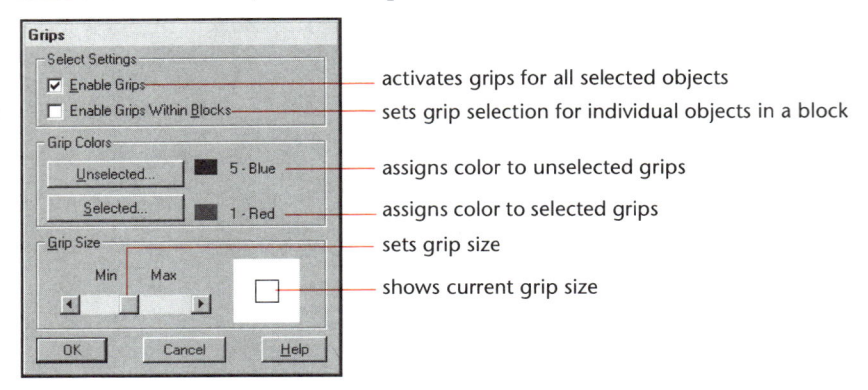

- activates grips for all selected objects
- sets grip selection for individual objects in a block
- assigns color to unselected grips
- assigns color to selected grips
- sets grip size
- shows current grip size

2 In the Grips dialog box, select Enable Grips and make any changes to color or size.

3 Choose OK.

Command line DDGRIPS

The two illustrations show the difference between having Enable Grips Within Blocks selected and cleared.

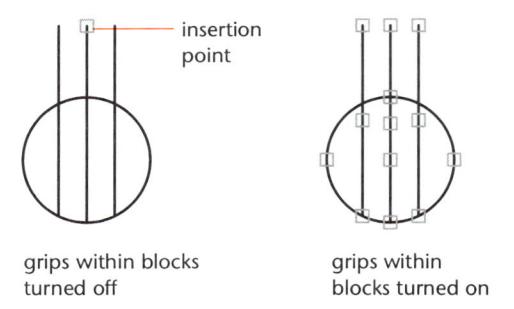

insertion point

grips within blocks turned off

grips within blocks turned on

Related The GRIPBLOCK system variable controls the assignment of grips within blocks. When GRIPBLOCK is 1, grips are assigned to all objects in the block. When GRIPBLOCK is 0, a single grip is assigned to the block's insertion point.

Editing with Grips

To use grips for editing, select a grip to act as the base point. This selected grip is known as the base grip. Then select one of the Grip modes: Stretch, Move, Rotate, Scale, or Mirror. You can cycle through these modes with the SPACEBAR or keyboard shortcuts. For example, to reach Stretch mode from another mode, enter **st** or keep pressing ENTER until Stretch appears. To exit Grip modes at any point and return to the Command prompt, enter **x** (Exit) or press ESC. For descriptions of these editing functions, see the sections on stretching, moving, rotating, scaling, and mirroring using grips.

Multiple Copy Mode

If you press SHIFT as you select the first new coordinate location, Multiple Copy mode is activated. For example, with Stretch mode, Multiple Copy mode stretches the object, such as a line, and copies it to wherever you specify in the graphics area. Another way to activate Multiple Copy mode is to use the Copy option at the Command prompt, and select a point or enter a coordinate for each copy's destination. Multiple Copy mode remains active until you select another option from the current grip mode or press ENTER to exit.

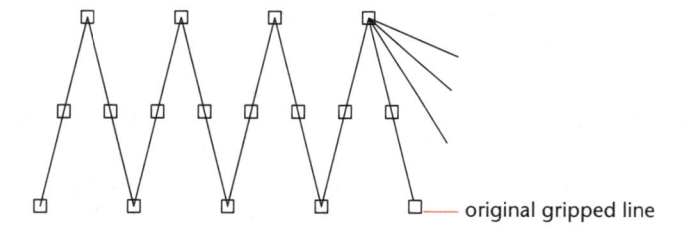

Stretch with multiple copy (grips and objects are not selected)

Multiple Copy Mode and Offset Snap Locations

If you hold down SHIFT continuously while you select multiple copy points on screen, the graphics cursor snaps to offset points based on the first two points you selected. For example, in the following illustration, the midpoint of line 1 is at the coordinate 8,5. Based on that midpoint, line 2 was copied using SHIFT with Stretch mode; its midpoint is at 9,5. Line 3 snaps to an offset based on these two coordinates, 10,5.

midpoint of line 1 at 8,5

midpoint of line 2 at 9,5

midpoint of line 3 at 10,5

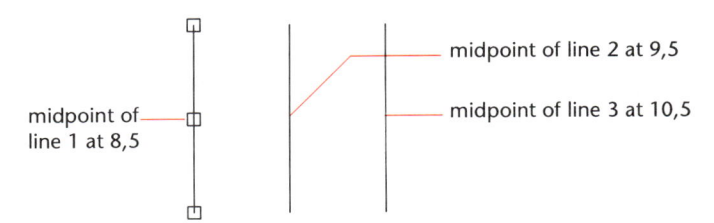

Stretch with multiple copy and automatic offset snap

Multiple Grips as Base Grips

You can use multiple grips as the base grips. This allows you to keep the geometry intact between the selected grips. Hold down the SHIFT key as you select the grips.

Using Groups

A group is a named selection set of objects. Unlike unnamed selection sets, groups are saved with the drawing. Group definitions are maintained when you use a drawing as an external reference or insert it in another drawing. However, until you have bound and exploded external references or exploded blocks, you cannot directly access groups that have been defined in an external reference or block.

When you create or edit a group, you can specify whether it is selectable. If a group is selectable, selecting one of its members selects all members in the current space that meet the selection criteria (for example, members on locked layers are not selectable). The ability to select groups is also affected by the PICKSTYLE system variable. When PICKSTYLE is off for group selection, you can individually select group members. In the following procedures, the groups that are used are selectable.

An object can be a member of more than one group. You can list all the groups to which a selected object belongs by using the Find Name option in the Object Grouping dialog box. Highlight all the members of a specified group with the Highlight option. Group members are numerically ordered and can be reordered. Reordering may be useful in some batch operations on objects or when it's important which object is "on top" for display purposes.

Creating Groups

When you create a group, you can give the group a name and description. If you copy a group, the copy is given the default name A*x* and is considered unnamed. Unnamed groups are not listed in the Object Grouping dialog box unless you select Include Unnamed.

If you choose a member of a selectable group for inclusion in a new group, all members of that selectable group are included in the new group. In the following example, you create a group consisting of the objects in the window. This group can then be copied multiple times.

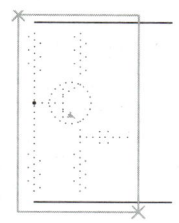

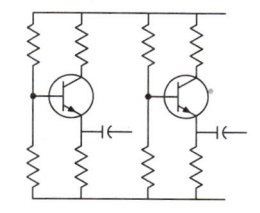

objects selected for grouping   group copied

To create a group

1 From the Tools menu, choose Object Group.

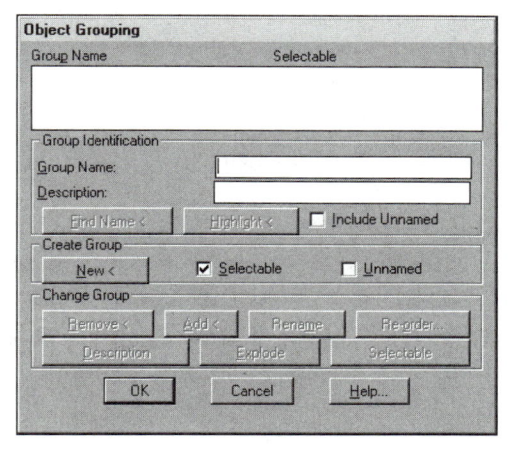

2 In the Object Grouping dialog box under Group Identification, enter a Group Name and a Description.
3 Choose New.
4 Select objects.
5 Choose OK.

Command line GROUP

Related -GROUP displays options on the command line.

Selecting Objects
241

Selecting Groups

You can select groups by name at the Select Objects prompt. If the PICKSTYLE system variable is set to 1 or 3 and you select any member of a selectable group, all group members that meet the selection criteria are selected. You can also toggle group selection on and off by pressing CTRL+A.

All members of selectable groups are also selected when you use object selection cycling, for example, if you want to select an object that lies directly behind another object (see "Selecting Objects Close Together" on page 233). Selecting an object that is a member of multiple selectable groups selects all the members of all the groups that contain that object. To select groups for editing with grips, use the pointing device to select the group at the Command prompt.

The following example shows how selecting objects works when the object you are selecting belongs to a selectable group.

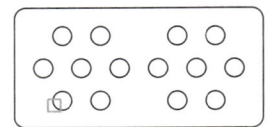

selected object belongs to a group

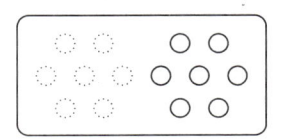

all group members are selected

To cycle through object and group selection

1 At the Command or Select Objects prompt, press CTRL and select the object.

This turns on object cycling.

Now select any point. An object within the original pickbox is selected. Press the pick button on your pointing device repeatedly until the objects you want are highlighted.

2 Press ENTER to turn off object cycling.

You can now continue to select objects normally.

NOTE To select individual objects without selecting the groups to which they belong, press CTRL+A to switch the PICKSTYLE system variable on and off.

Editing Groups

At any time, you can add or remove group members and rename groups. You can also copy, mirror, and array groups. Erasing a group member deletes that object from the group definition. When a group member is included in a deleted block, the object is deleted from the drawing and also from the group. If deleting an object or removing it from a group leaves the group empty, the group remains defined. You can remove the group definition by exploding the group. Exploding groups deletes them from a drawing. Objects that were part of the group remain in the drawing.

You can alter the group's member order, its description, and whether it's selectable. You can reorder group members in two ways: either change the numerical position of individual or ranges of group members or reverse the order of all members. The first object in each group is number 0 *not* number 1.

To delete a named group

1 From the Tools menu, choose Object Group.
2 In the Object Grouping dialog box, select the group name from the list of groups.
3 Under Change Group, select Explode.
4 Choose OK.
   The group is deleted.
   Command line GROUP

   Related -GROUP displays options on the command line.

To reorder group members

1 From the Tools menu, choose Object Group.
2 In the Object Grouping dialog box under Change Group, choose Re-order.
3 In the Order Group dialog box under Group Name, select the group to reorder.
4 To view the current order of this group, choose Highlight, and then choose Next. Choose OK when you have finished.
5 In the Order Group dialog box at Number of Objects, enter the object number or range of numbers to reorder.
6 At Remove from Position, enter the current position.
7 At Replace at Position, enter the new position.
8 Choose Reorder to update the group order.
9 Choose OK to exit each dialog box.

Editing Objects Using the Object Properties Toolbar

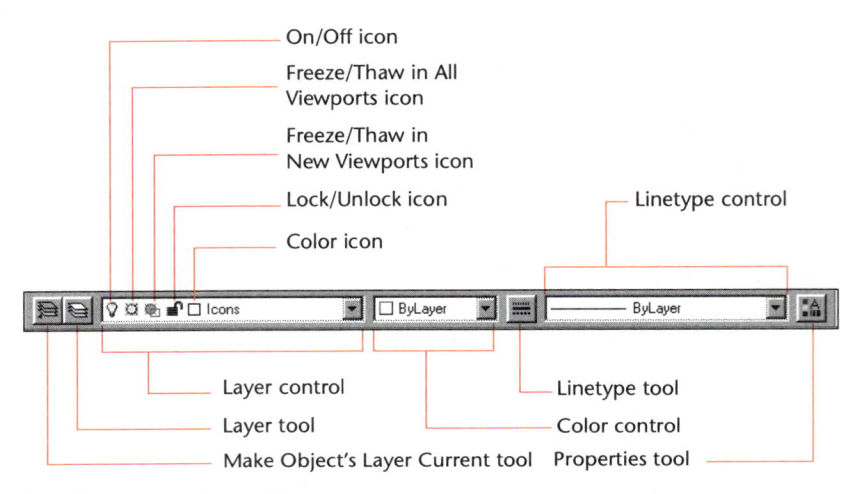

The Object Properties toolbar

Labels: On/Off icon; Freeze/Thaw in All Viewports icon; Freeze/Thaw in New Viewports icon; Lock/Unlock icon; Color icon; Linetype control; Layer control; Linetype tool; Layer tool; Color control; Make Object's Layer Current tool; Properties tool

You can use the controls on the Object Properties toolbar to quickly view or change an object's layer, color, and linetype. The layer, color, and linetype controls on the Object Properties toolbar consolidate the commands needed to view and edit an object's properties. Selecting any object when no command is active, dynamically displays its layer, color, and linetype in the controls on the toolbar.

NOTE You *cannot* change the properties of objects on locked layers.

All controls on the Object Properties toolbar support character matching: instead of scrolling through the lists to make a selection, you can enter the first character of the layer, color, or linetype name to select it. If the layer or linetype name is too long to be displayed within the control, it will be shortened with an ellipsis (...) in the middle of the name.

You can assign layer, color, and linetype properties to the individual components of complex objects such as blocks, xrefs, mtext, mlines, and raster images; however, when these properties are overriden, they cannot be viewed or edited by the layer, color, and linetype controls. For complex objects, the Layer, Color, and Linetype controls show the default properties assigned to the object in its entirety and not its individual parts.

Selecting an Object in PICKFIRST Mode

When the PICKFIRST system variable is on (set to 1), you can select an object with the pointing device before entering a command. When an object is selected with PICKFIRST turned on, solid lines become dashed lines and grips appear at key points as shown in the following example.

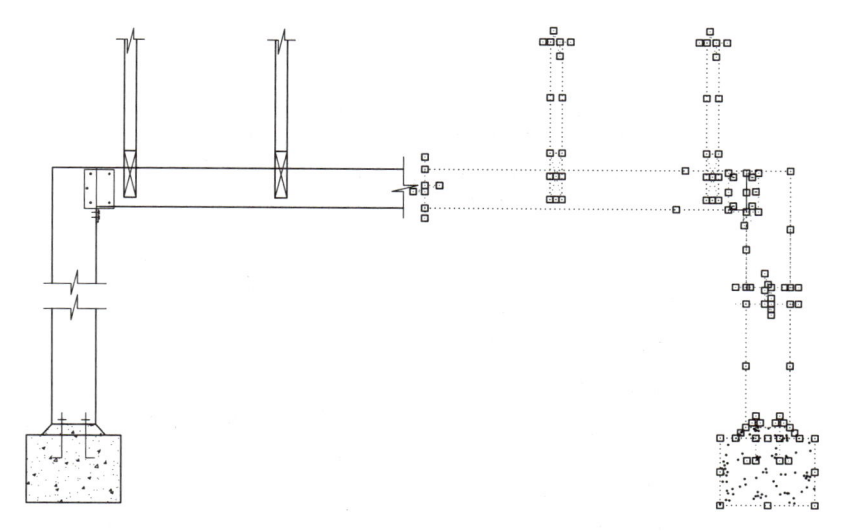

A selection made in PICKFIRST mode

PICKFIRST must be turned on to view or to change an object's properties with the Object Properties toolbar.

NOTE If the PICKADD system variable is set to 0, you can add objects to your selection set by holding down the SHIFT key and clicking with your pointing device.

Editing Layers

With the Layer control, you can make a layer current, view the layer of a selected object, and change an object's layer. You can also change a layer's properties by clicking on the icons in the Layer control. You can make an object's layer the current layer by choosing Make Object's Layer Current.

Editing Objects Using the Object Properties Toolbar

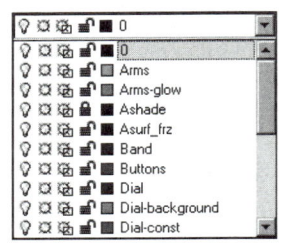

To make a layer current

1. On the Object Properties toolbar, click the Layer control.
2. Select the layer you want to make current. To quickly scroll to the desired layer, enter the first letter of the name.

NOTE Because frozen and xref-dependent layers cannot be made current, their names are grayed out in the Layer control.

To make an object's layer current

1. Select the object whose layer you want to make current.
2. On the Object Properties toolbar, click Make Object's Layer Current.

NOTE If you select a block or xref, the layer on which the block or xref is inserted becomes the current layer.

To change an object's layer

1. Select the objects whose layers you want to change.
2. On the Object Properties toolbar, select a layer in the Layer control.

   If one object is selected and no command is active, the Layer control displays the layer assigned to that object. If you've selected multiple objects on a variety of layers, the control is blank. Selecting a layer from the list changes all selected objects to that layer.

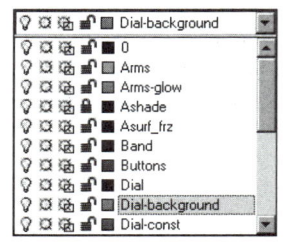

The Layer control

Chapter 7   Editing Methods

You can use the Layer control to transfer objects to locked, frozen, or turned off layers, but you cannot transfer an object to an xref-dependent layer. Xref-dependent layers appear grayed out in the list because they cannot be made current and you cannot edit objects on those layers. You can, however, still modify the properties on xref-dependent layers with the icons in the Layer control.

Editing Colors

With the Color control, you can make a color current, view the color of a selected object, and change an object's color.

The Color control displays seven standard colors and the four most recently used colors. If the desired color is not present in the list, select the Other option and choose the desired color from the Select Color dialog box.

To make a color current

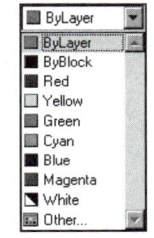

1 On the Object Properties toolbar, choose the Color control.

Select a color from the list. To quickly scroll to the desired color, enter the first letter of the name, or choose Other to select a color from the Select Color dialog box.

If you choose BYLAYER, new objects assume the color of the layer upon which they are drawn. If you choose BYBLOCK, new objects are drawn in the default color (white or black depending on your configuration) until they are grouped into a block. The objects in the block inherit the current color property.

NOTE If you insert a block on a layer whose color is set to the BYLAYER option, the block does not assume the layer's color if you have previously assigned a color to the block.

To change an object's color

1 Select the objects whose colors you want to change.
2 In the Color control on the Object Properties toolbar, select a color.

Editing Objects Using the Object Properties Toolbar

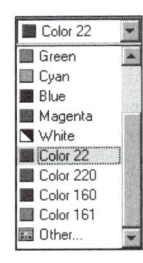

The Color control list

3   If you do not see the color that you want, choose Other.

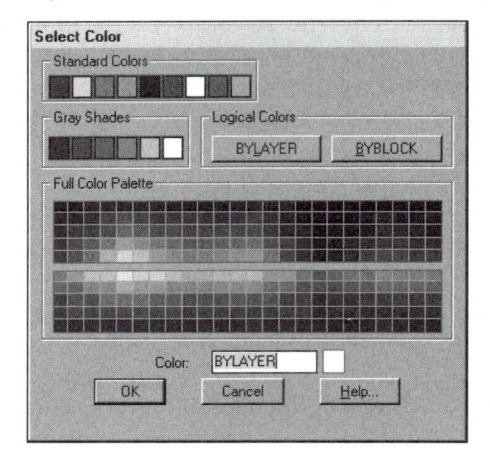

4   In the Select Color dialog box, select a color and choose OK.

If one object is selected and no command is active, the Color control list box displays the color assigned to that object. If you select multiple objects with a variety of colors, the display window of the Color control is blank. Selecting a color from the list changes all selected objects to that color.

NOTE When you select multiple objects from different layers, and the colors of the selected objects are set to the BYLAYER option, *BYLAYER* is displayed in the Color control without a color swatch if the color assigned to each layer varies.

Editing Linetypes

With the Linetype control, you can make a linetype current, view the linetype of a selected object, and change an object's linetype.

> **NOTE** Xref-dependent linetypes *cannot* be made current or assigned to objects, so their names are not displayed in the Linetype control.

To make a linetype current

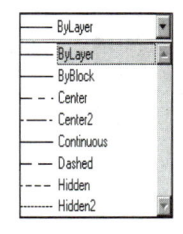

1 From the Object Properties toolbar, choose the Linetype control.
2 Select the linetype you want to make current. To quickly scroll to the desired linetype, enter the first letter of the name.

If you choose BYLAYER, new objects assume the linetype of the layer upon which they are drawn. If you choose BYBLOCK, new objects are drawn using the continuous linetype until they are grouped into a block. The objects in the block inherit the current linetype property.

To change an object's linetype

1 Select the objects whose linetypes you want to change.
2 From the Linetype control list box on the Object Properties toolbar, select a linetype.

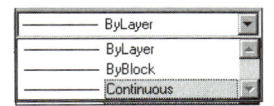

The Linetype control

If one object is selected and no command is active, the Linetype control list box displays the linetype assigned to that object. If you select multiple objects with a variety of linetypes, the display window of the Linetype control is blank. Selecting a linetype from the list changes all selected objects to that linetype.

> **NOTE** When you select multiple objects from different layers and the linetypes of the selected objects are set to the BYLAYER option, *BYLAYER* is displayed in the Linetype control. An example linetype is not displayed if the linetype that is assigned to each layer varies.

Editing Objects Using the Object Properties Toolbar

Matching Properties of Other Objects

You can copy some or all properties of one object to one or more objects using MATCHPROP. Properties that can be copied include color, layer, linetype, linetype scale, thickness, and in some cases, dimension, text, and hatch properties. This table lists the properties you can copy for each AutoCAD object.

Object properties you can change with Match Properties								
Object	Color	Layer	Linetype	Linetype scale	Thickness	Text properties	Dimension properties	Hatch properties
3dface	•	•	•	•				
Arc	•	•	•	•	•			
AttDef	•	•			•	•		
Body	•	•	•	•				
Circle	•	•	•	•	•			
Dimension	•	•	•	•			•	
Ellipse	•	•	•	•				
Hatch	•	•						•
Image	•	•	•	•				
Insert	•	•	•	•				
Leader	•	•	•	•			•	
LIne	•	•	•	•	•			
Mtext	•	•				•		
OLE object								
Point	•	•			•			
2D polyline	•	•	•	•	•			
3D polyline	•	•	•	•				

Chapter 7   Editing Methods

Object properties you can change with Match Properties (*continued*)

Object	Color	Layer	Linetype	Linetype scale	Thickness	Text properties	Dimension properties	Hatch properties
3D mesh	•	•	•	•				
Pface mesh	•	•	•	•				
Ray	•	•	•	•				
Region	•	•	•	•	•			
2D solid	•	•	•	•				
ACIS solid	•	•	•	•				
Spline	•	•	•	•				
Text	•	•	•	•	•	•		
Tolerance	•	•	•	•			•	
Trace	•	•	•	•	•			
Viewport	•	•						
Xline	•	•	•	•				
Xref	•	•	•	•				
Zombie	•	•	•	•				

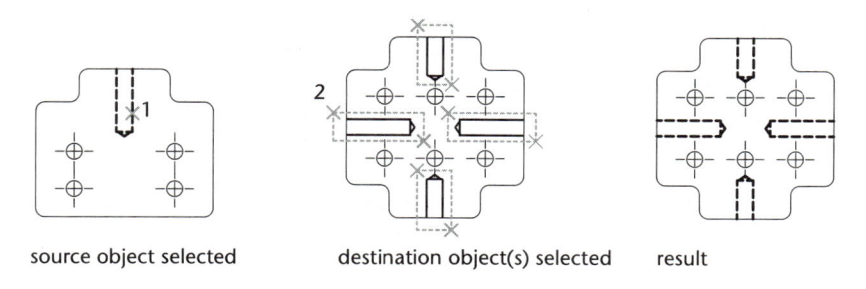

source object selected   destination object(s) selected   result

To copy properties from an object to one or more objects

1 From the Modify menu, choose Match Properties.
2 Select the object whose properties you want to copy (1).

Matching Properties of Other Objects

251

3   Select the objects to which you want to apply the properties (2).

   Command line   MATCHPROP

   By default, all applicable properties are automatically copied from the source object to the destination object.

   NOTE   Some properties may be accepted by the destination object, but are not visible after they are copied. For example, it is possible to copy a linetype to a text object and not see the text object updated with the linetype you copied. However, when the LIST command is used on the text object, the copied linetype is associated with the text.

   Use the settings option of the Match Properties command to change the properties that are copied.

To change the settings for matching properties

1   Enter **matchprop** on the command line.
2   Select the object whose properties you want to copy.
3   Enter **settings** on the command line.

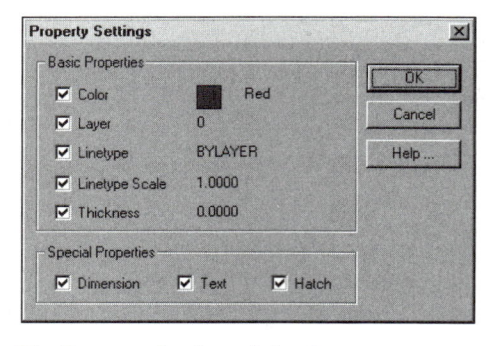

The Property Settings dialog box

4   In the Property Settings dialog box, select or clear boxes to turn properties on or off.

   The property settings are maintained for the duration of the AutoCAD session or until you change them.

Chapter 7   Editing Methods

252

Copying Objects

You can copy single or multiple objects within the current drawing, and you can copy between drawings or applications. Offsetting creates new objects at a specified distance from selected objects, or through a specified point. Mirroring creates a mirror image of objects in a specified mirror line. Arraying creates sets of copies in a rectangular or circular pattern.

Copying within a Drawing

To copy objects within a drawing, create a selection set and specify a starting point and an endpoint for the copy. These points are called the base point and the second point of displacement, respectively, and can be anywhere within the drawing.

To copy a selection set once

1. From the Modify menu, choose Copy.
2. Select the objects to copy and press ENTER.
3. Specify the base point (1).
4. Specify the point of displacement (2).

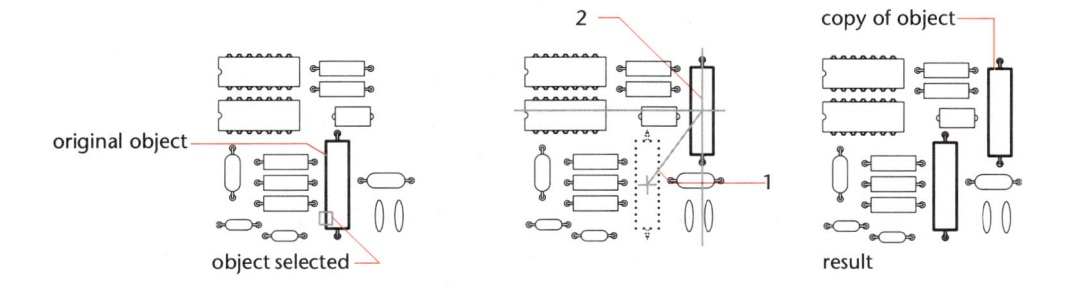

To copy a selection set multiple times

1. From the Modify menu, choose Copy.
2. Select the objects to copy and press ENTER.
3. Enter **m** (Multiple).
4. Specify the base point.
5. Specify the second point of displacement.
6. Specify the next point of displacement. Continue inserting copies, or press ENTER to end the command.

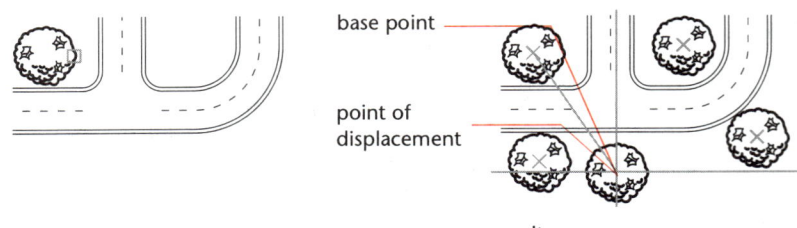

base point

point of displacement

object selected

result

To arrange multiple copies in a rectangular or circular pattern, see "Arraying Objects" on page 261.

Multiple Copying Using Grips

You can create multiple copies in any of the Grip modes. For example, you can rotate a selection set, leaving copies of the set at each location you specify with the pointing device. You can also make multiple copies of selection sets, which is a quick and simple way to create small arrays.

To make multiple rotated copies

1 Select the objects to rotate.
2 Select a base grip on one of the selected objects.
3 Enter **ro** to switch to Rotate mode.
4 Enter **copy**.
5 Drag the objects to a new location and click.

   The objects are copied and rotated around the base point.

6 Continue to drag and click for multiple copies, or press ENTER to end the command.

You can place multiple copies at regularly spaced intervals by creating an offset snap. The offset is defined by the distance between the original object and the first copy. In the following lighting layout, the first copy of the light fixture symbol is placed at an offset of two units. All subsequent copies are then placed two units apart.

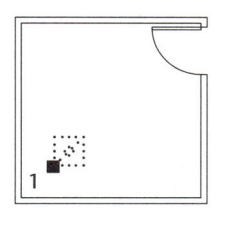

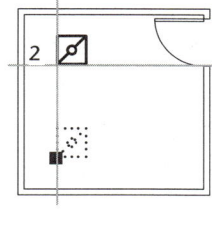

base grip selected   copy offset defined   result

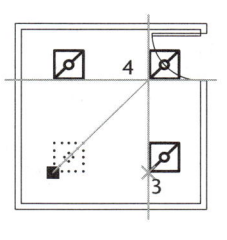

To create an offset snap for multiple copies

1 Select the objects to copy.
2 Select a base grip (1).
3 Enter **mo** (Move mode).
4 Enter **c** (Copy).
5 Select the first copy offset (2).

   The offset snap is the distance between points 1 and 2.
6 Hold down SHIFT and place additional copies (3, 4).

   These copies appear at the same offset snap from each other.
7 Press ENTER to exit Grip mode.

Copying with the Clipboard

When you want to use objects from another AutoCAD drawing or from a file created with another application, cut or copy these objects to the Clipboard and then paste them from the Clipboard into your drawing. Copying to and pasting from the Clipboard is different from copying objects from one location to another within a single drawing.

NOTE The color of the object doesn't change when copied to the Clipboard. If the objects are white, and they are pasted into an application with a white background, the objects won't be visible.

Cutting to the Clipboard

Cutting deletes the selected objects from the drawing and stores them on the Clipboard.

To cut objects to the Clipboard

1 Select the objects you want to cut.
2 From the Edit menu, choose Cut.

Command line   CUTCLIP

Related   Select the objects and press CTRL+X.

Copying to the Clipboard

Use the Clipboard to copy part or all of a drawing to another application. Updating the original does *not* update the embedded copy. Compare *copying* with *linking*, which is discussed in "Copying and Linking a View" on page 256.

To copy objects to the Clipboard

1 Select the objects you want to copy.
2 From the Edit menu, choose Copy, or press CTRL+C.

Command line   COPYCLIP

Copying Views

The COPYLINK command copies the current view rather than selected objects. If you select a viewport, AutoCAD copies the viewport contents. Otherwise, it copies the displayed graphics area.

Copying and Linking a View

You can copy the current AutoCAD view and link it to another file. Unlike embedding, linking creates a reference to the source. If the source view is updated, you have to update only the link to update all linked copies of the view.

To copy a view to the Clipboard

1 Select a viewport or display the view you want to copy.
2 From the Edit menu, choose Copy Link.

Command line   COPYLINK

Pasting Objects into AutoCAD

Applications use different internal formats to store information. When you copy objects to the Clipboard, AutoCAD stores information on all available formats. When you paste the Clipboard contents into an AutoCAD drawing, AutoCAD uses the format that retains the most information. However, you can override this setting and convert pasted information to AutoCAD format.

The AutoCAD format is the preferred format for copying objects to and from AutoCAD, because it is the easiest format to edit. It retains all relevant object information, including block references and 3D aspects.

ASCII text (in TXT files) is copied to AutoCAD as paragraph text. Paragraph breaks are retained, and the text can be edited using the MText editor. To retain the font and style characteristics of formatted text, specify the Windows metafile format (WMF).

The Windows metafile format, or picture format, contains screen vector information and can be scaled and printed without loss of resolution. Use this format to paste objects into Windows applications that support WMF files. Metafiles pasted into AutoCAD are of higher resolution than bitmap images but are less easily manipulated than AutoCAD objects. You can convert metafiles to AutoCAD objects by selecting Convert in the Paste Special dialog box.

Bitmapped images are raster images consisting of a pattern of pixels and are commonly used by paint applications. Bitmaps may lose clarity when scaled, so this format is pasted only if AutoCAD cannot correctly handle the format in another way. AutoCAD recognizes the standard Windows device-independent bitmap format (BMP files).

To paste objects from the Clipboard

- From the Edit menu, choose Paste.

The objects currently on the Clipboard are pasted into the drawing.

Command line PASTECLIP

Related Press CTRL+V to paste.

Converting to AutoCAD Format

When you convert a Windows metafile from another application to AutoCAD format, you can edit the file in the same way that you edit AutoCAD objects.

To convert pasted information to AutoCAD format

1 Copy the OLE metafile to the clipboard.
2 From the Edit menu, choose Paste Special.
3 In the Paste Special dialog box, select Paste.
4 Select Picture in the list of formats.
5 Choose OK.

lists the source application, file name, and internal object name

pastes a copy of the original information

establishes a reference link to the original information

identifies available formats

converts metafiles to AutoCAD objects

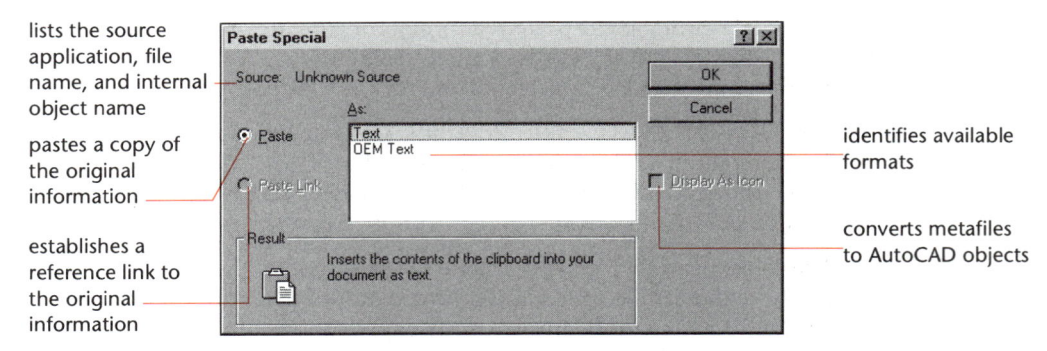

Command line PASTESPEC

Pasting to the Command Line
You can paste single- or multiline text from the Clipboard on the command line. For example, you could copy and paste a long command or text string to avoid entering it again.

Editing Pasted Information
If you convert pasted information to AutoCAD format, the pasted information becomes a true AutoCAD object and can be edited as such. The same is true for unformatted text and objects already in AutoCAD format. You cannot use all of AutoCAD's editing commands when modifying information in other formats.

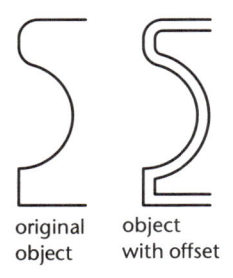

Offsetting Objects

Offsetting creates a new object that is similar to a selected object but at a specified distance. You can offset lines, arcs, circles, 2D polylines, ellipses, elliptical arcs, xlines, rays, and planar splines. Offsetting circles creates larger or smaller circles depending on the offset side. Offsetting outside the perimeter creates a larger circle. Offsetting inside creates a smaller one.

original object

object with offset

For information about offsetting splines, see "Editing Splines" on page 283.

To offset an object by specifying a distance

1 From the Modify menu, choose Offset.
2 Use the pointing device to specify the offset distance, or enter a value.
3 Select the object to offset.
4 Specify which side to offset.
5 Select another object to offset, or press ENTER to end the command.

Command line OFFSET

Chapter 7   Editing Methods

258

In the following example, you offset the polyline border of the room so that the wall aligns with the door frame.

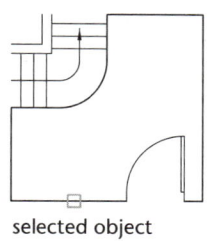

selected object 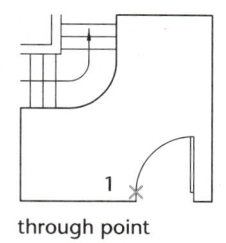   through point 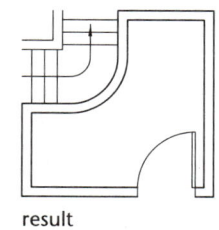   result

To offset an object through a point

1. From the Modify menu, choose Offset.
2. Enter **t** (Through).
3. Select the object to offset.
4. Specify the offset point (1).
5. Press ENTER to end the command.

NOTE OFFSET can be used only in plan view.

Mirroring Objects

You mirror objects around a mirror line, which you define with two points, as shown in the illustration. You can delete or retain the original objects. Mirroring works in any plane parallel to the *XY* plane of the current UCS. Although you can mirror a viewport object in paper space, doing so has no effect on its model space view or model space objects.

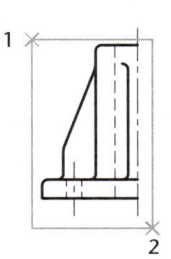

object selected with window 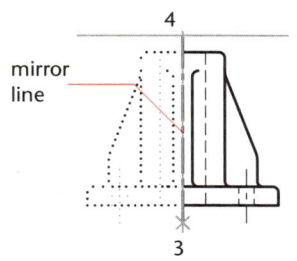   mirror line defined with two points 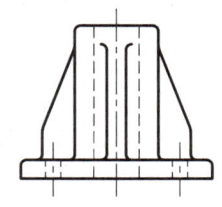   result with original object retained

Copying Objects

To mirror objects

1 From the Modify menu, choose Mirror.
2 Select the objects to mirror with a window (1, 2).
3 Specify the first point of the mirror line (3).
4 Specify the second point (4).
5 Press ENTER to retain the original objects.

Command line   MIRROR

Mirroring Text and Attributes

When you mirror text, attributes, and attribute definitions, they are reversed or turned upside down in the mirrored image. These mirrored objects are true mirror images of the original section of the object and follow the mathematical rules for reflection.

To prevent mirrored text from being reversed or turned upside down, set the MIRRTEXT system variable to 0. By default, MIRRTEXT is on. If you turn it off, the text has the same alignment and justification as before the mirroring. Compare the following illustrations.

before MIRROR   after MIRROR   after MIRROR
                     (MIRRTEXT = 1)   (MIRRTEXT = 0)

MIRRTEXT affects only text created with the TEXT, DTEXT, or MTEXT commands, attribute definitions, and variable attributes. Text and constant attributes within an inserted block are mirrored as a consequence of mirroring the entire block. These objects are inverted regardless of the MIRRTEXT setting. For more information, see chapter 11, "Using Blocks, Attributes, and Xrefs."

Mirroring with Grips

In the following example, you draw a valve by mirroring one half of the valve and retaining the original. Turning Ortho on helps you draw a vertical mirror line so that the object is mirrored horizontally.

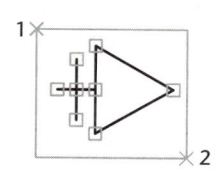

object to mirror selected with window

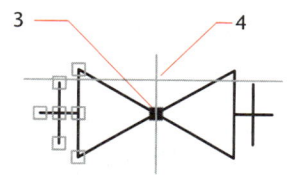

base grip and second point selected with Ortho on

result with original object retained

To mirror an object and retain the original

1. Select the original objects with a window (1, 2).
2. Select the base grip (3).
3. Enter **mirror** (Mirror Grip mode).
4. Turn on Ortho mode.
5. Hold down SHIFT and specify the second point of the mirror line (4). Select anywhere above or below the base point (on the vertical line of the crosshairs shown in the illustration).

Because Ortho is on, the mirror line is vertical and the object is mirrored horizontally.

Arraying Objects

You can copy an object or selection set in polar or rectangular arrays. For polar arrays, you control the number of copies of the object and whether the copies are rotated. For rectangular arrays, you control the number of rows and columns and the distance between them.

Creating Polar Arrays

In the following example, you surround a circular table with chairs by making a polar array of the original chair and rotating the copies as they are arrayed. Whether the array is drawn counterclockwise or clockwise depends on the Direction Control setting in the Units Control dialog box.

Copying Objects

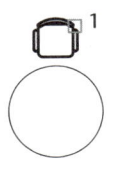

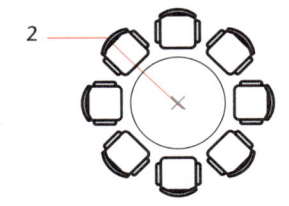

object selected

To create a polar array

1 From the Modify menu, choose Array.
2 Select the original object (1) and press ENTER.
3 Specify Polar.
4 Specify the center point of the array (2).
5 Enter the number of items in the array, including the original object.
6 Enter the angle the array is to fill, from 0 to 360.

   The default setting for the angle is 360 degrees.
7 Press ENTER to rotate the objects as they are arrayed.

Command line   ARRAY

Creating Rectangular Arrays
In this exercise, make a rectangular array of the chair. The array has two rows and four columns.

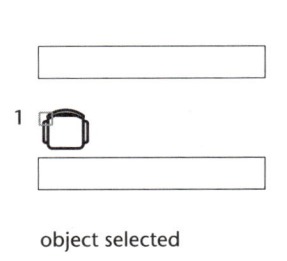

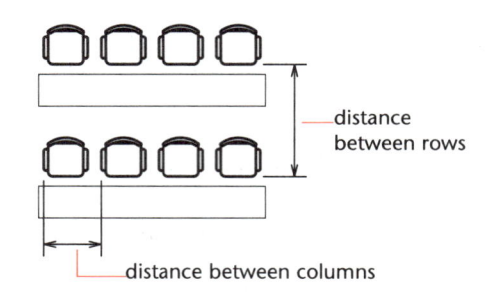

distance between rows

object selected   distance between columns

To create a rectangular array

1 From the Modify menu, choose Array.
2 Select the chair (1).
3 Specify Rectangular.
4 Enter the number of rows.

5 Enter the number of columns.
6 Enter the distance between the rows.
7 Enter the distance between the columns.

Creating Rotated Rectangular Arrays

AutoCAD builds a rectangular array along a baseline defined by the current snap rotation angle. This angle is zero by default, so the rows and columns of a rectangular array are orthogonal with respect to the *X* and *Y* drawing axes. However, you can change this angle and create a rotated array. Setting the snap rotation angle to a nonzero value rotates the screen crosshairs accordingly. You can consider all rectangular arrays to be constructed parallel to the crosshairs. Rows align with the *X* crosshair, and columns align with the *Y* crosshair.

In the following example, you rotate a rectangular array of chairs.

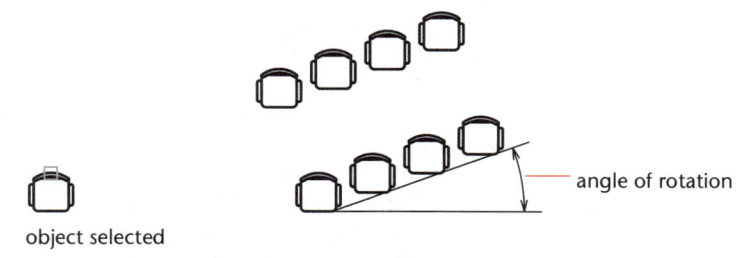

object selected

angle of rotation

To rotate a rectangular array

1 From the Tools menu, choose Drawing Aids.
2 In the Drawing Aids dialog box under Snap Angle, enter the angle by which you want to rotate the array.
3 Create the rectangular array as in the previous procedure.

   Related   Use the SNAPANG system variable to change the array rotation angle.

Moving Objects

When you move objects, you can rotate or align them or move them without changing orientation or size. Use snap, coordinates, grips, and object snap modes to move objects with precision.

In the following example, you move the window.

object selected   result

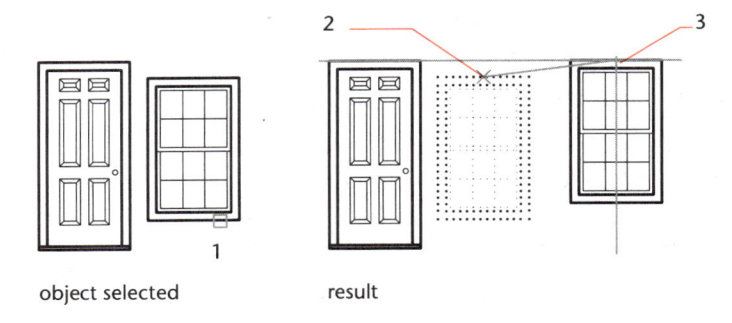

To move an object

1 From the Modify menu, choose Move.
2 Select the object to move (1).
3 Specify the base point for the move (2).
4 Specify the second point of displacement (3).

Command line   MOVE

Rotating Objects

You rotate objects by choosing a base point and a relative or absolute rotation angle. Specify a relative angle to rotate the object from its current orientation around the base point by that angle. Whether the objects are rotated counterclockwise or clockwise depends on the Direction Control setting in the Units Control dialog box. Specify absolute angles to rotate objects from the current angle to a new absolute angle.

In the following example, you rotate the plan view of a house, using the default relative angle method.

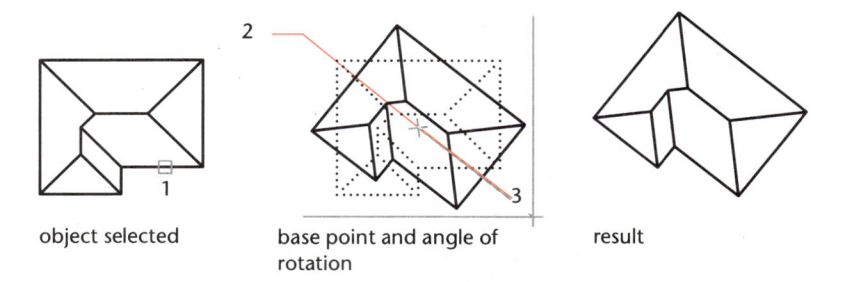

object selected   base point and angle of rotation   result

Chapter 7   Editing Methods

264

To rotate an object

1 From the Modify menu, choose Rotate.
2 Select the object to rotate (1).
3 Specify the base point for the rotation (2).
4 Specify the angle of rotation (3).

Command line   ROTATE

Related   DDUNITS sets the direction in which objects are rotated.

Rotating by Reference

Sometimes it's easier to rotate with absolute angles. For example, to align two objects when you know the absolute angles of both, use the current angle of the object to be rotated as the reference angle, and use the angle of the other object as the new angle. An easier way is to use the pointing device to select the object that you want to rotate and the object you want to align it with.

In the following example, you specify the reference angle by selecting two points on the object to rotate. The Intersection and Endpoint object snaps help you select precise points on this object. You then specify the new angle by selecting the object you want to align with.

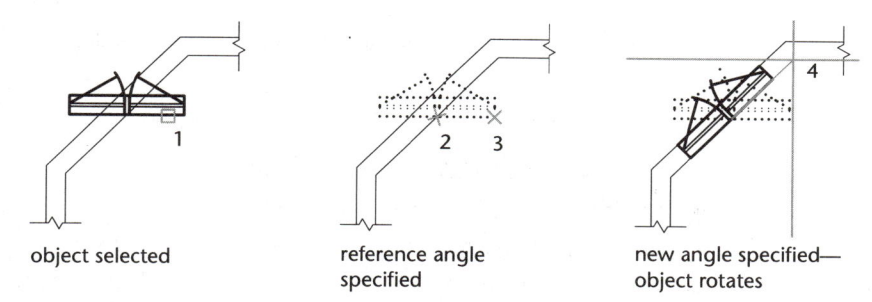

object selected   reference angle   new angle specified—
                        specified   object rotates

To rotate by reference

1 From the Modify menu, choose Rotate.
2 Select the object to rotate (1).
3 Select the object again to specify the base point for the rotation.
4 Enter **r** (Reference).

Moving Objects

Now define the reference and new angles by selecting the objects you're aligning.

1. Enter **int** (Intersection object snap).
2. Select the intersection point (2) to begin defining the reference angle.
3. Enter **endp** (Endpoint object snap).
4. Select the endpoint of the object you are rotating (3) to complete definition of the reference angle.
5. Enter **endp** again.
6. Select the endpoint of the object to align with (4).

Rotating with Grips

In the following example, you rotate a polygon using grips.

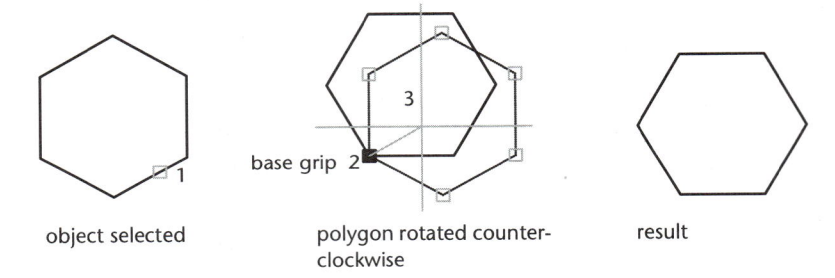

object selected   polygon rotated counter-clockwise   result

To rotate a polygon using grips

1. Select the object so it is marked with grips (1).
2. Select the base grip so it is highlighted (2).
3. Enter **ro** (Rotate mode).
4. Drag (3) to rotate the object and click or enter an angle to place the object in the new position.

Aligning Objects

You can move, rotate, or tilt an object so it aligns with another object. In the following example, align the pieces of piping using a window selection box to select the object to be aligned. Use the Endpoint object snap to align the pieces precisely.

object selected with window selection

source and destination points

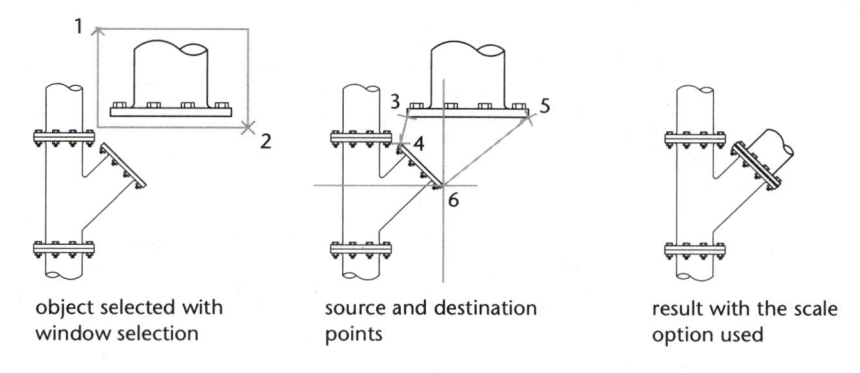

result with the scale option used

To align two objects

1 From the Modify menu, choose 3D Operation ➤ Align.
2 Select the objects you want to align.
3 Specify the first source point, then the first destination point.

If you press ENTER at this point, the objects are moved from the source point to the destination point.

4 Specify the second source point, then the second destination point.
5 Specify the third source point, or press ENTER to continue.
6 Specify whether you want to scale objects to the alignment points.

The objects are aligned (moved and rotated into position), then scaled. The first destination point is the base point of the scale, the distance between the first and second source points is the reference length, and the distance between the first and second destination point is the new reference length.

Erasing Objects

You can erase objects using all the available selection methods (see "Working with Named Objects" on page 228). In the following example, you use a window selection box to erase a section of piping. Only objects enclosed by the window are erased.

objects selected with window selection

selected objects

result

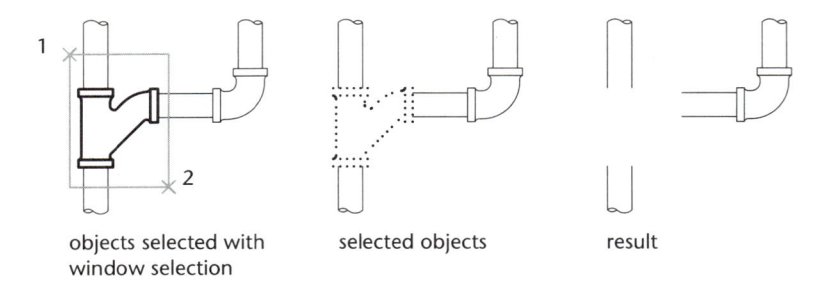

To erase a selection set

1 From the Modify menu, choose Erase.

2 Using a window selection box, select the objects to erase (1, 2).

Command line ERASE

Related The OOPS command restores all objects erased by the most recent use of ERASE. Enter l (Last) at the Select Objects prompt to erase the last object drawn.

Resizing Objects

You can resize objects by stretching, scaling, extending, lengthening, and trimming them.

Stretching Objects

To stretch an object, you specify a base point for the stretch and then two points of displacement. You can also select the object with a crossing selection and combine grip editing with object snaps, grip snaps, grid snaps, and relative coordinate entry to stretch with greater accuracy.

In this exercise, stretch the plan view of a house.

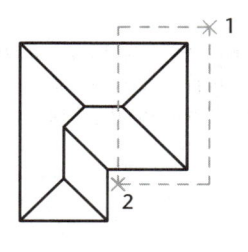

objects selected with a crossing selection

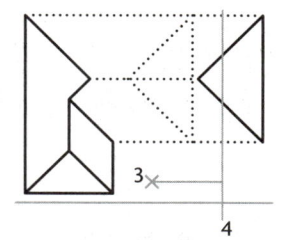

points specified for stretch

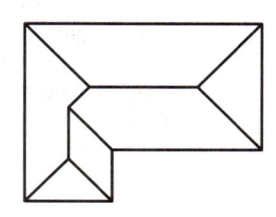

result

To stretch an object

1 From the Modify menu, choose Stretch.
2 Select the roof using a crossing selection (1, 2).
3 Specify the base point (3).
4 Specify the point of displacement (4).

Moving by Stretching

In the following example, you move a door from one part of a wall to another by stretching. Turning on Ortho helps you move the object in a straight line.

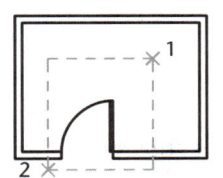

objects selected with crossing selection

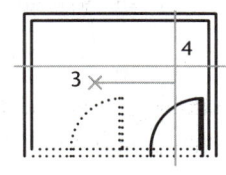

objects dragged with Ortho on

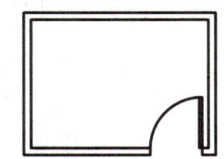

result

To move by stretching

1 Using a crossing selection, select the object to move (1, 2).
2 Enter **'ortho** to turn on Ortho mode transparently.
3 Drag the object and click to place it in the new position (3, 4).

The door and the door endpoint lie entirely within the selection window and thus move to the new location. The wall lines, on the other hand, merely cross the selection window and stretch in accordance with the movement of the door.

Resizing Objects
269

Stretching with Grips

You stretch an object by moving selected grips to new locations. Some grips move the object rather than stretching it. This is true of grips on text objects, blocks, midpoints of lines, centers of circles, centers of ellipses, and point objects.

To stretch an object using grips

1 Select the object so its grips appear.
2 Specify the base point by selecting a grip so it is highlighted.
3 Specify the new location to which you want the object stretched.

Before you start the grip modes and if you plan to use the Stretch grip mode, you can select more than one grip to stretch. In the following example, you stretch both lines that represent the pipe.

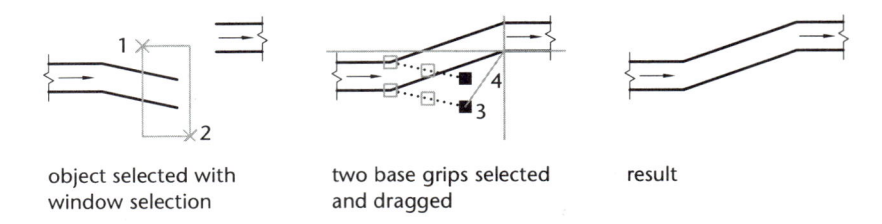

object selected with window selection

two base grips selected and dragged

result

To stretch more than one grip

1 Select both lines so their grips appear (1, 2).
2 Hold down the SHIFT key and select both end grips so they are highlighted (3, 4).
3 Release the SHIFT key and select either grip as the base grip (3).
4 Specify the new location for the objects.

Scaling Objects

You scale selection sets using the same scaling factor in the X and Y directions. Thus, you can make an object larger or smaller, but you cannot alter its aspect ratio. You can scale it by specifying a base point and a length, which is used as a scale factor based on the current drawing units, or by entering a scale factor directly. You can also specify the current length and a new length for the object.

Scaling a viewport object in paper space increases or decreases the area of model space visible in the viewport (see "Using Paper Space and Model Space" on page 476).

Scaling by a Scale Factor

Scaling by a scale factor changes all dimensions of the selected object. A scale factor greater than 1 enlarges the object. A scale factor less than 1 shrinks the object. In the following example, you decrease the size of the block by half, scaling it by a factor of 0.5.

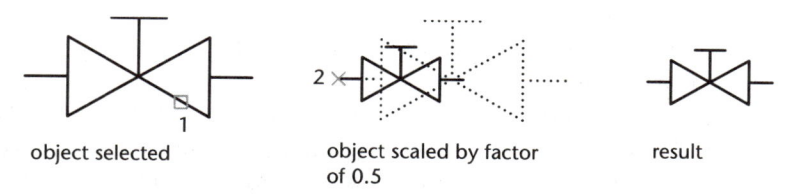

object selected object scaled by factor of 0.5 result

To scale a selection set by a scale factor

1. From the Modify menu, choose Scale.
2. Select the object to scale (1).
3. Specify the base point (2).
4. Enter **.5** (the scale factor).

Command line SCALE

Scaling by Reference

When you scale by reference you use the size of an existing object as a reference for the new size. To scale by reference, specify the current scale and then the new scale length. For example, if one side of an object is 4.8 units long and you want to expand it to 7.5 units, use 4.8 as the reference length and 7.5 as the new length. A quick way to change the length of open objects, such as lines, arcs, polylines, elliptical arcs, and splines, is to lengthen them (see "Changing the Length of Objects" on page 274).

You can also specify the reference length by selecting a base point and two reference points, and dragging to specify the new scale.

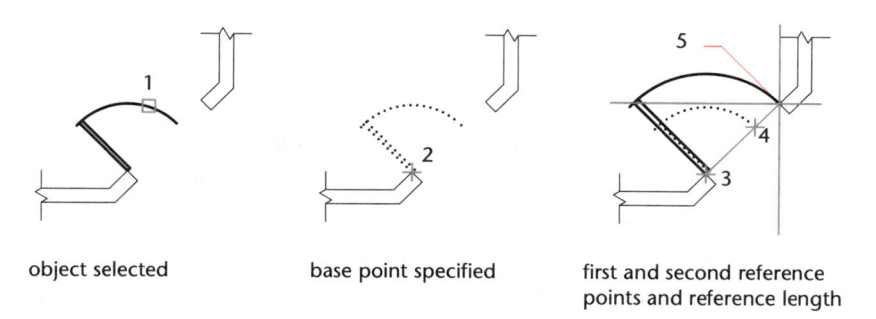

object selected base point specified first and second reference points and reference length

Resizing Objects

271

To scale by reference

1 From the Modify menu, choose Scale.
2 Select the object to scale (1).
3 Specify the base point (2).
4 Enter **r** (Reference).
5 Select the first and second reference points (3, 4), or enter a value for the reference length.
6 Drag the object and select a point (5), or enter a value for the new length.

You can use the Reference option to scale an entire drawing. For example, use this option when the original drawing units are inappropriate. Select all objects in the drawing. Then use Reference to select two points and specify the intended distance. All the objects in the drawing are scaled accordingly.

Scaling with Grips

You can use the Scale grip mode to scale objects. For example, you can increase the size of a circle by dragging outward from the base grip or decrease the size by dragging inward. Alternatively, you could enter a value for relative scaling. In the following example, the outlet symbol, which is defined as a block, is scaled down. When selected, blocks have a single grip at the insertion point. To scale the block, you select the insertion point as the base grip and move the cursor to resize the block.

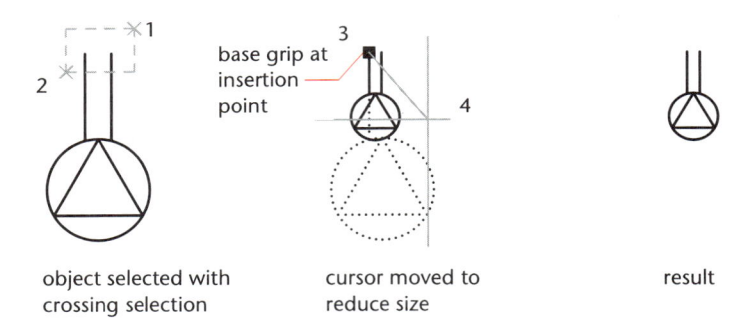

object selected with crossing selection

cursor moved to reduce size

result

To scale a block using grips

1 Select the block with a crossing selection (1, 2).

   A single grip appears at the block's insertion point.
2 Select the insertion point as the base grip (3).
3 Enter **sc** or cycle by pressing ENTER to get to the Scale grip mode.
4 Move the cursor to reduce the size of the block. Then click to specify the new size (4).

Extending Objects

You can extend objects so that they end precisely at a boundary defined by other objects. You can also extend objects to where they *would* intersect a boundary. This is called extending to an implied boundary. In the following exercise, you extend the lines precisely to a circle, which is the boundary.

boundary selected   objects to extend selected   result

To extend an object

1 From the Modify menu, choose Extend.
2 Select the object for the boundary.
3 Select the objects to extend and press ENTER.

Command line   EXTEND

Extending to an Implied Boundary

In this exercise, you extend the three horizontal lines to an implied boundary, which is where they would intersect the single line if it were extended.

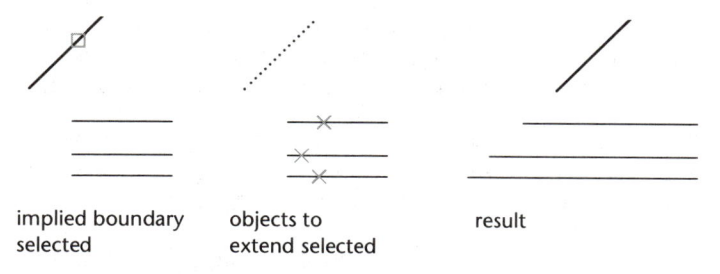

implied boundary   objects to   result
selected   extend selected

To extend to an implied boundary

1 From the Modify menu, choose Extend.
2 Select the object for the implied boundary and press ENTER.
3 Enter **e** (Edge).
4 Enter **e** (Extend), or press ENTER if Extend is the current option.
5 Select the lines to be extended and press ENTER.

Resizing Objects

Extending Polylines

You can extend only open polylines. Either the first or the last edge extends as if it were a line or arc object.

Wide polylines extend so the centerline intersects the boundary. Because the ends of wide polylines are at a 90-degree angle, part of the end extends past the boundary if the boundary is not perpendicular to the extended segment. If you extend a tapered polyline segment, the width of the extended end is corrected to continue the original taper to the new endpoint. If this correction gives the segment a negative ending width, the ending width is forced to 0.

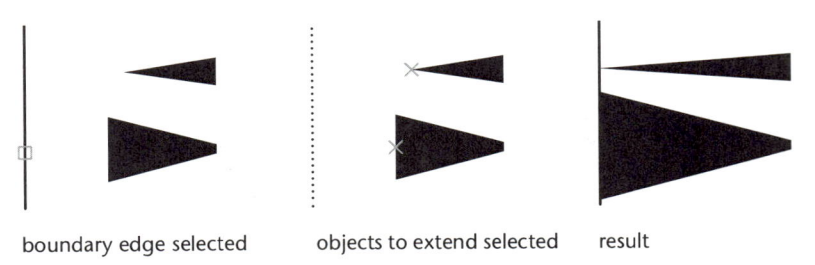

extending a wide polyline

boundary edge selected objects to extend selected result

Extending Infinite Lines

You can extend rays, but you *cannot* extend an xline. Like a circle, an xline is unbounded and has no endpoint. A ray is semibounded; therefore, a ray can be extended to a new start point.

Changing the Length of Objects

You can change the angle of arcs, and you can change the length of open lines, arcs, open polylines, elliptical arcs, and open splines. The results are similar to both extending and trimming. You can alter length in several ways:

- Dragging an object's endpoint (dynamically)
- Specifying a new length as a percentage of the total length or angle
- Specifying an incremental length or angle measured from an object's endpoint
- Specifying the object's total absolute length or included angle

To change an object's length by dragging

1   From the Modify menu, choose Lengthen.
2   Press ENTER or enter **dy** to enter Dynamic Dragging mode.

3 Select the object to lengthen.

4 Drag the endpoint closest to the point of selection, and specify a new endpoint using any point entry method.

Command line LENGTHEN

Trimming Objects

You can cut an object precisely at an edge defined by one or more objects. Objects you define as cutting edges do not have to intersect the object being trimmed; you can trim back to an implied intersection. Cutting edges can be lines, arcs, circles, polylines, ellipses, splines, xlines, rays, and viewports in paper space. Wide polylines are cut along their centerline.

In the following example, you join two walls smoothly by trimming the section where they intersect.

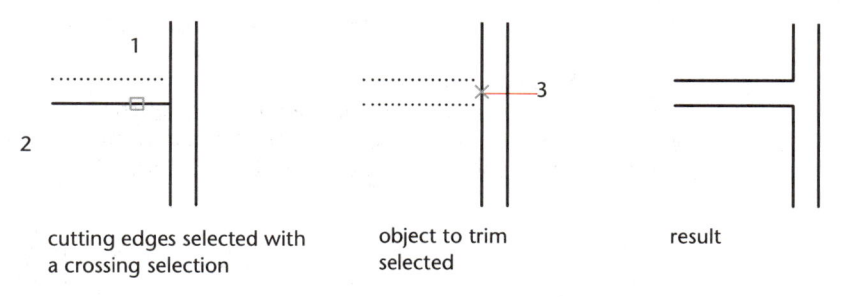

cutting edges selected with a crossing selection   object to trim selected   result

To trim walls where they intersect

1 From the Modify menu, choose Trim.

2 Select the cutting edges with a crossing selection (1, 2) and press ENTER.

3 Select the section of the wall you want trimmed (3) and press ENTER.

Command line TRIM

Trimming to an Implied Intersection

An implied intersection is the point where two objects would intersect if they were extended. You can trim objects using their implied intersection as the cutting edge. In the following example, you trim the vertical wall back to its implied intersection with the horizontal wall.

Resizing Objects

275

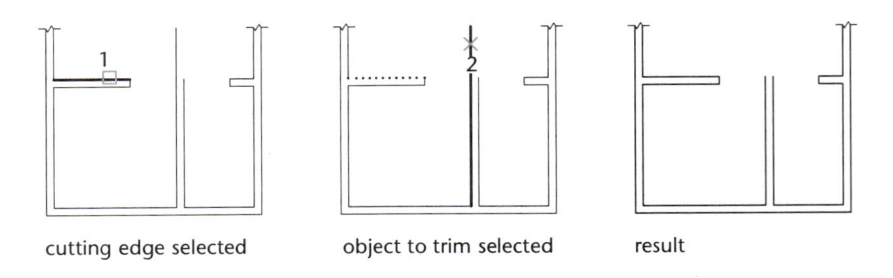

cutting edge selected   object to trim selected   result

To trim to an implied intersection

1. From the Modify menu, choose Trim.
2. Select the cutting edge (1) and press ENTER.
3. Enter **e** (Edge).
4. Enter **e** (Extend), or press ENTER if Extend is the current option.
5. Select the object to trim on the side you want trimmed (2) and press ENTER.

Trimming Complex Objects

An object can be one of the cutting edges *and* one of the objects being trimmed. For example, in the light fixture illustrated, the circle is a cutting edge for the construction lines and is also being trimmed.

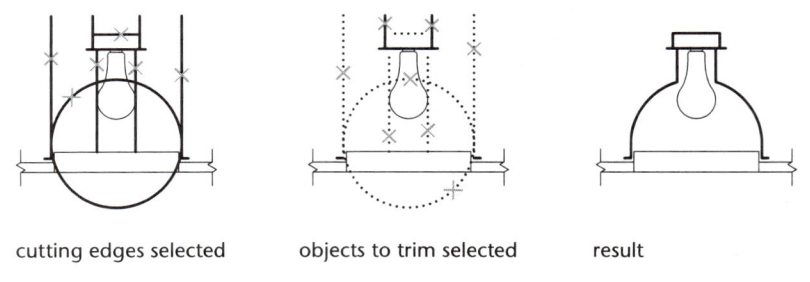

cutting edges selected   objects to trim selected   result

When trimming complex objects, using different selection methods can help you choose the right cutting edges and objects to trim. In the following example, the cutting edges are selected with a crossing window.

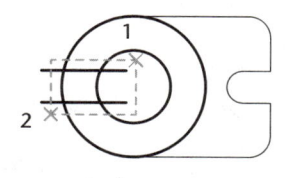

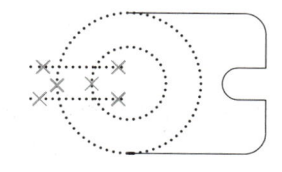

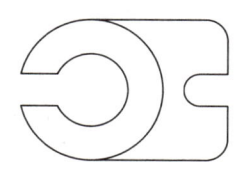

edges selected with   objects to trim selected   result
crossing selection

In the following example, fence selection is used to select a series of objects for trimming.

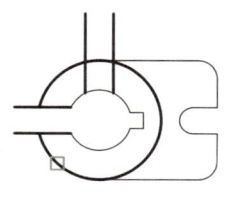

cutting edge selected   objects to trim selected   result
                             with fence selection

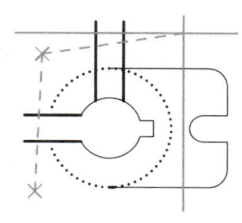

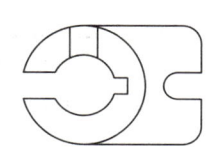

In paper space, you can use viewport borders as cutting edges. However, you cannot trim the viewports themselves.

Trimming to the Nearest Intersection

You can trim objects to their nearest intersection with other objects. When you select the objects to trim, AutoCAD automatically chooses the nearest selected objects as cutting edges. In the following example, the walls are trimmed so that they intersect smoothly.

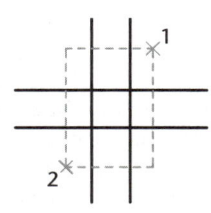

cutting edges selected   objects to trim selected   result
with crossing selection

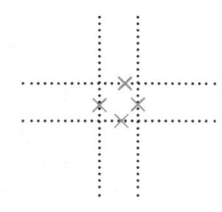

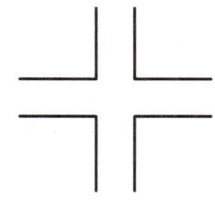

Resizing Objects

Inserting Breaks in Objects

You can remove part of an object with the BREAK command. You can break lines, circles, arcs, polylines, ellipses, splines, xlines, and rays. When breaking an object, you can either select the object at the first break point and then specify a second break point, or you can select the entire object and then specify the two break points.

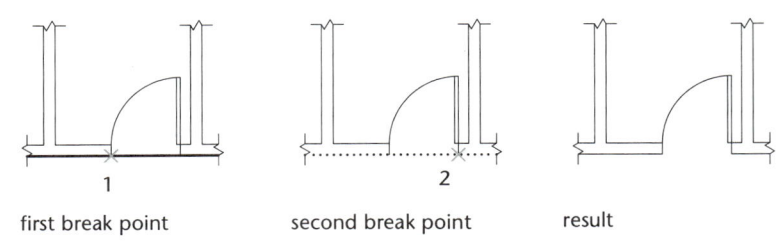

first break point   second break point   result

To break an object

1 From the Modify menu, choose Break.
2 Select the object to break (1).

By default, the point you select on the object will be the first break point. To choose a different first break point, enter **f** (First) and specify the new first break point.

3 Specify the second break point (2).

Command line BREAK

Exploding Objects

Exploding objects converts them from single objects to their constituent parts but has no visible effect. For example, exploding forms simple lines and arcs from polylines, rectangles, donuts, and polygons. It replaces a block reference or associative dimension with copies of the simple objects that compose the block or dimension. Groups explode into their member objects or into other groups.

To explode an object

1 From the Modify menu, choose Explode.
2 Select the objects to be exploded.

An exploded object doesn't look any different, but the colors and linetypes of objects can change as a result of floating colors, layers, or linetypes.

When you explode a polyline, AutoCAD discards the associated width information. The resulting lines and arcs follow the polyline's centerline. If you explode a block that contains a polyline, you need to explode the polyline separately. However, a nonuniformly scaled block can be exploded during an insert. If you explode a donut, its width becomes 0.

Blocks inserted with unequal *X*, *Y*, and *Z* scale factors may explode into unexpected objects. You cannot explode xrefs and their dependent blocks. If you explode a block with attributes, the attributes are deleted, but the attribute definitions from which they were created remain. The attribute values and any modifications made by the ATTEDIT or DDATTE commands are lost. For more information, see EXPLODE in the *Command Reference*.

Editing Polylines

Two-dimensional and three-dimensional polylines, rectangles, and polygons, and 3D polygon meshes are all polyline variants and are edited in the same way. For information about editing 3D polylines and polygon meshes, see "Editing in 3D" on page 556.

AutoCAD recognizes both fit polylines and spline-fit polylines. A spline-fit polyline uses a curve fit, similar to a B-spline. There are two kinds of spline-fit polylines, quadratic and cubic. Both of these polylines are controlled by the SPLINETYPE system variable. A fit polyline uses standard curves for curve fit and utilizes any tangent directions set on any given vertex.

You can edit polylines by closing and opening them and by moving, adding, or deleting individual vertices. You can straighten the polyline between any two vertices and toggle the linetype so that a dash appears before and after each vertex. You can set a uniform width for the entire polyline or control the width of each segment.

You can create a linear approximation of a spline curve from a polyline with the Fit and Spline options and then use Decurve to change the splined polyline back to a polyline. The illustration shows a polyline edited with the Spline option.

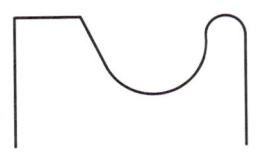

polyline

splined polyline

However, some editing actions, such as trimming, breaking, and any grip editing, remove the spline definition of a fit or splined polyline. For this reason, it is better to use a true spline, which maintains its spline definition.

You can join a line, arc, or other polyline to an open polyline if their ends touch. If a line crosses the end of a polyline in a T shape, the objects can't be joined. If two lines meet a polyline in a Y shape, AutoCAD selects one of the lines and joins it to the polyline. Joining also causes an implicit decurve, with AutoCAD discarding the spline information of the original polyline and any polylines being joined to it. Once the joining is completed, you can fit a new spline to the resulting polyline.

To modify a polyline

1 From the Modify menu, choose Object ➤ Polyline.
2 Select the polyline to modify.
3 Choose an option to modify the polyline.

Command line PEDIT

Related The SPLINETYPE, SPLFRAME, and SPLINESEGS system variables control spline-fit polylines.

In the following illustration, each polyline segment has a different starting and ending width, resulting in a taper.

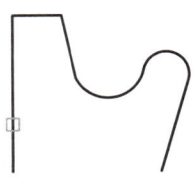

polyline selected

segments with different start and end widths

Chapter 7   Editing Methods

To taper the width of individual polyline segments

1 From the Modify menu, choose Object ➤ Polyline.
2 Select the polyline to edit.
3 Enter **e** (Edit Vertex).

The first vertex is marked with a cross.

4 Enter **w** (Width).
5 Enter different starting and ending widths.

Press ENTER to move to the next vertex. Or enter **n** for next.

6 Repeat steps 4 through 6 for each segment.
7 Enter **x** (Exit) to apply the new widths to all segments.

Related   PFACE creates polyface meshes.

Editing Multilines

You can edit a multiline by adding and deleting vertices and controlling the display of corner joints. You can make multilines intersect in various ways. You can also edit multiline styles to change the properties of individual line elements or the end caps and background fill of future multilines.

Adding and Deleting Multiline Vertices

You can add or delete any vertex in a multiline. In the following example, you delete a vertex from a multiline. Adding vertices works similarly.

vertex in multiline to delete

multiline with vertex deleted

To delete a vertex from a multiline

1 From the Modify menu, choose Object ➤ Multiline.
2 In the Multiline Edit Tools dialog box, select Delete Vertex and choose OK.
3 In the drawing, specify the vertex to delete and press ENTER.

Command line   MLEDIT

Related   -MLEDIT edits multilines from the command line.

Editing Multiline Intersections

If you have two multilines in a drawing, you can control the way they intersect. Multilines can intersect in a cross or a T shape, and the crosses or T shapes can be closed, open, or merged.

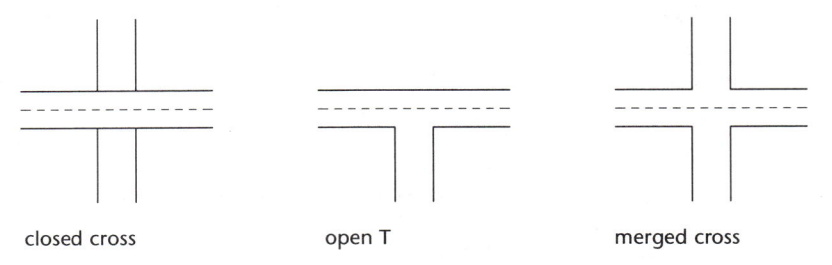

closed cross   open T   merged cross

To create a closed cross intersection

1. From the Modify menu, choose Object ➤ Multiline.
2. In the Multiline Edit Tools dialog box, double-click Closed Cross, and then choose OK.
3. Select the multiline for the foreground.
4. Select the multiline for the background.

   The intersection is modified. You can continue selecting intersecting multilines to modify, or press ENTER to end the command. Press ENTER again to redisplay the Multiline Edit Tools dialog box.

Editing Multiline Styles

Multiline styles control the number of line elements in a multiline and the color, linetype, and offset from the multiline origin of each element. You can change any of these properties. You can also modify the display of joints, end caps, and background fill. A modified multiline style retains the changes permanently.

In the following example, you delete a line element, modify the angle of the end cap lines and change the background fill of a multiline.

NOTE You *cannot* edit the element and multiline properties of the STANDARD multiline style or any multiline style that is being used in the drawing. If you try to edit the options in either the Element Properties dialog box or the Multiline Properties dialog box, the options are unavailable. To edit an existing multline style, you must do so *before* you draw any multilines in that style.

To edit a multiline style

1. From the Format menu, choose Multiline Style.
2. In the Multiline Styles dialog box, choose the style name from the list. Choose a style with more than two elements.
3. Choose Element Properties.
4. In the Element Properties dialog box under Elements, select the line element to delete, select Delete, and choose OK.
5. In the Multiline Styles dialog box, choose Multiline Properties.
6. In the Multiline Properties dialog box under Caps, enter the new angle for the start and end cap lines.
7. Under Fill, choose Color and select a new color from the Select Color dialog box, then choose OK twice.
8. In the Multiline Styles dialog box, choose Save to save the changes to the style in the MLN file.
9. Choose OK to save the modified symbol table entry and exit the dialog box.

Command line MLSTYLE

Editing Splines

You can delete fit points of a spline, add fit points for greater accuracy, or move fit points to alter the shape of a spline. You can open or close a spline and edit the spline start and end tangents. Spline direction is reversible. You can change the tolerance of the spline also. Tolerance refers to how closely the spline fits the set of fit points you specify. The lower the tolerance, the more closely the spline fits the points.

You can refine a spline by increasing the number of control points in one portion of the spline or by changing the weight of specific control points. Increasing the weight of a control point pulls the spline more towards that point. You can also refine a spline by changing its order. A spline's order is the degree of the spline polynomial + 1. A cubic spline, for example, has order 4. The higher a spline's order, the more control points it has.

Consider the following example. You have created a spline to represent a geographic contour. Grips are turned on, and you need to move the fourth fit point to increase accuracy. When you select the spline, grips appear at the control points. If you created the spline by fitting it through a set of points, you haven't purged this information using the Purge option, and you select the Fit Data option, grips appear at the fit points on the selected spline.

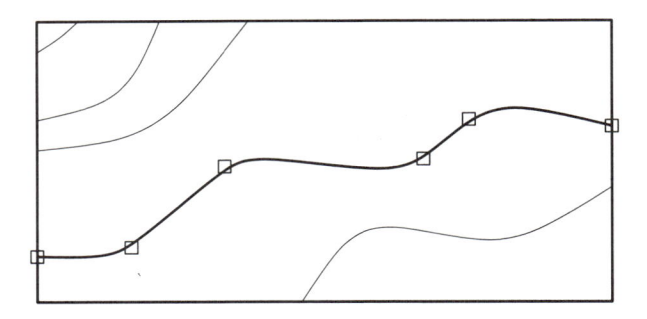

To move a spline fit point

1. From the Modify menu, choose Object ➤ Spline.
2. Select the spline.
3. Enter **f** (Fit Data).
4. Enter **m** (Move Vertex).
5. Repeatedly enter **n** to select the next vertex until the fourth control point is highlighted.

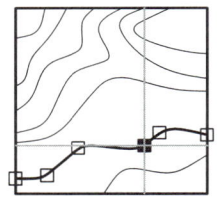

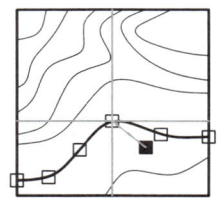

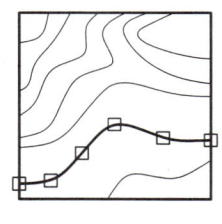

fourth fit point selected   fit point moved   result

6. Move the vertex with the pointing device or by entering the coordinate of the new location.
7. Enter **x** three times to exit and return to the Command prompt.

NOTE If any three consecutive control points are located at the same position, a degenerate case is created. In this situation, it is *not* possible to calculate a tangent at that position. AutoCAD can only offset curves that have a nonzero-length tangent vector at each point.

Command line   SPLINEDIT

Chamfering Objects

Chamfering connects two nonparallel objects by extending or trimming them to intersect or to join with a beveled line. You can chamfer lines, polylines, xlines, and rays. With the distance method, you specify the amount that each line should be trimmed or extended. With the angle method, you can also specify the length of the chamfer and the angle it forms with the first line. You can retain the objects as they were before the chamfer or trim or extend them to the chamfer line.

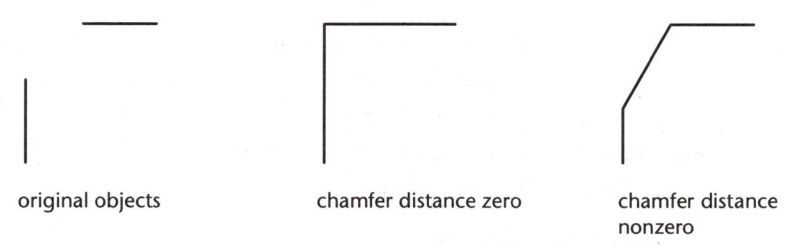

original objects   chamfer distance zero   chamfer distance nonzero

If both objects being chamfered are on the same layer, the chamfer line goes on that layer. Otherwise, the chamfer line goes on the current layer. The same rules apply to chamfer color and linetype.

If no intersection point is within the drawing limits and if limits checking is turned on, AutoCAD rejects the chamfering. For information about chamfering solids, see chapter 13, "Working in Three-Dimensional Space."

Chamfering by Specifying Distances

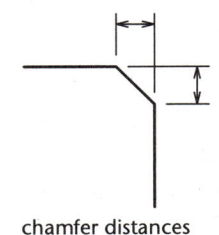

The chamfer distance is the amount each object is trimmed or extended to meet the chamfer line or to intersect the other object. If both chamfer distances are 0, chamfering trims or extends the two objects until they meet but does not draw a chamfer line.

The default setting for the first distance is the last distance specified. The default setting for the second distance is whatever you choose for the first distance, because symmetrical distances are common. However, you can reset the chamfer distances.

chamfer distances

In the following example, you set the chamfer distance to 0.5 for the first line and 0.25 for the second line. After you reset the distances, you are returned to the Command prompt.

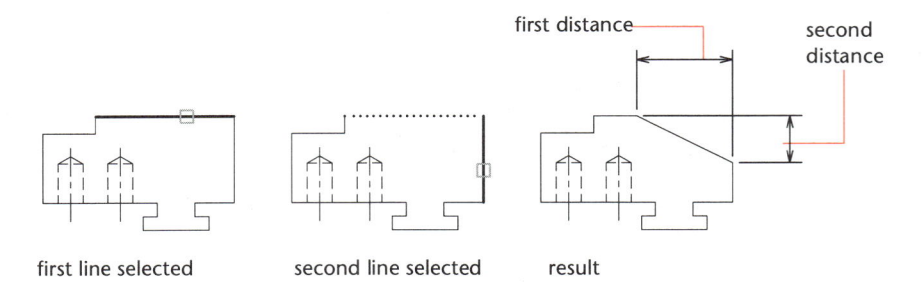

first line selected second line selected result

To reset chamfer distances

1 From the Modify menu, choose Chamfer.
2 Enter the first chamfer distance.
3 Enter the second chamfer distance.
4 Press ENTER to reenter the CHAMFER command.
5 Select the lines for chamfering.

Command line   CHAMFER

Related   Set the CHAMMODE system variable to 0 for the distance method. The CHAMFERA and CHAMFERB system variables store the first and second chamfer distances.

To chamfer two nonparallel lines

1 From the Modify menu, choose Chamfer.
2 Set the chamfer distances.
3 Select the first line.
4 Select the second line.

Command line   CHAMFER

Trimming Chamfered Objects

By default, objects are trimmed when chamfered, but you can use the Trim option to specify that they remain untrimmed.

To chamfer without trimming

1 From the Modify menu, choose Chamfer.
2 Enter **t** (Trim).
3 Enter **n** (No Trim).
4 Chamfer the objects.

Related Set the TRIMMODE system variable to 1 to trim the objects after chamfering. Set it to 0 to leave the objects untrimmed. A new setting takes effect with the next chamfer.

untrimmed chamfered objects

Chamfering by Specifying Length and Angle

You can chamfer two objects by specifying where on the first selected object the chamfer line starts. Then specify the angle the chamfer line forms with this object. In the following example, you chamfer two lines so that the chamfer line starts 1.5 units along the first line and forms an angle of 30 degrees with this line.

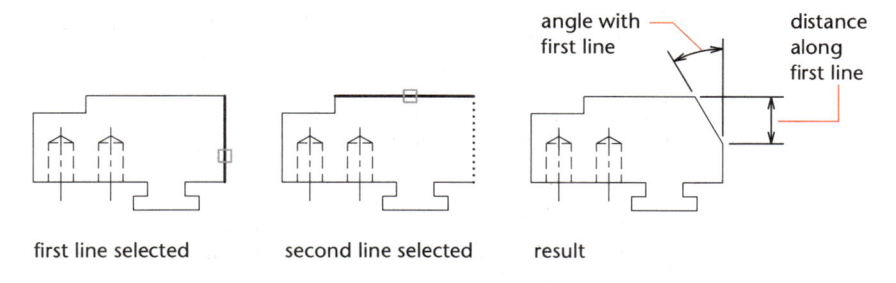

angle with first line
distance along first line

first line selected   second line selected   result

To chamfer by specifying chamfer length and angle

1 From the Modify menu, choose Chamfer.
2 Enter **a** (Angle).
3 Enter the chamfer length.
4 Enter the chamfer angle.
5 Press ENTER to reenter the CHAMFER command.
6 Select the first line and then the second line.

Related Set the CHAMMODE system variable to 1 for the angle method. The CHAMFERC system variable stores the chamfer length. The CHAMFERD system variable stores the chamfer angle.

Chamfering Objects

Chamfering Polyline Segments

If the two objects you select are segments of a polyline, they must be adjacent or separated by one arc segment.

Chamfering an Entire Polyline

You can chamfer an entire polyline so each intersection is chamfered. For best results, keep the chamfer distances equal. In this exercise, chamfer a closed polyline by setting both chamfer distances to equal values.

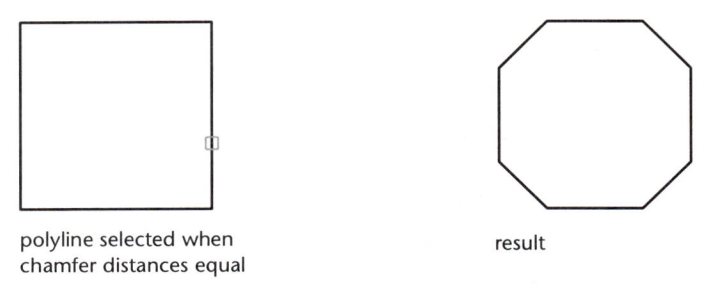

polyline selected when
chamfer distances equal

result

To chamfer an entire polyline

1 From the Modify menu, choose Chamfer.
2 Enter **p** (Polyline).
3 Select the polyline.

The polyline is chamfered using the current chamfer method and the default distances or angle.

When you chamfer an entire polyline, AutoCAD chamfers only the segments that are long enough to accommodate the chamfer distance. In the following illustration, some polyline segments were too short to be chamfered.

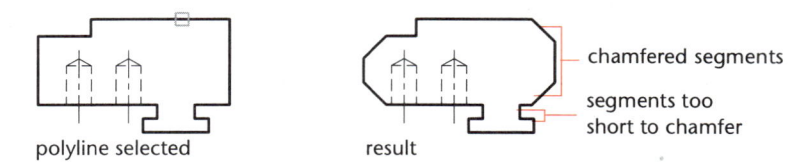

polyline selected   result   chamfered segments
                                 segments too
                                 short to chamfer

Chamfers added to a polyline become new segments of that polyline, even if the chamfer distance is 0.

Filleting Objects

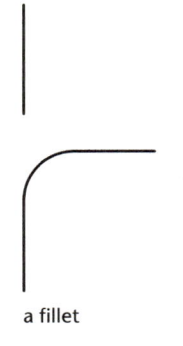

Filleting connects two objects with a smoothly fitted arc of a specified radius. Although an inside corner is called a fillet and an outside corner is called a round, AutoCAD treats both as fillets.

If both objects being filleted are on the same layer, the fillet line goes on that layer. Otherwise, the fillet line goes on the current layer. The same rules apply to fillet color and linetype.

You can fillet pairs of line segments, polyline line (not arc) segments, splines, xlines, rays, circles, arcs, and true (not polygon) ellipses. Lines, xlines, and rays can be filleted when parallel. You can fillet every vertex of a polyline at the same time. You can fillet a combination of lines and polylines and all true solids. See chapter 13, "Working in Three-Dimensional Space."

a fillet

Setting the Fillet Radius

The fillet radius is the radius of the arc that connects filleted objects. By default, the fillet radius is 0 or the last radius set. Changing the radius affects subsequent fillets but not existing ones. The FILLETRAD system variable stores the current fillet radius.

two lines filleted with zero radius

To set the fillet radius

1 From the Modify menu, choose Fillet.
2 Enter **r** (Radius).
3 Specify the fillet radius.
4 Press ENTER to reenter the FILLET command.
5 Select the objects to fillet.

In the following example, you fillet two line segments.

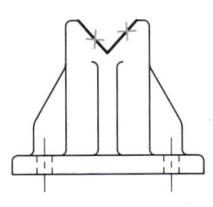

lines selected   result

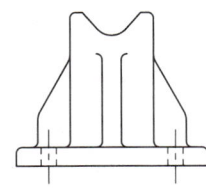

Filleting Objects

289

To fillet two line segments

1. From the Modify menu, choose Fillet.
2. Select the first line.
3. Select the second line.

Command line FILLET

Trimming Filleted Objects

By default, all objects except circles, full ellipses, closed polylines, and splines are trimmed when filleted. You can use the Trim option to specify that filleted objects remain untrimmed.

two lines filleted with the Trim option set

To fillet without trimming

1. From the Modify menu, choose Fillet.
2. Enter **t** (Trim).
3. Enter **n** (No Trim).
4. Fillet the objects.

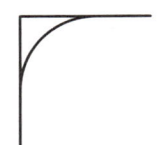

Related   Set the TRIMMODE system variable to 0 to leave the objects untrimmed. A new setting takes effect with the next fillet.

Filleting Circles and Arcs

two lines filleted with the No Trim option set

You fillet circles and arcs in the same way as lines. Depending on the points you specify, more than one possible fillet can exist between the objects. AutoCAD chooses the endpoints closest to the points you use to select the objects. Compare the following fillets.

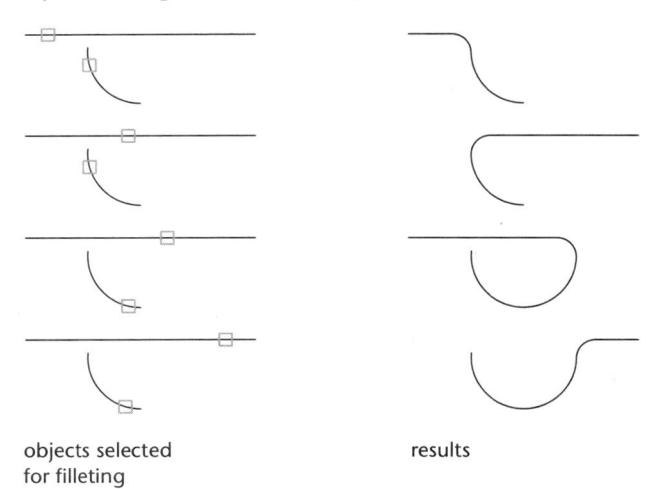

objects selected for filleting

results

Filleting Line and Polyline Combinations

For you to fillet line and polyline combinations, the line must intersect, or intersect when extended, one of the polyline's line segments. If the Trim option is turned on, the filleted objects and fillet arc join to form a single new polyline.

The illustration shows a fillet of a line and polyline with a fillet radius of 0.25 and the Trim option on.

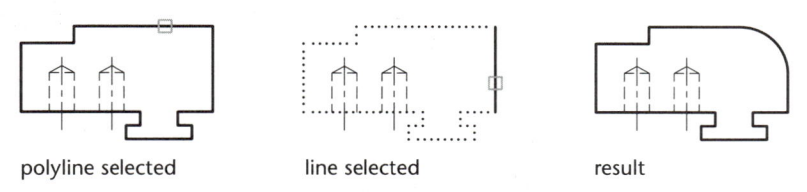

polyline selected   line selected   result

Filleting an Entire Polyline

You can fillet an entire polyline or remove fillets from a polyline. The polyline can contain arc segments, which have the same fillet radius as line segments in the polyline.

If you set a nonzero fillet radius, AutoCAD inserts fillet arcs at each vertex where two line segments meet if the segments are long enough to accommodate the fillet radius.

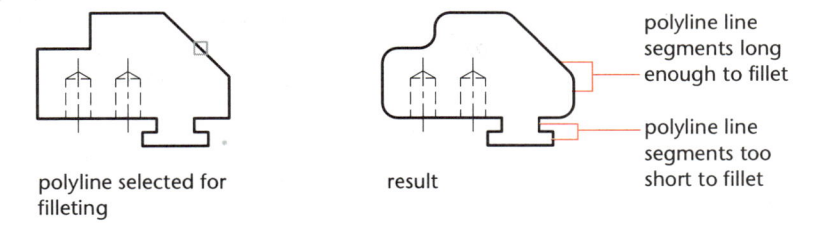

polyline selected for filleting   result   polyline line segments long enough to fillet

polyline line segments too short to fillet

To fillet an entire polyline

1. From the Modify menu, choose Fillet.
2. Enter **p** (Polyline).
3. Select the polyline.

   If two polyline line segments are separated by one arc segment and the two line segments converge as they approach the arc segment, AutoCAD removes the arc segment and replaces it with a fillet arc.

Filleting Objects

polyline arc segment

polyline line segment

polyline selected for filleting

fillet arc

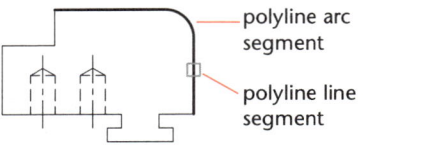

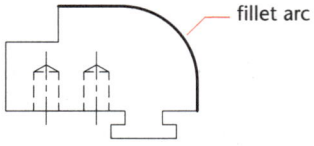

result—fillet arc replaces arc segment

If you set the fillet radius to 0, no fillet arcs are inserted. If two polyline line segments are separated by one arc segment, AutoCAD removes that arc and extends the lines until they intersect.

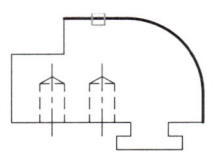

polyline selected for filleting

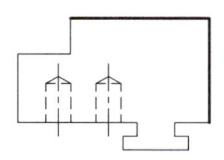

result—zero radius fillet replaces arc segment

This method provides a quick way to join two endpoints. However, if the lines do *not* converge as they approach the arc segment, no change occurs.

Filleting Parallel Lines

You can fillet parallel lines, xlines, and rays. Because two parallel lines uniquely determine a plane, the fillet arc is placed on that plane. The first selected object must be a line or ray, but the second object can be a line, xline, or ray. The fillet arc connects as shown in the following illustration.

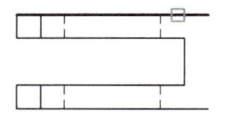

first parallel line selected

second parallel line selected

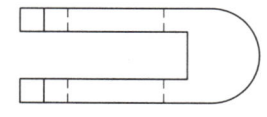

result

The diameter of the fillet arc is always equal to the distance between the lines. The current fillet radius is ignored and remains unchanged.

Editing Hatches

You can edit both hatch boundaries and hatch patterns. If you edit the boundary of an associative hatch, the pattern is updated as long as the editing results in a valid boundary (see "Editing Hatch Boundaries and Patterns" on page 293). Associative hatches are updated even if they're on layers that are turned off. You can modify hatch patterns or choose a new pattern for an existing hatch. You also can explode a hatch.

Selection of associative hatches and their boundaries depends on the setting of the PICKSTYLE system variable. To select an associative hatch without its associated boundary, set PICKSTYLE to 0 or 1. To select an associative hatch with its boundary, set PICKSTYLE to 2 or 3.

Removing Hatch Associativity

You can use the HATCHEDIT command to remove hatch associativity at any time.

To remove hatch associativity

1 From the Modify menu, choose Object ➤ Hatch.
2 Select an associative hatch pattern.
3 In the Hatchedit dialog box, clear Associative.

Command line   HATCHEDIT

Related   Use -HATCHEDIT to edit hatches from the command line.

> **NOTE**   Editing multiple associative hatch blocks can produce unpredictable results. For best results when editing hatched geometry, edit the boundary.

Editing Hatch Boundaries and Patterns

Hatch boundaries can be copied, moved, stretched, and so on. Associative hatches are updated to match any changes made to their boundaries. Non-associative hatches are not updated.

If you select a hatch pattern itself when editing its boundary geometry, the hatch pattern will disassociate unless the entire boundary is selected. If you want the hatch pattern to remain associative, you must select only the boundary geometry, not the hatch pattern.

If you delete the interior boundary geometry of an associative hatch, the hatch automatically updates. If all or part of the exterior boundary geometry is deleted, the hatch always disassociates. When you copy the polyline boundary of a hatch created with the Retain Boundaries option selected, the polyline is copied but the original boundary is not.

You can change the angle or spacing of an existing hatch pattern or replace it with a solid fill or one of the predefined patterns that AutoCAD offers. The Pattern option in the Boundary Hatch dialog box displays a list of these patterns. You can also explode hatch patterns into their composite lines and define new hatch patterns. To reduce file size, the hatch entity is defined in the drawing as a single graphic object.

Changing Existing Hatch Patterns

You can change the angle and spacing of a hatch. In the following example, you change the angle of the hatch.

NOTE If you are editing hatch patterns that were created using a previous version of AutoCAD, the hatch pattern will disassociate.

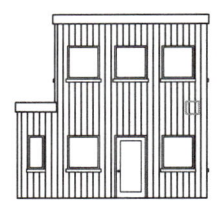

line hatch pattern
before editing

line hatch pattern
after editing

To change the angle of a hatch

1 From the Modify menu, choose Object ➤ Hatch.
2 Select the associative hatch pattern in your drawing to edit.
3 In the Hatchedit dialog box under Pattern Properties, Angle, enter the new angle.
4 Choose Apply.

Command line   HATCHEDIT

Erasing Hatch Patterns

Select hatch patterns for erasing with any of the standard selection methods. If the hatch is associative and the PICKSTYLE system variable is set to 2 or 3, you will also erase the boundary. If you want to retain the boundary, set PICKSTYLE to 0 or 1.

To erase a hatched area

1 From the Modify menu, choose Erase.
2 Select the hatch pattern to erase.

Command line   ERASE

Editing Hatches with Grips

Using grips, you can stretch, move, rotate, scale, and mirror hatch boundaries and their associated hatches just as you can other objects. If the editing results in a valid boundary, the associative hatch is updated.

Using Layers, Colors, and Linetypes

Layers are like transparent overlays on which you organize and group different kinds of drawing information. The objects you create have properties including layers, colors, and linetypes. Color helps you distinguish similar elements in your drawings, and linetypes help you differentiate easily between different drafting elements, such as centerlines or hidden lines. Organizing layers and objects on layers makes it easier to manage the information in your drawings.

In this chapter

- Creating and naming new layers
- Making a layer current
- Controlling the visibility of layers
- Assigning color to layers
- Loading linetypes and assigning them to layers
- Specifying linetype scales
- Assigning colors, linetypes, and layers to objects

Working with Layers

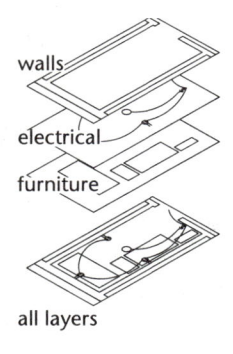

You are always drawing on a layer. It may be the default layer or a layer you create and name yourself. Each layer has an associated color and linetype. For example, you can create a layer on which you draw only centerlines and assign the color blue and the CENTER linetype to that layer. Then, whenever you want to draw centerlines you can switch to that layer and start drawing. You don't need to set up your linetype and color every time you want to draw a centerline. Also, if you don't want to display or plot the centerlines, you can turn off that layer. Using layers is one of the major advantages of creating drawings with AutoCAD instead of with paper and pencil.

In paper space, or when working in a floating viewport, you can specify layer visibility individually for each viewport. The same drawing limits, coordinate system, and zoom factor apply to all layers in a drawing. If you consistently use a specific layering scheme, you can set up a template drawing with layers, linetypes, and colors already assigned.

Sorting Layers and Linetypes

Once you've created layers and assigned them colors and linetypes, you can click each column head to sort layers. Layers can be sorted by name, visibility properties, colors, or linetype properties. Linetypes can be sorted by name and description. When linetypes are sorted, BYLAYER and BYBLOCK always appear at the top of the list. Layer and linetype names can be sorted in ascending or descending alphabetical order.

Creating and Naming Layers

You can create and name a layer for each conceptual grouping (such as walls or dimensions) and assign colors and linetypes to those layers. When organizing your layer scheme, choose layer names carefully.

When you begin a new drawing, AutoCAD creates a special layer named 0. By default, layer 0 is assigned the color number 7 (white or black depending upon your background color) and the CONTINUOUS linetype. Layer 0 cannot be deleted.

You can create new layers and assign color and linetype properties to those layers. To assign layers, colors, and linetypes to individual objects, see "Assigning Layers, Colors, and Linetypes to Objects" on page 317.

To create a new layer

1 From the Format menu, choose Layer.

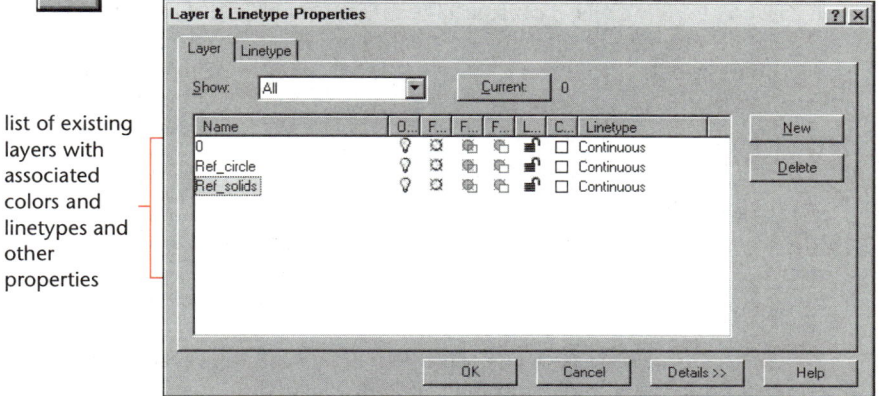

list of existing layers with associated colors and linetypes and other properties

2 In the Layer & Linetype Properties dialog box, choose New.

A new layer is displayed in the list with the temporary name Layer1.

3 Enter a new layer name.

The layer name can include up to 31 characters. Layer names can contain letters, digits, and the special characters dollar sign ($), hyphen (–), and underscore (_). Layer names *cannot* include blank spaces. If you attempt to enter an invalid character, AutoCAD displays an error message.

4 To create more than one layer, choose New again, enter the new layer name, and press ENTER.

5 Choose OK.

Each new layer is numbered sequentially, Layer1, Layer2, and so on. You can rename a layer by clicking it and entering a new name. The default color assigned to the new layer is white, and the default linetype is CONTINUOUS. You can accept the default settings or specify other colors and linetypes.

If an existing layer is highlighted when you create a new layer, the new layer will inherit the properties of the highlighted layer. You can modify the properties of the new layer as necessary.

NOTE You can also add multiple layers by entering a new name in the layer list followed by a comma. Each time you enter a comma, the new name is added to the list of layers.

Working with Layers

299

Making a Layer Current

You are always drawing on the current layer. When you make a layer current, you can create new objects on that layer. If you make a different layer current, any new objects you create are created on that new current layer and use its color and linetype. You cannot make a layer current if it is frozen or is an xref-dependent layer.

To make a layer current

1 From the Format menu, choose Layer.
2 In the Layer & Linetype Properties dialog box, select a layer and choose Current.
3 Choose OK.

NOTE You can also make a layer current by choosing the Layer control from the Object Properties toolbar and then clicking a layer from the list.

Command line LAYER

Related -LAYER changes the current layer from the command line. The CLAYER system variable sets the current layer.

Making an Object's Layer Current

To make the layer that is associated with an object the current layer, select the object and then choose Make Object's Layer Current on the Object Properties toolbar. The layer of the object you select becomes the current layer.

Controlling Layer Visibility

AutoCAD does not display or plot the objects drawn on invisible layers. If you need an unobstructed view when working in detail on a particular layer or set of layers, or if you don't want to plot certain details such as construction or reference lines, you can turn off layers or freeze layers.

The method you choose to control a layer's visibility depends on how you work and the size of your drawing. You can freeze layers that you want to be invisible for long periods.

You can only plot layers that are on and thawed. On most plotters, you can assign a different pen to each color number in the drawing. On single-pen plotters, AutoCAD pauses for pen changes. For more information about plotting, see "Layout and Plotting" on page 475.

Chapter 8   Using Layers, Colors, and Linetypes

Turning Layers On and Off

Turned-off layers are regenerated with the drawing but are not displayed or plotted. You can turn layers off rather than freezing layers if you are switching frequently between visible and invisible layers. By turning layers off, you avoid regenerating the drawing every time you thaw a layer. When you turn a layer on that has been turned off, AutoCAD redraws the objects on that layer.

AutoCAD surfaces and circles located on turned-off or frozen layers are invisible, but they still hide objects when you use HIDE, SHADE, or RENDER.

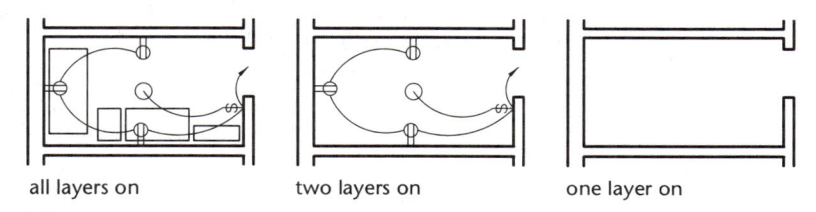

all layers on   two layers on   one layer on

To turn a layer on or off

1. From the Format menu, choose Layer.
2. In the Layer & Linetype Properties dialog box, select the layers you want to turn on or off.

   Use Select All on the cursor menu to select all layers simultaneously. (Right-click the pointing device to activate the cursor menu.)
3. Click the On/Off icon on or off.

   You can also choose Details and select or clear On to turn layers on or off.
4. Choose OK.

NOTE You can also turn layers on or off by choosing the Layer control on the Object Properties toolbar and then clicking the On/Off icon for each layer.

Command line   LAYER

Related   -LAYER turns layers on and off on the command line.

Freezing and Thawing Layers

You can freeze layers to speed up ZOOM, PAN, and VPOINT; improve object selection performance; and reduce regeneration time for complex drawings. AutoCAD does not display, plot, or regenerate objects on frozen layers. Freeze layers that you want to be invisible for long periods. When you "thaw" a frozen layer, AutoCAD regenerates and displays the objects on that layer.

Working with Layers

To freeze or thaw a layer

1 From the Format menu, choose Layer.

2 In the Layer & Linetype Properties dialog box, select the layers you want to freeze or thaw.

3 Click the Freeze/Thaw icon on or off.

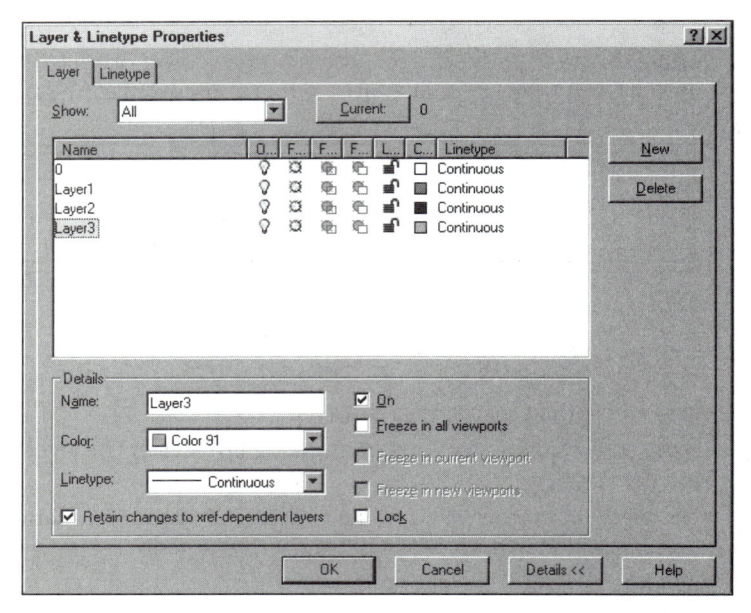

You can also choose Details and select or clear Freeze in All Viewports to freeze or thaw a layer.

4 Choose OK.

NOTE You can also freeze or thaw layers by choosing the Layer control on the Object Properties toolbar and then clicking the Freeze/Thaw icon on or off for each layer.

Command line LAYER

Related -LAYER displays the Layer & Linetype options. VPLAYER freezes and thaws layers in floating viewports (see "Controlling Visibility in Floating Viewports" on page 484).

Freezing or Thawing Layers in the Current Viewport

You can freeze or thaw layers in the current floating viewport without affecting other viewports. Frozen layers are invisible. They are not regenerated or plotted. This feature is useful, for example, if you want to create an annotation layer that is visible only in a particular viewport. Thawing restores the layer's visibility.

To freeze or thaw layers in the current floating viewport

1 From the Format menu, choose Layer.
2 In the Layer & Linetype Properties dialog box, select the layers to freeze or thaw.
3 Click the Freeze in Current Viewport icon on or off.
4 Choose OK.

Command line LAYER, VPLAYER

Freezing or Thawing Layers in New Viewports

You can set visibility defaults for specific layers in new floating viewports. For example, you can restrict display of dimensions by freezing the DIMENSIONS layer in all new viewports. If you create a viewport that requires dimensions, you can override the default setting by changing the current viewport setting. Changing the default for layers in new viewports does not affect layers in existing viewports.

To freeze or thaw layers in new viewports

1 From the Format menu, choose Layer.
2 In the Layer & Linetype Properties dialog box, select the layers to freeze or thaw.
3 Click the Freeze in New Viewports icon on or off.

You can also choose Details and select or clear Freeze in New Viewports to freeze or thaw layers in new viewports.

4 Choose OK.

Command line LAYER, VPLAYER

Controlling Visibility in Floating Viewports

You can control the visibility of objects in floating viewports using several methods:

- Freeze or thaw layers in individual viewports
- Turn viewports on and off
- Limit the number of viewports that can be active

These methods are useful for limiting screen regeneration and for emphasizing or hiding different elements of your drawing. You can freeze or thaw layers in the current viewport with the VPLAYER command. To enable floating viewports, set TILEMODE to 0. For more detailed information about defining layer properties for plotting, see "Controlling Visibility in Floating Viewports" on page 484.

Locking and Unlocking Layers

Locking layers is useful when you want to edit objects that are associated with particular layers but also want to view objects on other layers. You cannot edit the objects on a locked layer; however, they are still visible if the layer is on and thawed. You can make a locked layer current and you can add objects to it.

You can also use inquiry commands (such as LIST) and apply object snaps to objects on locked layers. You can freeze and turn off locked layers and change their associated colors and linetypes.

To lock or unlock layers

1 From the Format menu, choose Layer.
2 In the Layer & Linetype Properties dialog box, select the layers to lock or unlock.
3 Click the Lock/Unlock icon on or off.

Alternatively, under Details, you can select or deselect Lock to lock or unlock layers.

4 Choose OK.

NOTE You can also lock or unlock layers by choosing the Layer control on the Object Properties toolbar and then clicking the Lock icon on or off for each layer.

Command line LAYER

Assigning Color to a Layer

You can assign color to a layer from the Layer & Linetype Properties dialog box, either by clicking the Color icon in the Layer list, or by choosing Details and selecting Color. Selecting Color provides a list of the seven standard colors, along with the four most recently used colors and the Other option. You can choose Other to specify a new color in the Select Color dialog box.

Clicking the Color icon displays the Select Color dialog box. When specifying a color, you can enter the name of the color or its AutoCAD Color Index (ACI) number. Standard color names are available only for colors 1 to 7.

By default, AutoCAD assigns color number 7 (white or black depending on your drawing background) to newly created layers. You can assign an object a color that is different from the layer color.

If you expand the Color column in the Layer & Linetype Properties dialog box, the color name is displayed for the first seven colors. The remaining colors in the Color column contain a color number to identify them.

To assign a color to a layer

1 From the Format menu, choose Layer.

2 In the Layer & Linetype Properties dialog box, select a layer and click the Color icon.

You can also choose Details and select a color from the Colors list.

3 In the Select Color dialog box, select a color.

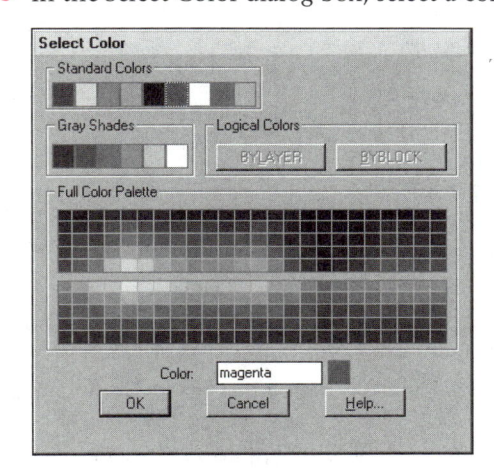

4 Choose OK.

Command line LAYER

Working with Layers

305

Assigning a Linetype to a Layer

When you're defining layers, linetypes provide another way to convey visual information. A linetype is a repeating pattern of dashes, dots, and blank spaces you can use to distinguish the purpose of one line from another.

The linetype name and definition describe the particular dash-dot sequence, the relative lengths of dashes and blank spaces, and the characteristics of any included text or shapes.

To assign an existing linetype to a layer

1 From the Format menu, choose Layer.
2 In the Layer & Linetype Properties dialog box, select a layer and then click the linetype that is associated with that layer.

You can also choose Details and select a linetype from the Linetype list.

3 In the Select Linetype dialog box, select a linetype from the list *or* select Load to load a linetype from a file.
4 Choose OK to exit each dialog box.

Filtering Layers

Sometimes you may want only certain layers to be listed. For instance, if you are working on a drawing that contains various layers of electrical information, you can use the Filter option to limit the layer names displayed to those electrical layers.

You can filter layers based on

- Names, colors, and linetypes
- Visibility
- Freeze or thaw status
- Locked or unlocked status
- Current usage
- Dependency on externally referenced (xref) drawings

To filter layers based on layer properties

1 From the Format menu, choose Layer.
2 In the Layer & Linetype Properties dialog box under Show, select Set Filter Dialog.
3 In the Set Layer Filters dialog box, select or enter layer property settings.

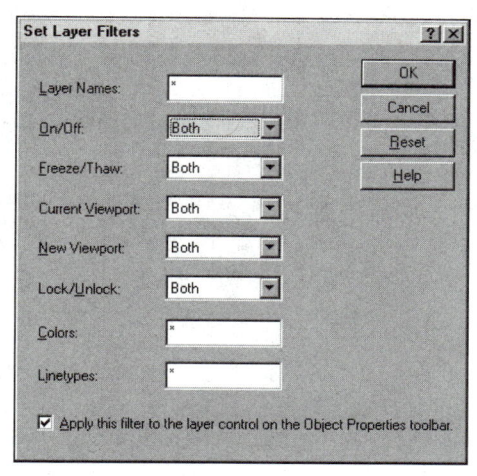

4   Choose OK.

In the Layer Names, Colors, and Linetypes boxes, you can enter a specific name or you can use a combination of wild-card symbols, numbers, or characters to filter similarly named objects all at once. The following table defines the wild-card characters you can use.

Valid wild-card characters	
Character	**Definition**
# (Pound)	Matches any numeric digit
@ (At)	Matches any alpha character
. (Period)	Matches any nonalphanumeric character
* (Asterisk)	Matches any string and can be used anywhere in the search string
? (Question mark)	Matches any single character; for example, ?BC matches ABC, 3BC, and so on
~ (Tilde)	Matches anything but the pattern; for example, ~*AB* matches all strings that don't contain AB
[...] (Ellipsis)	Matches any one of the characters enclosed; for example, [AB]C matches AC and BC

Working with Layers

307

Valid wild-card characters (*continued*)	
Character	Definition
[~...] (Tilde-Ellipsis)	Matches any character not enclosed; for example, [~AB]C matches XC but not AC
- (Hyphen)	Inside brackets; specifies a range for a single character; for example [A-G]C matches AC, BC, and so on to GC, but not HC
' (Reverse quote)	Reads next character literally; for example, '*AB matches *AB

Renaming Layers

You may want to rename a layer to better define how it's used in your drawing. You can rename a layer at any time during a drawing session.

NOTE You cannot rename layer 0 or an xref-dependent layer.

To rename a layer

1. From the Format menu, choose Layer.
2. In the Layer & Linetype Properties dialog box, select a layer to rename and then select it again and enter the new name.

    You can also choose Details and enter a new name.
3. Choose OK.

    Related DDRENAME renames a layer in a dialog box. RENAME renames a layer on the command line.

Deleting Layers

You can delete a layer at any time during a drawing session. You cannot delete the current layer, layer 0, an xref-dependent layer, or a layer that contains objects.

NOTE Layers referenced by block definitions, along with the special layer named DEFPOINTS, cannot be deleted even if they do not contain visible objects.

To delete a layer

1. From the Format menu, choose Layer.
2. In the Layer & Linetype Properties dialog box, select one or more layers, and then choose Delete.

   If the layer you select is referenced by a block, even an uninserted block, that layer cannot be deleted.
3. Choose OK.

Related   PURGE

Retaining Changes to Xref-Dependent Layers

If you want to view an externally referenced drawing with specific modifications, you can choose to retain the properties assigned to your externally referenced layers as currently edited.

To save changes to externally referenced layers

1. From the Format menu, choose Layer.
2. In the Layer & Linetype Properties dialog box, choose Details.
3. Select Retain Changes To Xref-dependent Layers.
4. Choose OK.

Related   Setting the VISRETAIN system variable to 1 saves changes to xref-dependent layers.

Working with Colors

You can assign colors to layers as well as to individual objects in a drawing. Each color is identified by a name or an AutoCAD Color Index (ACI) number, an integer from 1 through 255. Any number of objects and layers can have the same color number. You can assign each color number to a different pen on a pen plotter or use the color numbers to identify certain objects in the drawing even though you can't see the colors on your screen.

Specifying Colors

When specifying a color, you can enter the name of the color or its ACI number. The AutoCAD Color Index provides 255 color numbers. Standard color names are available only for colors 1 to 7.

Colors 1 to 7

Color number	Color name
1	Red
2	Yellow
3	Green
4	Cyan
5	Blue
6	Magenta
7	Black/White

Colors 8 to 255 must be assigned by a number or by selecting the color in a dialog box. The default color (7) is either white or black, depending upon your background color.

Setting the Current Color

You can assign a color to layers or objects that you create. You can define the current color as that of the current layer, or you can specify a different color.

If you choose BYLAYER, new objects assume the color of the layer upon which they are drawn. If you choose BYBLOCK, new objects are drawn in the default color until they are grouped into a block. The objects in the block inherit the current color setting.

To make a color current

1. From the Format menu, choose Color.
2. In the Select Color dialog box, select a color or enter the color name or number in the Color box.

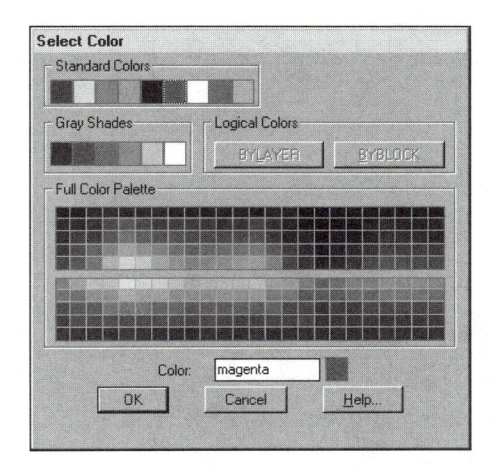

3 Choose OK.

> **NOTE** You can also make a color current by choosing Color on the Object Properties toolbar and then selecting a color from the list *or* selecting Other to display the Select Color dialog box.

Command line DDCOLOR

Related The CECOLOR system variable sets the color for new objects on the command line.

Working with Linetypes

A linetype is a repeating pattern of dashes, dots, and blank spaces. A complex linetype is a repeating pattern of symbols. The linetype name and definition describe the particular dash-dot sequence; the relative lengths of dashes and blank spaces; and the characteristics of any included text or shapes. You can create your own linetypes.

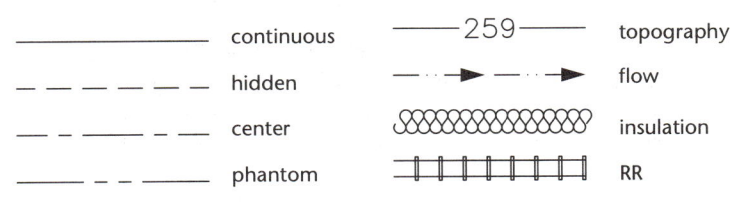

────────	continuous	──259──	topography
─ ─ ─ ─ ─	hidden	─·▶─··▶	flow
─ ─ ── ─ ─	center	∞∞∞∞∞	insulation
──── ─ ─ ────	phantom	▯▯▯▯▯▯▯	RR

Examples of linetypes

To use a linetype you must first load it into your drawing. A linetype definition must exist in a LIN library file before a linetype can be loaded into a drawing.

To load a linetype

1 From the Format menu, choose Linetype.

2 In the Layer & Linetype Properties dialog box, choose Load.

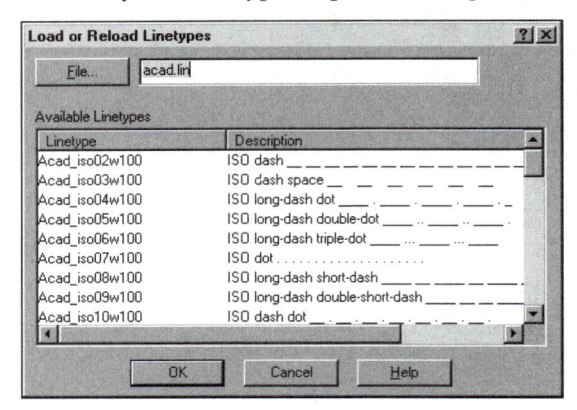

3 In the Load or Reload Linetypes dialog box, select one or more linetypes to load and then choose OK.

To select or clear all linetypes simultaneously, use Select All or Clear All on the cursor menu. (Right-click the pointing device to activate the cursor menu.)

The linetype you select is added to the linetype list in the Layer & Linetype Properties dialog box and to the Linetype Control on the Object Properties toolbar.

4 Choose OK.

Command line   LINETYPE

Related   -LINETYPE sets a layer's linetype.

NOTE   The linetypes used internally by AutoCAD should not be confused with the hardware linetypes provided by some plotters. The two types of dashed lines produce similar results. Do *not* use both types at the same time, however, because the results can be unpredictable.

Making a Linetype Current

To use a linetype to draw on the current layer, you must choose a linetype and make it current. All newly created objects are drawn using the current linetype.

NOTE Xref-dependent linetypes cannot be made current.

If you choose BYLAYER, new objects assume the linetype properties of the CURRENT linetype. If you choose BYBLOCK, new objects are drawn using that linetype until they are grouped into a block. The objects in the block inherit the current linetype properties.

To make a linetype current

1 From the Format menu, choose Linetype.
2 In the Layer & Linetype Properties dialog box, select a linetype and choose Current.
3 Choose OK.

NOTE You can also make a linetype current by choosing the Linetype list on the Object Properties toolbar and then selecting a linetype.

Command line LINETYPE

Related -LINETYPE changes the current linetype.

Renaming Linetypes

You may want to rename a linetype to more easily identify how it's used. You can rename a linetype at any time during the drawing session.

When you rename a linetype, you are renaming only the linetype definition in your drawing. The name in the LIN library file is not being updated to reflect the new name.

NOTE You cannot rename linetypes BYLAYER, BYBLOCK, or CONTINUOUS or xref-dependent linetypes.

Working with Linetypes

To rename a linetype

1. From the Format menu, choose Linetype.
2. In the Layer & Linetype Properties dialog box, select a linetype to rename, select it again to activate in-place editing, and then enter a new name.

   You can also choose Details and enter the new name at Linetype.
3. Choose OK.

   Command line   LINETYPE

   Related   DDRENAME

Deleting Linetypes

You can delete a linetype at any time during a drawing session; however, linetypes that cannot be deleted include BYLAYER, BYBLOCK, CONTINUOUS, the current linetype, and xref-dependent linetypes. Also, linetypes referenced by block definitions cannot be deleted, even if they contain no visible objects.

NOTE If a linetype is referenced by a layer while using a dialog box, you cannot delete that linetype until you close and reenter the Layer & Linetype Properties dialog box.

To delete a linetype

1. From the Format menu, choose Linetype.
2. In the Layer & Linetype Properties dialog box, select one linetype (or more), and then choose Delete.

   If the linetype you select is referenced by an uninserted block, that linetype cannot be deleted.
3. Choose OK.

   Command line   LINETYPE

Changing Linetype Descriptions

Linetypes can have a description associated with them. The description provides an ASCII representation of the linetype. You can assign or change a linetype description in the Layer & Linetype Properties dialog box.

To change a linetype description

1. From the Format menu, choose Linetype.
2. In the Layer & Linetype Properties dialog box, select a linetype and choose Details.
3. In the Details dialog box under Description, enter a new description for the linetype.
4. Choose OK.

Filtering Linetypes

Sometimes you may want only certain linetypes to be listed. You can use the Filter option to limit which linetypes are displayed. You can filter linetypes based on whether they're currently in use or whether they're xref-dependent.

To filter a linetype

1. From the Format menu, choose Linetype.
2. In the Layer & Linetype Properties dialog box under Show, select a linetype filtering option.
3. Choose OK.

Specifying Linetype Scale

You can specify the linetype scale for objects you create. The smaller the scale, the more repetitions of the pattern are generated per drawing unit. By default, AutoCAD uses a global linetype scale of 1.0, which is equal to one drawing unit.

To set the linetype scale for new objects

1. From the Format menu, choose Linetype.
2. In the Layer & Linetype Properties dialog box, choose the Linetype tab.
3. On the Linetype tab, choose Details.

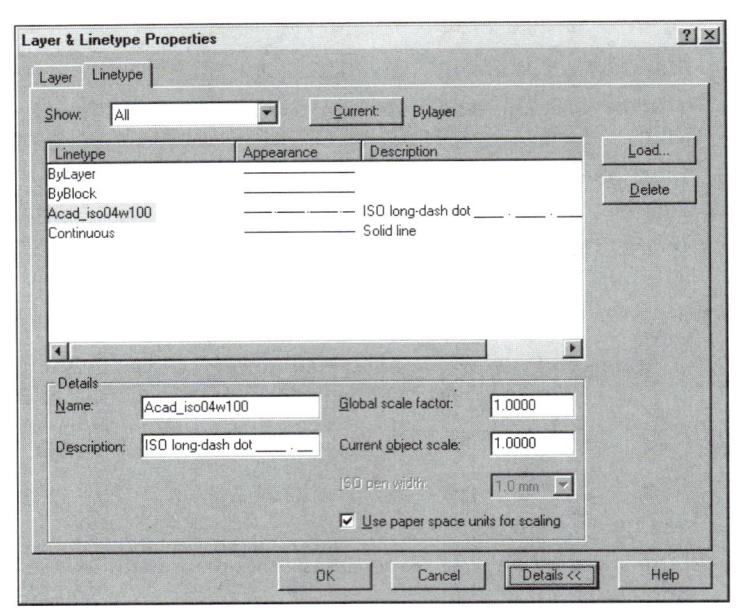

4 Under Details, enter the global scale factor and current object scale.

The global scale factor changes the scale factor for all new and existing linetypes. The current object scale modifies the linetype scale of any subsequently drawn objects relative to the current global scale setting.

5 Specify the ISO pen width by selecting a width from the list.

ISO pen width sets the linetype scale to one of a list of standard ISO values. The resulting scale is the global scale factor multiplied by the object's scale factor.

The ISO pen width list is available only for ISO linetypes. To activate the ISO pen width setting, the linetype must be set to current.

NOTE ISO linetypes are scaled larger than non-ISO linetypes. ISO linetypes are for use in metric drawings with an appropriate ISO pen-width setting.

6 Select Use Paper Space Units for scaling to activate paper space linetype scaling.

When selected, you can adjust the scaling of linetypes in different paper space viewports. For more information, see the PSLTSCALE system variable in the *Command Reference* and "Scaling Pattern Linetypes in Paper Space" on page 490.

7 Choose OK.

Command line LINETYPE

Chapter 8   Using Layers, Colors, and Linetypes

Related The CELTSCALE system variable sets the linetype scale for newly created objects. LTSCALE globally changes the linetype scale of existing objects as well as new objects.

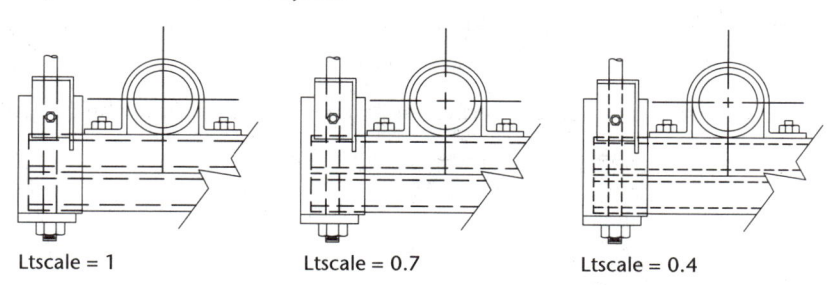

Ltscale = 1   Ltscale = 0.7   Ltscale = 0.4

Assigning Layers, Colors, and Linetypes to Objects

Once you've defined layers, colors, and linetypes, you can assign them to objects in your drawing. You can group associated components of a drawing by assigning objects to layers. You can control layer visibility, color, and linetype and specify whether objects on a layer can be edited. You can move objects from one layer to another and change the name of a layer.

The number of layers in a drawing and the number of objects per layer are virtually unlimited. You can assign a name to each layer and select any combination of layers for display.

Blocks can be defined from objects that were originally drawn on different layers with different colors and linetypes. You can preserve the layer, color, and linetype information of objects in a block. Then, each time you insert the block, you have each object drawn on its original layer with its original color and linetype.

For information about using the Object Properties toolbar to assign properties to objects, see "Editing Objects Using the Object Properties Toolbar" on page 244.

Changing an Object's Layer

Once you've created an object and assigned layer, color, and linetype properties to it, you may wish to change the object's layer. Changing an object's layer is useful if you accidentally create an object on the wrong layer or decide to change your layer organization later.

To change an object's layer

1 Select the objects whose layers you want to change.

NOTE If the PICKADD system variable is set to 0, you can hold down SHIFT to add objects to your selection set.

2 On the Object Properties toolbar, select a layer from the Layer list.

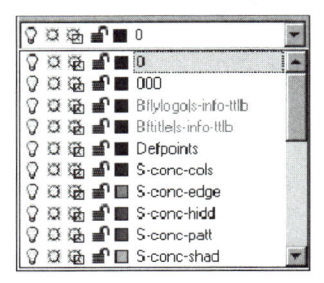

If the objects you've selected are on different layers, the first line of the list is blank. If the objects you've selected are all on the same layer, the layer name is highlighted. If the layer name is too long to fit in the control, it is shortened with an ellipsis. The object is updated to the selected layer.

Command line   DDMODIFY, DDCHPROP

Changing an Object's Color

You can assign colors to individual objects in a drawing. Each color is identified by an AutoCAD Color Index (ACI) number, an integer from 1 through 255. Standard color names are available only for colors 1 to 7. Setting a color for the object overrides the color setting for the layer on which the object resides.

AutoCAD assigns the current color to objects you create. If the current color is set to BYLAYER, objects are created in the color assigned to the current layer. The default setting for color is BYLAYER. If you choose BYLAYER, new objects assume the color of the layer upon which they are drawn.

If you choose BYBLOCK, new objects are drawn in the default color until they are grouped into a block. The objects in the block inherit the current color setting. When an xref or block is inserted into a drawing and the color list is set to BYLAYER, the xref or block inherits the color and properties assigned to the current layer in the drawing.

If you want to retain an object on a specific layer, but you don't want it to keep the color of that layer, you can change the object's color.

To change an object's color

1 Select the object whose color you want to change.
2 On the Object Properties toolbar, choose the Color list, and then select a color from the list *or* choose Other.
3 In the Select Color dialog box, select a color and choose OK.

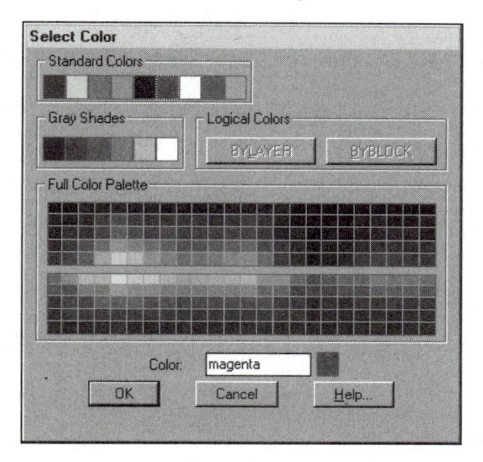

Command line DDMODIFY, DDCHPROP

Related The CECOLOR system variable sets the color for new objects on the command line. CHPROP and CHANGE change an existing object's color on the command line. LIST shows the color of selected objects.

Changing an Object's Linetype

Objects are created using the current linetype. If the current linetype is set to BYLAYER, objects are created using the linetype assigned to the current layer. The default setting for linetype is BYLAYER.

You can associate linetypes with all AutoCAD objects, but they are not displayed with text, points, viewports, xlines, rays, 3D polylines, and blocks. If a line is too short to hold at least one dash sequence, AutoCAD draws a continuous line between the endpoints.

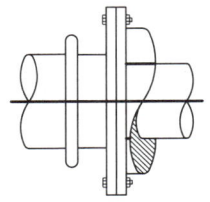

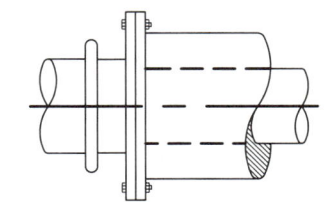

Short hidden and center linetypes continuous between endpoints

By default, objects inherit the linetype of the layer on which they are created. Use the following procedure to change an object's linetype.

For more information about assigning linetypes to objects, see "Editing Objects Using the Object Properties Toolbar" on page 244.

To change an object's linetype

1 Select the object whose linetype you want to change.
2 On the Object Properties toolbar, choose the Linetype list, and select a linetype from the list.

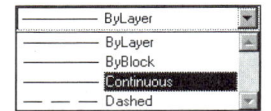

The linetype of all selected objects is changed to the new linetype.

Command line   DDMODIFY, DDCHPROP

Displaying Polyline Linetypes

You can specify whether a linetype pattern is centered on each segment or is continuous throughout the entire length of a 2D polyline. You do this by setting the PLINEGEN system variable. Compare the following illustrations.

PLINEGEN = 0

PLINEGEN = 1

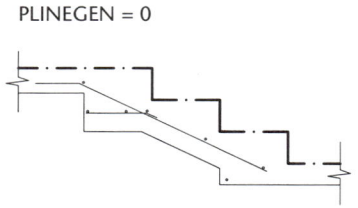

linetype centered on each 2D polyline segment

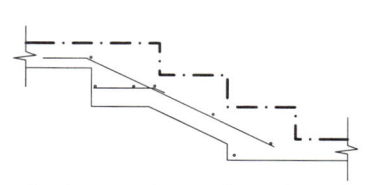

linetype continuous throughout the 2D polyline

The linetype is plotted the way it is displayed on the screen.

To set the linetype display of newly created 2D polylines

1 On the command line, enter **plinegen**.
2 Enter **1** to make the linetype continues throughout the 2D polyline. Enter **0** to center the linetype on each segment.

To change the linetype display of existing 2D polylines

1 From the Modify menu, choose Properties.
2 Select the 2D polyline whose linetype display you want to change.
3 In the Modify Polyline dialog box under Polyline, select LT Gen.
4 Choose OK.

Command line   DDMODIFY

Related   PEDIT changes the polyline linetype display.

Assigning Layers, Colors, and Linetypes to Objects

Adding Text to Drawings

In this chapter

- Creating and changing collections of formats known as styles
- Creating and editing single-line and multiline text
- Overriding text styles with formats, such as fonts and text height
- Changing existing text
- Using font mapping to substitute fonts
- Checking the spelling of text

Text conveys important information in your drawing. You use text for title blocks, to label parts of the drawing, to give specifications, or to make annotations.

AutoCAD provides various ways to create text. For short, simple entries, use line text. For longer entries with internal formatting, use multiline text. Although all entered text uses the current text style, which establishes the default font and format settings, you can use several methods to customize the text appearance.

Working with Text Styles

All text in an AutoCAD drawing has a style associated with it. When you enter text, AutoCAD uses the current text style, which sets the font, size, angle, orientation, and other text characteristics. Text style controls the attributes listed in the following table.

Style settings		
Setting	**Default**	**Description**
Style name	STANDARD	Name with up to 31 characters
Font file	*txt.shx*	File associated with a font (character style)
Big Font file	none	Special shape definition file used for a non-ASCII character set, such as kanji
Height	0	Character height
Width factor	1	Expansion or compression of the characters
Obliquing angle	0	Slant of the characters
Backwards	No	Backwards text
Upside-down	No	Upside-down text
Vertical	No	Vertical or horizontal text

The defaults for the current style are displayed at the prompts on the command line. You can use or modify the default style or create and load a new style. Once you've created a style, you can modify its attributes, change its name, or delete it when you no longer need it.

Creating and Modifying Text Styles

Except for the default STANDARD style, you must create any text style that you want to use. New text inherits height, width factor, obliquing angle, backwards, upside-down, and vertical alignment properties from the current text style. When you create or modify a text style, you use the Text Style dialog box or command line interface to assign or change the style name, assign a font to the style and set the font's width and angle, set the orientation of text, and preview the text style.

Style names can be up to 31 characters long. They can contain letters, numbers, and the special characters dollar sign ($), underscore (_), and hyphen (–). AutoCAD converts the characters to uppercase. If you don't enter a style name, AutoCAD automatically names the style Style*n*, where *n* is a number that starts at 1. Each new style is shown in increments of 1.

To create a text style

1 From the Format menu, choose Text Style.

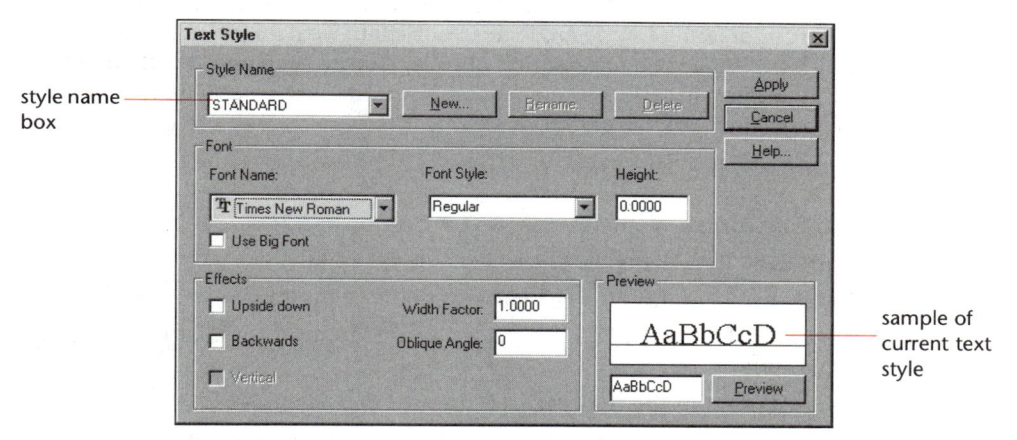

[Text Style dialog box shown, with "style name box" label pointing to the Style Name field and "sample of current text style" label pointing to the Preview area showing "AaBbCcD"]

2 In the New Text Style dialog box, choose New.

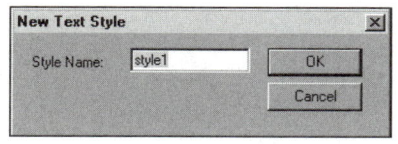

[New Text Style dialog box shown with Style Name: style1]

3 In the New Style dialog box, enter a name for the text style.

The new style you've created has all the characteristics shown in the Text Style dialog box. You can continue to change characteristics, such as the font, or you can do it later.

4 Choose OK to close the New Style dialog box.

5 If you have made any changes to the style characteristics, choose Apply to save them.

6 After you have made and applied all changes to the text style, choose Close. (Cancel becomes Close after you choose Apply.)

Working with Text Styles

325

For more information about modifying text style characteristics, see "Assigning Fonts" on page 326, "Setting Text Height" on page 330, "Setting Obliquing Angle" on page 331, and "Setting Horizontal or Vertical Orientation" on page 331.

Command line   STYLE displays the Text Style dialog box. -STYLE displays prompts at the command line.

You can modify an existing style in the Text Style dialog box by changing the settings. You can also update existing text of that style type to reflect the changes.

If you change an existing style's font or orientation, all text using that style is regenerated using the new font or orientation. Changing text height, width factor, and oblique angle does not change existing text but does change subsequently created text objects. However, changes to alignment, width, and rotation have no effect on multiline text objects (see "Creating Multiline Text" on page 339).

To modify a text style

1 From the Format menu, choose Text Style.
2 In the Text Style dialog box, select a style name.
3 Under either Font or Effects, change any of the options.

   The sample text in the Preview area is updated to show the changes you make to the style.
4 To update text in the drawing that uses the current style, choose Apply.

   When you choose Apply, changes to the style are applied, and can only be undone by changing the characteristics and choosing Apply again.
5 Choose Close.

Command line   STYLE or -STYLE

Assigning Fonts

Fonts define the shapes of the text characters that make up each character set. In AutoCAD, you can use TrueType fonts in addition to AutoCAD's own compiled shape (SHX) fonts.

A single font can be used by more than one style. If your company has a standard font type, you can modify other style settings to create a set of styles that use a standard font in different ways. The following illustration shows the same font used by different styles that have different obliquing settings to define the slant of the text.

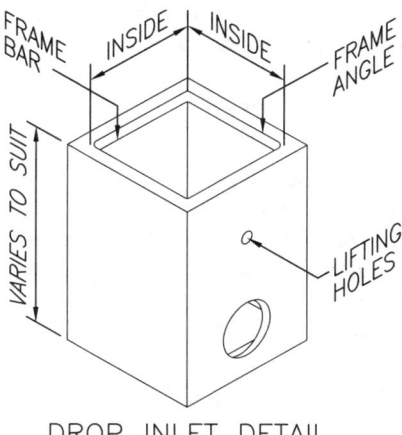

DROP INLET DETAIL

You can assign a font to a text style by selecting either a TrueType typeface name and its font style (bold or italic, for instance), or an AutoCAD compiled SHX font.

Using TrueType Fonts

TrueType fonts always appear filled in your drawing, however, when you plot, the TEXTFILL system variable controls whether the fonts are filled. By default TEXTFILL is set to 1 to plot the filled-in fonts. When you export the drawing with PSOUT and print it on a PostScript device, the font is plotted as designed.

To increase the speed and performance of TrueType fonts in this release of AutoCAD, the Windows operating system draws some TrueType text directly. Due to limitations in Windows, however, AutoCAD must draw TrueType text that is transformed in certain ways; for instance, text that is mirrored, upside-down, backward, oblique, has a width factor not equal to 1, or is in an orientation that is not co-planar with the screen. A general rule is that TrueType text that looks in AutoCAD as it does in a word processor is drawn by the Windows system; otherwise the TrueType text is drawn by AutoCAD. Text that has been transformed might appear slightly more bold in some circumstances, especially at lower resolutions. This difference is only in the display of the font and does not affect the plotted output. For more information on the effects of TrueType fonts in AutoCAD, see "Setting Text Height" on page 330.

The multiline text editor can display only fonts that are recognized by Windows. Because AutoCAD SHX fonts are not recognized by Windows, AutoCAD supplies a TrueType equivalent in the multiline text editor when you select an SHX or any other non-TrueType font for editing.

Using Unicode and Big Fonts

AutoCAD now supports the Unicode character-encoding standard. A Unicode font can contain 65,535 characters, with shapes for many languages. Unicode fonts contain many more characters than are defined in your system; therefore, to use a character not directly available from the keyboard, you can enter the escape sequence **\U+nnnn**, where *nnnn* represents the Unicode hexadecimal value for the character. All AutoCAD SHX shape fonts are now Unicode fonts.

The SHX fonts used in releases prior to Release 13 do *not* support the \U+*nnnn* sequence. However, you can continue to generate accented characters by using characters in the 128–256 range.

The text files for some alphabets, such as kanji, contain thousands of non-ASCII characters. To accommodate such text, AutoCAD supports a special type of shape definition known as a Big Font file. You can set a style to use both regular and Big Font files.

For samples of the standard fonts supplied with AutoCAD, see "Standard Libraries" in the *Command Reference*. AutoCAD also provides ways to substitute one font for another or to specify a default font (see "Substituting Fonts" on page 352).

When you specify fonts, AutoCAD assumes that the first name is the normal font and the second (separated by a comma) is the Big Font. If you enter only one name, AutoCAD assumes it's the normal font and removes any associated Big Font. By using leading or trailing commas when specifying the font file names, you can change one font without affecting the other, as shown in the following table.

Specifying fonts and Big Fonts on the command line	
Enter this...	To specify this...
font, big font	Both normal fonts and Big Fonts
font,	Only a normal font (Big Font unchanged)
,big font	Only a Big Font (normal font unchanged)
font	Only a normal font (Big Font, if any removed)

Specifying fonts and Big Fonts on the command line (continued)

Enter this...	To specify this...
ENTER (null response)	No change

☞ **NOTE** Long file names that contain commas are *not* accepted as font file names. The comma is interpreted as a separator for an SHX font–Big Font pair. For more information, see -STYLE in the *Command Reference*.

Proxy Fonts

For third-party or custom SHX fonts that have no TrueType equivalent, AutoCAD supplies up to eight different TrueType fonts called proxy fonts. Proxy fonts appear different in the multiline text editor from the font they represent to indicate that they are substitutions for the fonts used in the drawing.

A custom SHX font is not available for character formatting in the Character tab fonts list. To use a custom SHX font, you must define it using the STYLE command, and then apply that style to the text.

To assign a font to a text style

1 From the Format menu, choose Text Style.
2 In the Text Style dialog box under Style Name, select a style.
3 Under Font Name, enter the name of a font file or check Big Font to select an Asian-language big font.

When you check Use Big Font, the Font Style box changes to a Big Font Name box. Only SHX fonts are available for selection, and only Big Font names are shown in the Big Font box.

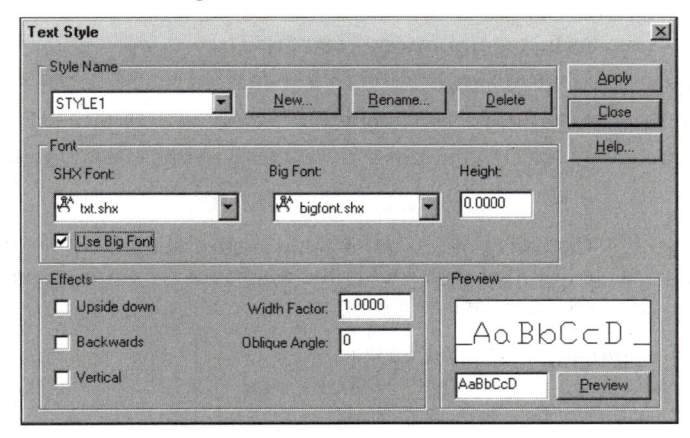

Working with Text Styles

329

4 To see the effects on different characters, enter a new text string in the sample text box, and then view the text under Preview.
5 To update text of the current style in the drawing, choose Apply.
6 Choose Close.

Command line   STYLE

Related   To set the style from the command line, use -STYLE.

Setting Text Height

Text height determines the size in drawing units of the letters in the font you are using. The value usually represents the size of the uppercase letters, with the exception of TrueType fonts.

For TrueType fonts, the value specified for text height might not represent the height of uppercase letters. The height specified represents the height of a capital letter plus an *ascent* area reserved for accent marks and other marks used in non-English languages. The relative portion of areas assigned to capital letters and ascent characters is determined by the font designer at the time the font is designed, and, consequently, will vary from font to font.

In addition to the height of a capital letter and the ascent area that comprise the height specified by the user, TrueType fonts have a *descent* area for portions of characters that extend below the text insertion line. Examples of such characters are y, j, p, g, and q.

If you specify a fixed height as part of a text style, AutoCAD bypasses the Height prompt when you create line text. When the height is set to 0 in the text style, AutoCAD prompts for the height each time you create line text. Set the value to 0 if you want to change the height as you create text.

To set text height in a text style

1 From the Format menu, choose Text Style.
2 In the Text Style dialog box, select a style from the Style Name list.
3 Under Font, enter the text height (in drawing units) in the Height box.
4 To update text of the current style in the drawing, choose Apply.
5 Choose Close.

NOTE   The height of text in the multiline text editor may be adjusted by AutoCAD to fit within the width of the dialog box. For more information, see MTEXT in the *Command Reference*.

Command line   STYLE or -STYLE

Setting Obliquing Angle

The obliquing angle determines the forward or backward slant of the text. The angle represents the offset from 90 degrees.

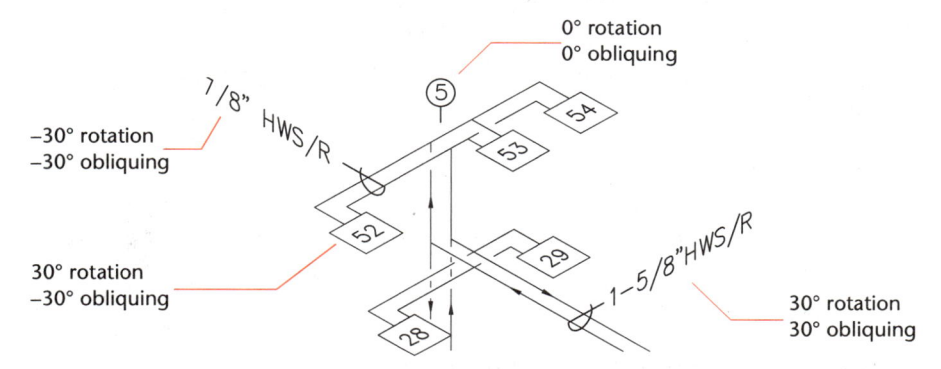

Text created using various obliquing and rotation angles

Entering a value between **-85** and **85** makes the text oblique. A positive obliquing angle slants text to the right. A negative obliquing angle slants text to the left.

To set the obliquing angle in a text style

1 From the Format menu, choose Text Style.
2 In the Text Style dialog box, select a style from the Style Name list.
3 Under Effects, enter an angle in the Oblique Angle box.
4 To update text of the current style in the drawing, choose Apply.
5 Choose Close.

Command line STYLE or -STYLE

Setting Horizontal or Vertical Orientation

AutoCAD orients line text to be vertical or horizontal. Text can have a vertical orientation only if the associated font supports dual orientation. You can create more than one line of vertical text. Each successive text line is drawn to the right of the preceding line. The normal rotation angle for vertical text is 270 degrees.

NOTE Vertical orientation is not supported for TrueType fonts.

vertical text

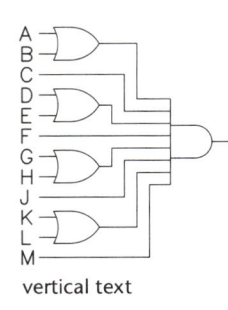

To set vertical orientation in a text style

1 From the Format menu, choose Text Style.
2 In the Text Style dialog box, select a style from the Style Name list.
3 Choose Vertical.
4 To update text of the current style in the drawing, choose Apply.
5 Choose Close.

Command line   STYLE

Making Another Text Style Current

If you want to create text using a different style, you can change the current text style.

To make another text style current

1 From the Format menu, choose Text Style.
2 In the Text Style dialog box, select a style from the Style Name list.
3 Choose OK.

Command line   STYLE or -STYLE

Related   The TEXTSTYLE system variable stores the name of the current text style.

Renaming a Text Style

You can rename an existing text style. Any text using the old name assumes the new text style name.

To rename an existing text style

1 From the Format menu, choose Text Style.
2 In the Text Style dialog box, select a style from the Style Name list.
3 Choose Rename.

The current name is displayed and selected in the Rename Text Style dialog box.

4 Enter a different name at Style Name.

Chapter 9   Adding Text to Drawings

332

5 Choose OK.

6 Choose Close to exit the Text Style dialog box.

Command line   STYLE

Related   DDRENAME and RENAME rename text styles on the command line.

Removing Unreferenced Text Styles

You can remove any styles not referenced in your drawing except the STANDARD text style. You can purge a text style at any time during your drawing session.

To remove unreferenced text styles

1 From the File menu, choose Drawing Utilities ➤ Purge ➤ Text Styles.

   AutoCAD displays prompts for each text style available for removal.

2 Enter **y** to delete the style or **n** to keep it.

Command line   PURGE

Related   From the STYLE dialog box, choose the style you want to delete (STANDARD cannot be deleted). Then choose Delete.

Using Styles with Previous Releases

In AutoCAD Release 13, you could display PostScript fonts in the drawing. AutoCAD Release 14 cannot display PostScript fonts in the drawing. Autodesk has supplied TrueType font equivalents in place of the PostScript fonts supplied with Release 13. The PostScript fonts supported in Release 13 are mapped to the equivalent TrueType file in a font mapping file supplied by AutoCAD. For more information on how to setup and use font mapping files, see "Substituting Fonts" on page 352.

Using Line Text

The text you add to your drawings conveys a variety of information. It may be a complex specification, title block information, a label, or even part of the drawing. For shorter entries that do not require multiple fonts or lines, create line text using DTEXT or TEXT. Line text is more convenient for labels.

Creating Line Text

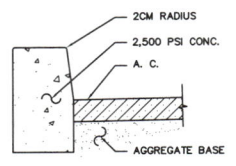

Use TEXT to create a single line of text. Use DTEXT to create one or more lines of text, ending each line when you press ENTER. Each text line is an object that you can relocate, reformat, or otherwise modify.

line and multiline text

To create line text

1 From the Draw menu, choose Text ➤ Single Line Text.
2 Specify the insertion point for the first character. If you press ENTER, AutoCAD locates the new text immediately below the last text object you created, if any.
3 Specify the height of the text. This prompt appears only if text height is set to 0 in the current text style.

   A "rubber band" is attached from the text insertion point to the pointing device cursor. To specify the height onscreen, click the pick button to set the height of the text to the distance specified by the length of the rubber band.

4 Specify a text rotation angle.

   You can specify the rotation angle by moving your pointing device or on the command line.

5 Enter the text. At the end of each line, press ENTER. Enter more text as needed.

   As you type, the text appears on the screen but is not displayed in its final position. If you select another point during this command, the cursor box moves to that point, and you can continue typing. This action creates a separate text object.

6 Press ENTER on a blank line to end text creation.

Command line   DTEXT

Related   TEXT creates text on the command line but does not display it in the graphics area until you complete the entry. You must enter the command again before you start a second line.

Formatting Line Text

When you create line text, you assign a style and set alignment from the command line. The alignment determines what part of the text character aligns with the insertion point. Style sets the default format characteristics. You *cannot* apply formats to individual words and characters.

Assigning a Style to Line Text

The styles used for line text are the same as those used for multiline text. When you create text, you can assign an existing style by entering its name at the Style prompt.

To specify a style when you create line text

1. From the Draw menu, choose Text ➤ Single Line Text.
2. Enter **s** (Style).
3. At the Style Name (or ?) prompt, enter an existing style name.
    If you first want to see a list of styles, enter **?**.
4. Continue creating text as described in "Creating Line Text" on page 334.

Command line DTEXT

Related TEXT

Aligning Line Text

As you create text, you can align it horizontally. That is, you can justify it with one of the alignment options shown in the following illustration. Left alignment is the default. To left align text, do not enter an option after the Justify prompt.

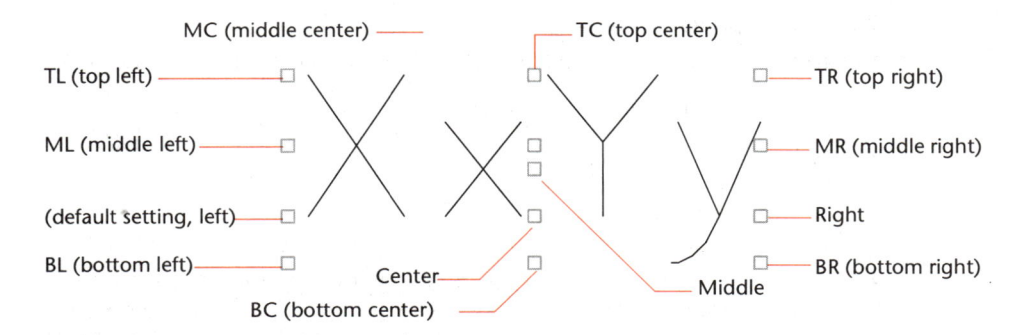

MC (middle center)
TC (top center)
TL (top left)
TR (top right)
ML (middle left)
MR (middle right)
(default setting, left)
Right
BL (bottom left)
Center
BR (bottom right)
BC (bottom center)
Middle

You also can fit line text between points that you specify. This option stretches or squeezes the text to fill the designated space. All of these alignment options are useful for creating text that must align with a specific insertion point or within geometric constructions.

Using Line Text

335

left-justified text   right-justified text

center-justified text

middle-justified text

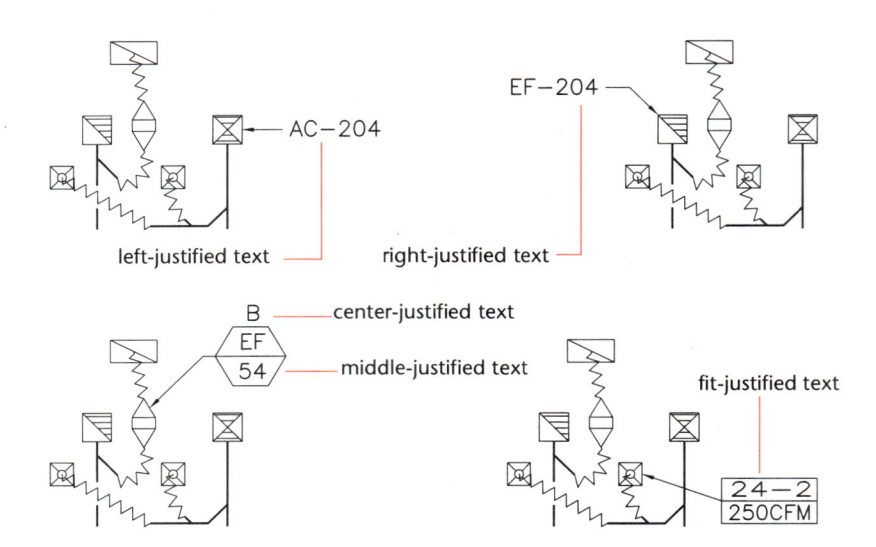

fit-justified text

To align line text as you create it

1 From the Draw menu, choose Text ➤ Single Line Text.
2 Enter **j** (Justify).
3 Enter an alignment option.
4 Continue creating text as described in "Changing Line Text" on page 336.

Command line   DTEXT

Related   TEXT

Changing Line Text

Like any other object, line text objects can be moved, rotated, erased, and copied. You also can mirror, or make a reverse copy of, text. If you do not want the text to be reversed when you mirror it, you can set the MIRRTEXT system variable to 0.

Text objects also have grips for stretching, scaling, and rotating. A line text object has grips at the lower-left corner of the baseline and at the alignment point.

EF—204
alignment point

grips for right-justified line text

EF
alignment point

grips for middle-justified line text

The effect of a command depends on which grip you choose.

You can change line text with DDEDIT and DDMODIFY. When used with line text, DDEDIT changes only the content. DDMODIFY, however, changes the content, along with the text insertion point and style, justification, size, and orientation properties.

Changing Line Text Content
Use DDEDIT when you need to change only the content of the text, not the formatting or properties.

To edit line text

1 From the Modify menu, choose Object ➤ Text.
2 Select the line text object you want to edit.

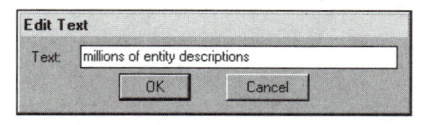

```
Edit Text
Text:  millions of entity descriptions
       [ OK ]   [ Cancel ]
```

3 In the Edit Text dialog box, enter the new text. Then choose OK.
4 Select another text object to edit, or press ENTER to exit the command.

Command line   DDEDIT

Changing Line Text Properties
Use DDMODIFY when you want to change content, style, location, orientation, or justification.

To modify line text objects

1 From the Modify menu, choose Properties.
2 Select a line text object.

Using Line Text

337

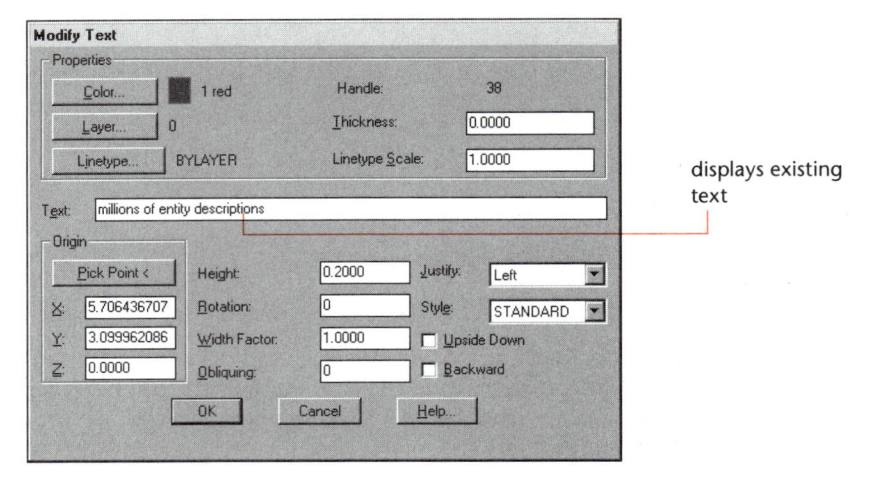

[Screenshot of the Modify Text dialog box with callout "displays existing text" pointing to the Text field containing "millions of entity descriptions"]

3 In the Modify Text dialog box, enter the new text.

4 Change format attributes and other settings as needed. These changes affect all the text in the text object.

5 Choose OK.

Command line DDMODIFY

Related CHANGE modifies text properties.

Using Multiline Text

For long, complex entries, create multiline text using MTEXT. Multiline text fits a specified width but can extend vertically to an indefinite length. You can format individual words or characters within the multiline text.

Multiline text consists of any number of text lines or paragraphs that fit within a width you specify. Regardless of the number of lines, each set of paragraphs created in a single editing session forms a single object, which you can move, rotate, erase, copy, mirror, stretch, or scale (see chapter 7, "Editing Methods").

Multiline text has more editing options than line text. For example, you can apply underlining, fonts, color, and text height changes to individual characters, words, or phrases within a paragraph.

Creating Multiline Text

You can create text in the Multiline Text Editor dialog box, on the command line, or with a third-party editor, which you can specify in the Preferences dialog box or with the MTEXTED system variable. The Multiline Text Editor dialog box provides a quick way to set properties that affect the entire object or formats that affect only selected text.

Before creating the text, you must define the paragraph's width. When text entry is complete, AutoCAD inserts the text entered in the dialog box within this width limit. You can apply the text height, justification, rotation angle, and style to the text object, or apply character formatting to selected characters. Justification determines where the text is inserted with respect to the text boundaries (see "Formatting Multiline Text Objects" on page 346).

By default mtext prompts for the first and second corner of a rectangle and place the text to fit within the sides of the rectangle. The text may flow beyond the top or bottom of the rectangle (or both) depending on the justification of the text.	By default mtext prompts for the first and second corner of a rectangle and place the text to fit within the sides of the rectangle. The text may flow beyond the top or bottom of the rectangle (or both) depending on the justification of the text.	By default mtext prompts for the first and second corner of a rectangle and place the text to fit within the sides of the rectangle. The text may flow beyond the top or bottom of the rectangle (or both) depending on the justification of the text.
left-justified	right-justified	middle-justified

The height of the multiline text object you create with MTEXT depends on the amount of text, not the height you specify when selecting the opposite corner of the boundary box on screen.

The following procedure describes how to create multiline text using the default properties and formats. For information about changing style and format, see "Formatting Multiline Text" on page 342.

To create multiline text

1 From the Draw menu, choose Text ➤ Multiline Text.

2 Specify the first corner of the rectangle.

3 Specify the width of the text boundary by dragging to the left or right of the insertion point, or enter a width value on the command line.

4 Specify the text flow direction by dragging up or down.

Arrows inside the boundary box indicate the direction entered text flows based on the current justification setting.

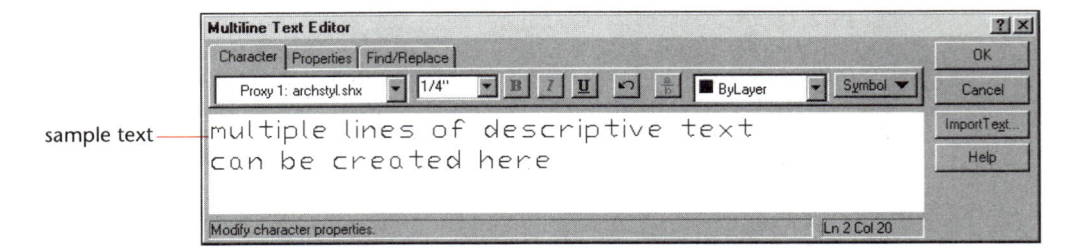

sample text — [Multiline Text Editor dialog box showing "multiple lines of descriptive text can be created here"]

5   In the Multiline Text Editor dialog box, enter the text, allowing it to wrap to the next line.

Words that extend beyond the bounding rectangle you specified when you create the MTEXT object wrap to the next line in the Multiline Text Editor.

You can use the standard Windows control keys described in the table to enter text.

Control keys used to edit text

Key	Description
CTRL+C	Copies selection to the Clipboard
CTRL+V	Pastes Clipboard contents over selection
CTRL+X	Cuts selection to the Clipboard
CTRL+SPACEBAR	Inserts a nonbreaking space
RETURN	Ends the current paragraph and starts a new line

6   Choose OK.

NOTE   If your monitor is set to display 256 colors or less, text objects that have colors assigned to them might not appear correctly in Multiline Text Editor.

Command line   MTEXT

Related   -MTEXT creates and formats multiline text on the command line only.

Using External Text Files

You can insert ASCII text files created in other word processors into your AutoCAD drawing. You can either import the text or drag a file icon from the Windows File Manager.

Importing Text Files

You can save time by importing ASCII or RTF files from other sources. For example, you can create a text file of standard notes that you include in drawings. Instead of entering this information each time you use it, you can import the file. The imported text becomes an AutoCAD text object, which you can edit as if you created it in AutoCAD. Imported text retains its original formatting properties.

To import text files

1 From the Draw menu, choose Text ➤ Multiline Text.
2 Specify the text boundary location and other properties as needed.
3 In the Multiline Text Editor dialog box, choose Import Text.
4 In the Open dialog box, navigate to and double-click on the file to import, or select the file and choose Open.
5 In the Inserting Text dialog box, choose the location for the imported text. Then choose Import.

   AutoCAD inserts the text at the cursor location in the Multiline Text Editor dialog box.

6 Change the text as needed. Then choose OK.

NOTE If the Clipboard contains text, you can choose Paste from the Edit menu to paste the Clipboard contents into AutoCAD.

Dragging a Text File into a Drawing

Use the drag-and-drop feature to insert ASCII or RTF text into a drawing. Inserted text uses the formats and fonts defined by the current AutoCAD text style. Its width is determined by line breaks and carriage returns in the original document. Imported text files are limited to a maximum of 16 KB. You can drag only files with a file extension of *.txt* or *.rtf* into an AutoCAD drawing.

To insert a text file using the drag-and-drop feature

1 Open the Windows File Manager, but make sure it doesn't fill the screen. Then display the directory that contains the TXT file you want.

2   Drag a TXT or RTF file icon onto the AutoCAD drawing.

AutoCAD draws the text as a text object at the point where you drop it.

3   Using the grips, you can move, rotate, and scale the text objects as needed.

To drag OLE objects into a drawing, see "Creating Compound Documents with OLE" on page 653.

Related   You can start DTEXT before dragging the file into AutoCAD. When you use this method, drag the file when you see the Text prompt.

Formatting Multiline Text

New text automatically assumes the characteristics of the current text style. The STANDARD text style is the default. You can override the default text style by applying formatting to individual characters and applying properties to the text object. You also can indicate formatting or special characters using the methods described in the following sections. For more information about special characters, see DTEXT in the *Command Reference*.

Formatting options such as underlining, stacked text, or fonts can be applied to individual words or characters within a paragraph. Properties such as style, justification, width, and rotation affect the entire text object. You can change both formats and properties in the Multiline Text Editor dialog box.

Formatting Individual Words or Characters

As you create multiline text, you can apply formats to selected text. The format changes affect only the characters you select. The current text style is not changed.

You can change the font and text height; apply boldface, italics, underlining, and color; and insert special characters, including Unicode characters for TrueType fonts.

Text height sets the height of capitalized text. This height establishes the default value for all the text in the text boundary. You can override it by specifying a different height for selected text. The change of text height displayed in the multiline text editor is proportional to the change in height of the actual characters displayed on-screen. For more information about how height is calculated, see MTEXT in the *Command Reference*.

To format characters using the dialog box

1. From the Draw menu, choose Text ➤ Multiline Text.
2. Specify the text boundary location and other properties as needed.
3. In the Multiline Text Editor dialog box, create text as described in "Creating Multiline Text" on page 339.
4. Choose the Character tab (visible by default).
5. Select text as follows:
   - To select one or more letters, click and drag the pointing device over the characters.
   - To select a word, double-click the word.
   - To select a paragraph, triple-click the paragraph.

6. Using the Character tab, change formatting as follows:
   - To change the font, select a font from the list. Then choose OK.
   - To change the height of selected text, enter a new value in the Height box.
   - To format text in a TrueType font with boldface or italics, or to create underlined text for any font, click the appropriate tool on the toolbar. SHX fonts do *not* support boldface or italics.
   - To apply color to selected text, choose a color from the Color list, or choose Other to display the Color dialog box. Select a color and then choose OK. The most recently used colors are displayed in the color list.

NOTE If you are working with a white background color, your Windows system palette is set to greater than 256 colors, and you have selected Smooth Edges of Screen Fonts from the Plus! tab on the Windows Control Panel, characters with angular lines (such as X) that are entered in the Multiline Text Editor dialog box appear grayed out. To correct this problem, set your Windows system palette to 256 colors or clear Smooth Edges of Screen Fonts.

color choices for selected text

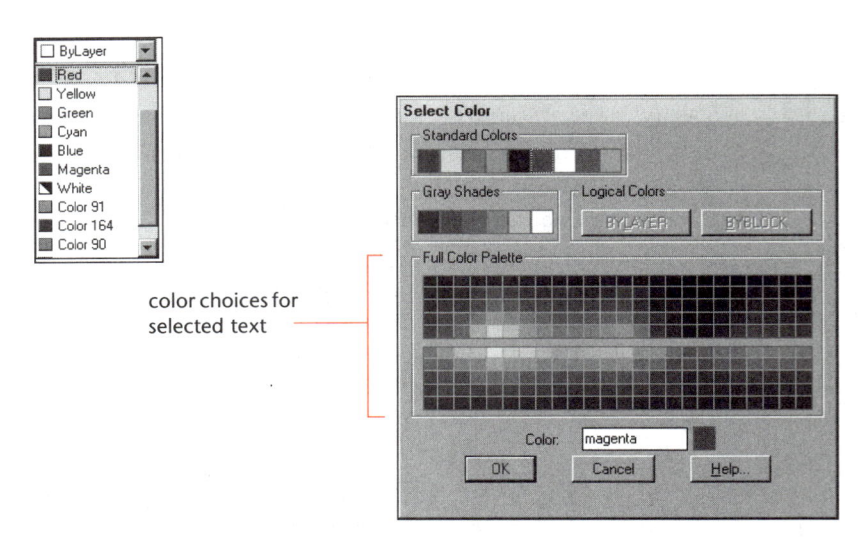

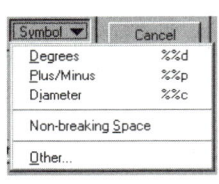

- To insert special characters, choose Symbol. Then choose an option from the Symbol menu.
- To insert Unicode characters for TrueType fonts, from the Symbol menu, choose Other.

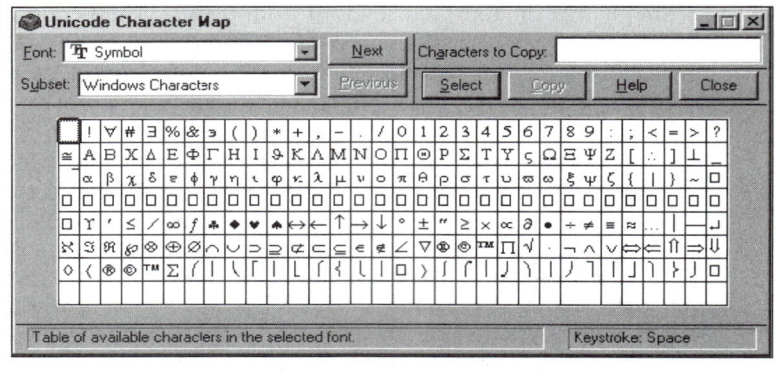

7 Choose OK.

NOTE To access the Unicode Character Map dialog box, you must have *charmap.exe* installed on your system. See Windows Help for adding programs to your system.

Command line MTEXT

Creating Stacked Text

Stacked text is text or fractions aligned vertically.

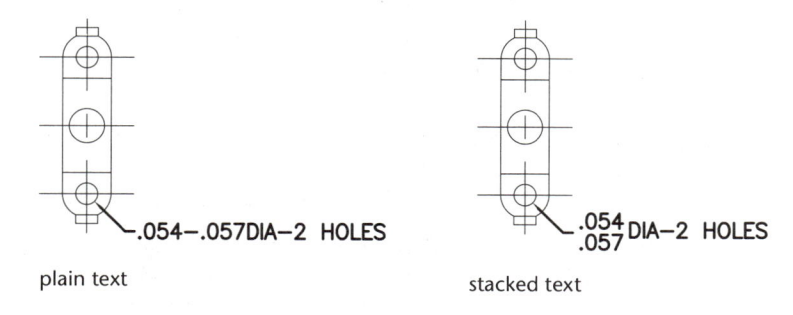

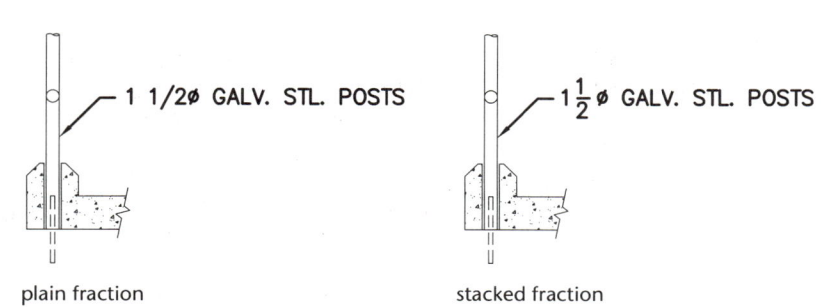

.054−.057DIA−2 HOLES

plain text

$\frac{.054}{.057}$DIA−2 HOLES

stacked text

1 1/2∅ GALV. STL. POSTS

plain fraction

1$\frac{1}{2}$ ∅ GALV. STL. POSTS

stacked fraction

AutoCAD uses the special characters slash (/) and caret (^) to indicate where selected text should be stacked. By default, stacked characters are vertically aligned at the midpoint of the text that precedes them. In the previous example, enter **054^057** to stack text as shown in the first example. Enter **1/2** to stack fractions as shown in the second example.

Text stacked in the text editor is always aligned with the text baseline. To top-align or center-align stacked text, see "Formatting Multiline Text in a Text Editor" on page 359.

To create stacked text

1 From the Draw menu, choose Text ➤ Multiline Text.
2 Specify the text boundary location and other properties as needed.
3 In the Multiline Text Editor dialog box, create text as described in "Creating Multiline Text" on page 339.
4 Insert a caret (^) symbol to indicate where to begin the lower line. For fractions, use a slash (/). Highlight the text that you want to align vertically and click the stack icon on the Character tab.

Using Multiline Text

345

When you are entering fractional numbers, the slash is converted to a horizontal bar the length of the longer number.

5 Choose OK.

Command line MTEXT

Formatting Multiline Text Objects

As you create multiline text, you can set the properties that control style, text justification, and the size and rotation of the text boundary. These settings affect all text within the text boundary, not specific words or characters.

You can set these properties on the command line before the Multiline Text Editor dialog box opens. If you already are in the Multiline Text Editor dialog box, choose the Properties tab and change the settings using Change Properties toolbar.

Style sets the default fonts and formatting characteristics for new text. As you create text, you can select which style you want to use from a list of existing styles. For information about creating and modifying styles, see "Working with Text Styles" on page 324.

When text is justified, the top, bottom, and middle settings are based on the border of the current multiline text object, not the height of the rectangle you specified when the text object was created.

When you change the style of a multiline text object that has character formatting applied to any portion of the text, the style is applied to the entire object, and some formatting of characters might not be retained. For instance, changing from a TrueType style to a style using an SHX font or to another TrueType font causes the text to use the new font for the entire object, and any character formatting is lost.

Effects of style change on character formatting

Formatting	Retained?
bold	No
color	Yes
font	No
height	No

Effects of style change on character formatting (*continued*)

Formatting	Retained?
italic	No
stacking	Yes
underlining	Yes

Justification controls both text alignment and text flow based on a specified justification point. Text is justified with respect to the left and right text boundaries. Text flows from the middle, the top, or the bottom of the paragraph with respect to the top and bottom text boundaries. The top and bottom boundaries are based on the top and bottom lines of the multiline text object. AutoCAD offers nine justification settings.

top left:
left-aligned

top center:
centered

top right:
right-aligned

middle left:
left-aligned

middle center:
centered

middle right:
right-aligned

bottom left:
left-aligned

bottom center:
centered

bottom right:
right-aligned

You can adjust line width by entering the line width (*not* the character width) in drawing units in the Width box. Width can also be adjusted with grips in the graphics window.

Rotation controls the angle of rotation of the text boundary.

To set multiline text properties

1   From the Draw menu, choose Text ➤ Multiline Text.
2   Specify the text boundary location and other properties as needed.
3   In the Multiline Text Editor dialog box, create text as described in "Creating Multiline Text" on page 339.
4   To change style, justification, text width, or rotation, choose the Properties tab.

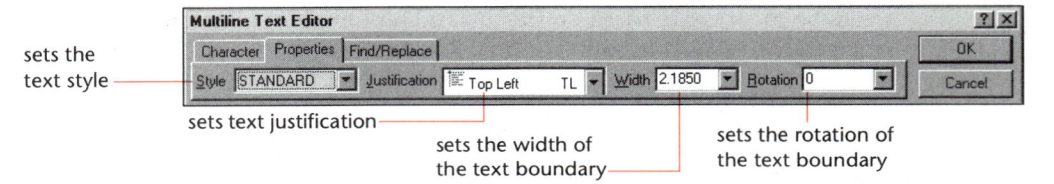

sets the text style — *sets text justification* — *sets the width of the text boundary* — *sets the rotation of the text boundary*

5   On the Properties tab, change the settings as required and choose OK.

Command line   MTEXT

Changing Multiline Text

As with line text, multiline text objects can be moved, rotated, erased, and copied. You also can mirror, or make a reverse copy of, text. If you do not want the text to be reversed when you mirror it, you can set the MIRRTEXT system variable to 0.

A multiline text object that has a nonzero width has grips at the four corners of the text boundary and, in some cases, at the justification point. A multiline text object that has an unspecified width has a single grip at the justification point. The effect of a command depends on which grip you choose.

After you create multiline text, you can change it with DDEDIT or DDMODIFY. DDEDIT changes content, formatting, and general object properties such as style and justification.

In addition to the settings available from DDEDIT, DDMODIFY changes the origin, or insertion point, of the object, as well as other object properties not specific to text objects.

Changing Text Content and Formatting

Use DDEDIT when you want to change either content or formatting of multiline text. The changes you make affect only the text you select, not the text style.

To edit multiline text in the Multiline Text Editor

1 From the Modify menu, choose Object ➤ Text.

2 Select the multiline text object you want to edit.

3 In the Multiline Text Editor dialog box, edit text by selecting it and then using the methods used to create it as described in "Creating Multiline Text" on page 339.

4 Change formats and justification as described in "Formatting Multiline Text" on page 342.

5 Choose OK.

Command line   DDEDIT, DDMODIFY

Related   Using DDEDIT, you can edit multiline text using the AutoCAD internal text editor. You can also use DDMODIFY to edit multiline text objects (see "Using Text Editors for Multiline Text" on page 357).

Using Other Text Editors

You can use the MTEXTED system variable to specify the text editor used by DDEDIT. If MTEXTED is set to Internal or is not set, DDEDIT uses the internal editor. You can also specify your own text editor, such as Notepad.

For information about specifying primary and secondary editors, see the MTEXTED system variable in the *Command Reference*.

To specify another text editor

1 From the Tools menu, choose Preferences.

2 In the Preferences dialog box, choose the Files tab.

3 On the Files tab, double-click Text Editor, Dictionary, and Font File Names.

4 Double-click Text Editor Application.

By default, the Internal editor is set.

5 Either double-click Internal, and then enter a text editor (such as Notepad) in the Select a File dialog box, or single-click Internal, and then single-click Internal, again, to enter the path and application name for another text editor.

Command line   MTEXTED

Changing Multiline Text Location

To move multiline text, use DDMODIFY. In the Modify MText dialog box, you can also edit content and change properties such as style, justification, and text boundary size.

To move a multiline text object

1 From the Modify menu, choose Properties.
2 Select the multiline text you want to change.

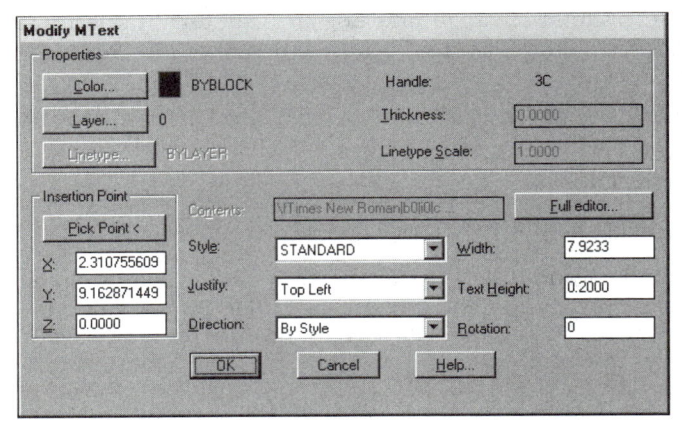

3 In the Modify MText dialog box, enter new coordinates in the X, Y, and Z boxes under Insertion Point.

If you want to specify the new insertion point by using the pointing device, choose Pick Point.

Related   MOVE can also be used to relocate text.

Changing Multiline Text Properties

Use DDMODIFY for changing general object properties such as color, linetype, and layer, as well as properties specific to text: style, justification, width, and rotation.

To change multiline text object properties

1 From the Modify menu, choose Properties.
2 Select the multiline text you want to change.
3 In the Modify MText dialog box, change general object properties as needed.

4 To change style, justification, rotation, or width, do *one* of the following:

- Continue to make changes within the Modify MText dialog box as necessary.
- Choose Full Editor.

5 Choose OK.

Command line   DDMODIFY

Finding and Replacing Multiline Text

To quickly search for and replace text on a word-by-word basis, use the multiline text editor's find and replace feature. Replacement is based on text content only; character formatting and text properties are unchanged.

To find text

1 From the Modify menu, choose Properties.
2 Select a multiline text object.
3 In the Modify MText dialog box, choose Full Editor.
4 In The Multiline Text Editor dialog box, choose the Find/Replace tab.

5 Enter the word that you want to change in the find box.

- To match the case of letters in a word, check Match Case.
- To find text that is not part of another word, check Whole Word.

6 To locate the word in the selected text, choose the Find tool.

When the text object has been completely searched, a message at the bottom of the dialog box is displayed to indicate that search is resuming at the beginning of the text object.

To replace text

1 In the Replace box, enter the word you want to replace the word in the Find box.
2 To locate the word in the Find box, choose the Find tool.
3 When you find the word you want to replace, choose the Replace tool.
4 Repeat steps 2 and 3 as for each occurrence of the word you want to change.
5 Choose OK.

Substituting Fonts

You can designate fonts to be substituted for other fonts or as defaults when AutoCAD cannot find a font specified in a drawing.

The fonts used for the text in your drawing are determined by the text style and, for multiline text, by individual font formats applied to sections of text. Sometimes you might want to ensure that your drawing uses only certain fonts, or perhaps you might want to convert the fonts you used to other fonts. You can use any text editor to create font mapping tables for both of these purposes.

You can use these font mapping tables to enforce corporate font standards, or to facilitate off-line printing. For example, if you share drawings with consultants, you may want to use a font mapping table to specify what font AutoCAD substitutes when it encounters a text object created with another font. Similarly, to edit the drawing using quicker-drawing SHX fonts, and then switch to more complex fonts for the final plot, you can set up a font mapping table that converts each SHX font to an equivalent.

The font mapping table is a plain ASCII text (FMP) file containing one font mapping per line. Each line contains the base name of the font file (with no directory name or path) followed by a semicolon (;) and the name of the substitute font file. The substitute file name includes a file extension such as *.ttf*.

For example, you could use the following entry in a font map table to specify that the *times.ttf* TrueType font file be substituted for the *romanc.shx* font file:

romanc.shx; times.ttf

AutoCAD comes with a default font mapping table (*acad.fmp*). You can edit this file using any ASCII text editor. You also can specify a different font mapping table file in the Preferences dialog box, or you can specify the font mapping file using the FONTMAP system variable.

To specify a font mapping table

1 From the Tools menu, choose Preferences.
2 In the list on the Files tab, double-click Text Editor, Dictionary, and Font File Names.

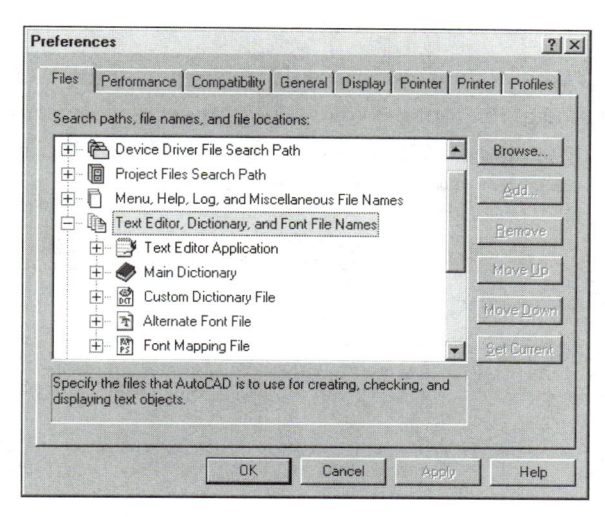

3 Double-click Font Mapping File.

acad.fmp is specified by default.

4 To change the font mapping file, double-click the arrow to specify a new file in the Select a File dialog box.

5 At the Command prompt, enter **regen** to convert existing text to the new font mappings.

Command line   PREFERENCES

Related   The FONTMAP system variable specifies the name of the current font mapping table.

Specifying an Alternative Default Font

If your drawing specifies a font that is not currently on your system, AutoCAD automatically substitutes the font designated as your alternate font. By default, AutoCAD uses the *simplex.shx* file. However, you can specify a different font if necessary. You enter the alternative font file name by changing the FONTALT system variable.

If you use a text style that uses a Big Font, you can map it to another font using the FONTALT system variable. This system variable uses a default font file pair of *txt.shx*, *bigfont.shx*.

Substituting Fonts

353

To specify a default alternative font

1. At the Command prompt, enter **fontalt**.
2. Enter the name of the font file you want to use as the alternative.

    The following table shows the font substitution rules used by AutoCAD when a font file cannot be located when a drawing is opened.

Font Substitution

File Extension	Mapping order			
ttf	Use FONTMAP value	Use font defined in text style	Windows substitutes a similar font	
shx	Use FONTMAP value	Use font defined in text style	Use FONTALT	Prompt for new font
pfd	Use FONTMAP value	Use FONTALT	Prompt for new font	

Checking Spelling

SPELL checks the spelling in your drawing, including spelling in dimension text. You use one of several main dictionaries, available in different languages. The main dictionaries use a standard word list, which you can customize.

To check spelling

1. From the Tools menu, choose Spelling.
2. Select the text objects you want to check, or enter **all** to select all text objects.
3. If AutoCAD does not find any misspelled words, it displays a message. If AutoCAD finds a misspelling, the Check Spelling dialog box identifies the misspelled word.

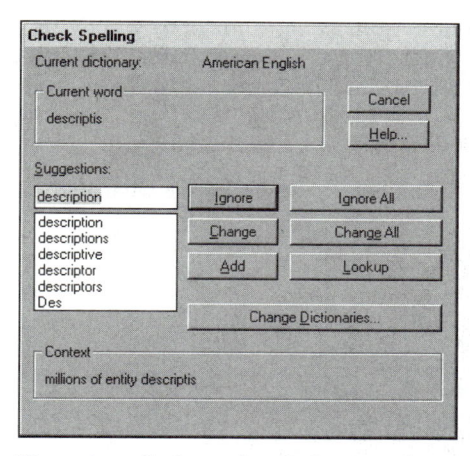

The misspelled word and the text that surrounds it are displayed under Context.

4 You can take *one* of the following actions:

- To correct a word, select an alternate word from the Suggestions list or type a word in the Suggestions box. Then choose Change or Change All.
- To leave a word unchanged, choose Ignore or Ignore All.
- To leave a word unchanged and add it to the custom dictionary, choose Add. (This option is not available unless a custom dictionary is specified.)

5 Choose Cancel to exit the dialog box.

Command line SPELL

Switching Dictionaries

During a spelling check, AutoCAD matches the words in the drawing to the words in the current main dictionary. Any words you add are stored in the custom dictionary that is current at the time of the spelling check. For example, you can add proper names so AutoCAD no longer identifies them as misspelled words.

To check spelling in another language, you can change to a different main dictionary. You also can create any number of custom dictionaries and switch to them as needed.

Checking Spelling

355

You can change dictionaries from a dialog box or by specifying the dictionary name in the DCTMAIN or DCTCUST system variable. For a list of the dictionary file names, see DCTMAIN in the *Command Reference*.

To switch main or custom dictionaries while checking spelling

1 In the Check Spelling dialog box, choose Change Dictionaries.

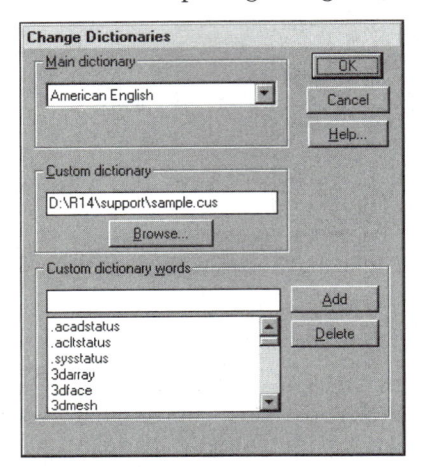

2 To change the main dictionary, select a dictionary from the Main Dictionary list.
3 To change the custom dictionary, enter a name under Custom Dictionary.
   To select from a list of dictionaries, choose Browse.
4 Choose OK.

Command line SPELL

Creating and Editing Custom Dictionaries

A custom dictionary is a list of spelling exceptions that you have identified. The files that contain them can be identified by the *.cus* file extension. You can use any ASCII text editor to add and delete words or to combine dictionaries. If a word is preceded by a tilde (~), AutoCAD always flags the word as incorrect.

You also can create and edit dictionaries from inside AutoCAD.

To create or edit custom dictionaries during a spelling check

1 In the Check Spelling dialog box, choose Change Dictionaries.
2 In the Change Dictionaries dialog box under Custom Dictionary, specify the dictionary you want to edit using one of these methods:

- To specify a dictionary, enter its name, using the *.cus* file extension.
- To select from a list of directories, choose Browse.
- To create a new custom dictionary, enter a new name. Use the *.cus* file extension.

3 To add a word, enter it under Custom Dictionary Words. Then choose Add.
4 To remove a word, select it from the list. Then choose Delete.
5 Choose OK.

Command line SPELL

Related You also can edit the CUS ASCII file. Each word in the CUS file must be on a line by itself.

Using Text Editors for Multiline Text

The default text editor is the Multiline Text Editor dialog box, but you can elect to use a third-party editor by setting the editor in the Preferences dialog box or the MTEXTED system variable to any ASCII editor.

Specifying a Multiline Text Editor

Your text editor may offer some formatting options that cannot be changed in the Multiline Text Editor dialog box. For best results, use the same text editor to edit text that you used when you created it.

To specify a text editor

1 From the Tools menu, choose Preferences.
2 In the Preferences dialog box, choose the Files tab.
3 Double-click Text Editor, Dictionary, and Font File Names.

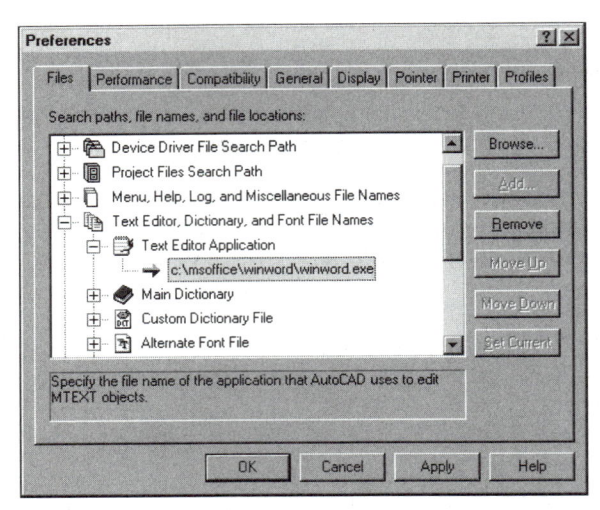

[Screenshot of the Preferences dialog box with the Files tab selected, showing Text Editor Application set to c:\msoffice\winword\winword.exe]

 4 Double-click Text Editor Application. Then double-click Internal.

   If you've previously changed the MTEXTED system variable to (.) for none, then the arrow appears beneath Text Editor Application, but Internal is not displayed. Double-click on the arrow or choose Browse to modify the text editor.

 5 In the Select a File dialog box, enter the name of the executable file for the ASCII text editor you want to use to create multiline text.

 6 Choose OK twice.

   Command line   PREFERENCES

   Related   Use the MTEXTED system variable to specify the name of an ASCII text editor to use to create multiline text. To use AutoCAD's internal text editor, specify Internal.

Creating Multiline Text in a Text Editor

If you use a third-party text editor for multiline text, you define general properties on the command line before you enter the text. AutoCAD then opens the text editor for entering text and uses format codes to format individual words and characters. When you close the text editor, AutoCAD inserts the text within the specified width limit.

When you import a file for MTEXT, load the file into the editor and save it using the name *AC000512*. (the period after "AC000512" is required). When you're prompted whether you want to overwrite the existing file of the same name, enter **y** (Yes).

The following procedure describes how to create multiline text in a text editor using the default properties and formats. For information about applying formats, see "Formatting Multiline Text in a Text Editor" on page 359.

To create multiline text in a text editor

1 From the Draw menu, choose Text ➤ Multiline Text.
2 Specify the first corner of the multiline text rectangle.
3 Specify the opposite corner of the multiline text rectangle.

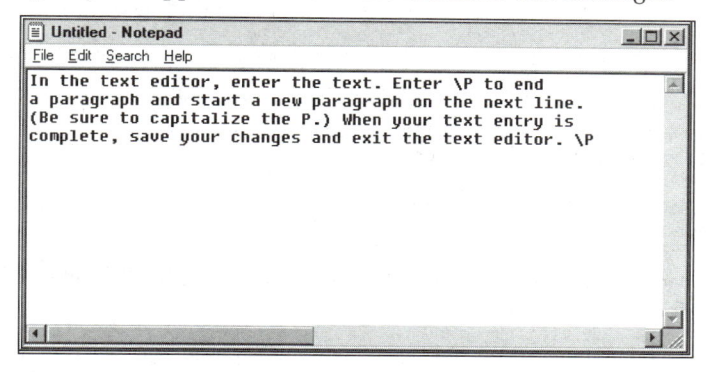

```
Untitled - Notepad
File  Edit  Search  Help
In the text editor, enter the text. Enter \P to end
a paragraph and start a new paragraph on the next line.
(Be sure to capitalize the P.) When your text entry is
complete, save your changes and exit the text editor. \P
```

4 In the text editor, enter the text. Enter **\P** to end a paragraph and start a new paragraph on the next line. (Be sure to capitalize the *P*.)
5 When your text entry is complete, save your changes and exit the text editor.

Command line MTEXT

Related Use -MTEXT to enter and format multiline text.

Formatting Multiline Text in a Text Editor

If you chose to use a third-party text editor, you can apply formatting by entering format codes. You can underline text, add a line over text, and create stacked text. You also can change color, font, and text height. You can change the spaces between text characters or increase the width of the characters themselves. To apply formatting, use the format codes shown in the following table.

Format codes for paragraphs

Format code	Purpose	Enter this...	To produce this
\O...\o	Turns overline on and off	You have \Omany\o choices	You have m̄ā̄n̄ȳ choices

Using Text Editors for Multiline Text

359

Format codes for paragraphs (continued)

Format code	Purpose	Enter this…	To produce this
\L…\l	Turns underline on and off	You have \Lmany\l choices	You have <u>many</u> choices
\~	Inserts a nonbreaking space	Keep these\~words together	Keep these words together
\\	Inserts a backslash	slash\\backslash	slash\backslash
\{…\}	Inserts an opening and closing brace	The \{bracketed\} word	The{bracketed}word
\C*value*;	Changes to the specified color	Change \C2;these colors	Change these colors
\F*ile name*;	Changes to the specified font file	Change \Ftimes;these fonts	Change these fonts
\H*value*;	Changes to the specified text height	Change \H2;these sizes	Change these sizes
\H*value*x;	Changes to multiple of mtext object's property	Change these\H3; sizes	Change these sizes
\S…^…;	Stacks the subsequent text at the \ or ^ symbol	1.000\S+0.010^-0.000;	+0.010 1.000 -0.000
\T*value*;	Adjusts the space between characters, from .75 to 4 times	\T2;TRACKING	T R A C K I N G
\Q*angle*;	Changes obliquing angle	\Q30;OBLIQUE	*OBLIQUE*
\W*value*;	Changes width factor to produce wide text	\W2;Wide	W I D E

Chapter 9   Adding Text to Drawings

Format codes for paragraphs (*continued*)

Format code	Purpose	Enter this...	To produce this
\A	Sets the alignment value; valid values: 0, 1, 2 (bottom, center, top)	\A1;Center\S1/2	`Center` $\frac{1}{2}$
\P	Ends paragraph	First paragraph\P Second paragraph	`First paragraph` `Second paragraph`

Multiline text objects use word wrap to break long lines into paragraphs. If you want AutoCAD to break lines automatically, you can create continuation lines by ending lines with either a backslash (\) or a space character.

For example, if you enter the following text into the text editor, AutoCAD treats the text as one long line and breaks the line based on the width allowed for the multiline text object:

**Note:\
See drawing C-12 for detail\
where curb meets ground.**

Use curly braces ({ }) to apply a format change only to the text within the braces, as shown in the following example:

Do {\H2\Ftimes.ttf;not} change this drawing.

Do ***not*** change this drawing.

Braces can be nested up to eight levels deep.

You also can enter control codes within lines or paragraphs to indicate formatting or special characters, such as tolerance or dimensioning symbols.

Using Text Editors for Multiline Text

361

To create the text in the following illustration from a text editor

```
Big text over text/under text

Baseline: 1 1/2

Center: 1 1/2

Topline: 1 1/2

Tolerances: 1.000 +0.010/-0.000

Architectural: 9-11/16"
```

1 From the Draw menu, choose Text ➤ Multiline Text.
2 You can change any or all of these options:

- To set justification, enter **j**. Then enter a text justification option.
- To assign a text style, enter **s**. Then specify a style. Enter **?** to see a list of style names.
- To set text boundary rotation, enter **r**. Then specify a rotation angle by entering a value on the command line or by specifying two points to define a rotation angle.
- To set text height, enter **h**. Then specify a character height (in drawing units) by entering a value on the command line or by using the pointing device to define a distance.

3 When you finish setting properties, specify an insertion point. Then define the text boundary by specifying a second point or by entering **w** and a width value or by entering **2p** and specifying two points.

4 When the text editor opens, enter each line below on a separate line in the text editor:

{\H1.5x; Big text} \A2; over text\A1;/\A0; under text}\P
{\A0;Baseline: 1 \S1/2;}\P
{\A1;Center: 1 \S1/2;}\P
{\A2;Topline: 1 \S1/2;}\P
{Tolerances: \A1;1.000\H.75x;\S+0.010^-0.000;}\P
{Architectural: 9-{\H.666x;\A2;11\A1;/\A0;16}\A2;"}\P

5 When the text entry is complete, save the changes and exit the text editor.

Command line   MTEXT

Related   Use –MTEXT to create and format multiline text on the command line.

Changing Text with an ASCII Text Editor

You can edit text using a third-party text editor by using the same format codes you used to create the original text. To avoid losing format information when you make changes to the text, use the same text editor you used to create the text.

To edit multiline text in a text editor

1 From the Modify menu, choose Object ➤ Text.
2 Select the multiline text you want to edit.
3 Enter the new text. For information about text formats, see "Formatting Multiline Text in a Text Editor" on page 359.
4 When your text entry is complete, save your changes and exit the text editor.

Command line   DDEDIT

Related   Use DDMODIFY to change the location or properties of multiline text.

To edit a multiline text object

1 From the Modify menu, choose Object ➤ Text.
2 Select the text to edit.

The text is displayed in the default full-screen editor (the Multiline Text Editor dialog box) or in a user-specified text editor.

3 To use the full-screen editor from the Multiline Text Editor dialog box, choose Full Editor.

Command line   DDEDIT

Related   MTEXTED sets the primary and secondary text editors to use for multiline text objects.

Dimensioning and Tolerancing

Dimensions add measurements to a drawing. Tolerances specify by how much a dimension can vary. With AutoCAD, dimensioning can be easily managed with dimension styles, style families, and overrides.

In this chapter

- Understanding dimensioning concepts
- Creating linear, radial, angular, and ordinate dimensions
- Adding dimensions
- Editing dimensions
- Using dimension styles, style families, and overrides
- Adding geometric tolerancing
- Creating arrowheads

Dimensioning Concepts

Dimensions show the geometric measurements of objects, the distances or angles between objects, or the *X* and *Y* coordinates of a feature. AutoCAD provides three basic types of dimensioning: linear, radial, and angular. Linear dimensions include horizontal, vertical, aligned, rotated, ordinate, baseline, and continued dimensions. A simple example of each is shown here.

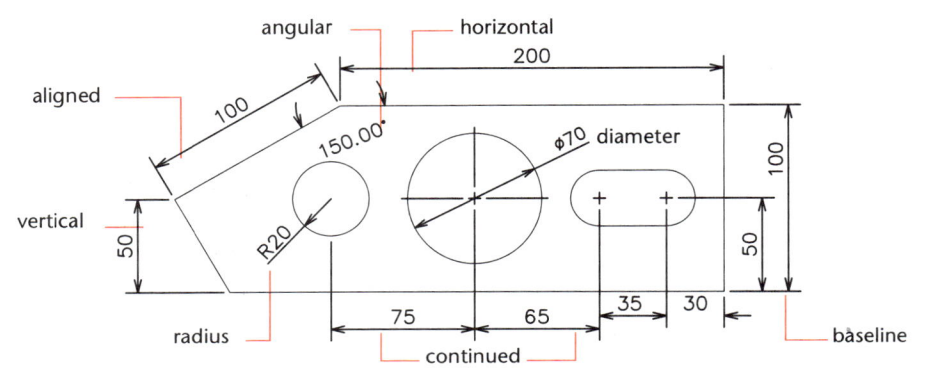

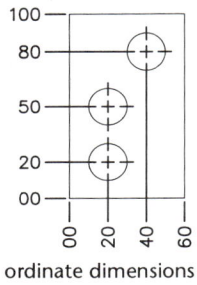

You can dimension lines, multilines, arcs, circles, and polyline segments by selecting the objects using object snaps, or you can draw dimensions that stand alone.

AutoCAD draws dimensions on the current layer. Every dimension has a dimension style associated with it, whether the default or one you define. The style controls characteristics such as color, text style, and linetype scale. Thickness information is not supported. Style families allow for subtle modifications to a base style for different types of dimensions. Overrides allow for style modifications to a specific dimension.

NOTE You can use the DIM command to access dimensioning mode as in previous releases. Dimensioning commands and variables are now available directly on the command line.

Parts of a Dimension

This section briefly defines the parts of a dimension.

Chapter 10 Dimensions and Tolerancing

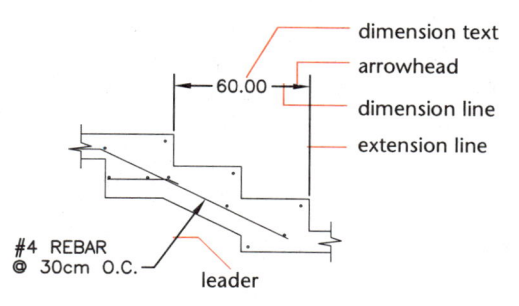

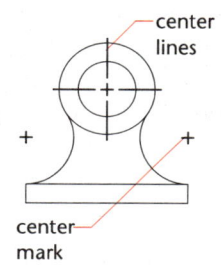

A dimension line is a line that indicates the direction and extent of a dimension. For angular dimensioning, the dimension line is an arc. Extension lines, also called projection lines or witness lines, extend from the feature being dimensioned to the dimension line. Arrowheads, also called *symbols of termination* or just *termination*, are added to each end of the dimension line. Dimension text is a text string that usually indicates the actual measurement. The text may also include prefixes, suffixes, and tolerances. A leader is a solid line leading from some annotation to the referenced feature. A center mark is a small cross that marks the center of a circle or arc. Centerlines are broken lines that mark the center of a circle or arc.

Dimensioning System Variables

The dimensioning system variables control the appearance of dimensions. You can set these variables on the command line or through the Dimension Style (DDIM) dialog boxes. For a full list of these variables and their functions and settings, see the *Command Reference*.

Dimension Text

Dimension text refers to any kind of text that is associated with dimensions, including measurements, tolerances (both lateral and geometric), prefixes, suffixes, and textual notes in single-line or paragraph form. You can use the default measurement computed by AutoCAD as the text, supply your own text, or suppress the text entirely. You can use dimension text to add information, such as special manufacturing procedures or assembly instructions.

Dimensioning Concepts

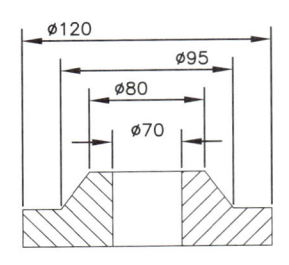

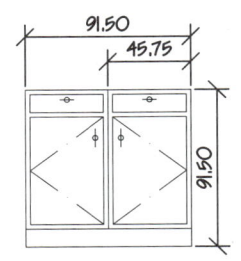

Different text styles

Single-line dimension text uses the text style you set in the DDIM Annotation dialog box. Paragraphs of text use the current style with any modifications you make in your text editor. For example, in the Multiline Text Editor dialog box, accessed with MTEXT or through the Text option of some dimensioning commands, you can underline text. See chapter 9, "Adding Text to Drawings."

Leader Lines

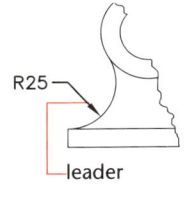

A default *leader line* is a straight line with an arrowhead that refers to a feature in a drawing. Usually, a leader's function is to connect annotation with the feature. Annotation in this case means paragraph text, blocks, or feature control frames. Such leader lines are different from the simple leader lines AutoCAD creates automatically for radial, diameter, and linear dimensions whose text won't fit between extension lines. For a description of these simple leader lines, see "Fitting Text within Extension Lines" on page 399.

Leader objects are associated with the annotation, so when the annotation is edited, the leader is updated accordingly. You can copy annotation used elsewhere in a drawing and append it to a leader, or you can create a new annotation using the LEADER command. You can also create a leader with no annotation appended (see "Leaders and Annotation" on page 377).

Associative Dimensions

Associative dimensions are dimensions in which all the lines, arrowheads, arcs, and text are drawn as a single-dimension object. The DIMASO system variable controls associative dimensioning and is on by default. If DIMASO is off, the dimension line, extension lines, arrowheads, leaders, and dimension text are drawn as separate objects. You can create a nonassociative dimension if you need to alter the dimension in ways that are not controlled by variables. In general, however, associative dimensions are easier to maintain because they can be modified as a single object.

Creating Dimensions

You can create dimensions by selecting an object to dimension (1) and specifying the dimension line location (2).

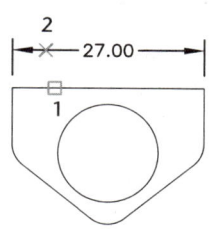

result of selecting a line to dimension

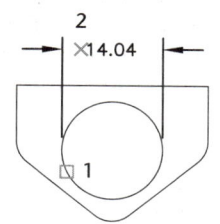

result of selecting a circle to dimension

You can also create dimensions by specifying the extension line origins. For lines, polyline segments, and arcs, the default extension line origins are the endpoints. For a circle, the endpoints of the diameter are used at the specified angle. You could also use the Quadrant snap mode, for example, to snap to adjacent quadrants of a circle.

As you create dimensions, you can modify the dimension text content and its angle relative to the dimension line. Before you create dimensions, you choose a dimension style. If you don't, the current style is used. If you haven't yet created a style, the dimension is assigned the default style, STANDARD. You can rename and modify this default style.

To select a dimension style

1 From the Dimension menu, choose Style.
2 Under Dimension Style, choose a style from the Current list.
3 Choose OK.

AutoCAD restores the style you choose and applies its settings to subsequent dimensions.

Command line DDIM

Related DIMSTYLE saves, restores, and previews dimension styles.

Linear Dimensions

Linear dimensions can be horizontal, vertical, aligned, or rotated. Aligned dimensions have the dimension line parallel to the line along which the extension line origins lie. Baseline (or parallel) and continued (or chain) dimensions are series of consecutive dimensions that can be based on a linear dimension. As you create linear dimensions, you can modify the text, the angle of the text, or the angle of the dimension line. You can also place text in any location using the User Defined option in the DDIM Format dialog box.

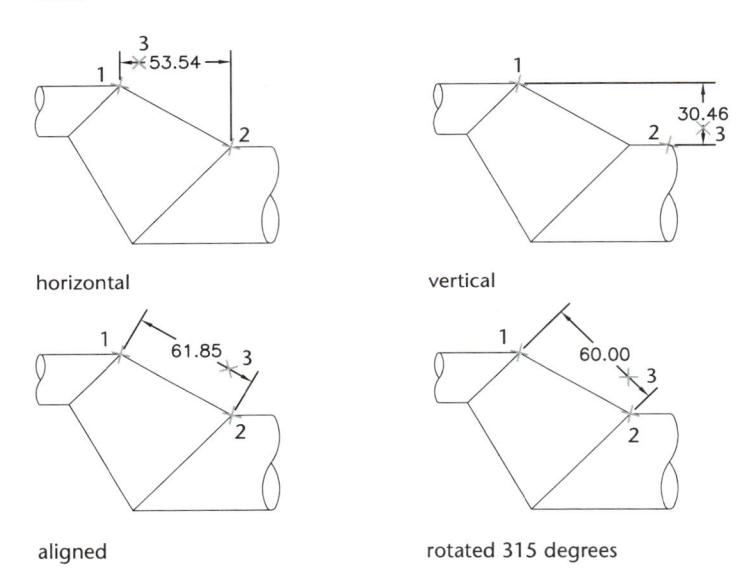

horizontal

vertical

aligned

rotated 315 degrees

In all four of these illustrations, the extension line origins are designated explicitly. The resulting dimension line location is also shown.

Horizontal and Vertical Dimensions

AutoCAD automatically applies a horizontal or vertical dimension, depending on the extension line origins you specify or the point where you select an object. However, you can override this as you create the dimension by specifying a horizontal or vertical dimension. For example, in the following illustration, a horizontal dimension is drawn by default unless you specify vertical.

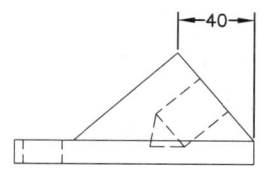

horizontal dimension
created by default

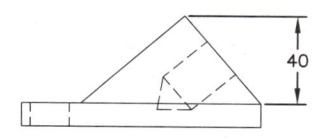

vertical dimension specified

As you create horizontal and vertical dimensions, you can modify the dimension line angle as well as the text content and angle.

To create a horizontal or vertical dimension

1 From the Dimension menu, choose Linear.
2 Press ENTER to select the object to dimension, or specify the first and second extension line origins.
3 Before specifying the dimension line location, you can override the dimension orientation and edit the text, the text angle, or the dimension line angle.

- To rotate the extension lines, enter **r** (Rotated). Then enter the dimension line angle.
- To override the default dimension orientation, enter **h** (Horizontal) or **v** (Vertical).
- To edit the text, enter **t** (Text).
- To edit text with the Multiline Text Editor, enter **m** (Mtext).
- In the Multiline Text Editor dialog box, add text in front of or after the dimension displayed between angle brackets (<>), or enter new dimension text by selecting the dimension text and entering new dimension text. Then choose OK.

  When you edit dimension text, the original text is deleted. To restore the original dimension text, enter <>.

- To rotate the text, enter **a** (Angle). Then enter the text angle.

4 Specify the dimension line location to complete the dimension.
   Command line   DIMLINEAR

Aligned Dimensions

In aligned dimensions, the dimension line is parallel to the extension line origins. The figure shows an example of aligned dimensioning. The object is selected (1), and the location of the aligned dimension is specified (2). The extension lines are drawn automatically.

Creating Dimensions

371

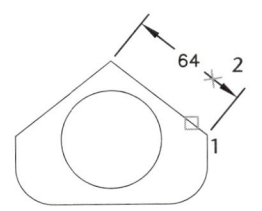

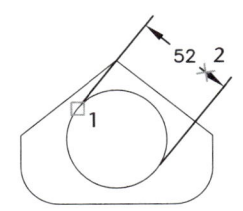

The circle uses the endpoints of the diameter for the origins of extension lines. The point where you select the circle defines one end of the diameter.

To create an aligned dimension

1. From the Dimension menu, choose Aligned.
2. Press ENTER to select the object to dimension or specify the first and second extension line origins.
3. Edit the text content or angle.
4. Specify the dimension line location.

Command line DIMALIGNED

Rotated Dimensions

In rotated dimensions, the dimension line is placed at an angle to the extension line origins. The following figure shows an example of rotated dimensioning.

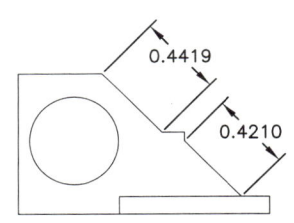

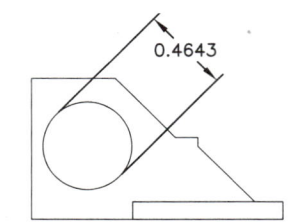

To create a rotated dimension

1. From the Dimension menu, choose Aligned.
2. Press ENTER to select the object to dimension or specify the first and second extension line origins.
3. To rotate the dimension text, enter **a** (Angle).
4. Specify the dimension line text angle.

Command line DIMALIGNED

Baseline and Continued Dimensions

Baseline dimensions are multiple dimensions measured from the same baseline. Continued dimensions are multiple dimensions placed end to end. There must already be a linear, ordinate, or angular dimension before you create baseline or continued dimensions.

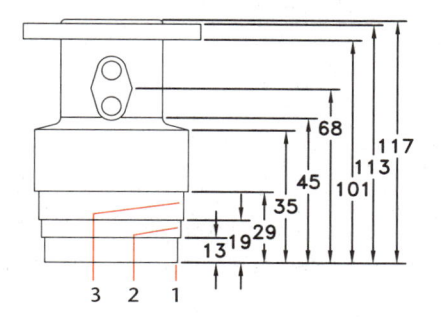

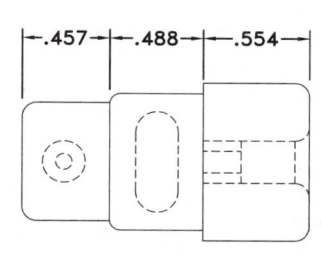

In the previous illustration, you create baseline dimensions from the initial vertical dimension (13 units). The initial vertical dimension (13 units) must be created from bottom to top. If the top extension line is created first, the baseline dimension starts from that point. For information about creating vertical dimensions, see "Horizontal and Vertical Dimensions" on page 370.

To create a baseline linear dimension

1. From the Dimension menu, choose Baseline.

   AutoCAD uses the origin of the base dimension's first extension line (1) and prompts for a second extension line origin.

2. Use the Endpoint object snap to select the end of the section (2) as the second extension line origin, or press ENTER to select any dimension as the base dimension.

   AutoCAD automatically places the second dimension above the first at the distance specified by the Spacing option in the DDIM Geometry dialog box.

3. Use the Endpoint object snap to select the next extension line origin (3).
4. Continue to select extension line origins.
5. Press ENTER twice to end the command.

   Command line   DIMBASELINE

   Related   DIMDLI controls the spacing of baseline dimension lines.

Creating continued dimensions is similar to creating baseline dimensions. The difference is that AutoCAD uses the origin of each dimension's second extension line as the origin for the next dimension's first extension line. The dimensions are aligned horizontally.

Creating Dimensions

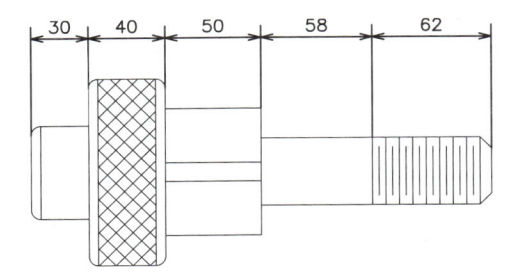

Continued dimensions

To create a continued dimension

1 From the Dimension menu, choose Continue.
2 Use the Endpoint object snap to select the end of the existing dimension as the first extension line origin.
3 Use the Endpoint object snap to select additional extension line origins.
4 Press ENTER twice to end the command.

Command line   DIMCONTINUE

Related   DIMFIT controls how text and arrowheads fit between extension lines.

Radial Dimensions

Radial dimensions measure the radii and diameters of arcs and circles with optional centerlines or a center mark. If the current style has the Fit option of Leader available, the dimension is applied with a leader line (see "Fitting Text within Extension Lines" on page 399).

To create a diameter dimension

1 From the Dimension menu, choose Diameter.
2 Select the arc or circle to dimension.
3 Enter **t** to edit the dimension text content (optional).
4 Enter **a** to edit the dimension text angle (optional).
5 Specify the dimension line location.

Command line   DIMDIAMETER creates diameter dimensions.

Related   DIMCEN controls whether center marks or lines are drawn and the size of what is drawn. (A negative value means lines are drawn at the size of the absolute value.) DIMRADIUS creates radius dimensions.

Angular Dimensions

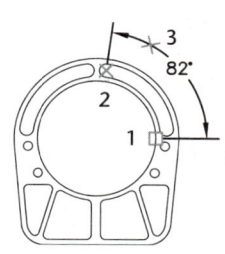

Angular dimensions measure the angle between two lines or three points. For example, you can use them to measure the angle between two radii of a circle. The dimension line forms an arc.

To dimension an angle on an arc, circle, or line, you select the object and specify the angle endpoints. You can also dimension an angle by specifying the angle vertex and endpoints. As you create the dimension, you can modify the text content and angle.

In the example, you dimension the angle by selecting the circle and specifying the angle's endpoints.

To create an angular dimension

1 From the Dimension menu, choose Angular.
2 Select the circle at the first endpoint of the angle (1).
3 Specify the second endpoint of the angle (2).
4 Enter **t** or **m** to edit the dimension text content (optional).
5 Enter **a** to edit the dimension text angle (optional).
6 Specify the dimension line arc location (3).

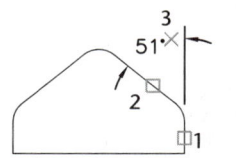

Command line   DIMANGULAR

Related   Use DIMADEC to control the number of places of precision displayed for angular dimensions.

To dimension the angle between two lines, select a line (1), a second line (2), and the location of the dimension line arc (3).

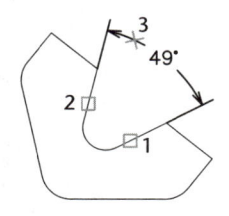

If you use two straight, nonparallel lines to specify an angle, the dimension line arc spans the angle between the two lines. If the arc doesn't meet one or both of the lines being dimensioned, AutoCAD draws one or two extension lines to intersect the dimension line arc. The arc is always less than 180 degrees.

If you use an arc or circle or select three points to specify an angle, AutoCAD draws the dimension line arc between the extension lines. The extension lines are drawn from the angle endpoints to intersect of the dimension line arc.

AutoCAD uses the location of the dimension line arc to choose between the minor and major angles specified by the angle vertex and extension lines.

Creating Dimensions

Ordinate Dimensions

Ordinate, or datum, dimensions measure the perpendicular distance from an origin point, called the datum, to a dimensioned feature, such as a hole in a part. These dimensions prevent escalating errors by maintaining accurate offsets of the features from the datum.

Ordinate dimensions consist of an *X* or *Y* ordinate with a leader line. *X*-datum ordinate dimensions measure the distance of a feature from the datum along the *X* axis. *Y*-datum ordinate dimensions measure the same distance along the *Y* axis. If you specify a point, AutoCAD automatically determines whether it is an *X*- or *Y*-datum ordinate dimension. This is called an *automatic* ordinate dimension. If the difference between the feature location and the leader endpoint is greater in the *Y* coordinate, the dimension measures the *X* coordinate. Otherwise, it measures the *Y* coordinate. AutoCAD uses the origin of the current UCS to determine the measured coordinates. The absolute value of the coordinate is used.

The text is aligned with the ordinate leader line regardless of the text orientation defined by the current dimension style. You can accept the default text or supply your own.

In the following procedure, you measure the coordinates of the circles' centers in relation to the datum (1) in the figure. In this case, the datum coordinates are (0,0).

To find out the *Y* ordinate of a datum

1 From the Dimension menu, choose Ordinate to start the DIMORDINATE command.
2 At the Select Feature prompt, enter **int** to use the Intersection object snap.
3 Specify the intersection (1).
4 Turn Ortho mode on to ensure straight ordinate leaders.
5 Enter **y** (Y Datum).
6 Specify the ordinate leader endpoint (2).
7 Press ENTER to accept the measured coordinate text (0.00).

To find out the *X* coordinate of the datum

1 From the Dimension menu, choose Ordinate to start the DIMORDINATE command.
2 At the Select Feature prompt, enter **int** to use the Intersection object snap.
3 Specify the intersection (1).
4 Specify the ordinate leader endpoint (3) and press ENTER.

You can now use ordinate dimensions to show the relative *X* and *Y* coordinates of the circles' centers. Using the circles you have created in the previous example, you can now use the Center object snap to specify the centers.

To create ordinate dimensions

1 From the Dimension menu, choose Ordinate.
2 At the Select Feature prompt, enter **cen** to use the Center object snap.
3 Select the first circle (4) to snap to its center.
4 Specify the leader endpoint (5).
5 Repeat steps 1 to 4 for the other two circles in the example.
6 To create *X*-datum ordinate dimensions for the circles' centers, repeat step 1, choosing X-datum instead of Y-datum. Then repeat steps 1 to 4 for each circle.

Command line   DIMORDINATE

Leaders and Annotation

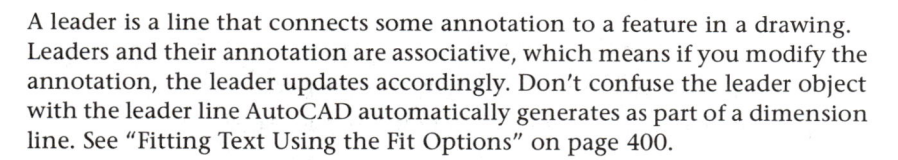

A leader is a line that connects some annotation to a feature in a drawing. Leaders and their annotation are associative, which means if you modify the annotation, the leader updates accordingly. Don't confuse the leader object with the leader line AutoCAD automatically generates as part of a dimension line. See "Fitting Text Using the Fit Options" on page 400.

Creating a Leader Line

You can create a leader line from any point or feature in a drawing and control its appearance as you draw it. Leaders can be straight line segments or smooth spline curves. Leader color is controlled by the current dimension line color. Leader scale is controlled by the overall dimension scale set in the current dimension style. The type and size of arrowhead, if one is present, is controlled by the first arrowhead defined in the current style.

A small line known as a hook line usually connects the annotation to the leader. Hook lines appear with multiline text and feature control frames if the last leader line segment is at an angle greater than 15 degrees from horizontal. The hook line is the length of a single arrowhead. If the leader has no annotation, it has no hook line. You can use the object snap modes to specify the start point of a leader accurately.

Adding the Annotation

Leader annotations can be multiline text, a feature control frame, or a block reference. You can create a new annotation, or you can append a copy of existing annotation.

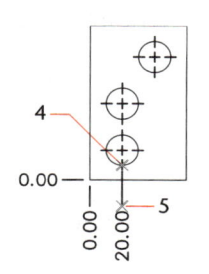

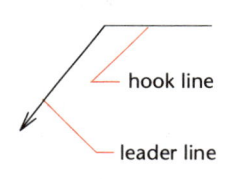

Creating Dimensions

377

Text annotation can be entered either on the command line a line at a time or in the Multiline Text Editor dialog box. If you enter text on the command line, it is created as *no word-wrap* text (its width is set to zero).

Text or feature control frame annotation is placed at a specified offset from the final endpoint of the leader. You specify this offset in the DDIM Annotation dialog box under Text Gap. Blocks are inserted at the location, scale, and rotation you specify. For more information, see "Inserting Blocks" on page 438.

Use the Vertical Justification options in the DDIM Format dialog box to align the annotation vertically with the leader. In the following figure, the vertical justification is Above.

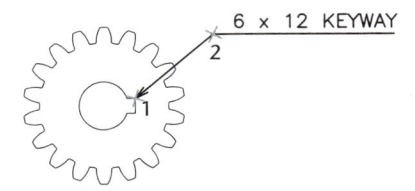

To create a simple leader with text

1 From the Dimension menu, choose Leader.
2 Specify the From and To points of the leader.
3 Press ENTER to end the point acquisition.
4 Enter the lines of text.
5 Press ENTER again to end the command.

NOTE After the LEADER command is completed, the text annotation becomes an Mtext object and cannot be edited using the DIMSTYLE or DIMOVERRIDE commands (see "Editing Leader Annotation" on page 380).

Command line LEADER

Related DIMCLRD controls leader color. DIMSCALE controls leader scale. DIMBLK controls the leader arrowhead if first and second dimension arrowheads are the same. DIMBLK1 controls the leader arrowhead if DIMSAH is on. DIMTXSTY controls the initial text style. DIMTXT controls its initial text height. DIMCLRT controls its initial text color.

The next procedure shows how to create a spline leader and append a paragraph of formatted text. The spline control points are determined by the leader vertices, each of which is given equal unit weight. To create and format the text paragraph, you can use the Multiline Text Editor dialog box or whatever editor you have set with the MTEXTED system variable (see "Using Multiline Text" on page 338).

To create a spline leader with a paragraph of formatted text

1 From the Dimension menu, choose Leader.
2 Specify the start point of the leader.
3 Specify the second point of the leader.
4 Enter **f** (Format).
5 Enter **s** (Spline).
6 Continue to specify points, or press ENTER to end the leader. You do not have to specify end tangent points as you do for ordinary splines.

Now add the paragraph of text.

1 At the Annotation prompt, press ENTER for the options.
2 Press ENTER to open the Multiline Text Editor dialog box and append paragraph text.
3 Using the text editor, format and enter the text.

When you exit the editor, the text is appended to the leader endpoint at the specified offset. Specify this offset in the DDIM Annotation dialog box under Text Gap.

NOTE DIMGAP controls the offset of paragraph text and feature control frames from the endpoint of the leader or hook line. To create a box around the text, set DIMGAP to a negative value. The offset between the box and the text is the absolute value of DIMGAP.

The next procedure shows how to append a feature control frame to a leader. The feature control frame is placed at an insertion point you specify and is associated with the leader. For information about how to create a feature control frame, see "Adding Geometric Tolerances" on page 424.

To append a feature control frame to a leader

1 From the Dimension menu, choose Leader.
2 Specify the start point of the leader.
3 Specify the second point of the leader.
4 Press ENTER twice to reach the Annotation options.
5 Enter **t** (Tolerance).
6 In the Symbol dialog box, select a symbol and choose OK.

7 In the Geometric Tolerance dialog box, continue to create the feature control frame. Then choose OK.

The feature control frame is attached to the endpoint of the leader.

Leader Associativity

Leaders are associated with their annotation so that when the annotation moves, the endpoint of the leader moves with it. As you move text and feature control frame annotation, the final leader line segment alternates between attaching to the left side and to the right side of the annotation according to the relation of the annotation to the penultimate (second to last) point of the leader. If the midpoint of the annotation is to the right of the penultimate leader point, then the leader attaches to the right; otherwise, it attaches to the left.

You can adjust the attach point of the leader by gripping the final leader endpoint and moving it. This point is retained through later edits of the annotation unless you move the annotation midpoint past the penultimate leader point, in which case the leader reattaches to the default point on the other side.

Removing either object from the drawing using ERASE, BLOCK, WBLOCK, or EXPLODE will break associativity. If the leader and its annotation are copied together in a single operation, the new copy will be associative. If they are copied separately, they will not be associative. If associativity is broken for any reason, for example, by copying only the leader object or by erasing the annotation object, the hook line will be removed from the leader.

Editing Leader Annotation

Except for the associativity relation between the leader and annotation, the leader and its annotation are entirely separate objects in your drawing. Editing of the leader does not affect the annotation, and editing of the annotation does not affect the leader.

Although text annotation is created using the DIMCLRT, DIMTXT, and DIMTXSTY system variables, to define its color, height, and style, it cannot be changed by these system variables, because it is not a true dimension object. Text annotation must be edited the same way as any other multiline text object.

Editing Leaders

Any modifications to leader annotation that change its position affects the position of the endpoint of the associated leader. Also, rotating the annotation causes the leader hook line (if any) to rotate.

Leaders can function as edges for TRIM and EXTEND, but they can't be trimmed or extended themselves. To resize a leader, you can stretch or scale it. Stretching modifies the offset between the leader endpoint and the annotation. Scaling updates only the scale of the selected object. For example, if you scale the leader, the annotation stays in the same position relative to the leader endpoint but isn't scaled.

Adding Dimensions

Dimensioning is the process of adding dimensions and tolerances to a drawing. Dimensions show the lengths of objects or the distances or angles between objects. AutoCAD provides five basic types of dimensioning: linear, angular, diameter, radius, and ordinate. Linear dimensions include horizontal, vertical, and aligned.

To create a horizontal dimension

1 From the Dimension menu, choose Linear.

2 Press ENTER and select the horizontal length to dimension (1).

AutoCAD dimensions a horizontal or vertical length, according to the dimension line location you specify. If horizontal is selected, a horizontal dimension is drawn.

3 Specify the dimension line location point (2).

Because you specified a point *below* the object, and not vertically to either side, AutoCAD places a horizontal dimension at this location with the default measurement text.

Command line DIMLINEAR

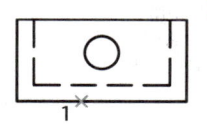

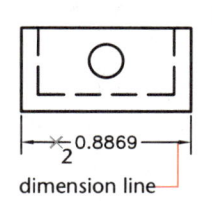

Editing Dimensions

You can edit dimensions with the AutoCAD editing commands and grip editing modes. Grip editing is the quickest and easiest way to modify dimensions. You can also modify dimensions by applying dimension style overrides (see "Using Style Overrides" on page 418).

When you edit dimensioned objects with the editing commands, you must include the relevant dimension definition points in the selection set in order for the dimensions to be updated correctly. Definition points are points that determine the dimension locations. For example, to scale a dimensioned polyline, select the polyline and definition points of the dimension with a crossing selection. Selecting the polyline with the pointing device does not update the associated dimension. To include definition points more easily, snap to them using the Node snap mode (see "Object Snaps" on page 164).

Grip points are located at the definition points, which is why grip editing is the simplest way to modify dimensions.

The definition points for each type of dimension are circled in the following illustrations. The middle point of the dimension text is also a definition point for all dimension types.

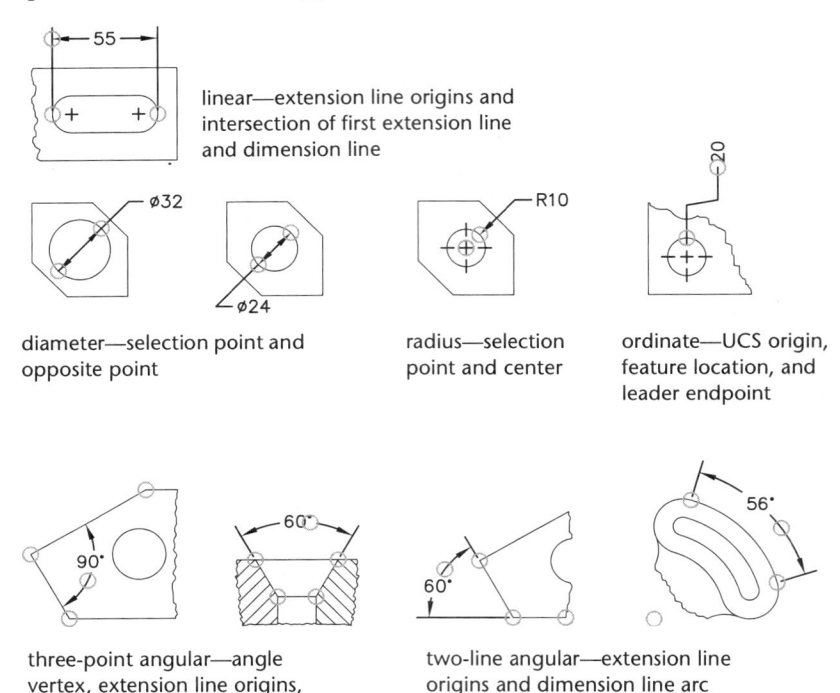

linear—extension line origins and intersection of first extension line and dimension line

diameter—selection point and opposite point

radius—selection point and center

ordinate—UCS origin, feature location, and leader endpoint

three-point angular—angle vertex, extension line origins, and dimension line arc

two-line angular—extension line origins and dimension line arc

If no angle vertex is shown, AutoCAD places definition points at the ends of the lines that form the angle. In the two-line angular example, because an arc is being dimensioned, AutoCAD places a definition point at the center of the arc.

Definition points are drawn on a special layer named DEFPOINTS that does not plot. If you want to plot definition points, rename the DEFPOINTS layer. AutoCAD creates a new DEFPOINTS layer for any subsequent dimensions in your drawing.

If you are dimensioning in paper space, note that associative dimensions are not associated with their model space objects and will not update when you modify these objects in paper space.

Chapter 10 Dimensions and Tolerancing

Some editing commands change the definition points of the dimension. For example, the definition points of a stretched or rotated dimension change because the object itself has changed. If the dimension is copied or arrayed, the definition points remain the same, because the dimensioned object has not been changed.

Stretching Dimensions

To stretch a dimension, you must include the appropriate definition point in the selection set, which you can most easily do by turning on grips and selecting the object so the grips are highlighted. For example, the center point of dimension text is a definition point, so you can move the dimension text anywhere as long as you select this point, as shown with the crossing window here.

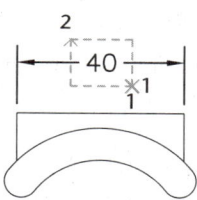

text definition point
selected to edit text

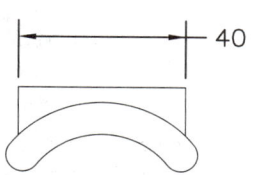

dimension line rejoined when
no longer split by text

If you move the text so that it no longer requires the dimension line to be split, the dimension line rejoins.

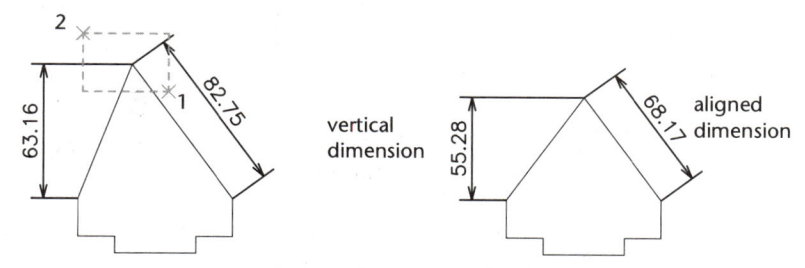

vertical
dimension

aligned
dimension

In the previous illustration, you stretch the top vertex of the triangle. You must include definition points for the aligned and vertical dimensions in the crossing selection window so that the dimensions are stretched as well.

Editing Dimensions

383

To stretch a dimension

1. From the Modify menu, choose Stretch.
2. Select the vertex of the triangle and definition points for each dimension by using a crossing selection window (1, 2).
3. Specify the top vertex of the triangle as the base point of displacement.
4. Specify the second point of displacement.

Command line   STRETCH

The dimension type (aligned, horizontal, or vertical) is retained after stretching. Notice that the aligned dimension realigns and is remeasured. The vertical dimension, however, still measures the vertical distance from the triangle base to the top vertex.

Trimming and Extending Dimensions

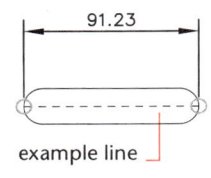

You can trim and extend all forms of linear and ordinate dimensions. To trim or extend a linear dimension, AutoCAD draws an example line between the two extension line definition points.

AutoCAD trims or extends the example line and then adjusts the dimension accordingly. To trim or extend an ordinate dimension, AutoCAD moves the feature location point (2) to the boundary edge perpendicular to the measured ordinate (1), so the ordinate value remains unchanged.

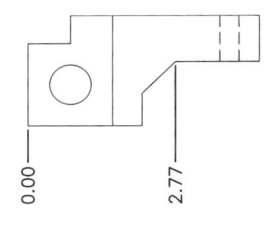

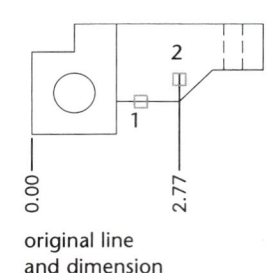

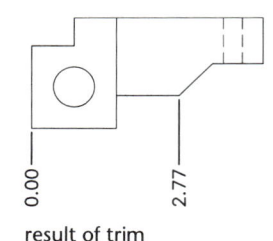

original line and dimension

result of trim

To extend a dimension

1. From the Modify menu, choose Extend.
2. Select the object that is the boundary edge (1).
3. Select the dimension as the object to extend (2).

Command line   EXTEND

If the edited object is not parallel to the dimension definition points, as shown in the following illustration, the imaginary line technique used by AutoCAD probably will not produce the result you want. The following figure illustrates extending a linear dimension. The dimension extends to where the imaginary line meets the selected feature (1).

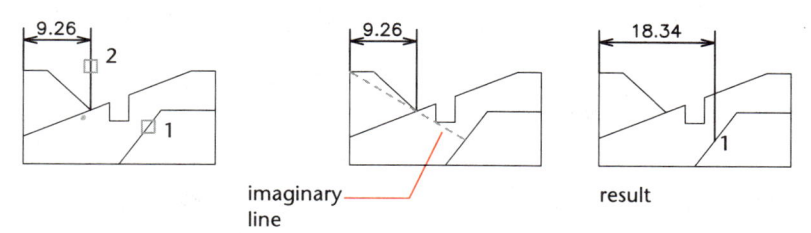

imaginary line

result

In these situations, stretch the dimension rather than trimming or extending it.

You cannot trim a dimension and split it in two by cutting a portion out of the middle.

Making Dimensions Oblique

AutoCAD creates extension lines perpendicular to the dimension line. However, if the extension lines conflict with other objects in a drawing, you can change their angle. New dimensions are not affected when you make an existing dimension oblique.

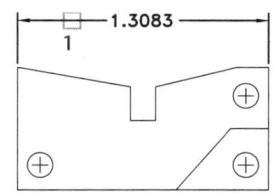

select an existing dimension

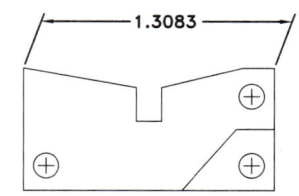

after entering an oblique angle of 70

To create oblique extension lines

1 From the Dimension menu, choose Oblique.
2 Select the dimension.
3 Enter the angle directly or by specifying two points.

Command line   DIMEDIT

Editing Dimension Text

Once you've created a dimension, you can rotate the existing text or replace it with new text. You can move the text to a new location or back to its home position, which is the position defined by the current style. In the following illustration, the home position is above and centered horizontally on the dimension line.

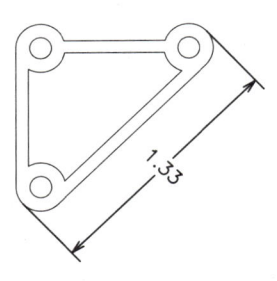

dimension text rotated

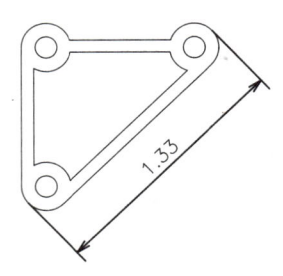

dimension text moved back to home position

When you rotate or replace dimension text, you specify the change first, for example, a rotation angle. You can then select any number of existing dimensions to apply this change to before pressing ENTER to end selection in the usual way. When you move dimension text, you can select only a single dimension.

To rotate dimension text

1 At the Command prompt, enter **dimedit**.
2 Enter **r** for rotate.
3 Enter the new angle for the text.
4 Select the dimensions to edit.

Related Rotate the dimension text of a single dimension with the Angle option of DIMTEDIT.

To return dimension text to its home position

1 From the Dimension menu, choose Align Text ➤ Home.
2 Select the dimension text to return to its home position.

To replace existing dimension text with new text

1 At the Command prompt, enter **dimedit**.
2 Enter **n** (New).
3 In the Multiline Text Editor dialog box, enter the new dimension text by adding text in front of or after the dimension displayed between angle brackets (<>) or by selecting the dimension text and entering a new dimension. Then choose OK.
4 Select the dimensions to apply the new text to.

You can move dimension text to the left, right, or center positions on the dimension line or to any position inside or outside the extension lines. A quick and simple way to do this is with grip editing. If you move text up or down, the current vertical justification of the text relative to the dimension line is not changed, so the dimension and extension lines are modified accordingly. The following illustration shows the result of moving text down and to the right. The text remains centered vertically on the dimension line.

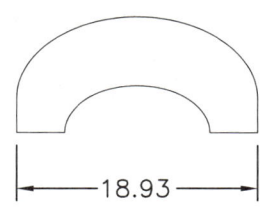

text centered vertically on the dimension line

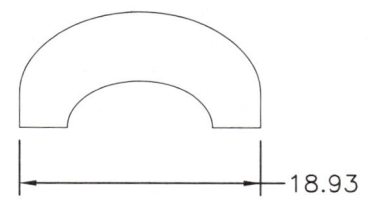

result of moving text down, to the right, and outside the extension lines

This procedure shows how to move the dimension text to the left of the dimension line.

To move dimension text to the left of the dimension line

1 From the Dimension menu, choose Align Text ➤ Left.
2 Select the dimension, and then use the preceeding illustration to move the dimension text.

If there is room for the text to move, it moves to the left on the dimension line.

Command line   DIMTEDIT

Related   Choose the Center or Right options to move the text to the center or right on the dimension line, or use grip editing to move the text to any location.

Editing Dimensions

Creating Dimension Styles

A named dimension style is a group of settings that determine the appearance of the dimension. Using named dimension styles, you can establish and enforce drafting standards for drawings.

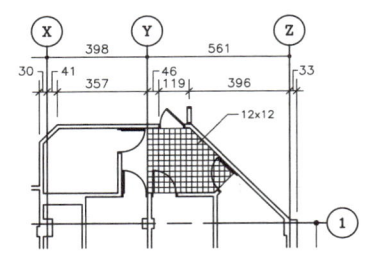

Dimension styles

All dimensions are created using the current style. If you don't define or apply a style before creating dimensions, AutoCAD applies the default style, STANDARD. The dimensioning system variables are controlled by the settings in the DDIM dialog boxes.

To set up a parent dimension style, you begin by naming and saving a style. The new style is based on the current style and will include all subsequent changes to the layout of the dimension parts (DDIM Geometry dialog box), the positioning of text (DDIM Format dialog box), and the appearance of annotation (DDIM Annotation dialog box). Annotation in this case means primary and alternate units, tolerances, and text.

To create a parent dimension style

1 From the Dimension menu, choose Style.

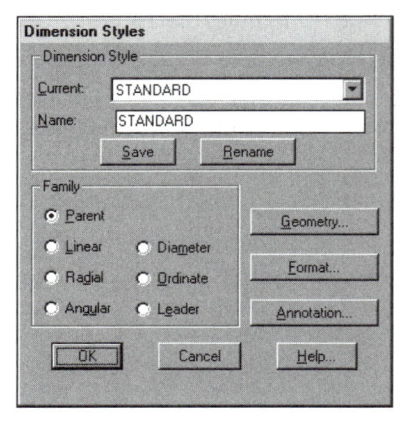

2 In the Dimension Styles dialog box, enter a style name and choose Save.

Note that under Family, Parent is selected by default, indicating that you're creating a parent style.

3 Choose Geometry to define the appearance and behavior of the dimension line, extension lines, arrowheads, and center marks or lines, and the scale of the dimension (see the next section, "Controlling Dimension Geometry").

4 Choose Format to define the positioning of the dimension text (see "Controlling Dimension Format" on page 398).

5 Choose Annotation to define the primary and alternate units, tolerances, text style, gap, and color and the rounding-off value (see "Controlling Dimension Text" on page 406).

6 In the Dimension Styles dialog box, select Save to save your changes to the new style. Then choose OK.

Command line   DDIM

Related   DIMSTYLE creates, saves, restores, applies, and displays the settings of dimension styles from the command line. The DIMSTYLE dimensioning system variable stores the name of the current dimension style. Use SETVAR to set this system variable.

Controlling Dimension Geometry

Dimension geometry refers to the extension lines, dimension lines, arrowheads, and center marks or lines. You control the appearance of these parts of the dimension in the DDIM Geometry dialog box.

You can also set the scale of the dimension sizes, distances, and offsets here. This scale setting does not affect tolerances, measured lengths, coordinates, or angles.

To control dimension geometry

1 From the Dimension menu, choose Style.

2 In the Dimension Styles dialog box, choose Geometry.

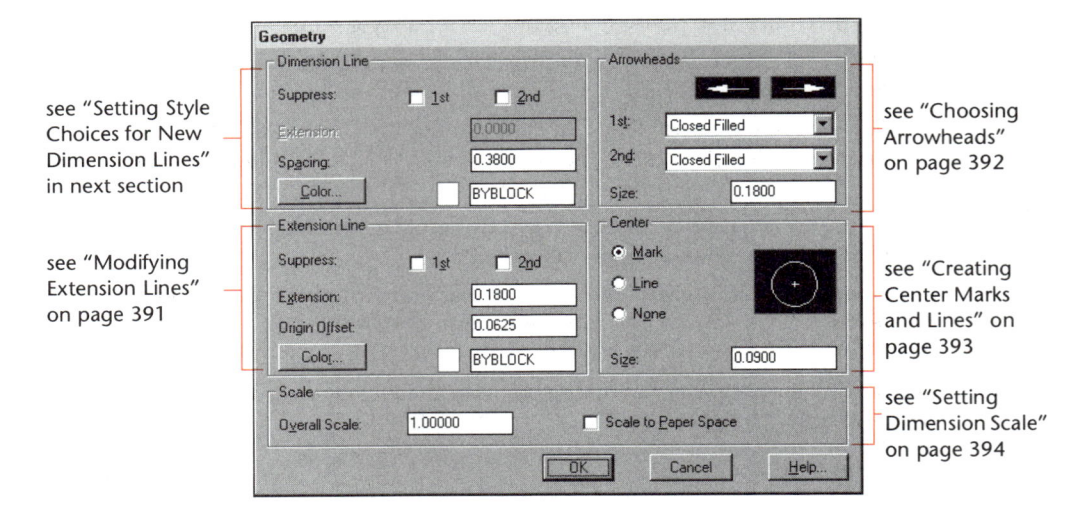

see "Setting Style Choices for New Dimension Lines" in next section

see "Modifying Extension Lines" on page 391

see "Choosing Arrowheads" on page 392

see "Creating Center Marks and Lines" on page 393

see "Setting Dimension Scale" on page 394

The following section describes the modifications you can make to dimension lines.

Setting Style Choices for New Dimension Lines

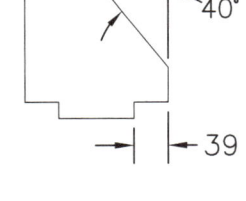

There are several aspects of the dimension line that you can control. When using oblique stroke arrowheads, you can set the distance which the dimension line extends beyond the extension lines. For baseline dimensions, you can control the spacing between successive dimension lines. If text divides a dimension line in two, you can control the visibility of each part of the dimension line. You can also give the dimension line a specific color.

The order of dimension lines is determined by the order of extension lines. The first extension line is on the side where you specify the first extension line origin. If the dimension line is split, the first dimension line is on this side too.

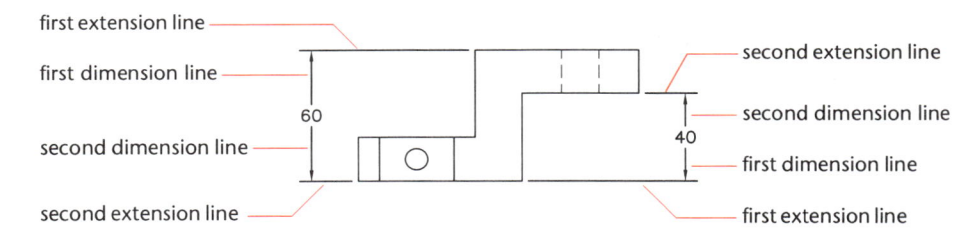

Chapter 10 Dimensions and Tolerancing

390

Use the following example illustration to set the dimension line spacing for baseline and continued dimensions so that the dimension text is easily readable.

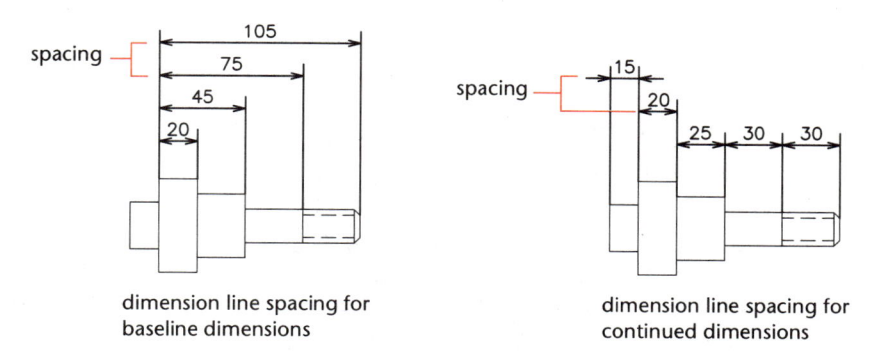

dimension line spacing for baseline dimensions

dimension line spacing for continued dimensions

To set dimension line spacing

1 From the Dimension menu, choose Style.
2 In the Dimension Styles dialog box, choose Geometry.
3 In the Geometry dialog box, under Dimension Line, enter a distance for spacing between dimension lines for baseline and continued dimensions.

Related DIMDLE controls the distance dimension lines extend beyond the extension lines when oblique stroke arrowheads are used. DIMDLI controls the spacing of dimension lines in baseline dimensions. DIMCLRD controls dimension line color.

Modifying Extension Lines

You can control several aspects of the extension lines. You can give them a specific color from the Select Color dialog box. If extension lines are unnecessary or there is no space for them, you can suppress one or both. You can specify how far beyond the dimension line the extension line extends. You can control the distance between the extension line origin and the start of the extension line, which is known as the extension origin offset.

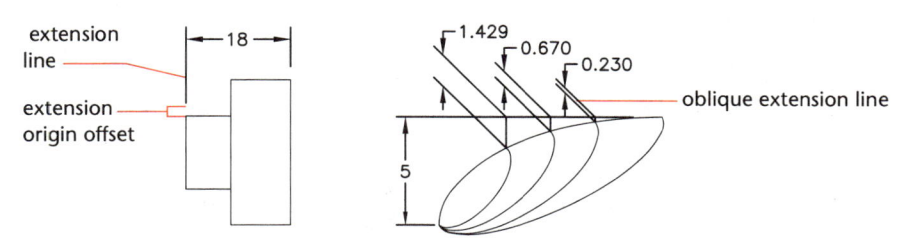

Creating Dimension Styles

391

Extension lines are normally perpendicular to the dimension line. However, when space is limited you can make linear dimensions oblique (see "Making Dimensions Oblique" on page 385).

To change the extension origin offset

1 From the Dimension menu, choose Style.
2 In the Dimension Styles dialog box, choose Geometry.
3 In the Geometry dialog box, under Extension Line, enter the new value for Origin Offset.

Related   DIMSE1 and DIMSE2 control suppression of first and second extension lines. DIMEXE controls the distance extension lines extend beyond the dimension line. DIMEXO controls extension origin offset. DIMCLRE controls extension line color.

Choosing Arrowheads

Drafting standards for termination symbols differ. AutoCAD provides eighteen standard types of arrowhead. You can apply a different type to each end of the dimension line and control the size of each. In the Geometry dialog box under Arrowheads, the first arrowhead is displayed in the *left* image tile and the second in the *right*. The order of arrowheads is determined by the order of extension lines. The first extension line is where you specify the first extension line origin when you are creating the dimension. For angular dimensioning, the second extension line is counterclockwise from the first. Leader lines use the first arrowhead (see "Leaders and Annotation" on page 377).

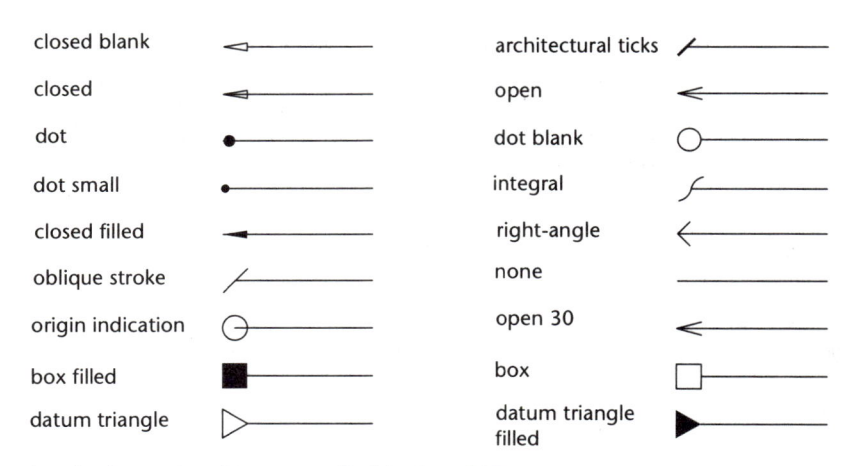

closed blank		architectural ticks	
closed		open	
dot		dot blank	
dot small		integral	
closed filled		right-angle	
oblique stroke		none	
origin indication		open 30	
box filled		box	
datum triangle		datum triangle filled	

Standard arrowhead types supplied by AutoCAD

The first arrowhead type automatically applies to the second arrowhead unless you select a different type for the second arrowhead. You can choose not to use any arrowhead or one arrowhead only. You can also create your own arrowheads (See "Creating and Modifying Arrowheads" on page 429).

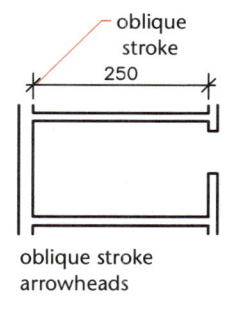

The following procedure shows how to choose oblique stroke arrowheads for both ends of the dimension line and how to set the stroke size. Oblique strokes, also known as tick marks, are short lines drawn where the dimension line meets the extension lines and at a 45-degree angle with respect to the dimension line. Arrowhead size is determined by the size set in the DDIM Geometry dialog box (DIMASZ) and is measured in the current units, which are set by the DDUNITS command.

When using oblique strokes, you can specify the distance that the dimension line extends past the extension line (see "Setting Style Choices for New Dimension Lines" on page 390).

To choose an arrowhead

1 From the Dimension menu, choose Style.

2 In the Dimension Styles dialog box, choose Geometry.

3 In the Geometry dialog box under Arrowheads, select the desired arrowhead style.

The second arrowhead is automatically set to the selected arrowhead style.

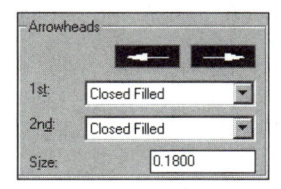

4 In the Size box, enter a size for the arrowhead.

Related   DIMBLK1 and DIMBLK2 control the first and second arrowhead types (if DIMSAH is on). DIMASZ controls the arrowhead size. DIMCLRD controls arrowhead color. DIMDLE controls the distance dimension lines extend beyond the extension lines. DIMTSZ specifies the size of oblique strokes drawn instead of arrowheads.

Creating Center Marks and Lines

Center marks and lines apply only to diameter and radius dimensions. They are drawn only if the dimension line is placed outside the circle or arc.

center marks

centerlines

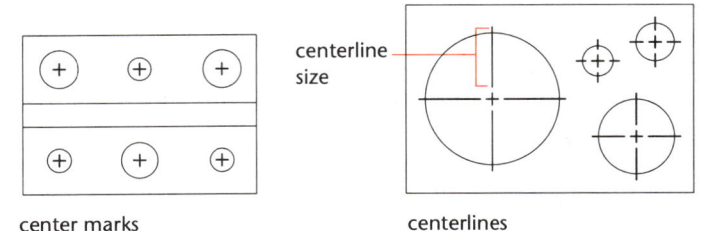

The size of the centerline refers to the length of the centerline segments extending from the center mark.

To create centerlines

1 From the Dimension menu, choose Style.
2 In the Dimension Styles dialog box, choose Geometry.
3 In the Geometry dialog box under Center, select Line.

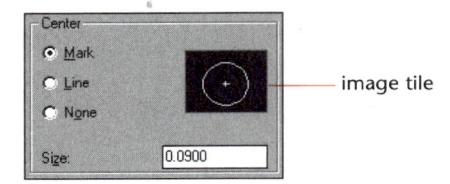

image tile

The image tile shows a sample of the selection. Click the image tile to cycle through the Center options.

4 In the Size box, enter the centerline size.
5 Choose OK to exit each dialog box.

Command line DIMCENTER

Related DIMDIAMETER and DIMRADIUS create center marks and lines if the dimension line is placed outside the circle or arc and the dimension style defines center marks or lines. DIMCEN stores the sizes of the center marks and lines. DIMCEN is 0 when no mark or lines are selected, positive when center marks are selected, and negative when centerlines are selected.

Setting Dimension Scale

Dimension scale is defined by the Overall Scale (the DIMSCALE system variable) value you set in the DDIM Geometry dialog box. It affects the size of the dimension geometry relative to the drawing, *not* the value of the dimension measurements, and it should be set according to the intended plot scaling. Dimension scale affects sizes, such as text height and arrowhead size, and offsets, such as the extension line origin offset. You should set these sizes and offsets to values that represent their actual plotted size. AutoCAD does not apply the overall scale factor to tolerances or measured lengths, coordinates, or angles. To scale these features, see "Adding Primary Units" on page 407.

You can also set a scale relative to paper space. This scale adjusts dimensions in model space to the scale of the paper space view. If you're working directly in paper space (TILEMODE is set to 0), AutoCAD uses the default scale factor of 1.0. If you choose to scale in paper space only, AutoCAD computes this scale automatically, and the overall scale option is not available.

The dimension scale is independent of the drawing scale, although they should be identical. For more information about the drawing scale, see "Determining the Scale Factor" on page 99. Changing the drawing scale might cause dimension text and arrowheads to appear at inappropriate sizes. For example, in a large facilities management drawing, arrowheads at the default size are invisible. Set text height and arrowhead size to the actual sizes you want. These values are then multiplied by the overall dimension scale.

You can set scalar dimension variables, such as dimension text and arrowhead sizes, to the actual size that you want in your plotted output. The following table shows the relationship of the dimension scale factor and the plot scale.

Relation between dimension scaling, plot scale, and output text height

Drawing text height (DIMTXT)	Dimension scale factor (DIMSCALE)	Plot scale (plotted units: drawing units)	Plotted text height
0.25	1	1:1	0.25
0.25	1	1:2	0.125
0.25	2	1:2	0.25
0.25	1	2:1	0.5

The relationship can be summarized as follows:

$$\text{PlottedHeight} = \text{DIMTXTX} \frac{\text{PlotUnits}}{\text{DrawingUnits}} \text{XDIMSCALE}$$

This relationship applies to other scalar dimension variables, such as arrowhead size.

Creating Dimension Styles

To set the overall dimension scale

1 From the Dimension menu, choose Style.
2 In the Dimension Styles dialog box, choose Geometry.
3 In the Geometry dialog box under Scale, enter a value for the overall scale.
4 Choose OK to exit each dialog box.

Related DIMSCALE stores the overall scale value. When the scale is relative to paper space, DIMSCALE is 0. DIMLFAC stores the global scale factor for linear dimensioning measurements. DIMLFAC has no effect on angular dimensions.

Dimensioning in Model Space and Paper Space

If you're dimensioning in paper space and the global scale factor for linear dimensioning (the DIMLFAC system variable) is set at less than zero, the distance measured is multiplied by the absolute value of DIMLFAC. If you're dimensioning in model space, the value of 1.0 is used even if DIMLFAC is less than zero. AutoCAD computes a value for DIMLFAC if you change the variable at the Dim prompt and select the Viewport option. AutoCAD calculates the scaling of model space to paper space and assigns the negative of this value to DIMLFAC.

Using the DIMLFAC dimensioning system variable, you can automatically adjust the dimension length scale factor to the zoom scale factor of a model space viewport. This is possible only from paper space, and you must enter dimensioning mode with the DIM command. This method does not work for ordinate dimensions.

To set dimension scale in paper space

1 Set TILEMODE to 0 (paper space).
2 At the Command prompt, enter **dimlfac**.
3 At the Current Value prompt, enter a new dimension scale value.

You can draw dimensions in both paper space and model space. However, if the geometry you're dimensioning is in model space, it's better to draw dimensions in model space, because AutoCAD places the definition points in the space where the geometry is drawn.

If you draw a dimension in paper space that describes geometry in your model, the paper space dimension does *not* change when you use editing commands or change the magnification of the display in the model space viewport. The location of the paper space dimensions also stays the same when you change a view from paper space to model space.

To dimension in floating viewports

1. Set the current layer to one that is visible only in the chosen viewport.
2. In the DDIM Geometry dialog box, select Scale to Paper Space.
3. Dimension the object.

NOTE Before you add dimensions, be sure you have zoomed to the correct scale factor. For information about scaling views relative to paper space, see "Scaling Views Relative to Paper Space" on page 488.

AutoCAD computes a scale factor based on the scaling between paper space and the current model space viewport.

You may prefer to work in model space but use the dimensioning capabilities of paper space. You can accomplish this by performing the following procedure.

To dimension in model space for layout in paper space

1. From the Dimension menu, choose Style.
2. In the Dimension Styles dialog box, choose Geometry.
3. In the Geometry dialog box under Scale, enter a value for the overall scale.

    For information about setting dimension scale, see "Setting Dimension Scale" on page 394.
4. Choose OK to exit each dialog box.
5. Add the dimensions to the drawing using the scale you've just defined.

When you're ready to view or plot your drawing in paper space, continue with the following steps.

1. Set TILEMODE to 0 (paper space).
2. Switch to a model space viewport.

Creating Dimension Styles

397

For more information on model space viewports, see "Creating Floating Viewports" on page 481 and "Scaling Views Relative to Paper Space" on page 488.

3 From the Dimension menu, choose Style.
4 In the Style dialog box, choose Geometry.
5 In the Geometry dialog box, select Scale to Paper Space.
6 Choose OK to exit each dialog box.
7 From the Dimension menu, choose Update, then select the dimensions that apply to your current view.

Controlling Dimension Format

Dimension format refers to placement of dimension text, arrowheads, and leader lines relative to the dimension and extension lines. For example, you can control how text is placed both horizontally and vertically relative to the dimension line and the extension lines. AutoCAD provides several justification settings that facilitate compliance with international standards, or you can choose your own location for the text.

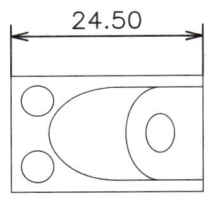

text centered above the dimension line

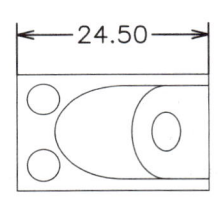

text centered vertically and horizontally on the dimension line

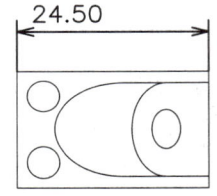

text left aligned above the dimension line

All these settings can be determined by the dimension style. Many of the settings are interdependent. Image tiles in the DDIM Format dialog box update dynamically to illustrate how text appears as you change the settings.

If you want to change, move, or rotate existing dimension text or return it to its default position according to the current style, use DIMEDIT or DIMTEDIT (see "Editing Dimensions" on page 381).

To control dimension format

1 From the Dimension menu, choose Style.
2 In the Dimension Styles dialog box, choose Format.

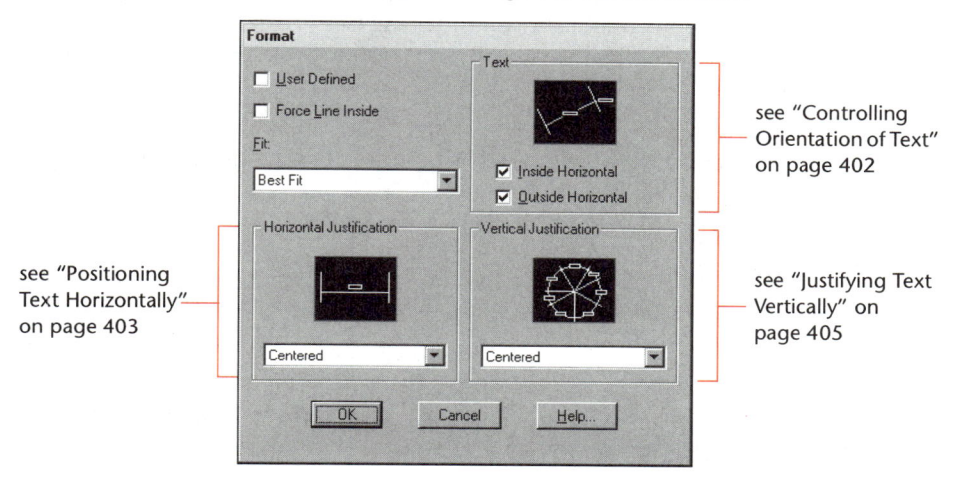

see "Controlling Orientation of Text" on page 402

see "Positioning Text Horizontally" on page 403

see "Justifying Text Vertically" on page 405

3 In the Format dialog box, specify whether you want the text to be Inside Horizontal or Outside Horizontal.
4 Under Horizontal Justification, select Centered.
5 Under Vertical Justification, select Centered, and then choose OK.
6 In the Dimension Styles dialog box, choose OK.

Command line DDIM

Fitting Text within Extension Lines

Many factors, such as space between extension lines and arrowhead size, influence how dimension text and arrowheads fit within the extension lines. In general, AutoCAD automatically applies the best fit given the available space. If possible, both text and arrowheads are accommodated between the extension lines, no matter what fit option you choose.

When creating new dimensions, you can place text by entering coordinates or by using the pointing device. This is known as user-defined text placement. Alternatively, you can allow AutoCAD to compute the text position. The options for automatic fitting of text and arrowheads are listed under Fit in the DDIM Format dialog box. For example, you can specify that text and arrowheads be kept together. In this case, if there is not room for both between the extension lines, they are both placed outside. Alternatively, you can specify that if there is room for only text *or* arrowheads, then either text only or arrowheads only are placed between the extension lines.

You can have a leader line created automatically if there is not room for text between the extension lines. This is useful in cases where text outside the extension lines would clash with other geometry, for example, in continued dimensions. Whether text is drawn to the right or the left of the leader is controlled by the horizontal justification setting (see "Positioning Text Horizontally" on page 403). Finally, you can fit text and arrowheads by changing their size.

Fitting Text Using the Fit Options

These examples show how AutoCAD applies a "best fit" for arrowheads and text.

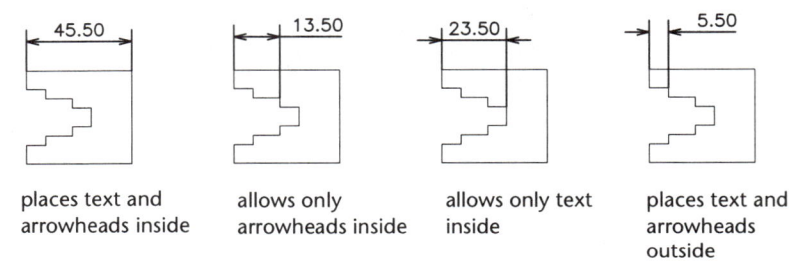

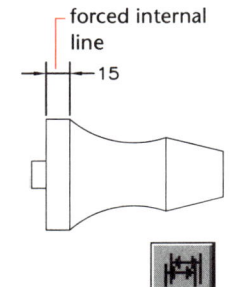

places text and arrowheads inside

allows only arrowheads inside

allows only text inside

places text and arrowheads outside

Even if the arrowheads are outside the extension lines, you can have a line drawn between the extension lines. This is called forcing an internal line and is illustrated on the left. In the following procedure, you force an internal line and choose to keep text and arrowheads together.

To force an internal line and choose a fit option

1 From the Dimension menu, choose Style.
2 In the Dimension Styles dialog box, choose Format.
3 In the Format dialog box, select Force Line Inside.
4 Under Fit, select Text and Arrows.
5 Choose OK to exit each dialog box.

Related   DIMFIT controls how text and arrowheads fit between extension lines. DIMUPT controls user-positioned dimension text. DIMTOFL controls whether an inside line is drawn.

You can draw several different styles of diameter dimensions depending on the horizontal settings for dimension text and whether you select Force Line Inside.

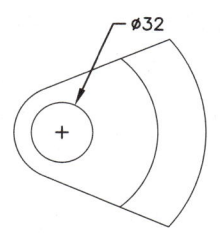

default horizontal placement—text outside circle, center mark, no forced interior line

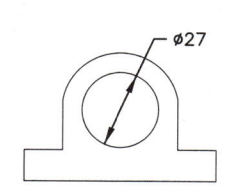

default horizontal placement—dimension line and arrows, no center mark, forced interior line

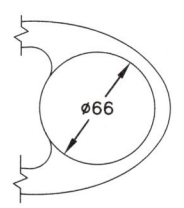

text and arrows inside with Inside Horizontal option selected

The rightmost previous illustration shows a combination of fit and orientation settings. The Text and Arrows and the Inside Horizontal options are both selected. The resulting text is inside the extension lines and forced to remain horizontal instead of aligning with the dimension line. For a description of orientation settings, see "Controlling Orientation of Text" on page 402.

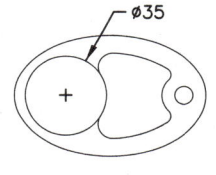

As shown in the illustration directly to the left, in the case of diameter dimensioning, AutoCAD places the text outside the circle and draws a leader line from the text to the circumference of the circle. If the Center Mark option in the DDIM Geometry dialog box is selected, a center mark is drawn inside the circle. In this case, the text is placed horizontally with no forced interior lines for the dimension line.

diameter dimensioning

Fitting Text and Arrowheads by Changing Their Size

If you want to fit text and arrowheads by changing their size yourself, you will need the information in this section. The figure illustrates the features of the dimension line and text that affect the fit of text and arrowheads.

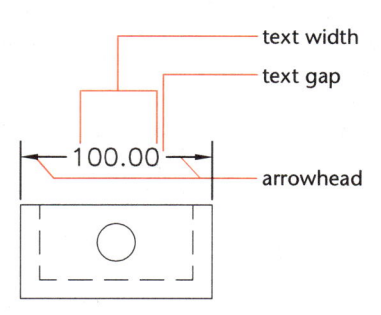

text width
text gap
arrowhead

Creating Dimension Styles

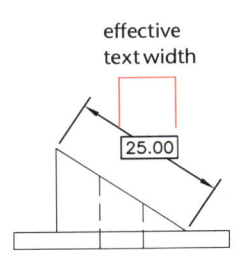

You need room for two arrowheads, the text gaps, and the text. Arrowheads must be at least as large as the text gap. The Oblique and None arrowhead types have zero width and are therefore useful when space is limited. When you place the text above the dimension line, the text gap is not required. A basic formula for determining the minimum width of text centered on the dimension line and within the extension lines is as follows:

effective text width

minimum width = 2 (overall scale) (text gap + arrowhead size) + effective text width

The effective text width is the size of the intersection of the dimension line with a box surrounding the dimension text, sometimes called a bounding box. The box is the size of the dimension text plus the text gap around that text. This box is identical to the box drawn around what is called a basic dimension. You set the text gap with the Gap option in the Annotation dialog box.

NOTE For simple vertical dimensions with no text rotation, the effective text width is twice the text gap plus the text height. The figure illustrates the effective text width when text has been rotated. In this case, basic dimensions have been used to outline the box surrounding the dimension text.

The simplest way to get the text to fit within extension lines is to reduce the size of the text gap or the arrowhead size. You can also reduce the overall dimension scale (see "Setting Dimension Scale" on page 394). You can also rotate the dimension text so that its orientation is close to perpendicular to the dimension line. Finally, you can reduce the length of the text itself by adjusting the appropriate unit settings or by using a text style that specifies a text width factor of less than one (see "Controlling the Appearance of Text" on page 415).

Controlling Orientation of Text

Whether text is inside or outside the extension lines, you can choose whether it is aligned with the dimension line or forced to remain horizontal. The following examples show two combinations of these options.

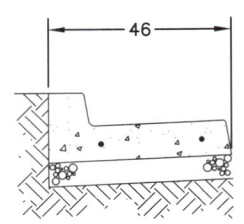

text inside extension lines oriented horizontally

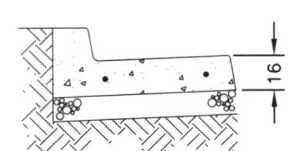

text outside extension lines aligned with dimension line

The AutoCAD default is horizontal dimension text, even for vertical dimensions.

To align text with the dimension line

1 From the Dimension menu, choose Style.
2 In the Dimension Styles dialog box, choose Format.
3 In the Format dialog box under Text, deselect Inside Horizontal.

Text inside the extension lines is aligned with the dimension line. The image tile reflects this setting.

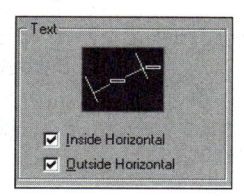

4 Clear Outside Horizontal.

Text outside the extension lines is aligned with the dimension line. The image tile reflects this setting.

5 Choose OK to exit each dialog box.

Related   DIMTIH controls the orientation of text inside extension lines. DIMTOH controls the orientation of text outside extension lines.

Positioning Text Horizontally

Horizontal Justification controls the position of the text along the dimension line. Use the User Defined option to place text yourself when you create a dimension. Use the Horizontal Justification options to automatically place text at the center of the dimension line, at either extension line, or over either extension line. The Vertical Justification settings further determine how the text appears when you select these options. For example, the following illustration shows the difference between text placed above the first dimension line when the Centered and Above Vertical Justification options are selected.

Creating Dimension Styles

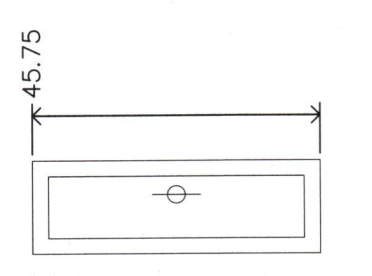

horizontal justification—
vertical justification—Centered

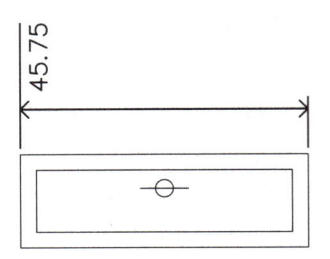

horizontal justification—
vertical justification—Above

First and second extension lines are defined by the order in which you specified the extension line origins. The exception is angular dimensions: their second extension line is counterclockwise from the first. In the next illustrations, the first extension line origin (1) and the second (2) are shown.

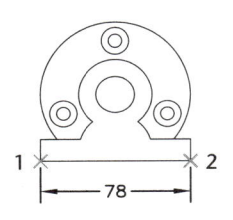

text horizontal and
centered along
dimension line

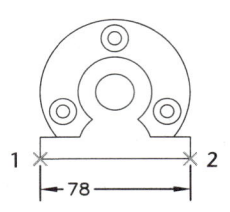

text horizontal at first
extension line

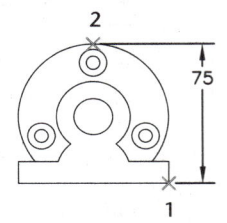

text horizontal at second
extension line

When text is at either extension line, it can be either vertical or horizontal. When it is over an extension line, it is always aligned with the extension line.

With the User Defined option, you can place the dimension text anywhere along the dimension line, inside or outside the extension lines, as you create the dimension. This option provides more flexibility and is especially useful when space is limited. However, it provides less accuracy and consistency between dimensions than the Horizontal Justification options.

To place text with the User Defined option

1 From the Dimension menu, choose Style.
2 In the Dimension Styles dialog box, choose Format.
3 In the Format dialog box, select User Defined.
4 Choose OK to exit each dialog box.

As you create dimensions, the text is movable along the dimension line. Use the pointing device or enter coordinates to specify the dimension line and text locations.

To justify text vertically at the second extension line

1 From the Dimension menu, choose Style.
2 In the Dimension Styles dialog box, choose Format.
3 In the Format dialog box under Horizontal Justification, select Over 2nd Extension.
4 Choose OK to exit each dialog box.

The image tile reflects your selection.

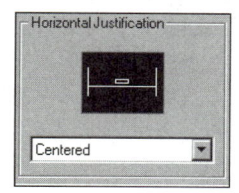

Related DIMUPT controls the user-defined horizontal text placement. DIMJUST controls horizontal justification of text.

Justifying Text Vertically

Vertical Justification controls the position of the text relative to the dimension line. Text can be placed above, below, or centered within the dimension line. In the ANSI standards, centered text usually splits the dimension line. In the ISO standards, it is usually above or outside the dimension line. Vertical Justification allows compliance with a variety of international standards. For example, the International Organization for Standardization (ISO) allows angular dimension text to appear in any of the following illustrated ways.

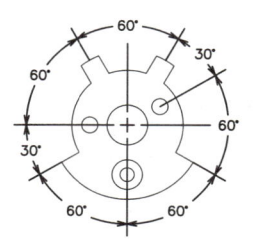

ANSI standard text centered on dimension line

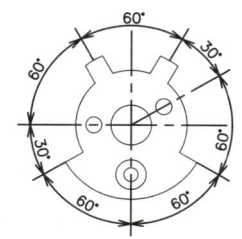

ISO standard text above dimension line

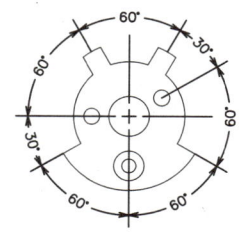

text aligned with and centered on the dimension line

Creating Dimension Styles

405

Other settings, such as Inside Horizontal and Outside Horizontal, affect the vertical justification of text. For example, if Inside Horizontal is selected, text centered on the dimension line is horizontal, as shown in the previous leftmost illustration, even if the dimension is rotated. If Inside Horizontal is selected, text above and outside the dimension line appears as shown in the following illustrations.

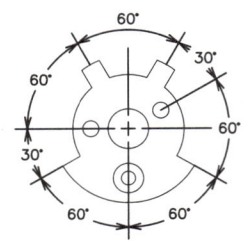

text above dimension line 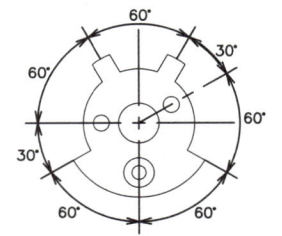   text outside dimension line

To place text above the dimension line

1 From the Dimension menu, choose Style.
2 In the Dimension Styles dialog box, choose Format.
3 In the Format dialog box under Vertical Justification, select Above.
4 Choose OK to exit each dialog box.

The image tile reflects the selection.

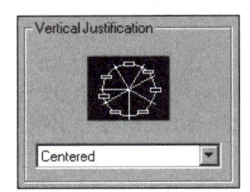

Related   DIMTAD controls the placement of dimension text above the dimension line. DIMTVP controls the vertical position of dimension text when DIMTAD is off.

Controlling Dimension Text

AutoCAD supports a mixture of user-supplied text, prefixes and suffixes supplied by the dimension style, and AutoCAD-generated measurements. For example, you could add a diameter symbol as a prefix to a measurement or add the word form for a unit, such as *mm*, as a suffix. Text in this context refers to all dimension text, prefixes and suffixes, primary and alternate units, and lateral tolerances. Geometric tolerances are controlled independently (see "Adding Geometric Tolerances" on page 424).

Dimension text is treated as a single string of text, which you create and format using your text editor.

To control dimension annotation

1 From the Dimension menu, choose Style.

2 In the Dimension Styles dialog box, choose Annotation.

3 In the Annotation dialog box, under Text, specify the style, height, gap, and color of the annotation text.

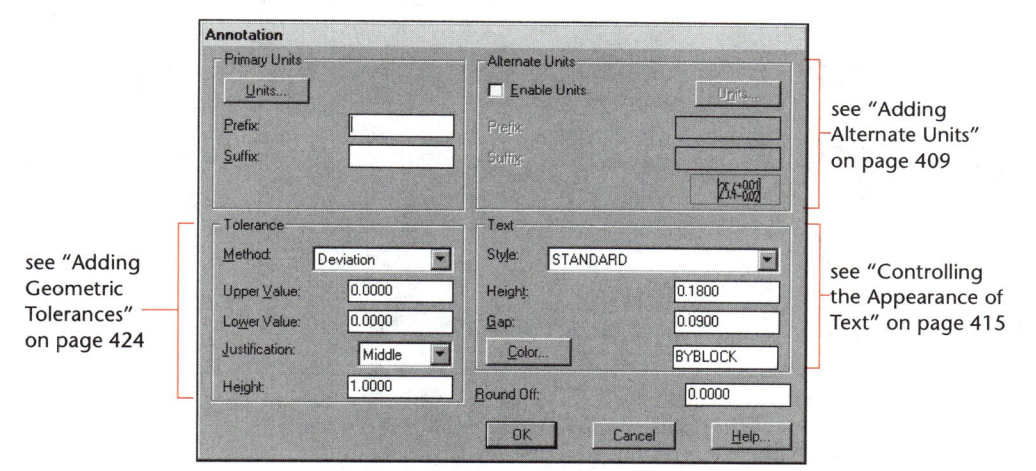

4 Choose OK to exit each dialog box.

Command line DDIM

Adding Primary Units

Primary units control the main dimension values. For example, you can enter the diameter symbol as a prefix, as shown in the illustration. Any prefix you specify replaces the prefixes normally used for diameter and radial dimensions (Ø and R, respectively).

To control suppression of zeros in primary and alternate units, see "Suppressing Zeros in Primary and Alternate Units" on page 411. To control zero suppression in tolerance values, see "Formatting Lateral Tolerances" on page 414.

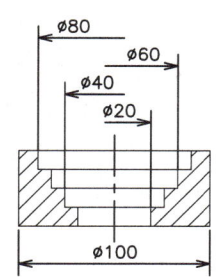

Creating Dimension Styles

407

You can set a global measurement scale for linear dimensions or a length-scaling value for dimensions created in paper space (see "Setting Dimension Scale" on page 394). The following procedure shows how to add and format primary units and any prefixes and suffixes.

To add and format primary units

1 From the Dimension menu, choose Style.
2 In the Dimension Styles dialog box, choose Annotation.
3 In the Annotation dialog box, under Primary Units, choose Units.

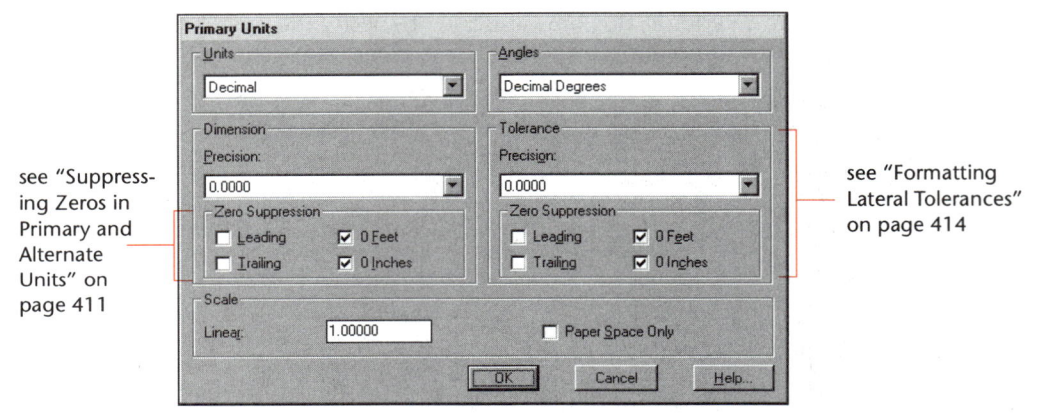

see "Suppressing Zeros in Primary and Alternate Units" on page 411

see "Formatting Lateral Tolerances" on page 414

4 In the Primary Units dialog box, under Units, select a unit type from the list for all dimension types except angular. For angular dimensions, select an angle type from the Angles list.
5 Under Dimension, select a precision value for the primary units.
6 Under Tolerance, select a precision value for any tolerance values.
7 Under Scale, set the units scale for primary units and choose OK.
8 In the Annotation dialog box under Primary Units, enter any prefix and suffix for the units.

An image tile displays a representation of the tolerance text depending on the current tolerance method (see "Adding Lateral Tolerances" on page 322).

9 Choose OK to exit each dialog box.

Related   DIMPOST stores the prefix and suffix values for the primary units. DIMUNIT controls the primary unit type for all dimension types except angular. DIMAUNIT controls the primary unit type for angular dimensions. DIMDEC controls the primary units precision. DIMADEC controls the

Chapter 10   Dimensions and Tolerancing

primary units for angular precision. DIMTDEC controls the primary units tolerance precision. DIMLFAC stores the global scale factor for linear dimensioning measurements.

Adding Alternate Units

You can create dimensions in two systems of measurement simultaneously. A common use of this feature is to add feet and inches dimensions to drawings created in metric units. The alternate units appear in square brackets [ ] in the dimensioned text. Alternate units cannot be applied to angular dimensions.

If alternate units dimensioning is turned on when you edit a linear dimension, the measurement is multiplied by the alternate scale value specified in the Alternate Units dialog box. Specify the alternate scaling value by entering the number of alternate units per current unit of measurement. The default value is 25.4, which is the number of millimeters per inch. The dimension would look like the figure shown on the left if you create a horizontal dimension of 1 inch while using architectural units for the primary units, and using decimal units for the alternate units with "mm" as the alternate units suffix. The number of decimal places is specified by the alternate units precision value.

To add and format alternate units

1 From the Dimension menu, choose Style.
2 In the Dimension Styles dialog box, choose Annotation.
3 In the Annotation dialog box, under Alternate Units, select Enable Units and choose Units.

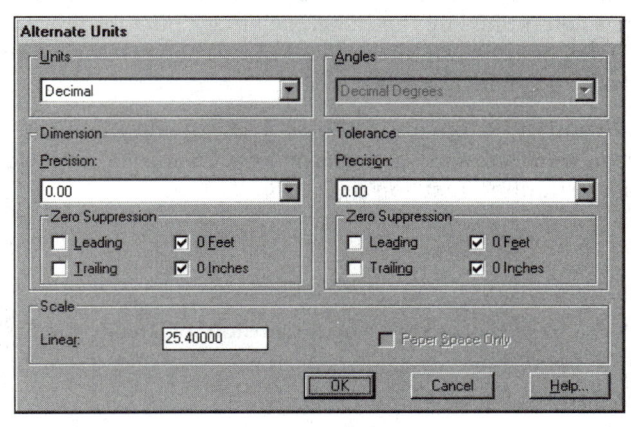

4 In the Alternate Units dialog box, under Units, select a unit type from the list for all dimension types except angular.

Creating Dimension Styles

409

5 Under Dimension, select a precision value for the alternate units.

6 Under Tolerance, select a precision value for any tolerance values.

7 Under Scale, set the units scale for alternate units. Then choose OK.

8 In the Annotation dialog box, under Alternate Units, enter any prefix and suffix for the units.

An image tile displays a representation of the tolerance text, depending on the current tolerance method (see "Adding Lateral Tolerances" on page 322).

9 Choose OK to exit each dialog box.

Related   DIMAPOST stores the alternate units prefix and suffix. DIMALTU controls the alternate units type for all dimension types except angular. DIMAUNIT controls the alternate units type for angular dimensions. DIMALTD controls the alternate units precision. DIMALTTD controls the alternate units tolerance precision. DIMALTF controls the alternate units scale factor.

Supplying User Text

In addition to the prefixes and suffixes specified for primary and alternate units, you can supply your own text as you create a dimension. Because the prefix, suffix, and user-supplied text form a single text string, you can represent tolerance stacks and apply changes to font, text size, and other characteristics using the text editor.

To add user text above and below the dimension line, use the formatting character \X. Text that precedes this symbol is aligned with and above the dimension line. Text that follows the \X formatting character is aligned with and below the dimension line. The space between the dimension line and the text is determined by the value you enter under Gap in the DDIM Annotation dialog box. To add further lines of text above or below the dimension line, use the formatting character \P.

The following procedure displays how to use the multiline text editor to add dimension text. For more information about using the multiline text editor, see "Using Multiline Text" on page 338.

To add text as you create a dimension

1 From the Dimension menu, choose Linear.

2 Press ENTER to select the object to dimension, or specify the first and second extension line origins.

3 Enter **m** (Mtext).

4 In the Multiline Text Editor dialog box, enter the text.

5 Choose the Properties tab to define text properties such as style, justification, width, and rotation.

6 Choose OK.

Command line   DIMLINEAR

Related   DIMGAP controls the space between the dimension line and expanded text format strings.

In the following example, the primary dimension measurement is 5.08, and the alternate dimension measurement is 2.00. The primary units have the suffix *H7/h6*, and the alternate units have the suffix *inches*. At the text prompt, while creating the dimension, you enter the format string

<>\XSee Note 26\P[]

The result is displayed as follows:

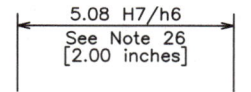

```
    5.08  H7/h6
   See Note 26
   [2.00 inches]
```

Suppressing Zeros in Primary and Alternate Units

If you suppress leading zeros in decimal dimensions, 0.500 becomes .500. If you suppress trailing zeros, 0.500 becomes 0.5. You can suppress *both* leading and trailing zeros so that 0.5000 becomes .5 and 0.0000 becomes 0.

To suppress zeros in decimal dimensions

1 From the Dimension menu, choose Style.

2 In the Dimension Styles dialog box, choose Annotation.

3 In the Annotation dialog box under Primary Units or Alternate Units, choose Units.

4 In the Primary Units or Alternate Units dialog box under Zero Suppression, select Leading to suppress leading zeros.

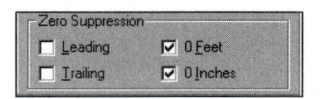

5 Select Trailing to suppress trailing zeros.

Related   DIMALTZ controls the suppression of zeros for alternate tolerance values.

Creating Dimension Styles

411

If you dimension your drawing using feet and inches, you can suppress the display of zero feet and zero inches. If you suppress feet, any dimension less than a foot shows just the inches portion. So 0'-6", for example, becomes 6". If you suppress inches, 1'-0" becomes 1'.

If feet are included with a fractional inch, the number of inches is indicated as zero, no matter which option you select. Thus, a dimension like 4'-3/4" is edited to 4'-0 3/4".

The table shows the effect of selecting each option and provides examples of the architectural units style.

Zero suppression for feet and inches

Option	Effect	Examples			
0 Feet and 0 Inches	Suppresses zero feet and zero inches	1/2"	6"	1'	1'-0 3/4"
No Options	Includes zero feet and zero inches	0'-0 1/2"	0'-6"	1'-0"	1'-0 3/4"
0 Inches	Suppresses zero inches (includes zero feet)	0'-0 1/2"	0'-6"	1'	1'-0 3/4"
0 Feet	Suppresses zero feet (includes zero inches)	1/2"	6"	1'-0"	1'-0 3/4"

To suppress zeros in feet and inches dimension text format

1 From the Dimension menu, choose Style.
2 In the Dimension Styles dialog box, choose Annotation.
3 In the Annotation dialog box, choose Units.
4 In the Primary Units dialog box under Zero Suppression, select 0 Feet to suppress display of 0 feet.

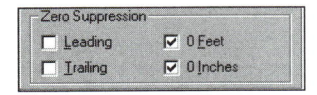

Chapter 10 Dimensions and Tolerancing

5 Select 0 Inches to suppress display of 0 inches.

6 Choose OK to exit each dialog box.

Related DIMZIN controls the suppression of zeros for feet and inches. DIMALTZ controls the suppression of zeros for alternate values.

Creating Lateral Tolerances

Lateral tolerances can be specified from theoretically exact measurements. These are called basic dimensions and have a box drawn round them. You can apply tolerances directly to a dimension by appending the tolerances to the dimension text. These dimension tolerances show the largest and smallest permissible size of the dimension.

If the dimension value can vary in both directions, the plus and minus values you supply are appended to the dimension value as deviation tolerances. If the deviation tolerance values are equal, AutoCAD displays them with a ± symbol and they are known as symmetrical. Otherwise, the plus value goes above the minus value.

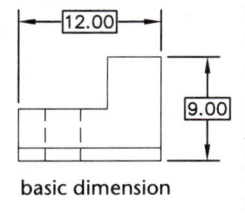

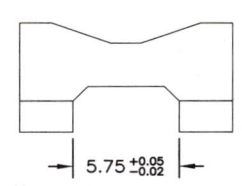

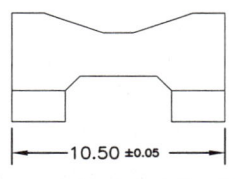

basic dimension

deviation tolerance

symmetrical deviation tolerance

If the tolerances are applied as limits, AutoCAD uses the plus and minus values you supply to calculate a maximum and minimum value. These values replace the dimension value. If you specify limits, the upper limit goes above the lower.

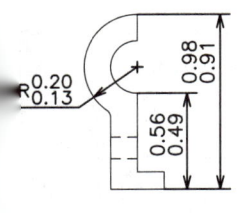

To specify limits

1 From the Dimension menu, choose Style.

2 In the Dimension Styles dialog box, choose Annotation.

3 In the Annotation dialog box, under Tolerance, select Limits from the Method list.

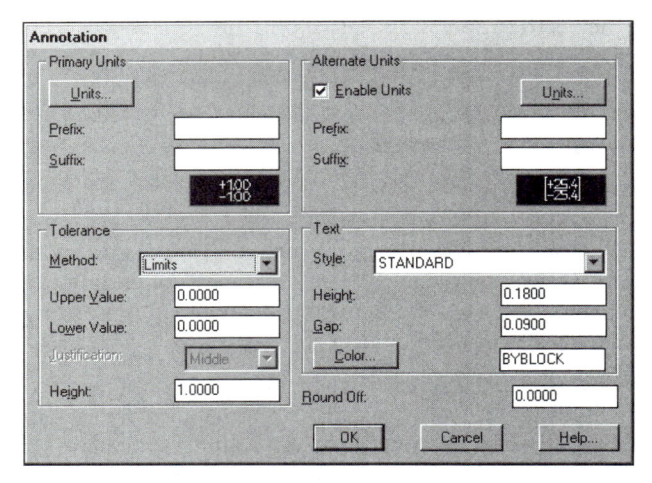

4 Enter the upper value.

5 Enter the lower value.

If you choose Symmetrical tolerances from the Method list, Lower Value is not available, because you need only one tolerance value. If you choose Basic, enter the gap between the text and its enclosing box under Text.

6 Choose OK to exit each dialog box.

Related DIMTOL controls whether tolerances are supplied. DIMLIM controls whether limits are supplied. DIMTOL and DIMLIM are mutually exclusive. DIMGAP controls the gap around basic dimension text. DIMTP and DIMTM control the upper and lower tolerance values, respectively. DIMTOLJ controls the justification of tolerances.

Formatting Lateral Tolerances

You can control the vertical placement of tolerance values relative to the main dimension text. Tolerances can align with the top, middle, or bottom of the dimension text.

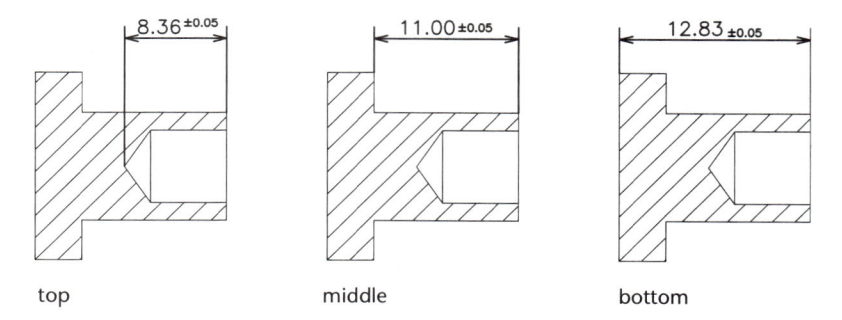

top   middle   bottom

Chapter 10 Dimensions and Tolerancing

You can also control zero suppression, as you can with the primary and alternate units. Suppressing zeros in lateral tolerances has the same effect as suppressing them in the primary and alternate units. If you suppress leading zeros, 0.5 becomes .5, and if you suppress trailing zeros, 0.5000 becomes 0.5.

To justify and suppress zeros in tolerance values

1. From the Dimension menu, choose Style.
2. In the Dimension Styles dialog box, choose Annotation.
3. In the Annotation dialog box under Tolerance, select a justification from the list.
4. Under Primary Units, choose Units to suppress zeros in primary units. Choose Units under Alternate Units to suppress zeros in alternate units.
5. In the Primary Units or Alternate Units dialog box under Tolerance Zero Suppression, select Leading to suppress leading zeros.
6. Select Trailing to suppress trailing zeros.
7. Choose OK to exit each dialog box.

Related DIMTOLJ controls the justification of tolerances. DIMTZIN controls zero suppression for primary units tolerances. DIMALTTZ controls zero suppression for alternate units tolerances.

Controlling the Appearance of Text

The appearance of dimension text is governed by the text style selected in the DDIM Annotation dialog box. You can choose a text style while creating a dimension style and specify a text color and specify a height independent of the current style's height setting. You can also specify the gap between base dimension text and the box that surrounds it. For information about creating text styles, see "Renaming a Text Style" on page 332.

To control text appearance

1. From the Dimension menu, choose Style.
2. In the Dimension Styles dialog box, choose Annotation.
3. In the Annotation dialog box, under Text, choose a text style from the Style list.

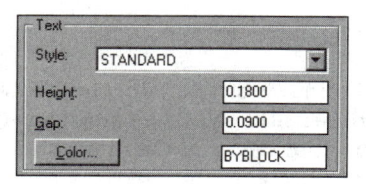

Creating Dimension Styles

415

4 Under Text, enter the height of dimension text in the Height box if the current text style doesn't have a fixed height.

5 Under Tolerance, enter a height for tolerance values in the Height box.

6 Under Text, enter a value for the gap around base dimension text.

7 Choose Color to select a color from the Select Color dialog box. Then choose OK to return to the Annotation dialog box.

8 Choose OK to exit each dialog box.

Related DIMTXSTY controls the dimension text style. DIMTXT controls dimension text height. DIMGAP controls the gap around base dimension text. DIMCLRT controls dimension text color.

Rounding Off Dimensions

You can round off all dimension values. For example, if you specify a round-off value of 0.25, all distances are rounded to the nearest 0.25 unit. The number of digits that appear after the decimal point depends on the precision set for primary and alternate units and lateral tolerance values.

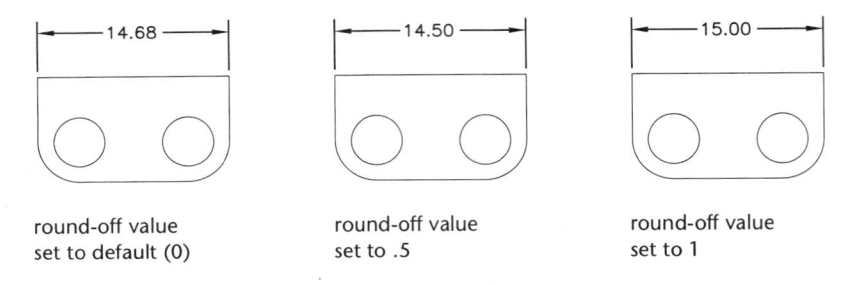

round-off value set to default (0)

round-off value set to .5

round-off value set to 1

To round off dimension values

- In the Annotation dialog box under Round Off, enter the rounded-off value.

Related DIMRND controls the rounded-off value. DIMADEC determines dimension values for angular dimensions.

Using Style Families

You can manage all the dimensioning system variables quickly and easily by setting up dimension styles. A dimension style is a named group of dimension settings that determines the appearance of the dimension. When you create a new style, it automatically becomes the *parent* style of a *style family*.

Style families are groups of styles based on a parent style with variations for different types of dimension. With dimension style families, you can design a dimension style and then specify variations on it for each dimension type, without having to set up and use an entirely new style.

For example, you may want to force a dimension line for radius and diameter dimensions only. Instead of creating a different style for each dimension type with only this option different, you create the parent style with Force Line Inside (or DIMTOFL) off, then create radius and diameter family members with Force Line Inside on. When dimensioning, you select the dimension base or parent style and AutoCAD automatically applies the appropriate family member style according to the type of dimension you're creating. In this case, AutoCAD forces a dimension line only when you create radial or diameter dimensions.

You can set up family member styles for linear, radial, angular, diameter, and ordinate dimensions and for leaders. Changes to a parent style after it has been created and saved are not applied to family members.

Dimension style families are related to one another by name. The child dimension styles are named with a numeric suffix that indicate the dimension type. The following is an example of valid suffixes:

ISO-25	ISO-25 parent dimstyle
ISO-25$0	Linear child of ISO-25 (both rotated and aligned types)
ISO-25$2	Angular child of ISO-25 (both 2-line and 3-point types)
ISO-25$3	Diameter child of ISO-25
ISO-25$4	Radius child of ISO-25
ISO-25$6	Ordinate child of ISO-25
ISO-25$7	Leader child of ISO-25 (also used for tolerance objects)

Families provide a set of permanent variations on the parent style. When you create a dimension, AutoCAD chooses the appropriate family member of the current style for the dimension you're creating. If there are no family styles defined, the parent style is applied.

NOTE Use the ? option of the DIMSTYLE command to view dimension style names.

Style families are used for different reasons than overrides. For example, you could use a style family member just for only ordinate dimensions to format units appropriately. However, the need to suppress extension lines usually arises in individual cases only and is thus a candidate for the use of overrides.

To create a family member style

1. From the Dimension menu, choose Style.
2. In the Dimension Styles dialog box under Family, select Parent.
3. Under Dimension Style, select from the Current style list the parent style for which you want to create a family member style.
4. Make the required modifications to the parent style.
5. Choose Save.
6. Choose OK.

The family member style is saved. When you next open the Dimension Styles dialog box, the Parent style is selected by default.

Command line   DDIM

Using Style Overrides

Overrides allow local changes to a dimension and changes to the settings of individual variables in the dimension style. You can apply overrides to a specific dimension. Once you apply an override to a style, the override applies to all dimensions created when that style was current. It's equivalent to changing the status of a dimension variable without changing the current dimension style. For example, if you change the color of extension lines in the DDIM Geometry dialog box, no change occurs in the current dimension style. However, the new value for the changed color is stored in the DIMCLRE system variable. The next dimension you create will have extension lines in the changed color.

Some dimension characteristics are common to a drawing or to a style of dimensioning and are therefore suited to be permanent style settings. Others generally apply on an individual basis and can more effectively be applied as overrides. For example, a drawing usually uses a single type of arrowhead, so it makes sense to define the arrowhead type as part of the style. Suppression of extension lines, however, usually applies in individual cases only and is more suited to a style override.

There are several ways to set up style overrides. You can change the options in the DDIM dialog boxes or the settings of individual dimensioning system variables on the command line. In this case, the style is based on the current style and displayed in the form +STYLENAME, indicating that overrides exist. The overrides apply to the dimension you are creating and all subsequent dimensions created with that style until you make a new style current. You can also use DDMODIFY or DIMOVERRIDE on the command line to set up overrides for an existing dimension style. You can use the Apply option of DIMSTYLE to apply overrides to a dimension you select.

The following example shows how to set up overrides using the DDIM dialog boxes.

To set up style overrides for a style

1 From the Dimension menu, choose Style.
2 In the Dimension Styles dialog box, select from the Current style list the style for which you want to create an override.
3 Make the changes to the style.
4 Choose OK.

The style and the overrides are stored in the form +STYLENAME in the style name list.

Command line   DDIM

The next example shows how to apply overrides to selected dimensions with DIMOVERRIDE. You can view the overrides by using LIST on the dimension object.

To apply style overrides to selected dimensions

1 At the Command prompt, enter **dimoverride**.
2 Enter the dimension variable whose setting you want to override.

For a list of variables, see "Listing Dimension Styles and Variables" on page 421.
3 Enter the new setting.
4 Repeat for as many dimension variables as necessary.
5 At the Dimension Variable to Override prompt, press ENTER.
6 Select the dimensions to apply overrides to.
7 Press ENTER to end the command.

Related   DDMODIFY

You can also set up overrides while you are creating a dimension by entering any dimension variable name at any dimension creation prompt. In this example, the dimension line color is changed in this way. The change will apply to subsequent dimensions until you make another style current.

Command: **dimlinear**
First extension line origin or ENTER to select: **dimclrd**
Current value < 4 (cyan) > New value: **5**
First extension line origin or ENTER to select:
Specify the first extension line origin or select an object to dimension

Working with Dimension Styles

You can apply any dimension style to an existing dimension. You can examine styles by comparing the current style settings with the style of a selected dimension or by listing the settings of a specified style's dimension variables. You can also list all the dimension styles in the current drawing.

Applying Styles to Existing Dimensions

When you create a dimension, the current dimension style is associated with that dimension. The dimension retains this style unless you apply a new one or set up overrides. You can restore an existing style by naming it or by selecting a dimension whose style you want to restore. You can also apply the current style, including any overrides, to selected dimensions.

To restore a dimension style

1 At the Command prompt, enter **dimstyle**.
2 Enter **r** (Restore).
3 Enter the name of the dimension style to restore, or press ENTER to select a dimension whose style you want to restore.

To apply a dimension style to existing dimensions

1 At the Command prompt, enter **dimstyle**.
2 Enter **a** (Apply).
3 Select the dimensions to apply the current style to.

Comparing Dimension Styles

You can compare the current dimension style with another style and see a list of the differences in settings or variables. When you use DIMSTYLE, AutoCAD lists any running overrides that apply to the current style.

In this example, you compare the STANDARD dimension style with the current style.

To compare dimension styles

1 At the Command prompt, enter **dimstyle**.
2 Enter **r** (Restore).
3 Enter **~standard**.

AutoCAD displays a listing like this one:

Differences between STANDARD and current settings:

	STANDARD	Current Setting
DIMASZ	0.1800	0.1000
DIMBLK1		_OPEN
DIMBLK2		_OPEN
DIMCLRD	BYBLOCK	3 (green)
DIMCLRE	BYBLOCK	3 (green)
DIMSAH	Off	On
DIMTAD	0	1
DIMTIH	On	Off

Listing Dimension Styles and Variables

You can list all dimensioning system variables and their current status, or you can list just the variables affected by a dimension style. You can also list the dimension styles in the current drawing.

To list all dimension variables for the current style

1 At the Command prompt, enter **dimstyle**.
2 Enter **st** (Status).

The dimensioning system variables are displayed in a scrolling list with their current settings and a brief description of each variable.

The following is a sample listing of the renamable default style, STANDARD.

Status of STANDARD

DIMADEC	-1	Decimal places for angular dimensions
DIMALT	Off	Alternate units selected
DIMALTD	2	Alternate unit decimal places
DIMALTF	25.4000	Alternate unit scale factor
DIMALTTD	2	Alternate tolerance decimal places
DIMALTTZ	0	Alternate tolerance zero suppression
DIMALTU	2	Alternate units
DIMALTZ	0	Alternate unit zero suppression
DIMAPOST		Prefix and suffix for alternate text
DIMASO	On	Create associative dimensions
DIMASZ	0.1800	Arrow size
DIMAUNIT	0	Angular unit format
DIMBLK		Arrow block name
DIMBLK1		First arrow block name
DIMBLK2		Second arrow block name
DIMCEN	0.0900	Center mark size
DIMCLRD	BYBLOCK	Dimension line and leader color
DIMCLRE	BYBLOCK	Extension line color
DIMCLRT	BYBLOCK	Dimension text color
DIMDEC	4	Decimal places for dimensions
DIMDLE	0.0000	Dimension line extension
DIMDLI	0.3800	Dimension line spacing
DIMEXE	0.1800	Extension above dimension line
DIMEXO	0.0625	Extension line origin offset
DIMFIT	3	Fit text
DIMGAP	0.0900	Gap from dimension line to text
DIMJUST	0	Justification of text on dimension line
DIMLFAC	1.000	Linear unit scale factor
DIMLIM	Off	Generate dimension limits
DIMPOST		Prefix and suffix for dimension text
DIMRND	0.0000	Rounding value
DIMSAH	Off	Separate arrow blocks
DIMSCALE	1.0000	Overall scale factor
DIMSD1	Off	Suppress the first dimension line
DIMSD2	Off	Suppress the second dimension line
DIMSE1	Off	Suppress the first extension line
DIMSE2	Off	Suppress the second extension line
DIMSHO	On	Update dimensions while dragging
DIMSOXD	Off	Suppress outside dimension lines
DIMSTYLE	STANDARD	Current dimension style (read-only)
DIMTAD	0	Place text above the dimension line

DIMTDEC	4	Tolerance decimal places
DIMTFAC	1.0000	Text height within tolerance objects
DIMTIH	On	Text inside extensions is horizontal
DIMTIX	Off	Place text inside extensions
DIMTM	0.0000	Minus tolerance
DIMTOFL	Off	Force line inside extension lines
DIMTOH	On	Text outside horizontal
DIMTOL	Off	Tolerance dimensioning
DIMTOLJ	1	Tolerance vertical justification
DIMTP	0.0000	Plus tolerance
DIMTSZ	0.0000	Tick size
DIMTVP	0.0000	Text vertical position
DIMTXSTY	STANDARD	Text style
DIMTXT	0.1800	Text height
DIMTZIN	0	Tolerance zero suppression
DIMUNIT	2	Unit format
DIMUPT	Off	User positioned text
DIMZIN	0	Zero suppression

To list variables affected by an existing dimension style

1 At the Command prompt, enter **dimstyle**.
2 Enter **v** (Variables).
3 Enter a style name or select a dimension whose style you want to examine.

The style name is followed by a scrolling list of affected variables, their settings, and a brief description of each. Overrides are not included.

To list dimension styles in the current drawing

1 At the Command prompt, enter **dimstyle**.
2 At the Dimension Style Edit prompt, enter **?**.
3 Press ENTER to list all styles, or use wild cards to specify a subset of styles.

Using Externally Referenced Dimension Styles

AutoCAD displays externally referenced dimension style names using the same syntax as for other externally dependent symbols. The name of the xref is combined with the dimension style name, and the two names are separated by the vertical bar (|) character. For example, if the drawing *baseplat.dwg* has a dimension style called FRACTIONAL-1 and you attach *baseplat.dwg* as an xref to a new drawing, then the dimension style appears in the new drawing as BASEPLAT|FRACTIONAL-1.

Externally referenced dimension styles can be examined, but they cannot be modified or made current. To use an externally referenced dimension style as a template for creating a new style, select the style from the Current list in the Dimension Styles dialog box and enter a new name in the Name box. All settings from the selected dimension style are used for the new style.

Adding Geometric Tolerances

Geometric tolerancing shows deviations of form, profile, orientation, location, and runout of a feature. You add geometric tolerances in feature control frames. These frames contain all the tolerance information for a single dimension.

You can copy, move, erase, stretch, scale, and rotate feature control frames. You can snap to them using the object snap modes. You can use DDEDIT. You can also edit them with grips (see "Editing with Grips" on page 239).

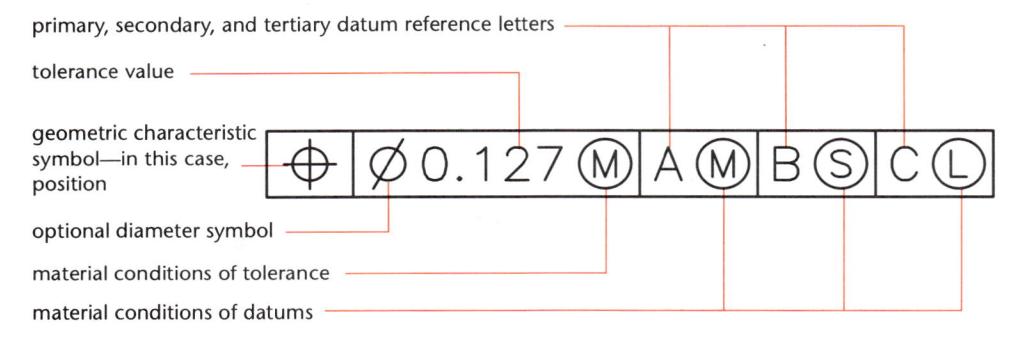

- primary, secondary, and tertiary datum reference letters
- tolerance value
- geometric characteristic symbol—in this case, position
- optional diameter symbol
- material conditions of tolerance
- material conditions of datums

⊕ | ⌀0.127 Ⓜ | A Ⓜ | B Ⓢ | C Ⓛ

A feature control frame consists of at least two compartments. The first contains a geometric characteristic symbol that represents the geometric characteristic to which a tolerance is being applied, for example, form, orientation, or runout. Form tolerances control straightness, flatness, circularity, cylindricity, and profiles of line and surface. In the previous illustration, the characteristic is position.

The second compartment contains the tolerance value. Where applicable, the tolerance value is preceded by a diameter symbol and followed by a material condition symbol.

To add geometric tolerances

1 From the Dimension menu, choose Tolerance.

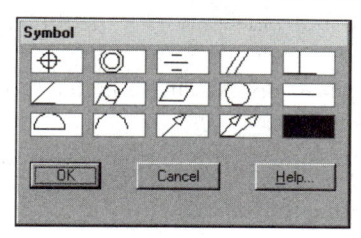

2 In the Symbol dialog box, select the required characteristic symbol.

3 Choose OK to display the Geometric Tolerance dialog box.

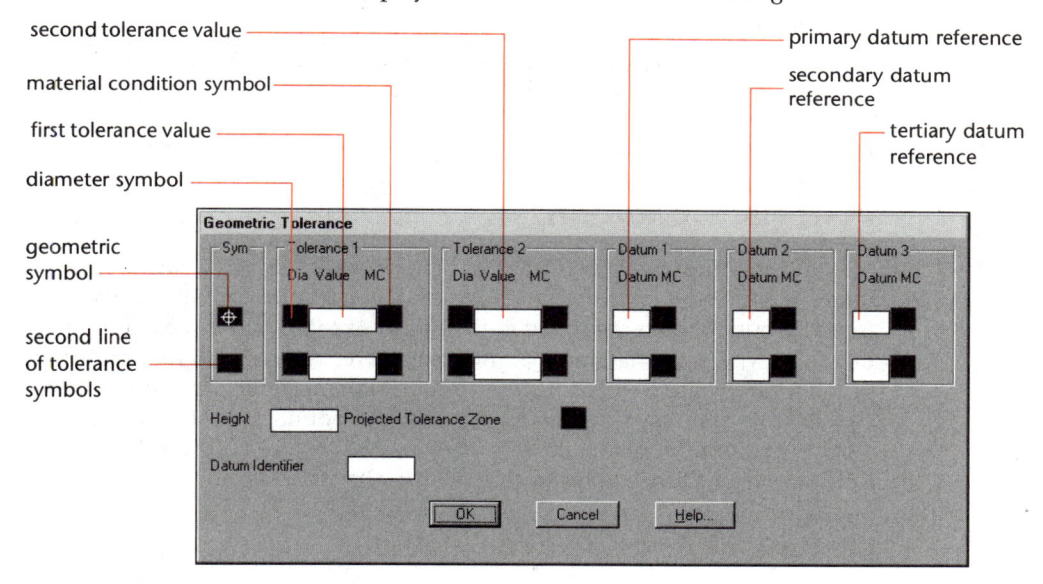

- second tolerance value
- material condition symbol
- first tolerance value
- diameter symbol
- geometric symbol
- second line of tolerance symbols
- primary datum reference
- secondary datum reference
- tertiary datum reference

Now add the tolerance values and their modifying symbols.

1 Under Tolerance 1, select Dia to insert a diameter symbol (optional).

2 Under Value, enter the first tolerance value.

3 Choose MC to add a material condition (optional).

4 In the Material Condition dialog box, double-click a material condition symbol to insert it.

5 Add a second tolerance value (optional) in the same way as the first tolerance value.

Adding Geometric Tolerances

425

Now add the datum reference letters and their modifying symbols (optional).

1. Under Datum 1, enter the primary datum reference letter.
2. Choose MC to insert a material condition symbol for the primary datum reference.
3. In the Material Condition dialog box, double-click a material condition symbol to insert it.
4. Add secondary and tertiary datums and modifying symbols in the same way.

Now add a projected tolerance zone (optional).

1. In the Height box, enter a height.
2. Select Projected Tolerance Zone to insert the Ⓟ symbol.
3. Choose OK.
4. In the drawing, specify a location for the feature control frame.
5. Choose OK to exit each dialog box.

Command line   TOLERANCE

Material Conditions

Material conditions apply to features that can vary in size. At maximum material condition (Ⓜ, also known as MMC), a feature contains the maximum amount of material stated in the limits. At MMC, a hole has minimum diameter, whereas a shaft has maximum diameter. At least material condition (Ⓛ, also known as LMC), a feature contains the minimum amount of material stated in the limits. At LMC, a hole has maximum diameter, whereas a shaft has minimum diameter. Regardless of Feature Size (Ⓢ, also known as RFS) means a feature can be any size within the stated limits.

Datum Reference Frames

The tolerance values in the feature control frame are followed by up to three optional datum reference letters and their modifying symbols. A datum is a theoretically exact point, axis, or plane from which you make measurements and verify dimensions. Usually, two or three mutually perpendicular planes perform this task best. These are jointly called the datum reference frame.

secondary datum plane

tertiary datum plane

primary datum plane

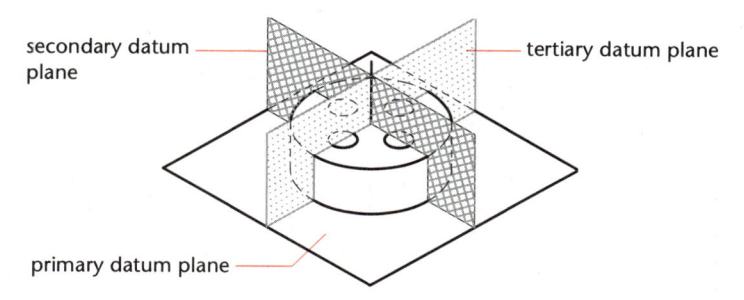

The previous illustration shows a datum reference frame verifying the dimensions of the part.

Projected Tolerance Zones

Projected tolerances are specified in addition to positional tolerances to make the tolerance more specific. Projected tolerances control, for example, the perpendicularity tolerance zone of an embedded part.

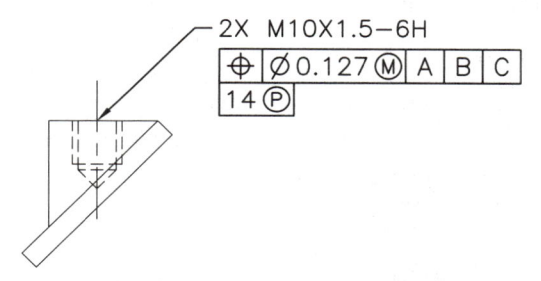

2X M10X1.5−6H

The symbol for projected tolerance (Ⓟ) is preceded by a height value, which specifies the minimum projected tolerance zone. The projected tolerance zone height and symbol appear in a frame below the feature control frame.

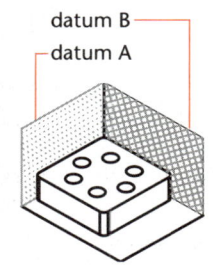

Composite Tolerances

datum B
datum A

A composite tolerance specifies two tolerances for the same geometric characteristic of a feature or features that have different datum requirements. One tolerance relates to a pattern of features and the other tolerance to each feature within the pattern. The individual feature tolerance is more restrictive than the pattern tolerance.

In the illustration, where datums A and B intersect is the datum axis, the point from which the position of the pattern is calculated. A composite tolerance could specify both the diameter of the pattern of holes and the diameter of each individual hole.

Adding Geometric Tolerances

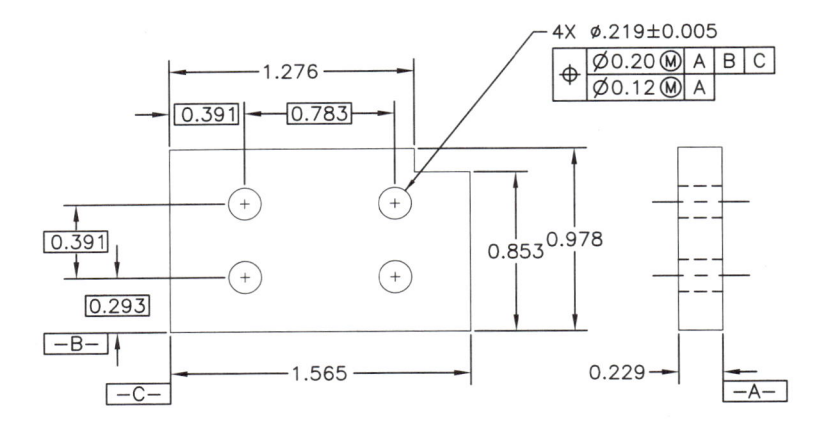

When you add composite tolerances to a drawing, you create the first line of a feature control frame and then choose the same geometric characteristic symbol for the second line of the feature control frame. AutoCAD extends the geometric symbol compartment over both lines. You can then create a second line of tolerance symbols.

To add composite tolerances

1 From the Dimension menu, choose Tolerance.
2 In the Symbol dialog box, select the composite tolerance symbol.

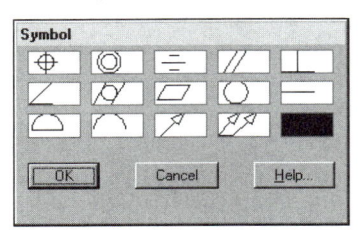

3 Choose OK.
4 In the Geometric Tolerance dialog box, create the first line of tolerance symbols.

Now, create the second line of tolerance symbols.

1 In the Geometric Tolerance dialog box, on the second line of the feature control frame, choose the geometric symbol button.
2 In the Symbol dialog box, select the same geometric characteristic symbol as for the first line and choose OK.

3 In the Geometric Tolerance dialog box under Tolerance 1, enter the tolerance value and any modifying symbols.

4 Choose OK, and then specify the location of the feature control frame in the drawing.

Command line   TOLERANCE

Creating and Modifying Arrowheads

The arrowheads AutoCAD uses are blocks. To define your own arrowhead, provide the name of an existing block created with the BLOCK command. For information on how to create a block, see "Defining Blocks" on page 437.

Arrowhead sizing relies on the overall dimension scale factor. When you create a dimension, AutoCAD inserts your block where the arrowheads would normally go. The object's *X* and *Y* scale factors are set to *arrowhead size* × *overall scale*. The dimension line is trimmed by *text gap* × *overall scale* units at each end. To trim the dimension line, AutoCAD inserts the rightmost block with a zero rotation angle for horizontal dimensioning. The leftmost block is rotated 180 degrees about its insertion point. If you use paper space scaling, AutoCAD computes the scale factor before applying it to the arrowhead size value.

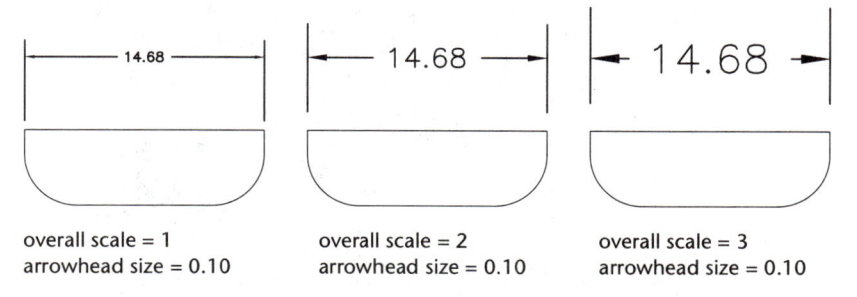

overall scale = 1
arrowhead size = 0.10

overall scale = 2
arrowhead size = 0.10

overall scale = 3
arrowhead size = 0.10

one drawing unit

insertion point

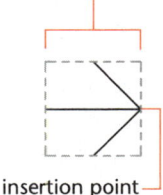

The following example shows how to create a custom three-stroke arrowhead and save it as a block. Setting Snap mode to half a drawing unit and Grid mode to one drawing unit makes it easier to create the block. You create the block for insertion as the *right* arrowhead of a horizontal dimension line.

The illustration shows a right-angle (or three-stroke) arrowhead with a one-unit grid for clarity. The insertion base point of the block is where the intersection of the dimension line and the extension line would be (in the illustration on the left, at the tip of the arrowhead).

The dimension line stops *arrowhead size × overall scale* drawing units away from the extension line. Consequently, the block consists of an arrowhead and a short horizontal tail line connecting to the dimension line.

To create your own arrowhead symbol

1 Draw the arrowhead so it measures exactly one drawing unit from the insertion base point at the tip of the arrowhead to the end of the tail.

2 From the Insert menu, choose Block.

3 Enter a block name.

4 For the insertion base point of the block, specify the point you want placed at the intersection of the dimension line and the extension line (where the tip of the default arrowhead would be).

5 Select the objects for inclusion in the block.

Command line BLOCK

To use your own arrowhead symbol

1 From the Dimension menu, choose Style.

2 In the Dimension Styles dialog box, choose Geometry.

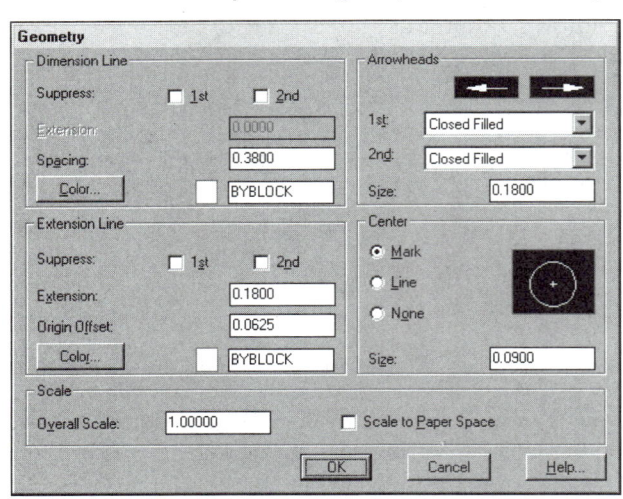

3 In the Geometry dialog box under Arrowheads, select User Arrow from the 1st Arrowheads list.

4 In the User Arrow dialog box, enter the name of your block. Then choose OK.

5 To choose a different custom arrowhead for the second arrowhead, repeat steps 3 and 4, choosing User Arrow from the 2nd Arrowheads list.

Related   DIMBLK controls the arrowhead type if both are the same. DIMBLK1 and DIMBLK2 control the first and second arrowhead types if they are different (when DIMSAH is on). DIMASZ controls arrowhead and hook line size.

Using Blocks, Attributes, and Xrefs

11

In this chapter

- Defining, inserting, and exploding blocks
- Using blocks with layers, colors, and linetypes
- Creating and editing attributes and extracting attribute information
- Managing external references

AutoCAD provides several features to help you manage objects in your drawings. With blocks you can organize and manipulate many objects as one component. Attributes associate items of information with the blocks in your drawings—for example, part numbers and prices.

Using AutoCAD external references, or xrefs, you can attach or overlay entire drawings to your current drawing. When you open your current drawing, any changes that have been made in the referenced drawing appear in the current drawing.

Specification sheets or bills of materials can also be created using this information.

Working with Blocks

A block is a collection of objects you can associate together to form a single object, or block definition. You can insert, scale, and rotate a block in a drawing. You can explode a block into its component objects, modify them, and redefine the block definition. AutoCAD updates all future instances of that block based on the block definition.

Blocks streamline the drawing process. For example, you can use blocks to

- Build a standard library of frequently used symbols, components, or standard parts. You can insert the same block numerous times instead of re-creating the drawing elements each time.
- Revise drawings efficiently by inserting, relocating, and copying blocks as components rather than individual geometric objects.
- Save disk space by storing all references to the same block as one block definition in the drawing database.

When you insert a block in your drawing, you are creating a block instance. Each time you insert a block instance, you assign a scale factor and rotation angle to the inserted block. You can also scale a block instance using different values in any coordinate (X, Y, Z) direction.

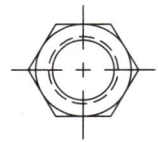

default values

X scale = .5
Y scale = 1

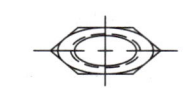

X scale = 1
Y scale = .5

rotation
angle = 45

For information about how to create a block, see "Defining Blocks" on page 437.

Blocks make it possible for you to organize your drawing tasks in a systematic way, so that you can set up, redesign, and sort the objects in your drawings and the information associated with them.

Working with Layers, Colors, and Linetypes

Blocks can be defined from objects that were originally drawn on different layers with different colors and linetypes. You can preserve the layer, color, and linetype information of objects in a block. Then, each time you insert the block, you have each object within the block drawn on its original layer with its original color and linetype.

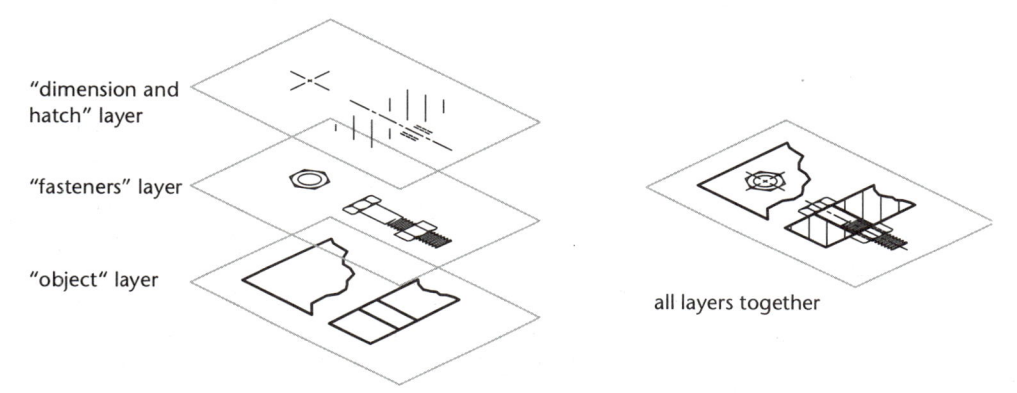

"dimension and hatch" layer

"fasteners" layer

"object" layer

all layers together

Layers separated and combined

When a block that consists of objects drawn on layer 0 and assigned the color and linetype BYLAYER is placed on the current layer, it assumes the color and linetype properties of the current layer. The current layer's properties override any color or linetype explicitly assigned to that block.

A block that consists of objects that have color or linetype specified with BYBLOCK is drawn with the color and linetype that are current when the block is inserted. If the color and linetype are not explicitly assigned, the block assumes the color and linetype of the layer.

Nesting Blocks

A block reference can contain other (nested) blocks. For example, you can insert a drawing of a mechanical assembly that contains a housing, a bracket, and fasteners, with each fastener composed of a bolt, washer, and nut. The only restriction on nested blocks is that you cannot insert or create blocks that reference themselves.

Working with Blocks

assembly block

blocks that are components of the assembly block

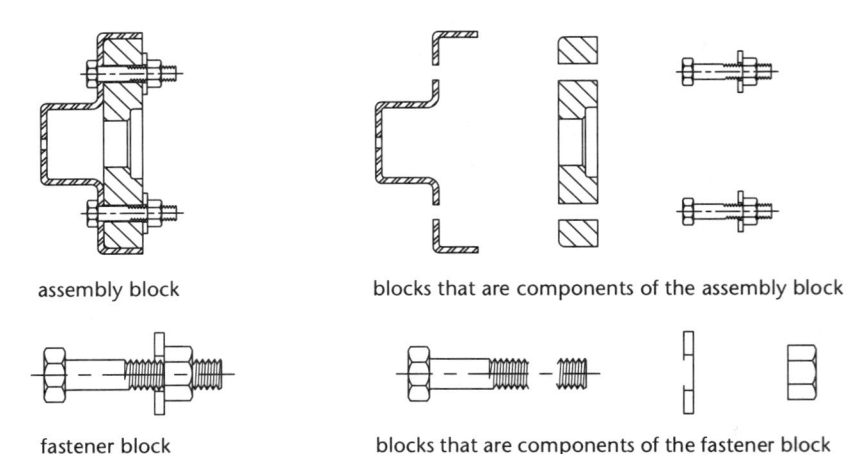

fastener block

blocks that are components of the fastener block

Nested blocks

Sometimes a nested block contains objects that are on layer 0 or that have color and linetype specified with BYBLOCK. Such objects are called floating objects, and their properties are determined by the block that contains them in the nested structure.

Although block nesting can be useful, floating layers, colors, and linetypes can make nesting complicated if they aren't used correctly. To minimize confusion, follow these guidelines:

If all instances of a particular block need the same layer, color, and linetype properties, assign properties explicitly to all objects in the block (including any nested blocks).

If you want to control the color and linetype of each instance of a particular block by using the color and linetype of the layer on which you insert it, draw each of the block's objects (including any nested blocks) on layer 0 with color and linetype set to BYLAYER.

If you want to control the color and linetype of each instance of a particular block using the current explicit color and linetype, draw each of its objects (including any nested blocks) with color and linetype set to BYBLOCK. Before creating a block, you can change the layer, color, and linetype of its constituent object with DDCHPROP.

Creating Unnamed Blocks

AutoCAD creates unnamed (also called anonymous) blocks to support hatch patterns, associative dimensioning, and PostScript images imported with PSIN. AutoCAD also creates unnamed blocks for objects that you cannot gain access to directly. You cannot insert unnamed blocks by name; however, you can create them in AutoLISP (see chapter 9, "Anonymous Blocks" in the *Customization Guide*).

Defining Blocks

You can define a block in three ways:

- Use BLOCK to group objects for use in the current drawing only.
- Use BMAKE TO GROUP OBJECTS FOR USE IN THE CURRENT DRAWING.
- Use WBLOCK to group objects in a separate drawing file. The drawing file can then be used as a block definition for other drawings. AutoCAD considers any drawing you insert into another drawing to be a block definition.

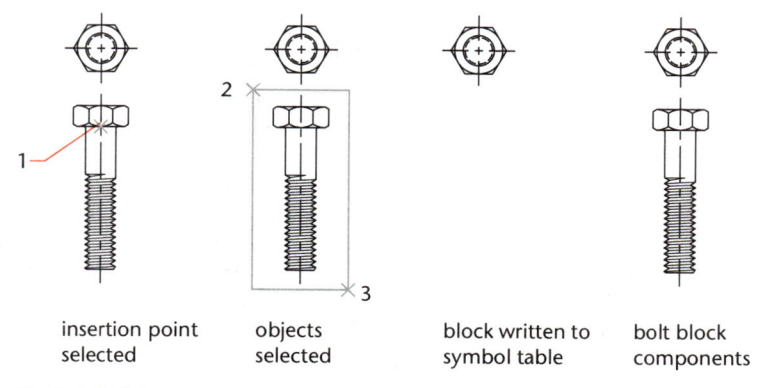

insertion point selected   objects selected   block written to symbol table   bolt block components

Block definition sequence

To define a block for the current drawing

1. From the Draw menu, choose Block ➤ Make.
2. Enter a name for the block. For example, enter **bolt**.
3. In the Block Definition dialog box, choose Select Point.
4. Select the insertion base point (1).

Working with Blocks

437

5   In the Block Definition dialog box, choose Select Objects.

6   Select the objects for the block (2 and 3). The block is now defined and named and exists in the current drawing only.

Command line BMAKE

To redefine a named block, use BLOCK again, entering the name of the existing block and selecting the new objects and insertion point. When you redefine a block, all the references to that block in the drawing are immediately updated to reflect the new definition.

To save a block as a separate drawing file

1   At the Command prompt, enter **wblock**.

2   In the Create Drawing File dialog box, enter the name of the drawing file.

3   Choose OK.

4   When prompted for the block name, use one of the following procedures:

- To save an existing block definition as a drawing file, enter the name of the block at the Block Name prompt. If the block name is the same as the file name you entered in step 2, enter an equal sign (=).
- To create a new block definition and save it as a drawing file, press ENTER at the Block Name prompt. Select the insertion base point and the objects.

The block definition is saved as a drawing file.

Command line WBLOCK

Inserting Blocks

You can insert blocks or entire drawings into the current drawing with DDINSERT and INSERT. When you insert a block or drawing, you specify the insertion point, scale, and rotation angle. This section explains inserting blocks into your drawing using DDINSERT.

When you insert an entire drawing into another drawing, AutoCAD treats the inserted drawing like any other block reference. Subsequent insertions reference the block definition (which contains the geometric description of the block) with different position, scale, and rotation settings, as shown in the following illustration. If you change the original drawing after inserting it, the changes have no effect on the inserted block. If you want the inserted block to reflect the changes you made to the original drawing, you can redefine the block by reinserting the original drawing. This can be done with the INSERT command by using a *<blockname>*= syntax at the Block Name prompt, or with the DDINSERT command by selecting the original DWG file.

If you want to insert a drawing but you don't want the file name to be the same as the block name, or if the file name is more than 31 characters or spaces, you can insert it using a *<blockname>* = *<filename>* syntax at the Block Name prompt.

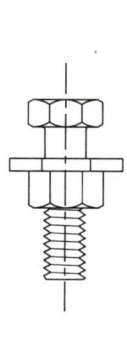

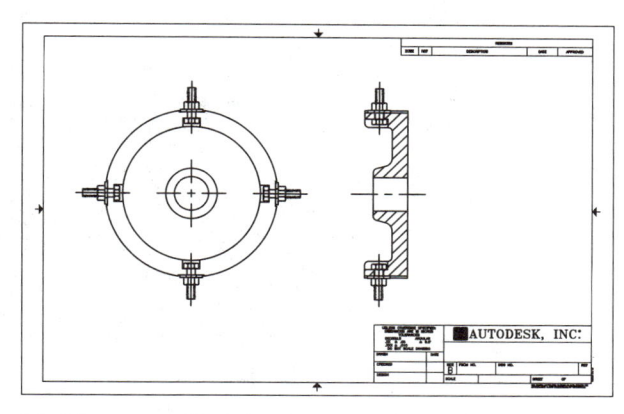

fastener

block instances of fastener

By default, AutoCAD uses the coordinate 0,0,0 as the insertion base point for inserted drawings. You can change the base point by opening the original drawing and using BASE to specify a different insertion base point. AutoCAD uses the new base point the next time you insert the drawing.

If the drawing you insert contains paper space objects, those objects are *not* be included in the current drawing's block definition. To use the paper space objects in another drawing, open the original drawing and use BLOCK to define the paper space objects as a block. This nested block definition is then included in the drawing database when you insert that drawing into another drawing. You can insert the drawing into either paper space or model space.

NOTE After insertion, the external file's WCS is aligned parallel to the *XY* plane of the current UCS in the current drawing. Thus, a block reference from an external file can be inserted at any orientation in space by setting the UCS before inserting it.

Working with Blocks

To insert a block reference

1   From the Insert menu, choose Block.

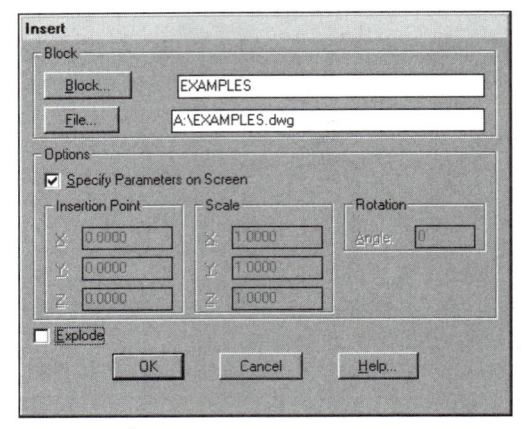

   [Insert dialog box screenshot showing Block name EXAMPLES, File A:\EXAMPLES.dwg, Specify Parameters on Screen checked, Insertion Point/Scale/Rotation fields, Explode checkbox, OK/Cancel/Help buttons]

2   In the Insert dialog box, specify the block name, where you want to insert it in the current drawing, and whether you want to explode it after insertion.

3   If you have modified the original drawing file for a block, you can redefine the block in the current drawing by choosing File to locate the file for the block.

    The block reference is updated in the current drawing.

4   Choose OK.

    Command line   DDINSERT

    Related   INSERT inserts a block on the command line. MINSERT inserts a block in a rectangular array.

Exploding a Block

Use EXPLODE to break a block instance. By exploding a block instance, you can modify the block or add to or delete the objects that define it.

To explode a block

1   From the Modify menu, choose Explode.
2   Select the block to explode.

    The block instance is broken into its component objects; however, the block definition still exists in the drawing's block symbol table.

    Command line   EXPLODE

Redefining a Block

You can use BLOCK or INSERT to redefine blocks and attribute definitions. Redefinition affects previous as well as future insertions of a block reference. Constant attributes are lost and replaced by any new constant attributes. Variable attributes remain unchanged, even if the new block definition has no attributes. When you insert the block with DDINSERT, specify a file in the Insert dialog box. For more information, see "To insert a block reference" on page 440.

Working with Attributes

An attribute provides an interactive label or tag for you to attach text to a block. Whenever you insert a block that has a variable attribute, AutoCAD prompts you to enter the data to be stored with the block. Examples of data are part numbers, prices, comments, and owners' names.

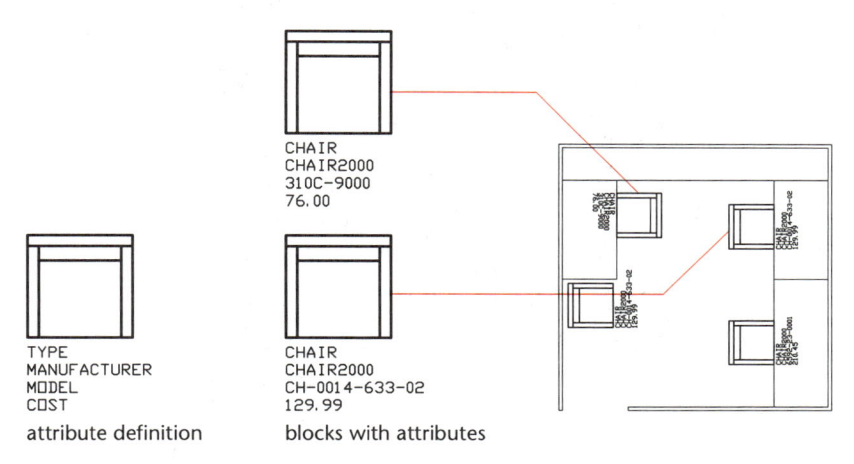

Blocks with attributes

You can extract attribute information from a drawing and use that information in a spreadsheet or database to produce items such as a parts list or bill of materials (BOM). You can associate more than one attribute with a block, provided that each attribute has a different tag. AutoCAD prompts you for the value of each attribute when you insert the block. You can also define constant attributes: because they have the same value in every occurrence of the block, AutoCAD does not prompt for a value when you insert the block.

Attributes can be invisible, which means the attribute is not displayed or plotted. However, information on the attribute is stored in the drawing file and written to an extract file by DDATTEXT and ATTEXT.

Creating Attributes

To create an attribute, you must first use DDATTDEF to create an attribute definition, which describes the characteristics of the attribute. The characteristics include the tag, prompt, value information, text formatting, location, and any optional modes.

To create an attribute definition

1   On the command line, enter **ddattdef**.

2   In the Attribute Definition dialog box, specify the insertion point and set the Attribute modes, tag, prompt, and text options.

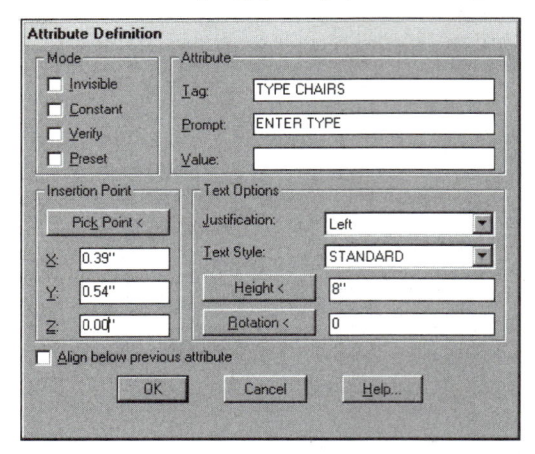

3   Choose OK.

After creating the attribute definition, you can select it as an object in a block definition. If the attribute definition is incorporated into a block, whenever you insert the block, AutoCAD prompts you with the text string you specified for the attribute. Each subsequent instance of the block can have a different value specified for the attribute.

If you want to use several attributes together, create each one separately and then include them in the same block. To control the order of prompts for multiple attributes, see DDSELECT in the *Command Reference*.

Related ATTDEF creates the attribute definition on the command line. The AFLAGS system variable also sets the DDATTDEF mode. ATTDISP globally controls the visibility of attributes. ATTREDEF redefines a block and updates associated attributes.

Editing Attribute Definitions

You can use DDEDIT to edit an attribute definition before it is associated with a block.

To edit an attribute definition before it is associated with a block

1 From the Modify menu, choose Object ➤ Text.
2 Select the attribute definition text to edit.

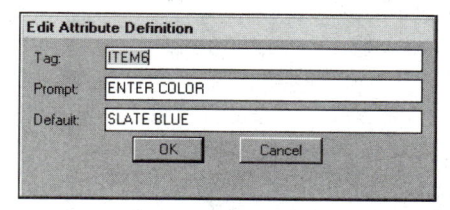

3 In the Edit Attribute Definition dialog box, specify the attribute tag, prompt, and default value. Then choose OK.

Command line DDEDIT

Related CHANGE changes the characteristics of existing attribute definitions.

Attaching Attributes to Blocks

You can attach attributes to a block when you define or redefine that block. When AutoCAD prompts you to select the objects to include in the block definition, include the desired attributes in the selection set. The order in which you select the attributes determines the order in which you are prompted for attribute information when you insert the block (see "Defining Blocks" on page 437).

Editing Attributes Attached to Blocks

You can edit attributes that are already attached to a block and inserted in a drawing.

To edit an attribute attached to a block

1. From the Modify menu, choose Object ➤ Attribute ➤ Single.
2. Select a block to edit.

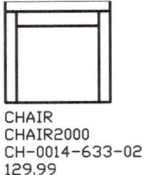

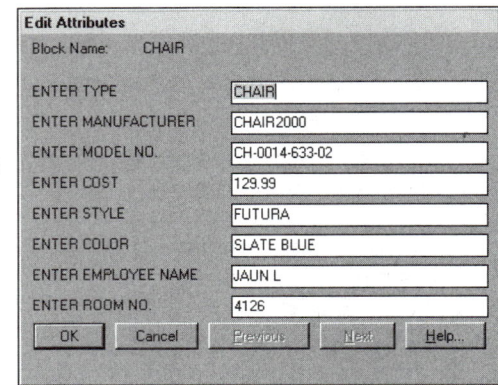

3. In the Edit Attributes dialog box, edit the attribute information as necessary.
4. Choose OK.

To control the order of prompts for multiple attributes, see DDSELECT in the *Command Reference*.

Command line DDATTE

Related ATTEDIT changes attribute information independently of the associated block reference. CHANGE changes the characteristics of existing objects.

Extracting Attribute Information

You can extract attribute information from a drawing and create a separate text file for use with database software. Extracting attribute information does not affect the drawing. You must create a template file to tell AutoCAD how to structure the file to contain the extracted attribute information. The template file contains all of the information associated with attribute tags, such as part name, model number, cost, or supplier, as shown in the illustration to the left of the table. After you create a template file, AutoCAD uses that file to determine what attribute information to extract from the drawing.

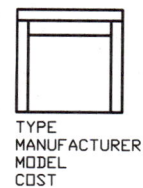

TYPE
MANUFACTURER
MODEL
COST

Template file information			
Attribute tag	(C)haracter or (N)umeric data	Maximum field length	Decimal places
Type	C	040	000
Manufacturer	C	006	000
Model	C	015	000
Cost	N	005	003

Each field in the template file extracts information from the drawing. Each line in the template file specifies one field to be written in the extract file, including the name of the field, its character width, and its numerical precision. Each record of the extract file includes all the specified fields in the order given by the template file.

The following template file displays the 15 possible fields.

BL: LEVEL	Nwww000	(*Block nesting level*)
BL: NAME	Cwww000	(*Block name*)
BL: X	Nwwwddd	(*X coordinate of block insertion point*)
BL: Y	Nwwwddd	(*Y coordinate*)
BL: Z	Nwwwddd	(*Z coordinate*)
BL: NUMBER	Nwww000	(*Block counter; same for* MINSERT)
BL: HANDLE	Cwww000	(*Block's handle; same for* MINSERT)
BL: LAYER	Cwww000	(*Block insertion layer name*)
BL: ORIENT	Nwwwddd	(*Block rotation angle*)
BL: XSCALE	Nwwwddd	(*X scale factor*)
BL: YSCALE	Nwwwddd	(*Y scale factor*)
BL: ZSCALE	Nwwwddd	(*Z scale factor*)
BL: XEXTRUDE	Nwwwddd	(*X component of block's extrusion direction*)
BL: YEXTRUDE	Nwwwddd	(*Y component*)
BL: ZEXTRUDE	Nwwwddd	(*Z component*)
numeric	Nwwwddd	(*Numeric attribute tag*)
character	Cwww000	(*Character attribute tag*)

Working with Attributes

The template file can include any or all of the BL:*xxx* field names listed above. The template file must include at least one attribute tag field. The attribute tag fields determine which attributes, hence which blocks, are included in the extract file. If a block contains some, but not all, of the specified attributes, the values for the absent ones are filled in with blanks (if characters) or zeros (if numeric). Block references that do *not* contain any of the specified attributes are excluded from the extract file. Each field can appear no more than once in the template file.

The comment fields should not be included in the template file.

To create a template file

1 Click Start on the Windows taskbar, and then choose Programs.

(In Windows 3.51, choose the Program Manager.)

2 From the Accessories program group, choose Notepad.

You can use any text editor or word processor that can save a text file in ASCII format.

3 Enter template information in Notepad and save with a *.txt* extension.

4 To extract data about a specific tag, insert the tag name in place of the "numeric" or "character" fields.

WARNING! Do *not* use tab characters when constructing the template file with a word processor. To align the columns, use ordinary spaces by using the SPACEBAR.

Attribute Information Files

An attribute is extracted only if its tag name matches the field name specified in the template file. DDATTEXT extracts the attribute information using one of the following formats:

- Comma-delimited file (CDF)
- Space-delimited file (SDF)
- Drawing interchange file (DXF)

The CDF format produces a file containing one record for each block reference in the drawing. A comma separates the fields of each record, and single quotation marks enclose the character fields. Some database applications can read this format directly.

The SDF format also produces a file containing one record for each block reference in a drawing. The fields of each record have a fixed width and employ neither field separators nor character-string delimiters.

The DXF format produces a subset of the AutoCAD drawing interchange file format containing only block references, attributes, and end-of-sequence objects. DXF format extraction requires no template. The file extension *.dxx* distinguishes the output file from normal DXF files.

The following is a sample template file.

BL: NAME	C008000	(*Block name, 8 characters*)
BL: X	N007001	(*X coordinate, format nnnnn.d*)
BL: Y	N007001	(*Y coordinate, format nnnnn.d*)
SUPPLIER	C016000	(*Manufacturer's name, 16 characters*)
MODEL	C009002	(*Model number, 9 characters*)
PRICE	N009002	(*Unit price, format nnnnn.dd*)

Using the previous template file information, you can extract attribute information with the DDATTEXT command, as in the following procedure.

To extract attribute information

1 On the command line, enter **ddattext**.

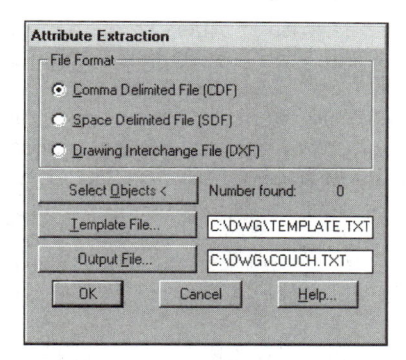

2 In the Attribute Extraction dialog box, specify the appropriate file format, the objects to extract attributes from, the template file to use, and the output file.

If you do not specify any objects, DDATTEXT extracts any attributed blocks in the entire drawing that match the template.

3 Choose OK.

Command line DDATTEXT

Related ATTEXT extracts attribute information from the command line. You can also associate information with objects using XDATA. For more information, see "Selection Set, Object, and Symbol Table Functions," in the *Customization Guide*.

Working with Attributes

447

Using External References

An external reference (xref) links another drawing to the current drawing. When you insert a drawing as a block, the block definition and all of the associated geometry is stored in the current drawing database. It is *not* updated if the original drawing changes. When you insert a drawing as an xref, however, it is updated when the original drawing changes. A drawing that contains xrefs, therefore, always reflects the most current editing of each externally referenced file.

Like a block reference, an xref is displayed in the current drawing as a single object. However, an xref does not significantly increase the file size of the current drawing and cannot be exploded. As with block references, you can nest xrefs that are attached to your drawing.

By attaching xrefs, you can

- Assemble a master drawing from component drawings that may undergo changes as a project develops.
- Coordinate your work with the work of others by overlaying other drawings on your drawing to keep up with the changes being made by other users.
- Ensure that the most recent version of the referenced drawing is displayed. When you open or plot your drawing, AutoCAD automatically reloads each xref, so it reflects the latest state of the referenced drawing file.
- Create clipped boundaries of xrefs, to display only a specific section of the xref file in the master drawing.

Updating Xrefs

When you open or plot your drawing, AutoCAD reloads each xref to reflect the latest state of the referenced drawing. After you make changes to an externally referenced drawing and save the file, other users can access your changes immediately by reloading the xref.

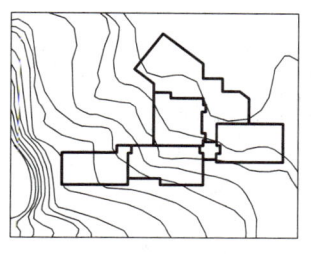

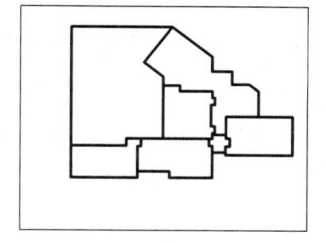

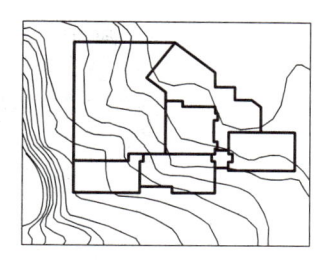

xref attached   edited xref file   xref updated

Updating Xrefs

Using the External Reference Dialog Box

With the External Reference dialog box, you can manage all of your externally referenced drawings. The External Reference dialog box displays the status of each xref and the relationship of xrefs to one another. In the dialog box, you can

- Attach a new xref
- Detach an existing xref
- Reload or unload an existing xref
- Change an attachment to an overlay or vice versa
- Bind the entire xref definition to the current drawing
- Change the xref path

You can view the xrefs from either a list view (flat listing) or a hierarchical tree view. To choose a view, click either the Tree View or the List View icon in the upper-left corner of the dialog box. The list view is displayed by default.

List View

When the External Reference dialog box is displayed, the list view displays an alphabetical list of the xref definitions in the current drawing. Each xref is defined by the following:

- Reference name
- Status
- File size
- Xref type (attachment or overlay)
- File date
- Saved path

Using External References

449

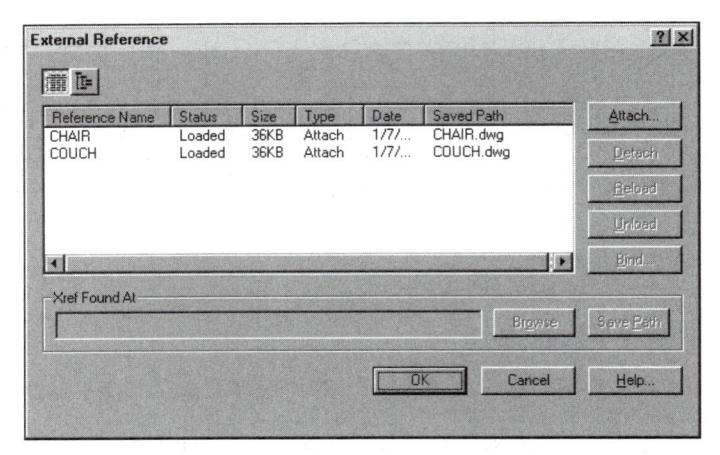

[Dialog box: External Reference, showing Reference Name, Status, Size, Type, Date, Saved Path columns with CHAIR and COUCH entries, both Loaded, 36KB, Attach, 1/7/..., CHAIR.dwg and COUCH.dwg. Buttons: Attach, Detach, Reload, Unload, Bind. Xref Found At field with Browse and Save Path buttons. OK, Cancel, Help buttons.]

The columns are aligned vertically and xrefs can be sorted by clicking the column headings in the list box. For example, to sort by name, click the Reference Name column heading. To sort by size, click the Size column heading.

You can edit the xref name by selecting the reference name on the list and then clicking the highlighted file name a second time. An xref name can include more than eight characters; however, it is recommended that you limit the number of characters to accommodate the symbol table length restrictions. For more information on symbol table name restrictions, see "Binding Xrefs to Drawings" on page 462.

Selecting any field in the list highlights the xref name. The xref name can be edited by selecting it a second time and then entering a new name. The Status column indicates the state of the xref definitions in the drawing or the action to be taken when the dialog is closed:

Loaded	Xref was found when the drawing was opened or reloaded.
Unloaded	Xref was unloaded by user.
Unreferenced	When an xref with nested xrefs is unloaded, not found, or unresolved, its nested xrefs become unreferenced because the parent xref is no longer present in the drawing. If a parent xref is unloaded, a message is displayed stating that its nested xrefs are "orphaned."
Not found	Xref was not found when the drawing was opened or reloaded.
Unresolved	Xref file was found but could not be read by AutoCAD.

The Type column indicates whether the xref is an attachment or an overlay. By double-clicking the Type column, you can switch an xref between an attachment and an overlay. The Date column contains the last date the referenced drawing file was saved. This column is only displayed if the xref is loaded. If an xref is not loaded, not found, or unreferenced, the date and size columns are blank. Changes take effect when you close the dialog box.

Tree View

When you click the Tree View icon, a hierarchical representation of the xrefs is displayed. The top level of the tree view is listed in alphabetical order. Xref information displayed includes the levels of nesting within xrefs, their relationship to one another, and whether they have been resolved.

The tree view displays only the relationships between xrefs. It does not display the number of attachments or overlays associated with the drawing. Repeated attachments of the same xref are not displayed in the tree view.

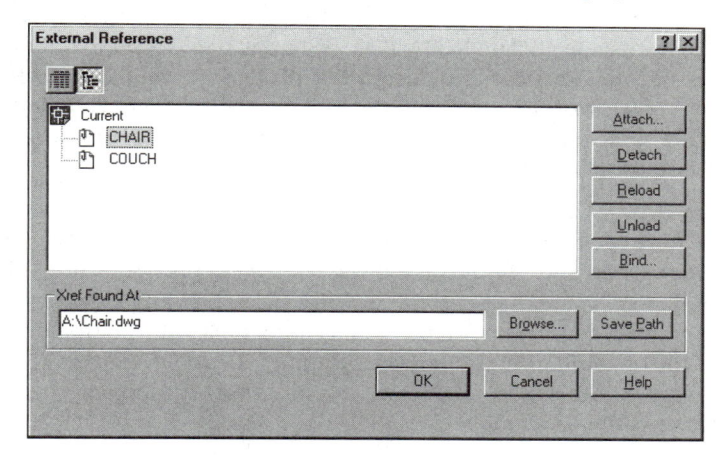

Attach

The Attach option links one drawing (the reference file, or xref) to the current drawing. An xref is a type of block. However, unlike regular blocks, where the block definition and the contents of the block are stored with the current drawing, only the definition of the xref is attached to the drawing. AutoCAD must read the reference drawing to determine what to display in the current drawing. If the reference file is missing or corrupt, its data is not displayed in the current drawing. All objects and xref-dependent symbol table information is loaded from the referenced file each time a drawing that contains the referenced file is opened. If VISRETAIN is on, AutoCAD stores locally any xref-dependent layer information that has been updated in the current drawing.

Detach

To remove xrefs from the current drawing, use XREF Detach. When you detach an xref from your drawing, all copies of the xref are erased, and the xref definition is deleted. When an xref is detached, it is removed from the tree view and the list view. All xref-dependent symbol table information (such as layers and linetypes) is deleted from the current drawing's symbol table. You cannot detach nested xrefs, nor can you detach a top level xref if it is defined as a nested xref of another top level xref in the xref tree.

Reload

When you reload an xref, the most recently saved version of the referenced file is read into the drawing, and the xref definition is updated to ensure that the current version of the reference is loaded.

If demand loading is turned on when the xref is loaded, the referenced drawing remains open during the current editing session, or a copy is created and remains open during the current editing session. When a demand loaded xref is reloaded, if the XLOADCTL system variable is set to 1, no one else can access the referenced drawing. If XLOADCTL is set to 2, AutoCAD loads a temporary copy of the most recently saved version of the referenced file. For more information about demand loading, see "Demand Loading and Maximizing Xref Performance" on page 453.

Unload

When an xref is unloaded from the current drawing, the drawing opens much faster and uses less memory. The xref definition is unloaded from the drawing file, but the pointer to the reference drawing remains. The xref is not displayed, and the xref-dependent symbol table information does not appear in the drawing. However, all the information can be restored by reloading the xref. If XLOADCTL (DEMAND LOADING) is set to 1, unloading the drawing unlocks the original file.

Unloading is recommended when a reference file is not needed in the current drawing session but may be used eventually for plotting. You can maintain a working list of unloaded xrefs in the drawing file that can be loaded as needed.

Bind

Binding an xref to a drawing makes the xref a permanent part of the drawing and no longer an externally referenced file. The externally referenced information becomes a block. When the externally referenced drawing is updated, the bound xref is *not* updated. You can bind the entire drawing's database, including all of its dependent symbols, by using XREF Bind. Or you can bind the dependent symbols such as layers or linetype styles individually with XBIND.

You can choose to bind an xref to a drawing using either the Bind option or the Insert option. The option you choose determines how the file names are defined in the symbol table when the definitions are merged from the reference file into the host drawing. If you use Bind, the symbol names are prefixed with a <blockname>x string, where x is an integer that is automatically incremented to avoid overriding existing block definitions.

If you use Insert, the symbol names are merged into the host drawing without the prefix. If duplicate symbols exist, AutoCAD uses the symbols already defined in the local drawing symbol table. If you are unsure whether your drawing contains duplicate symbol names, it is recommended that you use Bind, not Insert.

Demand Loading and Maximizing Xref Performance

Through a combination of demand loading and saving drawings with indexes, you can increase the performance of drawings with external references. Demand loading works in conjunction with the XLOADCTL and INDEXCTL system variables. When you turn on demand loading, if indexes have been saved in the referenced drawings, AutoCAD loads into memory only the data from the reference drawing that is necessary to regenerate the current drawing. In other words, referenced material is read in "on demand."

To realize the maximum benefits of demand loading, you need to save the referenced drawings with layer and spatial indexes. The performance benefits of demand loading are most noticeable when you

- Clip the xref to display a small fraction of it and a spatial index is saved in the externally referenced drawing
- Freeze several layers of the xref, and the externally referenced drawing is saved with a layer index

If demand loading is enabled, and you have clipped xrefs that were saved with spatial indexes, objects in the external reference database that are contained within the clip volume comprise the majority of the objects read into the drawing. If the clip volume is modified, more objects are loaded as required from the reference drawing. Similarly, if you have xrefs with many layers frozen that were saved with layer indexes, only the objects on those thawed layers are read into the current drawing. If those xref-dependent layers are thawed, AutoCAD reads in that geometry from the reference drawing as required.

Using External References

When demand loading is enabled, AutoCAD places a lock on all reference drawings so that it can read in any geometry it needs to on demand. Other users can open those reference drawings, but they cannot save changes to them. If you want other users to be able to modify an xref that is being demand loaded into another drawing, enable the demand loading with the Copy option.

If you turn on demand loading with the copy option, AutoCAD makes a temporary copy of the externally referenced file and demand loads the temporary file. You can then demand load the xref while allowing the original reference drawing to be available for modification. When you disable demand loading, AutoCAD reads in the entire reference drawing regardless of layer visibility or clip instances.

To turn on demand loading in the Preferences dialog box

1 From the Tools menu, choose Preferences.
2 In the Preferences box, choose the Performance tab.
3 On the Performance tab under External Reference File Demand Load, select Disabled, Enabled, or Enabled with Copy.

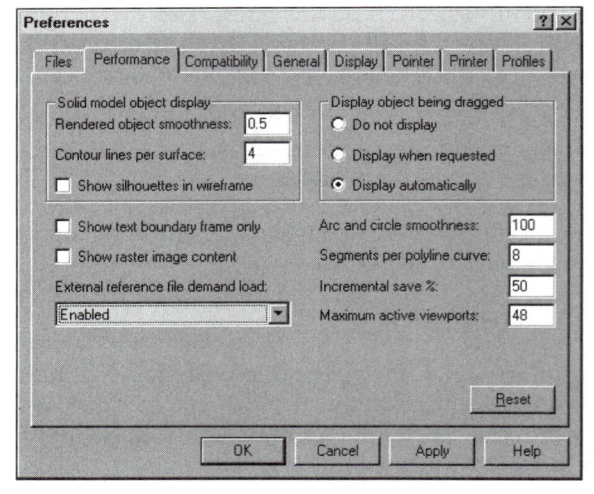

To receive the maximum benefit of demand loading, it is recommended that you save any drawings that are used as xrefs with layer and spatial indexes.

To turn on layer and spatial indexes

1 From the File menu, choose Save As.
2 In the Save As dialog box, choose Options.

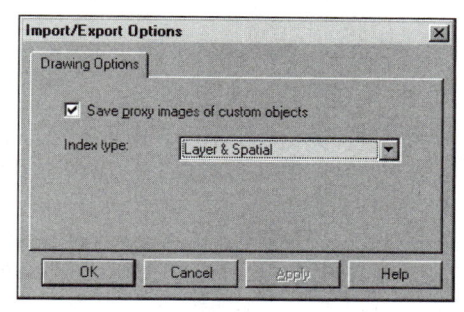

3 In the Import/Export Options dialog box, at Index type, select Layer, Spatial or Layer & Spatial, and then choose OK.

4 Choose OK to exit the Save As dialog box.

XLOADCTL

Another method of enabling demand loading for externally referenced files is to set the XLOADCTL system variable. Setting XLOADCTL to 0 turns off demand loading, which means that AutoCAD loads the entire externally referenced file into your host drawing. When XLOADCTL is set to 0, other users can also access and edit the referenced file.

By default, XLOADCTL is set to 1, which enables demand loading. AutoCAD keeps the original reference file open so it can demand load geometry from the reference drawing as necessary. Other users can open only that drawing file, and they cannot save changes.

Setting XLOADCTL to 2 turns on demand loading with the Copy option, which means that AutoCAD creates a temporary copy of the reference drawing and demand loads xref objects from the temporary copy. Also, because a temporary copy is created when XLOADCTL is set to 2, other users can modify the original file.

If you are externally referencing a drawing saved in a previous version of AutoCAD, and you have enabled demand loading, you will not see the same performance benefit as you would with a Release 14 drawing saved with layer and spatial indexes. Similarly, you will see little performance gain from demand loading a Release 14 drawing if layer and spatial indexes have not be saved with the drawing. For maximum performance, use demand loading in conjunction with reference drawings that have indexes saved with them, where you only need a small number of the xref-dependent objects visible in the current drawing.

XLOADPATH

When you set the XLOADCTL system variable to 2 (demand loading with copy), the XLOADPATH system variable can be used to indicate the path where copies of externally referenced files are to be placed. The path you specify remains in effect for all drawing sessions until you indicate a different path. If no value for XLOADPATH is specified, the temporary file copies are placed in the standard AutoCAD directory for temporary files.

NOTE If you find referencing drawings over a network to be slow, it is recommended that you set XLOADPATH to reference a local directory, and set XLOADCTL to 2 so that the externally referenced files are demand loaded from your local machine. Conversely, to minimize the number of temporary files created by multiple users referencing the same drawing, those users can set XLOADPATH to point to a common directory. In this manner, multiple sessions of AutoCAD can share the same temporary copies of reference drawings.

You can also use the Preferences dialog box to set XLOADPATH and indicate the path where copies of externally referenced files are to be placed.

To set XLOADPATH in the Preferences dialog box

1 From the Tools menu, choose Preferences.
2 In the Preferences dialog box, choose the Files tab.
3 On the Files tab, select the Temporary External Reference File Location folder.
    The expanded tree view displays the path where copies of xref files are placed. If no path is specified, AutoCAD places the temporary copies in the location specified by the Temporary External References File location.
4 Edit the path by selecting it and entering a new path.
5 Choose OK (or Apply) to set the path.

INDEXCTL

The INDEXCTL system variable determines whether Layer, Spatial or Layer & Spatial indexes are created when a drawing file is saved. Using layer and spatial indexes increases performance when AutoCAD is demand loading xrefs, but it may also slightly slow down saving, as well as increase drawing size. By default, INDEXCTL is set to 0, no indexes. The INDEXCTL setting is stored in the drawing.

If INDEXCTL is set to 1, a layer index is created. A layer index is a list showing which objects are on which layers. This list is used when AutoCAD is referencing the drawing in conjunction with demand loading to determine which objects need to be read in and displayed. Objects on frozen layers in an external reference are not read in if the external reference has a layer index and is being demand loaded.

If INDEXCTL is set to 2, a spatial index is created. The spatial index organizes objects based on their location in 3D space. This organization is used to efficiently determine which objects need to be read in when the drawing is being demand loaded and clipped as an external reference. If demand loading is enabled, and the drawing is attached as an xref and clipped, AutoCAD uses the spatial index in the externally referenced drawing to determine which objects lie within the clip boundary. It then reads only those objects into the current session.

If INDEXCTL is set to 3, both layer and spatial indexes are created and saved with the drawing. If the drawing you are working on is not going to be referenced by another drawing, it is recommended you set INDEXCTL to 0 (off). Spatial and layer indexes are best used in drawings that will be used as xrefs in other drawings where demand loading is enabled. Drawings that are not going to be used as xrefs will not benefit from layer and spatial indexing or demand loading.

The following settings apply to the INDEXCTL system variable:

- 0 = no indexes created
- 1 = layer index created
- 2 = spatial index created
- 3 = both spatial and layer indexes created

By default, INDEXCTL is set to 0 when you create a new AutoCAD drawing.

Attaching Xrefs

Using xrefs is an efficient way to manage drawings because the xref geometry is not saved in the host drawing. Instead, it is referenced and loaded when the host drawing is opened, which reduces the file size of the host drawing. When used with demand loading, using xrefs instead of blocks can greatly increase drawing performance.

Attached xrefs are designed to help you build drawings using other drawings. By attaching drawings as xrefs, as opposed to inserting drawing files as blocks, you can display changes to the externally referenced drawing in the host drawing each time it is opened; the host drawing always reflects the latest revisions made to the referenced files.

Xrefs can be nested within other xrefs. You can attach as many copies of an xref as you want, and each can have a different position, scale, and rotation. You can also control the dependent layers and linetype properties that are defined in that xref.

Because the symbol table length name is restricted to 31 characters, the name of an xref should be kept as short as possible. When an xref is attached, all of its dependent symbols (layers, linetypes, dimension styles, blocks, and text styles) are added to the current drawing's symbol table, prefixed with the xref's name and the pipe (|) character. For example, if you have an xref with the name THISISALONGFILE that has a layer in it named THISISALONGLAYER, the attachment is disallowed because the new xref-dependent layer name of THISISALONGFILE|THISISALONGLAYER exceeds 31 characters. If the drawing name contains any characters other than numbers, letters, dollar sign ($), underscore (_), or hyphen (-), AutoCAD prompts you to give the xref a different name from the drawing. If you are using the External Reference dialog box to attach an xref, AutoCAD prompts you for an alternate xref name if the drawing name exceeds eight characters.

The xref you attach to your drawing is included when your drawing is attached as an xref to another drawing. Because the geometry associated with the externally referenced drawing is visible in the current drawing, but stored in the external reference drawing, the drawing size does not increase significantly.

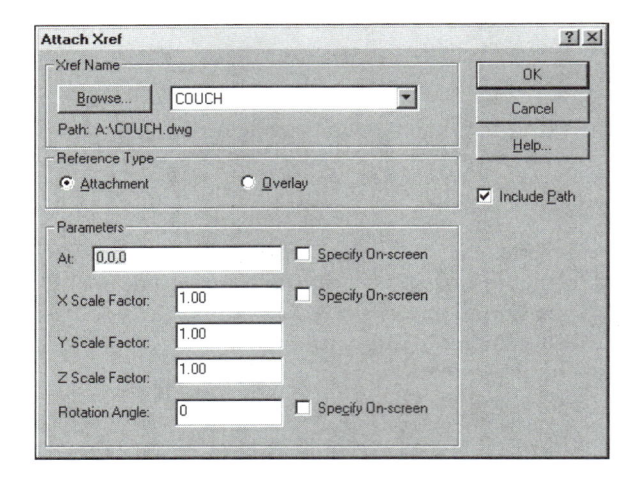

To attach a new xref

1. From the Insert menu, choose External Reference.
2. In the External Reference dialog box, choose Attach.

    The first time you attach an xref, the Select File dialog box is displayed. After you select a file to attach, the Attach Xref dialog box is displayed.

3. In the Attach Xref dialog box, choose Browse.
4. In the Select File to Attach dialog box, select a file and choose OK.

5 In the Attach Xref dialog box under Reference Type, select Attachment.

6 Specify the parameters, scaling factors, and rotation angle.

   You can also select Specify On-screen to specify parameters from the command line.

7 Choose OK.

Command line   XATTACH

Overlaying Xrefs

Overlaying is similar to attaching, except that when a drawing is attached or overlaid, any other overlays nested in it are ignored and, therefore, not displayed. In other words, nested overlays are *not* read in.

It is recommended that you use overlaying when you are referencing geometry that is not useful for other users to see when they reference your drawing. For example, you may have created a wiring plan for a house and need to reference the floor plan of the house. If you have chosen to overlay (rather than attach) the floor plan, then another user, who doesn't need to see the floor plan, could xref your wiring plan without the floor plan attached.

Overlaid xrefs are designed for data sharing. By overlaying an xref, you can see how your drawing relates to other drawings. Also, overlaying an xref reduces the possibility that you might create self-referencing drawings (circular xrefs).

To overlay an xref

1 From the Insert menu, choose External Reference.

   The first time you attach an xref, the Select File dialog box is displayed. After you select a file to attach, the Attach Xref dialog box is displayed.

2 In the External Reference dialog box, select an xref and then choose Attach.

3 In the Attach Xref dialog box under Reference Type, select Overlay.

4 Specify an insertion point.

5 Specify parameters, scaling factors, and rotation angle, or select Specify On-screen.

6 Choose OK.

Command line   XREF

Using External References

Deciding Whether to Attach or to Overlay an Xref

The following illustrations show the difference between attached and overlaid drawings. The upper illustrations show the type of xref used. The lower illustrations show what you see on your screen when you open each file.

In the "Attached xrefs" illustration, *trees.dwg* is attached to *topo.dwg*. *Topo.dwg* is either attached to or overlaid on *house.dwg*. Notice that when you open *house.dwg*, you also see both *trees.dwg* and *topo.dwg*. You see *trees.dwg* because it is attached. You see *topo.dwg* because it is overlaid and is no more than one level of xref from *house.dwg*.

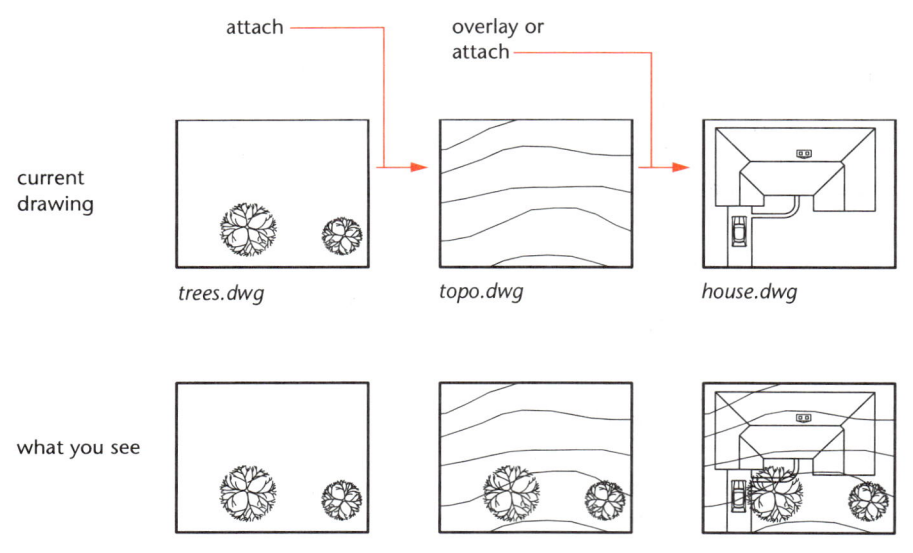

Attached xrefs

In the "Overlaid xrefs" illustration, *trees.dwg* is overlaid on *topo.dwg*. *Topo.dwg* is either attached to or overlaid on *house.dwg*. Notice that when you open *house.dwg*, you see only *topo.dwg* and *house.dwg*. You do not see *trees.dwg* because it is overlaid.

current drawing

overlay

trees.dwg

overlay or attach

topo.dwg

house.dwg

what you see

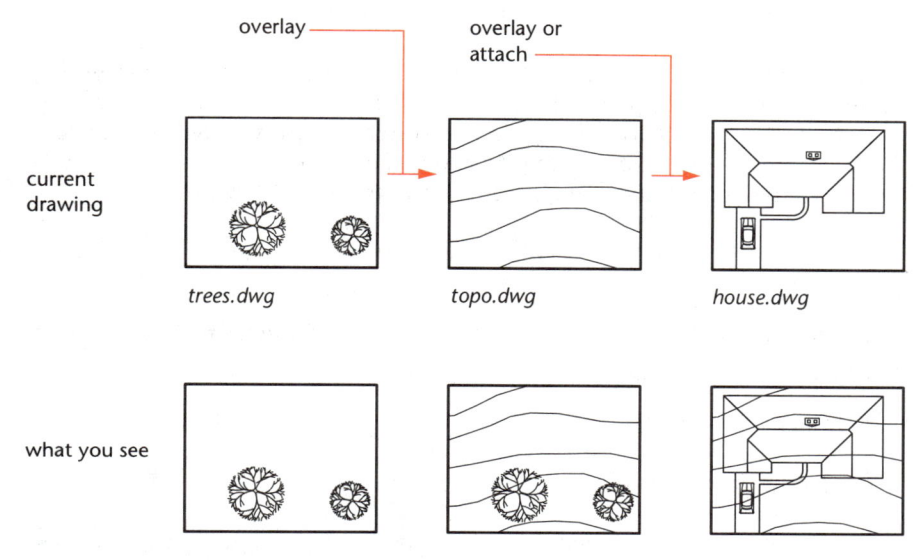

Overlaid xrefs

Detaching Xrefs

You can detach xrefs to completely remove them from your drawing. You can also erase the individual xref instances. Using the Detach option removes xrefs and all dependent symbols associated with that xref. If all the instances of an xref are erased from the drawing, AutoCAD removes the xref definition the next time the drawing is opened.

When an xref is detached, it is removed from the list view and tree view, along with any of its nested xrefs, unless the xref exists in another branch of the tree. You cannot detach a nested xref.

To detach an xref

1 From the Insert menu, choose External Reference.
2 In the External Reference dialog box, select an xref and then choose Detach.
3 Choose OK.

Command line XREF

Using External References

461

Reloading Xrefs

If someone modifies an externally referenced drawing while you are working on the host drawing to which that xref is attached, you can update that xref drawing using the Reload option. When you reload, the selected xref drawing is updated in your host drawing. Also, if you have unloaded an xref, you can choose to reload that externally referenced drawing at any time.

To reload an xref

1 From the Insert menu, choose External Reference.
2 In the External Reference dialog box, select an xref and then choose Reload.
3 Choose OK.

Command line   XREF

Unloading Xrefs

When you unload a referenced file that is not being used in the current drawing, AutoCAD's performance is enhanced by not having to read and display unnecessary drawing geometry or symbol table information. The xref geometry and that of any nested xrefs is not displayed in the current drawing until the xref is reloaded.

To unload an xref

1 From the Insert menu, choose External Reference.
2 In the External Reference dialog box, select an xref and then choose Unload.
3 Choose OK.

Command line   XREF

Binding Xrefs to Drawings

Binding xrefs to drawings is useful if you're archiving drawings and want to ensure that the xrefs do not change. It's also an easy way to send drawings to reviewers. Rather than send a master drawing plus each of the drawings it references, you can use the Bind option to convert those xrefs to blocks in the current drawing. Binding makes the reference a permanent part of the host drawing.

Only loaded xrefs can be bound. If you select an unloaded xref, the Bind button is disabled. You must reload the xref to bind it.

When final drawings that have xrefs are ready for archiving, either archive the xref drawing along with the master drawing or bind the xrefs to the master drawing. These procedures prevent unintentional updating of archived drawings by xrefs that are later changed.

You can choose to either bind an xref or insert it. When you bind an xref to a drawing, the symbol table definitions associated with the externally referenced drawing are permanently added to the host drawing. The names in the symbol table are prefixed with a *<blockname>x* string, where *blockname* is the name of the bound xref. When you insert an xref, the symbol table definitions are added to the host drawing without the prefix.

For example, if you have a drawing with a layer named BLUE and an externally referenced drawing called *xref* that also contains a layer named BLUE, and you bind *xref*, a new layer named XREF0BLUE is added to the host drawing. If you insert *xref*, no new layer is added to the host drawing because the layer named BLUE already exists.

It is recommended that you use the Insert option to bind xrefs when you are adhering to layer and symbol naming conventions. However, if you are inserting an xref that contains a block with the same name as one contained in the symbol table, the block definition in the externally referenced drawing will not be used. For example, if your current drawing contains a block named CHAIR, and you use the Insert option to bind an xref that also has a block named CHAIR, but with a different definition, the current drawing's block definition takes precedence.

To bind an xref to a drawing

1 From the Insert menu, choose External Reference.
2 In the External Reference dialog box, select an xref and then choose Bind.
3 In the Bind Xrefs dialog box, select Bind.
4 Choose OK to exit each dialog box.

To bind using insert

1 From the Insert menu, choose External Reference.
2 In the External Reference dialog box, select an xref, and then choose Bind.
3 In the Bind Xrefs dialog box, select Insert.
4 Choose OK to exit each dialog box.

The symbol table definitions associated with the externally referenced file are merged into the drawing without the prefix. With XBIND you can bind xref-dependent symbol table objects to the current drawing's symbol table without binding the entire xref.

The XBind dialog box provides a list of all xref definitions and their dependent symbols in the drawing. Each xref definition can be expanded to show its dependent symbols. Symbol table objects can be bound by highlighting the symbol name you want to xbind and choosing Add.

To bind dependent symbols to the current drawing

1 At the Command prompt, enter **xbind**.
2 In the XBind dialog box, expand the xref name and the symbol table. Highlight the dependent symbol you want to bind, then choose Add.

   The dependent symbols you select are added to the Definitions to Bind list.
3 Choose OK.

   The dependent symbols are added to your drawing and can be used the same way you use other named objects. AutoCAD removes the vertical bar character (|) from each dependent symbol name and replaces it with two dollar signs ($) separated by a number (usually zero), for example, STAIR0STEEL.

   Command line   -XBIND

Clipping Blocks and Xrefs

After attaching a drawing as an xref or inserting a block, you can define a clipping boundary by using XCLIP. A clipping boundary can define a portion of a block or xref while suppressing the display of geometry outside of the boundary. The portion of the xref or block within the clipped boundary remains visible, and the remainder of the xref or block becomes invisible. The referenced geometry is not altered, only the display of the xref is edited.

NOTE Clipping applies to an individual instance of an xref, not the xref definition itself.

You can use XCLIP to create a new clipping boundary, delete an existing boundary, or generate a polyline object coincident with vertices of the clipping boundary. Xref clipping can be turned on or off. When a clipping boundary is turned off, the boundary is not displayed and the entire xref is visible, provided that the geometry is on a layer that is on and thawed. When a clipping boundary is turned off, it still exists and can be turned on. However deleting a clipping boundary is permanent. For more information about XCLIP, see the *Command Reference*.

After an xref or block has been clipped, it can be edited, moved, or copied just like an unclipped xref or block. The boundary moves with the reference. If an xref contains nested clipped xrefs, they appear clipped in the drawing. If the parent xref is clipped, the nested xrefs are also clipped.

If you want to see the clipping boundary, you can turn on the XCLIPFRAME system variable. XCLIPFRAME determines whether the clipping boundary frame is displayed. When the clipping frame is on (set to 1), it can be selected as part of the object and plotted. For more information about the XCLIPFRAME system variable, see the *Command Reference*.

If the clipped xref is saved in Release 14 with a spatial index, the next time you open the drawing that contains that xref with demand loading enabled, AutoCAD loads only that portion of the drawing that lies within the clipping boundary. Because spatial indexes were not available in Release 13, performance when clipping Release 13 drawings may be slower. To improve performance, it is recommended you update your Release 13 drawings to Release 14.

Clipping Boundaries

An xref clipping boundary can be specified as a rectangular window or a polygonal boundary. You can also select a polyline to define the clipping boundary. The boundary can be specified anywhere in 3D space, but it is always applied planar to the current UCS. If a polyline is selected, the clipping boundary is applied in the plane of that polyline.

Rectangular Window Clipping Boundary

When you specify a rectangular clipping boundary, you are prompted for the corners of the window. The window is drawn parallel to the current UCS, and the clipping boundary is applied normal to the plane it lies on.

Polygonal Clipping Boundary

When you specify a polygonal clipping boundary, you are prompted to enter points to define the boundary. As you specify the clipping points, AutoCAD sketches the last segment of the polygon so that the boundary is closed at all times. When you apply polygonal clipping to images in externally referenced drawings, the clipping boundary is applied to the rectangular extents of the polygonal boundary, rather than to the polygon itself.

Polyline Clipping Boundary

When you specify a polyline clipping boundary, you are prompted to select a 2D polyline object. The clipping boundary is created coincident with the polyline. Valid boundaries are 2D polylines with straight or spline-curved segments. Polylines with arc segments, or fit-curved polylines, can be used as the definition of the clip boundary, but the clip boundary will be created as a straight segment representation of that polyline. An open polyline is treated as if it were closed.

Defining Clipdepth

The front and back clipping planes for xrefs can be set using the Clipdepth option. The xref must contain a clipping boundary before you can specify a clip depth. The clip depth is always calculated normal to the clipping boundary. When defining clip depth, you are prompted to specify a front and back point or distance relative to the clipped plane. Regardless of the current UCS, the clip depth is applied parallel to the clipping boundary.

To clip an xref

1. On the Command line, enter **xclip**.
2. Select objects.
3. At the prompt, select New Boundary by pressing ENTER.
4. Select a rectangular or polygonal clipping boundary, and then specify the corners or vertices of the boundary.

   AutoCAD clips the image based on the area that you specified and hides the portion of the xref outside the clipping boundary.

   Command line   XCLIP

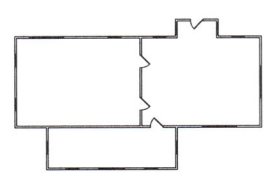

existing drawings

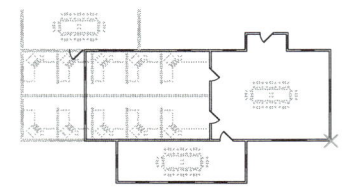

another similar drawing is referenced

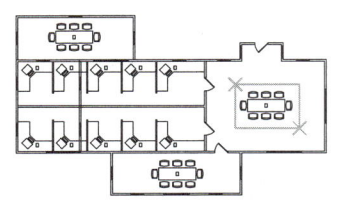

xref is clipped to show only the conference table

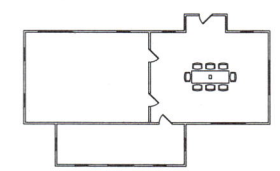

resulting clipped xref

Chapter 11 Using Blocks, Attributes, and Xrefs

Controlling Dependent Symbols

In addition to the drawing's objects, AutoCAD includes the drawing's dependent symbols (definitions of blocks, dimensioning styles, layers, linetypes, and text styles) in the xref definition. AutoCAD differentiates the names of these symbols from those of the current drawing by preceding their names with the name of the externally referenced drawing. The symbol name can contain up to 31 characters, and it consists of the dependent symbol information and the xref drawing name. For example, a layer named STEEL-HIDDEN in an externally referenced drawing entitled *stair.dwg* is listed as STAIR|STEEL-HIDDEN.

A dependent symbol's definition can change, or even disappear, if it is purged from the referenced drawing. Therefore, you cannot reference a symbol directly. For example, you cannot insert a dependent block or make a dependent layer the current layer and begin creating new objects on it. If you wish to add a dependent symbol to the current drawing, use XBIND.

You can't select dependent symbols, but you can control the visibility, color, and linetype of an xref's layers. The VISRETAIN system variable controls dependent layer properties. If the VISRETAIN system variable is set to 0, any changes you make apply only to the current drawing session. In other words, the next time the drawing is opened, the dependent layer settings revert back to the last saved settings in the original referenced file.

By default, VISRETAIN is set to 1, which means any dependent layer attributes set in the current drawing persist from session to session. When you save the file or use the XREF Reload option, the current layer visibility settings for dependent layers are saved with the current drawing. Reloading an xref doesn't alter layer settings you have overridden in the current drawing.

Changing Xref Paths

If you open a drawing that contains an xref that has been moved to a different directory other than the one that was saved with the xref, and it can't be found in the Project or AutoCAD search paths, the External Reference dialog box displays its status as "Not found" in the xref list, and the Xref Found At box is blank. When you choose Browse and select a new path and file name in the Select New Path dialog box, the new path and file name are displayed in the Saved Path column in the list view and also in the Xref Found At box.

You can remove the path from the file name or specify a relative path by directly editing the path in the Xref Found At box and then choosing Save Path.

You can change only one xref path at a time. If you select multiple xrefs, you cannot use the Path option.

To change an xref path

1. From the Insert menu, choose External Reference.
2. In the External Reference dialog box, select the xref whose path you want to edit.
3. Choose Browse.
4. In the Select New Path dialog box, enter a new path and then choose Open.
5. Choose OK to exit the External Reference dialog box.

The new path is displayed in the External Reference dialog box in the Saved Path field of the list view, and in the Found At box.

NOTE An alternate method of changing an xref path is to edit the path in the Xref Found At box, and then choose Save Path.

Command line -XREF PATH

Changing Nested Xref Paths

If the path of a nested xref is changed in the current drawing, the change is only saved if VISRETAIN is set to 1. If AutoCAD cannot save a changed nested xref path with the current drawing, the following message is displayed.

Warning: VISRETAIN must be On to save nested Xref path

When the drawing is reopened and the nested xref is loaded, AutoCAD attempts to find the xref in the original xref path first. If the xref is not found, AutoCAD searches the path saved in the current drawing and then searches the project path and Support File search path. This ensures that revisions made to the xref are reflected in the current drawing and also makes it possible for the xref to be found if its path has changed.

For example, the xref tree of the current drawing A is A>B>C, and the owner of drawing B changes the path of xref C to point to *C1.dwg*. When drawing A is reopened, it reflects the path change in drawing B and displays *C1.dwg*. However, if *C1.dwg* is not found, AutoCAD looks for xref C at the last location it was saved in drawing A.

Defining Alternate Xref Search Paths

Project names make it easier for you to manage Xrefs when drawings are exchanged between customers, or if you have different drive mappings to the same location on a server. The project name points to a section in the registry which can contain one or more search paths for each project name defined.

If AutoCAD cannot find an xref at the location specified by the hard-coded path, the prefix (if any) is stripped from the hard-coded path. If the drawing has a PROJECTNAME value set and a corresponding entry exists in the registry, AutoCAD searches for the file along the project search paths. If the xref still hasn't been located, the AutoCAD search path is searched again.

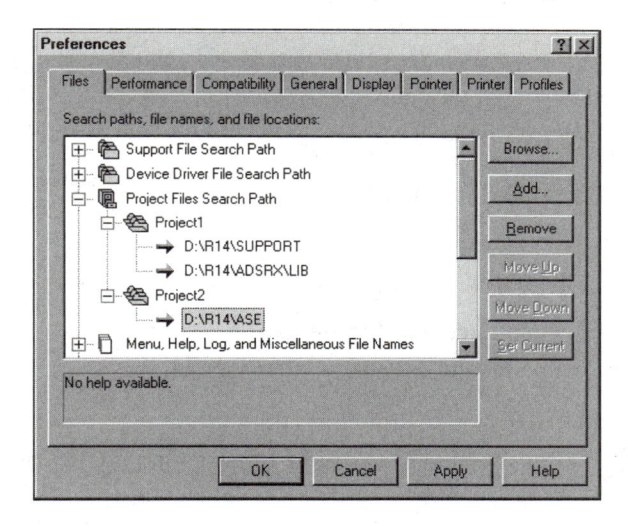

To display the currently defined project names

1. From the Tools menu, choose Preferences.
2. In the Preferences dialog box, on the Files tab, click Project Files Search Path.
3. Click each project name to display the search paths associated with the selected project name.
4. Choose OK or Apply.

Creating and Modifying Project Names

You can add, remove, or modify the project names that exist in the registry. The directory search paths beneath the project name can also be added, removed, or modified.

To add a project name

1. From the Tools menu, choose Preferences.
2. In the Preferences dialog box on the Files tab, double-click Project Files Search Path, and then choose Add.

   A folder named *projectx* (where *x* indicates the next available number) is created and indented beneath the *project* folder.

3. Either enter a new name, or press ENTER to accept *projectx*.

   The project name must be 31 characters or fewer, and it cannot contain leading spaces or terminating spaces.

4. Choose OK or Apply.

To remove a project name

1. From the Tools menu, choose Preferences.
2. In the Preferences dialog box on the Files tab, double-click Project Files Search Path.
3. Select a project name and then choose Remove.
4. Choose OK or Apply.

To modify a project name

1. From the Tools menu, choose Preferences.
2. Select a project name and then enter a new name.
3. Choose OK or Apply.

NOTE You can also modify a project name by selecting the name in the project folder and pressing F2.

Creating and Modifying Search Paths

The search paths beneath the project name can be added, removed, or modified in the same manner as the project name. The order in which the directories are searched can also be modified. Projects and their search paths can only be edited through the Files tab in the Preferences dialog box. There is no way to edit project names on the command line.

To add a search path

1. From the Tools menu, choose Preferences.
2. In the Preferences dialog box on the Files tab, select a project name, and then choose Add.

3 Add a new search path beneath the project name by entering a new path, or choose Browse and select a new path.

4 Choose OK or Apply.

The new path is indented and placed beneath the project name.

To delete a search path

1 From the Tools menu, choose Preferences.

2 In the Preferences dialog box on the Files tab, select a project name, and then choose Remove.

3 Choose OK.

To change a search path

1 From the Tools menu, choose Preferences.

2 In the Preferences dialog box on the Files tab, select a project name, and then choose Browse.

3 In the Choose Directory dialog box, select a new path.

4 Choose OK to exit each dialog box.

> **NOTE** You can also change a search path by selecting the project path and pressing F2.

Setting the Current Project

Once you have established a project name and the search paths you want associated with that project name, you can make that project name the currently active project. AutoCAD searches the paths associated with that currently active project for xrefs that were not found in the hard-coded path, the current drawing directory, or the AutoCAD support paths.

To set a project current

1 From the Tools menu, choose Preferences.

2 In the Preferences dialog box, on the Files tab, click Project Files Search Path.

3 Select a Project name, and then choose Set Current.

4 Choose OK or Apply.

> **NOTE** You can also set a project current by entering PROJECTNAME on the command line, and then entering the name of the project.

Using External References

471

To clear the current project

1 From the Tools menu, choose Preferences.
2 In the Preferences dialog box, on the Files tab, click Project Files Search Path.
3 Choose Clear Current.

   This clears the PROJECTNAME setting for the current drawing.
4 Choose OK or Apply.

NOTE You can also clear the current project by entering PROJECTNAME and then entering a period (.) at the prompt.

Handling Xref Errors

You may encounter two types of error messages when you use the external reference feature: messages indicating missing reference files or circular references.

Missing Reference Files

AutoCAD stores the file name of the drawing used to create the external reference. Each time you open or plot the drawing or use the XREF Reload option to update the external reference, AutoCAD checks the file name to determine the name and location of the associated drawing file. If the name of the drawing associated with the xref has changed, AutoCAD cannot read the external reference. If the drawing has been moved and doesn't exist in the AutoCAD support path, the current drawing directory, or in the directories specified by a current project, AutoCAD cannot resolve the xref.

If AutoCAD cannot load an external reference when it is opening your drawing, it displays an error message. In the following example of an error message, AutoCAD cannot find the xref *house*.

Resolve XREF House: \acad\dwg\house.dwg
Can't find \acad\dwg\house.dwg

For each insertion of the unresolved external reference, AutoCAD displays a single piece of text (at the insertion point, scale, and rotation angle of the original reference) that contains the path name of the missing xref, and the External Reference dialog box displays the xref as "Not found." You can use the XREF Path option to update or correct the path name.

Circular References

A reference file that contains a sequence of nested references that refers back to itself is considered a circular reference. For example, if drawing A attaches drawing B that attaches drawing C that attaches drawing A, the reference sequence A>B>C>A is a circular reference.

If AutoCAD detects a circular reference while attaching an xref, a warning is displayed asking you if you want to continue. If you respond with yes, AutoCAD reads in the xref and any nested xrefs to the point where it detects the circularity. If you respond with no, AutoCAD halts the process and the xref is not attached.

If AutoCAD encounters a circular reference while loading a drawing, it displays an error message and breaks the circular reference for the current session. For example, if you have the circular reference A>B>C>A, and you open *a.dwg*, AutoCAD detects and breaks the circularity between *c.dwg* and *a.dwg*. The following error message is displayed:

Breaking circular reference from C to current drawing.

Using the Xref Log File

AutoCAD can maintain a log of its actions when attaching, detaching, and reloading xrefs and when it loads a drawing containing xrefs. This log is maintained only if the XREFCTL system variable is set to 1. The system default setting is 0.

The log file is an ordinary ASCII text file. It has the same name as the current drawing, and its file extension is *.xlg*. If you load a drawing called *sample.dwg*, for example, AutoCAD searches for a log file named *sample.xlg* in the current directory. If the file does not exist, AutoCAD creates a new file with that name if XREFCTL is set to 1.

Once a log file has been created for a drawing, AutoCAD continues to append to it. If the log file becomes too large, you can delete it.

AutoCAD writes a title block to the log file each time the file is opened. This title block contains the name of the current drawing, the date and time, and the operation being performed.

```
==============================
Drawing: detail
Date/Time: 09/28/97 10:45:20
Operation: Attach Xref
==============================
```

When detaching or reloading xrefs, AutoCAD prints the nesting level of all affected xrefs immediately following the title block. To see a reference tree for a set of xrefs in your current drawing, choose Detach or Reload and check the resulting entries in the log file. In the following examples, the xref *entry_dr* contains two nested xrefs: *hardware* and *panels*. The xrefs *hardware* and *panels* also each contain two xrefs.

```
==============================
            Drawing: detail
Date/Time: 10/05/97 15:47:39
Operation: Reload Xref
==============================
Reference tree for ENTRY_DR:

ENTRY_DR            Xref
—HARDWARE           Xref
——LOCKSET           Xref
——HINGES            Xref
—PANELS             Xref
——UPPER             Xref
——LOWER             Xref
```

AutoCAD writes an entry in the log file for each dependent symbol temporarily added to the current drawing and for any errors that occur. Most error messages are written both to the screen and to the log file.

The following example shows a partial listing of the log file entries generated when the external reference *stair* is attached to the working drawing *test.dwg*. The log file lists the symbol table affected and the name of the symbol added, along with a status message.

```
==============================
            Drawing: test
Date/Time: 12/18/97 14:06:34
Operation: Attach Xref
==============================

Attach Xref STAIR: \ACAD\DWGS\STAIR.dwg

             Searching in ACAD search path

             Update block symbol table:
              Appending symbol: STAIR|BOLT
              Appending symbol: STAIR|BOLT-HALF
              ...
             block update complete.

             Update Ltype symbol table:
              Appending symbol: STAIR|DASHED
              Appending symbol: STAIR|CENTER
              Appending symbol: STAIR|PHANTOM
             Ltype update complete.

             Update Layer symbol table:
              Appending symbol: STAIR|STEEL-HIDDEN
              Appending symbol: STAIR|OAK
              ...
             Layer update complete.

STAIR loaded.
```

Layout and Plotting

After you've created your drawing with AutoCAD, you usually plot it on paper. A plotted drawing can contain a single view of your drawing or a more complex arrangement of views. In paper space, you can create windows called floating viewports, which display various views of the drawing. Depending on your needs, you can plot one or more viewports, or set options that determine what is plotted and how the image fits on the paper.

In this chapter

- Using paper space and model space
- Adding title blocks and borders
- Creating and using floating viewports
- Using named views in paper space
- Setting up the plot configuration
- Plotting to a file

Using Paper Space and Model Space

When you work with tiled viewports, you are in model space where you create the basic drawing, or model. If several tiled viewports are displayed, editing in one viewport affects all other viewports. However, you can set magnification, viewpoint, grid, and snap settings individually for each viewport.

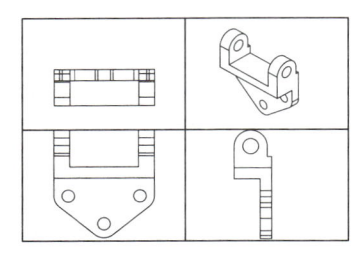

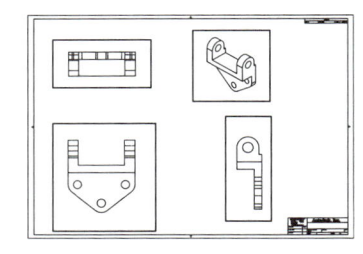

tiled viewports

floating viewports

The first time you switch to paper space, the graphics area displays a blank space that represents the "paper" on which you arrange your drawing. In this space, you create floating viewports to contain different views of your model. In paper space, floating viewports are treated as objects that you can move and resize in order to create a suitable layout. You are not restricted to plotting a single model space view, as you are with tiled viewports. Therefore, you can plot any arrangement of floating viewports. In paper space, you also can draw objects, such as title blocks or annotations, directly in the paper space view without affecting the model itself.

Because floating viewports are treated as objects, you cannot edit the model in paper space. To access the model in a floating viewport, you toggle from paper space to model space. As a result, you can work with the model while keeping the overall layout visible. In floating viewports, the editing and view-changing capabilities are almost the same as in tiled viewports. However, you have more control over the individual views. For example, you can freeze or turn off layers in some viewports without affecting others. You can turn an entire viewport display on or off. You can also align views between viewports and scale the views relative to the overall layout.

The following illustration shows how different views of a model can be displayed in paper space. Each of the paper space images represents a floating viewport with a different view. In one view, the dimensioning layer is frozen. Notice that the title block, border, and annotation, which are drawn in paper space, do not appear in the model space view. Also, the layer that contains the viewport borders has been turned off.

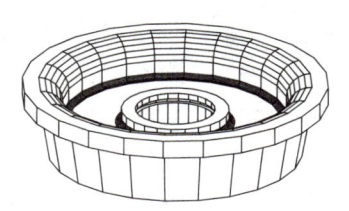

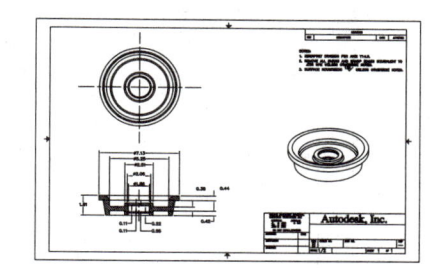

the model

the model displayed in paper space floating viewports

When you work in tiled viewports, the TILEMODE system variable is on. When TILEMODE is off, you can switch between paper space and model space as needed. Paper space, model space, and TILEMODE settings are interrelated as shown in the table.

Using paper space and model space		
Space	Status	Usage
Paper space	TILEMODE off	Arrange the layout by creating floating viewports and adding title block, borders and annotation. Editing does not affect the model.
Model space in floating viewports	TILEMODE off	Work within floating viewports to edit the model or change views. You can turn off or freeze layers in individual viewports.
Model space in tiled viewports	TILEMODE on	Split the screen into tiled viewports to edit different views of the model.

To switch from model to paper space, use the toggles on the status bar. The combined status of the Paper/Model and Tile toggles determines the current space.

Switching to Paper Space

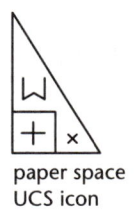

When you are in paper space, AutoCAD displays the paper space UCS icon in the lower-left corner of the graphics area. The crosshairs indicate that the paper space layout area (not the views in the viewports) can be edited.

paper space UCS icon

Using Paper Space and Model Space

477

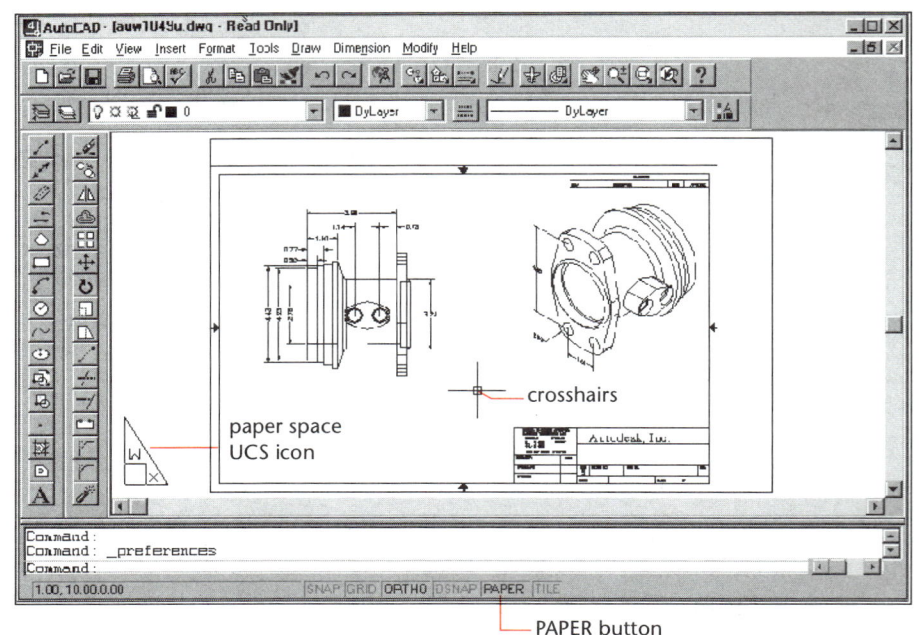

Paper space view

To turn on paper space

- On the status bar, double-click Model. The toggle changes to Paper. Also, you can choose Paper Space from the View menu.

Command line Turn off the TILEMODE system variable by setting it to 0.

Related If TILEMODE is off and model space is on, use the PSPACE command to turn on paper space.

Switching to Model Space

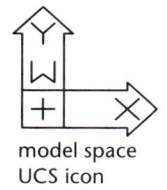

Once you have created floating viewports, you can edit the model itself by switching from paper space to floating model space. This switch allows you to edit the model within a floating viewport. In the following illustration, the crosshairs identify the current floating viewport. The model space UCS icon indicates that the view is in model space.

model space UCS icon

Chapter 12 Layout and Plotting

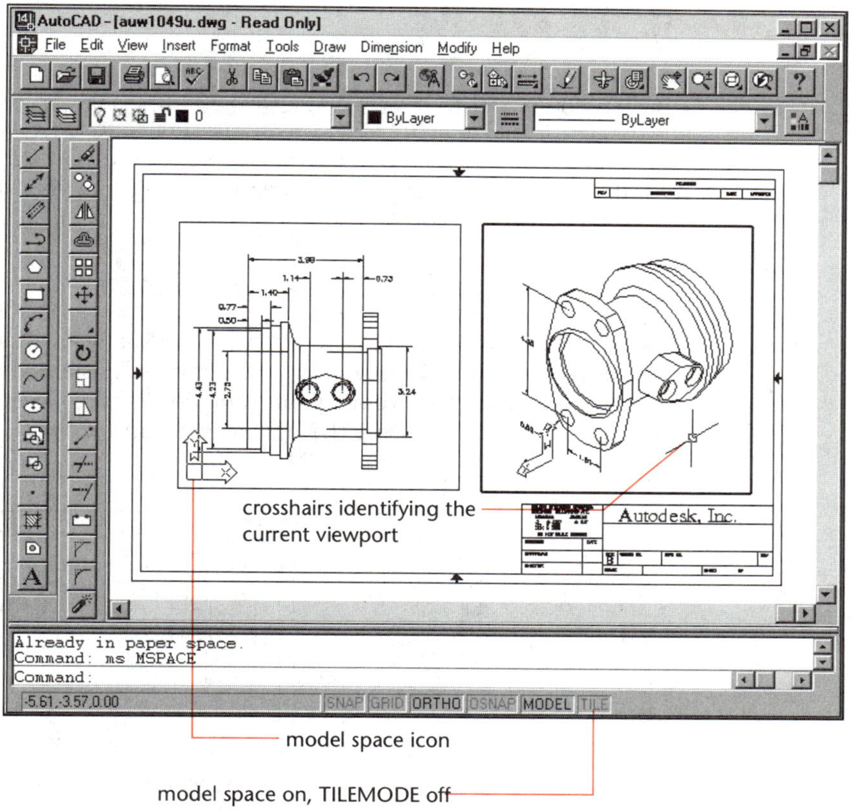

Floating viewports

If you switch to model space before you have created floating viewports, AutoCAD prompts you to use the MVIEW command to create viewports. See “Creating Floating Viewports” on page 481.

To work in floating viewports

- On the status bar, double-click PAPER. The toggle changes to MODEL. Also, you can choose Floating Model Space from the View menu.

Command line Turn off the TILEMODE system variable by setting it to 0. Then enter **mspace** to switch to model space.

Preparing a Layout

The arrangement of a drawing on paper is an important part of the drawing process. The initial drawing may consist of a single model; however, you can display this model in a myriad of ways. You can arrange it within a border, show it from different perspectives, magnify details that you want to emphasize, or hide insignificant details.

Adding a Title Block and Border

Because title blocks are part of the layout, they usually are drawn in paper space rather than model space. AutoCAD provides 13 standard title blocks, which you can insert into your layout using the Advanced Setup wizard. For more information about using the Advanced Setup wizard, see "Using the Advanced Setup Wizard" on page 94.

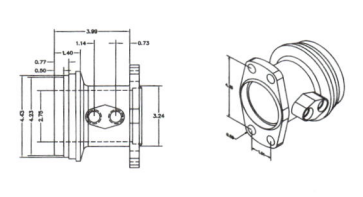

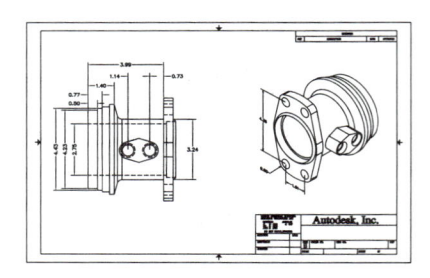

drawing   drawing with title block and border

To insert a title block and border

1 From the File menu, choose New.
2 In the Startup dialog box, choose Use a Wizard, and select Advanced Wizard.
3 Choose OK.
4 In the Advanced Setup dialog box, select Step 6: Title Block.
5 Select Title Block Description and Title Block File Name from the lists, then choose Add.
6 In the Select Title Block File dialog box, select a title block, then choose Open.
7 In the Advanced Setup dialog box, a sample of that title is displayed.
8 In the Advanced Setup dialog box, choose Done.

The title block you selected is added to your drawing.

Creating Floating Viewports

You create floating viewports using the MVIEW command. The MVSETUP command offers additional configuration choices, including a standard engineering configuration with different views in each viewport.

Standard Viewport Configurations

You can place the floating viewports you create anywhere in the drawing area. As with tiled viewports, you can choose one of several standard configurations. If you choose 1 Viewport in the following procedure, you can create a viewport that fits the entire graphics area or specify a size and shape. The illustrations show some of the options.

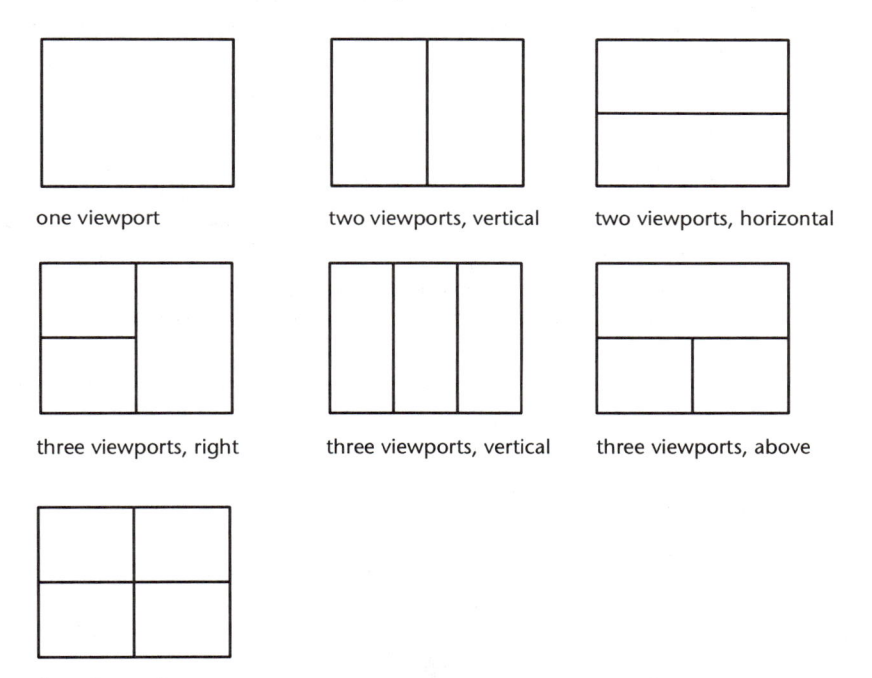

one viewport

two viewports, vertical

two viewports, horizontal

three viewports, right

three viewports, vertical

three viewports, above

four viewports

The configuration you choose depends on how you plan to use the floating viewports. If you are designing a layout, you may want to use the 1 Viewport option to place each viewport individually. If you expect to use the viewports to edit the model, one of the other configurations may be more useful.

Preparing a Layout

481

starting a layout with a single viewport

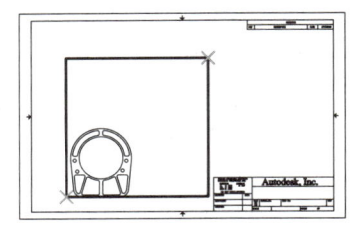

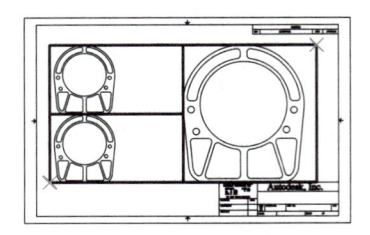

using three viewports for editing

After you specify the number of viewports you want to create, you define an area to contain them. Although these floating viewports are created simultaneously, they are separate objects that can be moved, resized, or erased as needed.

To create floating viewports

1. From the View menu, choose Floating Viewports. Then choose 1 Viewport, 2 Viewports, 3 Viewports, or 4 Viewports.
2. If you chose 2 Viewports or 3 Viewports, specify which configuration you want to use.

   If you chose 1 Viewport and want the viewport to fill the current graphics area, enter **f**. Otherwise, you'll specify the viewport border as described in step 3.
3. At each prompt, specify the corners of a rectangular area that will contain the viewports.

   The viewports fill the specified area.

   Command line   MVIEW

Other Viewport Configurations

When you use MVSETUP to create floating viewports, AutoCAD gives you several additional configuration options. As shown in the following illustrations, you can create viewports with top, isometric, front, and right-side views of the model, which you can then realign and scale to show a standard engineering configuration. You also can define an array of viewports by specifying the number of rows and columns in the configuration.

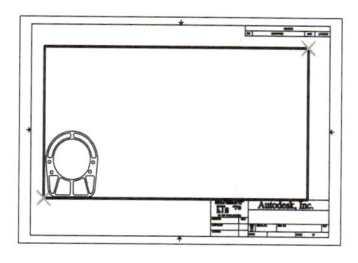

single viewport

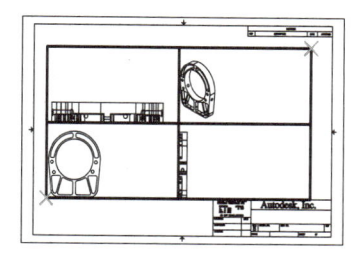

standard engineering viewports

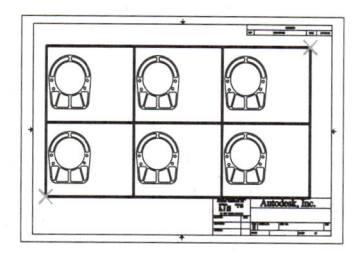

arrayed viewports

To create other floating viewport configurations

1. At the Command prompt, enter **mvsetup**.
2. Enter **c** (Create). Then press ENTER to continue.

   A list of viewport options is displayed.
3. Enter the number corresponding to the viewport option you want to use.
4. Specify the corners of the area that will contain the viewports.
5. If you are creating arrayed viewports, specify the number of columns (X) and rows (Y).
6. If you are creating engineering or arrayed viewports, specify the distance between the columns (X) and rows (Y).

Command line MVSETUP

Rearranging and Removing Floating Viewports

After you insert floating viewports, you can rearrange them according to your needs. You can snap to, copy, scale, stretch, erase, and move viewports using standard commands and most Grip modes. To use these commands, you must be in paper space, and the viewport borders must be visible.

When you scale a view within a viewport, you may need to resize the viewport. Scaling or stretching the viewport border does not change the view within the viewport, as shown in the following illustration.

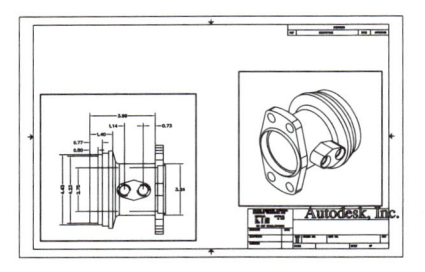

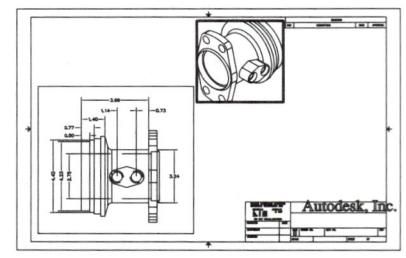

viewport to be moved and resized   resized viewport

By resizing the viewport borders, you can clip the view to display only a specific section of the drawing.

Controlling Visibility in Floating Viewports

You can control the visibility of objects in a floating viewport using several methods. You can

- Freeze or thaw layers in individual viewports
- Turn viewports on and off
- Limit the number of viewports that can be active

These methods are useful for limiting screen regeneration and for emphasizing or hiding different elements of your drawing.

Freezing or Thawing Layers in Existing Viewports

You can freeze or thaw layers in current and future floating viewports without affecting other viewports. Frozen layers are invisible. They are not regenerated or plotted. This feature is useful, for example, if you want to create an annotation layer that is visible only in a particular viewport. The following illustration shows a viewport in which the terrain layer has been frozen in one viewport.

viewport with terrain layer frozen

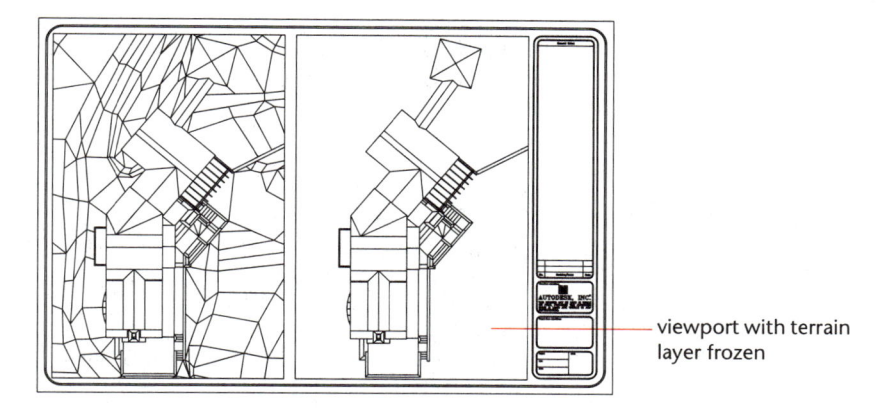

Thawing restores the layer visibility. You can freeze or thaw layers in the current viewport with the VPLAYER command. For more detailed information about defining layer properties for plotting, see "Working with Layers" on page 298.

To freeze or thaw layers in the current floating viewport

1 From the Format menu, choose Layer.
2 in the Layer & Linetype Properties dialog box, select the layers to freeze or thaw.
3 Under Details, select Freeze in current viewport.
4 Choose OK.

Command line LAYER

Freezing or Thawing Layers in New Viewports

You can set visibility defaults for specific layers in all new floating viewports. For example, you can restrict display of dimensions by freezing the DIMENSIONS layer in all new viewports. If you create a viewport that requires dimensions, you can override the default setting by changing the current viewport setting. Changing the default for new layers does not affect existing layers.

To freeze or thaw layers in all new viewports

1 From the Format menu, choose Layer.
2 In the Layer & Linetype Properties dialog box, select the layers to freeze or thaw.
3 Under Details, select Freeze in New Viewports.
4 Choose OK.

Command line LAYER

Preparing a Layout

485

Filtering Frozen Layers

When you need to know what layers are frozen in the current viewport, you can filter and list them. You can list frozen layers only for viewports whose borders are visible.

To filter and list layers that are frozen in a viewport

1 Make sure you are in paper space.
2 From the Format menu, choose Layer.
3 In the Layer & Linetype Properties dialog box under Show, select Set Filter Dialog.
4 In the Set Layer Filters dialog box under Freeze/Thaw, select Frozen.
5 Choose OK.

The names of the frozen layers in that viewport are displayed.

Command line   VPLAYER

Turning Floating Viewports On or Off

Displaying a large number of active floating viewports can affect your system's performance as the content of each viewport regenerates. You can save time by turning some viewports off or by limiting the number of active viewports. The following illustration shows the effects of turning off two viewports.

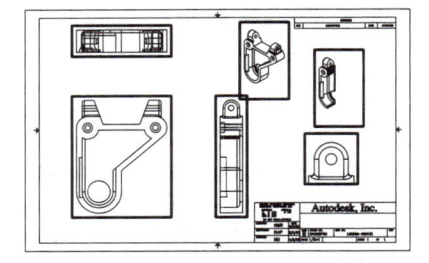

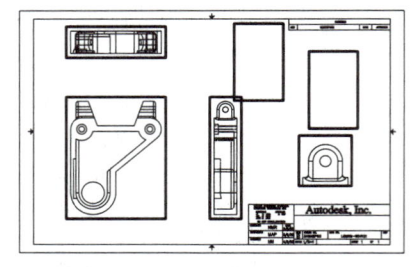

all viewports on   two viewports off

New viewports are turned on by default. If you turn off the viewports you aren't using, you can move or resize viewports without waiting for each one to regenerate. You also can turn off viewports that you don't want to plot.

Related   You can use the MAXACTVP system variable to control how many viewports you have on at a time.

To turn viewports on or off

1 From the View menu, choose Floating Viewports ➤ Viewports On or Viewports Off.
2 Select the viewports you want to turn on or off.

Command line   MVIEW

If you want to hide the viewport borders as you work or when you plot, create a special layer that you use for inserting viewports. Then, turn off or freeze that layer.

> **NOTE** All MVIEW viewports plot, whether they are on or off.

Limiting Active Viewports

A floating viewport is considered to be active when it is on, visible in the graphics area, and not part of an AutoCAD block. Viewports contained in blocks do not display model space views.

Your drawing can display an unlimited number of viewports. However, your operating system and display driver determine the number of viewports that are active. Active viewports are also limited by the maximum value set by the MAXACTVP system variable. Lowering this limit can improve performance, because inactive viewports are blank and their contents are not regenerated. The default limit is 48.

To set the maximum number of active viewports

1 At the Command prompt, enter **maxactvp**.
2 Enter the maximum number of viewports that can be active.

When the active viewport limit has been exceeded you can use MVIEW to turn on viewports that are blank. This activity will turn off other viewports.

Changing Viewport Views and Content

To change the view within a floating viewport, you must be in model space. Changes to the grid and snap settings, zoom values, or viewpoint direction affect only the current viewport.

Preparing a Layout

grid and UCS icon on in two viewports

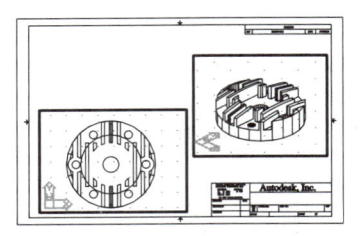

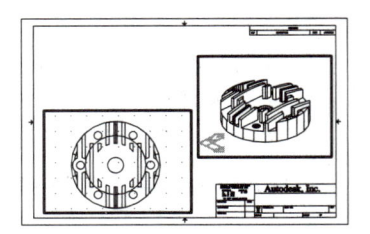

grid on in one viewport, UCS icon on in the other

To edit a drawing in a floating viewport

1   In model space, click inside the floating viewport that you want to edit to make it current.
2   Edit the drawing.

You also can create objects such as annotations, dimensions, and title blocks in paper space. You must, however, change TILEMODE to 0, and turn paper space on. Objects created in paper space are visible only in paper space.

Scaling Views Relative to Paper Space

Before you plot, you can establish accurate zoom scale factors for each section of your drawing. Scaling views relative to paper space establishes a consistent scale for each displayed view. For example, the following illustration shows a paper space view with several viewports—each set to different scales and views. To accurately scale the plotted drawing, you must scale each view relative to paper space, not relative to the previous view or to the full-scale model.

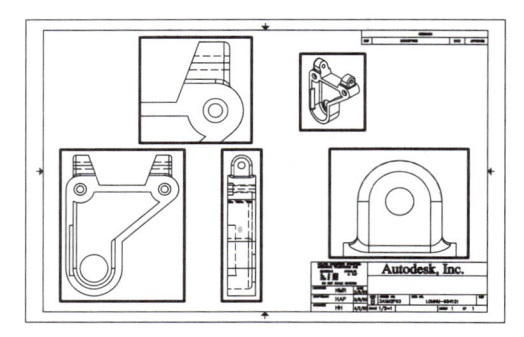

Viewports using different scales

When you work in paper space, the scale factor represents a ratio between the size of the plotted drawing and the actual size of the model displayed in the viewports. To derive this scale, divide paper space units by model space units. For a quarter-scale drawing, for example, you specify a scale factor of one paper space unit to four model space units (1:4).

You can use ZOOM to scale viewports relative to paper space units. The scale factor you enter is relative to the current paper space scale. As shown in the illustrations, if you enter a scale of **2xp**, the scale in the viewport increases to twice the size of the paper space units. A scale of **0.5xp** sets the scale to half the size of the paper space units. The model is plotted at half its actual size.

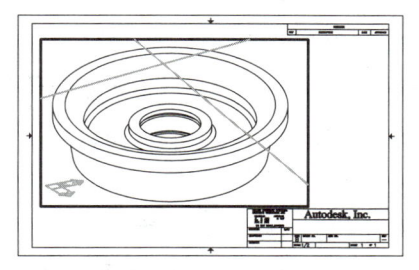

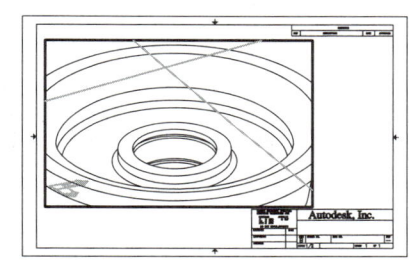

current view

zooming to 2xp

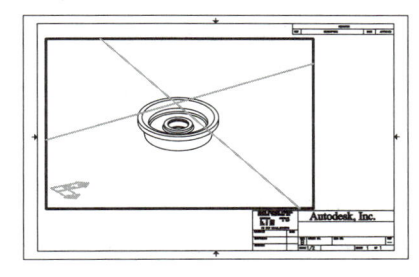

zooming to .5xp

Zooming to scale a view relative to paper space

To scale model space by zooming relative to paper space

1 From the View menu choose Zoom ➤ Scale.
2 Enter the scale factor followed by **xp**.

For a 1:4 ratio, for example, you would enter **0.25xp** or **1/4xp**. You derive the 0.25 value by dividing 1 by 4.

Command line   ZOOM Scale

Scaling Pattern Linetypes in Paper Space

In paper space you can scale any type of linetype in two ways. The scale can be based on the drawing units of the space in which the object was created (model or paper). For more information, see "Changing an Object's Linetype" on page 319. The linetype scale also can be a uniform scale based on paper space units. You can use the PSLTSCALE system variable to maintain the same linetype scaling for objects displayed at different zoom scales in different viewports. It also affects the line display in 3D views.

In the following illustration, the pattern linetype of the lines in model space has been scaled uniformly in paper space using the PSLTSCALE system variable. Notice that the linetype in the two viewports has the same scale, even though the objects have different zoom scales.

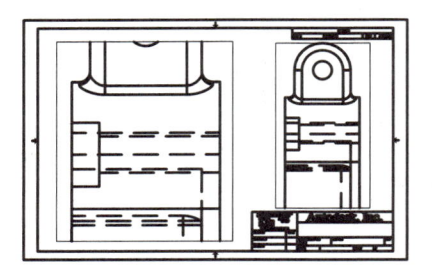

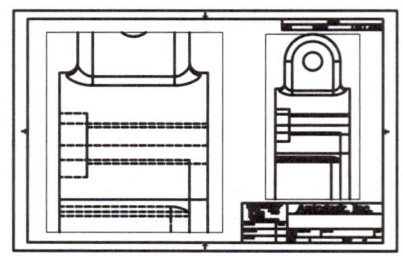

psltscale=1, dashes scaled to paper space   psltscale=0, dashes scaled to space where they were created

Scaled linetypes

To scale pattern linetypes globally in paper space

1 From the Format menu, choose Linetype.
2 In the Layer & Linetype properties dialog box under Details, specify the Global scale factor.
3 Choose OK.

Command line PSLTSCALE

Related The LTSCALE command sets the global linetype scale factor. The CELTSCALE command sets linetype scaling per object.

Aligning Views in Floating Viewports

You can arrange the elements of your drawing by aligning the view in one floating viewport with the view in another viewport. For angled, horizontal, and vertical alignments, you pan the view in one viewport in relation to a base point specified in another viewport.

To align objects between viewports

1 At the Command prompt, enter **mvsetup**.
2 Enter **a** (Align).
3 Choose one of the following alignments:
   - *Horizontal* aligns a point in one viewport horizontally with a base point in another viewport.
   - *Vertical* aligns a point in one viewport vertically with a base point in another viewport.
   - *Angled* aligns a point in one viewport at a specified distance and angle from a base point in another viewport.

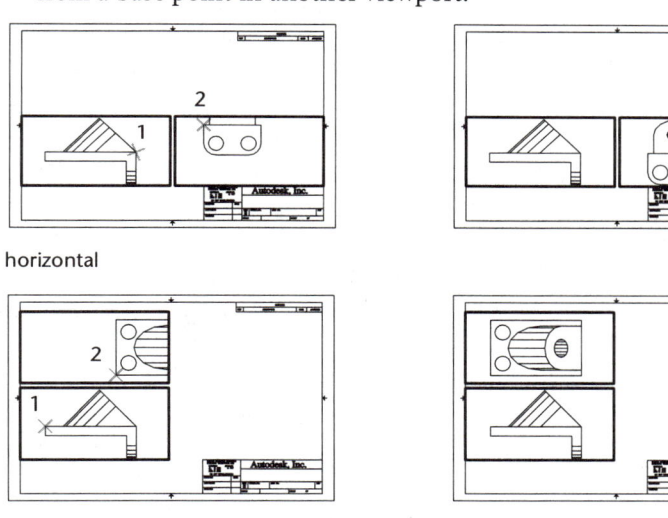

horizontal

vertical

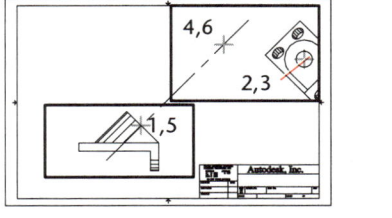

angled

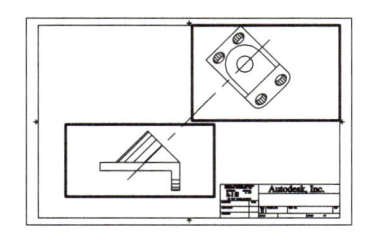

4 Make sure the viewport with the view that is to remain stationary is current. Then specify a base point (1).

5   Select the viewport with the view you want to realign. Then specify an alignment point in that view (2).

6   For angled alignments only, specify a distance and displacement angle from the base point to the alignment point in the second viewport.

The angled view in the previous illustration shows how the midpoint of the bracket in one viewport can be aligned with the center point of the hole shown from the top. After specifying the base point and alignment point (1, 2), you specify the distance (3, 4) and angle (5, 6) between the baseline and alignment point.

Rotating Views in Floating Viewports

You can rotate an entire view within a floating viewport. This feature differs from the ROTATE command, which rotates individual objects.

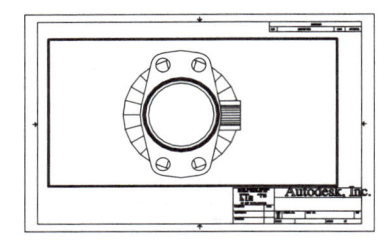

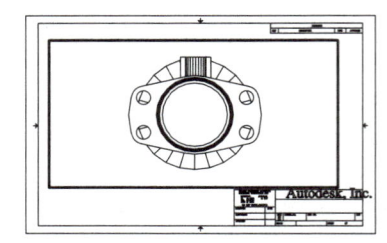

original view   rotated view

Notice that only the view, not the viewport borders, rotates.

To rotate a view

1   At the Command prompt, enter **mvsetup**.
2   Enter **a** (Align).
3   Enter **r** to rotate the view.
4   Select the viewport with the view you want to rotate.
5   Specify a base point for the rotation.
6   Specify the rotation angle.

The entire view rotates within the viewport.

Hiding Lines in Plotted Viewports

If your drawing contains 3D faces, meshes, extruded objects, surfaces, or solids, you can direct AutoCAD to remove hidden lines from specific viewports when you plot the paper space view. The Hideplot option of MVIEW affects only the plotted output, not the screen display. To remove hidden lines on the screen, use HIDE.

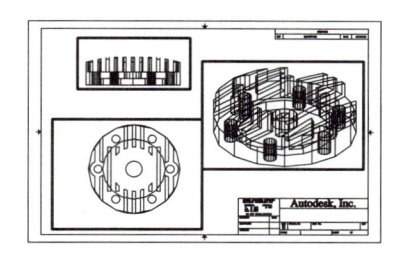

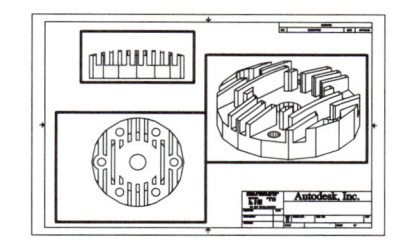

Hideplot off   Hideplot on

To turn hidden lines on or off when the paper space view is plotted

1 From the View menu, choose Floating Viewports ➤ Hideplot.
2 Enter **on** or **off**.
3 Select the viewports.

You do not see the effect of this command until you plot the drawing.

Command line   MVIEW HIDEPLOT

Related   The Hide Lines option in the Plot Configuration dialog box hides 3D lines in model space or paper space, whichever is current. You can use this option to hide lines when you plot from model space (see "Setting Plot Area and Output" on page 501).

Using Named Views in Paper Space

You can save views that you want to reuse or plot. Each view represents a specific pan and zoom position. For example, you can save a view of a room in a floor plan and then restore the view whenever you want to work on it.

In model space (tiled or floating), you save a view from a single viewport. When restored, the saved view replaces the view in the selected viewport. In paper space, a saved view may include one or more floating viewports. When you restore it, the zoom and pan position of the restored view replaces the current paper space display.

The procedure for saving the views in floating viewports and paper space is the same as for saving views in tiled viewports (see "Saving Views" on page 214).

Preparing a Layout

To restore a named view

1 From the View menu, choose Named Views.

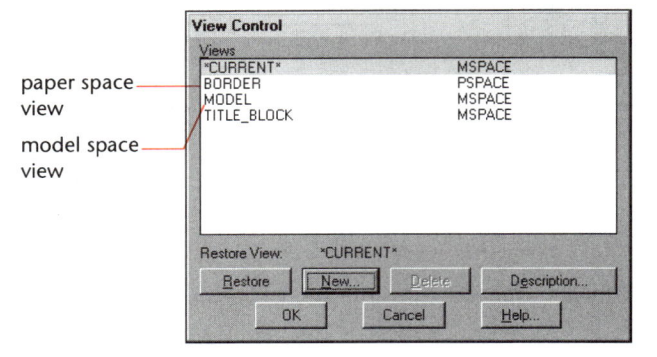

paper space view —
model space view —

[View Control dialog box showing Views list: *CURRENT* MSPACE, BORDER PSPACE, MODEL MSPACE, TITLE_BLOCK MSPACE. Restore View: *CURRENT*. Buttons: Restore, New..., Delete, Description..., OK, Cancel, Help...]

2 In the View Control dialog box under Views, select from the list the view you want to display. The column at the right indicates whether the view is a model space (MSPACE) or a paper space (PSPACE) view.

3 Choose Restore. Then choose OK.

The Restore option is unavailable when you are in model space and choose a paper space view.

4 If you selected a model space view, select a viewport to be replaced by the restored view.

If you selected a paper space view, that view replaces the current paper space view.

Command line DDVIEW

Plotting Your Drawing

You can configure AutoCAD for many devices, and store multiple configurations for a single device. AutoCAD can store up to 29 plotter configurations in the *acad14.cfg* file.

Each plotter configuration contains device-specific information such as the device driver name, device model name, the output port to which the device is connected, and various device-specific driver settings. A plotter configuration can also contain device-independent information including paper size, orientation, plot scale factors, pen parameters, optimization, plot origin, and rotation.

> **NOTE** AutoCAD does not store plotter configuration information in the drawing files. For each drawing, you can use the drawing editor to set up the view you want to plot. You can define the settings for the desired output by selecting an existing plotter configuration as a starting point modifying plotter settings in the Plot dialog box. Changes made in the Plot dialog box are saved as new default plotter settings only if a successful plot is completed using the new settings.

Preparing Your Plotter

Before you plot, make sure your plotter or printer is ready. Check to see whether it is turned on and properly connected to your computer. If you are using a pen plotter, check the pens. Are they seated properly in the pen holder? What pen width and color corresponds to each pen number? Run a self-test to see whether any of the pens are clogged or skipping. Check the paper. What size is loaded? Is it properly aligned?

Performing Basic Plotting

The following procedure describes how to plot quickly once you've configured your plotter. For more information about changing the plot configuration, see "Setting Up a Plotter Configuration" on page 498.

When you enter Plot Preview, the cursor changes to a magnifying glass with a plus and minus symbol. You can zoom in or out of the drawing by moving the cursor vertically up or down. Hold the pick button down at the midpoint of the drawing, and move the cursor vertically to the bottom (negative direction) of the window to zoom out 100 percent (.5x magnification). Hold the pick button down at the mid-point of the drawing and move the cursor vertically to the top (positive direction) of the window to zoom in 100 percent (2x magnification). You can continue to zoom in until you reach the zoom limits.

For more information on zooming, see "Using Zoom and Pan" on page 200.

The zoom-in capability of Plot Preview is limited by the resolution of your plotter. Plot Preview does not zoom in beyond the point where one pixel on your display is equal to one pixel (or plotter step) on your plotter; therefore, you can only zoom in to the level of detail that the plotter or printer is capable of plotting.

You can also use PREVIEW to plot a drawing using the current plotter configuration settings. After entering **preview** at the Command prompt and viewing your current drawing, display the cursor menu. From the cursor menu you can choose to pan, zoom, zoom previous, zoom window, exit plot preview, or plot. With this method, you cannot modify the plot configuration. You can change plotter configuration settings only when you use PLOT. For more information about previewing drawings and plotting, see PLOT and PREVIEW in the *Command Reference*.

To plot a drawing

1   From the File menu, choose Print.

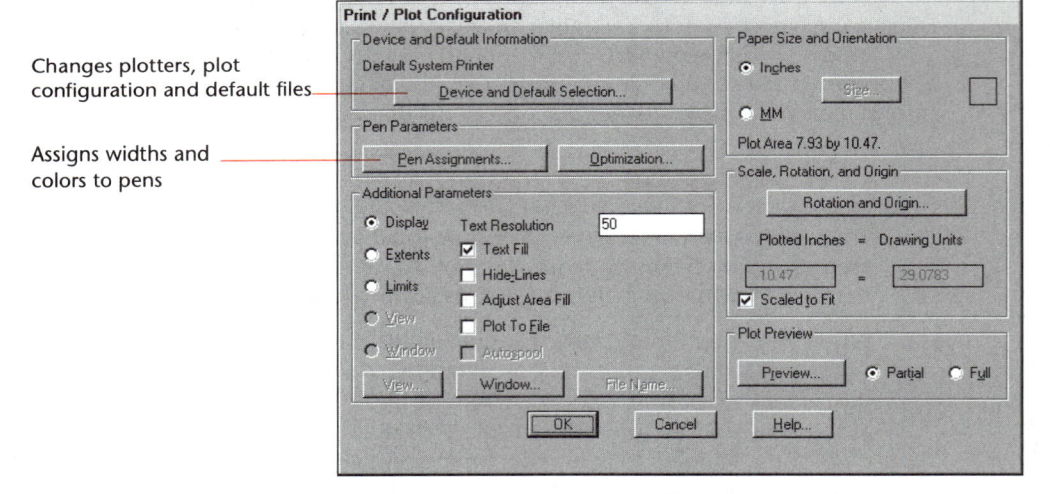

Changes plotters, plot configuration and default files

Assigns widths and colors to pens

2   In the Print/Plot Configuration dialog box, if you have configured more than one plotter, choose Device and Default Selection to display the current plotter.

3   In the Device and Default Selection dialog box, select the plotter you want to use. Then choose OK.

4   Select the area that you want to print.

Chapter 12 Layout and Plotting

5   In the Print/Plot Configuration dialog box, set the scale, and change the other settings as needed (see the following section, "Setting Up a Plotter Configuration").

6   To preview the final output, choose Plot Preview from the File menu.

If you choose Partial Preview, the Preview Effective Plotting Area dialog box is displayed, showing a simple preview of the plot position on paper.

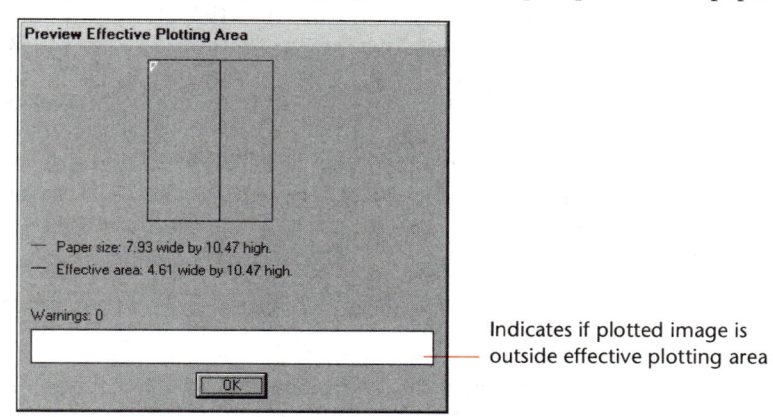

Indicates if plotted image is outside effective plotting area

If you choose Full Preview, a zoomable, detailed preview image of the plot is displayed.

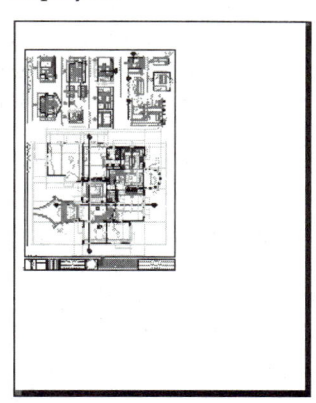

7   When you are ready to plot, choose OK.

Command line   PLOT

Related   To plot or set the plot configuration on the command line instead of in a dialog box, set the CMDDIA system variable to 0, and then use -PLOT.

Plotting Your Drawing

497

Setting Up a Plotter Configuration

The plotter configuration settings control the final output. These settings affect pen assignments, plot area, scale, paper size, and rotation. Understanding how to use these settings helps ensure that your drawing plots as expected.

Specifying some configurations can prove to be time consuming. For example, you can specify several parameters for up to 255 pens. To save time, you may want to save the more complicated or frequently used setups for a single plotter in partial plot configuration (PCP) files. A PCP file contains the device-independent configuration of a single plotter. Loading a PCP file changes the configuration but does not change the current device. For example, you can use PCP files to copy the pen parameters from one device's configuration to another or to save configurations for the same device with different paper sizes.

If you use several different plotters, you can use PC2 files to save your setups. A PC2 file contains a complete plotter configuration, including both device-dependent and device-independent settings. Loading a PC2 file changes the current device as well as its configuration. Use a PC2 file when you want to change devices, as in batch plotting. For more information about using PCP and PC2 files, see "Reusing a Plot Configuration" on page 508.

Setting Pen Assignments and Colors

Each object you create has an AutoCAD color that is assigned either by layer or specifically to the object. Although these colors can correspond to plotted colors, they more frequently are used to distinguish different layers on the screen. Colors also are used to assign line widths or weights. How you assign pens depends on whether you use a pen plotter or a raster printer.

Pen Width

For most pen plotters, the physical width of the pen determines the plotted line weight. However, some plotters can simulate a specified pen width by using multiple pen strokes. If you plot filled solids, wide polylines, or trace fills, be sure to configure the pen width to match the actual width of the pen.

Many plotter pens are marked with pen width in millimeters. Be sure that the pen width is accurately entered in the current units (inches or millimeters). If you are working in inches but your pen tip measurements are in millimeters, you can select Millimeters in the Plot Configuration dialog box, make your pen assignments, and then switch back to inches.

If you use a single-pen plotter, you can assign the same pen number, width, linetype, and speed to several screen colors, causing them to be drawn similarly. You can set the plotter configuration to prompt you to change pens each time a new color is needed. During configuration, answer **y** when you see this prompt: Do You Want to Change Pens While Plotting?

For raster printers such as laser or electrostatic printers, which do not have physical pens, you still can plot various line widths by assigning a pen width to a color. You may want to configure these widths to match the most common pen sizes: 0.18 mm, 0.25 mm, 0.35 mm, 0.50 mm, and 0.70 mm. If your printer allows you to specify pen widths on the hardware, be sure to change the hardware settings to read the software pen-width values.

For both pen plotters and raster printers, you can associate the same line width with several layers by assigning the same pen to more than one AutoCAD color. For example, suppose you set up a blue and a red layer. If pen 1 has a width of 0.25 mm (whether physical or assigned), you can plot 0.25 mm lines for all objects on those layers by assigning pen 1 to both blue and red. This assignment also causes those colors to be plotted in the same color on a multiple-pen plotter.

Plotter Linetypes

Some plotters support hardware linetypes. Hardware linetypes are faster, more device-dependent and less precise than software linetypes. They may be useful if you want to plot a different linetype without changing the linetype style in the drawing. Software linetypes are more precise. If you change hardware linetypes in the Plot Configuration dialog box, avoid unexpected results by making sure that the affected objects use the CONTINUOUS linetype. Hardware linetypes work best with narrow lines. Wide hardware linetypes produce unpredictable results on some devices.

Pen Speed

For some plotters, you can adjust pen speed on a pen-by-pen basis. This feature is useful, for example, for slowing down pens that are skipping. Each pen manufacturer recommends a pen speed for each type of media. For best results, use those values. You also can increase plotting efficiency by optimizing the pen (see "Optimizing Pen Motion" on page 515).

To set pen assignments

1 From the File menu, choose Print.
2 In the Plot Configuration dialog box, choose Pen Assignments.

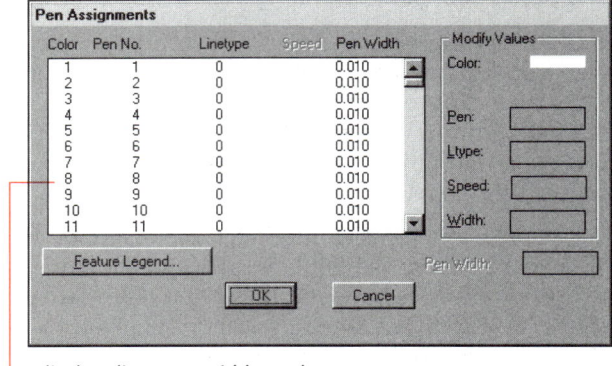

— displays linetype, width, and speed examples if applicable

The Pen Assignments dialog box is different for different plotter configurations. Options not supported by your plotter are unavailable in the dialog box.

3 In the Pen Assignments dialog box under Color, select an AutoCAD object color number. Under Modify Values, enter a pen number.

All AutoCAD objects with the selected color will be drawn with this pen. You can associate the same pen with more than one color.

4 If your plotter supports multiple pen widths, you can select a pen number and enter a pen tip width in the Width box. The same width then is used for all pens assigned to the same color.

If you use a plotter that does not support multiple widths, you can enter a single line width in the Width box. AutoCAD uses this value to correct area fills when you plot with the Adjust Area Fill option turned on.

5 If your plotter supports multiple linetypes, speeds, or widths, you can choose Feature Legend to see examples.

Examples vary depending on the plotter.

Feature Legend

Linetypes:
- 0 = continuous line
- 1 = ...
- 2 = ...
- 3 = ------------
- 4 = ...
- 5 = -- -- -- -- --
- 6 = --- --- --- ---
- 7 = ...
- 8 = _ _· _·· _·· _··_

Pen speed:

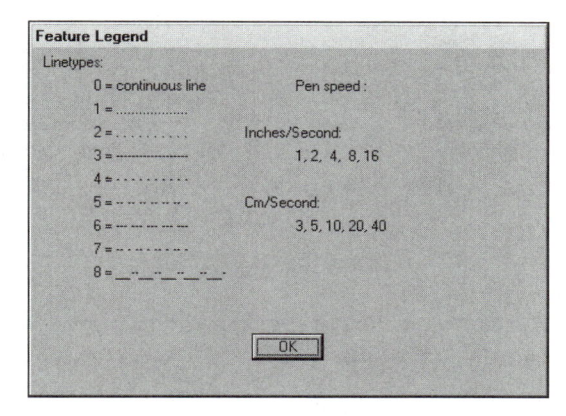

Inches/Second:
1, 2, 4, 8, 16

Cm/Second:
3, 5, 10, 20, 40

[OK]

6 In the Pen Assignments dialog box, enter values for Ltype, Speed, or Width.
7 Choose OK.

AutoCAD plots the drawing using the specified settings.

Setting Plot Area and Output

For any given drawing view, you can plot the current display, the extents of the objects, an area you define, the limits, or a named view. In model space, the options apply to the current viewport. If you are in paper space, the options apply to the paper space view.

If you are working with 3D meshes, extruded objects, surfaces, or solids, you also can specify whether hidden lines will plot. The Hide Lines option affects views in the current space only. If you are plotting from paper space and want to hide lines within specific viewports, use the Hideplot option of the MVIEW command (see "Hiding Lines in Plotted Viewports" on page 492).

When you plot 2D solids and wide polylines, AutoCAD uses the pen-width value specified in the Pen Assignments dialog box. The pen normally aligns with the center of the object boundaries. To ensure greater accuracy, you can use the Adjust Area Fill option in the Print/Plot configuration dialog box to move the pen inward by half a pen width.

pen position

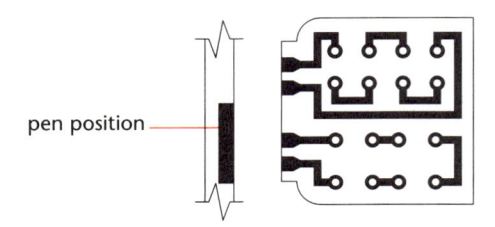

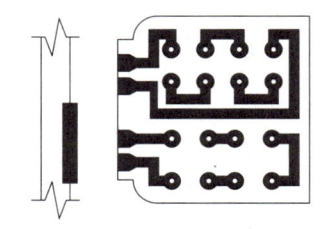

Adjust Area Fill on

Adjust Area Fill off

Use this option for drawings such as circuit diagrams in which the plot must be accurate to half the pen width.

To set the plot area and adjust the plotted display

1 From the File menu, choose Print.
2 In the Print/Plot Configuration dialog box under Additional Parameters, define the portion of the drawing to plot.

If you are in model space, the settings apply only to the current viewport. You can select one of the following options:

- Display plots the view in the graphics area.
- Extents plots all objects in the drawing.
- Limits plots the current drawing limits.
- View plots a saved view. Select the View option and then choose the View button to display the list of views.
- Window plots an area you define. Select the Window option and then choose the Window button to define the area.

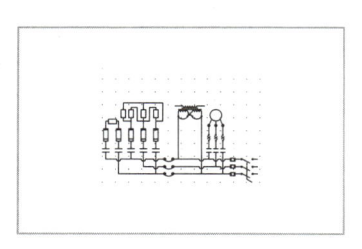

current graphics display, grid defining limits

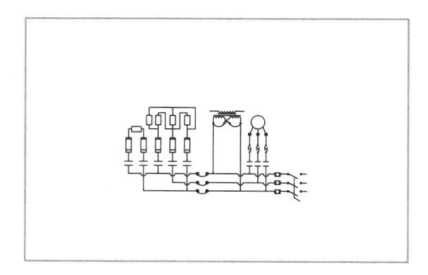

Display option

Chapter 12 Layout and Plotting

502

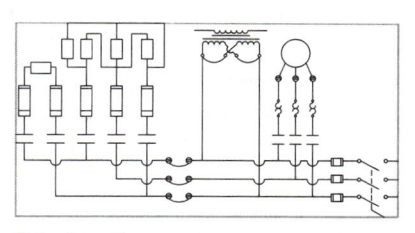

Extents option

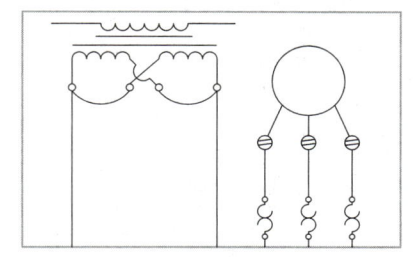

Limits option

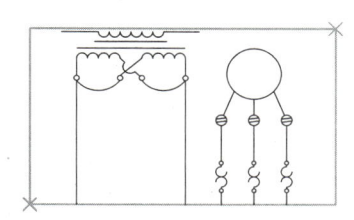

View option

Window option

3 To remove any hidden lines from the plotted output, select Hide Lines.

This option affects only objects in the current space.

4 To adjust the pen width inward for solids and wide polylines, select Adjust Area Fill.

5 Choose OK.

Command line PLOT

Setting Paper Size

You can choose a paper size from a standard list or create a custom size. You can base this size on millimeters or inches, depending on which option you choose. You also can specify the unit type used for plotting (millimeters or inches).

If you use a Windows system printer, the default paper size is specified in the Windows Control Panel by selecting Use Control Panel Defaults. You can change this by selecting Change Device Requirements. If your system printer is configured to use the Windows Control Panel defaults, these changes last for only one plot. If you clear Use Control Panel Defaults when configuring the system driver, any changes in paper are size saved.

Plotting Your Drawing

To set the paper size

1 From the File menu, choose Print.
2 In the Print/Plot Configuration dialog box, under Paper Size and Orientation, select either inches or millimeters as a basis for the measurement.
3 To display a list of the paper sizes that your plotter supports, choose Size.

   The width and height values displayed assume a 1/4" unplottable area around the edge of the page. You may need to define a user paper size if the unprintable area for your plotting device is different.

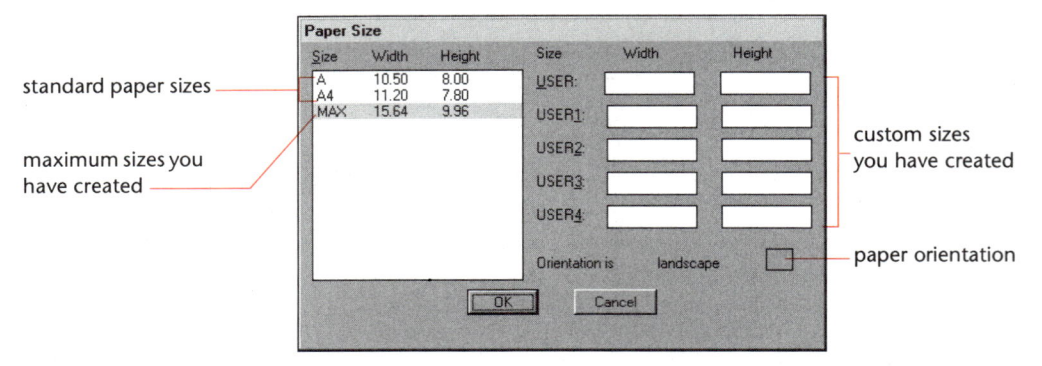

standard paper sizes

maximum sizes you have created

custom sizes you have created

paper orientation

4 In the Paper Size dialog box, select an existing size or enter a custom size at User.
5 Choose OK.

Command line PLOT

Positioning the View on the Paper

You can rotate the image to adjust its orientation on the paper. You also can reposition the image by changing its plot origin. The home position, or lower-left corner of the plotted area, is determined by your plotter. If necessary, you can change the plot origin (normally set to 0,0) to adjust the position of the plotted drawing relative to the home position. For example, the home position for pen plotters often is well within the edges of the paper. You can access the plot origin settings by choosing Rotation and Origin in the Print/Plot Configuration dialog box. To plot the lower-left corner of the drawing nearer to the lower-left corner of the paper, you might set X Origin to –1.0 and Y Origin to –0.5.

home position

lower-left corner of paper

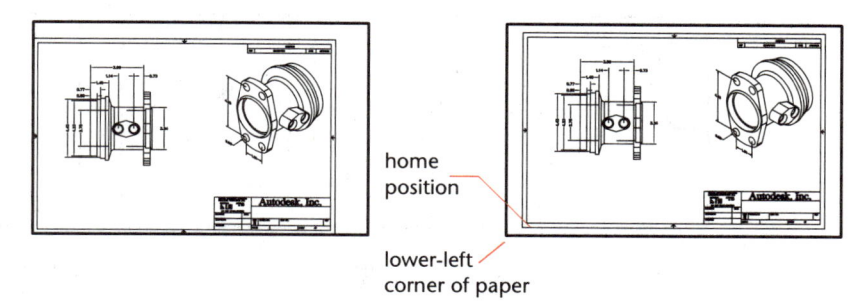

plot with origin 0,0   plot with origin -1.0, -0.5

For raster printers, the home position often is as close as 0.25 from each edge of the paper. However, many printers do not print that close to the edge. To avoid clipping off part of the drawing when you print, you can avoid drawing outside the printer-defined margins, or you can specify a new plot origin. For example, set X Origin and Y Origin to 0.5 to establish a plot margin 0.50 units in and up from the plotter's home position.

If you change the plot rotation, the home position remains in the lower-left corner of the rotated plot area. Positive plot-origin offsets shift the rotated image up or to the right. Negative plot-origin offsets shift the rotated image down or to the left.

The effect of the rotation and origin settings varies with the plotter you use. For information about the home position or clipping regions for your output device, see its documentation.

To set the plot rotation and origin

1 From the File menu, choose Print.
2 In the Print/Plot Configuration dialog box under Scale, Rotation, and Origin, choose Rotation and Origin.

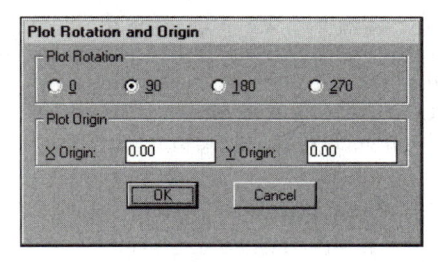

3 In the Plot Rotation and Origin dialog box, select a rotation.

Plotting Your Drawing

505

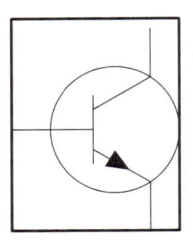

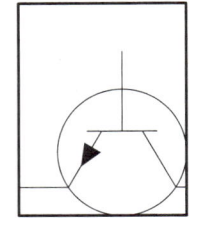

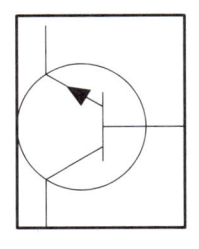

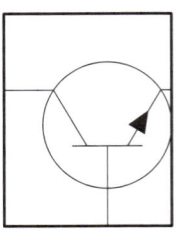

0° plot rotation   90° plot rotation   180° plot rotation   270° plot rotation

For Windows system printers, the rotation is affected by the settings in the Windows Control Panel.

4 Under Plot Origin, enter *X* and *Y* values to specify where on the paper the plot should begin. (These values use the unit type selected under Paper Size and Orientation.) Then choose OK.

5 In the Plot Configuration dialog box under Plot Preview, select Full or Partial. Then choose Preview to see the position of the image in the plotted drawing. Choose OK to close the window.

6 Repeat steps 2 to 6 to make adjustments. Then choose OK.

Command line   PLOT

Related   Set the PLOTROTMODE system variable to 0 to use the plot rotation method available in Release 12 or earlier. This method rotates the home position (from which the origin offsets are calculated) as you rotate the plot. When the variable is set to 1 (default) the home position stays in the lower-left corner when the plot is rotated.

Setting the Plot Scale

You generally draw objects at their actual size. When you plot the drawing, you either specify a precise scale or fit the image to the paper.

Most of your final drawings are plotted at a precise scale. To develop a scale, you enter the ratio of plotted units to drawing units under Scale, Rotation, and Origin in the Plot Configuration dialog box. You can choose the unit type, inches or millimeters, under Paper Size and Orientation. For example, if MM is selected, entering **1** under Plotted MM and **10** under Drawing Units produces a drawing in which each plotted millimeter represents 10 actual millimeters.

The following illustrations show a full-scale drawing scaled to fit a C-size sheet using both a 1:10 scale and the Scaled to Fit option.

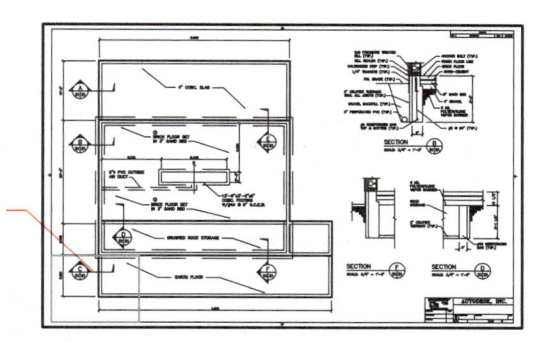

c-size paper compared with actual size

drawing shown at 1:1 scale

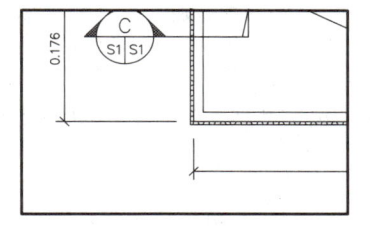

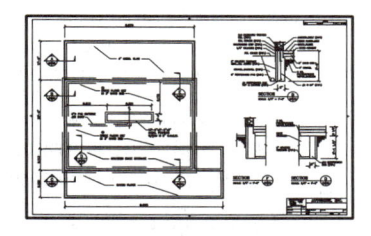

plotted at 1:10 on c-size paper

scaled to fit c-size paper

When you are reviewing drafts, a precise scale is not always important. You can use the Scaled to Fit option to plot the view at the largest possible size that fits the paper. AutoCAD fits either the horizontal or vertical dimension to the corresponding dimension of the paper. Perspective views are scaled to fit the paper, even when you enter a scale. Do *not* use Scaled to Fit with the long-axis plots that are available on some plotters.

When you choose the Scaled to Fit option, the text boxes change to reflect the actual ratio of plotted units to drawing units. AutoCAD updates this scale whenever you change the size of the plotted area, unit type, paper size, plotter, plot origin, or orientation.

To set the plot scale

1 From the File menu, choose Print.
2 In the Plot Configuration dialog box under Scale, Rotation, and Origin, enter a precise scale or choose Scaled to Fit.

Plotting Your Drawing

3 Choose OK.

Command line   PLOT

Related   If you plot from paper space, you can use ZOOM Scale to adjust the scaling in viewports relative to paper space. See "Scaling Views Relative to Paper Space" on page 488.

Reusing a Plot Configuration

For complex configurations with numerous pen assignments, using an existing complete plot configuration file can save time. You can create plot configurations for different drawings, for each available plotter, or for plotting the same drawing on the same plotter in different ways. By including complete plot configuration (PC2) files with drawing files that you send to another site, you can save other users from having to set up a detailed plot configuration. You can also use PC2 files for batch plotting.

You can save up to 29 plotter configurations in the *acad14.cfg* file. This file can contain configurations for 29 different plotters, or it can specify 29 configurations for a single plotter.

If you need more than 29 configurations, you can save an unlimited number of complete plot configuration (PC2*)* files. PC2 files contain the device-independent and device-dependent parts of a single plot configuration. If you plan to load a PC2 file from the Device and Default Selection dialog box, and you want to preserve the current default configuration, save it in another PC2 file before loading the new PC2 file. When you plot, you can choose the PC2 file you need.

Partial plot configuration (PCP) files can be used for exchanging device-independent plot configuration information with Release 12 or Release 13 users. PCP files can be used to merge pen parameters and device-independent settings from one device to another similar device's configuration.

Creating a Complete Plot Configuration File

You can create and save the current plot configuration directly to a complete plot configuration file. Complete plot configurations are saved with the *.pc2* file extension. When you save the PC2 file, it copies the plotter configuration information from one section of *acad14.cfg* to a separate PC2 file.

To create a complete plot configuration (PC2) file

1 From the File menu, choose Print.

2 In the Print/Plot Configuration dialog box, review the settings and make any necessary changes.

3   Choose Device and Default Selection.

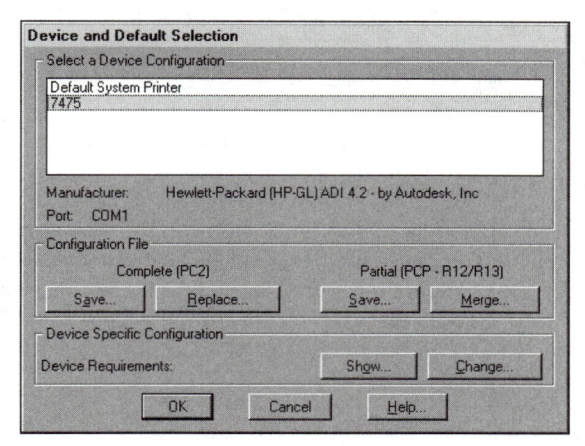

4   In the Device and Default Selection dialog box under Complete (PC2), choose Save.

5   In the Save PC2 File dialog box under File Name, enter a new file name. Specify a new directory if necessary.

6   Choose OK to exit each dialog box.

NOTE   You can also create PC2 files by choosing the Printer tab in the Preferences dialog box. Choose Save to save the current configuration to a PC2 file. The PC2 file configuration information is added to the *acad14.cfg* file.

Using a Complete Plot Configuration File

You can use the default configuration stored in a specific complete plot configuration file whenever you plot a drawing. Opening a PC2 file using the Device and Default Selection dialog box replaces your entire current plot configuration.

To use a complete plot configuration (PC2) file

1   From the File menu, choose Print.

2   In the Print/Plot Configuration dialog box, choose Device and Default Selection.

3   In the Device and Default Selection dialog box under Complete (PC2), choose Replace.

4   In the Replace from PC2 File dialog box, select the PC2 file you want to use.

    The PC2 file you select replaces the current default plotter configuration.

5   Choose OK.

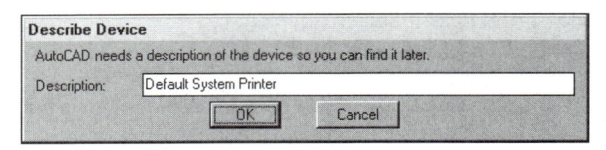

6 In the Describe Device dialog box, enter a unique description for the device.

7 Choose OK to exit each dialog box.

NOTE You can also add a configuration stored in the PC2 file by choosing the Printer tab in the Preferences dialog box. Choose Open to select the PC2 file you want. This adds the configuration stored in the PC2 file to the list of configurations in *acad14.cfg*. Unlike loading a PC2 file from the Device and Default Selection dialog box, loading it from the Printer tab does *not* replace the current configuration.

Creating a Partial Plot Configuration File

You can create and save the device-independent part of the current plot configuration directly to a partial plot configuration file. Partial configurations are saved with the *.pcp* file extension.

To create a partial plot configuration (PCP) file

1 From the File menu, choose Print.

2 In the Print/Plot Configuration dialog box, review the settings and make any necessary changes.

3 Choose Device and Default Selection.

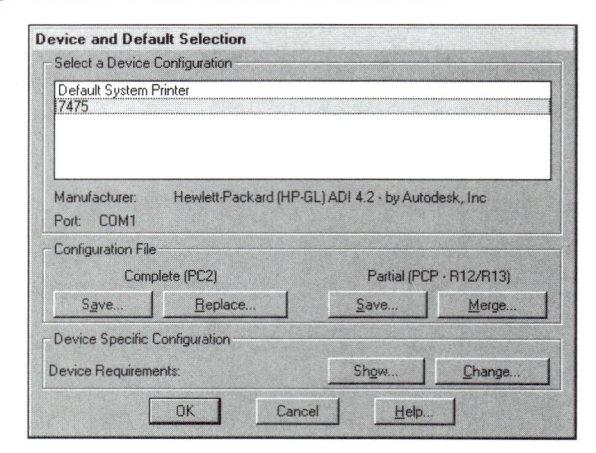

Chapter 12 Layout and Plotting

510

4   In the Device and Default Selection dialog box, under Partial (PCP-R12/R13), choose Save.

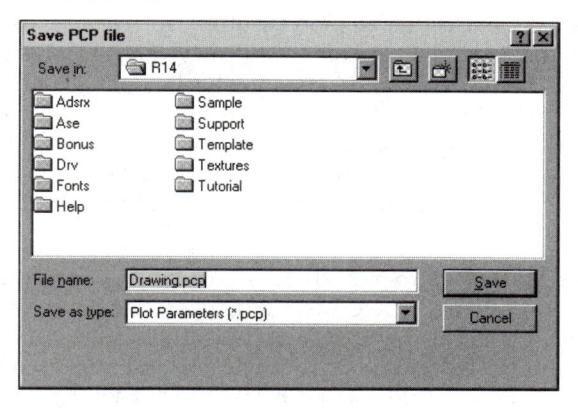

[Screenshot of Save PCP file dialog box showing folders Adsrx, Ase, Bonus, Drv, Fonts, Help, Sample, Support, Template, Textures, Tutorial in R14 directory. File name: Drawing.pcp. Save as type: Plot Parameters (.pcp).]*

5   In the Save to PCP File dialog box under File Name, enter a new file name. Change directories if necessary.

6   Choose OK to exit each dialog box.

Command line   PLOT

Related   Use any ASCII text editor to edit a plot configuration file.

Using a Partial Plot Configuration File

You can use the settings defined in a specific partial plot configuration file whenever you plot a drawing. The information in the PCP file is merged into your current plotter configuration, replacing existing settings for pen parameters, paper size and orientation, and plot scale and units.

To use a partial plot configuration (PCP) file

1   From the File menu, choose Print.

2   In the Print/Plot Configuration dialog box, choose Device and Default Selection.

3   In the Device and Default Selection dialog box under Partial (PCP-R12/R13), choose Merge.

4   In the Merge from PCP File dialog box, select the PCP file you want to use.

5   Choose OK to exit each dialog box.

Command line   PLOT

Plotting Your Drawing

511

Using BATCHPLT for Batch Plotting

BATCHPLT is a Visual Basic batch plotting utility you can use to construct lists of AutoCAD drawings to be plotted. After you've created a list of drawings using BATCHPLT, you can save the drawing list in a BPL (batch plot list) file. By default, BATCHPLT starts AutoCAD with a display window size of 640 × 480 pixels. This sets the default aspect ratio for any drawings plotted as DISPLAY. If you change the size or shape of the AutoCAD started by BATCHPLT and then save a BPL file, the new display size and shape is used when the BPL file is reloaded.

Before you use BATCHPLT to plot a batch of drawings, you should verify that all necessary fonts, external references, linetypes, and layer properties are available so that the drawings can be successfully loaded and viewed. If you want to plot more than one view of a single drawing, perhaps with different layers visible, you can create a series of "dummy" drawings, each of which externally references your drawing. Each dummy drawing can designate different zoom and layer visibility settings.

Because BATCHPLT plots each drawing's default display view, you should save each drawing with the view you want to plot as the current view. If you are plotting to a single plotter and using a single plot configuration, make the configuration you want current. When you plot, the drawings are plotted to the current plotter, unless you associate a PC2 file, which modifies the current plotter.

Once you've created a list of drawings using BATCHPLT, you can associate a PC2 or PCP file with each drawing. If you want to plot to more than one plotter, or if you want to use more than one plot configuration, you should save a PC2 file for each plot configuration you plan to use. If you want to merge device-independent settings from one device to another or from a similar device's configuration, you should save a PCP file for each plot configuration. Any drawing not associated with a PC2 or PCP file will plot to the device that was the default before you started BATCHPLT.

NOTE If you use a nonsystem driver to plot from another instance of AutoCAD to the same device that a batch plot is using, be sure to force the plot to be spooled by configuring a Windows system printer for the same device and port. For more information about plot spooling, see chapter 4, "Plot Spooling" in the *Installation Guide*.

To use BATCHPLT to plot several drawings to several devices

1 Open each drawing and save it with the view you want to plot displayed.

2 Set up each plot configuration you plan to use and save each to a PC2 file (see "Creating a Complete Plot Configuration File" on page 508).

3 Start BATCHPLT either from the command line or by double-clicking its icon in the AutoCAD program group.

NOTE You may want to resize the AutoCAD window and move the BATCHPLT window so that you can access other windows while the system is running the plotting utility.

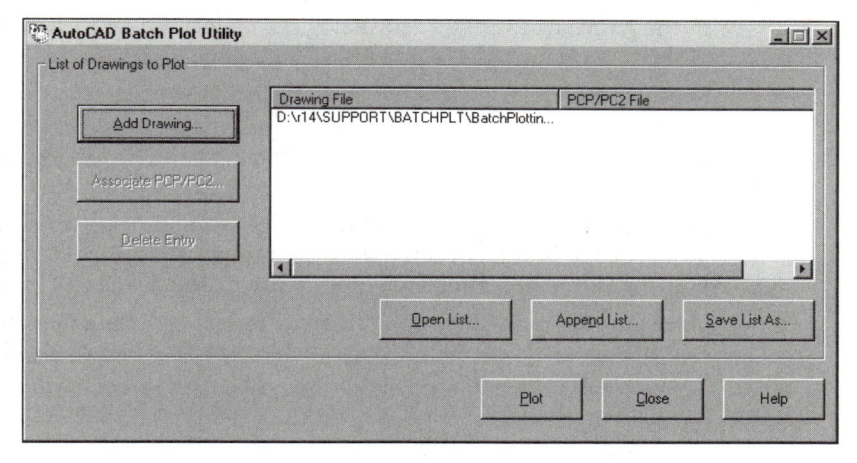

4 In the AutoCAD Batch Plot Utility dialog box, choose Add Drawing.

5 In the Add Drawing dialog box, select the first drawing and then choose Add.

Repeat the last two steps to add each drawing to the list, or you can select more than one drawing.

6 In the Add Drawing dialog box, select the first drawing, and then choose Associate PCP/PC2.

Plotting Your Drawing

513

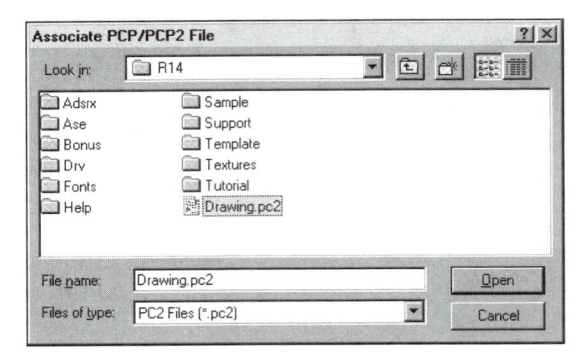

7   In the Associate PCP/PC2 File dialog box, select the PC2 file that holds the plot configuration you stored for this drawing.

    Repeat this step for each drawing in the list, or you can select more than one drawing.

8   Verify that all of the devices you are plotting to are ready, and then choose Plot.

    The Batch Plot Progress dialog box is displayed, indicating the drawing and its associated plot file. Each drawing is sent to the specified plotter. Once plotting is finished, the Batch Plot Utility dialog box is redisplayed.

9   Once plotting is finished, you can save the list of drawing files and associated PC2 files in a BPL file for reuse by clicking on Save List As, or you can leave BATCHPLT by choosing Close.

Plotting to a File

You can plot a drawing to a file rather than to a plotter or printer. Because you can plot this file later without opening AutoCAD, you can send the file to a plotting service or use a spooler to plot the file.

The plotted file uses the current drawing name with a different extension. Your plotter driver may specify a file extension automatically, or you can specify one when you plot. Otherwise, AutoCAD adds a *.plt* file extension.

To plot a drawing to a file

1   From the File menu, choose Print.
2   In the Print/Plot Configuration dialog box under Additional Parameters, select Plot to File.

3 To use a different name, choose File Name and enter a new file name. Change directories as needed. Then choose OK.

4 Choose OK.

Command line   PLOT

> **NOTE**   If you are plotting from a script or LISP routine, you are *not* prompted if an existing PLT file is overwritten. During interactive plotting, you are warned if an existing file is about to be overwritten.

Printing More Quickly

When plotting to a printer, AutoCAD scans your drawing from top to bottom, processing horizontal strips of the drawing. For many printers, AutoCAD can save time by truncating trailing blank space from the right end of each horizontal strip. A drawing without border lines often can be processed more quickly than the same drawing with border lines. If a drawing has borders, you can speed up plotting by placing the borders on a separate layer and turning them off before plotting.

If you use the Windows system printer, you also can speed up plotting performance by

- Setting a permanent, rather than temporary, swap file
- Turning off the Windows Print Manager
- Disabling spooling (to return to plotted output faster)

For more information about these procedures, see your Windows documentation.

Optimizing Pen Motion

You often can minimize wasted pen motion and reduce plot time by optimizing, or increasing the efficiency of, your pens. For example, you can prevent the pens from retracing duplicate lines. Also, if your drawing uses many colors or widths, you can reduce the time needed to change pens by turning on pen sorting. This option causes AutoCAD to plot every object that uses a particular pen before switching to another pen.

To optimize your pens

1 From the File menu, choose Print.
2 In the Print/Plot Configuration dialog box, choose Optimization.

Based on the current plotter, AutoCAD offers an appropriate optimization level.

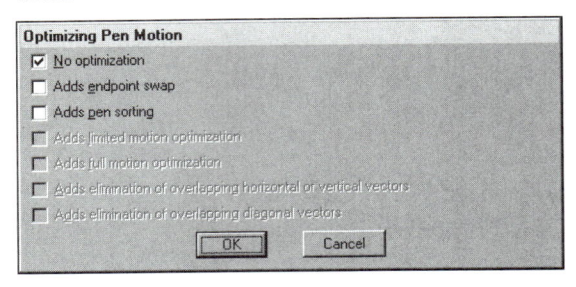

Each successive check box under No Optimization adds cumulatively to the optimization level. The two last options, which eliminate overlapping vectors, can save time if your drawing includes many overlapping lines.

3 In the Optimizing Pen Motion dialog box, select the options you want to change. Then choose OK.

Related To remove overlapping lines from 3D drawings, you can use the Hide Lines option in the Plot Configuration dialog box.

In some cases, optimizing can be counterproductive, depending on the speed of the computer, the plotter, and the plotter's pen change mechanism. This option generally has no effect on raster printers. It is *not* available for the Windows system printer.

Calibrating the Plotter

If your plotter meets the manufacturer's specifications for accuracy of scale, a 10-inch line in a drawing that is plotted at a scale of 1:1 should be exactly 10 inches long on the paper. If you need to correct scaling discrepancies, you can change the plotter calibration (see chapter 2, "Calibrating a Printer or Plotter" in the *Installation Guide*).

Multipen Plotting with a Single-Pen Plotter

If you use a single-pen plotter you can plot different colors by changing pens as you plot. You can turn on this plotter option with the CONFIG command. Enter **y** at the prompt Do You Want to Change Pens While Plotting? When this option is on, AutoCAD pauses when necessary during the plot and issues a prompt like this one:

Install pen number 2, color 3 (green)
Press ENTER to continue:

Wait for the plotter to stop, change the pen accordingly, and press ENTER to resume plotting.

Working in Three-Dimensional Space

13

In this chapter

- Specifying *X*, *Y*, and *Z* coordinates in a 3D coordinate system
- Controlling the user coordinate system (UCS)
- Defining 3D views
- Creating and editing wireframe models, surface models, and solid models

Most drawings consist of two-dimensional (2D) views of objects that are three-dimensional (3D). Though this method of drafting is widely used in the architectural and engineering communities, it is limited: the drawings are 2D representations of 3D objects and must be visually interpreted. Moreover, because the views are created independently, there are more possibilities for error and ambiguity. As a result, you may want to create true 3D models instead of 2D representations. You can use AutoCAD's drawing tools to create detailed, realistic 3D objects and manipulate them in various ways.

Specifying 3D Coordinates

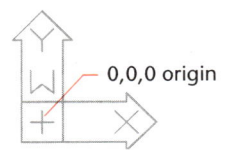

Specifying 3D coordinates is the same as specifying 2D coordinates with the addition of a third dimension, the Z axis. When drawing in 3D, you specify X, Y, and Z values of the coordinate in either the World Coordinate System (WCS) or the user coordinate system (UCS). The following illustration shows the X, Y, and Z axes of the WCS.

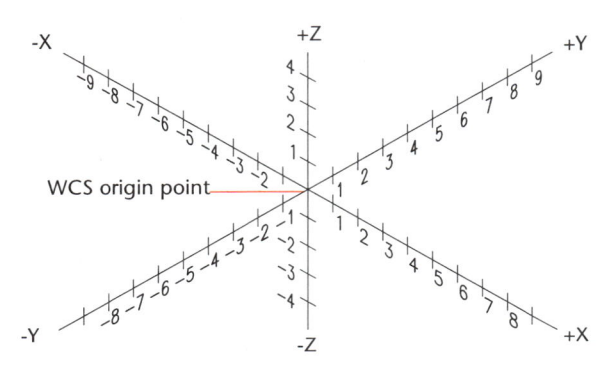

X, Y, and Z axes of the World Coordinate System

The Right-Hand Rule

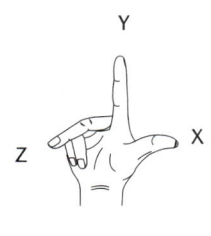

The right-hand rule determines the positive axis direction of the Z axis when you know the direction of the X and Y axes in a 3D coordinate system. The right-hand rule also determines the positive rotation direction about an axis in 3D space.

To determine the positive axis direction of the X, Y, and Z axes, place the back of your right hand near the screen. Point your thumb in the direction of the positive X axis. Extend your index and middle fingers as illustrated and point your index finger in the direction of the positive Y axis. Your middle finger indicates the direction of the positive Z axis.

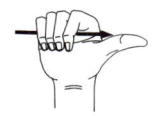

To determine the positive rotation direction about an axis, point your right thumb in the positive direction of the axis and curl your fingers as illustrated. Your fingers indicate the positive rotation direction about the axis.

Entering X,Y,Z Coordinates

Entering 3D cartesian coordinates (X,Y,Z) is similar to entering 2D coordinates (X,Y). In addition to specifying X and Y values, you specify a Z value. In the following illustration, the coordinate 3,2,5 indicates a point 3 units along the positive X axis, 2 units along the positive Y axis, and 5 units along the positive Z axis. You can enter absolute coordinate values, which are based on the origin, or relative coordinate values, which are based on the last point entered.

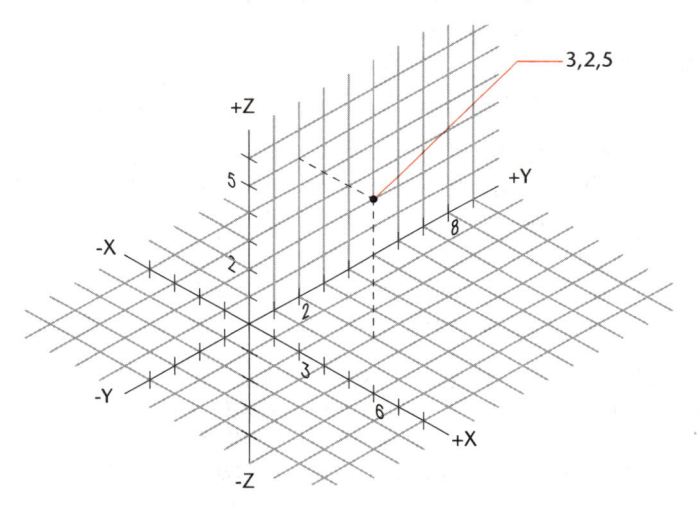

A 3D Cartesian coordinate

Using XYZ Point Filters

With *XYZ* point filters, you can extract coordinates from selected points and synthesize a new point using these coordinates. With this method, you can use known points to find an unknown point. On the command line, use the following format:

.coordinate_value

where coordinate_value is one or more of the letters X, Y, and Z. AutoCAD accepts the following filter selections: .X, .Y, .Z, .XY, .XZ, and .YZ. For example, if you enter **.x**, you are prompted for the Y and Z values.

Specifying 3D Coordinates

In the following example, you select midpoints on an object and use *XYZ* point filters to locate the center point of the object's cavity. In the illustration, HIDE has been used for clarity.

Command: *Enter* **point**
Point: *Enter* **.x**
of *Enter* **mid**
of *Select a point* (1)   (need YZ): *Enter* **.y**
of *Enter* **mid**
of *Select a point* (2)   (need Z): *Enter* **mid**
of *Select a point* (3)
Command:

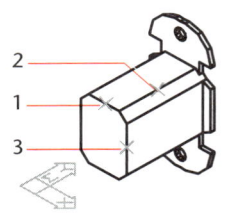

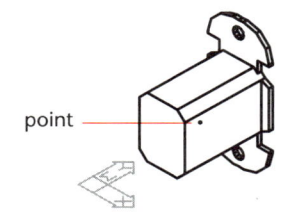

Entering Cylindrical Coordinates

Cylindrical coordinate entry is similar to 2D polar coordinate entry, but with an additional distance from the polar coordinate perpendicular to the *XY* plane. You locate a point by specifying its distance along an angle relative to the UCS *X* axis and its *Z* value perpendicular to the *XY* plane. In the following illustration, the coordinate 5<60,6 indicates a point 5 units from the origin of the current UCS, 60 degrees from the *X* axis in the *XY* plane, and 6 units along the *Z* axis. The coordinate 8<30,1 indicates a point 8 units from the origin of the current UCS in the *XY* plane, 30 degrees from the *X* axis in the *XY* plane and 1 unit along the *Z* axis.

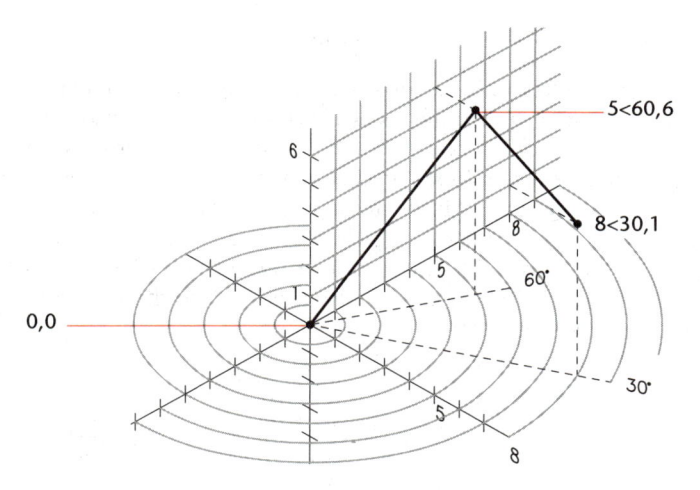

Absolute cylindrical coordinates

In the following illustration, the relative cylindrical coordinate @4<45,5 indicates a point 4 units in the *XY* plane from the last point entered, not from the UCS origin point, at an angle of 45 degrees from the positive *X* direction. The line extends to a *Z* coordinate of 5.

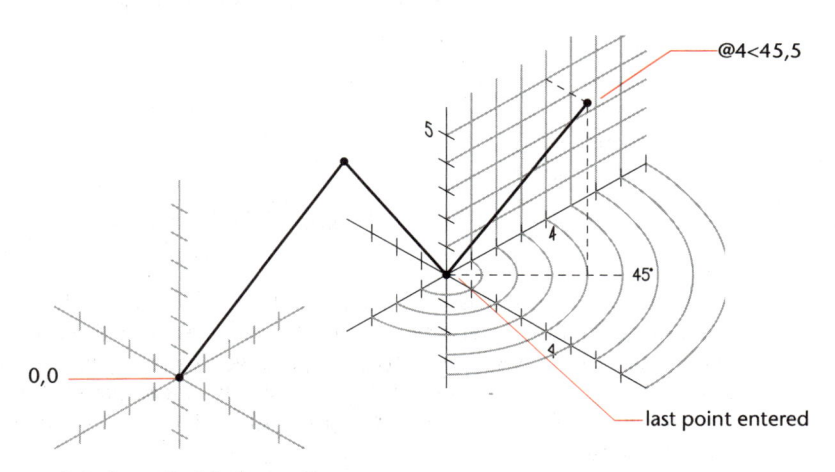

Relative cylindrical coordinate

Specifying 3D Coordinates

Entering Spherical Coordinates

Spherical coordinate entry in 3D is also similar to polar coordinate entry in 2D. You locate a point by specifying its distance from the origin of the current UCS, its angle from the *X* axis (in the *XY* plane), and its angle from the *XY* plane, each separated by an open angle bracket (<). In the following illustration, the coordinate 8<60<30 indicates a point 8 units from the origin of the current UCS in the *XY* plane, 60 degrees from the *X* axis in the *XY* plane, and 30 degrees up from the *XY* plane. The coordinate 5<45<15 indicates a point 5 units from the origin, 45 degrees from the *X* axis in the *XY* plane, and 15 degrees from the *XY* plane.

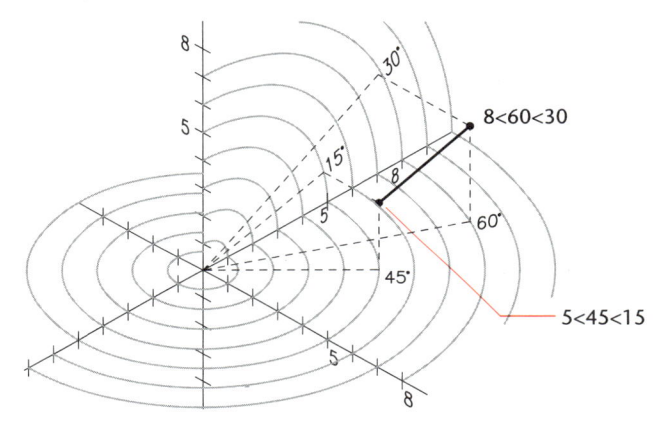

Spherical coordinates

Defining a User Coordinate System

You define a user coordinate system (UCS) to change the location of the 0,0,0 origin point and the orientation of the *XY* plane and *Z* axis. You can locate and orient a UCS anywhere in 3D space, and you can define, save, and recall as many user coordinate systems as you require. Coordinate input and display are relative to the current UCS. If multiple viewports are active, they share the same UCS.

If you plan to work extensively in 3D, you can define several user coordinate systems, each having a different origin and orientation for various construction requirements.

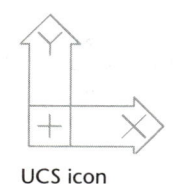

UCS icon

To indicate the origin and orientation of the UCS, you can display the UCS icon at the UCS origin point using the UCSICON command. See "Displaying the UCS Icon" on page 121.

UCSs are especially useful in 3D. You may find it easier to align the coordinate system with existing geometry than to figure out the exact placement of a 3D point.

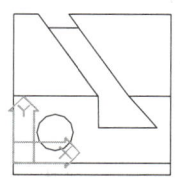

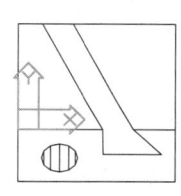

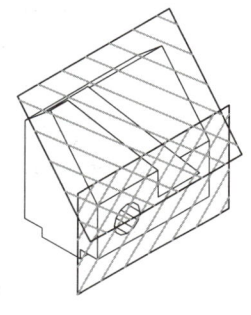

first UCS   second UCS   model with both UCSs

Multiple user coordinate systems

You can define a new UCS in paper space just as you can in model space; however, the UCSs in paper space are restricted to 2D manipulation. Although you can enter 3D coordinates in paper space, you cannot use such 3D viewing commands as DVIEW, VPOINT, and PLAN. AutoCAD keeps track of the last 10 coordinate systems created in model space and the last 10 in paper space.

The current elevation established by the ELEV command remains in effect as you change from one UCS to another, and it defines the drawing plane of the current UCS. AutoCAD maintains separate "current" elevation settings for paper space and model space. To avoid confusion, you can leave the elevation set to zero and control the *XY* plane of the current UCS with the UCS command. For more information, see "Setting Elevation and Thickness" on page 546.

You can define a user coordinate system in several ways:

- Specify a new origin, new *XY* plane, or new *Z* axis
- Align the new UCS with an existing object
- Align the new UCS with the current viewing direction
- Rotate the current UCS around any of its axes
- Select a preset UCS from a set of UCSs that AutoCAD provides

Defining a User Coordinate System

Defining a UCS in 3D Space

You can define a UCS in 3D space using the 3 Point option of the UCS command to specify the new UCS origin and the direction of its positive X and Y axes. The Z axis follows by applying the right-hand rule.

To define a UCS in 3D Space

1 From the Tools menu, choose UCS ➤ 3 Point.
2 Specify the origin point.
3 Specify a point on the positive portion of the X axis.
4 Specify a point anywhere on the positive Y portion of the new UCS XY plane.

Command line   UCS

Selecting a Preset UCS

The image tiles in the UCS Orientation dialog box represent the choices available to you to change the current UCS. After you select an image tile, AutoCAD changes the current UCS based on the setting of the Relative to Current UCS or Absolute to WCS options. Relative to Current UCS and Absolute to WCS are irrelevant if you restore the WCS or the previous UCS or set the UCS to the current view.

To select a UCS preset

1 From the Tools menu, choose UCS ➤ Preset UCS.
2 In the UCS Orientation dialog box, select a UCS.

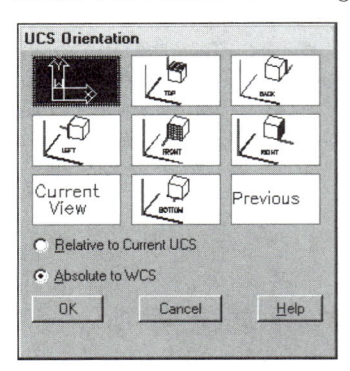

3 Choose OK.

Command line   DDUCSP

Chapter 13 Working in Three-Dimensional Space

526

The UCS Icon

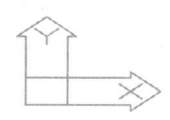

UCS rotated about the X axis

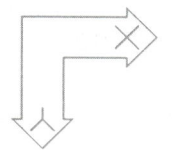

UCS viewed from below

Examples of UCS icon display in 3D space

broken pencil icon

A broken pencil icon appears when the edge of the *XY* plane of the current UCS is almost perpendicular to your viewing direction or display screen. This icon warns you that it is *not* recommended that you specify coordinates in this viewport by clicking with your pointing device.

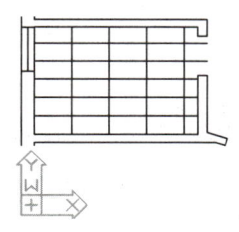

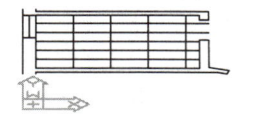

plan view
UCS=WCS

UCS rotated about the X axis

working plane perpendicular to the viewer

Examples of UCS icon display in 3D space

Viewing in 3D

In model space, you can view an AutoCAD drawing from any point. From a selected viewpoint, you can add new objects, edit existing objects, or generate a hidden line, shaded view, or rendered view. Also, you can define a parallel projection or perspective view.

If you are working in paper space, you *cannot* use the VPOINT, DVIEW, or PLAN commands to define paper space views. The view in paper space always remains a plan view.

In model space, you can set the viewing direction using DDVPOINT and VPOINT. A convenient way to view an AutoCAD drawing from any 3D point in model space is to use the compass and axis tripod feature of VPOINT (see "Setting a View with the Compass and Axis Tripod" on page 530).

Setting a Viewing Direction

Set a viewing direction when you begin work on a model or want to check a completed model from a particular viewpoint.

You can rotate a view using DDVPOINT. The following illustration shows a view defined by two angles relative to the *X* axis and the *XY* plane of the WCS.

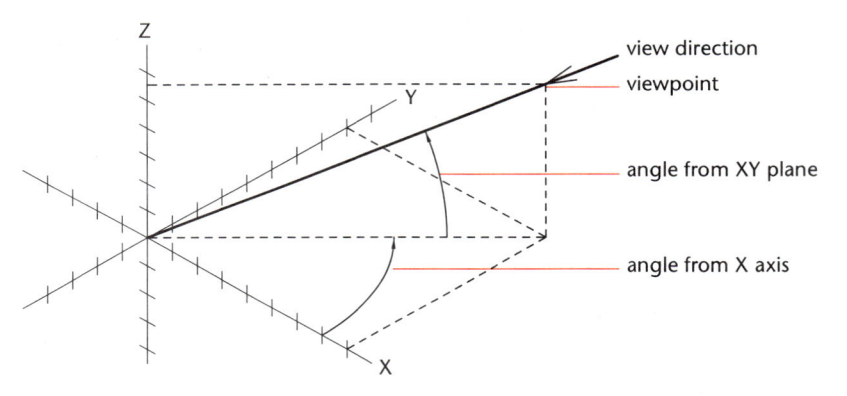

A viewing direction defined by two angles

To set the viewing direction

1 From the View menu, choose 3D Viewpoint ➤ Select.

viewing angles relative to the XY plane

viewing angles relative to the X axis

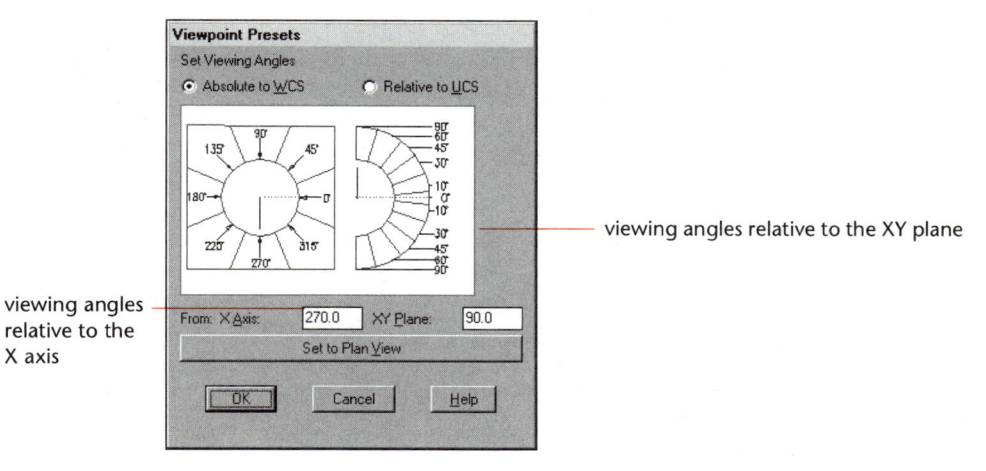

2   In the Viewpoint Presets dialog box, select viewing angles relative to the *X* axis and the *XY* plane by clicking your pointing device inside the image tiles, or enter the values directly for the *X* axis and *XY* plane.

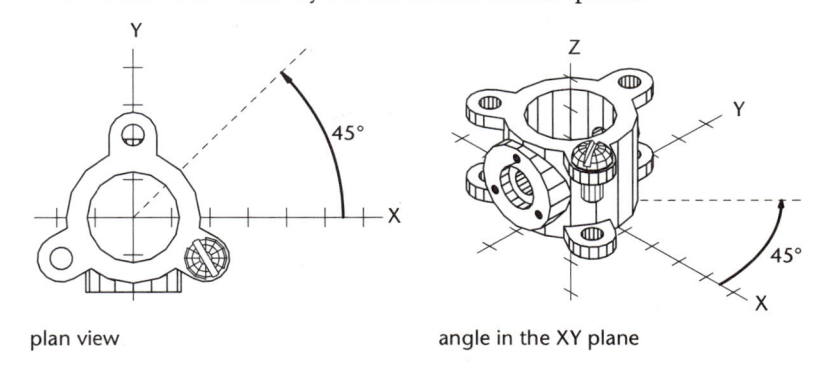

plan view

angle in the XY plane

Viewing angle relative to the *X* axis

Viewing in 3D

529

second angle result

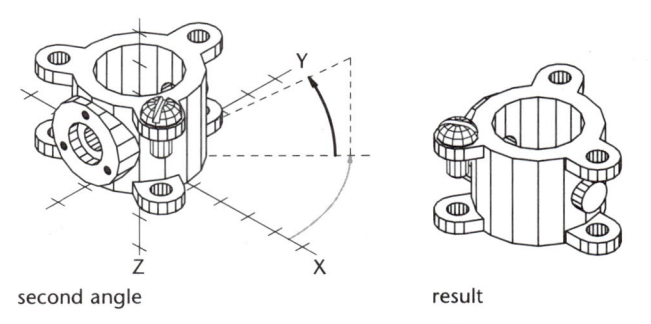

Viewing angle relative to the *XY* plane

To select the plan view of your drawing relative to the current UCS, choose Set to Plan View.

3 Choose OK.

Command line DDVPOINT

Related VPOINT sets the viewing position for a 3D visualization in the current viewport. It allows you to approximate a view using the compass and axis tripod or by entering coordinates directly.

Displaying a Plan View

You can use PLAN to change the current viewport to a plan view of the current UCS, a saved UCS, or the WCS in model space.

To change the current viewport to a plan view

1 From the View menu, choose 3D Viewpoint ➤ Plan View.
2 Choose either Current UCS (for the plan view), Named UCS (for a saved view), or World UCS.

Command line PLAN

Setting a View with the Compass and Axis Tripod

When you choose the Tripod option under 3D Viewpoint on the View menu, a compass and axis tripod are displayed on the screen. The compass represents a flattened globe. The center point of the compass indicates the north pole (0,0,1). The inner ring is the equator (*n,n,*0). The outer ring is the south

Chapter 13 Working in Three-Dimensional Space

pole (0,0,–1). Where you click in the compass determines the viewing angle relative to the *XY* plane. Where you click relative to the center point determines the *Z* angle. The axis tripod indicates the rotation of the *X*, *Y*, and *Z* axes as you move the viewpoint on the globe.

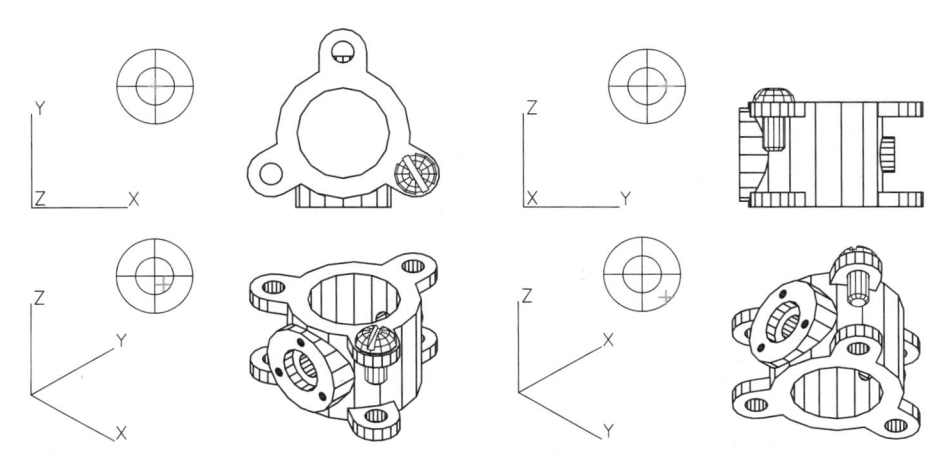

Examples of compass and axis tripod for various viewpoints

To set a view with the compass and axis tripod

1 From the View menu, choose 3D Viewpoint ➤ Tripod.
2 Choose a point inside the compass to specify the viewpoint.

Command line   VPOINT

Defining a Parallel Projection or a Perspective View

You can use DVIEW to create either a parallel projection or a perspective view. Also, you can use DVIEW to zoom, pan, and twist views. You can also use DVIEW to remove objects from in front of and behind a clipping plane and to remove hidden lines during a dynamic viewing operation. With DVIEW you can limit the number of objects displayed while creating a view magnification and orientation. When you end the command, all objects are displayed.

The following illustration shows a model in a parallel projection and in a perspective view. Both are based on the same viewing direction.

Viewing in 3D

531

parallel projection   perspective view

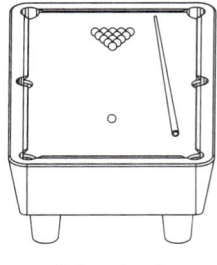

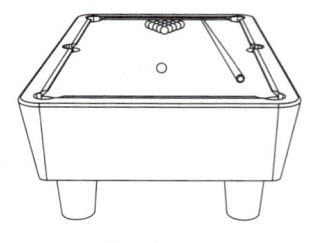

To create a parallel projection view

1. From the View menu, choose 3D Dynamic View.
2. Select the objects to display.
3. Enter **ca** (Camera).
4. Adjust the view as if you're aiming a camera. By default, AutoCAD sets the camera point at the center of the drawing. You can dynamically set the view by moving the crosshairs and clicking the return button of the pointing device, or you can adjust the view with one of two angle-input modes. To move between the modes, enter **t** (Toggle Angle).

   For Enter Angle From the XY Plane, you can enter the angle of the camera up or down relative to the *XY* plane of the current UCS. The default setting, 90 degrees, has the camera looking straight down from above.

   After you enter the angle, the camera is locked at that height and you can rotate the camera about the target with the rotation angle measured relative to the X axis of the current UCS.
5. To complete the parallel view, press ENTER.

   Command line   DVIEW

To create a perspective view

1. From the View menu, choose 3D Dynamic View.
2. Select the objects to display.

   For example, if you select only the outer walls of a building (not the interior layout plan), you can make adjustments to the perspective view much more quickly. AutoCAD applies the perspective view to the entire model.

   If you press ENTER without selecting objects, DVIEW displays a model of a small house instead of your actual drawing.
3. Enter **ca** (Camera).

4 Adjust the view as if you're aiming a camera. By default, AutoCAD sets the camera point at the center of the drawing. You can dynamically set the view by moving the crosshairs and clicking the return button on the pointing device, or you can adjust the view with one of two angle-input modes. To move between the modes, enter **t** (Toggle Angle).

For Enter Angle From the XY Plane, you can enter the angle of the camera up or down relative to the *XY* plane of the current UCS. The default setting, 90 degrees, has the camera looking straight down from above.

After you enter the angle, the camera is locked at that height and you can rotate the camera about the target with the rotation angle measured relative to the *X* axis of the current UCS.

Press ENTER to continue.

5 To turn on the perspective view, enter **d** (Distance).

slider bar of the Distance option

Use the slider bar to set the distance between the selected objects and the camera. As you move your pointing device on the slider bar, the distance changes. You can also enter a real number.

If the target point and the camera point are very close (or if the Zoom option is set high), you might see very little of your drawing. Use a larger distance value to adjust the view.

6 Specify a point along the slider bar, or press ENTER to complete the perspective view.

The Off option turns off perspective view.

NOTE Some commands are not available in perspective view.

Command line DVIEW

Setting View Clipping Planes

The Clip option of DVIEW removes objects from the front and back of a plane perpendicular to the view direction that you specify. You can move a pair of clipping planes perpendicular to the line of sight between the camera and target. The following figure shows how clipping planes work.

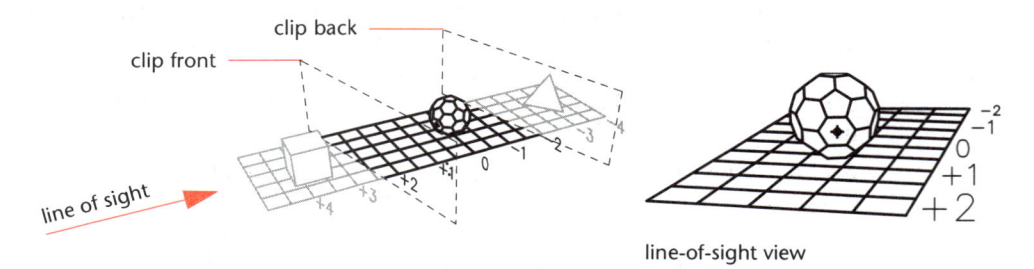

3D drawing with front and back clipping planes

To set the clipping planes

1. From the View menu, choose 3D Dynamic View.
2. Select the objects on which to base the view.
3. If necessary, set the view as described in "Defining a Parallel Projection or a Perspective View" on page 531.
4. Enter **cl** (Clip).
5. Enter **f** to set a front clipping plane or **b** to set a back clipping plane, or press ENTER to return to the DVIEW prompt.
6. Locate the position of the clipping plane by dragging the slider bar or entering a value for distance from the target.
7. Press ENTER to end the command.

Command line DVIEW

Removing Hidden Lines

The Hide option of DVIEW removes hidden lines from and creates a more realistic view of a 3D model. This option functions the same way as the HIDE command, but it's faster because it hides lines only in the objects on which the view is based.

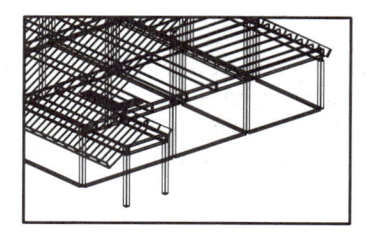

view without Hide option 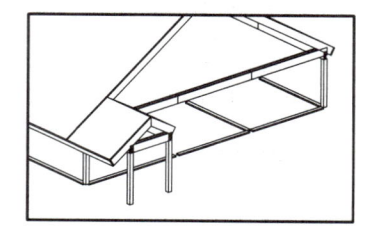   hidden-line view

To remove hidden lines

1. From the View menu, choose 3D Dynamic View.
2. Select the objects on which to base the hidden-line view.
3. If necessary, set the view as described in "Defining a Parallel Projection or a Perspective View" on page 531.
4. Enter **h** (Hide).
5. Press ENTER to end the command.

    The effect of the Hide option is temporary. AutoCAD regenerates the drawing after you exit DVIEW.

    Command line   DVIEW

    Related   HIDE removes hidden lines from the current view or viewport.

Creating 3D Objects

Although 3D models can be more difficult and time-consuming to create than 3D views, 3D modeling has several advantages. You can

- View the model from any vantage point
- Automatically generate reliable standard and auxiliary 2D views
- Remove hidden lines and do realistic shading
- Check interference
- Do engineering analysis
- Extract manufacturing data

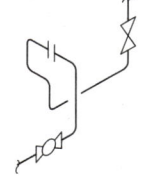

3D wireframe

mesh

AutoCAD supports three types of 3D modeling: wireframe, surface, and solid. Each type has its own creation and editing techniques.

A wireframe model is a skeletal description of a 3D object. There are no surfaces in a wireframe model; it consists only of points, lines, and curves that describe the edges of the object. With AutoCAD you can create wireframe models by positioning 2D (planar) objects anywhere in 3D space. AutoCAD also provides some three-dimensional wireframe objects, such as 3D polylines and splines. Because each object that makes up a wireframe model must be independently drawn and positioned, this type of modeling can often be the most time-consuming.

Surface modeling is more sophisticated than wireframe modeling in that it defines not only the edges of a 3D object, but also its surfaces. AutoCAD's surface modeler defines faceted surfaces using a polygonal mesh. Because the faces of the mesh are planar, the mesh can only approximate curved surfaces.

With the add-on AutoCAD product AutoSurf, you can create true curved surfaces. To differentiate these two types of surfaces, faceted surfaces are called meshes in this guide.

solid

Solid modeling is the easiest type of 3D modeling to use. With AutoCAD's solid modeler, you can make 3D objects by creating basic 3D shapes: box, cone, cylinder, sphere, wedge, and torus (donut). You then can combine these shapes to create more complex solids by joining or subtracting them or finding their intersecting (overlapping) volume. You can also create solids by sweeping a 2D object along a path or revolving it about an axis. With AutoCAD Designer, you can also define solids parametrically and maintain associativity between 3D models and the 2D views that you generate from them.

WARNING! Because each modeling type uses a different method for constructing 3D models and editing methods vary in their effect on the different model types, it is recommended that you *not* mix modeling methods. Limited conversion between model types is available from solids to surfaces and from surfaces to wireframes; however, you cannot convert from wireframes to surfaces or from surfaces to solids.

Creating Wireframes

With AutoCAD you can create wireframe models by positioning any 2D planar object anywhere in 3D space. You can position 2D objects in 3D space using several methods:

- Creating the object by entering 3D points. You enter a coordinate that defines the X, Y, and Z location of the point (see "Specifying 3D Coordinates" on page 520).
- Setting the default construction plane (XY plane) on which you will draw the object by defining a UCS (see "Defining a User Coordinate System" on page 524).
- Moving the object to its proper orientation in 3D space after you create it (see "Editing in 3D" on page 556).

Also, you can create some wireframe objects, such as polylines and splines, that can exist in all three dimensions. The following illustration is an example of a 3D modeling application using a combination of 3D polylines and 2D symbology positioned in 3D space.

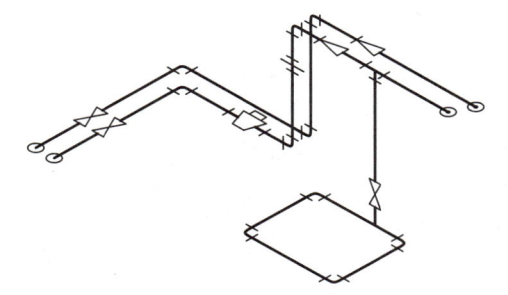

Piping diagram composed of 3D polylines and 2D symbology

Creating Meshes

A mesh represents an object's surface using planar facets. The mesh density, or number of facets, is defined in terms of a matrix of M and N vertices, similar to a grid consisting of columns and rows. M and N specify the column and row position, respectively, of any given vertex. You can create meshes in both 2D and 3D, but they are used primarily for 3D.

Use meshes if you don't need the level of detail about physical properties (that is, mass, weight, center of gravity, and so forth) that solids provide but you do need the hiding, shading, and rendering capabilities that wireframes don't provide. Meshes are also useful if you want to create geometry with unusual mesh patterns, such as a 3D topographical model of a mountainous terrain.

A mesh can be open or closed. A mesh is open in a given direction if the start and end edges of the mesh do not touch, as shown in the following illustration.

Creating 3D Objects

M open
N open

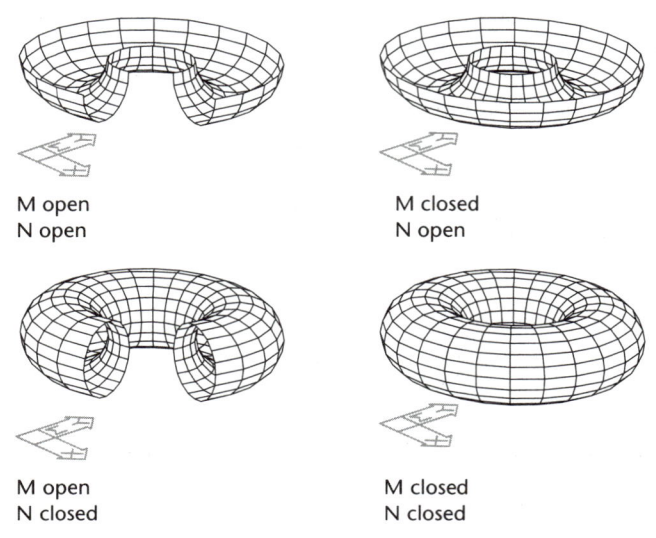

M closed
N open

M open
N closed

M closed
N closed

Open and closed meshes

AutoCAD provides several methods for creating meshes. Some of these methods can be difficult to use if you are entering the mesh parameters manually, so AutoCAD provides the 3D command, which simplifies the process of creating the basic surface shapes.

Creating a Predefined 3D-Surface Mesh

The 3D command creates the following 3D shapes: box, cone, dish, dome, mesh, pyramid, sphere, torus, and wedge. These are meshes that are displayed as wireframes until you use HIDE, SHADE, or RENDER.

To view the objects you are creating with the 3D command more clearly, set a viewing direction with VPOINT or DVIEW. The procedures for creating 3D shapes are similar to those creating 3D solids. For more information, see "Creating Solids" on page 548.

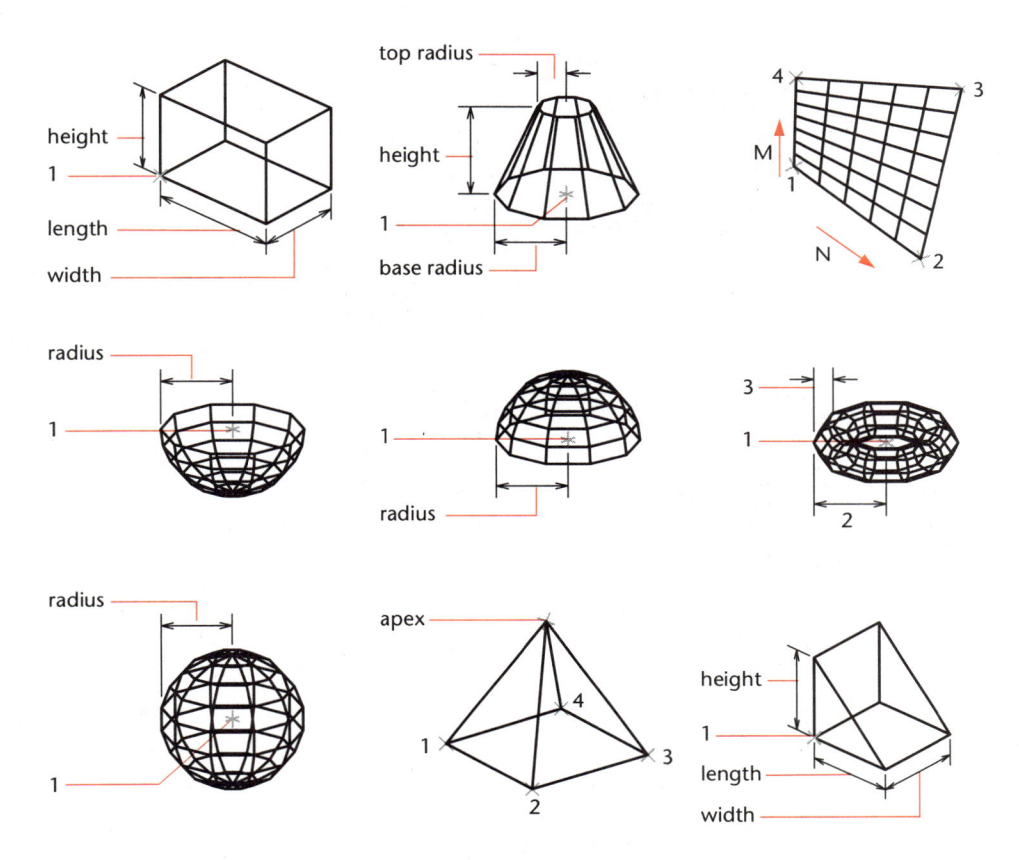

Surface meshes created with the 3D command

Creating a Rectangular Mesh

With the 3DMESH command you can create polygon meshes that are open in both the *M* and *N* directions (similar to the *X* and *Y* axes of an *XY* plane). You can close the meshes with PEDIT. You can use 3DMESH to construct very irregular surfaces. In most cases, you can use 3DMESH in conjunction with scripts or LISP routines when you know the mesh points.

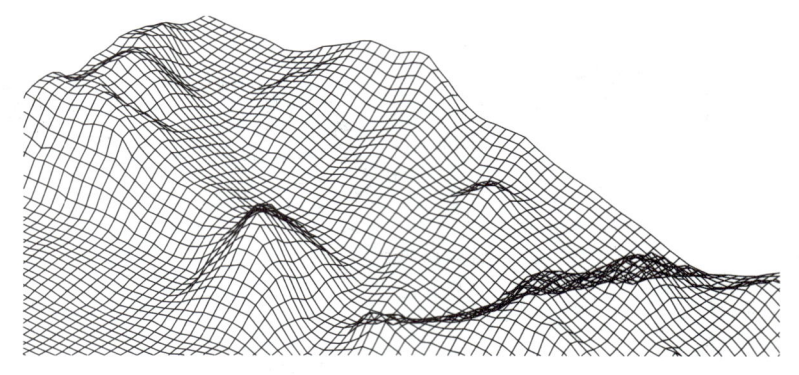

Example of rectangular mesh application

To create a rectangular mesh

1. From the Draw menu, choose Surfaces ➤ 3D Mesh.
2. Specify the *M* size, using an integer from 2 through 256.
3. Specify the *N* size, using an integer from 2 through 256.
4. Specify the vertex points as prompted. Specifying the last vertex point completes the mesh.

Example:

Command:	*Enter* **3dmesh**
Mesh M size:	*Enter* **4**
Mesh N size:	*Enter* **3**
Vertex (0, 0):	*Enter* **10,1, 3**
Vertex (0, 1):	*Enter* **10, 5, 5**
Vertex (0, 2):	*Enter* **10, 10, 3**
Vertex (1, 0):	*Enter* **15, 1, 0**
Vertex (1, 1):	*Enter* **15, 5, 0**
Vertex (1, 2):	*Enter* **15, 10, 0**
Vertex (2, 0):	*Enter* **20, 1, 0**
Vertex (2, 1):	*Enter* **20, 5, -1**
Vertex (2, 2):	*Enter* **20, 10, 0**
Vertex (3, 0):	*Enter* **25, 1, 0**
Vertex (3, 1):	*Enter* **25, 5, 0**
Vertex (3, 2):	*Enter* **25, 10, 0**

Command line 3DMESH

Related 3DFACE creates a 3D face. EDGE changes the visibility of 3D face edges. The Mesh option of 3D creates four-cornered planar meshes.

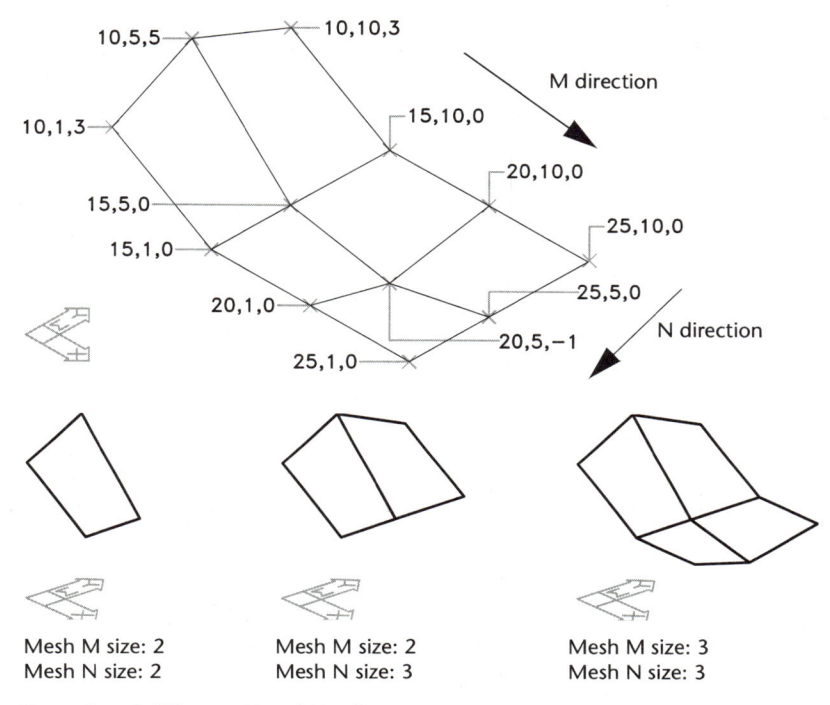

Mesh M size: 2 Mesh M size: 2 Mesh M size: 3
Mesh N size: 2 Mesh N size: 3 Mesh N size: 3

Examples of different *M* and *N* values

Creating a Polyface Mesh

The PFACE command produces a polyface (polygon) mesh, with each face capable of having numerous vertices.

Creating a polyface mesh is similar to creating a rectangular mesh. To create a polyface mesh, you specify coordinates for its vertices. You then define each face by entering vertex numbers for all the vertices of that face. As you create the polyface mesh, you can set specific edges to be invisible, assign them to layers, or give them colors.

To make the edge invisible, enter the vertex number as a negative value. For instance, to make the edge between vertices 5 and 7 invisible in the following illustration, you would enter the following:

Face 3, vertex 3: **–7**

Creating 3D Objects

In the illustration, face 1 is defined by vertices 1, 5, 6, and 2. Face 2 is defined by vertices 1, 4, 3, and 2. Face 3 is defined by vertices 1, 4, 7, and 5, and face 4 is defined by vertices 3, 4, 7, and 8.

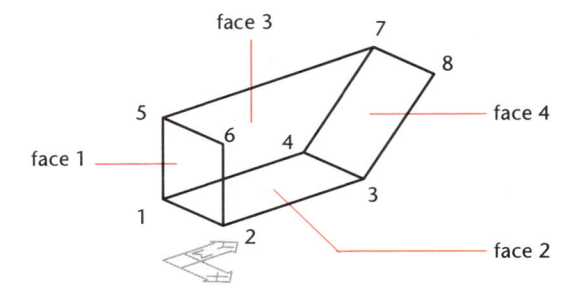

You can control the display of invisible edges with the SPLFRAME system variable. If SPLFRAME is set to a nonzero value, the invisible edges become visible and then can be edited. If SPLFRAME set to 0, the invisible edges remain invisible.

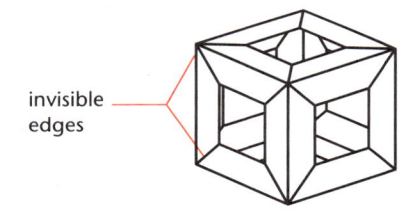

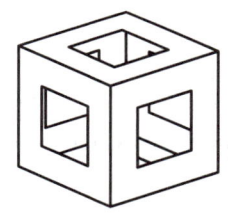

SPLFRAME = 1   SPLFRAME = 0

Display of invisible edges

Creating a Ruled Surface Mesh

With RULESURF, you can create a surface mesh between two objects. You use two different objects to define the edges of the ruled surface: lines, points, arcs, circles, ellipses, elliptical arcs, 2D polylines, 3D polylines, or splines. Pairs of objects to be used as the "rails" of a ruled surface mesh must both be either open or closed. You can pair a point object with either an open or a closed object.

To create a ruled surface

1 From the Draw menu, choose Surfaces ➤ Ruled Surface.
2 Select the first defining curve. Then select the second (1, 2).

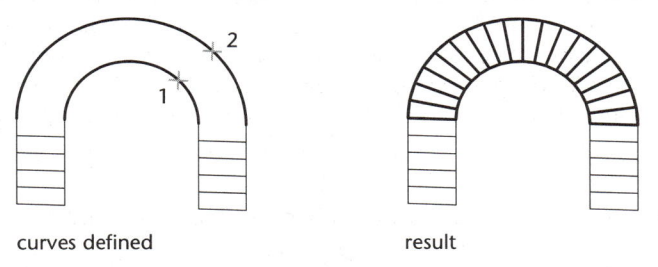

curves defined   result

3 Erase the original curve if necessary.

Command line   RULESURF

Related   The SURFTAB1 and SURFTAB2 system variables control mesh density (number of facets) in the *M* and *N* directions, respectively.

You can specify any two points on closed curves to complete RULESURF. For open curves, AutoCAD starts construction of the ruled surface based on the locations of the specified points on the curves.

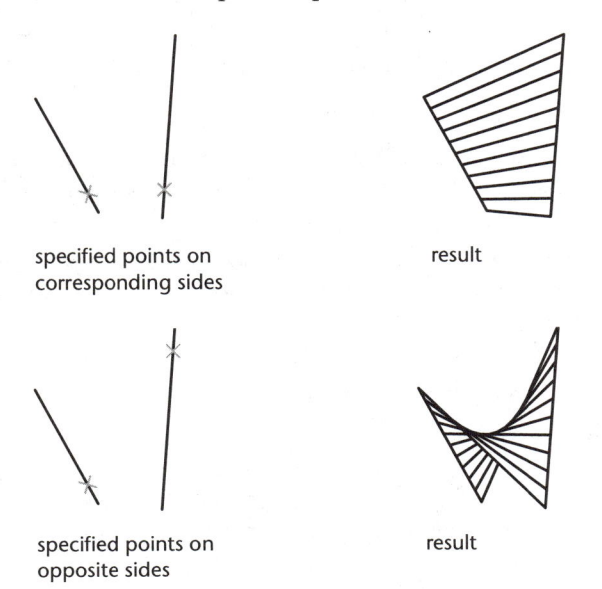

specified points on   result
corresponding sides

specified points on   result
opposite sides

Comparison of ruled surfaces created by specifying points on opposite sides

Creating 3D Objects
543

Creating a Tabulated Surface Mesh

With the TABSURF command you can create a surface mesh representing a general tabulated surface defined by a path curve and a direction vector. The path curve can be a line, arc, circle, ellipse, elliptical arc, 2D polyline, 3D polyline, or spline. The direction vector can be a line or an open 2D or 3D polyline. TABSURF creates the mesh as a series of parallel polygons running along a specified path. You must have the original object and the direction vector already drawn as shown in the following illustration.

To create a tabulated surface mesh

1 From the Draw menu, choose Surfaces ➤ Tabulated Surface.
2 Specify a path curve (1).
3 Specify a direction vector (2).
4 Erase the original objects if necessary.

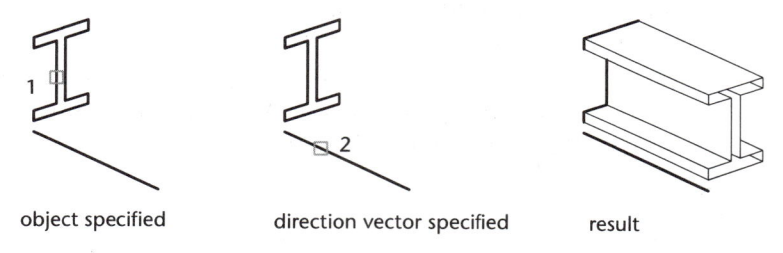

object specified   direction vector specified   result

Command line   TABSURF

Related   The SURFTAB1 and SURFTAB2 system variables control the mesh density (number of facets) in the *M* and *N* directions, respectively.

Creating a Surface of Revolution Mesh

Use REVSURF to create a surface of revolution by rotating a profile of the object about an axis. REVSURF is useful for surfaces with rotational symmetry.

To create a surface of revolution mesh

1 From the Draw menu, choose Surfaces ➤ Revolved Surface.
2 Specify a path curve (1).

The path curve, which defines the *N* direction of the mesh, can be a line, arc, circle, ellipse, elliptical arc, 2D polyline, 3D polyline, or spline. If you select a circle, closed ellipse, or closed polyline, AutoCAD closes the mesh in the *N* direction.

3   Specify the axis of revolution (2).

The direction vector can be a line or an open 2D or 3D polyline. If you choose a polyline, the vector sets the rotation axis from its first vertex to its last vertex. AutoCAD ignores any intermediate vertices. The axis of revolution determines the *M* direction of the mesh.

4   Specify the start angle. Then specify the included angle.

If you specify a nonzero start angle, AutoCAD generates the mesh at a position offset from the path curve by that angle. The included angle specifies how far about the axis of revolution the surface should extend.

5   Erase the original objects if necessary.

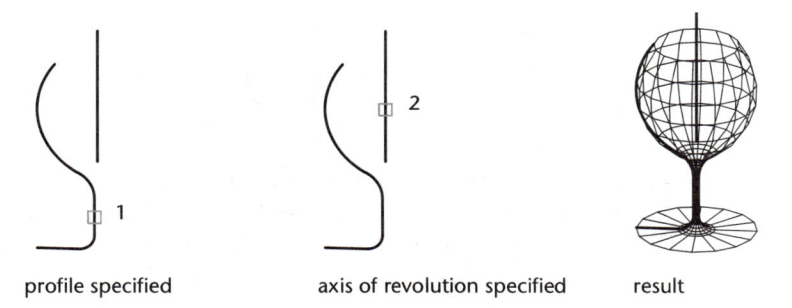

profile specified   axis of revolution specified   result

Command line   REVSURF

Related   The SURFTAB1 and SURFTAB2 system variables control mesh density (number of facets) in the *M* and *N* directions, respectively.

Creating an Edge-Defined Surface Mesh

With the EDGESURF command, you can create a Coons surface patch mesh shown in the following illustration, from four objects called edges. Edges can be arcs, lines, polylines, splines, and elliptical arcs and must form a closed loop and share endpoints. A Coons patch is a bicubic surface (one curve in the *M* direction and another in the *N* direction) interpolated between the four edges.

To create an edge-defined Coons surface patch mesh

1. From the Draw menu, choose Surfaces ➤ Edge Surface.
2. Select the four edges in any order (1–4).

   The first edge you select determines the mesh's *M* direction.

four edges selected

result

Command line   EDGESURF

Related   The SURFTAB1 and SURFTAB2 system variables control mesh density (number of facets) in the *M* and *N* direction, respectively.

Setting Elevation and Thickness

Thickness and elevation are methods of simulating meshes in AutoCAD. The advantage of using elevation and thickness instead of a mesh is that you can change them quickly and easily for both new and existing objects.

The elevation of an object is the *Z* value of the *XY* plane on which the object base is drawn. An elevation of 0 indicates the base *XY* plane of the current UCS. Positive elevations are above this plane, and negative elevations are below it.

The thickness of an object is the distance that object is extruded above or below its elevation. Positive thickness extrudes upward (positive *Z*), negative thickness extrudes downward (negative *Z*), and 0 thickness means no extrusion. An object with elevation 0 and a thickness of –1 unit appears identical to an object with an elevation of –1 and a thickness of 1 unit. The *Z* direction is determined by the orientation of the UCS at the time the object was created.

Thickness changes the appearance of certain geometric objects, such as circles, lines, polylines, arcs, 2D solids, and points. You can set the thickness of an object with the THICKNESS system variable. AutoCAD applies the extrusion uniformly on an object. A single object cannot have different thicknesses for its various points. Once you have set an object's thickness, you can visualize the results in any view other than the plan view.

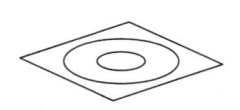

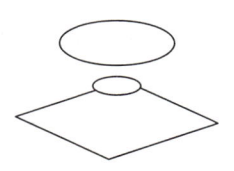

2D objects   elevation changed   thickness added

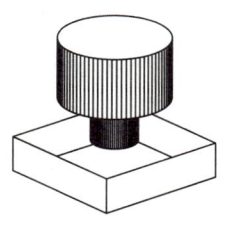

Like any other meshes, objects with thickness can be hidden, shaded, and rendered.

Consider the following when you change or set elevation and thickness:

- 3D faces, 3D polylines, 3D polygon meshes, dimensions, and viewports ignore the current thickness and cannot be extruded. Modifying the thickness of these objects with CHANGE does not affect their appearance.
- When you create new text or attribute definition objects, AutoCAD assigns the objects a 0 thickness regardless of the current thickness setting.
- Line segments produced by SKETCH are extruded after the Record option is selected.
- The current elevation established by the ELEV command remains in effect as you change from one UCS to another, and it defines the drawing plane of the current UCS.

You can set the elevation and thickness for new objects you create in AutoCAD. You can see the results in any view other than plan view.

To set the thickness of new objects

1. From the Modify menu, choose Properties.
2. In the Modify dialog box, enter the thickness settings, and then choose OK.
3. Draw the desired objects.

AutoCAD draws the objects at the current elevation and thickness. To change these settings for additional objects, repeat steps 1 and 2.

Command line   DDEMODES

Related   ELEV changes the elevation and thickness for new objects. The THICKNESS system variable controls the current thickness.

Creating 3D Objects

547

Any text objects you create with TEXT, DTEXT, and DDATTDEF or ATTDEF (either ordinary text or attribute definitions) are assigned a zero thickness regardless of the current thickness. You can assign these objects a nonzero thickness with DDMODIFY, DDCHPROP, CHPROP, or CHANGE.

You can change the elevation and thickness for existing objects. You can see the results in any view other than plan view.

To change the thickness of existing objects

1 On the command line, enter **chprop**.
2 Select the objects to change.
3 Enter **t** (Thickness).
4 Enter the new thickness in units.
5 Press ENTER to exit the command.

Command line   CHPROP

Related   CHANGE and DDMODIFY alter the characteristics of existing objects. To change the elevation of an existing object, move it in the Z direction. The THICKNESS system variable controls the current thickness.

Creating Solids

A solid object represents the entire volume of an object. Solids are the most informationally complete and least ambiguous of the 3D modeling types. Complex solid shapes are also easier to construct and edit than wireframes and meshes.

You create solids from one of the basic solid shapes of box, cone, cylinder, sphere, torus, and wedge or by extruding a 2D object along a path or revolving a 2D object about an axis.

Once you have created a solid in this manner, you can create more complex shapes by combining solids. You can join solids, subtract solids from each other, or find the common volume (overlapping portion) of solids. For more information, see "Creating a Composite Solid" on page 554.

Solids can be further modified by filleting and chamfering their edges. AutoCAD also provides commands for slicing a solid into two pieces or obtaining the 2D cross section of a solid (see "Editing 3D Solids" on page 561).

Like meshes, solids are displayed as wireframes until you hide, shade, or render them. Additionally, you can analyze solids for their mass properties (volume, moments of inertia, center of gravity, and so on). You can export data about a solid object to applications such as NC (numerical control) milling or FEM (finite element method) analysis. By exploding a solid, you can break it down to mesh and wireframe objects.

The ISOLINES system variable controls the number of tessellation lines used to visualize curved portions of the wireframe. The FACETRES system variable adjusts the smoothness of shaded and hidden-line objects.

Creating a Solid Box

You can use BOX to create a solid box. The base of the box is always parallel to the *XY* plane of the current UCS.

To create a solid box

1 From the Draw menu, choose Solids ➤ Box.
2 Specify the first corner of the base (1).
3 Specify the opposite corner of the base (2).
4 Specify the height (3).

Command line BOX

Related RECTANG or PLINE creates a rectangle or closed polyline from which you can create a box using EXTRUDE. 3D creates a box shape defined by surfaces only.

Creating a Solid Cone

You can use CONE to create a solid cone defined by a circular or an elliptical base tapering to a point perpendicular to its base. By default, the cone's base lies on the *XY* plane of the current UCS. The height, which can be positive or negative, is parallel to the *Z* axis. The apex determines the height and orientation of the cone.

To create a truncated cone or a cone that requires a specific angle to define its sides, draw a 2D circle and then use EXTRUDE to taper the circle at an angle along the *Z* axis. To complete the truncation, you can subtract a box from the tip of the cone with the SUBTRACT command.

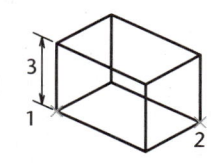

Creating 3D Objects

To create a solid cone with a circular base

1. From the Draw menu, choose Solids ➤ Cone.
2. Specify the base center point (1).
3. Specify the radius or diameter of the base (2).
4. Specify the height (3).

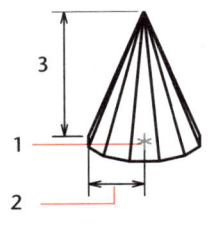

Command line   CONE

Related   CIRCLE creates a circle from which you can create a cone using EXTRUDE with its Taper option. 3D creates a conical shape defined by surfaces only.

Creating a Solid Cylinder

You can use CYLINDER to create a solid cylinder with a circular or an elliptical base. The base of the cylinder lies on the *XY* plane of the current UCS.

If you want to construct a cylinder with special detail, such as grooves along its sides, create a 2D profile of its base with a closed PLINE and use EXTRUDE to define its height along the *Z* axis.

To create a solid cylinder with a circular base

1. From the Draw menu, choose Solids ➤ Cylinder.
2. Specify the base center point (1).
3. Specify the radius or diameter of the base (2).
4. Specify the height (3).

Command line   CYLINDER

Related   CIRCLE creates a circle from which you can create a cylinder using EXTRUDE. 3D creates a cylindrical shape defined by surfaces only.

To create a solid cone with an elliptical base

1. From the Draw menu, choose Solids ➤ Cone.
2. Enter **e** (Elliptical).
3. Specify an axis endpoint.
4. Specify a second axis endpoint.
5. Specify the other axis distance.
6. Specify height, then press ENTER.

Chapter 13 Working in Three-Dimensional Space

Creating a Solid Sphere

You can use SPHERE to create a solid sphere based on a center point and a radius or diameter. Its latitudinal lines are parallel to the *XY* plane, and the central axis is coincident with the *Z* axis of the current UCS.

To create a dome or dish, combine a sphere with a box and use SUBTRACT. If you want to create a spherical object that has additional detail, create a 2D profile and use REVOLVE to define a rotation angle about the *Z* axis.

To create a solid sphere

1 From the Draw menu, choose Solids ➤ Sphere.
2 Specify the center of the sphere (1).
3 Specify the radius or diameter of the sphere (2).

Command line SPHERE

Related 3D creates a spherical shape defined by surfaces only.

Creating a Solid Torus

You can use TORUS to create a ring-shaped solid similar to the inner tube of a tire. The torus is parallel to and bisected by the *XY* plane of the current UCS.

To create a solid torus

1 From the Draw menu, choose Solids ➤ Torus.
2 Specify the center of the torus (1).
3 Specify the radius or diameter of the torus (2).
4 Specify the radius or diameter of the tube (3).

Command line TORUS

Related 3D creates a toroidal shape defined by surfaces only.

To create a lemon-shaped solid, use a negative torus radius and a tube radius of a positive number of greater magnitude. For example, if the torus radius is –2.0, the tube radius must be greater than 2.0.

A torus may be self-intersecting. A self-intersecting torus has no center hole because the radius of the tube is greater than the radius of the torus.

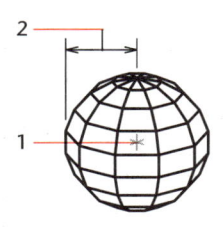

Creating a Solid Wedge

You can use WEDGE to create a solid wedge. The base of the wedge is parallel to the *XY* plane of the current UCS with the sloped face opposite the first corner. Its height, which can be positive or negative, is parallel to the *Z* axis.

To create a solid wedge

1. From the Draw menu, choose Solids ➤ Wedge.
2. Specify the first corner of the base (1).
3. Specify the opposite corner of the base (2).
4. Specify the height of the wedge (3).

Command line WEDGE

Related 3D creates a wedge shape defined by surfaces only.

Creating an Extruded Solid

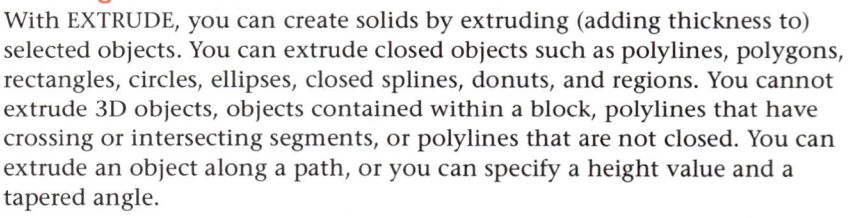

With EXTRUDE, you can create solids by extruding (adding thickness to) selected objects. You can extrude closed objects such as polylines, polygons, rectangles, circles, ellipses, closed splines, donuts, and regions. You cannot extrude 3D objects, objects contained within a block, polylines that have crossing or intersecting segments, or polylines that are not closed. You can extrude an object along a path, or you can specify a height value and a tapered angle.

Use EXTRUDE to create a solid from a common profile of an object, such as a gear or sprocket. EXTRUDE is particularly useful for objects that contain fillets, chamfers, and other details that might otherwise be difficult to reproduce except in a profile. If you create a profile using lines or arcs, use the Join option of PEDIT to convert them to a single polyline object or make them into a region before you use EXTRUDE.

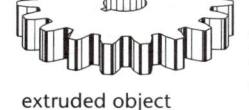

To extrude an object along a path

1. From the Draw menu, choose Solids ➤ Extrude.
2. Select the objects to extrude (1).
3. Enter **p** (Path).
4. Select the object to use as the path (2).

After the extrusion, AutoCAD deletes or retains the original object depending on the setting of the DELOBJ system variable.

Chapter 13 Working in Three-Dimensional Space

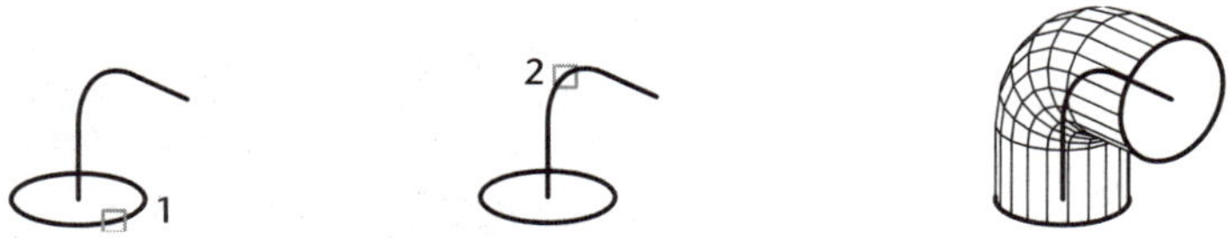

Command line EXTRUDE

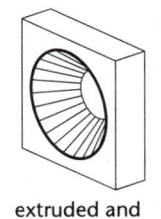

Tapering the extrusion is useful specifically for parts that need their sides defined along an angle, such as a mold used to create metal products in a foundry. Avoid using extremely large tapered angles. If the angle is too large, the profile can taper to a point before it reaches the specified height.

Creating a Revolved Solid

extruded and tapered circle

With REVOLVE, you can create a solid by revolving a closed object about the X or Y axis of the current UCS, using a specified angle. You can also revolve the object about a line, polyline, or two specified points. Similar to EXTRUDE, REVOLVE is useful for objects that contain fillets or other details that would otherwise be difficult to reproduce in a common profile. If you create a profile using lines or arcs that meet a polyline, use the PEDIT Join option to convert them to a single polyline object before you use REVOLVE.

You can use REVOLVE on closed objects such as polylines, polygons, rectangles, circles, ellipses, and regions. The same rules for polylines apply to EXTRUDE and REVOLVE. You cannot revolve objects in blocks or other 3D objects, and the object cannot intersect itself.

To revolve an object about an axis

1 From the Draw menu, choose Solids ➤ Revolve.
2 Select the objects to revolve.
3 Specify the start point and endpoint of the axis of revolution.

Specify the points so that the object is on one side of the axis points you specify. The positive axis direction is from the start point to the end point.

4 Specify the angle of revolution.

Creating 3D Objects

553

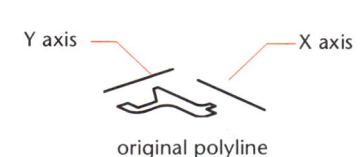

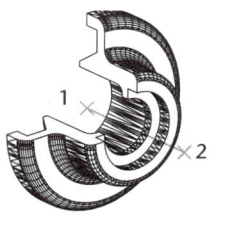

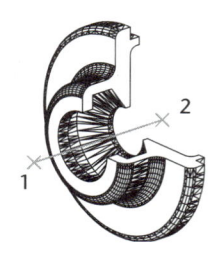

Y axis — X axis

original polyline   revolved about X axis   revolved about Y axis

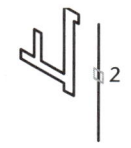

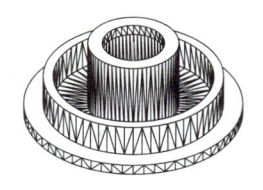

object to revolve selected   axis selected   result

Revolving by specifying an axis or by selecting an axis

Command line   REVOLVE

Creating a Composite Solid

This section describes how to combine, subtract, and find the intersection of existing solids to create composite solids.

With UNION, you can combine the total volume of two or more solids or two or more regions into a composite object.

To combine solids

1 From the Modify menu, choose Boolean ➤ Union.
2 Select the objects to combine (1, 2).

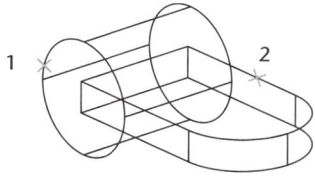

objects to be combined   result

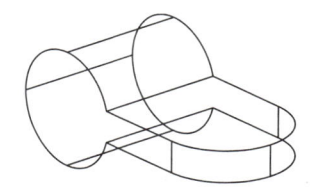

Chapter 13 Working in Three-Dimensional Space

With SUBTRACT, you can remove the common area of one set of solids from another. For example, you can use SUBTRACT to add holes to a mechanical part by subtracting cylinders from the object.

To subtract one set of solids from another

1 From the Modify menu, choose Boolean ➤ Subtract.
2 Select the objects to subtract from (1).
3 Select the objects to subtract (2).

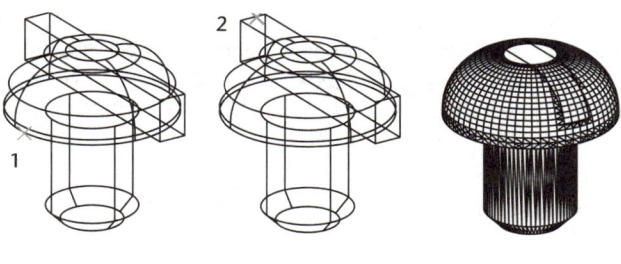

object to subtract from selected

object to subtract selected

result (lines hidden for clarity)

With INTERSECT, you can create a composite solid from the common volume of two or more overlapping solids. INTERSECT removes the nonoverlapping portions and creates a composite solid from the common volume.

To create a solid from the intersection of two or more other solids

1 From the Modify menu, choose Boolean ➤ Intersect.
2 Select the objects to intersect (1, 2).

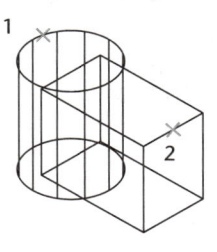

objects to intersect selected

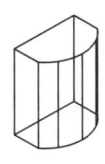

result

Related   INTERFERE performs the same operation as INTERSECT, but it keeps the original two objects.

Creating 3D Objects

Editing in 3D

This section describes how to edit 3D objects by, for example, rotating, arraying, mirroring, trimming, chamfering, and filleting. MOVE, COPY, ROTATE, MIRROR, and ARRAY can be used for 3D objects as well as 2D objects.

Rotating in 3D

With ROTATE, you can rotate objects in 2D about a specified point. The direction of rotation is determined by the current UCS. ROTATE3D rotates objects in 3D about a specified axis. You can specify the axis of rotation using two points; an object; the *X*, *Y*, or *Z* axis; or the *Z* direction of the current view. To rotate 3D objects, you can use either ROTATE or ROTATE3D.

To rotate a 3D object about an axis

1 From the Modify menu, choose 3D Operation ➤ Rotate 3D.
2 Select the object to rotate (1).
3 Specify the start point and endpoint of the axis about which the objects are to be rotated (2, 3).

   The positive axis direction is from the start point to the end point, and the rotation follows the right-hand rule.
4 Specify the angle of rotation.

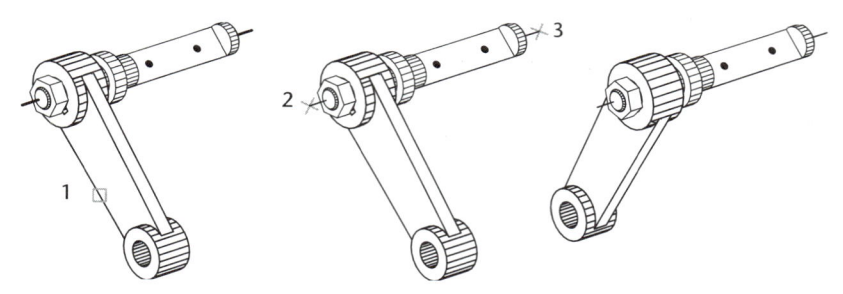

object to rotate selected   axis of rotation specified   result

Command line   ROTATE3D

Arraying in 3D

With 3DARRAY, you can create a rectangular array or a polar array of objects in 3D. In addition to specifying the number of columns (*X* direction) and rows (*Y* direction), you also specify the number of levels (*Z* direction).

To create a rectangular array of objects

1. From the Modify menu, choose 3D Operation ➤ 3D Array.
2. Select the object to array (1).
3. Specify Rectangular.
4. Enter the number of rows.
5. Enter the number of columns.
6. Enter the number of levels.
7. Specify the distance between rows.
8. Specify the distance between columns.
9. Specify the distance between levels.

Command line 3DARRAY

object to array selected result

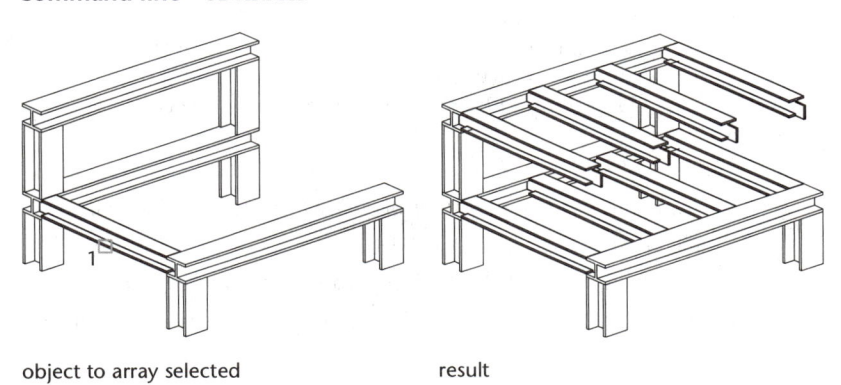

To create a polar array of objects

1. From the Modify menu, choose 3D Operation ➤ 3D Array.
2. Select the object to array (1).
3. Specify Polar.
4. Enter the number of items to array.
5. Specify the angle that the arrayed objects are to fill.
6. Press ENTER to rotate the objects as they are arrayed, or enter **n** to retain their orientation.
7. Specify the start point and endpoint of the axis about which the objects are to be rotated (2, 3).

Command line 3DARRAY

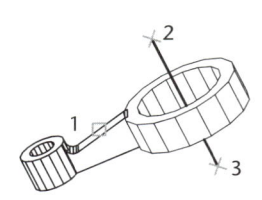

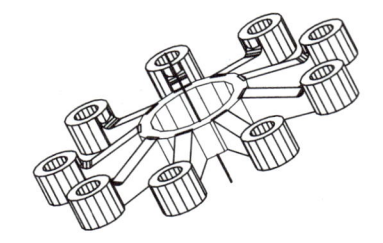

Mirroring in 3D

With MIRROR3D, you can mirror objects along a specified mirroring plane. The mirroring plane can be one of the following:

- The plane of a planar object
- A plane parallel to the *XY*, *YZ*, or *XZ* plane of the current UCS that passes through a point you select
- A plane defined by three points that you select

To mirror objects in 3D

1. From the Modify menu, choose 3D Operation ➤ Mirror 3D.
2. Select the object to mirror (1).
3. Specify three points to define a mirroring plane (2–4).
4. Press ENTER to retain the original objects, or enter **y** to delete them.

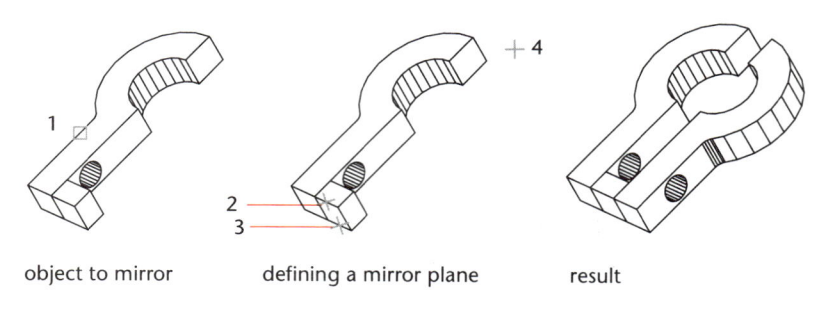

object to mirror   defining a mirror plane   result

Command line MIRROR3D

Trimming and Extending in 3D

You can trim or extend an object to any other object in 3D space, regardless of whether the objects are on the same plane or parallel to the cutting or boundary edges. By using the PROJMODE and EXTEDGE system variables, you can choose one of three projections for trimming or extending: the *XY* plane of the current UCS, the current view plane, or true 3D, which is not a projection.

In a true 3D trimming or extending, objects must intersect with the boundaries in 3D space. If the two do not intersect when you trim or extend an object in the current UCS *XY* plane, the trimmed or extended object might not end precisely at the boundary in 3D space. The following procedures illustrate trimming and extending using the three projection options.

To extend using an *XY* plane of the current UCS

1 From the Modify menu, choose Extend.
2 Select the boundary edge for extending (1).

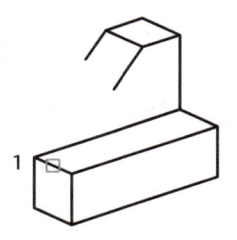

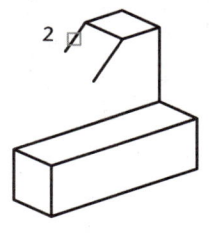

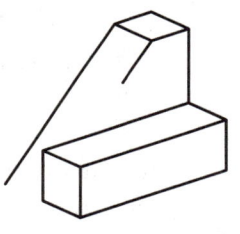

3 Enter **e** (Edge).
4 Enter **e** (Extend).
5 Enter **p** (Project).
6 Enter **u** (UCS).
7 Select the object to extend (2).

Command line EXTEND

To trim using the current view plane

1 From the Modify menu, choose Trim.
2 Select the cutting edge for trimming (1).

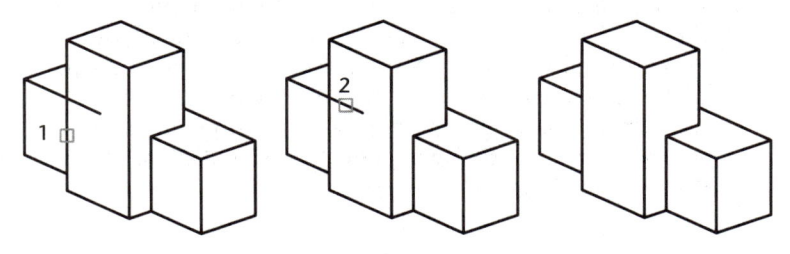

Editing in 3D

3 Enter **p** (Project).
4 Enter **v** (View).
5 Select the object to trim (2).

Command line TRIM

To trim using true 3D

1 From Modify menu, choose Trim.
2 Select the cutting edges to use for trimming (1, 2).

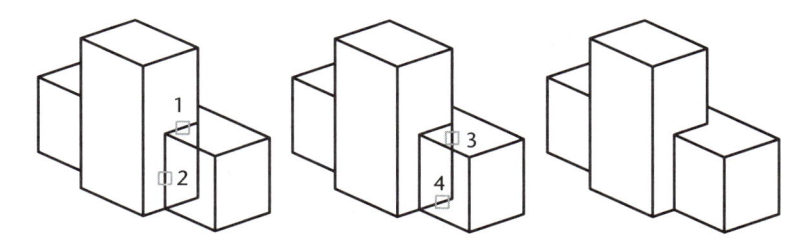

3 Enter **p** (Project).
4 Enter **n** (None).
5 Select the object to trim (3, 4).

Command line TRIM

Filleting in 3D

You can fillet coplanar objects with extrusion directions not parallel to the Z axis of the current UCS. AutoCAD determines the extrusion direction for the fillet arc in 3D space as follows.

For objects on the same plane with the same extrusion direction normal to that plane, the fillet arc is on that plane and has the same extrusion direction.

If the objects are on the same plane but have opposite or different extrusion directions, the fillet arc is placed on that object plane with an extrusion direction normal to the object plane and inclined towards the positive Z direction of the current UCS. For example, suppose two arcs, A and B, are on the same plane in 3D space but have opposite extrusion directions (0, 0.5, 0.8) and (0, –0.5, –0.8) relative to the current UCS. The fillet arc adopts the extrusion direction (0, 0.5, 0.8).

Editing 3D Solids

This section describes how to chamfer, fillet, section, and slice 3D solid objects.

Chamfering Solids

CHAMFER bevels the edges along the adjoining faces of a solid.

To chamfer a solid object

1 From the Modify menu, choose Chamfer.

2 Select the edge of the base surface to chamfer (1).

AutoCAD highlights one of two surfaces adjacent to the selected edge.

3 To select a different surface, enter **n** (Next) or choose OK to use the current surface.

4 Specify the base surface distance.

The base surface distance is measured from the selected edge to a point on the base surface. The other surface distance is measured from the selected edge to a point on the adjacent surface.

5 Specify the adjacent surface distance.

Loop selects all edges around the base surface and Select Edge selects individual edges.

6 Specify the edges to chamfer (2).

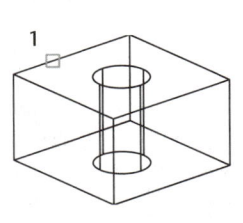

base surface selected   edge to chamfer selected   result

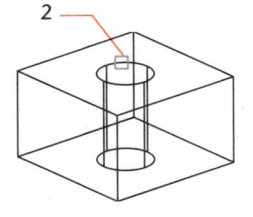

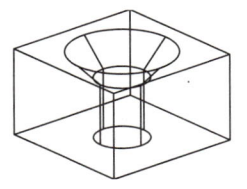

Command line   CHAMFER

Filleting Solids

With FILLET, you can add rounds and fillets to selected objects. The default method is specifying the fillet radius and then selecting the edges to fillet. Other methods specify individual measurements for each filleted edge and fillet a tangential series of edges.

To fillet a solid object

1 From the Modify menu, choose Fillet.
2 Select the edge of the solid to fillet (1).
3 Specify the fillet radius.
4 Select additional edges or press ENTER to fillet.

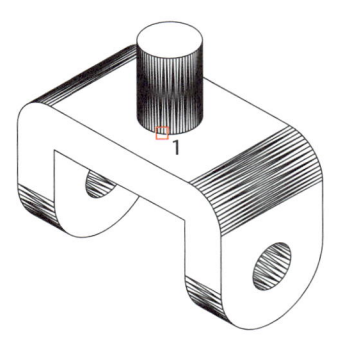

edge to fillet selected   result

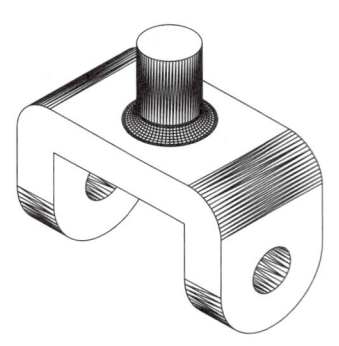

Command line   FILLET

Sectioning Solids

With SECTION, you can create a cross section through a solid as a region or an anonymous block. The default method is specifying three points to define the plane. Other methods define the cross-sectional plane by another object, the current view, the Z axis, or the XY, YZ, and ZX planes. AutoCAD places the cross-sectional plane on the current layer.

To create a cross section of a solid

1 From the Draw menu, choose Solids ➤ Section.
2 Select the objects to cross-section.
3 Specify three points to define the cross-sectional plane.

The first point defines the origin (0,0,0) of the cutting plane. The second point defines the X axis, and the third point defines the Y axis.

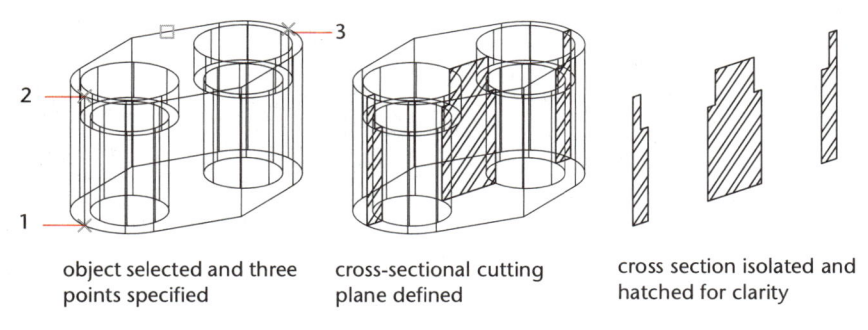

object selected and three points specified

cross-sectional cutting plane defined

cross section isolated and hatched for clarity

Command line SECTION

Slicing Solids

With SLICE, you can create a new solid by cutting the existing solid and removing a specified side. You can retain one or both halves of the sliced solids. The sliced solids retain the layer and color properties of the original solids. The default method of slicing a solid is to specify three points that define the cutting plane and then select which side to retain. You can also define the cutting plane by using another object, the current view, the Z axis, or the XY, YZ, and ZX plane.

To slice a solid

1 From the Draw menu, choose Solids ➤ Slice.
2 Select the objects to slice.
3 Specify three points to define the cutting plane.

The first point refers to the 0,0,0 origin of the cutting plane. The second point defines the positive X axis, and the third point defines the positive Y axis.

4 Specify which side to retain, or enter **b** to retain both sides.

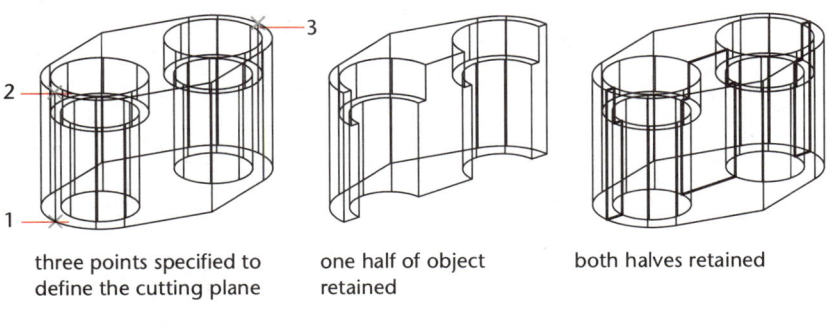

three points specified to define the cutting plane

one half of object retained

both halves retained

Command line SLICE

Editing 3D Solids

563

Creating Three-Dimensional Images

14

Most drafting time is spent working on wireframe representations of a model. On occasion, however, you might need to see a more realistic image involving color and perspective—for example, when verifying your design or when presenting a final drawing.

In this chapter

- Producing hidden-line images, shaded images, and renderings
- Preparing models for generating 3D images
- Using basic and photorealistic rendering
- Using lights, views, and scenes
- Applying materials
- Saving, displaying, and printing renderings
- Using AutoCAD's rendering features with other Autodesk applications

Using 3D Image Types

Creating realistic three-dimensional images helps you visualize your final design much more clearly than you can with wireframe representations. In the wireframe, because all edges and tessellation lines are visible, it's hard to tell whether you're viewing the model from above or below. The hidden-line image makes it easier to visualize the model because the back faces are not displayed. Shading and rendering can greatly enhance the realism of the image.

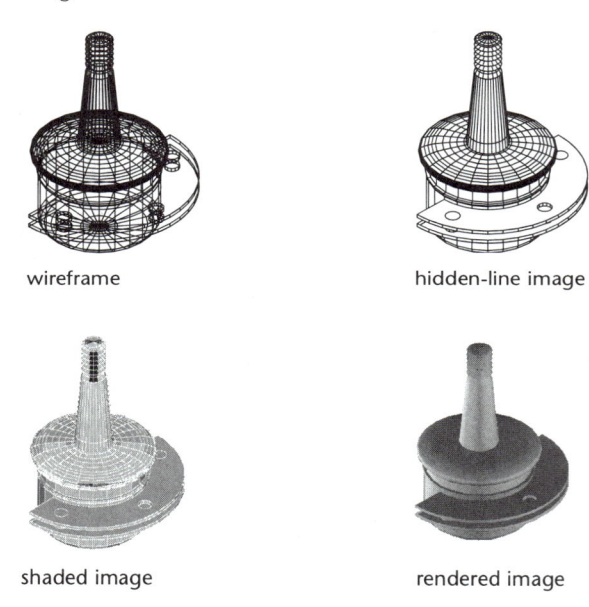

wireframe

hidden-line image

shaded image

rendered image

Ways to display 3D models

Of the image types, hidden-line images are the simplest. Shading removes hidden lines and assigns flat colors to visible surfaces. Rendering adds and adjusts lights and attaches materials to surfaces to produce realistic effects.

To decide what type of image to produce, you need to consider factors such as purpose and time. For a presentation, a full rendering might be appropriate. If time is limited, or if your display and graphics equipment cannot produce varied gradations and colors, you might not need a detailed rendering. If you want a quick check of the integrity of a design, a simple hidden-line or shaded image is sufficient.

Drawing 3D Models

When performing hidden-line, shading, and rendering operations on 3D objects, AutoCAD treats different surfaces in different ways. This section discusses surfaces, specifically extrusions, 3D faces, solids, polygon meshes, closed polylines, and text.

Surfaces

You begin drawing models by using objects that represent surfaces. For example, to draw a cube you could use one of several methods. You could draw six 3D faces, use the BOX command to create a 3D solid, or change the thickness of a 2D solid, trace, or wide polyline segment. But if you draw a cube by using twelve lines, you *cannot* generate a hidden-line, shaded, or rendered image. It would always look like a frame made of wires.

To produce a shaded or rendered image, AutoCAD always goes through a line-hiding process first. The descriptions of hiding lines that follow apply equally to the shading and rendering processes.

Solid 3D objects such as cylinders have top and bottom surfaces. However, AutoCAD puts top and bottom surfaces on some extruded objects but not others. In general, if the 2D object being extruded encloses a planar region, the extruded object has a top and a bottom surface. As a result, AutoCAD treats this object as a solid. If the one- or two-dimensional object is not closed, then its extrusion is considered to be a zero-thickness vertical sheet. A model comprising such objects, such as a cylinder made up of two extruded semicircular arcs, would lack a top and bottom.

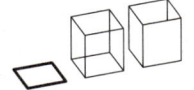

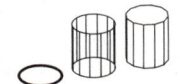

extrusions before and after HIDE

Objects with Thickness

Solid fills, traces, circles, and wide polyline segments are treated as surfaces with tops and bottoms when they are given thickness and shaded. The Thickness option of CHANGE and CHPROP makes 2D objects look like 3D objects. EXTRUDE creates true 3D solid objects.

A solid or a trace becomes a prism with three or four faces when given thickness. A circle becomes a vertical pole, and shades as a solid cylinder. Each segment of a wide polyline is treated separately. Segments with nonzero width have tops and bottoms, but those with zero width are represented as the same lines and arcs with thickness.

Solids, 3D Faces, and Polygon Meshes

Visually, AutoCAD treats a cube formed by 3D faces or a 2D solid with thickness as a solid object. A polygon mesh or 3D face cannot have a thickness; however, such objects define a surface for hiding, shading, or rendering. All other objects produce one- or two-dimensional surfaces in space. Where such an object touches any other object, hiding lines may produce unexpected results.

Closed Polylines

No special treatment is given to zero-width closed polylines when thickness is applied to them. During hiding, shading, or rendering, the region bounded by a closed polyline, whether or not it has thickness, is *not* treated as a top or a bottom surface.

Text

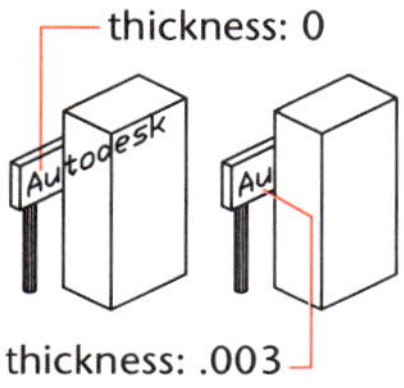

thickness: 0

thickness: .003

Text is ignored by HIDE unless it is given a thickness. The thickness can be as great as you want or as small as 0.001 units.

During regeneration of text, attribute, and attribute definition objects, AutoCAD processes the text without considering its visibility. If you put textual information on distinct layers, you can later suppress it by turning off those layers.

Abutting and Intersecting Objects

The hiding process may present problems in two cases: objects that exactly abut or objects that intersect in space. Because no two objects can actually occupy the same point, drawings of objects that touch or intersect must allow for the effects of shading or rendering. Many of these problems can be avoided by using Boolean operations with true 3D solid objects.

Touching Objects

Objects can abut at a point, along a line, or along a plane. However, when two objects occupy the same space, AutoCAD treats one of them as hiding the other.

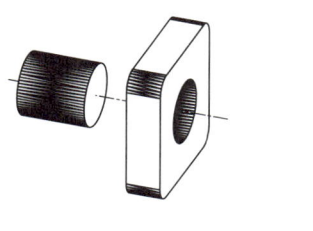

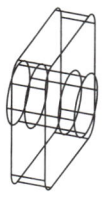

separate objects   before HIDE   after HIDE

Even a very small round-off error in calculating the relative positions of two touching objects can result in an incorrect determination of where one obscures the other.

Intersecting Objects

It is not uncommon to draw two objects with intersecting boundaries—for example, a cylinder solid intersecting a rectangular solid.

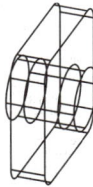

before HIDE   after HIDE

Intersecting objects

A very slight round-off error could make the two objects appear to be one object. To compensate for this effect, shorten one of the objects where it would otherwise penetrate the second object, or break one of two intersecting objects into two objects, one on either side of the surface of the intersecting object.

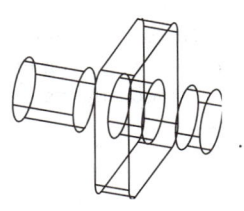

before HIDE   after HIDE

Broken objects

Alternatively, separate the objects by reducing or increasing the size of one of the objects by a small amount, such as 0.001 units.

Intersecting Lines and Turned-Off Layers

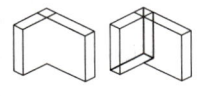

A drawing of two walls meeting at a corner demonstrates intersecting lines. If hidden lines are being suppressed and the two walls are on the same layer, it doesn't matter which of the two intersecting edges is hidden. However, objects on layers that are turned off affect the hiding process. Objects on layers that are invisible obscure objects on visible layers. Objects on frozen layers do not affect hiding.

Drawing 3D Models

Creating Hidden-Line Images

When creating or editing a drawing, you work on the wireframe representation of an object or surface and use the hiding process only to verify the current placement of those surfaces. When viewed or plotted as wireframes, complex drawings often appear too cluttered to convey useful information. Hiding background objects that in reality would be obscured by objects in the foreground simplifies the display and clarifies the design.

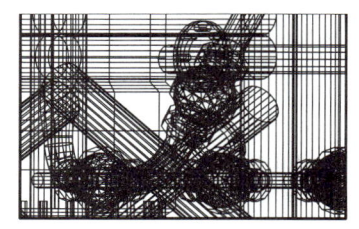

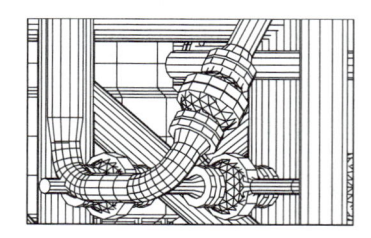

before HIDE   after HIDE

Not displaying those lines makes the display much clearer; however, you can't edit hidden-line, shaded, or rendered views.

Calculating and obscuring hidden lines can be time-consuming, but you can speed up the process in several ways. For example, you can avoid drawing details that won't be visible at the scale at which you're displaying or plotting the image. You can also zoom into a part of the drawing that excludes objects from the hiding process. You can also hide selected objects in the drawing.

Hiding Lines of All Objects

You can use HIDE on every object in a drawing.

To hide lines in the whole drawing

- From the View menu, choose Hide. The lines remain hidden until you perform an action that regenerates the drawing and redisplays a wireframe view.

Command line   HIDE

Related   You can plot hidden-line views generated by HIDE (see "Hiding Lines in Plotted Viewports" on page 492).

Hiding Lines of Selected Objects

You can remove hidden lines on one or more objects in a drawing that you select. Selecting specific objects on which to hide lines is one way to speed up the process.

To hide lines of one or more objects

1 From the View menu, choose 3D Dynamic View.
2 Select an object or objects in your drawing.
3 Enter **h** (Hide).

AutoCAD does not display lines hidden by foreground objects. The hidden lines are obscured only temporarily and are redisplayed when you exit DVIEW and the drawing regenerates.

Command line   DVIEW Hide

Related   HIDE removes hidden lines on all objects in the drawing.

Hiding Solid Objects

When solid objects are hidden, AutoCAD generates and hides the solid by creating a mesh. If the DISPSILH system variable is set to on (1), AutoCAD suppresses drawing the mesh, and only draws silhouette lines of the solid.

Creating Shaded Images

Although obscuring hidden lines enhances the drawing and clarifies the design, flat shading produces a more realistic image of your model. In the shading process, AutoCAD hides lines before creating a flat-shaded picture of the drawing in the current viewport. It uses light coming from a single light source located directly behind you (an "over-the-shoulder" light) and two factors to compute the shade (brightness) of each surface: the angle of the surface to the current view and the setting of the SHADEDIF system variable.

- The steeper the angle of the surface to your viewpoint, the darker the surface shading. Distance from your viewpoint has no effect on shading.

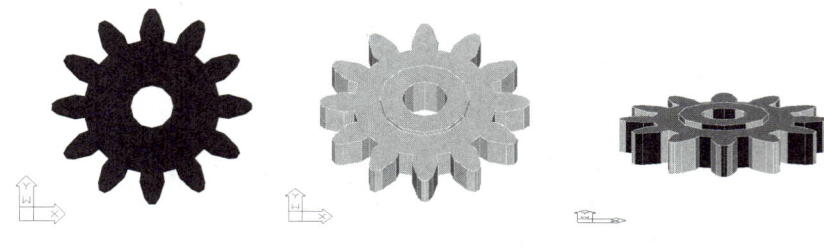

vertical view   tilted view   near horizontal view

Different viewpoints produce different shading effects. Experiment with different views until you achieve the effect you want.

- The higher the value of the SHADEDIF system variable, the greater the contrast in your image (see "Setting Diffuse Reflection" on page 573).

Shading Models

When you use SHADE, you cannot produce highlights, move the light, or add more lights. For greater control over lighting, you must render the model (see "Creating Rendered Images" on page 574). The smaller the area of the screen, the faster the shading process. Use smaller viewports to speed up shading.

To create a shaded image

1 Make current the viewport that contains the view you want to shade.
2 From the View menu, choose Shade, and then select the color option.

AutoCAD displays a shaded image of your model in the current viewport.

Command line SHADE

Related RENDER uses lights and materials to create a more realistic three-dimensional rendered image.

You cannot edit a shaded image. Use REGEN, or a command such as ZOOM, to regenerate and replace the shaded image with the original wireframe. Using UNDO on the shaded image has no effect.

Setting a Shading Method

The shading process uses one of four shading methods, which you set with the SHADEDGE system variable.

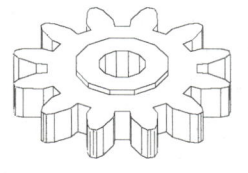

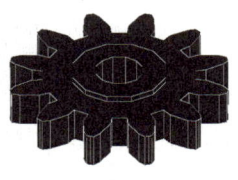

SHADEDGE=0   SHADEDGE=1   SHADEDGE=2   SHADEDGE=3

Option 0 creates shaded faces with no edge highlighting. Option 1 creates shaded faces with the edges highlighted in the background color. You need a 256-color or better display with the standard AutoCAD 256-color map to see the full effects of options 0 and 1. Option 2 paints the surfaces of polygons in the background color and colors the visible edges in the object's color. Option 3, the default, does *not* shade faces but draws them in their original color and colors the edges in the background color with no lighting effect.

To set the shading method

1 On the command line, enter **shadedge**.
2 Enter **0**, **1**, **2**, or **3**.

Setting Diffuse Reflection

The SHADEDIF (shade diffuse) system variable controls the amount of diffuse reflection AutoCAD uses to calculate the shade of each surface.

SHADEDIF=0   SHADEDIF=70   SHADEDIF=100

The default for SHADEDIF is 70. This value signifies that 70 percent of the light reflected from the surface is light reflected diffusely from the over-the-shoulder light source, and that the remaining 30 percent is ambient light.

To set diffuse reflection

1. On the command line, enter **shadedif**.
2. Specify a value between 0 and 100.

   Increasing the value (up to a maximum of 100) increases the contrast between surfaces in the image. Setting SHADEDIF to 0 turns off diffuse reflections.

Creating Rendered Images

Rendering can make a design clearer than a simple hidden-line or shaded image can. Traditional rendering of architectural, mechanical, and engineering drawings involves watercolors, colored crayons and inks, and air-brush techniques to produce a final presentation-quality rendering.

Rendering is often what requires the most computer time in a 3D project. It generally involves four steps:

- Preparing models for rendering includes following proper drafting techniques, removing hidden surfaces, constructing meshes for smooth shading, and setting view resolution
- Illuminating includes creating and placing lights and creating shadows
- Adding color includes defining the reflective qualities of materials and associating these materials with the visible surfaces
- Rendering usually includes rendering objects at intermediate steps to check your preparation, illumination, and colors

These steps are conceptual and aren't usually implemented as discrete steps during the rendering process, nor must they occur in the order presented.

Rendered image

AutoCAD uses geometry, lighting, and materials to render a realistic image of a model.

Preparing Models for Rendering

There are several factors to bear in mind when you are creating a model that you are going to render.

Drawing Outward-Facing Surfaces and Removing Hidden Surfaces

An important step in the rendering process is to remove hidden surfaces, because rendering hidden surfaces and back faces wastes time. AutoCAD uses the *normal* on each face to ascertain which is a front face and which is a back face. A normal is a vector that is perpendicular to each polygon face on the model and points outward toward space.

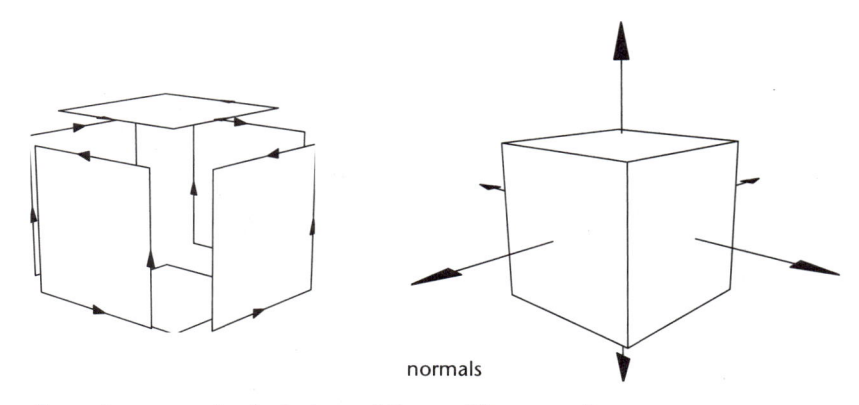

Faces drawn counterclockwise and the resulting normals

Normals are determined by the way a face is drawn in a right-handed coordinate system such as AutoCAD's: if you draw the face counterclockwise, the normals point outward; if you draw the face clockwise, the normals point inward. You should draw faces consistently. Mixing methods produces unexpected results. AutoCAD calculates all the normals in the drawing during rendering. The renderer searches for all normals that point away from the viewpoint and removes the associated polygons from the scene. This step is called back-face removal.

After the back faces have been removed, the renderer uses a Z buffer to compare relative distances along the Z axis. If the Z buffer indicates that one face overlaps another, the renderer removes the face that would be hidden.

To discard faces with normals pointing away from viewpoint

1 From the View menu, choose Render ➤ Preferences.
2 In the Rendering Preferences dialog box, under Rendering Options, choose More Options.
3 In the Photo Real Render Options dialog box, under Face Controls, select Discard Back Faces, then choose OK.
4 Choose OK to exit the Rendering Preferences dialog box.

Command line   RPREF

The back faces are removed because they wouldn't be visible from your viewpoint. AutoCAD compares relative distances between each surface and your viewpoint, decides which faces obscure other faces, and discards obscured faces.

The time saved is in proportion to the number of faces discarded out of the total number of faces.

Sometimes you may want to skip the back-face removal step and leave back faces in (for example, if an object is transparent, or if you can see two sides of it because of its shape and orientation, or if an open object will be rendered with a view angle that lets you see inside). Transparency also affects whether one face should hide another.

You can also choose to render back faces instead of front faces. Do this by turning off the Back Face Normal is Negative option, found in the applicable Render Options dialog box under Face Controls. This can be useful if you've created a drawing without being aware of the counterclockwise convention for normals in AutoCAD drawings.

If you're rendering a drawing that wasn't created with rendering in mind, you might have to leave Discard Back Faces turned off or even turn off Back Face Normal is Negative.

NOTE Solid objects created with the Advanced Modeling Extension (AME) have meshes and normals correctly oriented, which can be an aid to creating models for rendering. For more information, see "AME" on page 629.

Following Proper Drafting Techniques

Be consistent in your method of drawing. For example, avoid creating a building with walls that are a mixture of faces, extruded lines, and wireframe meshes.

The more faces a model has, the longer it takes to render. Keep the geometry of your drawing simple to keep rendering time to a minimum. Use the fewest faces possible to describe a plane. The simpler the surface, the less computation time to calculate the color of each pixel in the face. When you want to display a complicated detail, modeling the detail with a bitmap often renders more quickly than modeling it in the geometry.

The complexity of an AutoCAD object is a function of the number of its vertices and faces. Certain kinds of geometry, described in this section, create special rendering problems. The photorealistic renderers (Photo Real and Photo Raytrace) provide controls for handling such geometry. For more information about creating a model that will render well, see "Constructing Meshes for Smooth Shading."

Intersecting faces in a model occur when two faces pass through each other. While intersecting faces are unrealistic in real-world terms, it's sometimes easier to use them in an AutoCAD model than to ensure that the faces model disjoint objects. However, they can render incorrectly unless the renderer explicitly checks for them. The photorealistic renderers always check for intersections; however, rendering artifacts can appear at the intersection points, particularly with low-resolution renderings.

Faces that overlap and lie in the same plane can produce ambiguous results, especially if the materials attached to the two faces differ.

Faces that self-overlap due to a 180-degree twist can also produce ambiguous results, because the normal for the face is not well defined. Avoid this problem by not allowing boundary lines to intersect.

Constructing Meshes for Smooth Shading

AutoCAD drawings have two types of faces: a regular face and an *M*-by-*N* mesh made up of many faces.

Mesh components include normals, vertices, faces, and edges. These components are defined as follows:

- A normal is a vector perpendicular to the face and pointing outward.
- A vertex is a point that forms the corner of a face.
- A face is a triangular or quadrilateral portion of a surface object.
- An edge is the boundary of a face.

In an AutoCAD drawing, all faces have four vertices, except faces in polyface mesh, which are treated as adjoining triangles. For rendering purposes, each quadrilateral face is a pair of triangular faces that share one edge.

If you use the Smooth Shading option for basic rendering in either the Render or the Rendering Preferences dialog box, set the density of the mesh so that the angle between the normals of any two adjoining faces of the mesh is less than the smoothing angle. If the angle is greater than the smoothing angle, an edge appears between those faces when you render your model, even with Smooth Shading turned on. You control Smoothing Angle in the Render dialog box (RENDER) and the Rendering Preferences dialog box (RPREF).

When the Smooth Shading option is turned off, Render assigns a color or material to each face based on the light that strikes the base of the normal (that is, at the face's centroid). Because this shading is uniform across the faces, edges between faces are often visible.

When Smooth Shading is turned on, AutoCAD can either calculate the shading at each vertex and then average the shading across each face (Gouraud shading), or calculate the shading at each pixel (Phong shading). Phong shading generates more realistic highlights; it is the only method used by the photorealistic renderers.

In addition to hiding and smoothing, the appearance of a face depends on the light that reaches it and the material assigned to it.

You must explicitly turn AutoSurf surfaces into meshes before you render them, as described in "AutoSurf and AutoCAD Designer" on page 629. If the mesh is not dense enough to render well, increase the size of your drawing by a factor of 10 to 50, and then use the Surface Display option on the AutoSurf menu to generate new meshes. The finer meshes will render more smoothly.

Controlling Resolution and Display Accuracy

VIEWRES Command

The value you set with VIEWRES controls the display accuracy of circles, arcs, and ellipses. AutoCAD draws these objects on the screen using many short straight line segments. The higher the value set in VIEWRES, the smoother the arc or circle looks but the longer it takes to regenerate. If the circles look like polygons in the drawing, they'll look like polygons when rendered. To increase performance while you're drawing, set a low value with VIEWRES. However, to make sure you get a good-quality rendering, raise the value before rendering drawings containing arcs or circles.

To raise the resolution value, start VIEWRES and enter a high number (up to 20,000) for Circle Zoom Percent. (You can ignore the prompt about fast zooms if you only want to make circles and arcs in the drawing look better for your rendering.) See VIEWRES in the *Command Reference*.

FACETRES System Variable

The FACETRES system variable controls the smoothness of shaded and rendered curved solids. It is linked to the value set by VIEWRES: when FACETRES is set to 1, there is a one-to-one correspondence between the viewing resolution of circles, arcs, and ellipses and the tessellation of solid objects. For example, when FACETRES is set to 2, the tessellation will be twice the tessellation set by VIEWRES. The default value of FACETRES is 0.5. The range of possible values is 0.01 to 10.

When you raise and lower the value of VIEWRES, objects controlled by both VIEWRES and FACETRES are affected. When you raise and lower the value of FACETRES, only solid objects are affected.

Creating Rendered Images

Configuring Render for Different Displays

When you first use a rendering command such as RENDER, LIGHT, or SCENE, AutoCAD automatically configures AutoCAD Render. For a full explanation of AutoCAD configuration, see the *Installation Guide*.

In the Render or Rendering Preferences dialog box, you can choose to render to a viewport, to a separate Render window, or to a file.

Render to the Render window to take advantage of the capabilities of that window. You can copy images to the Clipboard for use in other applications, and you can print easily to the system printer or render to a file using several formats.

Screen resolution is a function of the number of pixels displayed. The resolution is inversely related to the displayed pixel size; that is, the greater the screen resolution, the smaller the pixels (given the same size screen). Like color depth, resolution depends on your display driver, and you can select it only at configuration time.

NOTE The highest possible resolution for photorealistic rendering is 4096 × 4096 at the maximum color depth for the selected file format (for example, 24 bits for PostScript).

Anti-aliasing

Because the image on a monitor is made up of discrete picture elements (or pixels) on a fixed grid, straight or curved edges can appear to be jagged or stepped. This effect is known as aliasing.

The greater the resolution (and thus the smaller the pixels), the less apparent aliasing is. However, it is often best to reduce the effect further by a technique known as anti-aliasing. Anti-aliasing shades pixels adjacent to the main pixels that define a line or boundary.

Anti-aliasing involves at least two trade-offs:

- Extra calculation: pixels in the offending line or boundary and neighboring pixels in the background must be analyzed so that intermediate shades can be added
- Thicker lines: although an antialiased line appears smoother, it must be thicker than a jagged one

You have to decide how much time you want to spend rendering and how good you want the final rendering to be. These trade-offs will depend partly on the hardware you're using and partly on the audience for your work.

The photorealistic renderers offer four levels of anti-aliasing control. Photo Raytrace provides a further refinement of the speed and quality trade-off called adaptive sampling. (To view these selections, choose More Options in the Render or Rendering Preferences dialog box while Photo Real or Photo Raytrace is the selected rendering type.)

- Minimal applies an analytic horizontal anti-aliasing algorithm to each scan line.
- Low enhances the horizontal algorithm by computing a maximum of 4 samples for each pixel; the samples are averaged to produce the final pixel value.
- Medium further enhances the algorithm by using a greater number of samples (up to 9 per pixel).
- High establishes a maximum of 16 samples per pixel.

Each successive level is slower to compute. The anti-aliasing algorithm makes the process more efficient by allowing AutoCAD to decide for any given pixel that fewer samples need to be computed.

With Photo Raytrace, you can specify a value between 0.0 and 1.0. With a low setting, small differences between initial sample values force more samples to be taken. At a higher setting, the sample value differences must be greater to force more sampling. This increases rendering speed at the expense of image quality.

Bitplanes

The number of bitplanes (also called color depth or pixel depth) refers to the number of bits of information available to define a pixel's shade or color. With a bitplane of 1, a pixel can be only black or white (on or off), and only one bit of information is required to define its state.

With a bitplane of 8, a pixel can be any of 256 shades (calculated by raising 2 to the eighth power), and 8 bits of information are required to define its color state. A bitplane of 24 requires 24 bits of information but can display almost 16.8 million shades (2 raised to the 24th power).

You select bitplane settings for your rendering device when you configure. A bitplane of at least 8 bits is required for reasonable rendering results, and a bitplane of 24 or 32 bits produces the best results.

Using Render

AutoCAD Render provides three rendering types:

- Render, the basic AutoCAD rendering option for best performance
- Photo Real, the photorealistic scanline renderer, which can display bit-mapped and transparent materials and generate volumetric and mapped shadows
- Photo Raytrace, the photorealistic raytraced renderer, which uses ray tracing to generate reflections, refraction, and more precise shadows

Both photorealistic renderers generate images one horizontal scanline at a time.

Using the basic Render option, you can render your model without adding any lights, applying any materials, or setting up a scene. When you render a new model, the AutoCAD renderer automatically uses a virtual "over-the-shoulder" distant light. You cannot move or adjust this light.

Loading, Unloading, and Stopping

AutoCAD Render is automatically loaded into memory when you choose an option on the Render toolbar or enter an AutoCAD command such as RENDER, LIGHT, FOG, or SCENE. To free memory, you can unload AutoCAD Render.

To unload AutoCAD Render

1. At the Command prompt, enter **arx**.
2. Enter **unload**.
3. When prompted for an ARX file, enter **render**.

   Rendering is unloaded.

   You can stop the rendering process by pressing ESC.

Setting Rendering Conditions

The following sections describe some of the conditions that can affect rendering quality.

Setting the Rendering Background Color

Rendering to a viewport always renders against the background color you set for the AutoCAD graphics area. The Render window background color matches the AutoCAD background color.

To set the Render window background color

1 From the View menu, choose Render ➤ Preferences.
2 In the Rendering Preferences dialog box, choose Background.
3 In the Background dialog box, under Colors, select the color you want to modify (Top, Middle, Bottom), then choose Select Custom Color.
4 In the Color dialog box, select a color, then choose OK.
5 Choose OK to exit the Background dialog box.
6 In the Rendering Preferences dialog box, under Destination, select Render Window.
7 Choose OK.

To view the new color, you must apply Render to an object or scene. The Render Window is displayed with the new background color.

For more information about setting background types and images, see RENDER in the *Command Reference*.

Rendering All Objects

The default rendering choice is to render all objects in the current scene in the drawing. If no scene is defined or selected, AutoCAD renders the current view (see "Using Scenes in Rendering" on page 618). The rendering process is faster when you render to a smaller area of the screen. If you have configured AutoCAD to render to a viewport, use VPORTS or MVIEW to make a small viewport for rendering. Or, use the Crop Window option in the Render dialog box to specify a portion of the screen to be rendered. To display the Render toolbar, from the View menu choose Toolbars and then choose Render.

To render a model

1 Make sure you have a 3D view of your model.
2 From the View menu, choose Render ➤ Render.
3 In the Render dialog box, set options or accept the defaults.

Using Render

583

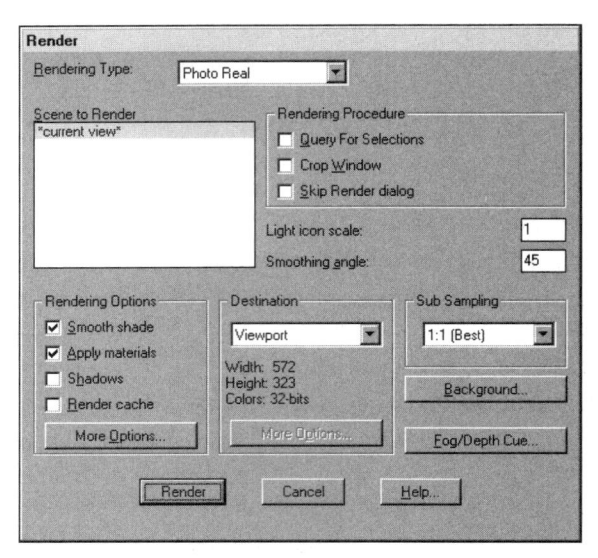

For example, under Rendering Options, select Smooth Shading to smooth the edges between polygon faces.

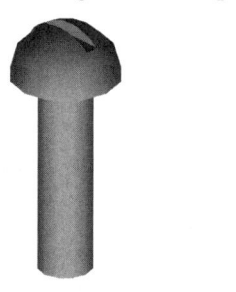

Smooth Shading on   Smooth Shading off

Related to Smooth Shading is Smoothing Angle, which sets the angle at which AutoCAD interprets an edge. The default angle setting is 45 degrees. Angles less than 45 degrees are smoothed, angles greater than 45 degrees are considered edges.

In the Rendering Options box, choose More Options. Then in the appropriate Render Options dialog box under Quality, choose Phong or Gouraud shading.

Phong shading, available for Photo Real and Photo Raytrace, produces higher-quality renderings with more accurate highlights. Gouraud renderings, available for the basic Render only, are slightly lower in quality but faster. For information about the options in the Render dialog box, see RENDER in the *Command Reference*.

4 To render the image to the screen, make sure that in the Render dialog box, Rendering Destination is set to Window or Viewport.

If you set Rendering Destination to File, the image is sent directly to a file; there is no screen display.

5 Select a scene or *current view*.

6 Choose Render.

Depending on the size of your drawing, after a short or long pause AutoCAD displays a rendered image of your model.

Command line RENDER

Related RPREF displays the Rendering Preferences dialog box, in which you can choose additional rendering options. STATS displays information about your last rendering, such as the time it took to render the image.

Rendering Selected Objects

Rendering can be a time-consuming process. You can save time by first rendering selected objects rather than the whole model.

To render selected objects

1 Make sure you have a current 3D view of your model.

2 From the View menu, choose Render ➤ Render.

3 In the Render dialog box, choose Query for Selections and select Render.

4 Select one or more objects in the drawing.

5 Press ENTER to complete your selection.

AutoCAD renders only the objects you select.

Command line RENDER

Accessing the Render Window

If your rendering destination is set to the Render window, it displays a bitmap image of your rendering.

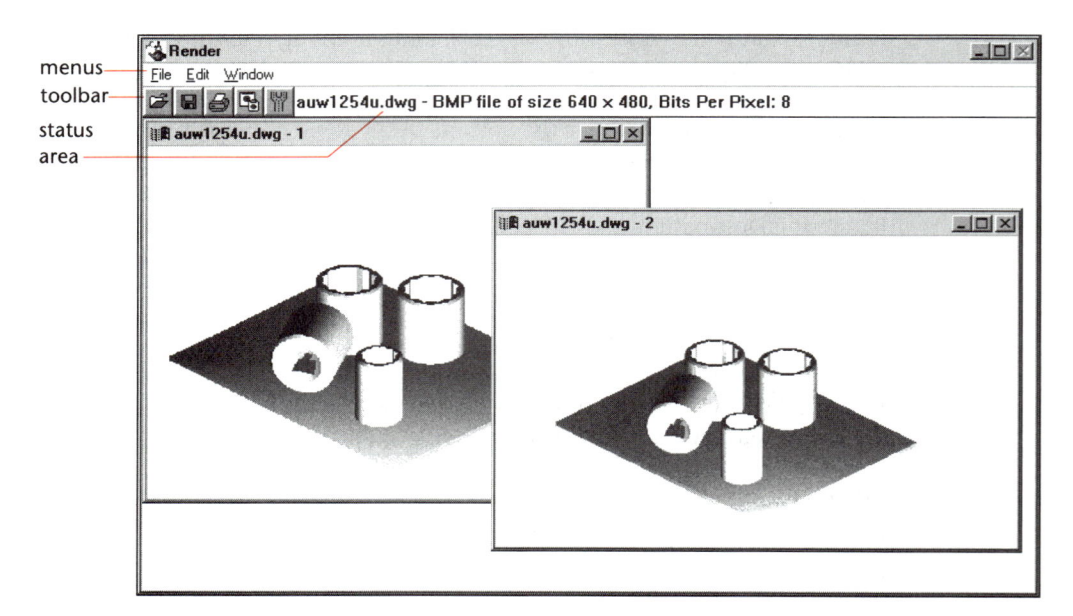

(menus, toolbar, status area — labels pointing to Render window screenshot)

For a complete description of the Render window Window menu and the Render window toolbar, see RENDER in the *Command Reference*.

At full screen display, the AutoCAD graphics area sometimes hides the Render window. In this situation, you cannot select the Render window with your pointing device to bring it to the front. You can press ALT+TAB to select the Render window from the active tasks.

Merging a Rendering with a Background

One method of creating special effects is to merge a rendering of one or more selected objects with a background image. For example, for presentation purposes you might want to import a landscape or a sky scene and use it as a background for your model.

TIFF image

rendered model

merged rendering

Instead of clearing the image from the display, AutoCAD renders the selected objects against the image.

Use REPLAY to display a BMP, TGA, or TIFF image in a viewport. (You *cannot* merge images in the Render window.)

To merge a rendering with a background image

1. From the View menu, choose Render ➤ Render.
2. In the Render dialog box, select Background.
3. In the Background dialog box, select Image.
4. Specify the background image file to be used by selecting Find File in the Image Name box.

When you use Merge, the wireframe edge of the object shows against the background image. For additional information about creating and editing landscapes, see the LSNEW, LSEDIT, and LSLIB commands in the *Command Reference*.

NOTE You can also use the REPLAY command to import a landscape or sky scene as a background image.

Changing Color Depth for Rendering

When you render to the Render window, your rendering may be displayed in fewer colors or be of lower quality than you expect. This probably means that you have 8-bit color depth selected in the Windows Render Options dialog box, or that you have an 8-bit color Windows display. If your system supports it, you may want to change to 16-bit or 24-bit color depth for your Windows display and render using 24-bit color in the Render window.

When rendering to a viewport, Render uses the current Windows color depth.

To change color depth for bitmap files in the Render window

1. From Start on the Window's taskbar, choose the Render icon.
2. From the Render window Files menu, choose Options.
3. In the Windows Render Options dialog box under Color Depth, select 24-Bit.
4. Choose OK.

Using Lights in Rendering

You are using the real power of rendering when you insert and manipulate lights in your drawing and assign material properties, such as shiny plastic or dull metal, to surfaces in your model.

Adding lights to your drawing is the simplest way to improve the appearance of your models. You can use lights to illuminate a whole model or to highlight selected objects and parts of objects in your drawing.

AutoCAD recognizes four types of light: ambient light, distant light, point lights, and spotlights. Light from these sources passes through faces and by default does not cast shadows. To create shadows, use the Photo Real or Photo Raytrace renderer, Autodesk 3D Studio, or a third-party application.

Ambient Light

Light that provides a constant illumination to every surface in a model is ambient light; it comes from no particular source and has no direction.

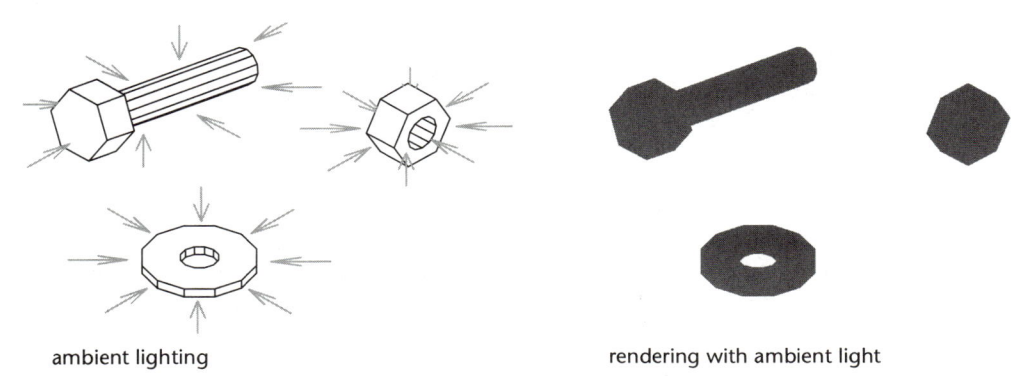

ambient lighting

rendering with ambient light

You can set the intensity of ambient light or turn it off. Keep ambient light low; otherwise, it tends to saturate your image and give it a washed-out look. Turn off ambient light to simulate a dark internal room or a scene at night.

By itself, ambient light does not produce realistic images. Adjoining faces are indistinguishable because all are equally illuminated. Use ambient light to provide fill light to surfaces not directly illuminated by a directional light source such as a spotlight (see the figure "Effects of different types of reflection" on page 598).

Distant Light

A distant light emits uniform parallel light rays in one direction only. Light rays extend infinitely on either side of the point you specify as the light source. The intensity of distant light does not diminish over distance; it is as bright at each face it strikes as it is at the source.

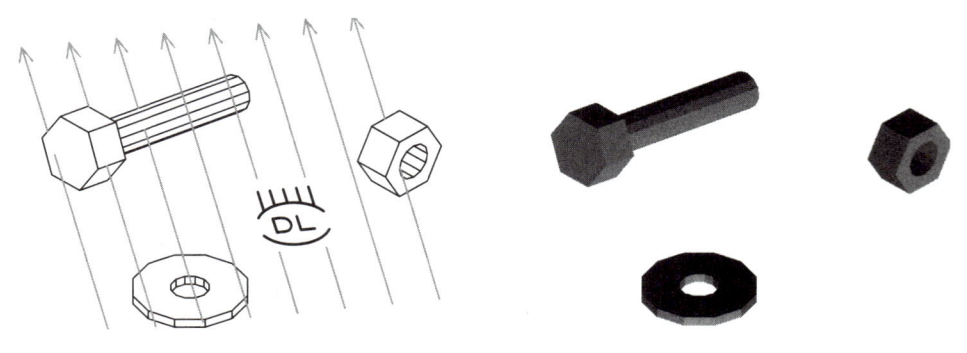

distant light

rendering with distant light

The direction of a distant light in a drawing is more critical than its location. All the objects are lighted, including any "behind" the light. A distant light acts as if it were outside the drawing. To avoid confusion, it's recommended that you position distant lights at the extents of your drawing.

Distant lights are useful for lighting objects or a backdrop uniformly and for simulating sunlight. A single distant light simulates the sun. Although the sun radiates in all directions, because of its size and distance, by the time its rays reach the earth they are effectively parallel. Because a distant light is so frequently used to simulate the sun in this way, especially in architectural renderings, the photorealistic renderers provide a special sun angle calculator that calculates the sun's position based on both the hour of the day and geographic location.

Point Lights

A point light radiates light in all directions from its location. The intensity of a point light diminishes over distance according to its rate of attenuation (see "Distance of Faces from Lights" on page 595).

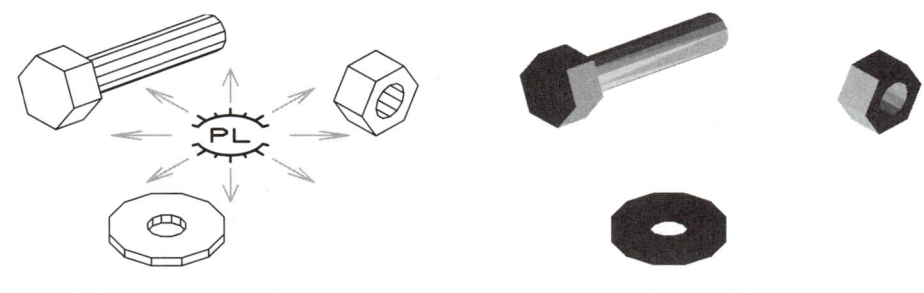

point light

rendering with point light

A point light is useful for simulating light from a light bulb. Use point lights for general lighting effects. Combine point lights with spotlights for what we generally think of as "lighting effects." Point lights are an alternative to ambient light for providing fill in a localized area.

Spotlights

A spotlight emits a directional cone of light. You can specify the direction of the light and the size of the cone. Like that of point lights, the intensity of spotlights diminishes over distance (see "Distance of Faces from Lights" on page 595). Spotlights have hotspot and falloff angles that together specify how light diminishes along the edge of the cone. When light from a spotlight falls on a surface, the area of maximum illumination is surrounded by an area of lesser intensity.

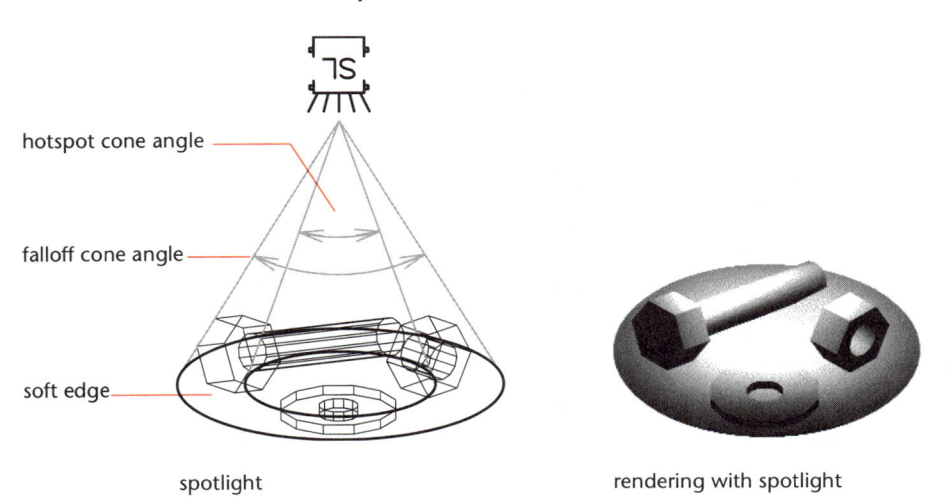

hotspot cone angle

falloff cone angle

soft edge

spotlight

rendering with spotlight

Using Render
591

- The hotspot cone angle defines the brightest part of a light beam. This is also known as the beam angle.
- The falloff cone angle defines the full cone of light. This is also known as the field angle.

The region between the hotspot and falloff angles is sometimes referred to as the rapid decay area.

The greater the difference between the hotspot and falloff angles, the softer the edge of the light beam. If the hotspot and falloff angles are equal, the edge of the light beam is sharp. Both values can range from 0 to 160 degrees. You cannot set the hotspot angle to be greater than the falloff angle.

Spotlights are useful for highlighting specific features and areas in your model.

Using Shadows in Rendering

When you create or modify a photorealistically rendered light, you can use the Shadow On option. Lights generate shadows when you render a scene using the Photo Real or the Photo Raytrace renderer—provided the global Shadows option in the Rendering Options section of the Render dialog box is turned on (see RENDER in the *Command Reference*). Shadows increase rendering time but can also increase a scene's realism.

The photorealistic renderers can generate shadows in three different ways: volumetric shadows, shadow maps, and raytraced shadows.

Volumetric Shadows

The Photo Real and the Photo Raytrace renderers can generate volumetric shadows. The renderers compute the volume of space cast by the shadow of an object and generate a shadow based on this volume.

Volumetric shadows are hard edged, but their outlines are approximate. Volumetric shadows cast by transparent or translucent objects are affected by the color of the object.

To generate volumetric shadows

1 From the View menu, choose Render ➤ Render.
2 In the Render dialog box, make sure you have selected Shadows under Rendering Options and the rendering type of Photo Real or Photo Raytrace.
3 In the dialog box for any light, select Shadow On and choose Shadow Options.
4 In the Shadow Options dialog box, select Shadow Volumes/Raytraced Shadows.

Shadow Maps

The Photo Real and Photo Raytrace renderers can both generate shadow maps during a prerendering pass of the view to render. For each light, you can set the size of the shadow map it generates, from 64 to 4,096 pixels square. The larger the shadow map, the greater its accuracy.

Shadow maps do not show the color cast by transparent or translucent objects, but shadow maps are the only way to generate soft-edged shadows with the photorealistic renderers. You can adjust the softness of the shadow's edge. (With spotlights, the relationship between the shadow map size and the falloff area determines the final resolution of the shadow.)

To generate a shadow map

1 From the View menu, choose Render ➤ Preferences.
2 In the Render dialog box, make sure you have selected Shadows under Rendering Options and the rendering type of Photo Real or Photo Raytrace.
3 In the dialog box for any light, select Shadow On and choose Shadow Options.
4 Clear Shadow Volumes/Raytraced Shadows. Shadow-mapped shadows override the default shadows (volumetric for Photo Real or raytraced for Photo Raytrace).
5 In the Shadow Options dialog box, adjust the light's shadow map size if necessary (default is 128).

Raytraced Shadows

Raytraced shadows (like other raytraced effects of reflection and refraction) are generated by tracing the path of light beams or rays sampled from a light source.

Raytraced shadows have hard edges and accurate outlines; they also transmit color from transparent and translucent objects.

If you've selected the Shadows option and you choose the Photo Raytrace renderer, raytraced shadows are generated for each light that has shadows turned on except lights that are set to generate shadow-mapped shadows.

Shadows and Rendering Speed

Shadows always increase rendering time, sometimes considerably. Volumetric shadows tend to be quicker than raytraced shadows for simple geometry. For more complex geometry with a large number of faces, however, raytraced shadows can be quicker to generate than volumetric shadows.

Shadow maps are particularly costly in terms of render time. You can save some time by hand-selecting objects for shadow casting (see LIGHT in the *Command Reference*).

Understanding Lighting Principles

The way light strikes each surface in a model is affected by the angle of the face to the light, and for point lights and spotlights, the distance of the face from the light. Reflection of light from a surface is affected by the reflective qualities you set for the surface's material (see "Defining Materials" on page 606).

Angle of Faces to Lights

The more a surface inclines away from a light source, the darker the surface appears. Faces perpendicular to a light source appear the brightest; the farther a face is from a 90-degree angle, the darker it is. The following figure illustrates how the angle of a light source affects brightness: each face is the same length; each light source emits eight beams of light. The brightness of each face depends solely on its angle to the light source.

Face 1 is perpendicular to the light source and is struck by all 8 beams of light. It is the brightest of the three faces.

Face 2 is at the greatest angle to the light source and receives only 4 beams of light. It is the darkest of the three faces.

Face 3 is at a slight angle to the light source and receives only 6 beams of light. It is darker than Face 1.

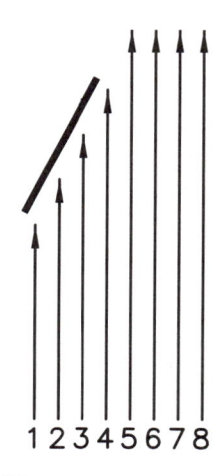

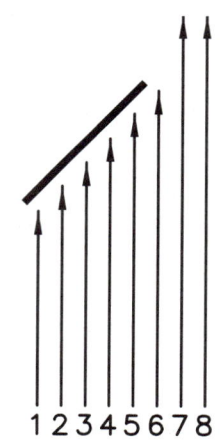

Effects of angle upon brightness

When you use a distant light that emits parallel beams in one direction, all faces that present the same angle to that light have the same brightness.

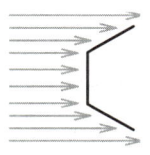

Object rendered using a distant light source

Distance of Faces from Lights

Objects far from point lights and spotlights can be defined to appear darker. Objects closer can appear brighter. Distant lights are unaffected by distance. The effect of light diminishing over distance is known as attenuation or falloff. You can choose between two rates of attenuation: inverse linear and inverse square. You can also specify no attenuation.

- Inverse linear: Illumination decreases in *inverse* proportion to the *distance* from the light source. Thus, as light travels 2, 4, 6, and 8 units, its brightness becomes 1/2, 1/4, 1/6, and 1/8 as strong.
- Inverse square: Illumination decreases in *inverse* proportion to the *square of the distance* from the light source. Thus, as light travels 2, 4, 6, and 8 units, its brightness becomes 1/4, 1/16, 1/36, and 1/64 as strong.

inverse linear attenuation

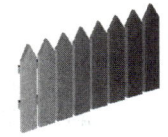

inverse square attenuation

Objects become darker earlier when you use inverse square as compared with inverse linear. The option you choose depends on the effect you're trying to achieve. For example, assume you want to produce a brightly lighted surface. If the light-to-object distance is 8 units, and the rate of falloff is inverse linear, you need to set light intensity to 8 for the light to have an intensity of 1 when it strikes the target surface.

Lighting Color Systems

To set the color of lights and the surface reflection of those lights, you can use one of two color systems: a primary red, green, and blue (RGB) light color system or a hue, lightness, and saturation (HLS) system.

Mixing primary RGB light colors yields the following secondary colors: yellow (red and green), cyan (green and blue), and magenta (red and blue). All light colors together produce white; the absence of any light color produces black. When you use an HLS system, you choose a color from a range of hues and then vary its lightness (brightness) and saturation (the amount of black the hue contains).

Reflection

Photorealistic rendering uses two kinds of reflection—diffuse and specular.

Diffuse Reflection

Surfaces such as blotting paper or matte-painted walls exhibit diffuse reflection. Light hitting a totally diffuse surface is dispersed equally in all directions. The following figure shows three beams of light hitting a matte surface. The surface reflects light in many different directions. Viewpoints 1, 2, and 3 can all display the reflection of the light.

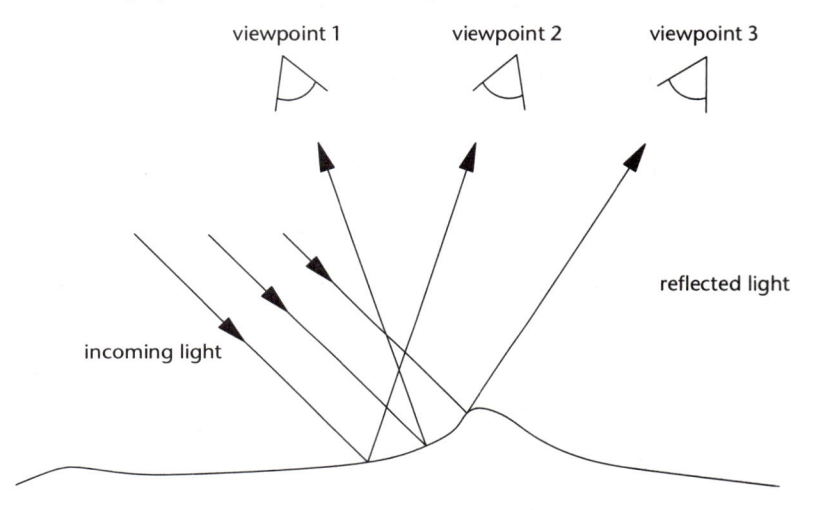

diffuse reflection of three beams of light

No matter where your viewpoint is, the reflection of the surface is the same. Therefore, when the Photo Real or Photo Raytrace renderer measures diffuse reflection, it does not adjust for the position of your viewpoint.

Specular Reflection

Specular reflection reflects light in a narrow cone. A beam of light striking a perfectly specular surface, such as a mirror, reflects light in one direction only. In the following figure, only viewpoint 3 can display the reflection of the incoming light beams.

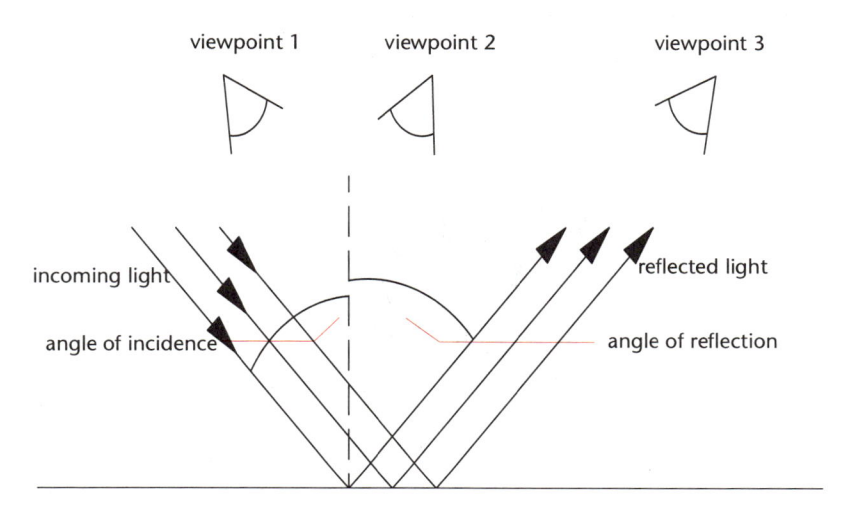

specular reflection of three beams of light

The angle of incidence is the angle between an incoming beam of light and the surface normal. The angle of reflection is the angle between a reflected beam of light and the surface normal. Specular reflection is visible only from a viewpoint where the two angles are equal.

This principle explains why the area of specular reflection is the shiniest spot on an egg, for example, when a light shines on it. If you move around the egg, the highlight—the point of reflection—moves to mirror your viewpoint.

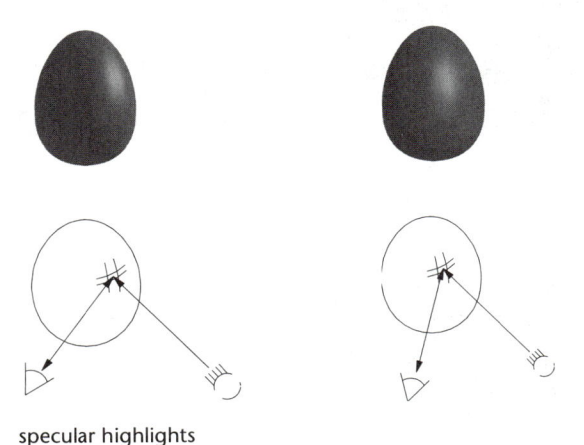

specular highlights

Using Render

With diffuse reflection, Render considers only the angle of the surface to the light source. With specular reflection (controlled by the Reflection and Roughness rendering attributes), the angle of the surface to both the light source and your viewpoint is considered.

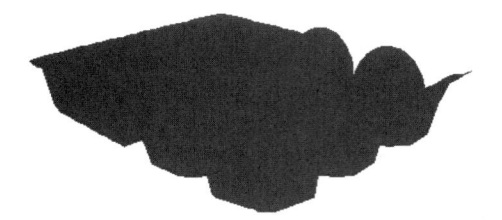

reflection of ambient light—uniform lighting of all surfaces with no contrast and no highlights

diffuse reflection—no highlights; contrast due solely to differences in the angle of surfaces to the light source

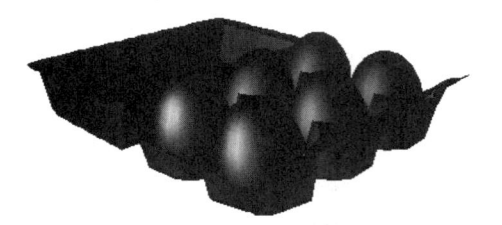

specular reflection—darker scene with highlights on surfaces where the angle of the surface to the light is the same as the angle of the surface to your viewpoint

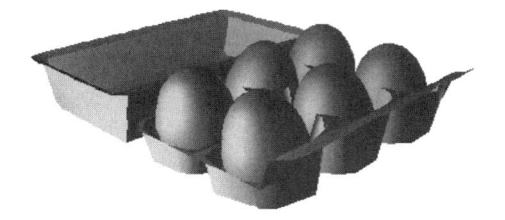

ambient, diffuse, and specular reflection combined

Effects of different types of reflection

With only ambient light, there is no contrast at all. With only diffuse reflection, there are no highlights. With the model set up for only specular reflection, the image displays highlights but is very dark. The combined effects of ambient, diffuse, and specular reflection produce the greatest realism.

Roughness

With the photorealistic renderers, you can control the size of the specular reflection area by using a roughness value. You can think of differences in roughness as the difference between a new, highly polished metal ball bearing and a ball bearing that is used and scuffed. Both surfaces are shiny and exhibit a high degree of specular reflection; however, they have different roughness.

With a photorealistic rendering material, the greater the roughness, the larger the size of the highlight.

low roughness   high roughness

Distance and Attenuation

As light travels from its source, it becomes less bright; therefore, the greater an object's distance from a light source, the darker it appears. When you use a flashlight in a dark room, objects close to the light are bright; against a distant wall, the light is barely visible. The phenomenon of light diminishing over distance is known as attenuation. The photorealistic renderers calculate attenuation for all light types.

As described in "Distance of Faces from Lights" on page 595, with the photorealistic renderers you can choose one of three methods for calculating attenuation: no attenuation (None), Inverse Linear, or Inverse Square. Actual light attenuates at the inverse square rate, but this does not always give the rendering effect you want.

Using Render

Adding Lights

You can add any number of lights to a drawing. You can set the color, location, and direction of each light you create. For point lights and spotlights, you can also set attenuation.

To add a new light to the drawing

First, you choose a light type and set the color and intensity of ambient light.

1 From the View menu, choose Render ➤ Light.
2 In the Lights dialog box, set the ambient light color and intensity.

   For most purposes, an intensity value of 0.3 is satisfactory. Setting higher values produces a washed-out, low-contrast image.

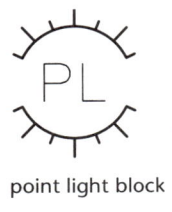

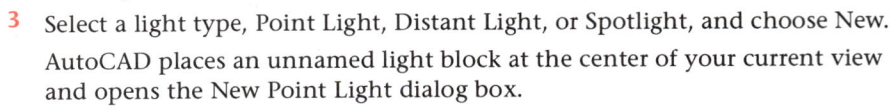

3 Select a light type, Point Light, Distant Light, or Spotlight, and choose New.

   AutoCAD places an unnamed light block at the center of your current view and opens the New Point Light dialog box.

4 In the New Point Light dialog box, enter a name for the light.

   The name must be unique and have no more than eight characters.

To set the intensity and location of the light.

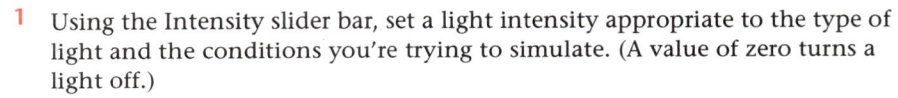

1 Using the Intensity slider bar, set a light intensity appropriate to the type of light and the conditions you're trying to simulate. (A value of zero turns a light off.)

   The default light intensities are designed to give reasonable illumination to your model. Render first using the defaults and then adjust the lights until you achieve the effect you want.

   The default setting for point lights and spotlights is determined by the Attenuation setting and the extents of the drawing. If Attenuation is None, the default intensity is 1. If Attenuation is set to Inverse Linear, the default intensity is the value of half the extents distance. If Attenuation is set to Inverse Square, the default intensity is the square of half the extents distance. Distant lights have no attenuation, and the default intensity is 1.

2 Set the appropriate hotspot and falloff angles for spotlights.

   To produce a sharp circle of light, make the hotspot cone angle equal to the falloff cone angle. To produce a fuzzy edge to the light, make the falloff angle a few degrees larger than the hotspot angle (see "Spotlights" on page 591).

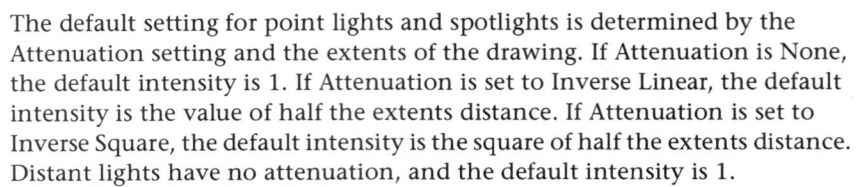

3 Accept or change the X,Y,Z coordinate of the Light Target and/or Location. By default, AutoCAD places the light in the center of the current viewport. To change the light position, under Position, choose Modify (see the procedure "To change a light's position" on page 602).

4 Choose OK.

AutoCAD confirms the insertion of the new light by displaying the light name in the center of the light block, returning you to the Lights dialog box, and displaying the name of the new light in the list.

5 Select New again to add another light, or choose OK to exit the dialog box.

Command line   LIGHT

Related   SCENE creates a combination of lights and a named view.

Don't worry about creating too many lights; you can always delete them, exclude them from the current scene, or turn them off by setting their intensity to zero. Excluding them from the current scene is the recommended method (see "Defining Scenes" on page 619). To ensure that you do not create lights with duplicate names, do not add lights to blocks.

Deleting and Modifying Lights

You can delete a light or modify its position, color, and intensity. The only change you *cannot* make is to the light type. For example, you cannot change a point light to a spotlight. Instead, you must delete the point light and insert a new spotlight.

To delete or modify a light

1 From the View menu, choose Render ➤ Lights.

2 In the Lights dialog box, select one of the lights listed.

3 To delete the light, select Delete and confirm the deletion.

4 To modify the light, select Modify.

5 In the Modify Light dialog box, change the values as needed. Then choose OK.

To modify the position of a light, see the following procedure, "To change a light's position."

6 Select another light and choose Delete or Modify again.

7 Choose OK.

Command line   LIGHT

Related   SCENE creates a combination of lights and a named view.

After your initial light setup you will often want to modify the position of lights in the drawing.

Using Render
601

To change a light's position

1 From the View menu, choose Render ➤ Lights.
2 In the Lights dialog box, choose Modify.
3 Do one of the following:

- In the Modify Point Light or Modify Spotlight dialog box under Position, choose Modify.
- In the Modify Distant Light dialog box under Light Source Vector, choose Modify.

AutoCAD closes the dialog box and displays the drawing. Depending on the type of light you are modifying, AutoCAD displays a vector that stretches from the current light location or light target to the crosshair. In the case of a distant light, it shows the light direction. As you move the crosshair, the vector stretches, helping you to reposition the light accurately.

4 Use your pointing device to change the position of the light. (The default target for distant lights and spotlights matches the current view direction.)

- For a point light, specify a new location for the light.
- For a spotlight, specify a new target for the light. Then specify a new location for the light.
- For a distant light, under To, specify a new target point for the light. Then, under From, specify a new location for the light to determine the direction of the light.

The drawing displays the light in its new position, and AutoCAD redisplays the appropriate Modify Light dialog box.

5 Choose OK.

After you change the location of the light, you may want to change its intensity.

Command line   LIGHT

Related   SCENE creates a combination of lights and a named view.

If you have difficulty establishing the correct coordinates for your lights, try using different viewpoints and inserting the lights at those viewpoints. AutoCAD automatically positions the light at the center of your viewpoint.

Using VPORTS, you can also set up different views in different viewports.

To position a light using views

1 Use DDVIEW to save your current viewpoint to a named view.
2 Use VPOINT to set up a view that you want the light to see. You can also name and save that view if you wish.
3 Add a light at that position.

   AutoCAD positions the light at the center of your viewpoint.
4 Use DDVIEW again to return to your original named view.

   You'll see the light in the position you want, shining on the object you intended it to shine on.
5 To fine-tune the light position, use the Modify Position option in the Modify Light dialog box.

Command line LIGHT

Related SCENE creates a combination of lights and a named view.

To position a distant light, you can use the Azimuth and Altitude controls in the New Distant Light and Modify Distant Light dialog boxes.

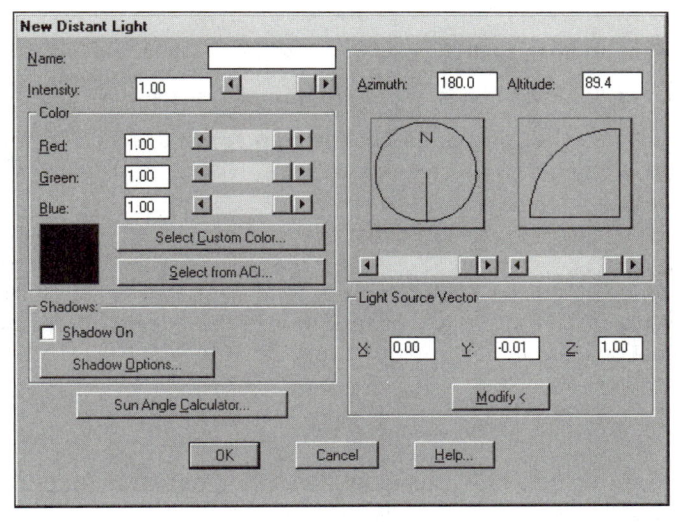

You can also use a distant light to simulate the position of the sun in relation to your model.

Using Render
603

To position a distant light to simulate sunlight

1 Align your model in relation to the points of the compass: North, South, East, and West. By default, the *Y* axis points north.

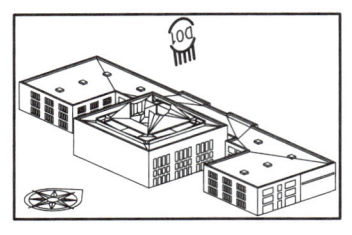

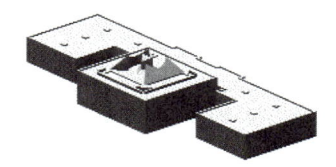

aligned and lighted   rendered view at noon

2 Add a new distant light.
3 Assuming you want to simulate the sun's position at noon in the northern hemisphere, enter **180** for Azimuth, that is, due south.
4 Enter an appropriate angle for the Altitude of the sun at noon for your particular location. For example, enter **80** degrees to put the sun almost overhead at noon.

Command line   LIGHT

Related   SCENE creates a combination of lights and a named view.

To produce the appropriate shadows, you must use the Photo Real or Photo Raytrace renderer.

Using Materials in Rendering

To lend still greater realism to your renderings, apply materials such as steel and plastic to the surfaces of your model. You can attach materials to individual objects, all objects with a specific AutoCAD Color Index (ACI) number, blocks, or layers.

Using materials involves several steps:

- Defining materials, including their color, reflection, or dullness
- Attaching materials to objects in the drawing
- Importing and exporting materials to and from material libraries

Creating color, shading, and patterning is different on a computer than with traditional media such as paints and crayons.

Color

When you look at objects around you, most colors you see are pigment colors. When sunlight hits a red rose petal, for example, the petal absorbs all the colors of the spectrum except red, which reflects back to your eyes. If an object reflects the entire spectrum, you see white; if it reflects no color, you see black. The primary pigment colors are red, yellow, and blue. The secondary colors, which are an equal mix of two primary colors, are orange (red and yellow), green (yellow and blue), and purple (red and blue). When painters mix oils on a palette, they are working with pigment color.

If an object is a source of light, it emanates color rather than reflects it. In a computer monitor, you see not pigment color but light color. The primary light colors are red, green, and blue. For this reason, computer color systems are often referred to as "RGB" systems. The secondary light colors are yellow (red and green), cyan (green and blue), and magenta (red and blue). All light colors together produce white; the absence of any light color is black.

An addition to the RGB light color system is the HLS system (hue, lightness, saturation). Instead of mixing primary colors, you choose the color from a range of hues and then vary its lightness (brightness) and saturation (purity).

Surface Color Variations

One of the key components of materials is their surface color variation.

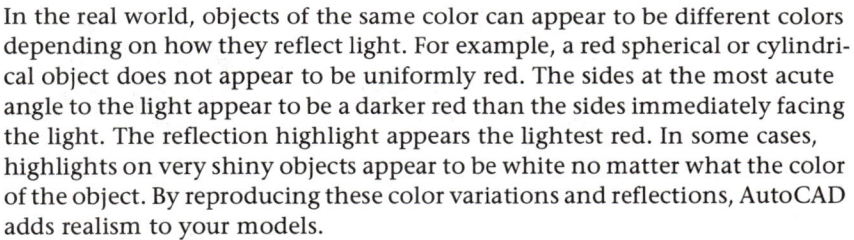

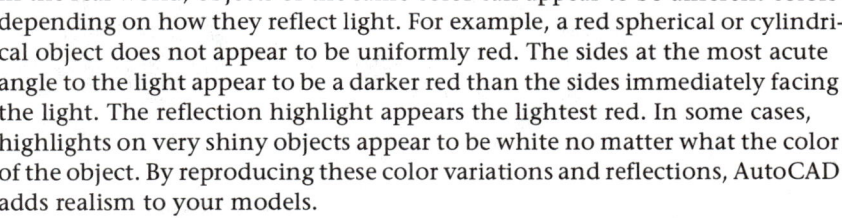

In the real world, objects of the same color can appear to be different colors depending on how they reflect light. For example, a red spherical or cylindrical object does not appear to be uniformly red. The sides at the most acute angle to the light appear to be a darker red than the sides immediately facing the light. The reflection highlight appears the lightest red. In some cases, highlights on very shiny objects appear to be white no matter what the color of the object. By reproducing these color variations and reflections, AutoCAD adds realism to your models.

white highlight

AutoCAD is flexible in the way it treats lighting color. You can specify the color of the light reflected from the surface of an object irrespective of the color of the object or the color of the light shining on the object. For example, you can simulate a blue light shining on a red sphere giving off maroon reflection highlights.

Because of surface color variations, each rendered material actually specifies three color variables:

- The object's main color (also known as its diffuse color)
- Its ambient color, which appears on those faces lighted by ambient light alone

- Its reflection color (or specular color), which is the color of a highlight on a shiny material (the size of the highlight depends on the material's roughness)

When you define a material, you can adjust all of these variables.

Transparency

If you want to make all or part of an object transparent or translucent, you can adjust a material's degree of transparency from 0 to 1.0. Transparency increases rendering time. Multiple layers of transparent objects increase rendering time for each multilayered transparent pixel.

You can set the refraction index of transparent materials. Photo Raytrace rendering generates refractive effects: bending light rays as they pass through the refractive material, and thus shifting the objects that are visible through it.

Defining Materials

You define a material by specifying the color of the material and its reflective qualities, such as shiny or dull, and whether the surface of an object should reflect highlights when the material is applied to that object.

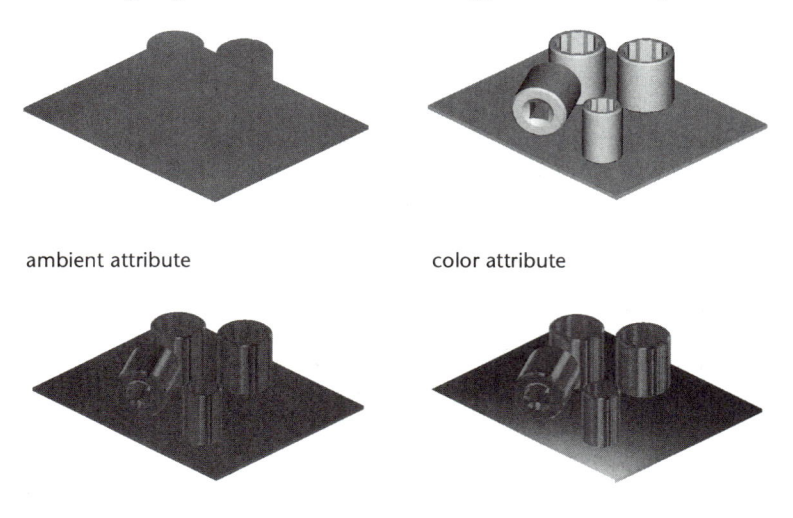

ambient attribute

color attribute

reflection attribute

ambient, color, and reflection attributes

Different types of light and reflection effects

With only ambient light, you see no contrast and no highlights. With only the color attribute, you see no highlights; contrast is due solely to differences in the angle that surfaces present to the light source. With only the reflection attribute, the image displays highlights but is very dark.

When you preview your materials, Preview always shows a sphere from a default orientation. If the object you're attaching the material to is a cube, the preview sphere does not show you exactly how the material is rendered, but it does give you a good idea. Some preview panels provide a list of geometry, so you can view your materials on a flat or curved surface.

To define a new material

1 From the View menu, choose Render ➤ Materials.

2 In the Materials dialog box, choose New.

3 In the New Standard Materials dialog box, enter a name in the Material Name box.

The name must be unique and have no more than sixteen characters.

4 Set the color and specify a value for each of the following material attributes: Color/Pattern, Ambient, Reflection, Roughness, Transparency, Refraction, and Bump Map. For each attribute, you can make the color the same as the object color or a different color.

You can set the color of each attribute by using the RGB (red, green, and blue) or HLS (hue, lightness, and saturation) slider bars, the color wheel, or the AutoCAD Color Index (ACI) number of the object itself. For information about manipulating RGB and HLS color values, see "Lighting Color Systems" on page 595.

- Set the color and value for Color/Pattern.
  Color is the base color reflected by the object, also known as diffuse reflection. The main (diffuse) color of the material can be viewed in the Preview area. You can adjust the color with the Value and Color controls. For a dull, matte-finish effect, set the value for Color to around 0.7 and set the value for Reflection to 0.3. To make this material a pattern instead of a color, enter a file name in the Bitmap Blend area.

- Set the color and value for Ambient.
  The settings for Ambient determine the color reflected from ambient light. Generally, keep the ambient light value in the Lights dialog box below 0.3 (or keep the value at the default setting of 0.1). A high ambient light setting tends to give your renderings a washed-out appearance.

- Set the color and value for Reflection.

  The Reflection settings determine the color of the reflected highlights, also known as specular reflection. The material's reflective (highlight or specular) color can be viewed in the Preview area. You can adjust the color with the Value and Color controls. Shiny surfaces such as polished metals reflect light in a narrow direction. When light shines on a spherical or cylindrical object, the highlight is the shiniest spot on the object.

  For Photo Raytrace, Value specifies the material's coefficient of reflectivity. This is the amount of a reflected ray's color to add to a surface where the ray strikes.

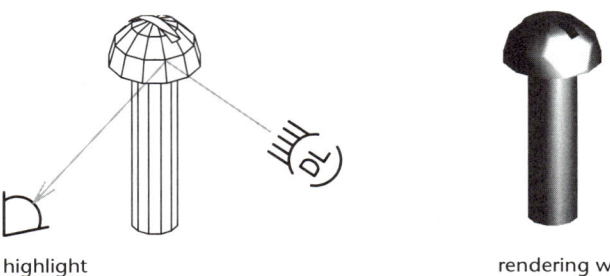

  highlight

  rendering with highlight

  For a shiny effect, set the value for Reflection to 0.7, and set the value for Color to 0.3. If you want the color of the highlight to be white, move the Red, Green, and Blue slider bars until each has a value of 1.

- Set the value for Roughness.

  The Roughness setting determines the size of the reflected highlight. Roughness is similar to the difference between a highly polished steel ball bearing and one that is scuffed with glass paper. Because a smoother, less rough surface produces a smaller highlight, the lower the roughness value, the smaller the size of the highlight. Roughness values have no effect unless you enter a value for Reflection.

- Set the value for Transparency.

  The Transparency setting lets you make all or part of an object transparent or translucent. You can adjust a material's degree of transparency from 0 to 1.0. Transparency increases rendering time (see RMAT in the *Command Reference* for a discussion of bitmap blend).

- Set the value for Refraction.

  The Refraction setting lets you set a refraction index for transparent materials. Refraction values have no effect unless you enter a value for Transparency.

- Set the value for Bump Map.
  The Bump Map setting determines the brightness of a bump map object. Bump Map values are translated into apparent changes in the height of the surface of an object.

5 Choose Preview to see if the values you specified produce the effect you want.

A small sphere appears, rendered with the material values that you have specified. If the object you're attaching the material to is a cube, the preview sphere does not show you exactly how the material is rendered, but it does give you a good idea. Some preview panels provide a list of geometry so you can view your materials on a flat or curved surface.

6 Change the values and continue to preview your changes until you're satisfied with the material's appearance. Then choose OK.

Command line   RMAT

Modifying Materials

You can duplicate and modify a material at any time using Duplicate and Modify in the Materials dialog box. A fast way to define a new material is to select an existing material in the Materials dialog box and choose Duplicate. Then in the New Materials dialog box, provide a new name for the material and modify the fields. You will find it easier to modify the existing fields than to create everything from scratch.

You can easily change the Color and Reflection parameters, for example, to change a material from dull to shiny.

To change a material from matte to shiny

1 From the View menu, choose Render ➤ Materials.
2 In the Materials dialog box, select a material from the Materials list.
3 Choose Modify.
4 In the Modify Materials dialog box, enter a low value (0.3 or lower) for Color.
5 Enter a high value (0.7 or higher) for Reflection and a low value (0.3 or lower) for Roughness.
6 Choose Preview to see the difference.
7 Choose OK.

Command line   RMAT

Attaching Materials

Having defined a material, you can apply or attach it to one or more objects in the drawing. You can attach materials to individual objects, to all objects with a specific AutoCAD Color Index (ACI) number, or to layers.

To attach a material

1   From the View menu, choose Render ➤ Material.
2   in the Materials dialog box, select a material from the list or choose Select to select a material already attached to an object in the drawing.

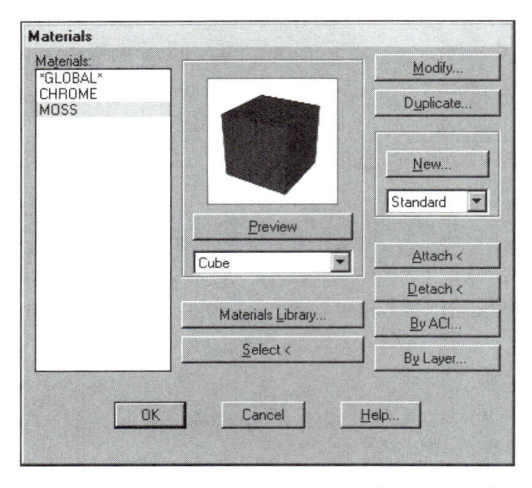

3   Apply a material directly to an object, to all objects with a specific ACI number, or to all objects on a specific layer.

- To attach a material directly to one or more objects, choose Attach. Then select the objects in the drawing.
- To attach a material to all objects in the drawing with a specific ACI number, choose By ACI. In the Attach by AutoCAD Color Index dialog box, select an ACI number.
- To attach a material to all objects on a specific layer, choose By Layer. In the Attach by Layer dialog box, select a layer.

4   Choose OK.

Render the model again to see the effect.

Command line   RMAT

To detach a material attached to an object, choose Detach in the Materials dialog box. To detach a material attached by ACI, choose Detach in the Attach by AutoCAD Color Index dialog box. To detach a material attached by layer, choose Detach in the Attach by Layer dialog box.

Using Materials, Blocks, and Layers

AutoCAD renders materials on objects according to a hierarchy based on how the material is attached. Materials explicitly attached have the highest priority, then materials attached by ACI, and finally materials attached by layer. If no material is attached, the global (*GLOBAL*) material is used.

If you attach materials (explicitly, by ACI, or by layer) to objects and then use those objects to form a block, the block is rendered according to the materials of its component objects. For example, a basin with a porcelain material attached and two faucets with a chrome material attached might be combined into a sink block. When the sink block is rendered, the two separate materials are distinctly displayed.

If you then attach a material to the layer on which the sink block resides, the hierarchy ensures that the materials attached to the sink block still are displayed. For example, if the component basin is drawn on a porcelain layer and the component faucets on a chrome layer, and if the sink block is placed on a red layer, the two separate materials are still displayed when the sink block is rendered.

If some components of a block have materials attached and other components have no materials attached, attaching a material to the block affects only those objects with no materials attached. For example, assume a stool block is composed of two elements: legs with the metal material attached, and a seat with no material attached. If you attach no material to the chair block, the legs are rendered metal and the seat is rendered with the global material. If you attach red to the block, the legs are rendered metal and the seat is rendered red.

If you're including blocks with materials attached from another drawing, you must import the materials from that drawing into the list of materials in your current drawing.

Mapping

In the context of rendering, mapping means projecting a 2D image onto the surface of a 3D object. Photorealistic rendering maps are 2D images in one of several file formats, including BMP, TGA, TIFF, and JPEG.

Mapping coordinates are also referred to as *UV* coordinates. (The letters *UV* are used because these coordinates are independent of the *XY* coordinates used to describe the AutoCAD geometry.)

Photorealistic rendering supports the following kinds of maps:

- Texture maps define surface colors, as if the bitmap image were painted onto the object. For example, you might apply an image of a checkerboard pattern to a horizontal flat surface to create the appearance of a parquet floor.
- Reflection maps simulate a scene reflected on the surface of a shiny object (also known as environment maps).
- Opacity maps specify areas of opacity and transparency. For example, if your bitmap image is a black circle in the middle of a white rectangle and you apply it as an opacity map, the surface appears to have a hole in it where the circle maps onto the object.
- Bump maps create an embossed or bas-relief effect.

For bitmap effects, you must render using the Photo Real or Photo Raytrace renderer.

Mapping involves two steps (performed in either order):

- Attaching a material with bitmaps to an object
- Assigning mapping coordinates to the object so that the renderer can position the maps

Reflection maps do not require mapping coordinates.

WARNING! The mapping coordinates you assign in the Mapping dialog box apply to the entire selection set and remain with the selection set. When you move the geometry, the mapping coordinates and other mapping attributes (such as bitmap scaling) move with it.

Unless you take advantage of tiling (see the next section, "Tiling and Cropping"), try to apply your material maps in a 1:1 relationship (the default) to your geometry so that the map projection is effective and takes less time. For example, if you have a 512 by 480 checkerboard pattern, you should not scale the mapping so small that the checkerboard merely makes your object seem gray, nor should you scale the mapping so large that the object becomes either all black or all white.

To counter bitmap aliasing when you get close to or far away from a mapped object, the renderer performs some filtering operations to obtain the best appearance. For example, when the viewpoint is close to the mapped object, the renderer interpolates new pixels to smooth out the map's jagged edges; when the viewpoint is distant, the renderer samples the map to approximate an overall image. (You can select the bitmap sampling technique; see RENDER in the *Command Reference*.) These filtering operations increase rendering time.

You can apply maps in combination. For example, apply a wood grain bitmap as both a bump map and a texture map on a paneled wall to give the wall both the "feel" and the color of wood. Then apply an opacity map to punch a hole in the wall.

All maps have a blend value that specifies how much they affect the rendering. For example, a texture map with a blend value less than the maximum (1.0) allows some of the material's surface colors to show through. Lower blend values reduce the bitmap's effect. For bump maps, a low blend value usually gives the best effect.

Tiling and Cropping

When you project a bitmap onto an object, you can choose to create either a tiled or a cropped ("decal") effect if the image is scaled smaller than the object.

If the scale of bitmap to object is less than 1:1, tiling repeats the image or pattern until the entire object is covered. For example, you can use this effect to project a checkerboard onto a sphere with only a 2 by 2 starting image or to wallpaper a room scene with a very small bitmap. Tiling is adjustable to obtain different tiling values along the mapping axes, U and V.

With cropped projection, you can place an image in a single location on an object. The rest of the object is rendered with the colors of the material—its main color, reflection color, and ambient color. Also, areas within the decal can let the object's main material color show through. For more information, see RMAT in the *Command Reference*.

Texture Maps

A texture map is the projection of an image (such as a tile pattern) onto an object (such as a table or chair). Because of the interaction of the texture map with an object's surface characteristics and the light and shadow, this technique can produce highly realistic images.

Reflection Maps

A reflection map (also known as an environment map) simulates the effect of a scene reflected on the surface of an object. For reflection maps to render well, the material should have low roughness (see "Roughness" on page 599), and the reflection bitmap itself should have a high resolution (at least 512 by 480 pixels).

NOTE Reflection maps ar distinct from raytraced reflections, which are generated by the Photo Raytrace renderer without mapping.

Opacity Maps

Opacity maps are projections of opaque and transparent areas onto objects, creating the effect of a solid surface with holes or gaps. Opacity maps use the brightness value of the mapping image to determine opacity. Pure white areas in an opacity map are completely opaque, while pure black areas are transparent. If an opacity map is in color, the equivalent gray-scale values of the colors supply the opacity translation.

Bump Maps

The brightness values of a bump map image are translated into apparent changes in the height of the surface of an object. A simple example is white text on a black background. Bump mapping that image gives the white text the appearance of being raised (or embossed) against a flat background, even though the geometry has not changed.

If the bump map image is in color, the translated gray-scale value of each of the colors is used to supply the height translation. You can select any image for mapping onto an object to create an embossed or bas-relief effect.

Bump mapping increases rendering time significantly.

Solid Materials

Photorealistic rendering also supports three special or procedural materials—marble, granite, and wood. At rendering time, these materials generate a 3D pattern in two or more colors and apply it to an object. The pattern is controlled by parameters that vary with the kind of material. These materials are also known as template materials.

WARNING! You *cannot* export procedural materials to other applications, such as 3D Studio.

Mapping Projection Types

With photorealistic rendering, you can select how to project a map image onto an object. As detailed in the following sections, you can use the following projection types:

- Planar
- Cylindrical
- Spherical
- Solid

Generally, the effect is best if the projection type corresponds roughly to the shape of the object onto which you're mapping, although you might need to experiment to find the best result in different situations. The Preview box in the Photorealistic Mapping and Adjust Projection dialog boxes can help you see the effect of mapping before you do a full rendering.

When tiling is turned on, the extents of the projection geometry have no effect on projection. This is true even though the Adjust Planar, Cylindrical, and Spherical dialog boxes represent the projection systems by geometry—based either on the extents of the current selection set or on points you specify yourself using the pointing device. They do not limit where the bitmap is rendered, unless you also turn on cropping.

Planar Projection

Planar projection maps the texture onto the object with a one-to-one correspondence, as if you were projecting the texture from a slide projector onto the surface. This does not distort the texture; it just scales the image to fit the object.

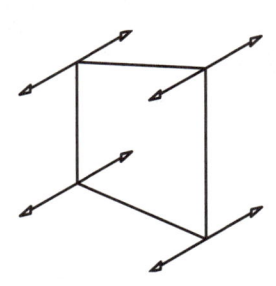

Cylindrical projection maps an image onto an object with a cylindrical projection; the horizontal edges are wrapped together but not the top and bottom edges. The height of the texture is scaled along the cylinder's axis.

Spherical Projection
Spherical projection warps the texture both horizontally and vertically. The top edge of the texture map is compressed to a point at the "north pole" of the sphere, as is the bottom edge at the "south pole."

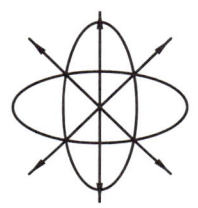

Solid Projection
Because solid materials are three-dimensional, they have three mapping coordinates, *U*, *V*, and *W*, and can be applied from any angle. You do not always need to specify the mapping coordinates for these materials, but you can. For example, you might want to change the material's orientation for a particular rendering or skew a pattern along one dimension. For more information, see SETUV in the *Command Reference*.

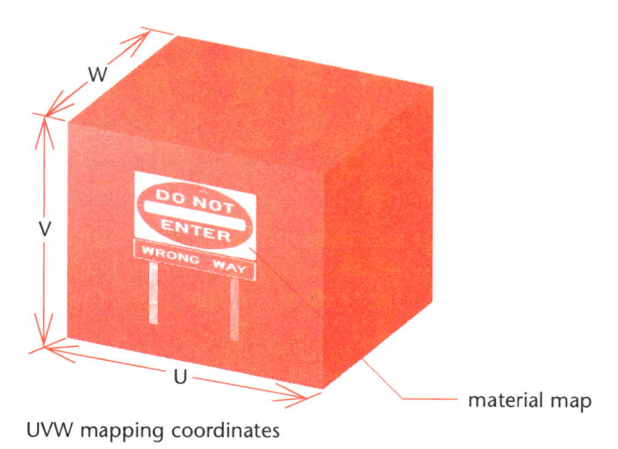

UVW mapping coordinates

Chapter 14 Creating Three-Dimensional Images

Importing and Exporting Materials

In a new drawing, only the *GLOBAL* material, the set of default material values, is listed in the Materials List. Rather than create a material from scratch, you might want to import a predefined material from a library of materials supplied with AutoCAD. You can use the material as is or modify it and save it under a new name for use in any drawing.

To import or export a material

1 From the View menu, choose Render ➤ Materials Library.

In the Materials Library dialog box, the Materials List contains materials in the drawing; the Library List contains materials in the library.

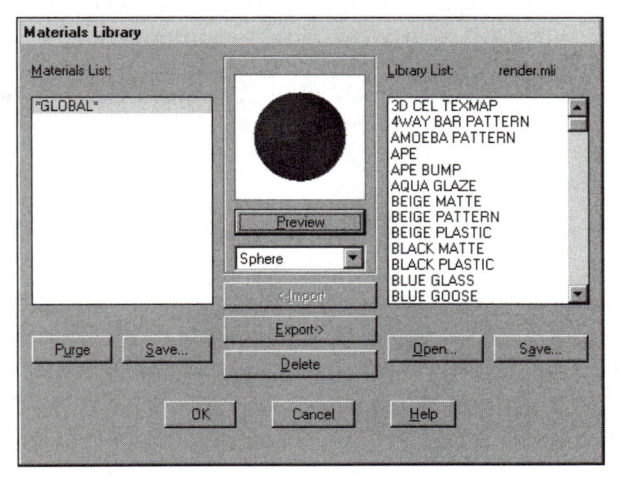

2 Choose Preview to see a rendering of the material on a small sphere in the preview image tile before you import or export the material.

3 To add a material to the list of materials in the drawing, select a material from the Library List. Then choose Import.

The material appears under Materials List. Importing a material copies that material and its parameters to the list of materials in the drawing; it does not delete the material from the library.

4 To export a material from the drawing to the library of materials, select a material from the Materials List. Then choose Export.

The material appears under Library List.

Using Render
617

5 Under Materials List, choose Save to save the materials in the current drawing to a named materials library (MLI) file that you can use with other drawings.

6 Choose OK.

Command line MATLIB

You can use AutoVision and 3D Studio materials library (MLI) files in AutoCAD. To access other library files, choose Open in the Materials Library dialog box.

Using Scenes in Rendering

Named views are important to rendering because you can quickly and easily go to preset viewpoint positions. Set up views using VPOINT and DVIEW and save named views using DDVIEW. (For more information, see chapter 6, "Controlling the Drawing Display.") For rendering purposes, you can also create scenes. A scene is a combination of a named view and one or more lights.

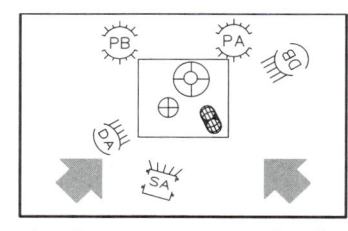

view A   view B

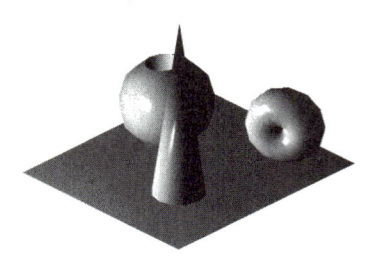

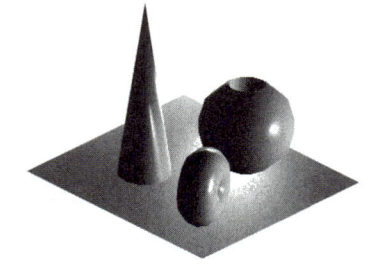

scene 1   scene 2
view A   view B
lights DA, PA, SA   lights DB, PB

Scenes save you time because you don't have to set up your viewpoint and lights from scratch every time you render.

Defining Scenes

A scene is composed of one named view and one or more lights. You can have up to 500 lights in a scene. You can set the lights in the scene any way you wish, including turning them off.

Before setting up a new scene, create one or more named views using VPOINT, DVIEW, or DDVIEW and if you haven't already done so, insert one or more lights in the drawing (see "Adding Lights" on page 600).

To set up a new scene

1 From the View menu, choose Render ➤ Scene.
2 In the Scenes dialog box, choose New.
3 In the New Scene dialog box, enter a name for the scene.
   The name must be unique and have no more than eight characters.
4 Select a named view or *CURRENT* from the list of views.
5 Select one or more lights or *ALL* from the list of lights. Then choose OK.
6 Choose New again to create another scene, or choose OK to exit the dialog box.

Command line SCENE

Related LIGHT creates lights. DDVIEW creates named views.

Deleting and Modifying Scenes

Once you've set up a scene, you can delete or modify it at any time. You can modify the scene by changing its name or its associated view or by changing the lights in the scene.

To delete or modify a scene

1 From the View menu, choose Render ➤ Scene.
2 In the Scenes dialog box, select one of the scenes listed.
3 To delete the scene, choose Delete and confirm the deletion.
4 To modify the scene, choose Modify.
5 In the Modify Scene dialog box.

- To rename a scene, enter a new Scene Name.
- To change the scene viewpoint, select another view.
- To add another light to the scene, select a light that is not highlighted.
- To remove a light from the scene, select a highlighted light. Removing a light from the scene does *not* delete the light from the drawing.

6 Choose OK.

Command line SCENE

Related LIGHT creates lights. DDVIEW creates named views.

Saving and Redisplaying Renderings

After creating a rendering, you can save the image for redisplay at a later time. Rendering can be a time-consuming process, but redisplaying a previously rendered image is instantaneous.

To save a rendered image, you can render directly to a file, or you can render to the screen and then save the image. You can redisplay (replay) these images at any time.

Saving a Rendering Directly to a File

No matter how your display is configured, you can bypass the screen and redirect your rendering to a file. An advantage of not rendering to the screen is that you can render to higher resolutions than your current display configuration permits. You can then replay that image on other systems with higher-resolution displays. You can render your images to several file formats, including BMP, TGA, TIFF, PCX, and PostScript.

To render an image directly to a file

1 From the View menu, choose Render ➤ Render.
2 In the Render dialog box under Rendering Destination, choose File and then More Options.
3 In the File Output Configuration dialog box, select a file type and the options you want. Then choose OK.
4 In the Render dialog box, choose Render.
5 In the Rendering File dialog box, name the file and choose OK.

After some time, your rendered image is created and saved as a file. There is no screen display.

Command line RENDER

Related REPLAY redisplays a BMP, TGA, or TIFF format file in a viewport. SAVEIMG saves a rendered screen image in a viewport to a BMP, TGA, or TIFF format file.

Saving a Viewport Rendering

After rendering a model to a viewport, you can use SAVEIMG to save the screen image to one of the following file formats: BMP, TGA, or TIFF.

To save a rendered image from the viewport display

1. Render the model to a viewport.
2. From the Tools menu, choose Display Image ➤ Save.
3. In the Save Image dialog box, select a file format: BMP, TGA, or TIFF.
4. Accept the default full screen size or specify the size and offsets for the image. (For an explanation of each option in the Save Image dialog box, see SAVEIMG in the *Command Reference*.) Then choose OK.
5. In the Image File dialog box, enter a file name. Then choose OK.

   AutoCAD saves the image in the selected file format.

   Command line   SAVEIMG

   Related   REPLAY redisplays a BMP, TGA, or TIFF file in a viewport.

   To save a rendering directly to a file with no screen display, use RENDER and choose File as the Rendering Destination in the Render dialog box.

Saving a Render Window Rendering

After rendering a model to the Render window, you can save the rendered image to a bitmap (BMP) file. Note that when scaled down, bitmap images lose information; when scaled up, images become blocky and do not print well.

To save a rendered image as a bitmap file

1. Select the rendered image.
2. From the File menu, choose Save.
3. In the Save File dialog box, enter a file name.
4. Choose OK.

   AutoCAD saves the image in the BMP file format.

   To save or copy rendered images to the Clipboard, make the Render window active, and then choose Copy from the Edit menu.

   To save PostScript format images from the Render window, you must export your image to a PostScript file (see "Saving Render Window Images in PostScript Format" on page 626).

Redisplaying a Rendered Image

Having saved your rendered screen image, you can redisplay that rendering at any time. If you saved the screen image in BMP, TGA, or TIFF format, use REPLAY to redisplay the image.

To redisplay a rendered image in a viewport

1 From the Tools menu, choose Display Image ➤ View.

2 In the Replay dialog box, enter a file name or select a file.

3 In the Image Specifications dialog box, accept the default full screen size or specify the size and offsets for displaying the image. (To specify size and offsets, see the next two procedures: "To crop a rendered image in a viewport" and "To offset a rendered image in a viewport.")

4 Choose OK.

AutoCAD displays the image.

Command line   REPLAY

The default size of the image in the Image box reflects the entire display size measured in pixels. Rather than display the whole image, you can choose a portion of the image to display.

To crop a rendered image in a viewport

1 From the Tools menu, choose Display Image ➤ View.

2 In the Replay dialog box, enter a file name or select a file.

3 In the Image Specifications dialog box, specify two diagonal points to define the area you want to display.

AutoCAD draws a box to mark the bounds of the cropped image.

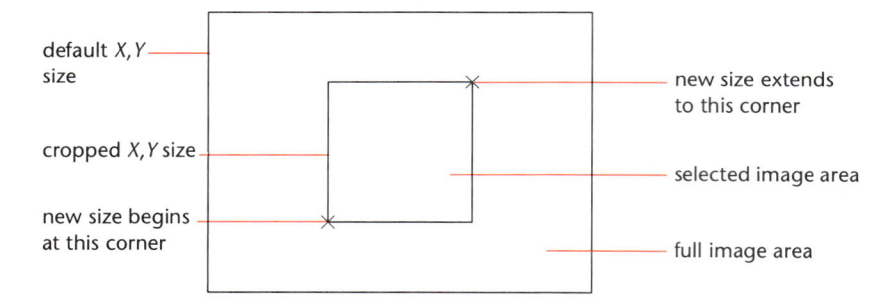

- default X,Y size
- cropped X,Y size
- new size begins at this corner
- new size extends to this corner
- selected image area
- full image area

After cropping the image size in the Image box, AutoCAD updates the values of the coordinates and displays a representation of the cropped image size in the Screen box in the dialog box.

The X,Y coordinate defines the lower-left corner of the saved image area—by default, 0,0. You can change the location of the image in your display, that is, offset the image.

To offset a rendered image in a viewport

1 From the Tools menu, choose Display Image ➤ View.
2 In the Replay dialog box, enter a file name or select a file.
3 In the Image Specifications dialog box under Image, specify two diagonal points to crop the image size and define the area you want to display.

   AutoCAD draws a boundary box in the Image box to mark the bounds of the cropped image area and displays the reduced image in the Screen box.

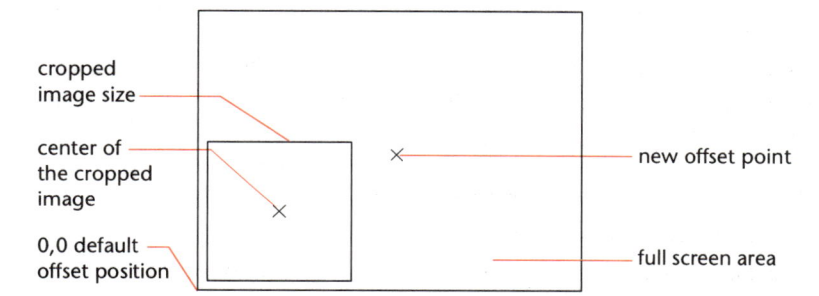

- cropped image size
- center of the cropped image
- 0,0 default offset position
- new offset point
- full screen area

4 Select a point in this box to offset the center of the image to that point.

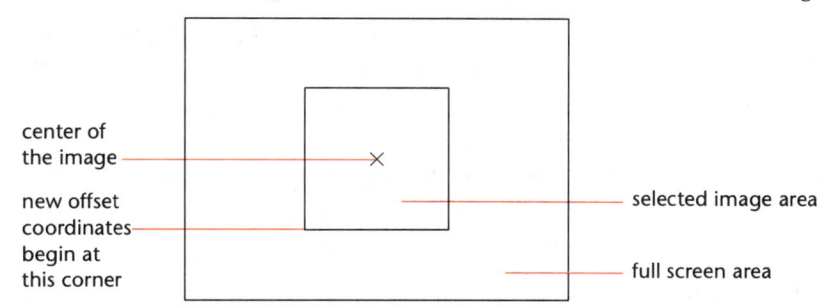

- center of the image
- new offset coordinates begin at this corner
- selected image area
- full screen area

   AutoCAD automatically redraws the image size boundaries to mark the new offset.

   You can move this boundary box in the Screen box by clicking and dragging the boundary box to the desired location inside the window.

new offset coordinates begin at this corner

center of the image

only this part of the image is displayed on the screen

full screen area

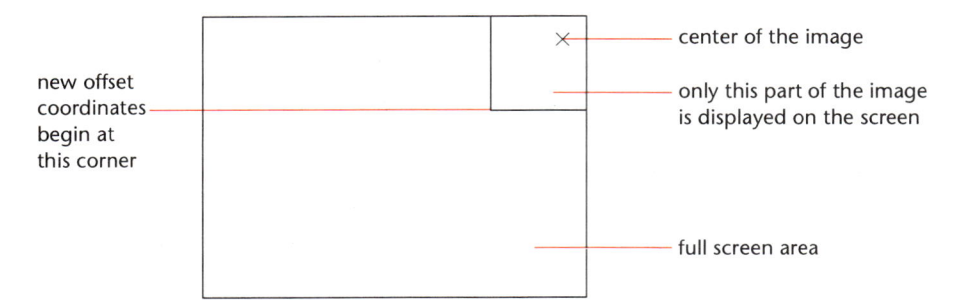

If you saved the screen image in bitmap file format, use REPLAY or choose the Open option from the Render window File menu to display the bitmap image in the Render window.

To redisplay a rendered image to the Render window

1   From the File menu, choose Open.
2   In the Select File dialog box, enter the name of the bitmap file, or select a file.
3   Choose OK.

The image is displayed on screen.

If you saved your renderings directly to a file format other than BMP, TGA, or TIFF format, see the *Installation Guide* for more information about importing those files into your drawing.

Copying Images to the Clipboard

You can copy images to the Clipboard from the Render window for use in desktop publishing and other applications.

To copy a rendered image to the Clipboard

1   Select the rendered image.
2   From the Edit menu, choose Copy.

The bitmap image is copied to the Clipboard.

To place that image in another application, you don't need to quit AutoCAD. Simply start another application, open a document, and use that application's Paste command to insert the image from the Clipboard.

Printing Rendered Images

You can print rendered images that are displayed in the Render window or in a viewport. You can also use other applications to print rendered images that you sent directly to a file.

Printing Render Window Images

You can print any displayed image to your currently configured Windows printer. To select paper size, paper orientation, and a printer, use the Windows printing controls. For more information, see your Windows documentation.

To print a Render window image

1 Make sure you've configured Windows correctly for your printer.
2 Render to the Render window.
3 From the Render window File menu, choose Print.

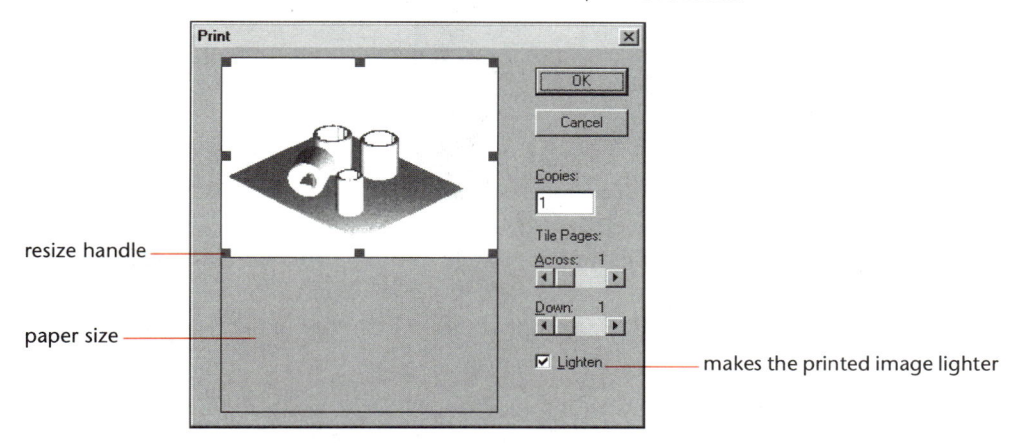

resize handle

paper size

makes the printed image lighter

A small picture of your rendered image is displayed in the Print dialog box on a representation of the paper size using the orientation (portrait or landscape) you selected.

In the Print dialog box, you can alter the image in the following ways:

- By changing the position of the image on the page.
  Click anywhere inside the image area, hold down the pick button on the pointing device, and drag the image to the desired location on the page.

- By changing the size of the image on the page using the resize handles. Move the cursor to a handle on the boundary of the image area until the cursor changes shape to a double-headed arrow. Hold down the pick button on the pointing device and drag to stretch the image to the desired size.

- By printing the image on a single page or by tiling across several pages. Use tiling to print large, poster-size images.

Select the number of tiled pages by moving the Tile Pages Across and Tile Pages Down sliders. The image is redisplayed, but the aspect ratio of the image is maintained.

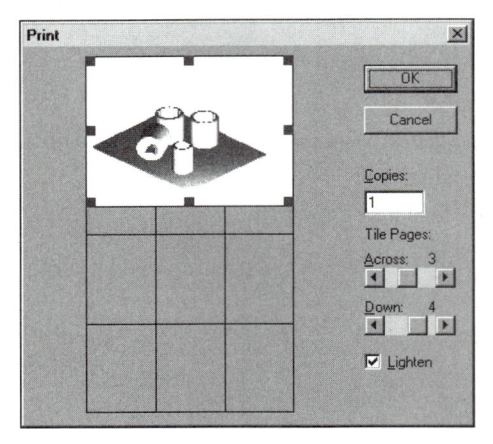

After defining the number of tiled pages, move the image and use the handles to stretch or reduce the image until it covers the number of pages you want.

4 After making your changes, choose OK to print the image.

Saving Render Window Images in PostScript Format

You can save a Render window image as a PostScript file for use in a word processing, desktop publishing, or other application by using the AutoCAD Export Data feature.

To save a rendered image as a PostScript file

1 From the View menu, choose Render ➤ Render.
2 In the Options.
3 In the File Output Configuration dialog box, select PostScript as the file type. Then choose OK.
4 In the Render dialog box, choose Render.
5 In the Rendering File dialog box, name the file and choose OK.

The image is save in PostScript format.

Printing Viewport Images

To print an image that is currently displayed in a viewport, use SAVEIMG to save the image as a BMP, TGA, or TIFF file and then print that file (see "Saving a Viewport Rendering" on page 620). To save to other file formats, you must set Rendering Destination to File in the Render dialog box or the Rendering Preferences dialog box and print directly to a file. The image is not displayed on the screen (see "Saving a Rendering Directly to a File" on page 620).

Comparing Render Window and Viewport Features

The availability of several rendering features depends on whether you are rendering to the Render window or rendering to a viewport. For example, you can save to BMP file format from a viewport or from the Render window.

The following table lists features unique to the Render window.

Render window features		
Feature	Render window menu	Description
Copy to Clipboard	Edit ➤ Copy	Copies a Render window image to the Clipboard
Save image	File ➤ Save	Saves a Render window image to bitmap format
Display saved image	File ➤ Open	Displays a bitmap format image
Print	File ➤ Print	Prints contents of the Render window to the Windows system printer

The following table lists features unique to viewports.

Viewport features		
Feature	Render toolbar or Tools menu	Description
Save image	Tools ➤ Image ➤ Save	Saves a partial or whole viewport image to BMP, TGA, or TIFF file format
Replay	Tools ➤ Image ➤ View	Redisplays an image that can be cropped and moved in the viewport

Using Render

Updating Existing Drawings

You can open a drawing containing AutoShade information, such as lights, scene blocks, and camera blocks, without any problems.

When you load AutoCAD Render, AutoCAD updates any old block information into the new AutoCAD Render block types and makes the following changes to pre–AutoCAD Release 13 Render blocks (camera, light, scene blocks) in the drawing.

Camera	Converts the information in camera blocks to named views using the camera name and deletes the camera blocks. If a view already exists with the same name, AutoCAD appends numbers automatically until the view name is unique.
Overhead, Direct, Sh_Spot	Retains the light blocks as originally inserted. The *overhead.dwg* file is the block for point lights, *direct.dwg* is the block for distant lights, and *sh_spot.dwg* is the block for spotlights.
Clapper	Deletes these blocks.
Shot	Converts the information in shot blocks to defined scenes and deletes the shot blocks.

Using Render with Related Applications

Several Autodesk products have links with the AutoCAD renderer, including 3D Studio, Advanced Modeling Extension (AME), AutoSurf, and AutoCAD Designer.

3D Studio

If you want to use AutoCAD geometry and rendering data with 3D Studio, you can export a drawing from the menu File ➤ Export (or 3DSOUT), or import a 3D Studio file from the menu Insert ➤ 3DStudio (or 3DSIN).

AME

If you have drawings that contain AME-created objects, use AMECONVERT to convert them to AutoCAD objects before using AutoCAD RENDER. You do not have to have AME running to render these objects. Attached AME material definitions are not brought into the drawing with the converted objects. Use RMAT to attach new materials to the objects.

AutoSurf and AutoCAD Designer

If you want to use AutoCAD geometry and rendering data with AutoSurf or AutoCAD Designer, you can export a drawing using File ➤ Export, or import a file using Insert ➤ Drawing Exchange Binary.

NOTE If you need to adjust surface smoothness, you can use FACETRES to control the density of the facets.

Using Render with Related Applications

Using Raster Images

15

With AutoCAD you can add raster images to your vector-based AutoCAD drawings, and then view and plot the resulting file. There are a number of reasons for combining raster images with vector files, including scanning documents, faxes, or microfilm drawings; using aerial and satellite photographs; using digital photographs; creating effects such as watermarks and logos; and adding computer-rendered images created by visualization programs like AutoVision.

In this chapter

- Attaching and scaling raster image files
- Managing image links
- Clipping images
- Controlling image brightness, contrast, and fade
- Managing image support preferences

Raster Images in Drawings

Raster images consist of a rectangular grid of small squares or dots known as pixels. For example, a photograph of a house is made up of a series of pixels colorized to represent the appearance of a house. A raster image references the pixels in a specific grid.

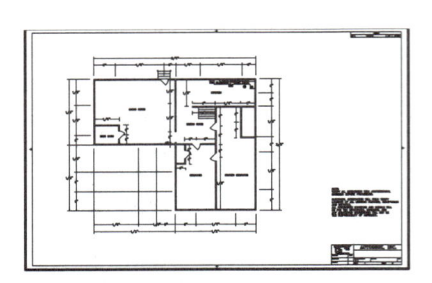

Raster images, like many other AutoCAD drawing objects, can be copied, moved, or clipped. You can modify an image with grip modes, adjust an image for contrast, clip the image with a rectangle or polygon, or use an image as a cutting edge for a trim.

The image file formats supported by AutoCAD include the most common formats used in major technical imaging application areas: computer graphics, document management, and mapping and geographic information systems (GIS). Images can be bitonal, 8-bit gray, 8-bit color, or 24-bit color.

Several image file formats support images with transparent pixels. When image transparency is set to on, AutoCAD recognizes those transparent pixels and allows graphics on the AutoCAD screen to "show through" those pixels. (In bitonal images, background pixels are treated as transparent.) Transparent images can be gray-scale or color.

Although the file extension is listed, AutoCAD determines the file format from the file contents not from the file extension.

Supported file formats		
Type	Description and versions	File extension
BMP	Windows and OS/2 bitmap format	.bmp, .dib, .rle
CALS-I	Mil-R-Raster I	.gp4, .mil, .rst, .cg4, .cal

Supported file formats (*continued*)

Type	Description and versions	File extension
GIF	CompuServe Graphics Exchange Format	.gif
JFIF		.jpg
FLIC	Animator FLIC	.flc, .fli
PCX		.pcx
PICT		.pct
PNG		.png
TARGA		.tga
TIF/LZW		.tif

Attaching and Scaling Raster Images

Images can be placed in drawings files, but, like xrefs, they are not actually part of the drawing file. The image is linked to the drawing file through a path name or a data management document ID. Linked image paths can be changed or removed at any time. By attaching images using linked image paths, you can place images in your drawing, only slightly increasing the drawing file size.

Once you've attached an image, you can reattach it multiple times treating it as if it were a block. Each insertion has its own clip boundary and its own settings for brightness, contrast, fade, and transparency. A single image can be cut into multiple pieces that can be rearranged independently in your drawing.

You can set the raster image scale factor when you attach the image so that the image's geometry scale matches the scale of the geometry created in the AutoCAD drawing. The default image scale factor is 1, and the default unit for all images is "Unitless." When you select an image to attach, the image is inserted at a scale factor of 1 image unit of measurement to 1 AutoCAD unit of measurement. To set the image scale factor, you need to know the scale of the geometry on the image, and you need to know what unit of measurement (inches, feet, and so on) you want to use to define 1 AutoCAD unit. The image file must contain resolution information defining the DPI, or dots per inch, and number of pixels in the image.

If an image has resolution information, AutoCAD combines it with the scale factor and the AutoCAD unit of measurement you supply to scale the image in your drawing. For example, if your raster image is a scanned blueprint on which the scale is 1 inch equals 50 feet or 1:600, and your AutoCAD drawing is set up so that 1 unit represents 1 inch, then in the Attach Image dialog box, you click Details and select Inches from the Current AutoCAD Unit list. To set the scale factor of the image, you then enter 600 in the Scale Factor box. AutoCAD then inserts the image at a scale that brings the geometry in the image into alignment with the vector geometry in the drawing.

NOTE If no resolution information is defined with the attached image file, the Current AutoCAD Units list is forced to Unitless. When the Units field is set to Unitless, AutoCAD calculates the image's original width to be one unit. After insertion, the image width in AutoCAD units is equal to the scale factor. If you want to dynamically scale and place the image into the drawing, set Current AutoCAD units to Unitless.

To attach and scale an image

1 From the Insert menu, choose Raster Image.

2 In the Image dialog box, choose Attach.

If the drawing contains attached images, the Image Attach dialog box is displayed. Otherwise, the Attach Image File dialog box is displayed.

3 If the drawing contains attached images, in the Image Attach dialog box, select an image from the list and choose OK, or choose Browse to select a new image.

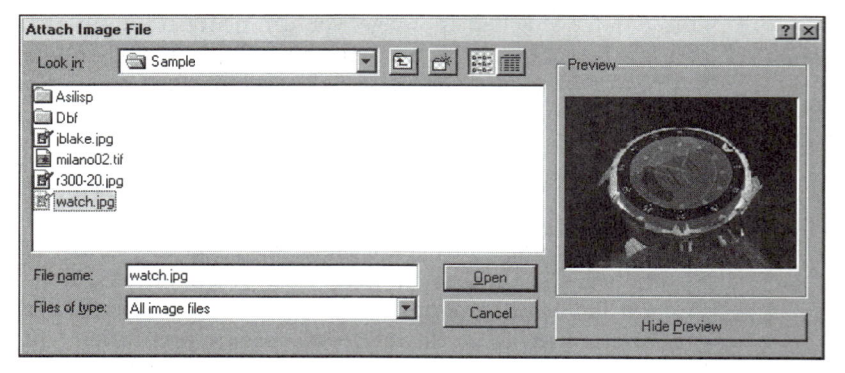

4 In the Attach Image File dialog box, select a file name from the list or enter the name of the image file in the File Name box. Then choose Open.

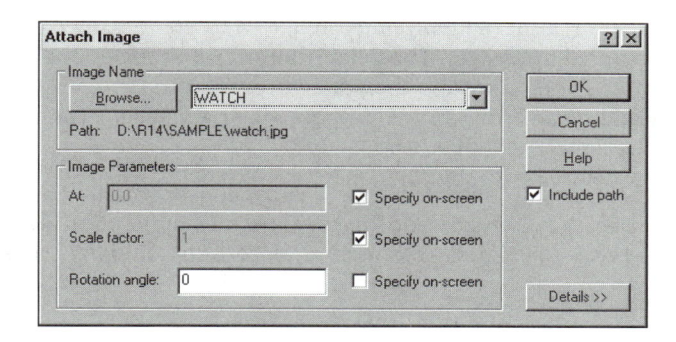

[Screenshot of Attach Image dialog box showing Image Name, Path, Image Parameters (At, Scale factor, Rotation angle) with Specify on-screen checkboxes, and Include path option.]

> **NOTE** By default, the Specify On-screen check boxes are checked for At (insertion point data) and Scale Factor. To specify the insertion point and scale factor in the dialog box, clear the check boxes, and enter values for an insertion point and scale factor in the boxes provided.

5 Choose Details to specify the unit of measurement for the scale factor.

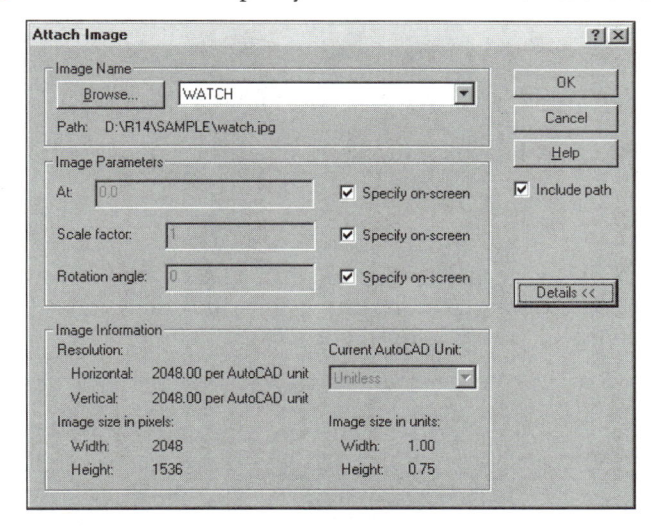

[Screenshot of expanded Attach Image dialog box showing additional Image Information section with Resolution (Horizontal: 2048.00 per AutoCAD unit, Vertical: 2048.00 per AutoCAD unit), Current AutoCAD Unit (Unitless), Image size in pixels (Width: 2048, Height: 1536), and Image size in units (Width: 1.00, Height: 0.75).]

6 Select the corresponding measurement unit from the Current AutoCAD Unit list in the Image File Details dialog box.

7 Enter a rotation angle in degrees. Then choose OK.

The default rotation angle value is 0.

8 If prompted (see previous Note), enter an insertion point and scale factor at the command line.

AutoCAD uses a special temporary image swap file to reduce the amount of RAM occupied by images. The default location of the temporary swap file that is used is the Windows *temp* directory. You can specify a different directory by adding an entry under Temporary Drawing File Location on the Files tab in the Preferences dialog box.

NOTE To specify image location, scale, or angle of rotation by dragging the image, select the corresponding Specify On-screen option. You are prompted to drag the image to the desired location, scale, or angle after the dialog box closes.

Command line   IMAGE

Related   IMAGEATTACH

Managing Raster Images

You can view image information and manage image status, names, and paths using the Image dialog box.

To view the Image dialog box

- From the Insert menu, choose Raster Image.

    The Image dialog box is displayed.

Viewing Image Information

You can view image information either as a list or a tree. To control how the information is displayed in the Image dialog box, select one of the two icons in the upper-left corner of the dialog box.

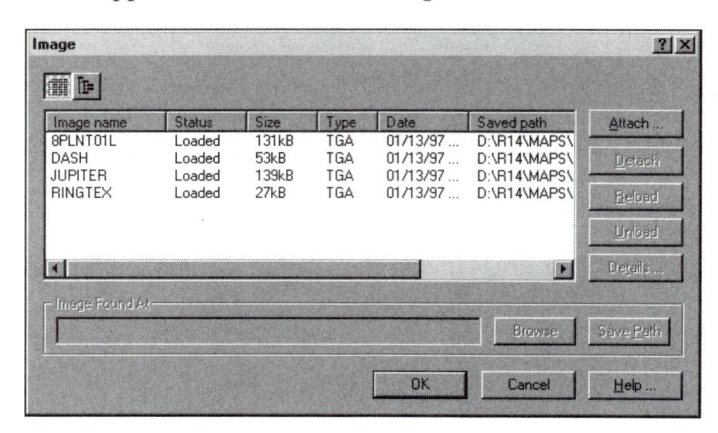

Image name	Status	Size	Type	Date	Saved path
8PLNT01L	Loaded	131kB	TGA	01/13/97 ...	D:\R14\MAPS\
DASH	Loaded	53kB	TGA	01/13/97 ...	D:\R14\MAPS\
JUPITER	Loaded	139kB	TGA	01/13/97 ...	D:\R14\MAPS\
RINGTEX	Loaded	27kB	TGA	01/13/97 ...	D:\R14\MAPS\

List View

In the List View, the columns are aligned vertically and can be sorted by column by clicking the column heading in the list box. You change the width of a column by dragging its border to the right or left. The list view displays the images attached to the current drawing, but it does not specify the number of instances. To view the number of instances, enter **–image** on the command line.

The information displayed includes

- Image name
- Image status
- Image file size
- Image file type
- Image file date and time
- Name of the saved path

If an image is not found by AutoCAD, its status is listed as Not Found. If the image is not loaded, its status is Unloaded. Images with a status of Unloaded or Not Found are not displayed in the drawing.

List View is the default.

To display a list of the images attached to the drawing

1 From the Insert menu, choose Raster Image.
2 In the Image dialog box, choose List View.

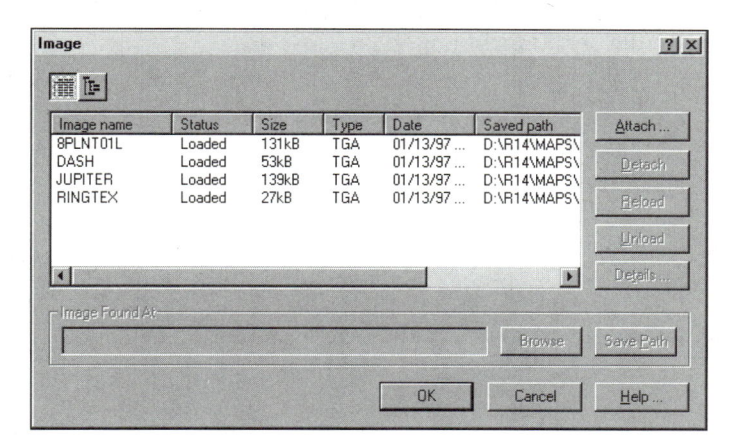

Managing Raster Images

637

Tree View

The top level of the Tree View is listed in alphabetical order. In most cases an image file is linked directly to an existing drawing and exists at the top level only. However, if an xref or a block contains a linked image, AutoCAD displays additional levels.

To display image names and their nesting levels within xrefs and blocks

1 From the Insert menu, choose Raster Image.
2 In the Image dialog box, choose Tree View.

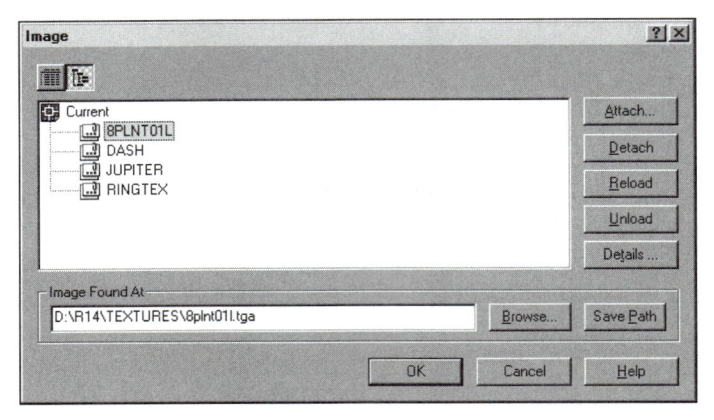

Accessing Image File Details

From the Image dialog box you can preview a selected image and access image file details including

- Image name
- Saved path
- Active path (where the image is found)
- File creation date
- File size
- File type
- Color
- Color depth
- Image size (pixel width and height, resolution and default size)

To preview an image and access attached image file details

1 From the Insert menu, choose Raster Image.
2 In the Image dialog box, select the name of the image.
3 Choose Details.

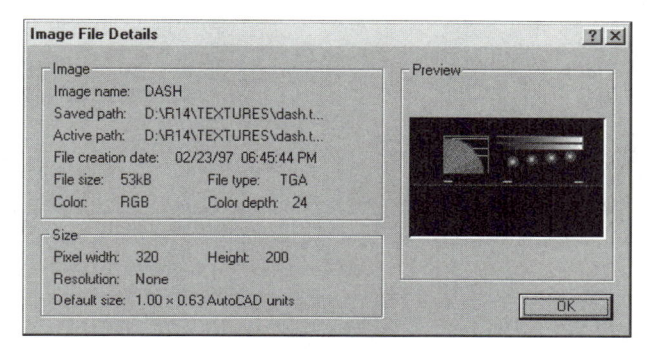

The Image File Details dialog box displays a preview of the selected image and available details of the image file. If image resolution is not saved with the image file, then the Resolution option is None.

To preview an image that has not been attached

1 From the Insert menu, choose Raster Image.
2 In the Image dialog box, choose Attach.
3 In the Attach Image File dialog box, choose an image to display a preview.
4 Select Open.
5 In the Attach Image dialog box, choose Details.

Viewing Image Information on the Command Line

You can view image information on the command line. Command line image information includes image name, image path, and the number of instances of the image attached to the drawing.

To view image information on the command line

1 At the Command prompt, enter **–image**.
2 Enter **?** (List).

The AutoCAD Text Window displays image information as a list.

Managing Raster Images

639

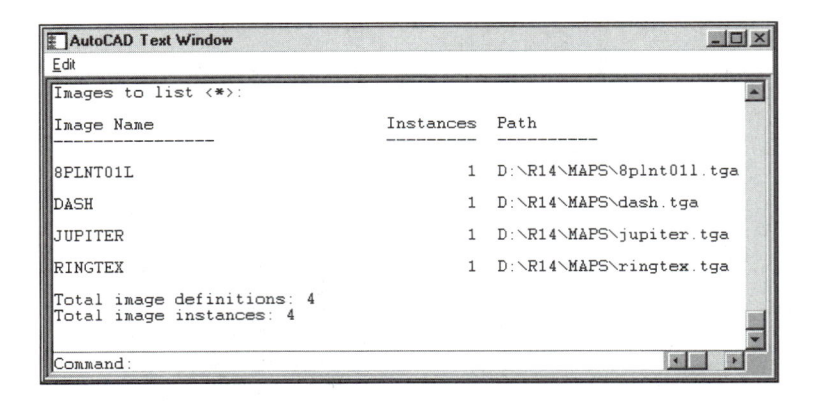

```
AutoCAD Text Window
Edit
Images to list <*>:
Image Name                          Instances  Path
----------                          ---------  ----
8PLNT01L                                1      D:\R14\MAPS\8plnt01l.tga
DASH                                    1      D:\R14\MAPS\dash.tga
JUPITER                                 1      D:\R14\MAPS\jupiter.tga
RINGTEX                                 1      D:\R14\MAPS\ringtex.tga
Total image definitions: 4
Total image instances:   4

Command:
```

Changing Image File Paths

When you open a drawing with an attached image, the path of the selected image is displayed at the bottom of the Image dialog box under Image Found At. The path displayed is the actual path where AutoCAD found the image file.

If you open a drawing that contains an image that is not in the saved path location or in any of the defined search paths, the Image dialog box displays "Not found" in the image list, and the Image Found At box is blank.

To locate the image, AutoCAD first searches the standard AutoCAD search path for the image's saved path. (For more information, see "Support File Search Path" on page 45 in the *Installation Guide*.) If AutoCAD cannot locate the drawing (for example, if you have moved the file to a different directory than the one that was saved with the image), it removes relative or absolute path information from the name (for example, \images\tree.tga or c:\my project\images\tree.tga becomes *tree.tga*) and searches the paths you have defined in the Project Files Search Path in the Preferences dialog box. If a project has been defined in the Project Files Search Path, and the PROJECT-NAME system variable has been specified (by default, it is Empty), the project name is displayed at the top of the Image dialog box. If the drawing is not located in the paths specified in the Project Files Search Path, it attempts the first search path again. If the saved path doesn't specify a file extension, all image file extensions are searched.

You can remove the path from the file name or specify a relative path by directly editing the path in the Image Found At box, and then choosing Save Path. It may be different from the current "Found at" path.

For more information about using project files and alternate search paths, see "Creating and Modifying Project Names" on page 469 and "Defining Alternate Xref Search Paths" on page 469. Also see PROJECTNAME in the *Command Reference*.

Changing the path in the Image dialog box does not affect the Project Files Search Path settings.

To change the image path

1 From the Insert menu, choose Raster Image.
2 In the Image dialog box, select an image whose path you want to change. Then choose Browse.
3 In the Attach Image File dialog box, select a new path, and then choose Open.
4 In the Image dialog box, choose Save Path to save the new path.
   The new path is displayed in the Saved Path column.
5 Choose OK.

Command line   -IMAGE Path

Naming Images

Image names are not necessarily the same as image file names. When you attach an image to a drawing, AutoCAD uses the file name without the file extension as the image name. You can change the image name without affecting the name of the file.

To change an image name

1 From the Insert menu, choose Raster Image.
2 In the Image dialog box, select the image name.
3 Select the image name again, then modify the name.
4 Choose OK.

NOTE   You can also change the image name by pressing F2 and editing the name.

Unloading and Reloading Images

You can improve performance by unloading images when you do not need them in the current drawing session. Unloaded images are not displayed or plotted; only the drawing boundary is displayed. Image links are not altered when you unload images.

In the Image dialog box, you can use Reload either to reload an unloaded image or to update a loaded image to ensure you are viewing the most recent version of the image file.

To unload or reload images

1 From the Insert menu, choose Raster Image.
2 In the Image dialog box, select the image, and then choose Unload or Reload.
   The status of the selected image changes.
3 Choose OK.
   All instances of the selected attached images are unloaded or reloaded.

   Command line   IMAGE

   Related   From the Image dialog box, select the image name and then double-click on the status to update the status from Unload to Reload, or from Loaded or Reload to Unload.

   NOTE If a drawing is closed after an image is unloaded, AutoCAD does not load the image file when the drawing is next opened; you must reload it.

   To display a specific image instance without unloading the image (and all image instances), select the image, then clear Show Image in the Modify Image dialog box. If the image was not found (for instance, if you changed the path), the status becomes Not Found when you reenter the Image dialog box.

   For more information about displaying images, see "Improving Drawing Redraw Speed" on page 584.

Detaching Images

You can detach images that are no longer needed in a drawing. When you detach an image, all instances of the image are removed from the drawing, the image definition is purged, and the link to the image is removed. The image file itself is not affected.

To detach an image

1 From the Insert menu, choose Raster Image.
2 In the Image dialog box, select the image name.
3 Choose Detach.

The image is no longer linked to the drawing file, and all instances of the image are removed from the drawing.

Command line   -IMAGE Detach

NOTE Erasing an individual instance of an image is not the same as detaching an image. An image must be detached to remove the link from your drawing to the image file.

Modifying Images and Image Boundaries

All images have an image boundary. You can select an image by clicking this boundary; clicking in the middle of an image will not select the image. You cannot use the pointing device to select an image if its boundary is not displayed. With boundaries turned off, you can still select images by layer, by object name, and so on.

When you attach an image to a drawing, the image boundary inherits the current property settings, including color, layer, linetype, and linetype scale. If the image is a bitonal image, the image color and boundary color are the same.

As with other AutoCAD objects, you can modify images and their boundary properties, including:

- Image layer, boundary color, and linetype
- Display of image boundaries
- Location
- Scale, rotation, width, and height
- Image transparency
- Image brightness, contrast, and fade
- Quality and speed of image display

Showing and Hiding Image Boundaries

You can hide image boundaries. Hiding an image boundary ensures that the image cannot accidentally be moved or modified and prevents the boundary from being plotted or displayed. When image boundaries are hidden, clipped images are still displayed to their specified boundary limits; only the boundary is affected. Showing and hiding image boundaries affects all images attached to your drawing.

image with boundaries off   *image with boundaries on*

To show and hide image boundaries

1 From the Modify menu, choose Object ➤ Image ➤ Frame.
2 To show image boundaries, enter **on**; to hide image boundaries, enter **off**.

NOTE When an image frame is turned off, you cannot select images using the Pick or Window options of SELECT.

Changing Image Layer, Boundary Color, and Linetype

You can change the color and linetype of image boundaries and the layer of an image.

To change the image layer, boundary color, or linetype

1 From the Modify menu, choose Properties.
2 Select the image to modify.
3 In the Modify Image dialog box, choose Color, Layer, or Linetype.
4 In the Select Color, Select Layer, or Select Linetype dialog box, make the changes you want.
5 To close each dialog box, choose OK.

Command line DDMODIFY

For more information about using the Modify Image dialog box, see DDMODIFY in the *Command Reference*.

Changing Image Location

You can change the location of the image by using Grip mode. To move the image to a precise location, use the Modify Image dialog box. For information about using Grip modes, see "Editing with Grips" on page 239.

To change image location

1. From the Modify menu, choose Properties.
2. Select the image to move.
3. In the Modify Image dialog box, to move the image to a precise location, enter coordinate values for *X*, *Y*, or *Z*. Choose OK.

   If you choose Pick Point, the dialog box closes, and you are prompted to use the pointing device to specify the new location for the image. When the dialog box is redisplayed, choose OK.

   Command line DDMODIFY

For more information about using the Modify Image dialog box, see DDMODIFY in the *Command Reference*.

Changing Image Scale, Rotation, Width, and Height

As with any AutoCAD drawing object, you can change image scale, rotation, width, and height.

To change image parameters

1. From the Modify menu, choose Properties.
2. Select the image to modify.
3. In the Modify Image dialog box, to change image scale, rotation, width, or height, enter a value in the appropriate box.

   Rotation is in degrees, and scale, width, and height are based on the drawing's unit of measurement.
4. Choose OK.

For more information about using the Modify Image dialog box, see DDMODIFY in the *Command Reference*.

Command line   DDMODIFY

Related   You can modify images with Grip modes. For more information on Grip modes, see "Editing with Grips" on page 239.

Modifying Bitonal Image Color and Transparency

Bitonal raster images are images consisting only of a foreground color and a background color. When you attach a bitonal image, the foreground pixels in the image inherit the current layer settings for color. In addition to the modifications you can make to any attached image, you can modify bitonal images by changing the foreground color and by turning on and off the transparency of the background.

NOTE   Bitonal images and bitonal image boundaries are always the same color.

To change the color and transparency of a bitonal image

1. From the Modify menu, choose Properties.
2. Select the image to modify.
3. In the Modify Image dialog box, to change image color, choose Color.
4. In the Select Color dialog box, specify a color and choose OK.
5. To change the background of the selected image to transparent, or from transparent to opaque, select or clear Transparency.
6. Choose OK.

To change only the transparency of a bitonal image

1. From the Modify menu, choose Object ➤ Image ➤ Transparency.
2. Select the image to modify.
3. To change the background of the selected image to transparent, or from transparent to opaque, enter **on** or **off** on the command line.
4. Choose OK.

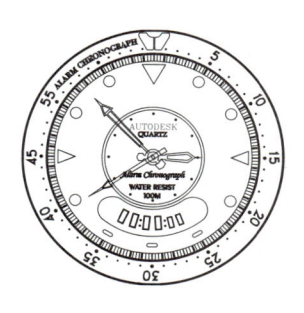

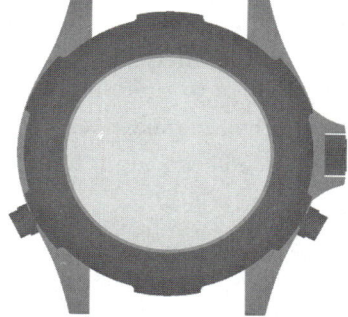

layout of a watch face drawn in AutoCAD

conceptual rendering of the watch case constructed and rendered in 3D Studio MAX

result after importing the face layout into AutoCAD, making it transparent, and then placing it over the rendering

Command line TRANSPARENCY

Adjusting Image Brightness, Contrast, and Fade

You can adjust image brightness, contrast, and fade in AutoCAD to the display of the image as well as to plotted output without affecting the original raster image file. Adjust brightness to darken or lighten an image. Adjust contrast to make poor-quality images easier to read. Adjust fade to make vectors easier to see over images, and to create a watermark effect in your plotted output.

To adjust brightness, contrast, and fade of an image

1 From the Modify menu, choose Object ➤ Image ➤ Adjust.
2 Select the image to modify.

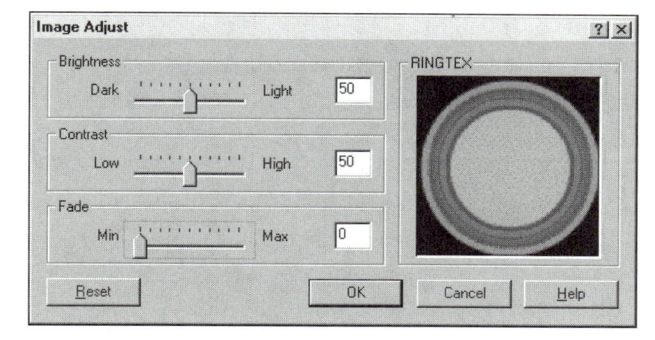

Modifying Images and Image Boundaries

647

3   In the Image Adjust dialog box, to adjust brightness or contrast, use the appropriate slider bar.

The default value for both brightness and contrast is 50. You can adjust to a maximum brightness of 100 or to a minimum of 0.

4   To adjust image fade, use the Fade slider bar.

The default fade value is 0. You can adjust to a maximum fade of 100.

5   Choose OK.

NOTE   Bitonal images *cannot* be adjusted for brightness, contrast, or fade. Images fade to the current screen background when displayed, and fade to white (the color of most paper) when plotted.

Command line   IMAGEADJUST

Related   To change the brightness, contrast, or fade values of an image, use DDMODIFY.

Changing Quality and Speed of Image Display

To increase the display speed of images, you can change image display quality from the default high quality to draft quality. Draft-quality images may appear more grainy, but they are displayed more quickly than high-quality images. Changing the image quality setting affects all images attached to your drawing.

You can also increase redrawing speed by clipping the image so that only the parts of the image you want visible are displayed. If you want to display more than one piece of the image, create additional insertions of the image, each with a different clip boundary.

To change the image display quality

1   At the Command prompt, enter **imagequality**.
2   Enter **d** (Draft) or **h** (High).

Images are displayed at the specified quality.

You can increase redrawing speed by hiding images you do not need in the current drawing session. Hidden images are not displayed or plotted; only the drawing boundary is displayed. You can choose to hide an image regardless of the current viewport coordinate system, or specifically when the image is not orthogonal (aligned) with the current viewport coordinate system.

NOTE For information about improving performance when working with drawings containing raster images, see "Unloading and Reloading Images" on page 642.

To hide or show an image

1. From the Modify menu, choose Properties.
2. Select the image to modify.
3. To hide or show the image, clear or select Show Image.

   To hide or show an image that is not orthogonal to the current viewport coordinate system, clear or select Show Non-Ortho Image.
4. Choose OK.

Related   DDMODIFY

For more information about using the Modify Image dialog box, see DDMODIFY in the *Command Reference*.

Clipping Images

You can define a region of an image for display and plotting by clipping the image. The clipping boundary can be a rectangle or a two-dimensional polygon with vertices constrained to lie within the boundaries of the image. Multiple instances of the same image can have different boundaries.

NOTE To clip an image, the image boundary must be visible. For more information, see "Showing and Hiding Image Boundaries" on page 644.

rectangular clipping boundary applied

image after clipping boundary is applied

To clip an image

1 From the Modify menu, choose Object ➤ Image Clip.
2 Select the image to clip by clicking the image boundary.
3 Enter **n** (New Boundary).
4 Enter **p** (Polygonal) or **r** (Rectangular), and then draw the boundary on the image.

If you are drawing a polygonal boundary, you are prompted to draw consecutive vertices. To finish drawing a polygon, right-click anywhere.

Command line   IMAGECLIP

Changing the Clipping Boundary

You can change the boundary of a clipped image.

To change the boundary of a clipped image

1 From the Modify menu, choose Object ➤ Image Clip.
2 Select the image to clip by clicking the image boundary.
3 Enter **n** (New Boundary), and then enter **y** (Yes) to delete the old boundary.
4 Enter **p** (Polygonal) or **r** (Rectangular), and then draw the new boundary on the image.

If you are drawing a polygonal boundary, you are prompted to draw consecutive vertices. To finish drawing a polygon, press ENTER anywhere.

Related   You can modify clipped boundaries with Grip modes. For more information, see "Editing with Grips" on page 239.

Showing and Hiding the Clipping Boundary

You can display a clipped image using the clipping boundary, or you can hide the clipping boundary and display the original image boundaries.

To show or hide the clipped portion of an image

1. From the Modify menu, choose Properties.
2. Choose the clipped image to show or hide.
3. In the Modify Image dialog box, clear or select Show Clipped Image.
4. Choose OK.

Command line   IMAGECLIP

Related   Use DDMODIFY to show or hide clipping boundaries on more than one image. For more information about using the Modify Image dialog box, see DDMODIFY in the *Command Reference*.

Deleting a Clipping Boundary

You can delete the clipped boundary of an image. When you delete a clipping boundary, the original image boundary is displayed.

To delete the boundary of a clipped image

1. From the Modify menu, choose Object ➤ Image Clip.
2. Select the clipped image with the boundary to delete.
3. Enter **d** (Delete).

The clipped image boundary is deleted, and the original image boundary is restored.

Command line   IMAGECLIP

Creating Compound Documents with OLE

16

In this chapter

- Understanding OLE terminology
- Determining the difference between linking and embedding
- Using AutoCAD information in other applications
- Using information from other applications in AutoCAD

With the OLE (object linking and embedding) Windows feature, you can copy or move information from one application to another while retaining the ability to edit the information in the original application.

You can use OLE to create compound documents containing information from two or more applications: for example, an Adobe PageMaker layout containing an AutoCAD view, a Microsoft Word document containing AutoCAD objects, or an AutoCAD drawing containing all or part of a Microsoft Excel spreadsheet.

Understanding OLE Terminology

OLE terminology can be confusing because each term has many counterparts. For clarity, this chapter uses the following terms:

- A source application is called the *server* and creates the OLE *objects* that you embed or link. Although an AutoCAD object can be used as an OLE object, the terms are not synonymous.
- A destination application is called the *container* and creates the *compound document* that accepts OLE objects created with the server.

For information about alternate OLE terminology, as well as general OLE concepts, see your Windows documentation.

Linking and Embedding

The relationship between embedding and linking is similar to that between AutoCAD INSERT and XREF. Both linking and embedding insert information from one document into another document, and with both you can edit the source information from within the compound document. Linking and embedding differ in the way they store information.

The linking function of OLE creates a reference between the source information and the compound document. Linking is a good way to use the same information in several documents, because if you change the source information, you need to update only the links in order to update the compound documents. Most container applications can be set to update links automatically.

When you link a drawing, you need to maintain access to the server application and document. If you rename or move either of them, you may need to reestablish the link.

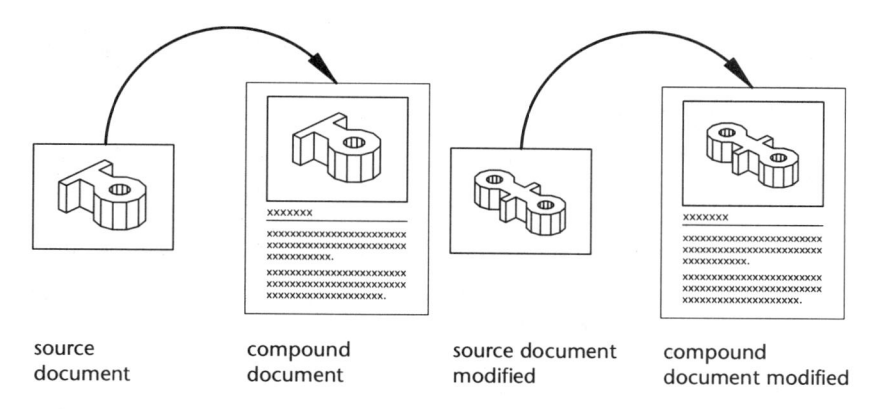

| source document | compound document | source document modified | compound document modified |

Updating of linked documents

The embedding function of OLE stores a copy of the source information in the compound document. The embedded copy is no longer associated with the original document. You still can edit embedded data in the compound document, using the application that created it, but the source document remains unaltered.

When you embed objects, there's no link to the original file. Embed objects if you do not want the source document to be updated when you edit information in the compound document.

| source document | compound document | compound document modified | source document unmodified |

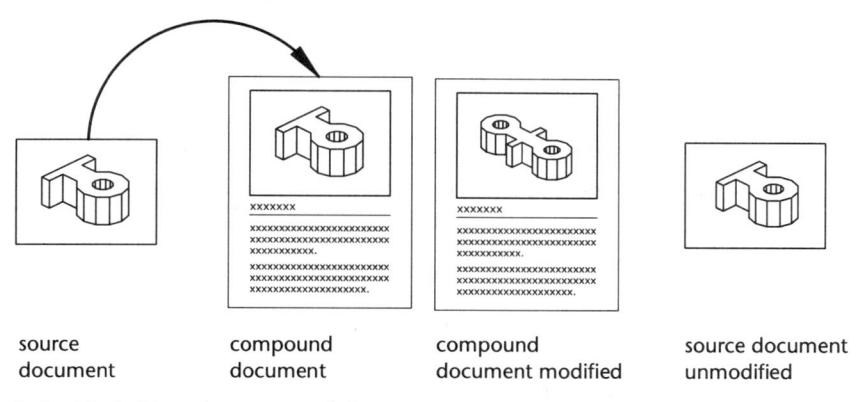

Embedded objects in compound documents

Linking and Embedding

655

Using AutoCAD Information in Other Applications

An AutoCAD drawing can be a server document with links to one or more compound documents. AutoCAD uses the following commands to export information to other applications for linking and embedding:

- COPYLINK: The Copy Link option on the Edit menu. Copies the current view to the Clipboard.
- COPYCLIP: The Copy option on the Edit menu. Copies AutoCAD objects to the Clipboard.
- CUTCLIP: The Cut option on the Edit menu. Moves AutoCAD objects to the Clipboard, removing them from the drawing.

Linking AutoCAD Views to Other Documents

The COPYLINK command copies the view in the current viewport in both model space and paper space of the AutoCAD drawing to the Clipboard. With a single viewport, AutoCAD uses the current view. You can then paste the view into a document created in another application.

To link an AutoCAD view to another document

1 Save the AutoCAD drawing you want to link.
2 If multiple viewports are displayed, click inside the viewport that contains the view you want to link.
3 From the Edit menu, choose Copy Link.

   AutoCAD copies the view to the Clipboard.
4 Start the container application and open a new or existing document.
5 Paste the Clipboard contents into the document, following the container application's instructions for inserting linked data.

   If you paste an unsaved, unnamed view into the compound document, AutoCAD assigns a view name, such as *ole1*. If you then exit the drawing, AutoCAD prompts you to save your changes to the newly named view. You must save the drawing to establish the link and to save the view name *ole1*.

Editing Linked Views

The compound document stores a reference or link that identifies the AutoCAD drawing file's location. You can edit a linked drawing both in the compound document and in AutoCAD. AutoCAD must be loaded on the system containing the compound document you're editing.

When you double-click a linked object and AutoCAD is operating, the image in the compound document is displayed with diagonal lines through it. This indicates that the active image is the one in AutoCAD.

To edit a linked drawing in the compound document

1. Open the document that contains the linked AutoCAD drawing (for example, a Microsoft Word file).
2. Double-click the linked drawing.

    The drawing opens in AutoCAD.
3. Modify the drawing as necessary.
4. From the AutoCAD File menu, choose Save to save the changes to the original drawing.
5. From the AutoCAD File menu, choose Exit to return to the compound document.

To edit a linked drawing in AutoCAD

1. Start AutoCAD and open the linked drawing.
2. Modify the drawing and view as necessary.
3. From the AutoCAD File menu, choose Save to save the changes to the drawing in AutoCAD.
4. Update the link in the compound document if necessary. How the link is updated in the compound document depends on the application the document was created in. Some applications support automatic updating of links; others require you to update the links manually.

Embedding AutoCAD Objects in Other Documents

You can select AutoCAD objects and embed them in other documents. Embedding places a copy of the objects in the compound document. However, editing the objects in the compound document does not update the objects in the original AutoCAD drawing.

To embed AutoCAD objects in another document

1. Select the objects you want to embed.
2. From the Edit menu, choose Copy.

   The selected objects are copied to the Clipboard.
3. Start the container application, and open a new or existing document.
4. Paste the Clipboard contents into the document, following the container application's instructions for inserting embedded data.

   You edit embedded AutoCAD objects by selecting them from within the compound document. For example, AutoCAD objects might be embedded in a report created by a word processor.

To edit embedded AutoCAD objects

1. Open the document that contains the embedded AutoCAD objects (for example, a Microsoft Word file).
2. Double-click the embedded objects to start AutoCAD and display the objects.
3. Modify the objects as necessary.
4. From the AutoCAD File menu, choose Update to save changes to the embedded objects.
5. From the AutoCAD File menu, choose Exit to close AutoCAD.

Using Information from Other Applications in AutoCAD

You can link or embed information from a server document to an AutoCAD drawing, which serves as the compound document. For example, you might want to insert a schedule that you can update periodically or a company logo that was created with another application. You also can install multimedia icons that are activated by double-clicking.

AutoCAD uses the following commands to link and embed information from other applications:

- OLELINKS: The Links option on the Insert menu. Updates, modifies, and cancels existing links. Specifies whether links are updated automatically.
- INSERTOBJ: The Insert OLE Object option on the Insert menu. Imports objects to be linked and embedded from within an AutoCAD drawing.

- PASTECLIP: The Paste option on the Edit menu. Inserts data from the Clipboard into an AutoCAD drawing.
- PASTESPEC: The Paste Special option on the Edit menu. Inserts data from the Clipboard and controls the format of the data.

Dragging Objects into AutoCAD

drag-and-drop cursor

You can drag selected data and graphics into AutoCAD from another active application window. Both AutoCAD and the other application must be running and visible on your screen. The other application must also support ActiveX to drag-and-drop information between applications. Objects dragged into AutoCAD are embedded, not linked.

Dragging data is the same as cutting and pasting. The data is *permanently* removed from the server document and pasted into the compound document. Pressing CTRL while dragging is the same as copying and pasting: it creates a copy in the compound document and leaves the original intact.

Linking Information to AutoCAD Drawings

You can link data to an AutoCAD drawing with the PASTESPEC command. You can also use INSERTOBJ to link an entire server file to a drawing from within AutoCAD.

To link objects to an AutoCAD drawing

1. Start the server application and open a new or existing document.
2. Select the data you want to link and copy it to the Clipboard.
3. Open the AutoCAD drawing.
4. From the AutoCAD Edit menu, choose Paste Special.

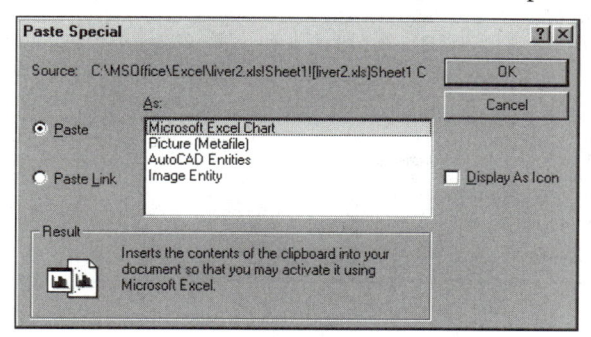

5. In the As list, select the data format you want to use. Picture uses a metafile format, primarily vector graphics.

Using Information from Other Applications in AutoCAD

659

6 Choose Paste Link to paste the contents of the Clipboard into the current drawing and to create a link to the original file. (If you choose Paste, the Clipboard contents will be embedded instead of linked.)

7 Choose OK.

You can also use the INSERTOBJ command to link an entire file to a drawing from within AutoCAD.

To link a server file starting from within AutoCAD

1 Open the AutoCAD drawing.
2 From the AutoCAD Insert menu, choose OLE Object.
3 In the Insert Object dialog box, select Create from File.

The contents of the dialog box change so that you can select a server file.

4 Check Link and choose Browse.
5 In the Browse dialog box, select the file you want to link and choose OK.
6 In the Insert Object dialog box, choose OK.

Updating Links

You can set AutoCAD to update links either automatically or manually when information in the server document changes. By default, AutoCAD updates links automatically. Use the AutoCAD OLELINKS command to change this setting.

To update a link manually

1 From the Edit Menu, choose OLE Links.

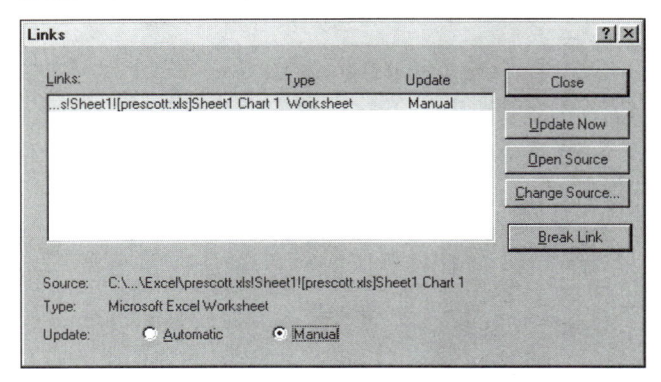

2 In the Links dialog box, select the link you want to update.
3 Select Update Now.
4 Choose Close.

Reconnecting Links

Because a link references the location of the server information, you need to reconnect the link if the server file location changes or is renamed. You also reconnect links when you need to substitute new information or objects containing links.

To change links

1 In the AutoCAD drawing, select the linked object you want to update.
2 From the Edit menu, choose OLE Links.
3 In the Links dialog box, choose Change Source.

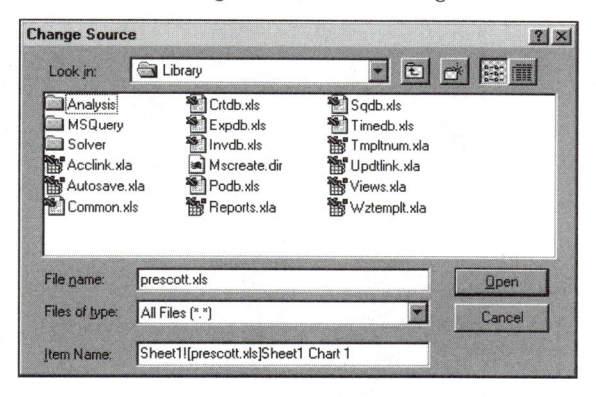

4 In the Change Source dialog box, search the directories to find the file name or file location.
5 Select the server file and choose OK.

If you select a file without a link, AutoCAD tries to find the file. If the file did not originate in the same application, or if the application can't find the named object, the link will fail.

6 Choose OK.

Breaking Links

Breaking a link does not remove the inserted information from the AutoCAD drawing. Instead, it removes the *connection* to the server document. You can break a link when you no longer need it.

To break a link

1 Select the information whose link you want to break.
2 From the Edit menu, choose OLE Links.
3 In the Links dialog box, choose Break Link.
4 Choose OK.

Embedding Objects in AutoCAD Drawings

You can embed an object in an AutoCAD drawing by pasting the contents of the Clipboard. Most non-AutoCAD objects are pasted in as embedded OLE objects. ASCII text is pasted in as an AutoCAD MTEXT object.

To embed an existing object in an AutoCAD drawing

1 Start the server application and open a new or existing document.
2 Select the data you want and copy it to the Clipboard.
3 Open the AutoCAD drawing.
4 From the AutoCAD Edit menu, choose Paste.

Command line   PASTECLIP

Related   You can also use the AutoCAD INSERTOBJ command to open the server application from within AutoCAD and create or select the information.

To create and embed an object starting from AutoCAD

1 Open the AutoCAD drawing.
2 From the Insert menu, choose OLE Object.

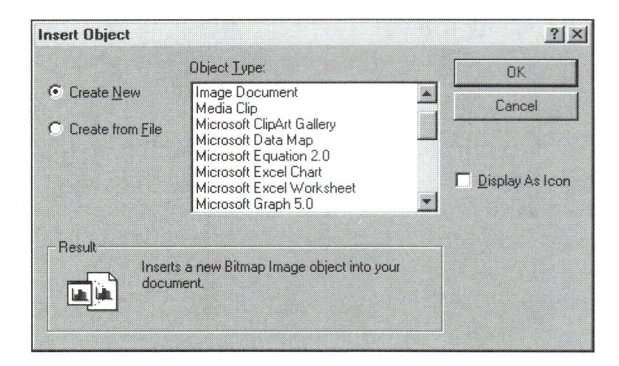

Chapter 16 Creating Compound Documents with OLE

3 In the Insert Object dialog box, under Object Type, select the application you want to use from the list of applications on your computer that support linking and embedding. Then choose OK.

The application opens.

4 Create the information you want to insert, and save a copy of the document in the server application.

5 From the server application's File menu, choose Update.

6 Close the application.

The object is inserted in the AutoCAD drawing.

You can edit information embedded in an AutoCAD drawing by opening the server application from within AutoCAD.

To edit an object embedded in AutoCAD

1 From within AutoCAD, do one of the following to open the object in its own application.

- Double-click the object.
- Move the cursor over the object frame until the move cursor appears (four arrows). Then right-click the pointing device to display the cursor menu.

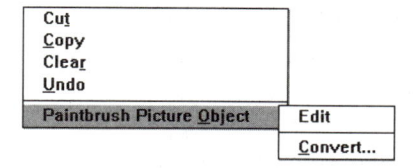

```
Cut
Copy
Clear
Undo
Paintbrush Picture Object    Edit
                             Convert...
```

Choose Object (this option name changes to reflect the type of object you select) and then Edit.

The application that created the object opens.

2 Modify the object as needed.

3 From the server application's File menu, choose Update to save changes to the object embedded in the AutoCAD drawing.

Using Information from Other Applications in AutoCAD

663

Working with OLE Objects

AutoCAD commands and snap modes generally do not work with OLE objects. However, you can resize and scale those OLE objects using the pointing device.

You can cut, copy, or clear an OLE object using the cursor menu that opens when you right-click the pointing device on an OLE object. You can also use the cursor menu to control the drawing order, display, and selection of OLE objects.

To stretch or scale an OLE object

1 Select the object.
2 Drag a sizing handle to change the size of the object.

- Dragging a middle handle stretches the object in one direction.
- Dragging a corner handle scales the object proportionately, maintaining the width-to-height ratio.

To restore an OLE object to its original size

1 Right-click the OLE object.
2 From the cursor menu, choose Cut.
3 Use the Object Properties toolbar or LAYER command to change the current layer.
4 From the Edit menu, choose Paste.

The OLE object is pasted back into the drawing at its original size.

To move an OLE object

1 Move the cursor over the object frame until the move cursor appears.
2 Drag the OLE object to the new location.

To cut, copy, or clear an OLE object

1 Select the embedded object. Right-click the pointing device.
2 From the cursor menu, choose the option you want to use.

- Cut permanently removes the object from the drawing and places it on the Clipboard.
- Copy places a copy of the object on the Clipboard.
- Clear removes the object from the drawing without placing it on the Clipboard.

- Object (this option name changes to reflect the type of object you select) displays the Edit and Convert options. Edit opens the object in its original server application. Convert displays the Convert dialog box, in which you can convert objects.
- Undo cancels the last action.

For information about copying, cutting, and pasting images using the Clipboard, see chapter 7, "Editing Methods."

You can control the display of OLE objects in both paper space and model space.

To move OLE objects behind or in front of AutoCAD objects

1 Move the cursor over the object frame until the move cursor appears. Then right-click the pointing device.
2 From the cursor menu, select Bring to Front or Send to Back, as applicable.

Clicking inside an OLE object selects it, even when the OLE object is behind an AutoCAD object. To select the AutoCAD object, you need to suppress the selection of the OLE object.

To change the layer of an OLE object

1 Right-click the OLE object.
2 From the cursor menu, choose Cut.
3 Use the Object Properties toobar or LAYER command to change the current layer.
4 From the Edit menu, choose Paste.

The OLE object is pasted into the new layer, reverting to its original size.

To control the display of OLE objects

1 At the Command prompt, enter **ole hide**.
2 Enter one of the following values:

   0—displays OLE objects in both paper space and model space

   1—displays OLE objects in paper space only

   2—displays OLE objects in model space only

   3—does not display OLE objects

OLEHIDE affects both display and plotting.

You can control whether OLE objects are displayed and printed behind or in front of AutoCAD objects.

Using Information from Other Applications in AutoCAD

665

To turn off selection of an OLE object

1. Move the cursor over the object frame until the move cursor appears.
2. From the cursor menu, choose Selectable.

Selectable is a toggle that turns selection of the OLE object on and off.

Limitations of OLE Objects in AutoCAD

OLE objects in AutoCAD are subject to the following limitations:

- They are not displayed or plotted in inserted blocks and drawings.
- They are not displayed or plotted in externally referenced drawings.
- They are not displayed or plotted in versions of AutoCAD running on platforms other than Windows.
- In most cases, they are not plotted on plotters driven by non-Windows drivers. They appear on the screen but print only on Windows system printers. Configure your plotter to be the system printer.
- On Windows system printers, they do not respond to changes in PLOT rotation. Use the system printer's landscape mode instead.
- Excel spreadsheets pasted into AutoCAD use only the Picture (metafile) format. If a spreadsheet is too large, only part of it is pasted into the drawing.

Accessing External Databases

In this chapter

- Connecting to existing databases
- Accessing data without using SQL
- Associating database rows with AutoCAD objects
- Creating text objects from database rows
- Selecting objects using nongraphic search criteria
- Exporting associated data
- Accessing external data with SQL

Using external databases to store nongraphic attributes for objects can reduce the size of drawings, simplify reporting, and enable you to edit external data.

AutoCAD can associate, or link, nongraphic attributes stored in external database programs such as dBASE III, ORACLE, and Microsoft Access (using ODBC) with graphic objects in your AutoCAD drawing. You can use all of the external database feature without prior knowledge of databases or query languages. However, it is helpful to be familiar with the standard structured query language ANSI SQL.

Connecting to Existing Databases

When you install AutoCAD and select Full installation, or choose External Databases after selecting Custom installation, AutoCAD will be installed and configured for connecting to the sample database. For information on installing the External Database Configuration utility, see chapter 9, "Accessing External Databases," in the *Installation Guide*. You can also connect AutoCAD to the sample database during an AutoCAD session. If you want to access either the ORACLE or ODBC databases using the supplied DBMS drivers, run the configuration program by double-clicking the External Database Configuration icon in the AutoCAD program folder.

All procedures in this chapter are based on the sample dBASE III driver, environment, and database tables that are installed with AutoCAD and configured by the External Database Configuration utility. If you are not connected to the dBASE III database, use the following procedure. When you have completed the procedure, you will be connected to a database, catalog, schema, and table.

To connect to dBASE III

1 From the Tools menu, choose External Database ➤ Administration.

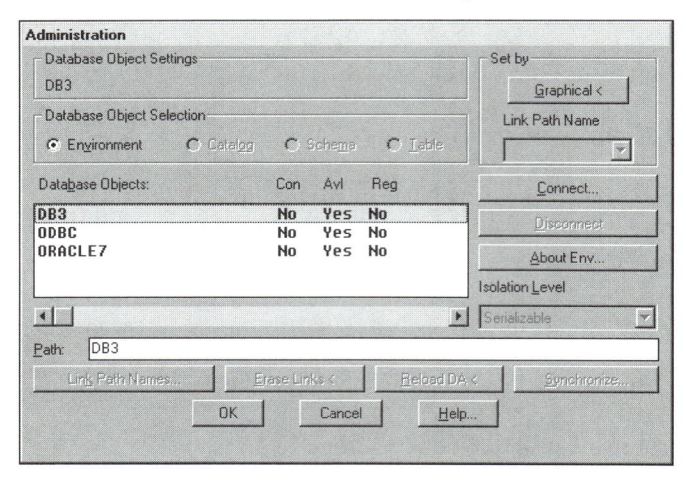

2 In the Administration dialog box under Database Objects, select DB3 to turn on the Environment database object. Then choose Connect.

NOTE You can have more than one environment connected to the same database driver. In this example, the environment name associated with the dBASE III driver is DB3.

3   In the Connect to Environment dialog box, choose OK (User Name and Password are *not* required).

    The External Database Configuration utility specifies the default catalog and default schema, and Table automatically becomes the current database object. If the default catalog and schema have not been specified, follow the remaining steps.

4   In the Administration dialog box under Database Object Selection, select Catalog.

5   Select ASE in the Database Objects list to make it current.

6   Repeat steps 4 and 5, but instead of selecting Catalog, select Schema and then Table. Then double-click an entry in the Database Objects list.

    At this point you have connected AutoCAD to a database table using the default catalog and schema, and you are able to view data in your external databases from within AutoCAD. For information on connecting to other databases, see the External Database Configuration utility's online help.

    You can dynamically add and remove catalogs and schema using the External Database Configuration utility. The database objects are cached. To make them available, you must select a different environment, and then select the original environment. This action updates the cache. However, when you add or remove environments using the External Database Configuration utility, the changes are not made available to the external database commands—ASEADMIN, ASEROWS, ASELINKS, ASESELECT, ASEEXPORT, and ASESQLED—until you unload and reload the external database command set. You can unload them at the Command prompt by entering

    arx u ase

    and then reload them by issuing any external database command.

Accessing Databases from AutoCAD

Once you are connected to the external database, you can access its data by using the external database command set. You can change the current database object selection by using any of the external database commands.

Viewing External Data

All operations that require selecting a row are accessible from the ASEROWS command. Some operations change only the database and have no effect on the drawing. These operations include viewing a row, adding a row, deleting a row, or changing the values of the data, and creating selection sets. Other operations affect the drawing directly by changing the graphic information or by adding links to the drawing database.

Before you can use database data, you need to set the cursor state and specify whether data can be modified. The cursor state determines the accessibility of table rows that belong to the set. The cursor is a mechanism that identifies the current position in the table for a set of rows that meet a query condition. In AutoCAD, the cursor has one of three states: scrollable, updatable, or read-only. With a scrollable cursor, you can navigate the rows in a forward or backward direction. With updatable and read-only cursors, the cursor moves only in the forward direction. You cannot update read-only rows, but you can use the SQL UPDATE command on updatable rows. For more information, see ASESQLED in the *Command Reference*.

To determine whether the driver in use supports updatable cursors

1 From the Tools menu, choose External Database ➤ Administration.
2 In the Administration dialog box under Database Objects, select an environment name from the list of database objects. Then choose Connect.
3 In the Connect to Environment dialog box, enter your login name and password, if required.
4 Choose About Env.
5 Scroll down the list until the following lines are displayed in the Capabilities list.

- Delete: positioned
- Update: positioned

A *yes* or *no* in the right-hand column indicates whether updatable cursors are supported by the driver. Each ODBC driver has its own set of capabilities.

You can operate on only one row at a time. The row you select for manipulating is the *current* row. The simplest way to make a row current is to select all rows (this is equivalent to SELECT * FROM <current table> in SQL) and then locate a particular row using the First, Last, Next, and Previous options for scanning the table. Another way is to use a key to search for a row or rows using an SQL WHERE clause. You can also select a row graphically by selecting the object it is linked to.

To view a table row

1 Make sure you are connected to an environment as described in "Connecting to Existing Databases" on page 668.

2 From the Tools menu, choose External Database ➤ Rows.

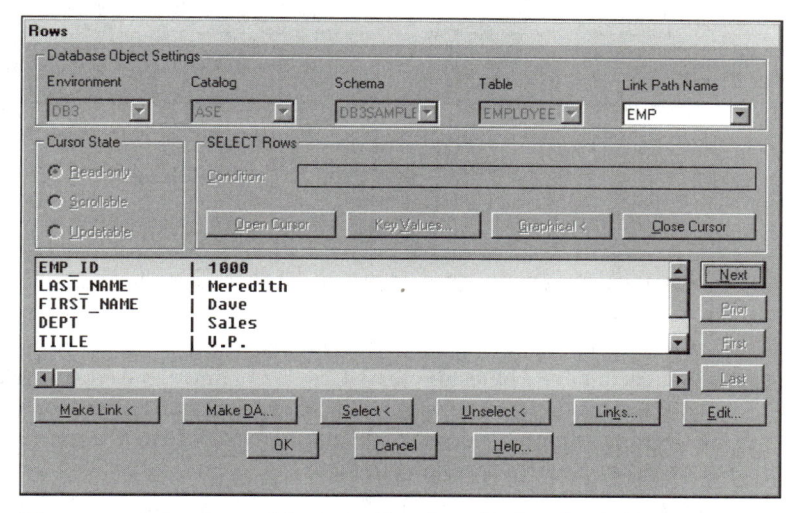

The current database objects are listed under Database Object Settings. In the lists, select the database objects you want to edit.

3 In the Rows dialog box under Database Object Settings, select INVENTRY from the Table list.

4 Under Cursor State, select Read-Only so that the data is not modifiable.

5 Under SELECT Rows, enter condition **mfr='Baby bell'**.

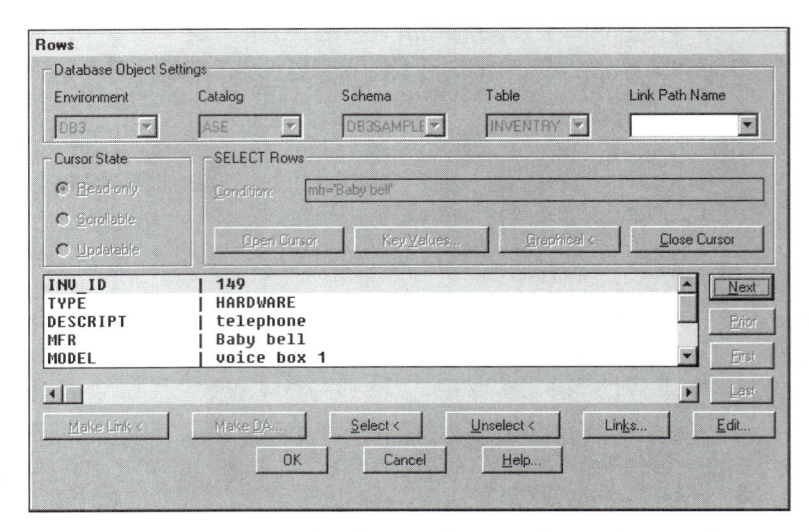

6 Use the Next key to view the data, and notice that only rows that match the condition you specified are selected.

Command line ASEROWS

Viewing and Accessing New Databases Dynamically

If a new database object is created, such as a new table created with a CREATE TABLE statement from the SQL Editor or from another user or application on a network, that table or other database object will *not* be immediately visible in the lists in the ASE dialog boxes.

To view or access the new database object, you must select a different superior database object, and then select the new database object. Selecting the new database object adds it to the database objects list. For example, if your current database object settings are DB3.CAT.SCH.TABLE1 and a new TABLE2 was just added to the SCH schema, you should choose a different schema, catalog, or environment. The new table will be contained in the lists the next time they are viewed. If only one schema, catalog, and environment are contained in the lists, disconnect and reconnect to the environment.

You can also set an environment by

- Using Set By in the Administration dialog box; you select the database object by selecting the AutoCAD object linked to it
- Using Path in the Administration dialog box, when Catalog and Schema are turned off (the current driver does not support catalog and schema)

Modifying External Data

The data in your database is likely to require updating eventually. For example, a database containing an EMPLOYEE table might contain the names of employees whose addresses have changed. To edit information in the table, first choose the row that contains the data. Then, make that the current row. In the AutoCAD user interface, the current row is the one that appears on the screen or in a list box.

To edit a table row

1 From the Tools menu, choose External Database ➤ Rows.

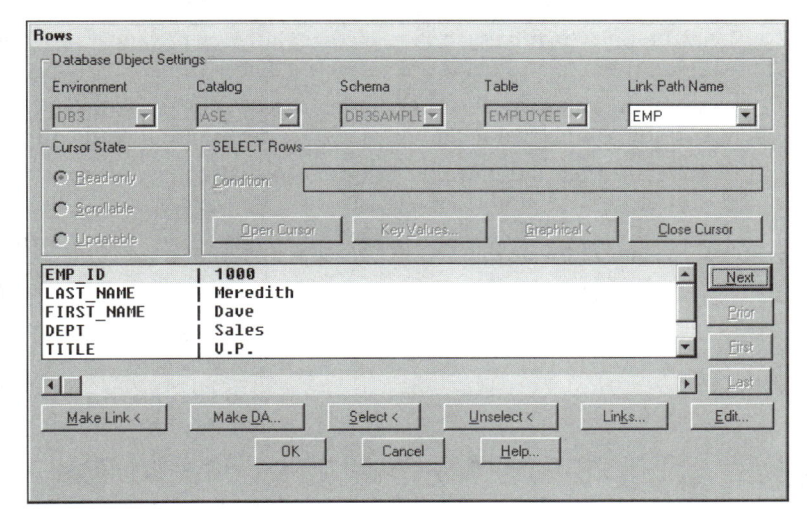

2 In the Rows dialog box, the current database objects are listed under Database Object Settings. In the lists, select the database objects you want to edit.

3 Under Cursor State, select Updatable so that all rows are accessible and modifiable.

4 Under SELECT Rows, select Open Cursor to select all rows in the table.

Accessing Databases from AutoCAD

673

5   Use the Next, Prior, First, and Last options alongside the box to scroll through the list of table rows. Select a row to practice on. You can cancel your changes after you make them.

6   Choose Edit.

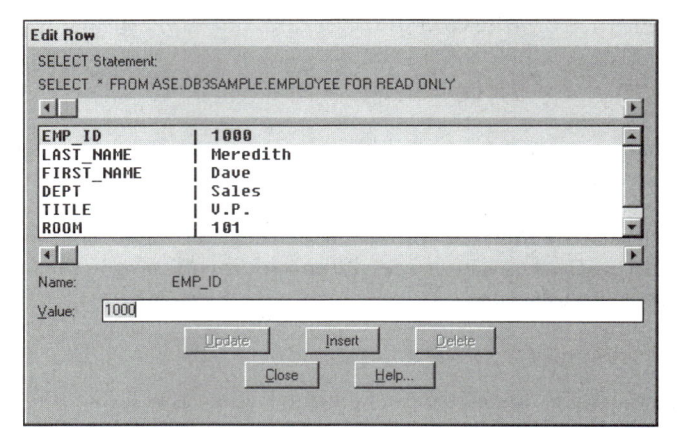

7   In the Edit Row dialog box, select a column name and value in the list. The column name and value are displayed below the list.

8   Select the value in the box and enter a new value. Pressing ENTER updates the current column value and displays the next column value in the Value box.

9   To retain the original value, choose Close. If you want to save the change, choose Update, and then choose Close.

Command line   ASEROWS

You can also change the database by deleting rows from the table. For example, if an employee leaves the company, you can delete the relevant personnel information.

To delete a row from a table

1   From the Tools menu, choose External Database ➤ Rows.

2   In the Rows dialog box under Cursor State, select Updatable so that all rows are accessible and modifiable.

3   Under SELECT Rows, choose Open Cursor.

4   Choose Edit.

5 In the Edit Rows dialog box, choose Delete.

In the Confirm dialog box, choose Cancel to cancel the delete operation. Then choose Close.

6 Choose OK to close the Rows dialog box.

You can make changes to the database by adding rows to the table. For example, when a new employee joins the company, you can add information about the employee—name, room, extension, and so on—to the database.

To add a row to a table

1 From the Tools menu, choose External Database ➤ Rows.
2 In the Rows dialog box, under Cursor State, select Scrollable so that all rows can be navigated in both directions.
3 Choose Edit.
4 The Edit Row dialog box is displayed. Because a cursor was not opened, no values appear next to their column names in the list. The column name is displayed below the list. A period (.) indicating a null value appears in the Value box.
5 Select a column in the list.
6 In the Value box, select the period and enter a new value. Pressing ENTER updates the current column value and displays the next column value (a period for null) in the Value box.
7 Repeat step 5 for each column in the table.
8 If you want to insert the row, choose Insert. Then choose Close.

Related You can add a row by first editing the fields in an existing row. Follow steps 1 through 7 for the procedure "To edit a table row" on page 673, but choose Insert instead of Update in step 8.

To complete any of the remaining procedures in this chapter, you must first set up your environment using ASEADMIN.

Associating Database Rows with AutoCAD Objects

In addition to setting up the database objects in your environment, you also need to define key columns and set link paths.

Defining Key Columns

When you link an AutoCAD object with data in an external database, you specify the row or rows in the database table by using a key. The key specifies a column or set of columns in the table and a value against which the column values are matched. A key is used to search for and select specific information in the database. For example, in the sample table below, if the key column is Inv_ID and a value of 173 is specified, the Inv_ID column of the table must have a value of 173 to match. The key identifies one or more database rows to attach to the object.

Inventory table						
INV_ID	TYPE	DESCRIPT	MFR	PRICE	ROOM	EMP_ID
1	furniture	6x3 couch	FutonsRu	800	101	1000
119	furniture	file cabinet	MetalWork	35	118	1024
173	hardware	telephone	Baby Bell	150	118	1024

A unique key is one that matches only one row in a table. A key that is not unique can identify more than one row in a table. The uniqueness of a key depends upon the data in the table.

A compound key consists of more than one column, for example, Type = furniture and Price = 800. A compound key does not guarantee a unique key.

A unique compound key is a key that is based on more than one column and that locates only one row in the table. For example, two rows in the previous inventory table both contain the Type column value furniture. In the first row, the value for a second column called Room is 101. In the second row, the value for the same column is 118.

If you search for the Type column value furniture with a key based on Type only, the query retrieves two rows; the first has a value for Room of 101, the second a Room value of 118. If, however, you search using a compound key based on both Inv_ID and Rooms the query retrieves the first row encountered (because you created a unique compound key).

In the preceding example, a query would have returned only the first row if both rows had a Type of furniture and a Room of 101. You must be familiar with the data in the table to determine which columns to use for creating a unique key.

Setting Link Paths

A link path identifies the database object hierarchy: *environment.catalog.schema.table*. A link path name specifies key columns for the current table identified by its link path. You might register it by selecting LAST_NAME and FIRST_NAME as the key columns. A link path name is used to distinguish between multiple instances of a registered table. A link path name is an alias for the link path. It is recommended that key values and link path names be determined by their relevance to a particular project and that all drawings use the same scheme so that they can be used together.

In the following example, the link path name is DB3.CAT.SCH.Employee (Employee_Name).

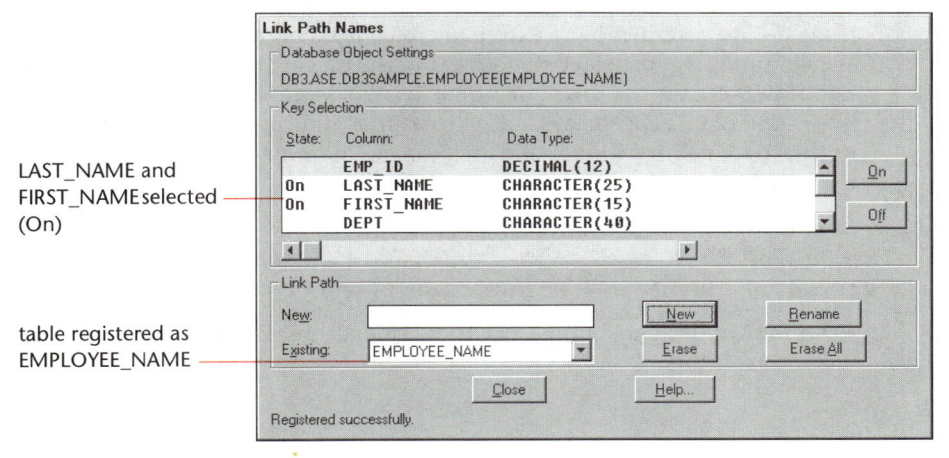

LAST_NAME and FIRST_NAME selected (On)

table registered as EMPLOYEE_NAME

In the following example, the link path name is DB3.ASE.DB3SAMPLE.EMPLOYEE (EMPLOYEE_NAME).

Associating Database Rows with AutoCAD Objects

677

LAST_NAME and TITLE selected (On) —

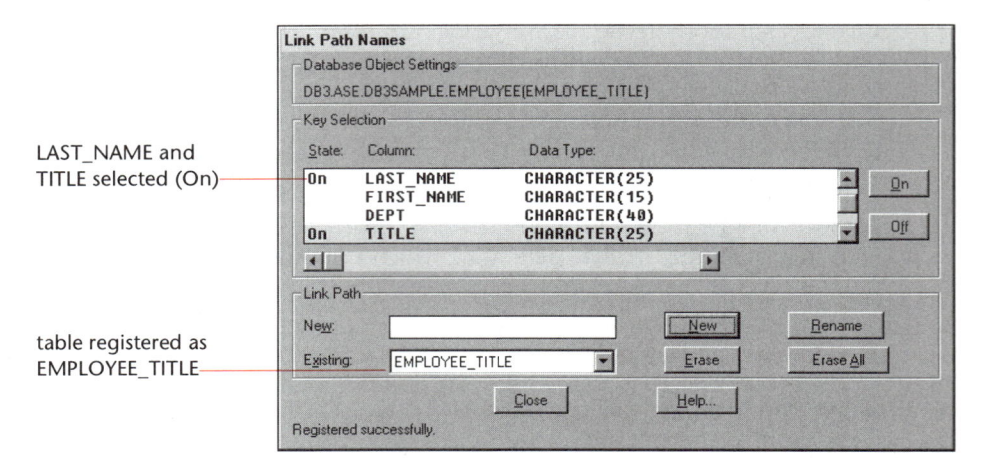

table registered as EMPLOYEE_TITLE —

The same link path name can be used in multiple drawings. It can define the same link path, or it can define different link paths.

For example, if in a block the name for the link path having LAST_NAME and ROOM as key columns is EMPLOYEE_NAME instead of EMPLOYEE_LOCATION, and that block is imported into a drawing with links to EMPLOYEE_NAME, all links in the block would be discarded. To avoid losing any link information, you should give unique link path names to the block before it is included in the drawing.

If the link path resides in an externally referenced drawing and has the same key columns, it is considered identical to the link path in the current drawing. However, if it has the same link path name and different key column information, it is considered a duplicate. To avoid confusion with the same link path name in the main drawing, the link path name is given a prefix of the attached drawing name.

Next you define a link path name by selecting key columns.

To set up link path names and register tables

1   From the Tools menu, choose External Database ➤ Administration.

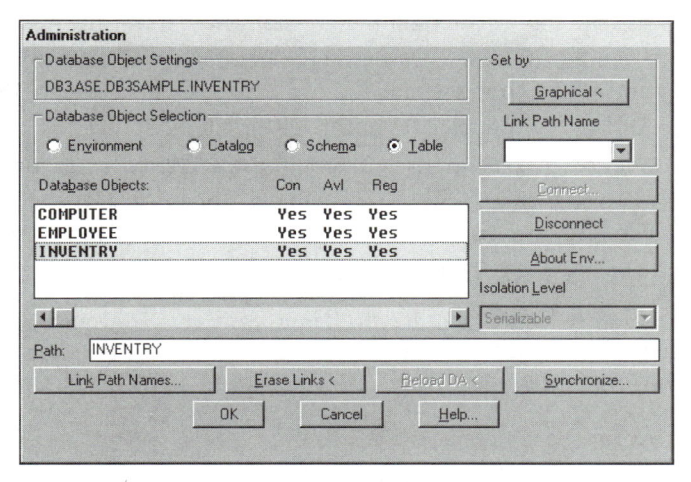

2 Make sure you are connected to a database driver and that a default catalog and schema have been specified for the tables you want to access.

3 From the list of Database Objects, select an environment, catalog, schema and table.

4 In the Administration dialog box, select Link Path Names so that you can define key columns for the current table.

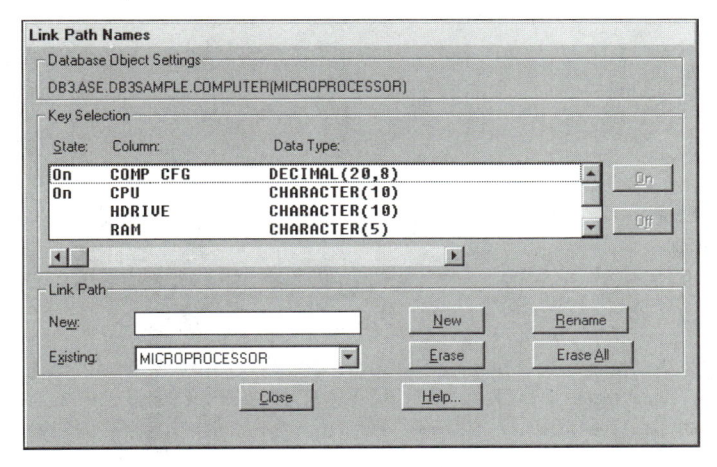

5 In the Link Path Names dialog box, select a column that will be part of the link path for the table. Then choose On.

Associating Database Rows with AutoCAD Objects

679

6   Repeat step 3 for each column you want in the link path.

7   Under Link Path, enter a new link path name for the selected column or columns. Then choose New.

The link path name appears in the Existing box.

8   Choose Close. Then choose OK to end the ASEADMIN command.

After you've defined link paths for a table, the table becomes registered, and you can link it to AutoCAD objects in your drawing.

Command line   ASEADMIN

Once you've created a link path name, you can retrieve rows based on key values. To use the method of selecting a row based on its key value, use the following procedure.

To view a row based on key values

1   From the Tools menu, choose External Database ➤ Rows.

2   In the Rows dialog box under Cursor State, select Updatable so that all rows are accessible and modifiable.

3   Under Select Rows, choose Key Values.

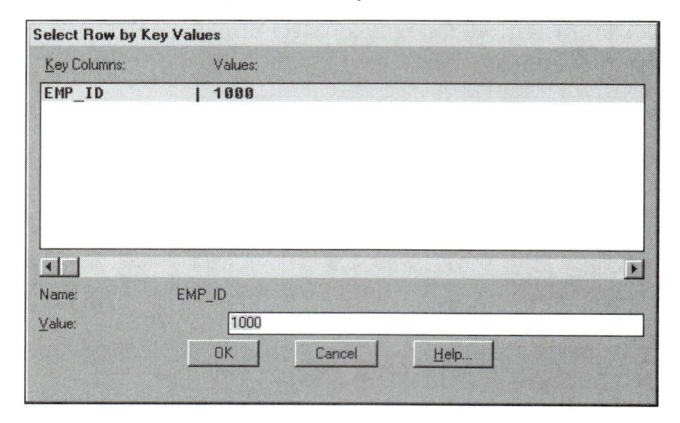

4   In the Select Row by Key Values dialog box, enter a value for the key column in the Value box. Use a unique key so that DBMS software retrieves only one row in the table.

5   The Rows dialog box displays the selected row.

6   To view another key column, repeat step 4.

7   In the Rows dialog box, choose Close.

Defining Primary and Secondary Link Path Names

You can create a single link from one object to multiple tables (within a DBMS) that share the same key columns by creating two link path names that have the same key column or columns. You make one a primary link path name and the other a secondary link path name. The secondary link path name becomes an alias or a map to the first (primary) link path name. Thus, a single link points to multiple tables that have the same key column definition and there is no need to create duplicate links for each table.

For example, the following Water table has the key field PIPE_ID. The link path name for this table is WATER_LPN.

Water table		
PIPE_ID	MATERIAL	AGE
1234	Cast Iron	25
2123	Cast Iron	30
3215	PVC	10

Suppose you make a link from an object to the first row with a key value of 1234. You can then select the object and view this linked row. A second table, called Maint, has the same key column as the Water table—PIPE_ID.

Maint table		
PIPE_ID	DATE	MAINT_DESC
1234	0494	Replaced Pipe
2123	0392	Fixed Break
3215	0893	Replaced Pipe

Because both tables have the same key column, you can create a secondary link path name for the Maint table. This new link path name is called MAINT_LPN. You can then access the data in the Maint table using either the primary or the secondary link path name without having to relink the object to the Maint table, thus without having to duplicate link data.

When you link a drawing object to a database record using either the primary or the secondary link path name, the primary link path name's key values are always used. When you create a link using a secondary link path name, you will not be able to access records from tables referenced through the primary link path name by using this link. In order to access multiple tables from one link path name, all links must be created using the primary link path name.

Using secondary link path names, you can use a single link to access rows from multiple tables. To create a secondary link path name with the tables provided, use the following procedure.

To create a primary link path name that shares key column information

1. From the Tools menu, choose External Database ➤ Administration.
2. Under Database Object Selection, choose Table. Then select EMPLOYEE.
3. Choose Link Path Names.
4. Under Key Selection in the Link Path Names dialog box, select ROOM. Then choose On.
5. Under Link Path in the New box, enter **emproom**. Then choose New.
6. Choose Close.
7. Do *not* choose OK yet. Continue with the next procedure.

To create a secondary link path name

1. Under Database Object Selection, choose Table. Then select INVENTRY.
2. Choose Link Path Names.
3. Under Key Selection in the Link Path Names dialog box, select ROOM. Then choose On.
4. Under Link Path, in the New box, enter **invroom**. Then choose New.
5. In the Select Primary Link Path Name dialog box, choose EMPROOM.
6. Choose Select.
7. Choose Close, and then choose OK.

Choosing Isolation Levels

Isolation levels refer to the integrity of the data retrieved in an SQL statement when multiple users are accessing the data simultaneously. Depending on the isolation level, results of a query can be affected in different ways. For more information on isolation levels, see ASESQLED in the *Command Reference*.

Linking Objects to the Database

You can link more than one AutoCAD object to a single row. Furthermore, using databases and tables from one or several DBMS programs, you can link more than one row to one AutoCAD object.

NOTE You *cannot* create links to OLE objects.

The following diagram shows the relationship between AutoCAD and DBMS drivers.

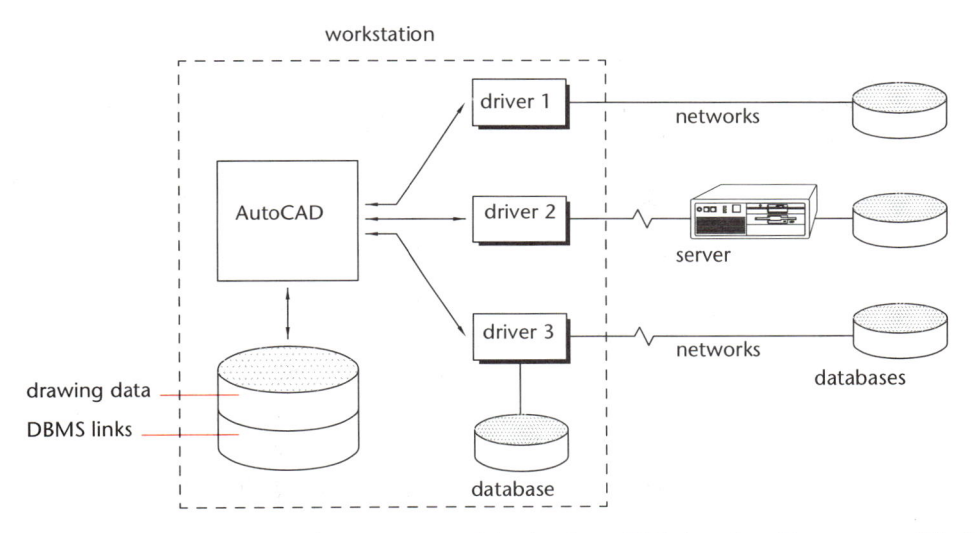

Links to databases are stored in the AutoCAD drawing. You can modify links only when the drawing is loaded into AutoCAD, but you can modify the linked database values and view them from either the DBMS or AutoCAD. The data is stored in the native external database format and is available to the DBMS even when the drawing is not loaded in AutoCAD.

One advantage of using external database commands is being able to manipulate database data from AutoCAD. Another is the ability to link that data to graphic objects in the drawing. By linking external data to AutoCAD objects, you can manipulate data more quickly by selecting the AutoCAD objects that are linked to the data. (You can link more than one AutoCAD object to a single row and link more than one row to a single AutoCAD object.) The greatest advantage is that, in storing links to the external database, you can avoid storing that data in your drawing. Many drawings can share the data in a database.

In addition to maintaining link information in the main drawing, AutoCAD can access links to objects in xrefs and blocks. You can create a link to one or more objects and then later include them in a block or an xref. Furthermore, you can have multiple levels of nesting by including a block that contains a link within another block.

To link an AutoCAD object to a row

1. From the Tools menu, choose External Database ➤ Rows.
2. In the Rows dialog box, use one of the three methods—Select, Key Values, or Graphical—to select a row in the current table.
3. Choose Make Link.
4. Select the objects you want to link to the row. (The Select Objects prompt is displayed only if the current table is registered.)

Command line   ASEROWS

To link an AutoCAD object to a table row with a shared link path name

1. Make sure you have completed the procedures "To create a primary link path name that shares key column information" on page 682 and "To create a secondary link path name" on page 682.
2. From the Tools menu, choose External Database ➤ Rows.
3. In the Rows dialog box, under Database Object Settings, select EMPLOYEE for the table name and EMPROOM for the link path name.
4. Under Select Rows in the Rows dialog box, choose Open Cursor. Then select any row in the EMPLOYEE table.
5. Choose Make Link.
6. Select the objects you want to link to the row. (The Select Objects prompt is displayed only if the current table is registered.)

Command line   ASEROWS

Referencing Link Path Names in Blocks and Xrefs

Links to blocks and external references (xrefs) are established using link path names just as they are for objects in the main drawing. The current database object settings in the main drawing are not affected by the link path name attached to the block or xref. However, the names of the database objects in the block or xref appear in the database objects list as available. A link path name in a block or xref attached to the main drawing has one of the following characteristics:

Unique   The incoming link path name is contained in the block or xref only and no link path with the same name exists in the main drawing.

Identical The incoming link path name is already contained in the main drawing, and both link path names have the same structure (same link path and key columns).

Duplicate The incoming link path name is already contained in the main drawing but has a different structure—the same link path name, but a different link path and/or key columns.

Certain operations, such as detaching xrefs or manipulating link path names of the main drawing, can change the characteristic of an xref's link path name and put it into a different category. However, its original characteristic will be maintained throughout an ASE editing or xref session.

Using Identical or Unique Link Path Names
If a block or xref contains a unique link path name (not defined in the main drawing), it is displayed the same as any other link path name of the main drawing. If a block or xref contains a link path name identical to one in the main drawing, these xref link path names are combined into one operable link path name in the main drawing. This one link path name then supports common operations such as linked object selection and links export across multiple xrefs. In this way, many identical link path names that are attached to a drawing only need to be listed once as a single link path name and can be easily selected and used in filtering. There is no difference in how you access and view links in blocks or xrefs and links in the main drawing as long as they have unique or identical link path names.

Using the Bind option of XREF may cause problems when you are attempting to rename or erase a link path name in the main drawing if it is from, or also used in, an attached xref. Use the Detach option of XREF on the xref before renaming or erasing link path names.

Associating Database Rows with AutoCAD Objects

Using Duplicate Link Path Names in Xrefs

If an xref contains a duplicate link path name (having the same name as the main drawing, but a different link path and/or key columns), AutoCAD displays the link path names with a prefix of the xref file name, as it does for blocks. Thus, they are temporarily unique during their attachment. However, duplicate link path names should be the exception rather than the rule.

Using Duplicate Link Path Names in Blocks

When a block contains a link whose link path name is identical to the name stored in a drawing that references the block object, all link information is retained. If the link paths identify different key columns, the link information for the block is not retained when it is included in the drawing, and all links to the blocks are discarded.

Creating Links to Xrefs

You can create links directly to objects and then include them in xrefs, and you can make links directly to xrefs, but you cannot make links directly to objects nested within an xref. For example, you can make links to objects within *office.dwg*, and then from your main drawing *floorplan.dwg*, you can attach the drawing *office.dwg* as an xref. You can then make a link to *office.dwg* itself, but not to an object within the xref. You can then change the links so that they associated with another xref.

AutoCAD cannot create, delete, or modify links to objects nested within xrefs. If a drawing has objects that already contain links, and the drawing is later attached as an xref, the links to those objects nested in the xref can be viewed (read) only. However, they can be created, deleted, or modified after the drawing attached as an xref is detached from the main drawing.

You can use the Bind option of XREF on xrefs whose link path names are duplicated in the main drawing. However, the duplicated link path names from the xref and their associated link information are lost after execution. To prevent their loss, load the xref as a separate drawing and rename the corresponding link path names. A link path name from the main drawing can be erased or renamed if there is a duplicate link path name.

Creating Links to Blocks

You can create links directly to objects and then include them in blocks, and you can make links to a block, but you cannot make links directly to objects within a block. For example, you can create links to objects, and then from those objects make a block called *office.dwg*. From your main drawing, *floorplan.dwg*, you include the block *office.dwg*. You can make a link to the block itself (as described in "To link an AutoCAD object to a row"), but not to any objects within the block. You can then change links from one block to another block.

When a block is inserted into a drawing, AutoCAD creates a block definition. If the block contains nested objects with links, these links are stored in the block definition. If a link is made to a block reference (an instance of the block), the link is stored with the block reference, not the block definition.

Block link information becomes accessible as soon as the block is inserted into the current drawing. Block link information becomes inaccessible (detached) as soon as the block is purged.

A block definition and its associated link information is maintained when you use WBLOCK. Objects containing links that become nested within a block maintain their link information after the block is exploded.

If a block has objects that already contain links and the block is later included in a drawing, the links to those objects nested in the block can be viewed (read), deleted, and modified.

Editing Links

You can edit and delete links in the main drawing and to blocks included in the drawing using ASELINKS. When you change a link, you specify the scope of the change: all links to the object or only those within the environment, catalog, schema, or table. You select the object in the drawing whose link you want to modify. Then you select the row you want to link the object to. Changing a link does not change the data in the external database.

To edit a link

1 From the Tools menu, choose External Database ➤ Links.

2 At the Select Objects prompt, select the object whose link you want to change.

The Key Values list in the Links dialog box displays the key value of the row linked to the object. If the selected object has more than one link, you can use the navigation buttons to scroll through the list of links until you find the link information you want to edit.

3 If you want to filter the links displayed, under Database Object Filters, choose the database object that specifies the scope of the change. You can change links for all environments or change links within a specific environment, catalog, schema, table, or link path name.

4 Choose Rows.

5 In the Rows dialog box, use the navigation keys to select the row you want to link the object to.

6 To update the link, choose OK in the Rows dialog box.

Related If you know the row's key value, you can omit steps 4 and 5, manually edit the link field to update the key value, and then choose OK in the Links dialog box. When you update a row, AutoCAD always checks for the existence of the row.

Command line ASELINKS

To view a link to a row that contains a primary and secondary link path name

1 From the Tools menu, choose External Database ➤ Links.

2 At the Select Objects prompt, select the object you chose in the procedure "To link an AutoCAD object to a table row with a shared link path name."

3 Make sure that EMPROOM is the current link path name.

EMPROOM is the link path name you created in the procedure "To create a primary link path name that shares key column information." The Key Values list in the Links dialog box displays the key value of the row linked to the object.

4 Choose Rows.

In the Rows dialog box, the row in the EMPLOYEE table that is linked to the selected object is displayed.

5 Choose Close Cursor.

6 Under Database Object Filters, choose INVROOM.

7 To view the row in the INVENTRY table with the same link value as the row in the EMPLOYEE table, choose Open Cursor.

8 Choose OK to return the Links dialog box.

Using the navigation keys, you can view all the furniture (rows) that is in the Room number you chose in the EMPLOYEE table.

To delete a link to the selected object

1 From the Tools menu, choose External Database ➤ Links.

2 At the Select Objects prompt, select the object whose link you want to delete.

3 In the Links dialog box, if the selected object is linked to more than one row, use the navigation buttons to find the link information you want to delete. If the object has only one link, the navigation buttons are not available.

link to be deleted

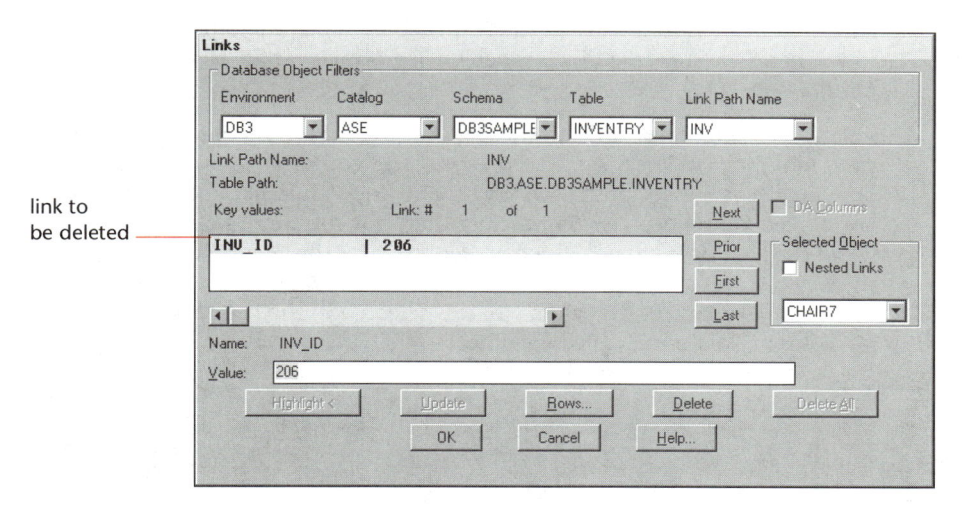

4 Choose Delete to delete the link information listed under Key Values, or choose Delete All to delete all link information if more than one link has been created for the selected object.

Command line ASELINKS

You can also delete a link by selecting the row an object is linked to instead of selecting the object.

To delete a link to the current row

1 From the Tools menu, choose External Database ➤ Rows.
2 In the Rows dialog box, select from the list the row whose link you want to delete.
3 Choose Links.
4 In the Links dialog box, choose Delete to delete the link from the object connected to the current row.

Command line ASEROWS

Accessing Links in Xrefs and Blocks

If you want to view or change links to an object that is nested in an xref or a block, use the Selected Object list in the Links dialog box to view its linked values. The list shows the name of the base object within the selected object and all parent block or xref names, regardless of whether the selected object contains a link.

Associating Database Rows with AutoCAD Objects

689

For example, you might select Chair, which contains the link to the current row. Chair is nested in a block called Office, which is part of an xref called *furnitur.dwg*.

AutoCAD searches for links to the highest level of nested objects—in this case, *furnitur.dwg*. The Selected Object list will contain a hierarchical list of drawing objects associated with Chair. The Key Values list does not display any linked values because *furnitur.dwg* does not contain links. Similarly, when the base object Line, which is used to create the Chair block, is selected, the Key Columns list remains empty because Line is not linked to a row. Key values are displayed only when Chair is selected in the list or when Nested Links is checked under Selected Object.

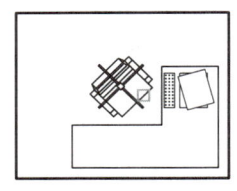

selected chair

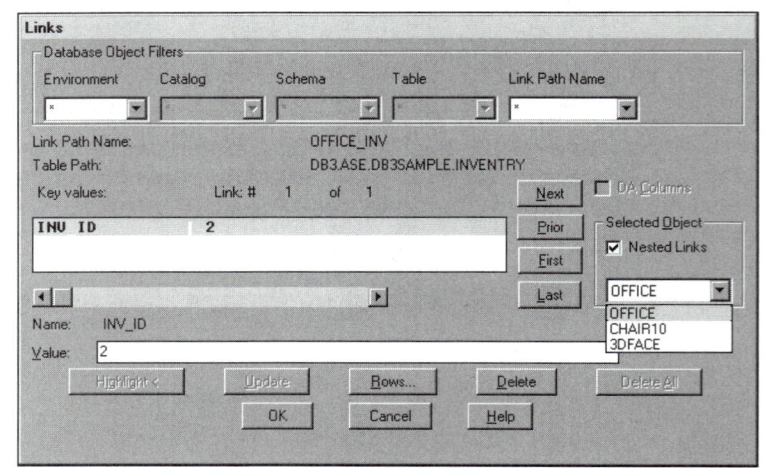

Rows can have links to an xref or a block and separate links to nested objects within that xref or block. The Office block can be linked to one row, Chair to another row, and Line to a third row.

By default, you can view links only to the selected object and not to its nested objects. If you want to change or delete links in a block or to view links to nested objects, select Nested Links. All links are displayed in the Key Values list. You cannot create, change, or delete links in xrefs.

NOTE Updating or deleting links in a block changes the links for every insertion of that block.

Editing Rows Linked to Objects

Links between AutoCAD objects and external data are used for a variety of purposes, including updating the external database from within AutoCAD, exporting link data to database files, and selecting objects linked to nongraphic data. The simplest and most common use of external data is to view it with the graphic objects it relates to. Use either ASEROWS or ASESQLED to modify rows.

Several important issues arise when objects are linked to a row in a table (see "To edit a table row" on page 673):

- When you edit a row, all objects linked to that row reflect the changes.
- If you edit a row linked to a displayable attribute, use the Reload DA option of the ASEADMIN command to update the displayable attributes with the new values (see "To create a displayable attribute" on page 692).
- If you edit a column, ASEROWS prompts you to update the links. If you edit a column using ASESQLED, the links between the drawing objects and the external data are *not* maintained.
- If you want to change data for only one of the linked objects, use ASEROWS to create a new row for that object only and enter the new information. Once you have created a new row, you must use ASELINKS to link that object to the new row.

Creating Text Objects from Database Rows

After you have created a link between the drawing object and a row in the external database, you may find it helpful to add a visual link near the linked drawing object so that you know which row it is linked to. A displayable attribute is an AutoCAD block containing text that is linked to a row in the database. Adding displayable attributes to your drawing is similar to using attributes with blocks, as described in "Creating Attributes" on page 442. The text reflects the attribute values in the linked row. You can store the displayable attribute in the drawing near the object it describes.

To create a displayable attribute

```
38
FURNITURE
adjustable chair
comp pro
200.00
129
1017
```

1 From the Tools menu, choose External Database ➤ Rows.
2 In the Rows dialog box, select a row for which you want to create displayable attributes.
3 Choose MakeDA.

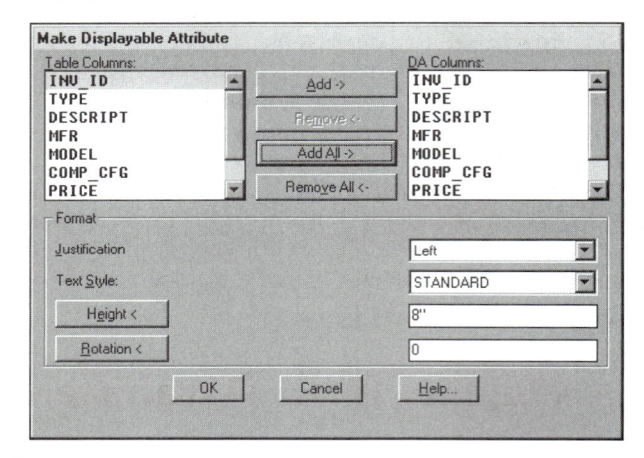

4 In the Make Displayable Attribute dialog box, under Table Columns, select a column. Then select Add.

The column is displayed in the DA Columns list.

5 Repeat step 4 for each column that you want to use as a displayable attribute. Select Add All to make all columns displayable attribute columns.

To format and place the displayable attribute

1 In the Make Displayable Attribute dialog box, select the type of justification in the Justification list.
2 Select the text style in the Text Style list.
3 Enter values for height and rotation.

4 Choose OK.

5 On the screen, specify the point where you want the displayable attribute to be displayed.

The displayable attribute is displayed at the specified location in the drawing.

Command line   ASEROWS

Inventory table						
INV_ID	TYPE	DESCRIPT	MODEL	PRICE	ROOM	EMP_ID
1	furniture	6x3 couch	lounger	800	101	1000
38	furniture	adjustable chair	comp pro	200	129	1017
119	furniture	file cabinet	fc 15x27d	35	118	1024

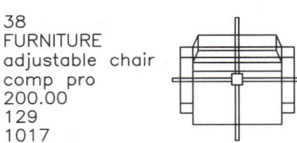

```
38
FURNITURE
adjustable chair
comp pro
200.00
129
1017
```

If you modify the data in the external database, you can update the displayable attributes by selecting Reload DA in the Administration dialog box.

To update a displayable attribute after changing a database row

1 Follow the procedure "To create a displayable attribute" on page 692.

2 Edit the value for the row you selected by editing the external database directly.

> **NOTE**   If you edit the row values using ASEROWS, the displayable attribute is automatically updated.

3 From the Tools menu, choose External Database ➤ Administration.

4 To update the displayable attribute in the drawing, choose Reload DA.

5 Select the displayable attribute to update. Then choose OK.

The new values are displayed after the dialog box is closed.

Creating Text Objects from Database Rows

Selecting Objects Using Nongraphic Search Criteria

You can use linked nongraphic data to find and select graphic objects in the drawing. For example, you can find all the vacant offices in a building or a specific fastener in an assembly. You can select graphic objects by their nongraphic attributes, highlight the selected objects, or create a selection set of objects.

Two options in the Rows dialog box—Select and Unselect—add highlighted objects to or removes them from the selection set. Displaying highlighted objects makes it easy to see when you have the correct row selected.

To create a selection of objects linked to the current row

1 From the Tools menu, choose External Database ➤ Rows.
2 In the Rows dialog box, use one of the three methods, Select, Key Values, or Graphical, to select a row linked to an object.
3 Choose Select to highlight and add to a selection set the objects that are linked to the current row.
4 Choose Unselect to remove objects from the selection set.

Command line ASEROWS

ASESELECT gives you more flexibility; you can create a selection set based on a combination of graphic and nongraphic data. This command creates a selection set from sets A and B: graphically selected linked AutoCAD objects and AutoCAD objects linked to search criteria in the current table.

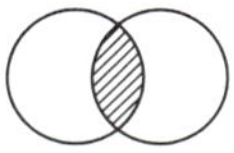

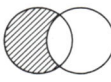

A Intersect B	A Intersect B	Creates the selection set of objects belonging to both selection sets.
A Union B	A Union B	Creates a selection set made up of all AutoCAD objects linked to rows meeting search criteria and all the selected graphic objects.
Subtract A-B	Subtract A-B	Creates a selection set of objects based on the results of subtracting the second selection set from the first selection set.
Subtract B-A	Subtract B-A	Creates a selection set of objects based on the results of subtracting the first selection set from the second selection set.

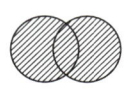

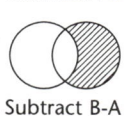

For example, executive offices have been upgraded with new couches. You can use ASESELECT to locate executive offices. The office layout in the following illustration shows furniture in each of the offices. To locate inventory, you link all the fixtures in the drawing to the row with a matching INV_ID in the INVENTRY table.

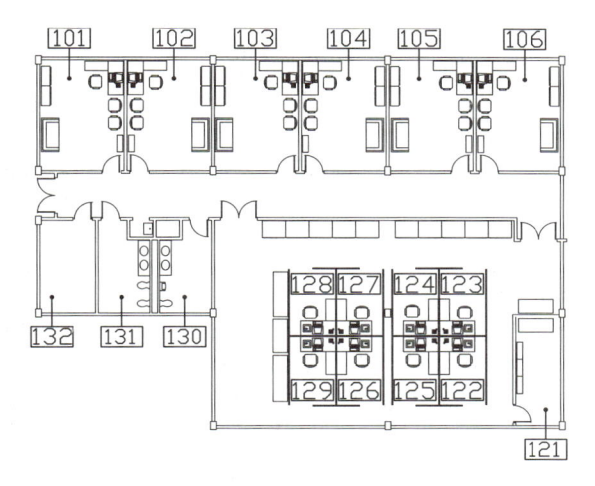

To create a selection set from graphic and nongraphic data

1 Make sure you are connected to an environment as described in the procedure "To connect to dBASE III" on page 668.
2 Make sure have created a link path name as described in the procedure "To set up link path names and register tables" on page 678.
3 From the Tools menu, choose External Database ➤ Select Objects.

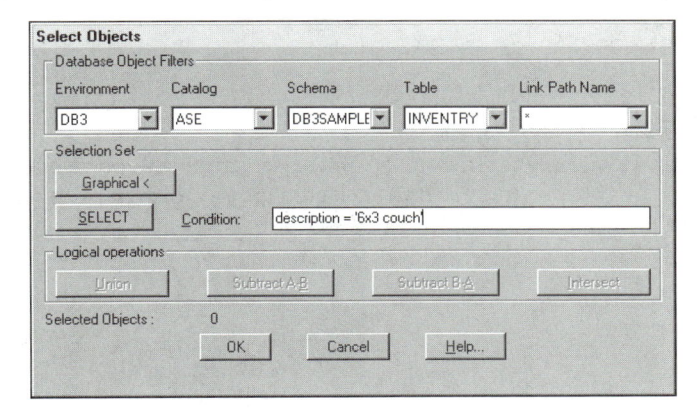

4 Under Database Object Filters, select a link path name.

Selecting Objects Using Nongraphic Search Criteria

695

5 Open the file *sample\asesmp.dwg*.

6 In the Select Objects dialog box, confine the scope of your database object to the table level by specifying an environment, catalog, schema, and table, but not a link path name.

7 Enter the SELECT statement: **descript = '6x3 couch'**. This textual select statement creates selection set A, which includes all the objects in the drawing linked to rows in which 6x3 couch is the description.

8 Under Logical Operations, select Intersect.

9 Choose Graphical.

10 At the Select Objects prompt, select all offices by using a window selection box. Then press ENTER. This graphical operation creates selection set B.

AutoCAD creates a selection set based on the intersection of selection set A and selection set B: all objects from set B linked to rows in which 6x3 couch is the description.

If the selected object has multiple links, the Links dialog box is displayed. Use the navigation buttons to select the link you want to use.

The selection set resulting from the intersection of A and B redefines selection set A for any subsequent logical operations.

If the PICKFIRST system variable is set to 1 (on), at the end of the operation, the resulting selection set of objects is highlighted with grips and can be selected using any standard selection method.

Command line   ASESELECT

If the PICKFIRST system variable is set to 0 (off), use the Previous option of SELECT to obtain the selection set created with either ASESELECT or ASEROWS.

To view a selection set

1 At the Command prompt, enter **select**.

2 Enter **p** (Previous).

AutoCAD highlights the objects in the selection set you previously created from the intersection of all the selected graphic objects with all the linked rows in which 6x3 couch is the description.

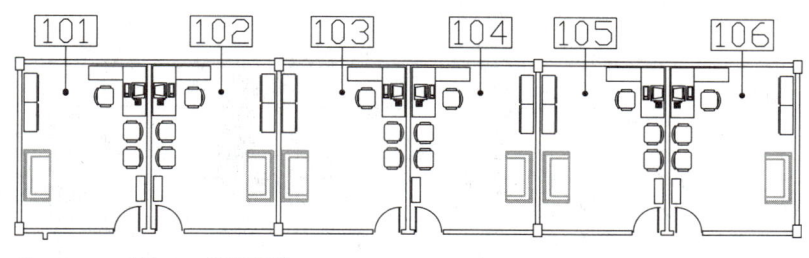

Command line   SELECT

Exporting Associated Data

With external database commands, you can produce reports and materials lists based on information linked to your drawings. AutoCAD does not provide direct reporting capability. Reports are generated by the products best suited to the task—the DBMS and report-writer software. However, AutoCAD's external database commands simplify the process.

With AutoCAD you could structure your data so that each object in the drawing is linked to only one row and each row is linked to only one object. Although tables do not store information on the objects linked to them, you can produce reports easily because each row represents one object in the drawing.

With external database commands you can link more than one object to a single row, which reduces the size of your database when objects do not have unique attributes. If you have structured your data this way—with shared rows—there is no way to know how many objects are linked to a single row from the DBMS. ASEEXPORT provides a way to retrieve that count information by exporting link information in the drawing, and in any xrefs and blocks it contains, in various formats (the format native to your DBMS, comma-delimited format, or space-delimited format). You can combine this information with the data in the tables to produce a report.

To export links to a file

1   From the Tools menu, choose External Database ➤ Export Links.

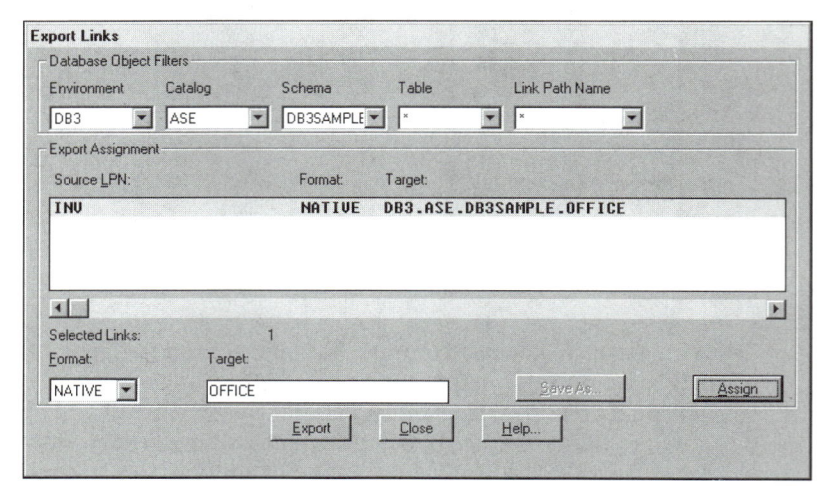

```
Export Links
┌─ Database Object Filters ─────────────────────────────────────┐
│  Environment   Catalog      Schema        Table    Link Path Name │
│  [DB3    ▼]  [ASE    ▼]  [DB3SAMPLE▼]  [*    ▼]  [*        ▼]    │
└───────────────────────────────────────────────────────────────┘
┌─ Export Assignment ───────────────────────────────────────────┐
│  Source LPN:              Format:    Target:                  │
│  INV                      NATIVE    DB3.ASE.DB3SAMPLE.OFFICE  │
│                                                               │
│                                                               │
│  ◄                                                          ► │
│  Selected Links:     1                                        │
│  Format:       Target:                                        │
│  [NATIVE ▼]   [OFFICE              ]   [ Save As ]  [ Assign ]│
└───────────────────────────────────────────────────────────────┘
              [ Export ]   [ Close ]   [ Help... ]
```

2   At the Select Objects prompt, select the objects whose link information you want to export.

3   In the Export Links dialog box under Database Object Filters, select the scope of the linked data to be generated in the report.

You can export links associated with an environment, catalog, schema, table, or link path name within a table. By default, asterisks (*) appear in all the lists, indicating that all links associated with the environment will be exported. For each database object in which you replace an asterisk with a name from the list, you narrow the scope of the links to be exported to that particular database object.

4   Select a link path name in the list.

NOTE If you specified a link path name in step 3, only one selection is available.

5   Under Selected Links, select Native as the file format of the exported information.

6   Under Target, enter the name of the table you want to create.

By default, the catalog and schema for the specified link path name are used to define the path name for the table when Native is selected.

7   Choose Assign to assign the specified file format and target path name to the selected link path name.

8   Repeat steps 3 through 7 for each link path name whose links you want to export.

9   Choose Export.

The export operation is repeated for each link path name assignment.

The following table shows sample file contents generated by the ASEEXPORT command.

Sample file contents generated by ASEEXPORT

Key value	Handle
1014	117F
0	117C
1017	117E
1016	117D
1013	117A
0	1119
1012	117B

Command line   ASEEXPORT

Accessing External Data with SQL

The external database commands available through AutoCAD are primarily for querying the database as it relates to objects in a drawing. However, you might need to manipulate data as it relates to other tables within the database. When you need greater data manipulation capabilities, you can issue SQL statements from AutoCAD to query external databases directly. For example, to add rows to an external database table directly without using the Edit or Insert options of ASEROWS, you could include these two lines in a text file:

insert into employee values (1035, 'Park', 'John', 'Sales', 'Coordinator', '','')
insert into employee values (1036, 'Burns', 'Julie', 'Engineering', 'Programmer', '', '')

To query external databases

1 From the Tools menu, choose External Database ➤ SQL Editor.

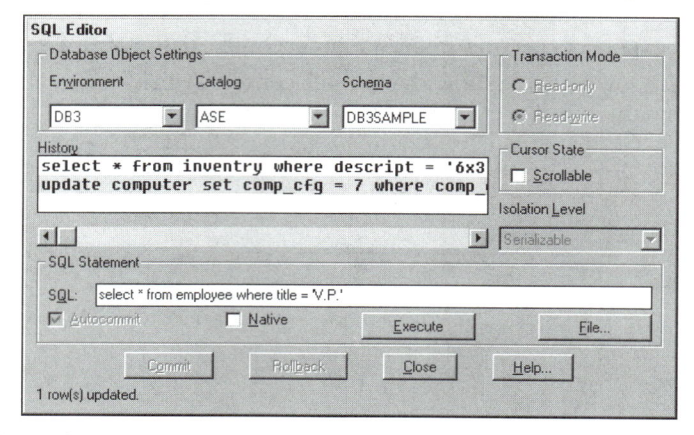

2 In the SQL Editor dialog box, enter an SQL SELECT statement.

3 Choose Execute.

The database is queried directly. The results are displayed in the SQL Cursor dialog box.

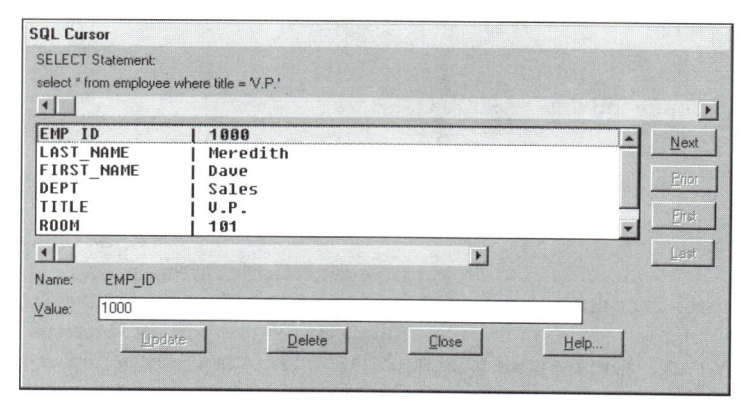

4 Use the navigation buttons to scroll through the selected rows to view the data.

Command line ASESQLED executes SQL statements interactively on the command line or in batch form from a text file.

All external database commands except ASESQLED have options you can use to change the current database objects. ASESQLED changes only the environment, catalog, and schema. All tables within the selected schema are accessible using SQL statements (see "Opening Files Containing Links" on page 702).

Checking Data Integrity

Conflicts between an external database and a drawing can occur if the objects in the drawing or the data in the database are altered in some ways. These conflicts are the result of a loss of data integrity when links still exist to a record that has been deleted from the database. This problem occurs when you do any of the following:

- Delete a record from a database when the drawing to which it's linked is not loaded in AutoCAD or when AutoCAD is not loaded. AutoCAD is a single drawing file environment, and the database management systems are not aware of the graphics links stored in the AutoCAD drawing.
- Use an SQL DELETE FROM statement in ASESQLED. The SQL DELETE statement is processed directly by the driver, and AutoCAD does not know which rows have been deleted.
- Use an SQL UPDATE statement for a key value in ASESQLED or outside of AutoCAD. The SQL DELETE statement is processed directly by the driver, and AutoCAD does not know which rows have been deleted.
- Choose Delete in the ASESQLED SQL Cursor dialog box. If you delete the row by using ASEROWS, then AutoCAD removes associated links to the deleted row automatically.

To report on and restore data integrity, use ASEADMIN with the Synchronize option. This option is available only for synchronizing links that do *not* have secondary link path names. If they do, you must first delete the secondary link path name and then resynchronize the database with the drawing.

To check data integrity

1 From the Tools menu, choose External Database ➤ Administration.
2 Determine the scope of links you want to fix or report.

You can fix or report on all links in the database; links within an environment, catalog, schema, or table; or links associated with a link path name.

3 In the Administration dialog box, choose Synchronize.

![Synchronize Links dialog box]

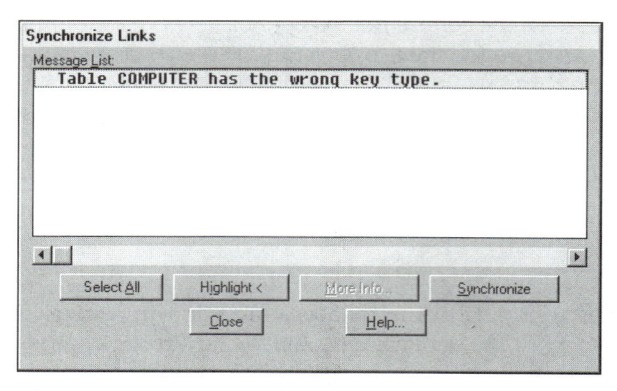

The message list shows messages from the synchronization report.

4 In the Synchronize Links dialog box, select a message in the Message List.
5 Choose Highlight to view objects whose links are invalid.
6 Choose Synchronize.

AutoCAD removes links from objects linked to deleted rows and erases displayable attributes linked to deleted rows.

Command line   ASEADMIN

To ensure drawing integrity, you can limit a specific operator's ability to edit external data by using the access permission capabilities of your DBMS or operating system. With AutoCAD, you can use user names and passwords for DBMS products that support them.

Opening Files Containing Links

AutoCAD loads external database commands automatically so that it can track the changes made to the linked objects. If you won't be working with links in the current drawing session, you can unload the external database commands after using ASEADMIN and ASESQLED by entering at the Command prompt

arx u ase

(Unloading the external database set of commands generates a message that proxy objects have been created. The proxy objects are handled by default according to the selections on the Compatibility tab in the Preferences dialog box. You can choose to change how they are handled at this time.) To access link information already stored in drawings, ASE must first be loaded before the drawing is opened. To ensure that it is loaded first, do one of the following:

- Manually load *ase.arx* with the ARX command by entering

  arx ase

- Run an external database command before opening the drawing

If a drawing that contains links is loaded and external database commands are not loaded, no link information will be recognized, although it is still stored in the drawing.

DXFIN and DXFOUT also require that external database commands be loaded first, otherwise link information will not be read or written.

AutoCAD Release 12 drawings opened in AutoCAD Release 13 and Release 14 retain their link information. However, Release 13 links *cannot* be saved back to Release 12 with SAVEASR12. You can convert Release 12 drawing links into a Release 14 format by running the External Database Configuration utility in the directory or folder where you installed AutoCAD.

To convert Release 12 links to Release 14 links

1. Save a copy of the original Release 12 drawing.
2. In the External Database Configuration utility, follow the procedure described in "Converting Release 12 Links" in the configuration utility's online help.
3. From the Tools menu, choose External Database ➤ Administration.
4. Connect to the environment whose links you want to convert.
5. Open the Release 12 drawing containing the links to be converted.

   When the drawing is opened, the links are converted.

To remove unneeded data from the Release 12 links

1. In the Administration dialog box, under Database Objects, select Schema.
2. Choose Synchronize.
3. In the Synchronize Links dialog box, choose Select All. Then choose OK.
4. At the command line, enter **wblock**.
5. In the Create New Drawing dialog box, enter a new name for the drawing. Then choose Save.
6. When prompted for a new block name, press ENTER.
7. When prompted to select objects, enter **all**.
8. Delete the original drawing, and then rename the new block name you created with the original drawing name.

If a Release 12 drawing is attached as a block or xref, associated links are converted to Release 14 links in memory. If the Release 12 drawing contains a bound xref, AutoCAD saves link information as stated above. Convert Release 12 drawing links by running the External Database Configuration utility.

You cannot edit links for objects on locked layers. In these cases, AutoCAD displays a Warning dialog box with a message that the selected object is on a locked layer. The corresponding layer name and object handle are displayed in the Diagnostic Parameters list. You must unlock the layers before editing the links. This also applies to reading AutoCAD Release 12 drawings that contain objects with links on locked layers.

Using Unicode Fonts

When you open drawings that are created in other countries, you may need to be familiar with Unicode fonts and their use. Understanding Unicode fonts is also required if you frequently enter hexadecimal equivalents of Unicode characters while using one of the text commands. The information in this appendix describes what Unicode fonts are and how they are used with AutoCAD.

In this appendix

- Using Unicode fonts with AutoCAD
- Using the Code Page independent format
- Using the interchange Multibyte Independent format

Unicode Fonts

AutoCAD supports the Unicode character encoding standard. A Unicode font can contain 65,535 characters, with glyphs for many languages, including the most common European languages. Unicode fonts contain many more characters than are defined in your system code page. Most AutoCAD fonts are Unicode encoded; exceptions are listed in the following table.

Fonts not Unicode encoded
Fonts
Syastro
Symath
Symeteo
Symbol
Symusic
Symap

Code Page Independent Format (CIF)

The code page that is current is dependent upon the operating system. To change the code page, you must refer to your operating system documentation. When a drawing is opened in AutoCAD that contains fonts or characters not supported by your operating system, the fonts or characters are converted to control characters with the format \U+*xxxx* before a text string is actually drawn. U represents the Unicode shape number, and *xxxx* is the hexadecimal value of the Unicode character.

You can enter Unicode hexadecimal values for all Unicode-encoded fonts using any of the text commands.

The Code Page Independent format (CIF) enables drawings to be opened both in the language the drawing was created and in the language of a different country to which the drawing might be sent without any loss of information.

For example, if the phrase,

JA, DET ÄR DANS PÅ BRÄNNÖ BRYGGA

were converted to CIF, it would look like this:

JA, DET \U+00C4R DANS PA BR\U+00C4NN\U+00D6 BRYGGA

Converting this string back to its original Unicode font would bring back all the original characters.

> **NOTE** These control characters are also used by the AutoCAD database handler. Any Unicode shape numbers not representable in the current code page are converted to such control codes.

Characters in text strings that are not available in the current font are displayed as question marks. This also includes any Unicode control characters. However, Unicode control characters are not interpreted if the current font does not support Unicode. In that case, the control characters are displayed literally.

You can use Unicode fonts (as the normal font) in conjunction with Big Fonts.

The special dimensioning symbols degree sign (°), plus-or-minus sign(±), and diameter symbol (∅) in a font are assigned to the hexadecimal Unicode values in the following table.

Special symbol values

Symbol	Value
Degree sign	0x00B0
Plus or minus sign	0x00B1
Diameter symbol	0x2205

> **NOTE** You can also use the (degree sign) **%%d** (°), (plus or minus sign) **%%p** (±), and (diameter symbol) **%%c** (∅) with Unicode fonts, as with regular AutoCAD fonts. These symbols can also be accessed from the symbols menu in the multiline text editor.

You can mix \U+ (CIF) sequences with normal text, for example

`"A \U+0074ext string"`

This string is displayed as

"A text string"

Because "t" exists in every system code page, the sequence is converted to a real character when the object is regenerated.

The Multibyte Interchange Format (MIF)

The Multibyte Interchange format (MIF) is used to convert Asian language character strings. The following string represents an Asian character displayed on a system other than the native one:

\M+*nxxxx*   Multibyte shape number. The *n* is a digit identifying the originating multibyte code page ID. The *xxxx* is the hexadecimal value of the multibyte character.

The code page identifications AutoCAD supports are listed in the table.

Supported code page identification

Code page ID	Code page number	Language
0	undefined	Undefined
1	932	Japanese (Shift-JIS)
2	950	Traditional Chinese (Big 5)
3	949	Wansung (KS C-5601-1987)
4	1361	Johab (KS C-5601-1992)
5	936	Simplified Chinese (GB 2312-80)

If a Big Font is used, the sequence is converted to a 16-bit value, and if a character exists for it, it is drawn in the graphics window.

Characters that do not readily map in the system-character representation appear in DXF as \U+*xxxx* sequences or as \M+*nxxxx* sequences for multibyte code pages (non-Unicode mapped). Also, 8-bit and multibyte characters, as well as \U+*xxxx* and \M+*nxxxx* sequences, are accepted in symbol table names.

WARNING! If you are using CIF or MIF sequences as symbol table names, they must be entered correctly; otherwise, you can corrupt your drawing.

Code Page Information

You can find out which code page or language is installed on your operating system by choosing the Regional Settings icon in the Control Panel. (On some platforms you need to choose the International Settings icon.) For more information, see your Windows documentation.

To find out which code page AutoCAD is referencing, enter **syscodepage** at the Command prompt.

The following table lists all the ANSI code pages supported by Windows.

ANSI code pages supported by Windows

Identifier	Meaning
874	Thai
932	Japanese
936	Chinese (PRC, Singapore)
949	Korean
950	Chinese (Taiwan, Hong Kong)
1200	Unicode (BMP of ISO 10646)
1250	Windows 3.1 Eastern European
1251	Windows 3.1 Cyrillic
1252	Windows 3.1 Latin 1 (U.S., Western Europe)
1253	Windows 3.1 Greek
1254	Windows 3.1 Turkish
1255	Hebrew
1256	Arabic
1257	Baltic

Unicode Fonts

Customizing Toolbars

AutoCAD has a set of standard toolbars. You can customize these toolbars and create your own to give you easier and more efficient access to the AutoCAD commands you use most frequently. (For information about customizing menus, see chapter 4, "Custom Menus," in the *Customization Guide*.)

In this appendix

- Creating custom toolbars
- Modifying, positioning, displaying, and hiding toolbars
- Creating and editing tools

Creating and Modifying Toolbars

AutoCAD toolbars provide access to frequently used commands, settings, and modes. A subset of the AutoCAD toolbars, called top level toolbars, is displayed by default. You can add tools to these default toolbars, remove tools you use infrequently, and rearrange the organization of tools and toolbars to best suit your needs. Or you can create your own toolbars.

You can display multiple toolbars at once, and they can be either docked or floating. Docked toolbars lock into place along the top, bottom, or sides of the screen. Floating toolbars do not lock into the AutoCAD screen. You move them around using your pointing device and they can overlap other floating and docked toolbars. You can also hide toolbars until you need them.

The Customize Toolbars dialog box provides a list of tool categories that correspond to categories of AutoCAD commands. Each category has a set of tool icons. You can use these tool icons or create your own.

Creating a New Toolbar

To create a new toolbar, you first create an empty toolbar. Then, from the Customize Toolbars dialog box, you drag tools onto the new toolbar. You can modify existing toolbars by adding, deleting, and rearranging tools. To create or modify toolbars, you start in the Toolbars dialog box.

To create a toolbar

1 From the View menu, choose Toolbars.

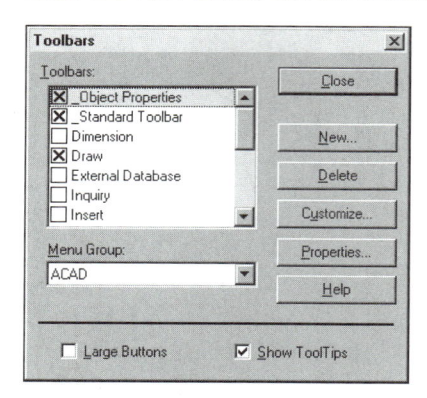

The Toolbars dialog box lists all available toolbars. The menu group determines the file to which your toolbar configuration is saved. For more information, see chapter 4, "Custom Menus" in the *Customization Guide*.

2 In the Toolbars dialog box, choose New.

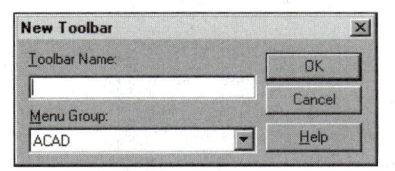

3 In the New Toolbar dialog box, specify a name for the toolbar.
4 Under Menu Group, specify the menu group associated with the toolbar.
5 Choose OK.
6 Choose Close in the Toolbars dialog box.

The new, empty toolbar is displayed. You can now add tools to the toolbar (see "Adding, Deleting, Moving, and Copying Tools" on page 714).

Command line   TOOLBAR

To delete a toolbar

1 From the View menu, choose Toolbars.
2 In the Toolbars dialog box, select the toolbar name you want to delete, then choose Delete.
3 Choose OK.

AutoCAD prompts you to confirm the procedure. You cannot undo this action.

Command line   TOOLBAR

Displaying Toolbar Properties

Each toolbar has an associated alias that AutoCAD uses internally. This name appears in the Toolbars Properties dialog box. You must use this alias when you use TOOLBAR to display and position toolbars.

To display toolbar properties

1   From the View menu, choose Toolbars.
2   In the Toolbars dialog box, select a toolbar, and then choose Properties.

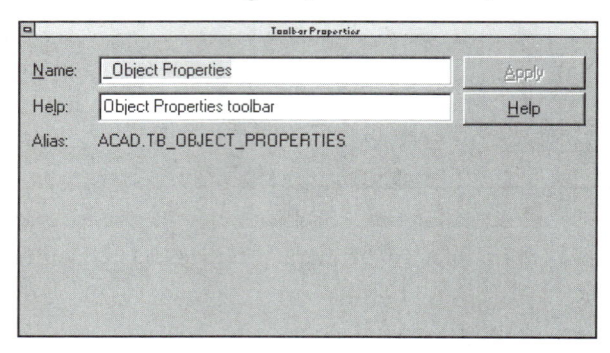

	Toolbar Properties	
Name:	_Object Properties	Apply
Help:	Object Properties toolbar	Help
Alias:	ACAD.TB_OBJECT_PROPERTIES	

The Toolbar Properties dialog box displays the toolbar's alias.

3   Exit the Toolbar Properties dialog box, and then choose Close to exit the Toolbars dialog box.

Command line   TOOLBAR

Adding, Deleting, Moving, and Copying Tools

You use the Customize Toolbars dialog box to add tools to a toolbar from a menu category, and to copy or move tools from one toolbar to another. You can also delete tools. You can also create a new toolbar by dragging a tool from the Customize Toolbars dialog box, and dropping it onto the screen.

To add a tool to a toolbar

1   Make sure the toolbar you want to customize is displayed.
2   From the View menu, choose Toolbars.
3   In the Toolbars dialog box, choose Customize.

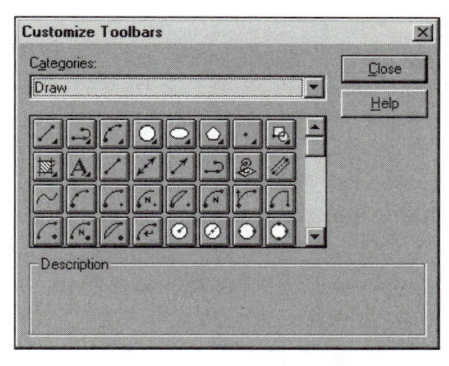

4   In the Customize Toolbars dialog box, under Categories, select the category from which you want to drag an icon.

The tools for the selected category are displayed below the Categories box.

5   Drag the tool to the toolbar.

The toolbar resizes to fit the tool added.

Command line   TOOLBAR

To delete a tool from a toolbar

1   Make sure the toolbar you want to customize is displayed.

2   From the View menu, choose Toolbars.

3   In the Toolbars dialog box, choose Customize.

4   Drag the tool off the toolbar.

If you delete a default tool from a toolbar, you can restore it from the Customize Toolbars dialog box. If you delete a tool you have customized, you cannot restore it.

Command line   TOOLBAR

To move or copy a tool from another toolbar

1   Make sure the toolbars you want to customize are displayed.

2   From the View menu, choose Toolbars.

3   In the Toolbars dialog box, choose Customize.

4   Do *one* of the following:

- To move a tool from another toolbar, drag the tool to the new toolbar.
- To copy a tool from another toolbar, press CTRL and drag the tool to the new toolbar.

Displaying Toolbars

You can display all toolbars, or only the ones you use frequently. You can also hide a toolbar while you use a tool.

To display a toolbar

1 From the View menu, choose Toolbars.

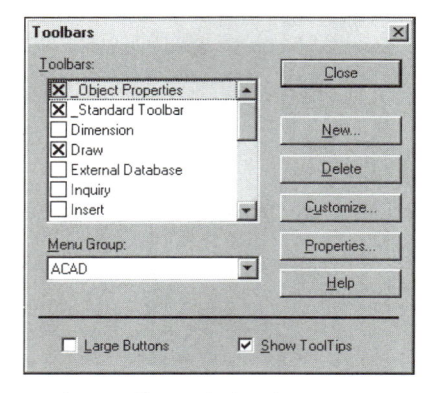

2 In the Toolbars dialog box, select the box next to the toolbar you want to display.

3 Choose Close.

Command line   TOOLBAR

> **NOTE** Entering **-toolbar** at the Command prompt initiates the Release 13 version of TOOLBAR.

To hide a toolbar

1 From the View menu, choose Toolbars.

2 In the Toolbars dialog box, clear the box next to the toolbar you want to hide.

To hide all toolbars, including the Standard and Object Properties toolbars, choose Toolbars from the View menu. Then deselect all toolbars in the Toolbars dialog box.

Command line   TOOLBAR

Positioning a Toolbar

You can dock toolbars along the top, bottom, or sides of the AutoCAD screen, or you can float toolbars anywhere on the screen. You position a toolbar by dragging it into place. Docked toolbars have a gray area, or grab region, around the tool icon.

To dock a floating toolbar

1 Position the cursor on the area that contains the toolbar name and press the pick button on the pointing device.

As you move the toolbar, an outline of the toolbar shows how it will look in the new location. As you drag the outline of the floating toolbar, the outline changes weight once the toolbar reaches a dockable location. The floating toolbar docks vertically along the left or right sides, and horizontally along the top and bottom.

2 Drag the toolbar to a docking location at the top, bottom, or sides of the screen.

3 When the outline of the toolbar appears in the docking area, release the pick button.

If you release the toolbar in a docking area, it locks to that location. If you release the toolbar anywhere else on the screen, it floats in that location.

Related   Enter **-toolbar** at the Command prompt and provide the toolbar name. Then enter **left**, **right**, **top**, or **bottom**.

To float a docked toolbar

1 Position the pointing device over a grab region on the toolbar, and press the pick button on your pointing device.

2 Drag the toolbar away from the docked location.

3 Release the pick button when the toolbar is in the desired location.

Related   Enter **-toolbar** at the Command prompt and provide the toolbar name. Then enter **float**.

Modifying a Toolbar

You can reposition tools on a toolbar, add space between them, and adjust the toolbar's shape. You can also change the name of the toolbar. A toolbar changes size automatically when tools are added or deleted. You can, however, change the shape of the toolbar vertically or horizontally.

The Large Buttons option in the Toolbars dialog box changes the size of tools from 16 × 15 pixels to 24 × 22 pixels. The Show ToolTips option displays the name associated with a tool.

To reposition tools on a toolbar

1. From the View menu, choose Toolbars.
2. In the Toolbars dialog box, choose Customize.
3. Drag the tool to the new position.

    You must drag the tool more than halfway across the tool that already exists in the proposed new location.

To add space between tools on a toolbar

1. From the View menu, choose Toolbars.
2. In the Toolbars dialog box, choose Customize.
3. In the toolbar, drag the tool to the left or right edge of the tool beside it, but not past the middle.

To rename a toolbar

1. From the View menu, choose Toolbar.
2. In the Toolbar dialog box, select the toolbar name, then choose Properties.
3. In the Toolbar Properties dialog box, at Name, enter a new name.
4. To change the text displayed in the status line, enter new text at Help, then choose Apply.
5. From the Toolbars dialog box, choose Close.

To change the shape of a floating toolbar

- Drag the bottom border of a toolbar to create a vertical toolbar.
- Drag the side border of a toolbar to create a horizontal toolbar.
- Drag the border of a floating toolbar to reshape its configuration.

A docked toolbar cannot be reshaped. You must float it and then reshape it.

To display tooltips

1 From the View menu, choose Toolbars.
2 In the Toolbars dialog box, select Show ToolTips, and choose Close.
   Related   Use the TOOLTIPS system variable to turn tooltips on and off.

To change the size of tools

1 From the View menu, choose Toolbars.
2 In the Toolbars dialog box, select Large Buttons and choose Close.

Creating and Editing Tools

After you create a toolbar, you can add tools supplied with AutoCAD, or you can create your own by modifying existing tools. Under one tool icon, you can create or modify a set of tools called a flyout. You can customize the appearance of tools to suit your needs.

Creating a Tool

AutoCAD commands are organized into categories in the Customize Toolbars dialog box. You can select a category to display a set of icons that represent a group of commands. AutoCAD also provides blank icons that you can assign to any command or macro.

Most commands begin with ^C^C to cancel a command that may be running and display the command prompt. An underline character (_) enables commands to work on international versions of AutoCAD. An apostrophe (') enables the command to work in conjunction with another command. If you associate a series of commands with a tool, separate them with semicolons or spaces. You create button macros the same way you create menu macros. For more information about entering commands in macros, see chapter 4, "Custom Menus," in the *Customization Guide*.

To create a tool

1 From the View menu, choose Toolbars.
2 Right-click on any tool icon from an existing toolbar.
   The Button Properties dialog box is displayed.

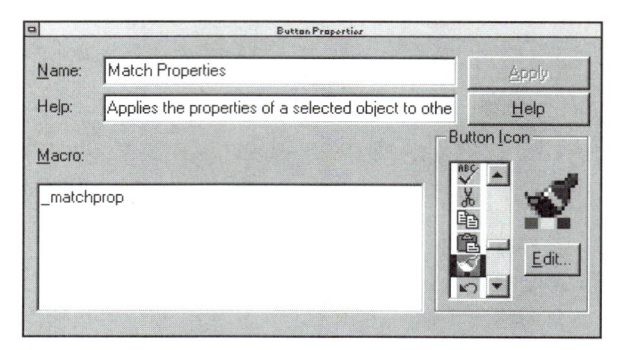

3   In the Button Properties dialog box, at Name, enter a new name for the tool.

4   At Help, enter the explanatory text you want to be displayed on the status line.

5   To associate a command with the tool, enter the command in the box under Macro.

6   Under Button Icon, select an icon for the tool.

7   To modify the tool icon, choose Edit.

8   After making any changes to the icon, choose Save or Save As, or choose Close to exit the Button Editor dialog box.

9   To apply the new tool and properties to the toolbar, choose Apply in the Button Properties dialog box. Then choose Close to exit the Toolbars dialog box.

For more information, see "Editing Tool Icons" on page 722.

To add the newly created tool to a toolbar, see "Adding, Deleting, Moving, and Copying Tools" on page 714.

Changing the Command Assigned to a Tool

In addition to changing a tool associated with a command, you can change a command associated with a tool.

To change a command

1   From the View menu, choose Toolbars.

2   Right-click on any tool icon from an existing toolbar.

3   In the Button Properties dialog box, edit the command information in the Macro area to specify a new command for the tool.

4 Choose Apply.

5 From the Toolbars dialog box, choose Close.

Command line TOOLBAR

Creating a Flyout

A flyout is a set of icons nested under a single icon on a toolbar. Flyout icons are defined by a black triangle in the lower-right corner. To create a flyout you create the flyout icon and associate a toolbar with it.

To create a flyout

1 From the View menu, choose Toolbars.

2 In the Toolbars dialog box, choose Customize.

3 In the Customize Toolbars dialog box, from Categories, select Custom.

4 Drag the flyout icon (denoted by a black triangle) from the Customize Toolbars dialog box to the destination toolbar.

If you don't have a destination toolbar, AutoCAD creates one when you drop the icon anywhere except on another toolbar.

5 Right-click the newly created flyout from the toolbar icon.

The Flyout Properties dialog box is displayed.

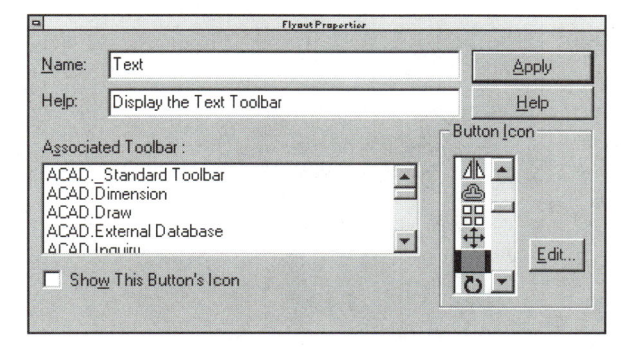

6 In the Flyout Properties dialog box, from Associated Toolbar, select the toolbar to associate with the flyout.

NOTE You should always create a toolbar before you create a flyout. If you don't associate a toolbar with the flyout button you create, AutoCAD issues a warning beep when you select that flyout button.

Creating and Editing Tools

721

7   To specify an icon for the flyout, select one under Button Icon.

    You can modify the icon by choosing Edit to display the Button Editor. For more information, see the following section, "Editing Tool Icons."

8   To display the icon you specified, select Show This Button's Icon.

    If you select this option, AutoCAD uses the icon you just specified for the flyout. The first tool in the associated toolbar will always be the current tool (this tool is invoked if you click on the flyout icon). If you do not select this option, the first tool in the associated toolbar is displayed until you use a different tool from the flyout. Each time you use a different tool from the flyout, that tool becomes the current tool in the flyout.

9   Choose Apply. Then from the Toolbars dialog box, choose Close.

Editing Tool Icons

AutoCAD provides standard tool icons to start AutoCAD commands. You can create custom icons to run custom macros. You can modify an existing icon or create your own. AutoCAD saves buttons as BMP (bitmap) files.

To edit or create a flyout icon

1   From the View menu, choose Toolbars.

2   Right-click a flyout from the toolbar icon to display the Flyout Properties dialog box.

3   In the Flyout Properties dialog box, under Button Icon, select a button, then choose Edit.

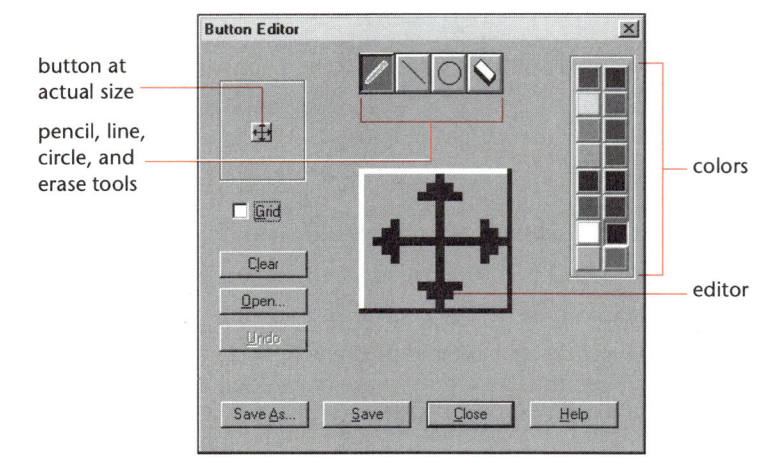

button at actual size

pencil, line, circle, and erase tools

colors

editor

Appendix B Customizing Toolbars

The Button Editor dialog box provides a close-up view of the button icon. If you turn on Grid, AutoCAD divides the view into a grid. Each grid box represents one pixel. The Button Editor dialog box displays the button icon at its actual size in the upper-left corner.

You can open an existing button using Open.

4. Use the Pencil, Line, Circle, and Erase tools to create or edit the button icon.

   To use color, select a color from the color palette.

   The Pencil tool edits one pixel at a time in the selected color. You can drag the pointing device to edit several pixels at once.

   The Line tool creates lines in the selected color. Press the return button on the pointing device to set the first endpoint of the line. Drag to draw the line. Then release the return button to complete the line.

   The Circle tool creates circles in the selected color. Press the return button on the pointing device to set the center of the circle. Then drag to set the radius. Release the return button to complete the circle.

   Drag the Erase tool to set pixels to the background color. Double-click the Erase tool with the pointing device to set all pixels to the background color.

5. To save the customized button, choose Save As. Then specify a file name and choose Save.

   Or, to overwrite the original button, choose Save.

6. Choose Close.

Using Other File Formats

AutoCAD provides many options for importing or exporting other file formats. This chapter defines the file formats that can be used for importing or exporting, including DXF, ACIS, WMF, BMP, and PostScript. It also includes information about the VSLIDE and MSLIDE commands, and how to create and use slides for a presentation.

In this appendix

- Creating and using slides
- Importing other file formats
- Creating and exporting other file formats
- Creating and importing PostScript images

Working with Slides

AutoCAD offers many ways to share data created with other applications. With the slides feature, you can quickly display different views from different drawings. With the import function, you can open files from other applications for use by AutoCAD. With the export function, you can convert AutoCAD drawings to a format that can be used by other applications.

A slide is a snapshot of an AutoCAD drawing. Although it contains a picture of the drawing at a given instant, it is not a drawing file. You can not import a slide file into the current drawing, nor can you edit or print a slide. You can only view it.

You can use slide files to

- Make presentations using other Autodesk products
- Reference a snapshot of a drawing while working on a different drawing
- Exchange images with other graphics and desktop publishing programs

When you view a slide file, it temporarily replaces objects on the screen. You can draw on top of it, but when you change the view (by redrawing, panning, or zooming), the slide file disappears, and AutoCAD redisplays only what you drew and any preexisting objects.

You can display slides singly or in sequence (when used with scripts). Slides also can be used on custom menus. For example, if you create scripts that insert blocks containing frequently used mechanical parts, you can design a menu that shows a slide of each part. When you select the slide image from the menu, AutoCAD inserts the block into the drawing.

Creating Slides

You create a slide by saving the current view in slide format. In model space, the slide shows only the current viewport. In paper space, the slide shows all visible viewports and their contents. Slides show only what was visible. They do not show objects in layers that have been turned off or frozen or in viewports that have been turned off.

You cannot edit a slide; you must change the original drawing and remake the slide. If you use a low-resolution graphics monitor when creating a slide file and later upgrade to a higher-resolution monitor, you can still view the slide. AutoCAD adjusts the image accordingly. The slide does not take full advantage of the new monitor, however, until you remake the slide file from the original drawing.

To make a slide

1 In the graphics area, display the view you want to use for the slide.
2 At the Command prompt, enter **mslide**.

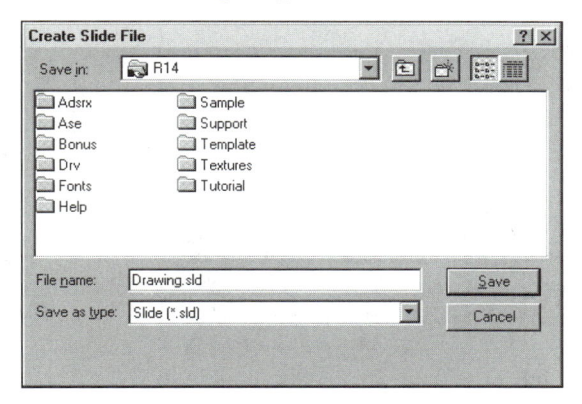

3 In the Create Slide File dialog box, enter a name for the slide.

   AutoCAD offers the name of the drawing as a default name for the slide. It automatically appends the file extension *.sld*.

4 Choose OK.

Viewing Slides

You can view slides individually using VSLIDE. To view a series of slides for a presentation, use a script file. For information about creating scripts, see chapter 6, "Command Scripts" in the *Customization Guide*.

NOTE Be careful about using editing commands as you view a slide, which looks like an ordinary drawing. Editing commands affect the current drawing underneath the slide, but not the slide itself.

Some commands, such as MENU and SCRIPT, do not affect the slide or the current drawing. Other commands, such as TIME and STATUS, can by used but may force redrawing, which removes the slide.

The layer/color relationships, zoom magnification, and other conditions in effect when you view a slide do not affect the appearance of the slide.

To view a slide

1 At the Command prompt, enter **vslide**.

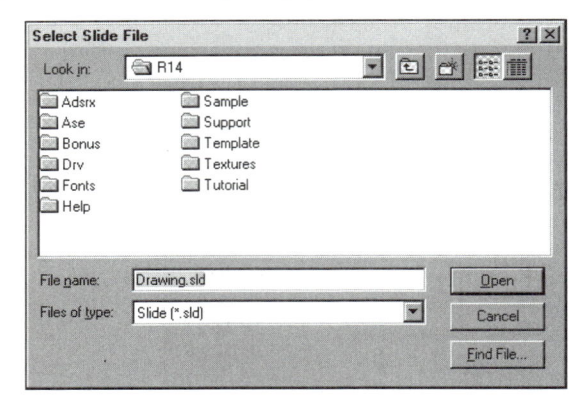

2 In the Select Slide File dialog box, select a slide to view.
3 Choose OK.

The slide image is displayed in the graphics area.

4 To remove the slide from the display, redraw the screen by choosing Redraw from the View menu.

Viewing Slide Libraries

The slidelib utility provides a way of organizing your slide files. If you have set up slide libraries using the *slidelib* utility, you can view slides by specifying the library and slide names. For information about creating slide libraries, see SLIDELIB in the *Command Reference*.

To view a slide in a library

1 At the Command prompt, enter **vslide**.
2 In the Select Slide dialog box, enter a file name, then choose Open.
3 On the command line, enter **library (*slidename*)** to specify the slide.

For example, enter **house1(balcony)** to open the *balcony* slide file, which is stored in the *house1* library file.

4 To remove the slide from the display, redraw the screen by choosing Redraw from the View menu.

Creating Other File Formats

If you need to use an AutoCAD drawing in another application, you can convert it to a specific format. For all platforms, you can convert the formats by using commands associated with each file type.

Creating a DWF File

You can export your drawing in AutoCAD's Drawing Web Format (DWF). A DWF file is a highly compressed 2D vector file that you can use to publish your AutoCAD drawing on the World Wide Web. Using a Web browser, such as Netscape Navigator or Microsoft Internet Explorer, and the *WHIP!* plug-in provided by Autodesk, others can view your drawings via the Internet (provided you have posted them to an Internet server and the viewer has Internet access). The *WHIP!* plug-in provides dynamic pan and zoom capabilities.

The AutoCAD Internet Utilities (provided as a bonus application) let you embed URLs (Universal Resource Locators) into your AutoCAD drawings, which become hyperlinks to other Web pages when the drawing is saved as a DWF file. For more information, see Internet Utilities in the online *Command Reference*.

You can set the precision of your DWF files between 16 and 32 bits, with the default being 20 bits. For simple drawings there's little visual difference. However, for more complex drawings and fine details, you'll need higher precision.

The DWF file uses the background color from the original drawing file. To keep file size down, you can use a default color map and reduce file size by 1K if the background color is black or white.

Only data within the current view is saved to the DWF file. Geometry outside of a zoomed area isn't included in the DWF file.

NOTE The DWFOUT command is disabled in paper space.

To create a DWF file

1. From the File menu, select Export.
2. In the Export Data dialog box, enter a file name.
3. At Save As Type, select Drawing Web Format (*.dwf), and then choose Save.

Command line DWFOUT

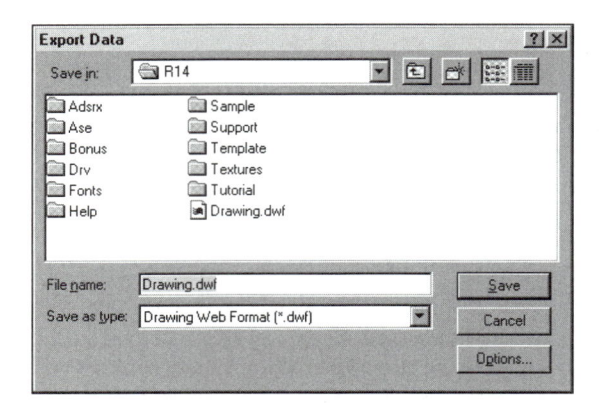

Creating a DXF File

You can export a drawing in Release 12, Release 13, or Release 14 DXF format. The DXF file is a text file that contains drawing information that can be read by other CAD systems or programs. If you are working with consultants who use a CAD program that accepts DXF files, you can share a drawing by saving it in DXF format.

You can specify a precision of up to 16 places for floating-point numbers and save the drawing in either ASCII or binary format. If you do not want to save the entire drawing, you can save selected objects. This feature helps you remove extraneous material when you want to save only specific blocks or areas of the drawing.

NOTE To create and export attribute extract files, select DXX Extract (*.dxx) from Save as Type in the Export Data dialog box. For more information about attribute extract files, see ATTEXT in the *Command Reference*.

To create a DXF file

1 From the File menu, choose Export.
2 In the Export Data dialog box, enter a file name.
3 At Save As Type, select DXF (*.dxf) and version, and then choose Save.

You can also choose Options to specify format, precision, and whether to select specific objects or write the entire file.

Command line DXFOUT

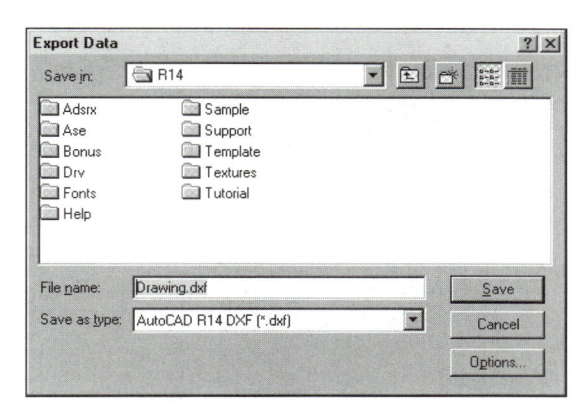

AutoCAD automatically appends the file extension *.dxf* to the file name.

Creating an ACIS File

You can export AutoCAD objects representing trimmed NURB surfaces, regions, and solids to an ACIS file in ASCII (SAT) format. Other objects, such as lines and arcs, are ignored.

To create an ACIS file

1 From the File menu, choose Export.
2 In the Export Data dialog box, enter a file name.
3 At Save As Type, select ACIS (*.sat), and then choose Save.
4 Select the objects you want to save as an ACIS file.

AutoCAD automatically appends the file extension *.sat*.

Command line ACISOUT

Creating a 3DS File

You can create a file in the 3D Studio format (3DS). This procedure saves 3D geometry, views, lights, and materials. 3DSOUT exports circles, polygonal meshes, polyface meshes, and objects with surface characteristics. For a complete list of criteria, see 3DSOUT in the *Command Reference*.

To create a 3DS file

1. From the File menu, choose Export.
2. In the Export Data dialog box, enter a file name.
3. At Save As Type, select 3D Studio (*.3ds), and then choose Save.
4. Select the objects you want to export.
5. In the Create 3D Studio Output File dialog box, enter a file name.

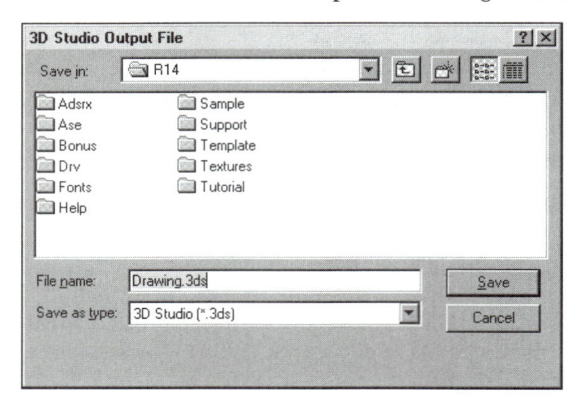

6. Choose Save.

   AutoCAD automatically appends the file extension *.3ds* to the file name.

   Command line   3DSOUT

Creating a Windows WMF File

A Windows metafile format (WMF) file contains screen vector graphics and raster graphic formats. Use WMFOUT to save selected AutoCAD objects in a WMF file.

To create a WMF file

1. From the File menu, choose Export.
2. In the Export Data dialog box, enter a file name.
3. At Save As Type, select Metafile (*.wmf), and then choose Save.
4. Select the objects to export.

   AutoCAD automatically appends the file extension *.wmf* to the file name.

   Command line   WMFOUT

Creating a BMP File

You can use BMPOUT to create a bitmap image of the objects in your drawing.

To create a bitmap file

1 From the File menu, choose Export.
2 In the Export Data dialog box, enter a file name.
3 At Save As Type, select Bitmap (*.bmp), and then choose Save.
4 Select the objects you want to save as bitmaps.

   AutoCAD automatically appends the file extension *.bmp* to the file name.

   Command line   BMPOUT

Creating a PostScript File

You can create a PostScript file consisting of all or some of your drawing. When you use PSOUT to create an Encapsulated PostScript (EPS) file, some AutoCAD objects are specially rendered into PostScript. For a description of how different objects are treated, see the table "How exporting in PostScript format affects objects" on page 734.

To create a PostScript file

1 From the File menu, choose Export.
2 In the Export Data dialog box, enter a file name.
3 At Save As Type, select Encapsulated PS (*.eps), and then choose Options.

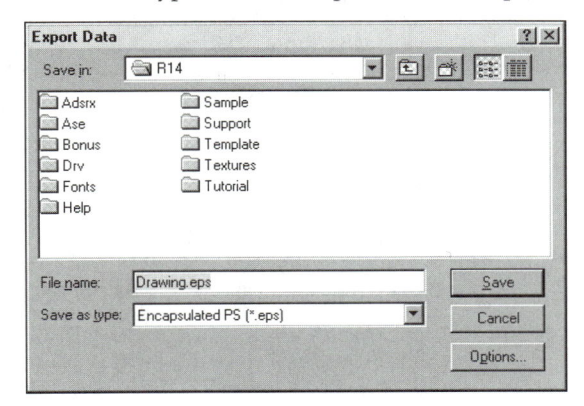

4 In the Import/Export Options dialog box under What to Plot, select an option to specify the area in the drawing to use for the PostScript file.

Creating Other File Formats

733

5   Under Preview, specify whether you want to include an EPSI or TIFF screen preview or no preview for desktop publishing applications.
6   Under Size Units, specify whether to use inches or millimeters.
7   Under Scale, specify a scale for the EPS output using one of these methods:

   - Specify a custom scale based on the size of the plotted output compared with the actual size represented in the drawing. For example, entering **1=10** produces output in which each plotted inch represents 10 actual inches.
   - Select Fit to Paper to scale the output to fill the paper.

8   Under Paper Size, specify a standard paper size or a custom size that you have defined in the Plot Configuration dialog box.
9   Choose OK. Then choose Save to exit the Create PostScript File dialog box.

Command line   PSOUT

How PostScript Format Affects Objects

When you use PSOUT to create an EPS file, various AutoCAD objects are specially rendered into PostScript, as described in the following table.

How exporting in PostScript format affects objects

Object	Effect
Text, attribute definitions, attributes	You can render into PostScript both text objects and AutoCAD objects that contain attributes and attribute definitions. If you specify the font file for rendering the text objects in the font substitution map of *acad.psf*, AutoCAD plots the text using the PostScript font you specified. Otherwise, AutoCAD renders the text using outlined characters. The *acad.psf* file must be in a directory on the AutoCAD library search path.
Extruded text, text control codes	If an AutoCAD text object has a thickness greater than 0 or contains control codes (such as %%O or %%D), it is not plotted as PostScript text, although the text is accurately rendered. International and special symbols (such as %%213) are output as PostScript text.
ISO 8859 Latin/1 character set	When AutoCAD text objects use character codes in the 127 to 255 range, the text is interpreted according to the ISO 8859 Latin/1 character set. If such a character appears in a text object that can be mapped to PostScript, AutoCAD generates a version of the font with an encoding vector remapped to represent the ISO character set. The resulting text is output in PostScript in a form compatible with the font.

Appendix C Using Other File Formats

How exporting in PostScript format affects objects (*continued*)

Object	Effect
Circles, arcs, ellipses, elliptical arcs	Except when they are extruded, AutoCAD translates arcs and circles into the equivalent PostScript path objects. This translation occurs regardless of the 3D projection in effect in the active view when you start PSOUT.

Using the PostScript Support File

The AutoCAD PostScript Support file (*acad.psf*) is the master support file for PSOUT and PSFILL. This editable ASCII file is divided into sections that control font substitution and define PostScript fill patterns. It also includes *prolog* sections that consist of PostScript-coded procedure definitions and constants.

The PSPROLOG system variable instructs PSOUT to reference an additional prolog section that you create in the *acad.psf* file. By creating a prolog section and placing PostScript code in it, you can customize the appearance of PostScript output in a number of ways. This is useful if you want to perform output functions such as assigning different line widths for different colors or creating special linetypes with the PostScript setdash function. A single prolog section can contain many PostScript functions. For more information about the PostScript Support file, see chapter 3, "PostScript Support," in the *Customization Guide*.

Writing a Solid in Stereolithograph Format

You can write AutoCAD solid objects in a file format compatible with Stereolithograph Apparatus (SLA). The solid data is transferred to SLA as a faceted mesh representation consisting of a set of triangles. The SLA workstation uses the data to define a set of layers representing the part.

To store solids in an SLA file

1 From the File menu, choose Export.

2 In the Export Data dialog box, enter a file name.

3 At Save As Type, select Lithography (*.stl), and then choose Save.

4 Select one or more solid objects. All objects must be entirely within the positive *XYZ* octant of the WCS. That is, their *X*, *Y*, and *Z* coordinates must be greater than zero.

5   Press ENTER to create a binary file.

AutoCAD automatically appends the file extension *.stl* to the file name.

Command line   STLOUT

Related   You can use the FACETRES system variable to control the resolution of the mesh that is created by these triangles.

Using Files Created in Other Formats

You can use drawings or images from other applications by opening them in specific formats. AutoCAD handles some form of conversion for DXF, DXB, SAT, 3D Studio, WMF, and PostScript. For all versions, you can import the file by using the commands associated with each file type.

Using DXF Files

A DXF (drawing exchange) file is an ASCII description of the AutoCAD drawing file. It is used to share drawing data with other applications. DXF files can be opened using the OPEN command.

To open a DXF file

1   From the File menu, choose Open.

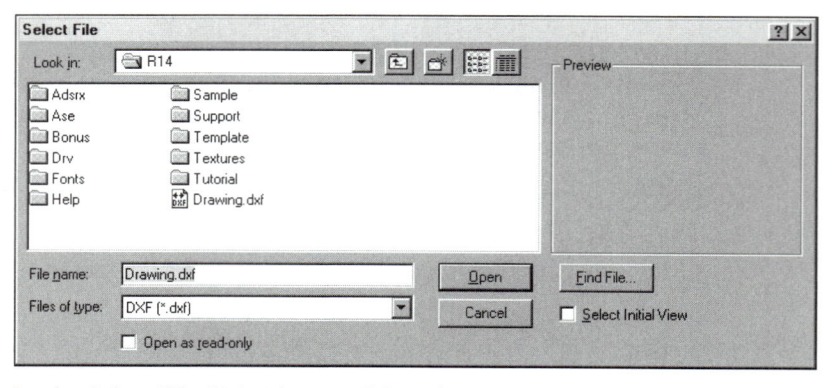

2   In the Select File dialog box, at Files of Type, select DXF (*.dxf).
3   Find and select the DXF file you want to import.
    Or enter the name of the DXF file at File Name.

4 Choose Open.

A new drawing is created, and the DXF file is imported into the drawing.

Command line OPEN

Related IMPORT, DXFIN. DXFOUT saves files with the DXF format for use with other programs.

Using DXB Files

DXBIN opens a specially coded binary DXB file produced by programs such as AutoShade.

To open a DXB file

1 From the Insert menu, choose Drawing Exchange Binary.
2 In the Select DXB File dialog box, find and select the DXB file you want to import.
3 Choose Open.

The file opens in AutoCAD.

Command line DXBIN

Using ACIS SAT Files

You can import geometry objects stored in SAT (ASCII) files. AutoCAD converts the model to a body object or to solids and regions if the body is a true solid or a true region.

To import an ACIS file

1 From the Insert menu, choose ACIS Solid.
2 In the Select ACIS File dialog box, select the file you want to import.
3 Choose Open.

Command line ACISIN

Using 3D Studio Files

You can import a file created with Autodesk 3D Studio. 3DSIN reads 3D Studio geometry and rendering data, which includes meshes, materials, mapping, lights, and cameras. 3DSIN cannot import 3D Studio procedural materials or smoothing groups.

To import a 3DS file

1 From the Insert menu, choose 3D Studio.
2 In the 3D Studio File Import dialog box, find and select the file you want to import.
3 Choose Open.

Command line 3DSIN

Using Windows WMF Files

With AutoCAD for Windows, you can import Windows metafiles into AutoCAD as a block. Unlike bitmaps, WMF files can be scaled and printed without losing resolution. If the WMF file contains solids or wide lines, you can turn off their display to increase drawing speed. See the following section, "Hiding Solid Fills or Wide Lines in Metafiles."

To import a WMF file in AutoCAD

1 From the Insert menu, choose Windows Metafile.
2 In the Import WMF dialog box, select the WMF file you want to open. Then choose Open.
3 Specify an insertion point for the file.
4 Specify the scaling with one of these options:

- Enter a scale to set the *X* and *Y* scale settings. You can set different horizontal and vertical scales. Enter **1** to retain the current scale. Enter a higher number to enlarge the metafile image. Enter a positive number less than 1 to shrink the image.
- Enter **c** (for corner) to specify an imaginary box whose dimensions correspond to the scale factor. To avoid inserting a mirror image, the second point should be above and to the right of the insertion point.
- Enter **xyz** to specify 3D scale factors.

5 Specify the rotation angle.

Command line WMFIN

Hiding Solid Fills or Wide Lines in Metafiles

You can speed up the metafile import process by first turning off the display of solid fills or wide lines.

To control the display of solid fills and wide lines in metafiles

1. From the Insert menu, choose Windows Metafile.
2. In the Import WMF dialog box, choose Options.
3. In the Import/Export Options dialog box, select Wire Frame (No Fills) and Wide Lines to set the display of solid fills and wide lines. By default, these options are selected.
4. Choose OK.
5. Import the WMF file in the normal manner.

Command line WMFOPTS

Using PostScript Files

PSIN imports Encapsulated PostScript images. The graphic is inserted into the drawing as an anonymous block that represents the size and shape of the image.

To import a PostScript file

1. From the Insert menu, choose Encapsulated PostScript.
2. In the Select PostScript File dialog box, select the name of the PostScript file.
3. Choose Open.

   AutoCAD attaches the PostScript description of the image to the block as extended object data.
4. Specify the insertion point or press ENTER to insert the graphic at 0,0.
5. Specify the scale by specifying a point or a value.

NOTE Any discrepancies in the scale size of the imported file can be adjusted by using the SCALE command.

Command line PSIN

Controlling the Quality of the PostScript Display

AutoCAD renders the PostScript graphic according to the quality index set in the PSQUALITY system variable. If the quality index is zero, AutoCAD displays a PostScript object as a bounding rectangle and file name. Nonzero numbers determine the resolution (the number of pixels per AutoCAD drawing unit) of the PostScript image. AutoCAD draws the image as either a solid or an outline (PostScript paths without filling).

To change the PostScript display quality

1 At the Command prompt, enter **psquality**.
2 Enter a quality index.

Displaying PostScript Fills in 2D Polylines

PSFILL fills a 2D polyline outline. You can use any PostScript fill patterns defined in the AutoCAD PostScript support file (*acad.psf*). AutoCAD does not display the patterns on screen, but PSOUT recognizes and exports them. The definition of fill patterns can contain arguments or parameters that control the appearance of the pattern.

To fill 2D polylines with a PostScript fill pattern

1 At the Command prompt, enter **psfill**.
2 Select a wide polyline.

   If the object was previously filled with a PostScript pattern, AutoCAD displays the current pattern name as the default.

3 To list the PostScript fill patterns defined in *acad.psf*, enter **?**.

   AutoCAD displays a list of available patterns.

4 Enter the name of the pattern you want to use.

   By default, PSOUT plots patterns with the polyline outline. If you do *not* want the outline to appear, precede the pattern name with an asterisk (*).

5 Respond to the prompts for any parameters or arguments required by the pattern you chose. Patterns can have up to 25 arguments.

Using Font Mapping When Importing PostScript Files

The AutoCAD font map file (*fontmap.ps*) is a catalog, or font map, of all fonts known to the AutoCAD PostScript interpreter (*acad.ps*). When you import a PostScript image, this ASCII file maps PostScript language font names to the names of their respective font definition (PFB) files. Any font to be loaded automatically should be declared in *fontmap.ps*. You can place the fonts in any directory on the ACAD search path.

When you import an EPS file with PSIN, *acad.ps* uses *fontmap.ps* to locate PFB files corresponding to fonts named in the EPS file. If *acad.ps* finds a PFB file in *fontmap.ps* but not in your system, it displays a warning and substitutes a default font. Consequently, it's not harmful to declare fonts you have not installed.

The *fontmap.ps* file references a set of Type 1 fonts supplied with AutoCAD, as well as the fonts distributed with the Adobe Type Manager for Windows, Adobe Plus Pack, and Adobe Font Pack 1. If you've purchased additional fonts, you can edit the font map file and declare them the same way the existing fonts are declared.

Color Mapping for Imported PostScript Images

The AutoCAD PostScript rendering program, *acad.ps*, matches a requested color as closely as possible to one of AutoCAD's 256 standard colors. If you've set up AutoCAD to use nonstandard colors (for example, 8- or 16-color displays that replicate the first 8 or 16 colors in the 256-color range), the full-color PostScript files may be displayed incorrectly but usually are recognizable. PostScript files that use only the colors in the standard AutoCAD 8-color set are displayed properly on such displays.

If you've set a white screen background, PostScript objects drawn in white are mapped to another color, such as black. You may want to map requests to render in white to AutoCAD color 255, the brightest of the six gray-scale values.

For imported PostScript images, the display color assignments are overridden when you render or replay an image using the Best Map/Fold or Best Map/No Fold color maps, which are set in the Rendering Preferences dialog box.

Glossary

Commands associated with definitions are shown in parentheses at the end of the definition.

absolute coordinates   Coordinate values measured from a coordinate system's origin point. *See also* **origin, relative coordinates, user coordinate system (UCS), world coordinates,** *and* **World Coordinate System (WCS).**

adaptive sampling   A method to accelerate the antialiasing process within the bounds of the sample matrix size. *See also* **antialiasing**.

ADI   For *Autodesk Device Interface*. An interface specification for developing device drivers that are required for peripherals to work with AutoCAD and other Autodesk products.

affine calibration   A tablet calibration method that provides an arbitrary linear transformation in two-dimensional space. Affine calibration requires three calibration points to allow a tablet transformation that combines translation, independent X and Y scaling, rotation, and some skewing. Use affine calibration if a drawing has been stretched differently in the horizontal or vertical direction. (TABLET)

alias   A shortcut for an AutoCAD command. For example, *CP* is an alias for COPY, and *Z* is an alias for ZOOM. You define aliases in the *acad.pgp* file.

aliasing   The effect of discrete picture elements, or pixels, aligned as a straight or curved edge on fixed grid appearing to be jagged or stepped. *See also* **anti-aliasing**.

aligned dimension   A dimension that measures the distance between two points at any angle. The dimension line is parallel to the line connecting the dimension's definition points. (DIMALIGNED)

ambient color   A color produced only by ambient light.

ambient light   Light that illuminates all surfaces of a model with equal intensity. Ambient light has no single source of direction and does not diminish in intensity over distance.

angular dimension   A dimension that measures angles or arc segments and consists of text, extension lines, and leaders. (DIMANGULAR)

angular unit   The unit of measurement for an angle. Angular units can be measured in decimal degrees, degrees/minutes/seconds, grads, and radians.

annotations Text, dimensions, tolerances, symbols, or notes.

anonymous block An unnamed block that supports associative dimensions.

ANSI For *American National Standards Institute*. Coordinator of voluntary standards development for both private and public sectors in the United States. Standards pertain to programming languages, Electronic Data Interchange (EDI), telecommunications, and the physical properties of diskettes, cartridges, and magnetic tapes.

anti-aliasing A method that reduces aliasing by shading the pixels adjacent to the main pixels that define a line or boundary.

approximation points Point locations that a B-spline must pass near, within a fit tolerance. *See also* **fit points** *and* **interpolation points**.

array 1. Multiple copies of selected AutoCAD objects in a rectangular or polar (radial) pattern. (ARRAY) 2. A collection of data items, each identified by a subscript or key, arranged so a computer can examine the collection and retrieve data with the key.

arrowhead A terminator, such as an arrowhead, slash, or dot, at the end of a dimension line showing where a dimension begins and ends.

ASCII For *American Standard Code for Information Interchange*. A common numeric code used in computer data communications. The code assigns meaning to 128 numbers, using seven bits per character with the eighth bit used for parity checking. Nonstandard versions of ASCII assign meaning to 255 numbers.

aspect ratio Ratio of display width to height.

associative dimension A dimension that adapts as the associated geometry is modified.

associative hatching Hatching that conforms to its bounding objects such that modifying the bounding objects automatically adjusts the hatch. (BHATCH)

attenuation The diminishing of light intensity over distance.

attribute definition An AutoCAD object that is included in a block definition to store alphanumeric data. Attribute values can be predefined or specified when the block is inserted. Attribute data can be extracted from a drawing and inserted into external files. (DDATTDEF, ATTDEF)

attribute extraction file An ASCII text file to which extracted attribute data is written. The contents and format are determined by the attribute extraction template file.

attribute extraction template file An ASCII text file that determines which attributes are extracted and how they are formatted when written to an attribute extraction file.

attribute prompt The text string displayed when you insert a block with an attribute whose value is undefined. *See also* **attribute definition, attribute tag,** *and* **attribute value**.

attribute tag A text string associated with an attribute that identifies a particular attribute during extraction from the drawing database. *See also* **attribute definition, attribute prompt,** *and* **attribute value**.

attribute value The alphanumeric information associated with an attribute tag. *See also* **attribute definition, attribute prompt,** *and* **attribute tag**.

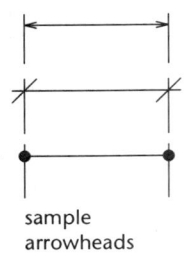

sample arrowheads

AutoCAD library search path   The order in which AutoCAD looks for a support file: current directory, drawing directory, directory specified in the support path, and directory containing the AutoCAD executable file, *acad.exe*.

Autodesk Device Interface   *See* **ADI**.

axis tripod   Icon with *X*, *Y*, and *Z* coordinates that is used to visualize the viewpoint (view direction) of a drawing without displaying the drawing. (VPOINT)

back face   The opposite side of a front face. Back faces are not visible in a rendered image. *See also* **front face**.

baseline   An imaginary line on which text characters appear to rest. Individual characters can have descenders that drop below the baseline.

baseline dimension   Multiple dimensions measured from the same baseline. Also called *parallel dimensions*.

base point   1. In the context of editing grips, the grip that changes to a solid color when selected to specify the focus of the subsequent editing operation. 2. A point for relative distance and angle when copying, moving, and rotating objects. 3. The insertion base point of the current drawing. (BASE) 4. The insertion base point for a block definition. (BLOCK)

Bezier curve   A polynomial curve defined by a set of control points, representing an equation of an order one less than the number of points being considered. A Bezier curve is a special case of a B-spline curve.

bitmap   The digital representation of an image having bits referenced to pixels. In color graphics, a different value represents each red, green, and blue component of a pixel.

blip marks   Temporary screen markers displayed in the AutoCAD graphics area when you specify a point or select objects. (BLIPMODE)

block   A generic term for one or more AutoCAD objects that are combined to create a single object. Commonly used for either block definition or block reference. *See* **block definition** *and* **block reference**. (BLOCK)

block definition   The name, base point, and set of objects that are combined and stored in the symbol table of a drawing. (BLOCK) *SEE* **block**. *SEE ALSO* **block reference**.

block reference   A compound object that is inserted in a drawing and displays the data stored in a block definition. Also called *instance*. *See* **block**. *See also* **block definition**. (INSERT)

block table   The nongraphic data area of a drawing file that stores block definitions. *See also* **symbol table**.

B-spline curve   A blended piecewise polynomial curve passing near a given set of control points. (SPLINE)

bump map   A map in which brightness values are translated into apparent changes in the height of the surface of an object.

button menu   The menu for a pointing device with multiple buttons. Each button on the pointing device (except the pick button) can be defined in the AutoCAD menu file *acad.mnu* in the BUTTONS*n* and AUX*n* sections.

BYBLOCK A special object property used to specify that the object inherits the color or linetype of any block containing it. *See also* **BYLAYER**.

BYLAYER A special object property used to specify that the object inherits the color or linetype associated with its layer. *See also* **BYBLOCK**.

circular external reference An externally referenced drawing (xref) that references itself directly or indirectly. AutoCAD ignores the xref that creates the circular condition.

clipping planes The boundaries that define or clip the field of view. (DVIEW)

CMYK For *cyan, magenta, yellow, and key color*. A system of defining colors by specifying the percentages of cyan, magenta, yellow, and the key color, which is typically black.

color map A table defining the intensity of red, green, and blue (RGB) for each displayed color.

command line A text area reserved for keyboard input, prompts, and messages.

construction plane A plane on which planar geometry is constructed. The *XY* plane of the current UCS represents the construction plane. *See also* **elevation** *and* **user coordinate system**.

continued dimension A type of linear dimension that uses the second extension line origin of a selected dimension as its first extension line origin, breaking one long dimension into shorter segments that add up to the total measurement. Also called *chain dimension*. (DIMCONTINUE)

control frame A series of point locations used as a mechanism to control the shape of a B-spline. These points are connected by a series of line segments for visual clarity and to distinguish the control frame from fit points. The SPLFRAME system variable must be turned on to display control frames.

control point *See* **control frame**.

coordinate filters Functions that extract individual *X*, *Y*, and *Z* coordinate values from different points to create a new, composite point. Also called *X,Y,Z point filters*.

CPolygon A multisided area specified to select objects fully or partially within its borders. *See also* **crossing window** *and* **WPolygon**.

crosshairs A type of cursor consisting of two lines that intersect. Also called *graphics cursor*.

crosshairs

crossing window A rectangular area drawn to select objects fully or partly within its borders. *See also* **CPolygon**.

cursor A pointer on a video display screen that can be moved around to place textual or graphical information. Also called *graphics cursor*. *See also* **crosshairs**.

cursor menu The menu that is displayed in the graphics area at the cursor location when you hold down SHIFT and press the return button on a pointing device. The cursor menu is defined in the POP0 section of *acad.mnu*.

default A predefined value for a program input or parameter. Default values and options for AutoCAD commands are denoted by angle braces <>.

default drawing *See* **initial environment**.

definition points Points for creating an associative dimension. AutoCAD refers to the points to modify the appearance and value of an associative dimension when the associated object is modified. Also called *defpoints* and stored on the special layer DEFPOINTS.

dependent symbols Symbol table definitions that are brought into a drawing by an external reference. *See also* **symbol table**.

DIESEL For *Direct Interpretively Evaluated String Expression Language*. A macro language for altering the AutoCAD status line with the MODEMACRO system variable and for customizing menu items.

diffuse color In AutoCAD, an object's predominant color.

dimension line arc An arc (usually with arrows at each end) spanning the angle formed by the extension lines of an angle being measured. The dimension text near this arc sometimes divides it into two arcs. *See also* **angular dimension**.

dimension style A named group of dimension settings that determines the appearance of the dimension and simplifies setting dimension system variables. (DDIM)

dimension text The measurement value of dimensioned objects.

dimension variables A set of numeric values, text strings, and settings that control AutoCAD dimensioning features. (DDIM)

direct distance entry A method to specify a second point by first moving the cursor to indicate direction and then entering a distance.

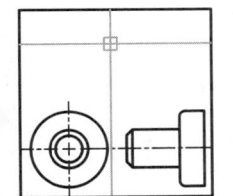

dithering Combining color dots to give the impression of displaying more colors than are actually available.

drawing extents The smallest rectangle that contains all objects in a drawing, positioned on the screen to display the largest possible view of all objects. (ZOOM)

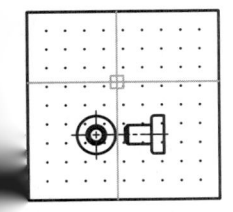

drawing limits The user-defined rectangular boundary of the drawing area covered by dots when the grid is turned on. Also called *grid limits*. (LIMITS)

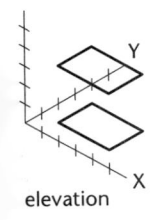

DWF For *drawing Web format*. A highly compressed file format that is created from a DWG file. DWF files are easy to publish and view on the Web.

DWG Standard file format for saving vector graphics from within AutoCAD.

DXF For *drawing interchange format*. An ASCII or binary file format of an AutoCAD drawing file for exporting AutoCAD drawings to other applications or for importing drawings from other applications.

edge The boundary of a face.

elevation The default *Z* value above or below the *XY* plane of the current user coordinate system, which is used for entering coordinates and digitizing locations. (ELEVATION)

embed To use object linking and embedding (OLE) information from a source document in a destination document. An embedded object is a copy of the information from a source document that is placed in the destination document and has no link to the source document. *See also* **link**.

environment variable A setting stored in the operating system that controls the operation of a program. In AutoCAD the ACADSERVER environment variable must be set for the License Manager. Typically, ACADSERVER is set as a *system* (not *user*) environment variable.

explode To disassemble a complex object, such as a block, solid, or polyline, into simpler objects. In the case of a block, the block definition is unchanged. The block reference is replaced by the components of the block. *See also* **block, block definition,** *and* **block reference.** (EXPLODE)

extents *See* **drawing extents.**

external reference (xref) A drawing file linked (or attached) to another drawing. (XREF)

extrusion A 3D solid created by sweeping an object that encloses an area along a linear path.

face A triangular or quadrilateral portion of a surface object.

feature control frame Specifies the tolerance that applies to specific features or patterns of features. Feature control frames always contain at least a geometric characteristic symbol to indicate the type of control and a tolerance value to indicate the amount of acceptable variation.

fence A multisegmented line specified to select objects it passes through.

fill A solid color covering an area bounded by lines or curves. (FILL)

filters *See* **coordinate filters.**

fit points Locations that a B-spline must pass through exactly or within a fit tolerance. *See also* **interpolation points** *and* **approximation points.**

fit tolerance The setting for the maximum distance that a B-spline can pass for each of the fit points that define it.

floating viewports Rectangular objects that are created in paper space that display views. *See also* **paper space.** (MVIEW)

font A character set, comprising letters, numbers, punctuation marks, and symbols, of a distinctive proportion and design.

freeze A setting that suppresses the display of objects on selected layers. Objects on frozen layers are not displayed, regenerated, or plotted. Freezing layers shortens regenerating time. *See also* **thaw.** (LAYER)

front faces Faces with their normals pointed outward.

graphics area The area of the AutoCAD screen for creating and editing a drawing.

graphics cursor *See* **crosshairs** *and* **cursor.**

graphics screen *See* **graphics window.**

graphics window The graphics area, its surrounding menus, and the command line.

grid An area on the graphics display covered with regularly spaced dots to aid drawing. The spacing between grid dots is adjustable. Grid dots are not plotted. *See also* **drawing limits.** (GRID)

grip modes The editing capabilities activated when grips are displayed on an object: stretching, moving, rotating, scaling, and mirroring.

grips Small squares that appear on objects you select. After selecting the grip, you edit the object by dragging it with the mouse instead of entering commands.

handle   A unique alphanumeric tag for an object in the AutoCAD database.

home page   The main navigating screen for a Web site.

HLS   For *hue, lightness, and saturation*. A system of defining color by specifying the amount of hue, lightness, and saturation.

IGES   For *initial graphics exchange specification*. An ANSI-standard format for digital representation and exchange of information between CAD/CAM systems.

initial environment   The variables and settings for new drawings as defined by the default template drawing, such as *acad.dwg* or *acltiso.dwg*. *See also* **template drawing**.

instance   *See* **block reference**.

interpolation points   Defining points that a B-spline passes through. *See also* **approximation points** *and* **fit points**.

island   An enclosed area within a hatched area.

ISO   For *International Standards Organization*. The organization that sets international standards in all fields except electrical and electronics. Headquarters are in Geneva, Switzerland.

isometric snap style   An AutoCAD drafting option that aligns the cursor with two of three isometric axes and displays grid points, making isometric drawings easier to create.

layer   A logical grouping of data that are like transparent acetate overlays on a drawing. You can view layers individually or in combination. (LAYER)

limits   *See* **drawing limits**.

line font   *See* **linetype**.

linetype   How a line or type of curve is displayed. For example, a continuous line has a different linetype than a dashed line. Also called *line font*. (LINETYPE)

link   To use object linking and embedding (OLE) to reference data in another file. When data is linked, any changes to it in the source document is automatically updated in any destination document. *See also* **embed**.

mirror   To create a new version of an existing object by reflecting it symmetrically with respect to a prescribed line or plane. (MIRROR)

mode   A software setting or operating state.

model   A two- or three-dimensional representation of an object.

model space   One of the two primary spaces in which AutoCAD objects reside. Typically, a geometric model is placed in a three-dimensional coordinate space called model space. A final layout of specific views and annotations of this model is placed in paper space. *See also* **paper space**. (MSPACE)

named view   A view saved for restoration later. (VIEW)

node   An object snap specification to locate points, dimension definition points, and dimension text origins.

normal   A vector perpendicular to a face.

noun-verb selection   Selecting an object first and then performing an operation on it rather than entering a command first and then selecting the object.

NURBS For *nonuniform rational B-spline curve*. A B-spline curve or surface defined by a series of weighted control points and one or more knot vectors. *See* **B-spline curve**.

object One or more AutoCAD graphical elements, such as text, dimensions, lines, circles, or polylines, treated as a single element for creation, manipulation, and modification. Also called *entity*.

Object Snap mode Methods for selecting commonly needed points on an object while you create or edit an AutoCAD drawing. *See also* **running object snap** *and* **object snap override**.

object snap override Turning off or changing a running object snap mode for input of a single point. *See also* **Object Snap modes** *and* **running object snap**.

OLE For *object linking and embedding*. An information-sharing method in which data from a source document can be linked to or embedded in a destination document. Selecting the data in the destination document opens the source application so that the data can be edited. *See also* **embed** *and* **link**.

opacity map Projection of opaque and transparent areas onto objects, creating the effect of a solid surface with holes or gaps.

origin The point where coordinate axes intersect. For example, the origin of a Cartesian coordinate system is where the *X*, *Y*, and *Z* axes meet at 0,0,0.

orthogonal Having perpendicular slopes or tangents at the point of intersection.

Ortho mode An AutoCAD setting that limits pointing device input to horizontal or vertical (relative to the current snap angle and the user coordinate system). *See also* **snap angle** *and* **user coordinate system**.

pan To shift the view of a drawing without changing magnification. *See also* **zoom**. (PAN)

paper space One of two primary spaces in which AutoCAD objects reside. Paper space is used for creating a finished layout for printing or plotting, as opposed to doing drafting or design work. Model space is used for creating the drawing. *See also* **model space**, *and* **viewport**. (PSPACE)

personalization Customizing the AutoCAD executable file, *acad.exe*, during installation by entering the user name, company, and other information.

photorealistic rendering Rendering that resembles a photograph.

pick button The button on a pointing device that is used to select objects or specify points on the screen. For example, on a two-button mouse, it is the left button.

planar projection Mapping of objects or images onto a plane.

plan view A view orientation from a point on the positive Z axis toward the origin (0,0,0). (PLAN)

pline *See* **polyline**.

point 1. A location in three-dimensional space specified by *X*, *Y*, and *Z* coordinate values. 2. An AutoCAD object consisting of a single coordinate location. (POINT)

point filters *See* **coordinate filters**.

polar array Objects copied around a specified center point a specified number of times. (ARRAY)

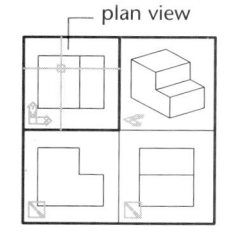

polygon window   A multisided area specified to select objects in groups. *See also* **CPolygon, crossing window,** *and* **WPolygon.**

polyline   An AutoCAD object composed of one or more connected line segments or circular arcs treated as a single object. Also called *pline*. (PLINE, PEDIT)

procedural materials   Materials that generate a 3D pattern in two or more colors, and apply it to an object. These include marble, granite, and wood. Also called *template materials*.

prompt   A message on the command line that asks for information or requests action such as specifying a point.

redraw   To quickly refresh or clean up the current viewport without updating the drawing's database. *See also* **regenerate**. (REDRAW)

reflection color   The color of a highlight on shiny material. Also called *specular color*.

reflection mapping   Creates the effect of a scene reflected on the surface of a shiny object.

regenerate   To update a drawing's screen display by recomputing the screen coordinates from the database. *See also* **redraw**. (REGEN)

relative coordinates   Coordinates specified in relation to previous coordinates.

return button   The button on a pointing device used to accept an entry. For example, on a two-button mouse, it is the right button.

RGB   For *red, green, and blue*. A system of defining colors by specifying percentages of red, green, and blue.

rubber-band line   A line that stretches dynamically on the screen with the movement of the cursor. One endpoint of the line is attached to a point in your drawing, and the other is attached to the moving cursor.

running object snap   Setting an object snap mode so it continues for subsequent selections. (OSNAP) *See also* **Object Snap modes** *and* **object snap override.**

script file   A set of AutoCAD commands executed sequentially with a single SCRIPT command. Script files are created outside AutoCAD using a text editor, saved in text format, and stored in an external file with the extension *.scr*.

selection set   One or more AutoCAD objects specified for processing as a unit.

selection window   A rectangular area drawn in the AutoCAD graphics area to select objects in groups. *See also* **CPolygon, crossing window, polygon window,** *and* **WPolygon.**

slide file   A file that contains a raster image or snapshot of the display on the graphics screen. Slide files work with Autodesk Animator and Animator Pro and have the file extension *.sld*. (MSLIDE, VSLIDE)

slide library   A collection of slide files organized for convenient retrieval and display. Slide library names have the extension *.slb* and are created with the *slidelib.exe* utility.

smooth shading   Smoothing of the edges between polygon faces.

snap angle   The angle that the snap grid is rotated.

snap grid   The invisible grid that locks the graphics cursor into alignment with the grid points according to the spacing set by Snap. Snap grid does not necessarily correspond to the visible grid, which is controlled separately by Grid. (SNAP)

Snap mode   A mode for locking a pointing device into alignment with an invisible rectangular grid. When Snap mode is on, the screen crosshairs and all input coordinates are snapped to the nearest point on the grid. The snap resolution defines the spacing of this grid. *See also* **Object Snap mode**. (SNAP)

snap resolution   The spacing between points of the snap grid.

specular reflection   The light in a narrow cone where the angle of the incoming beam equals the angle of the reflected beam.

symbol table   A nongraphic AutoCAD object definition that is stored in the drawing, also known as a *named object*. Symbols can include definitions of blocks, dimensioning styles, layers, linetypes, and text styles.

system variable   A name that AutoCAD recognizes as a mode, size, or limit. Read-only system variables, such as DWGNAME, cannot be modified directly by the user.

template drawing   A drawing file with preestablished settings for new drawings such as *acad.dwg* and *acadiso.dwg*; however, any drawing can be used as a template. *See also* **initial environment**.

temporary files   Data files created during an AutoCAD session. AutoCAD deletes the files by the time you end the session. If the session ends abnormally, such as during a power outage, temporary files might be left on the disk.

tessellation lines   Lines that help you visualize a curved surface.

text style   A named, saved collection of settings that determines the appearance of text characters—for example, stretched, compressed, oblique, mirrored, or set in a vertical column.

texture map   The projection of an image (such as a tile pattern) onto an object (such as a chair).

thaw   A setting that displays previously frozen layers. *See also* **freeze**. (LAYER)

thickness   The distance certain objects are extruded to give them a 3D appearance. (CHPROP, DDCHPROP, ELEV, THICKNESS)

tiled viewports   A type of display that splits the AutoCAD graphics area into one or more adjacent rectangular viewing areas. *See also* **floating viewports**, **TILEMODE**, *and* **viewport**. (VPORTS)

TILEMODE   A system variable that controls whether viewports can be created as movable, resizable objects (floating), or as nonoverlapping display elements that appear side-by-side (tiled). *See also* **viewport**.

toolbar   Part of the AutoCAD interface containing icons that represent commands.

tracking   A way to locate a point relative to other points on the drawing. (TRACKING)

transparent command   A command started while another is in progress. Precede transparent commands with an apostrophe.

UCS   *See* **user coordinate system**.

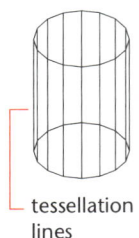

UCS icon   An icon that indicates the orientation of the UCS axes. (UCSICON)

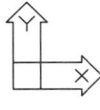

user coordinate system (UCS)   A user-defined coordinate system that defines the orientation of the *X*, *Y*, and *Z* axes in 3D space. The UCS determines the default placement of geometry in a drawing. *See also* **World Coordinate System** (UCS).

UCS icon

vector   A mathematical object with precise direction and length but without specific location.

vertex   A location where edges or polyline segments meet.

view   A graphical representation of a model from a specific location (viewpoint) in space. (VPOINT, DVIEW, VIEW)

viewpoint   The location in 3D model space from which you are viewing a model. (DVIEW, VPOINT)

viewport   A bounded area that displays some portion of the model space of a drawing. The TILEMODE system variable determines the type of viewport created. 1. When TILEMODE is off (0), viewports are objects that can be moved and resized. (MVIEW) 2. When TILEMODE is on (1), viewports are noneditable, nonoverlapping screen displays. *See also* **floating viewport** *and* **TILEMODE**. (VPORTS)

viewport configuration   A named collection of tiled viewports that can be saved and restored. (VPORTS)

virtual screen display   The area in which AutoCAD can pan and zoom without regenerating the drawing.

volumetric shadows   A photorealistically rendered volume of space cast by the shadow of an object.

WCS   *See* **World Coordinate System**.

wireframe model   The representation of an object using lines and curves to represent its boundaries.

working drawing   A drawing for manufacturing or building purposes.

world coordinates   Coordinates expressed in relation to the World Coordinate System.

World Coordinate System (WCS)   A coordinate system used as the basis for defining all objects and other coordinate systems.

WPolygon   A multisided polygon area specified to select objects contained completely within its borders. *See also* **crossing window** *and* **CPolygon**.

WCS icon

xref   *See* **external reference**.

X,Y,Z point filters   *See* **coordinate filters**.

zoom   To reduce or increase the apparent magnification of the graphics display. (ZOOM)

Glossary

753

Index

Symbols

< (angle bracket, open), polar coordinate delimiter, 117
<> (angle brackets), command prompt delimiters, 73
>> (angle brackets, double close), transparent command prompt indicator, 77
' (apostrophe), transparent command character, 76, 719
* (asterisk)
    mathematical operator, 188
    polyline outline deletion character, 740
    wild-card character, 230, 307
@ (at sign)
    relative/polar coordinate specifier, 117
    wild-card character, 230, 307
\ (backslash), word wrap character, 361
^ (caret)
    mathematical operator, 188
    stacked text indicator, 345
^C^C, cancel command prefix, 719
{ } (curly braces), format change characters, 361
° (degree sign), Unicode value, 707
Ø (diameter symbol), Unicode value, 707
$$ (dollar signs), bound xref name characters, 463, 464
[...] (ellipsis, enclosed), wild-card character, 230, 307
= (equal sign), block name symbol, 438
- (hyphen)
    dialog box suppression character, 78
    wild-card character, 230, 308
- (minus sign)
    mathematical operator, 188
    zoom cursor, 201
( ) (parentheses), mathematical operators, 188
. (period), wild-card character, 230, 307
+ (plus sign)
    mathematical operator, 188
    UCS icon symbol, 121
    zoom cursor, 201
± (plus-or-minus sign)
    lateral tolerance symbol, 413
    Unicode value, 707

(pound sign), wild-card character, 230, 307
' (prime symbol), feet specifier, 118
Ⓟ, projected tolerance symbol, 427
? (question mark)
    noncurrent font display character, 707
    wild-card character, 230, 307
" (quotes, double), long file name delimiters, 77
' (reverse quote), wild-card character, 230, 308
/ (slash, forward)
    mathematical operator, 188
    stacked text indicator, 345
[ ] (square brackets), alternate units delimiter, 409
~ (tilde)
    dialog box display character, 78
    wild-card character, 230, 307
[~...] (tilde-ellipsis, enclosed), wild-card character, 230, 308
_ (underscore), foreign language translation character, 719
| (vertical bar)
    dependent symbol name character, 464
    dimension style xref name separator, 423
2D (two dimensions), drafting limitations, 519
2D Cartesian coordinates (X,Y coordinates)
    absolute, 116
    locating points with, 114, 195
    relative, 46, 116
    specifying, 114, 115
2D coordinates
    specifying, 114–118
    See also 2D Cartesian coordinates (X,Y coordinates); polar coordinates
2D images
    background images, 586–588
    mapping onto 3D object surfaces, 611–616
2D objects
    positioning in 3D space, 536
    See also objects

2D polylines
    linetypes, 320
    PostScript fills, 740
2D Solid option (Surfaces, Draw menu), 147
2D solids. *See* solid-fills
2D space, drafting limitations, 519
3 Point option (UCS, Tools menu), 120, 526
3 Points option (Arc, Draw menu), 139
3D (three dimensions). *See* 3D space
3D Array option (3D Operation, Modify menu), 557
3D Cartesian coordinates (*X,Y,Z* coordinates)
    extracting from selected points, 521
    locating points with, 195
    specifying, 521
3D command, 538, 549–552
3D coordinates
    cylindrical, 522
    specifying, 55, 115, 118, 520–524
    spherical, 524
    See also 3D Cartesian coordinates (*X,Y,Z* coordinates)
3D Dynamic View (View menu), 532–535, 571
3D faces
    creating, 540
    removing/plotting hidden lines, 492, 501
    surfaces defined by, 568
3D images, 565–629
    lighting, 588–604
    removing overlapping lines, 516
    smoothness, 549, 579
    types, 566
    See also 3D views; hidden-line images; hiding hidden lines; rendered images; rendering; shaded images; shading
3D Mesh option (Surfaces, Draw menu), 540
3D meshes. *See* meshes (faceted surfaces)
3D modeling, 55, 535–555, 567–569
    abutting objects and, 568–569
    drafting techniques, 577
    drawing surfaces, 575
    intersecting faces and, 578
    intersecting objects and, 568–569
    methods, 535, 567
    overlapping faces and, 578
    removing hidden surfaces, 575
    surfaces defined for, 567–568
    See also 3D objects
3D models. *See* 3D objects
3D objects
    abutting (touching) objects, 568
    arraying, 556
    complexity, 577
    creating, 535–555

3D objects (*continued*)
    editing, 556–563
    export file format, 731
    extending, 558
    filleting, 560
    intersecting objects, 568, 569
    mapping 2D images onto, 611–616
    mirroring, 558
    preparing for rendering, 575–579
    rotating, 556
    top and bottom surfaces, 567
    trimming, 558, 559
    types, 535
        converting between, 536
    wireframes, 535, 536, 566, 753
    See also 3D images; 3D views; extruded objects; hiding hidden lines; meshes; rendering; shading; solids; surfaces
3D Operation (Modify menu), options, 556, 557, 558
3D shapes, 536, 538, 548
3D solids. *See* solids
3D space
    defining user coordinate systems (UCSs) in, 525
    positioning 2D objects in, 536
    simulating, 162
    viewing drawings in, 527–535
    working in, 519–563
    See also 3D objects; 3D views
3D Studio, exporting/importing drawings/files to/from, 628
3D Studio files
    creating, 628, 731
    importing, 628, 737
3D Viewpoint (View menu), options, 528, 530
3D views (in 3D model space), 527–535
    changing to a plan view, 530
    dynamic viewing, 531–535
    export file format, 731
    parallel projections (of 3D views), 531
    perspective views, 507, 531, 532
    removing hidden lines, 534
    rotating, 528
    setting, 528–535
        camera points/angles, 532, 533
        clipping planes, 533
        with the compass and axis tripod, 530
3DARRAY command, 556
3DFACE command, 540
3DMESH command, 539
3DS files. *See* 3D Studio files
3DSIN command, 628, 737
3DSOUT command, 628, 731

A

absolute coordinates, 116, 743
    2D (X,Y), 116
    cylindrical, 522
acad.mnu file, 68, 85
acad.ps (AutoCAD PostScript interpreter), 740
acad.psf file, 735
acad14.cfg file, 494, 508
accelerator keys, reassigning, 72
accuracy. *See* precision
ACI (AutoCAD Color Index) numbers, 309, 318
ACIS files
    creating, 731
    importing, 737
actions
    marking, 80
    redoing, 80
    undoing, 45, 80
ActiveX Automation Guide, 34
adaptive sampling, 743
ADI (Autodesk Device Interface) specification, 743
Adjust Area Fill option (Plot Configuration dialog box), 501
Adjust option, Image option (Object, Modify menu), 647
Administration dialog box
    connecting to existing databases, 668, 670
    setting environments, 673
Adobe PostScript fonts. *See* PostScript fonts
Advanced Modeling Extension application. *See* AME (Advanced Modeling Extension application)
Advanced Setup wizard
    adding title blocks, 103
    customizing title blocks, 104
    setting up new drawings, 37, 94, 96, 97, 99, 101
Aerial View, 210–214
    displaying the entire drawing, 213
    Fast Zoom mode and, 210
    panning with, 212
    resizing the image, 213
    updating of, 214
    zooming with, 211
    See also Aerial View window
Aerial View (View menu), 211
Aerial View toolbar, illustrated, 211
Aerial View window
    illustrated, 211
    opening/closing, 211
    pan box, 213
    view box, 211
affine calibration, 743
AFLAGS system variable, 443
aliases, 743
    toolbar aliases, 713

aliasing, 580, 743
    filtering (in rendering), 613
Align Text (Dimension menu), options, 386, 387
Aligned (Dimension menu), 372
aligned dimensions, 370, 743
    creating, 371
    illustrated, 366, 370, 372
    stretching, 384
    See also dimensions; linear dimensions
aligning
    floating viewport views, 490
    the grid, 160–164
    objects, at intervals, 181
    the snap, 160–164
    text. *See* text alignment
All option (ZOOM command), 208
ALT+letter keys, choosing menu options, 68
alternate scale value, 409
alternate units (for dimensions), 409
    illustrated, 409
    suppressing zeros, 411
Alternate Units dialog box, 409
alternate xref search paths, defining, 469–471
ambient color, 605, 607, 743
ambient light, 589, 743
    reflection of, 598
AME (Advanced Modeling Extension application), 629
AME objects, 577, 629
AMECONVERT command, 629
American National Standards Institute. *See* ANSI (American National Standards Institute)
American Standard Code for Information Interchange (ASCII), 744
ANGBASE system variable, 99, 117
ANGDIR system variable, 99, 117, 143
angle brackets (<>)
    command prompt delimiters, 73
    double close, transparent command prompt indicator, 77
    single open, polar coordinate delimiter, 117
angle of incidence, 597
angle of reflection, 597
angles
    calculating, 194
    camera angle, 532, 533
    chamfering objects by specifying, 287
    dimensioning, 375
    direction, specifying, 98
    of faces to lights, 594
    falloff angle, 591, 592, 600
    hotspot angle, 591, 592, 600
    of incidence, 597
    for polar coordinates, 117
    reference angles, 265
    of reflection, 597
    relative angles, 264

angles (*continued*)
    smoothing angle, 578
    snap angle, 160, 751
    snap rotation angles, 263
    specifying type, precision, and direction, 98
    spotlight angles, 591, 592, 600
    text obliquing angle, 331
    See also angular dimensions; angular units
Angular (Dimension menu), 375
angular dimensions, 375, 743
    creating, 375
    definition points (illustrated), 382
    extension line order, 404
    illustrated, 366, 375
    See also dimensions
angular units, 743
    setting, 98
    types, 115
Annotation dialog box, 407–410, 411, 413–416
annotations, 744
    adding, 476
        in paper space, 488
    for leader lines, 368, 377, 380
    See also dimension text
anonymous blocks, 437, 744
ANSI (American National Standards Institute), 744
    code pages supported by Windows, 709
antialiasing, 580, 744
    adaptive sampling, 581
    control levels, 581
    in image mapping, 613
apostrophe ('), transparent command character, 76, 719
Apparent Intersection (APP or APPINT) object snap, 166
apparent intersections, snapping to, 166
applications
    AutoCAD Render-related, 628–629
    destination, 654
    source, 654
    using AutoCAD information in other applications, 656–658
    using information from other applications in AutoCAD, 658–666
Apply option (DIMSTYLE command), 419, 420
approximation points, 744
    See also fit points
Arc (Draw menu), options, 139, 140
ARC command, 139
Arc option (Ellipse, Draw menu), 143
architectural units, specifying, 118
archiving drawings, 462
arcs
    converting donuts into, 144
    dimension line arcs, 747
    dimensioning, 374, 375

arcs (*continued*)
    drawing, 139–141
        in polylines, 126
    elliptical, 142
    extension line origins, 369
    filleting, 290
    joining to polylines, 280
    as rendered into PostScript, 735
    See also objects
AREA command, 190–194
Area option (Inquiry, Tools menu), 190–194
areas
    calculating, 190–194
    combined, 192
    hatching, 150–157
    See also plot area
Array (Modify menu), 262
ARRAY command, 262, 556
arraying
    2D objects, 253, 261–263
    3D objects, 556
arrays, 744
    3D, 556
    creating, 261–263
    polar, 261, 557, 750
    rectangular, 261, 262
arrow keys, moving the cursor, 71, 74
arrowheads, 367, 744
    choosing, 393, 430
    creating, 429–431
    defining, 429
    illustrated, 367, 744
    for leader lines, 377
    oblique stroke, 390, 393
    order, 392
    resizing, 401
    sizing, 429
    types, 392
arrows. *See* arrowheads
ARX (AutoCAD Runtime Extension), 57
ASCII (American Standard Code for Information Interchange), 744
ASCII text files. *See* text files
ASE (AutoCAD SQL Environment) commands. *See* external database commands (ASE commands)
ASEADMIN command, 680, 701
ASEEXPORT command, 697–699
ASELINKS command, 687–689
ASEROWS command, 670, 672, 674, 684, 689, 691, 693, 694
ASESELECT command, 694–697
ASESQLED command, 691, 700
Asian fonts, 329
    converting character strings, 708
    See also Big Fonts
aspect ratio, 744

Index

associative dimensions, 368, 744
   See also definition points (of dimensions)
associative hatches
   creating, 151
   removing associativity, 151, 293
   selecting, 293
   updating of, 293
associative hatching, 744
asterisk (*)
   mathematical operator, 188
   polyline outline deletion character, 740
   wild-card character, 230, 307
at sign (@)
   relative/polar coordinate specifier, 117
   wild-card character, 230, 307
Attach Image dialog box, 634
Attach Image File dialog box, 634
Attach option (External Reference dialog box), 451
Attach Xref dialog box, 458
attaching
   attributes to blocks, 443
   materials, 610–611
   raster images, 633
   xrefs, 451, 457–461
   See also linking
ATTDEF command, 443
ATTDISP command, 443
ATTEDIT command, 444
attenuation of light, 590, 599, 744
   rate options, 595, 599
   See also falloff angle (of spotlights)
ATTEXT command, 447
ATTREDEF command, 443
Attribute Definition dialog box, 442
attribute definitions, 744
   creating, 442
   editing, 443
   mirroring, 260
   redefining, 441
   as rendered into PostScript, 734
   specifying viewports with, 105
   thickness, 548
   for title blocks, 105
Attribute Extraction dialog box, 447
attribute information extract files
   formats, 446
   See also template files (for extracting attribute information)
Attribute option (Object, Modify menu), options, 444
attribute tag fields, in extract template files, 446
attribute tags, 744
attribute values, 744

attributes, 45, 433, 441–447
   attaching to blocks, 443
   block redefinitions and, 441
   characteristics, 442
   constant, 441
   creating, 442
   editing, 444
   extracting attribute information, 441, 444–447
   and hatch lines, 156
   invisible, 442
   mirroring, 260
   multiple, 441, 442
   as rendered into PostScript, 734
   variable, 181, 441
   See also displayable attributes
AUNITS system variable, 99
AUPREC system variable, 99
Auto Viewport (Options menu, Aerial View window), 214
AutoCAD
   advanced features, 55–56
   basic concepts, 39–55, 59–90
   and DBMS drivers, 683
   documentation, 33–37
   earlier releases
      drawing order in Release 12, 146
      link information in, 703
      PostScript fonts in Release 14, 333
      updating of pre-Release 14 Render blocks, 628
   exiting, 90
   installing, 60–62
   learning tools, 35
   new features, 35, 465
   personalizing, 750
   programming language support, 57
   starting, 42, 62
   system requirements, 60
   using AutoCAD information in other applications, 656–658
   using information from other applications in, 658–666
   See also AutoCAD environment; performance improvements
AutoCAD Color Index (ACI) numbers, 309, 318
AutoCAD environment
   accessing commands, 72–80
   customizing, 56, 81–87
   interface, 66–72
   redrawing the screen, 81, 751
   undoing actions, 80
   See also Help
AutoCAD format, 256
   converting WMF files to, 257

AutoCAD interface, 66–72
  See also Aerial View window; command line; command window; dialog boxes; graphics window (graphics area); menus; text window; toolbars
AutoCAD Internet Utilities, 56, 729
AutoCAD library search paths, 84, 745
AutoCAD objects. *See* objects (AutoCAD)
AutoCAD PostScript interpreter, 740
AutoCAD PostScript support file. *See* PostScript support file
AutoCAD Render. *See* Render renderer
AutoCAD Runtime Extension (ARX), 57
AutoCAD SQL Environment (ASE) commands, 56
AutoCAD Window Colors dialog box, 83
AutoCAD window. *See* main window
Autodesk Device Interface (ADI) specification, 743
AutoLISP, 57
automatic save option, 83, 90
AutoSnap, 174–176
AutoSurf, 536
AutoSurf surfaces
  converting into meshes, 579
axes
  of ellipses, 141
  right-hand rule, 520
  in the World Coordinate System, 119
axis tripod (in 3D model space), 530, 745
  setting 3D views, 530
Axis, End option (Ellipse, Draw menu), 142

B

back faces (of 3D objects), 745
  leaving in, 577
  removing, 575
  rendering, 577
Back option (UNDO command), 80
background color, setting for rendering, 583
background images, merging renderings with, 586–588
background objects, hiding for hidden line hiding, 570
backgrounds, bitonal image transparency, 646
backslash (\), word wrap character, 361
BACKSPACE key, deleting characters, 74
base grips, 239, 240
base point, 745
  for copying objects, 253
  insertion base point, 437, 439
  snap base point, 160
Baseline (Dimension menu), 373
baseline dimensions, 370, 373, 745
  creating, 373
  dimension line spacing, 390
  extension line origins, 373

baseline dimensions (*continued*)
  illustrated, 366
  See also dimensions
baselines, 745
basic dimensions, 413
batch plotting, 512–514
BATCHPLT utility, 512–514
beam angles of spotlights (hotspots), 591, 592
Beep on Error option (Preferences dialog box), 72, 82
beeps, turning on/off, 72, 82
beveling objects. *See* chamfering objects
Bezier curves, 745
BHATCH command, 148, 150, 151, 157
Big Fonts, 328
  code page identifications, 708
  mapping to other fonts, 353
  specifying, 328, 329
  and Unicode fonts, 707
bills of materials (BOMs). *See* parts lists
Bind option (External Reference dialog box), 452, 686
Bind option (XREF command), 452, 463, 686
Bind Xrefs dialog box, 463
binding
  dependent symbols to drawings, 452, 463
  drawing databases, 452
  xrefs to drawings, 452, 462–464, 686, 745
bitmaps, 745
  displaying, 587, 620
  mapping onto 3D object surfaces, 611–616
  pasting into AutoCAD, 257
  saving, 627
  See also aliasing; antialiasing; BMP files
bitonal raster images, 643, 646, 648
bitplanes, and rendering, 581
Blip mode, turning on/off, 225
BLIPMODE system variable, 195
blips, 195, 225, 745
  turning on/off, 225
Block (Draw menu), options, 437
Block (Insert menu), 430, 440
BLOCK command, 148, 430, 437, 438, 441
block definitions, 47, 434, 745
  creating, 437–438
  saving, 49, 438
block objects
  assigning properties to, 436
  colors, 435, 436
  layers, 435
  linetypes, 435, 436
block references, 47, 434, 435, 437, 745
  exploding, 440
  inserting, 77, 438–440
  scaling, 434
  updating, 438, 440
  See also blocks

Index
760

blocks, 49, 433, 434–441, 745
    anonymous, 437, 744
    arrowheads as, 429
    attaching attributes to, 443
    base point, 437, 439
    colors, 310, 318
    colors of objects in, 435, 436
    database links to, 686
        accessing, 689–690
    defining, 437–438
    exploding, 49, 279, 440, 748
    grips within, 237, 238
    inserting, 49, 434, 438–440
        at intervals, 180–183
    layers of objects in, 435
    linetypes of objects in, 435, 436
    nesting/nested, 435
    redefining, 438, 440, 441
    referencing link path names in, 684–686
    rendering, 611
    saving, 438
    scaling, 272
    selecting, 181
    unnamed (anonymous), 437, 744
    updating, 438, 440
    updating of pre-Release 14 Render blocks, 628
    uses, 434
    versus xrefs, 448
    See also block definitions; block references; displayable attributes; named objects; title blocks
BMP files, 745
    creating, 733
    saving rendered images to, 620, 627
    See also bitmaps
BMPOUT command, 733
bold typeface, formatting text in, 343, 346
BOMs (bills of materials). *See* parts lists
borders (of title blocks), adding, 103, 480
borders (of viewports)
    as cutting edges, 277
    hiding, 487
boundaries
    creating regions from, 148
    polyline, 148
    specifying boundary corners for zooming, 202
    See also clipping boundaries; drawing limits; hatch boundaries; raster image boundaries
Boundary (Draw menu), 149
BOUNDARY command, 148, 149, 152
Boundary Hatch dialog box, 151, 153, 154, 157
boundary sets
    defining, 153–155
    highlighting objects in, 154

bounding box (dimension text), 402
BOX command, 549
Box option (Solids, Draw menu), 549
boxes
    bounding box, 402
    pickbox, 231
    solid boxes, 549
    target box (object snap), 172, 174
    view box (Aerial View), 211
BPL files, 512
braces (curly) ({}), format change characters, 361
brackets. *See* angle brackets (<>); square brackets ([])
Break (Modify menu), 180, 278
BREAK command, 180, 278
breaking
    links, 661
    objects, 180, 278
Bring Above Object option (Display Order, Tools menu), 146
Bring to Top option (Display Order, Tools menu), 146
broken pencil icon, 122, 527
Browse/Search dialog box, 88
browser (drawing browser), 88
BROWSER command, 56
browsing
    through drawing files, 88
    the Web, 56
B-spline curves, 745
    Bezier curves, 745
bump maps, 612, 614, 745
Button Editor, 722
button icons. *See* tool icons
button menus, 745
Button Properties dialog box, 719–721
buttons
    button menus, 745
    mouse buttons, 64
    on pointing devices, 64, 68
    saving, 722
    See also tools
BYBLOCK property, 746
    color specification, 310, 318, 436
    linetype specification, 313, 436
BYLAYER property, 746
    color specification, 248, 310, 318, 436
    linetype specification, 249, 313, 436

C

CAL command, 188–190
calculating
    angles, 194
    areas, 190–194
    circumferences, 191
    distance, 194

calculating (*continued*)
    evaluating expressions, 188
    perimeters, 191
    points, 188, 189
    values, 188
camera (in 3D model space)
    setting distance, 533
    setting point and angle, 532, 533
camera blocks (pre-Release 14), updating of, 628
canceling commands, 41, 75
caret (^)
    mathematical operator, 188
    stacked text indicator, 345
Cartesian coordinate systems, 114
Cartesian coordinates. *See* 2D Cartesian coordinates (X,Y coordinates); 3D Cartesian coordinates (X,Y,Z coordinates)
catalogs
    adding/removing, 669
    exporting links associated with, 698
^C^C, cancel command prefix, 719
CDF (comma-delimited file) format, 446
CECOLOR system variable, 311, 319
CELTSCALE system variable, 317, 490
CELTYPE system variable, 109, 133
Center (CEN) object snap, 168
center marks, 367, 393
    creating, 393
Center option (ZOOM command), 208
center points, snapping to, 168
Center, Radius option (Circle, draw menu), 138
centering views on points, 207
centerlines, 367, 393
    creating, 393
chain dimensions. *See* continued dimensions
Chamfer (Modify menu), 286, 287, 288, 561
CHAMFER command, 286, 561
CHAMFERA system variable, 96, 286
CHAMFERB system variable, 96, 286
CHAMFERC system variable, 287
CHAMFERD system variable, 287
chamfering objects, 53, 285–288
    distance method, 285
    length and angle method, 287
    solids, 561
    without trimming, 286
chamfers, 285
CHAMMODE system variable, 286, 287
CHANGE command, 319, 338, 443, 444, 548, 567
Change Dictionaries dialog box, 356, 357
Change Source dialog box, 661
character matching, in Object Properties toolbar lists, 244, 246
Character tab (Multiline Text Editor dialog box), formatting text, 343

characters
    converting Asian character strings, 708
    formatting, 334, 342–344
        text style changes and, 346
    inserting Unicode characters for TrueType fonts, 344
    ISO 8859 Latin/1 character set as rendered into PostScript, 734
    \M+ character sequences, 708
    noncurrent font character display, 707
    \U+ character sequences, 706, 707
    unsupported font Unicode character conversion, 706
    See also special characters
Check Spelling dialog box, 354
child dimension styles
    creating, 416
    suffixes, 417
CHPROP command, 319, 548, 567
CIF (Code Page Independent format), 706–708
Circle (Draw menu), options, 138
CIRCLE command, 138, 550
circles
    calculating areas/circumferences, 191
    dimensioning, 374, 375
    drawing, 73, 137–139
        tangent to objects, 138, 171
    drawing polygons from, 132
    export file format, 731
    extension line origins, 369
    filleting, 290
    isometric, 143
    offsetting, 258
    as rendered into PostScript, 735
    scaling, 272
    solid-filled, 143
    surfaces defined by added thickness, 567
    See also objects
circuit diagrams, plotting, 502
circular references (between xrefs), 472, 746
circumferences, calculating, 191
circumscribed polygons, drawing, 133
clapper blocks (pre-Release 14), updating of, 628
CLAYER system variable, 300
Clipboard (Windows), 255–258
    copying command history to, 79
    copying objects to, 255
    copying rendered images to, 624
    copying views into other documents, 656
    cutting objects to, 255
    pasting objects from, 256
    pasting text from, 79, 258, 341
clipdepth (xrefs), specifying, 466
clipping
    raster images, 648, 649–651
    xrefs, 464–466

clipping boundaries (raster images), 649–651
    changing, 650
    deleting, 651
    showing/hiding, 651
clipping boundaries (xrefs), 464–466
    and clipdepth, 466
    displaying, 465
    loading xrefs with, 465
    specifying, 465
    types, 465
clipping planes, 746
    for xrefs, 466
clipping planes (in 3D views), setting, 533
CMDDIA system variable, 78, 497
CMLSTYLE system variable, 131
CMYK color system, 746
Code Page Independent format (CIF), 706–708
code pages
    ANSI code pages supported by Windows, 709
    identifications, 708
    identifying installed, 709
codes. *See* control codes (text)
Color (Format menu), 310
color depth (for bitmaps), 581
    editing, 588
Color dialog box, 343
color mapping, for imported PostScript images, 741
color maps, 746
color names, 305, 310
color numbers, 309
color systems, 595
coloring
    bitonal raster images, 646
    dimension lines, 390
    dimension text, 416
    materials, 607
    multilines, 131
    objects, 48, 317
    raster image boundaries, 644
    text, 83, 343, 350, 359
    See also colors
colors, 309–311
    ambient color, 605, 607, 743
    assigning to layers, 305
    assigning to objects, 317
    assigning to pens/penwidths, 106, 300, 309, 498, 499, 500
    AutoCAD interface, 83
    of block objects, 435, 436
    color names, 305, 310
    color numbers, 309
    color systems, 595
    copying, 250
    default color, 305, 310
    depth, 581, 588

colors (*continued*)
    diffuse color, 605, 607, 747
    in DWF files, 729
    editing, 244, 247, 318, 319
    of highlights, 605
    HLS color system, 595, 605
    identifying, 309
    light colors, 605
    making current, 247, 310
    of materials, 605
    pigment colors, 605
    reflection color, 605, 608
    RGB light colors, 595, 605
    saturation, 595
    specifying, 248, 305, 310
    text, 83
    in xref layers, 467
    See also coloring; layer colors; object colors
columns (in database tables), editing, 691
comma-delimited file (CDF) format, 446
command history
    copying to the Clipboard, 79
    displaying, 70
    navigating, 71
    redisplaying lines on the command line, 76
command keys
    editing keys, 340
    navigation keys, 71, 74, 75
command line, 746
    controlling dialog box display, 78
    copying text to, 75, 79
    editing text on, 74
    entering commands on, 73
    entering object snaps on, 172
    illustrated, 40
    pasting text to, 258
    plotting from, 497
    redisplaying command history lines, 76
    spaces in, 76
    specifying fonts on, 328
    using, 73
    viewing raster image information on, 639
    See also command window; prompts (command line)
Command prompt, entering commands at, 73
Command Reference, 34, 35, 36
command shortcuts
    entering, 74
    See also command keys
command window, 69, 70
    docking/undocking, 70
    illustrated, 40, 69
    navigating in, 74
    resizing, 69
    toggling with the text window, 71
    See also command line; prompts (command line); scripts

Index
763

commands
    accessing, 41, 72–80
    associating with tools, 719–721
    cancel command prefix, 719
    canceling, 41, 75
    command history, 70, 79
    context-sensitive Help, 41
    displaying commands associated with tools, 718, 719
    editing commands, 727
        selecting objects after choosing, 230–236
    entering, 70, 73
    executing commands, 74
        last-used command, 41, 75
        two at once, 76
    options, 41
    repeating, 41, 75
    running with scripts, 78
    shortcuts, 74
    system variables and, 79
    in Tablet mode, 65
    transparent commands, 76, 752
    See also command line; external database commands; scripts; tools; *and names of specific commands*
compass (in 3D model space), 530
    setting 3D views, 530
complete plotter configuration files. *See* PCP files
complex objects, trimming, 276
complex solids, 149, 536
composite regions, creating, 149
composite solids, creating, 554
composite tolerances, 427
compound documents, 654, 656, 657
    editing linked drawings in, 657
CONE command, 549
Cone option (Solids, Draw menu), 550
cones (solid), creating, 549
CONFIG command, 517
constant attributes, 441
Construction Line (Draw menu), 184
construction lines, 48
    creating, 184–186
construction plane, 115, 746
containers (destination applications), 654
context-sensitive Help, 41
continued dimensions, 370, 373, 746
    creating, 373
    dimension line spacing, 391
    extension line origins, 373
    illustrated, 366, 374
    See also dimensions
control codes (text)
    for formatting multiline text, 359–362
    as rendered into PostScript, 734

control keys. *See* command keys
control points, 746
conventions, as used in this manual, 37
converting
    Asian language character strings, 708
    donuts into arcs, 144
    drawing units, 86
    splined polylines into spline curves, 136
    unsupported font Unicode character conversion, 706
    WMF files to AutoCAD format, 257
Coons surface patch meshes, creating, 545
coordinate display (status bar), 64, 115
    cycling through, 115
    illustrated, 115
    options, 115
coordinate filters. *See* point filters (coordinate filters)
coordinate systems, 46
    Cartesian, 114
    specifying points with, 46, 114–118
    types, 119
    See also coordinates; user coordinate systems (UCSs); World Coordinate System (WCS)
coordinates
    determining, 115
    displaying, 115, 195
        See also coordinate display, 709
    for image mapping, 612
    locating points with, 114, 195
    specifying, 46, 114–118
        broken pencil icon warning, 122, 527
        one value at a time, 177
    world, 753
    See also 2D coordinates; 3D coordinates; absolute coordinates; coordinate systems; origin; point filters (coordinate filters); points (geometric); relative coordinates
COORDS system variable, 115
Copy (Edit menu), 256, 624, 656, 658
Copy (Modify menu), 253
COPY command, 253, 556
Copy Link (Edit menu), 256, 656
COPYCLIP command, 256, 656
COPYHIST command, 79
copying
    command history, 79
    hatch boundaries, 293
    multiple copies, 239, 253
    objects, 52, 253–263
        to the Clipboard, 255
        with grips, 239, 254
    OLE objects, 664
    properties, 250–252
    rendered images, 624

Index

copying (*continued*)
    text, 340
        to the command line, 75
    tools, 715
    views, into other documents, 656
    xrefs for demand loading, 455
    See also arraying; mirroring; offsetting; pasting
COPYLINK command, 256, 656
correcting mistakes, 80
CPolygons (crossing polygons), 232, 746
Create 3D Studio Output File dialog box, 732
Create Drawing File dialog box, 438
Create DXF File dialog box, 730
Create New Drawing dialog box, 62, 93, 110
Create Slide File dialog box, 727
cropping
    in image mapping, 613
    rendered images, 622
cropping the screen in rendering, 583
crosshairs, 41, 746
    illustrated, 40, 231, 746
    in model space, 478
    in paper space, 477
        illustrated, 478
    specifying colors for, 83
crosshatching. *See* hatching
crossing polygons. *See* CPolygons (crossing polygons)
crossing selections, 231, 381, 746
crossing windows. *See* crossing selections
CTRL+A keys, toggling group selection, 242
CTRL+B keys, toggling Snap mode, 37, 103
CTRL+C keys
    copying selections to the Clipboard, 340
CTRL+D keys, cycling through coordinate display types, 115
CTRL+drag procedure, copying and pasting, 659
CTRL+E keys, cycling through isometric planes, 163
CTRL+F keys, turning running object snaps on/off, 174
CTRL+G keys, toggling Grid mode, 102
CTRL+SHIFT+END keys, moving the cursor, 75
CTRL+SHIFT+HOME keys, moving the cursor, 75
CTRL+SHIFT+PGDN keys, moving the cursor, 75
CTRL+SHIFT+PGUP keys, moving the cursor, 75
CTRL+SPACEBAR keys, inserting a nonbreaking space, 340
CTRL+TAB keys, accessing the Render Window, 585–586
CTRL+V keys
    pasting Clipboard contents, 340
    pasting text, 71, 74
CTRL+X keys, cutting selections to the Clipboard, 256, 340
curly braces ({}), format change characters, 361

Current UCS option, Plan View option (3D Viewpoint, View menu), 530
cursor, 746
    constraining, 163
    current location display, 115
    drag-and-drop cursor, 659
    in external databases, 670
    in interactive zooming/panning, 200–202
    magnifying glass, 495
    minus sign, 201
    move cursor, 664
    navigation keys, 71, 74, 75
    plus sign, 201
    rubber-band line, 163, 751
    target box, 172, 174
    See also crosshairs; cursor menu
cursor menu, 68, 664, 746
    choosing object snaps, 173
    displaying, 64, 68, 179
    starting tracking from, 179
    using point filters from, 177
cursor state, in external databases, 670
curved objects. *See* curves
curved surfaces, 535
curve-fit polylines. *See* splined polylines
curves
    creating meshes between, 542
    creating regions from open curves, 148
    drawing, 135–144
    See also arcs; circles; donuts; ellipses; objects; spline curves; splined polylines
CUS files, editing, 357
custom dictionaries, creating and editing, 356
custom menus, specifying, 85
custom objects, 157
Customization Guide, 34, 35, 36
Customize Toolbars dialog box, 712, 714–715, 719, 721
customizing
    the AutoCAD environment, 56, 81–87
    menus, 711
    object selection, 234
    title blocks, 104
    toolbars, 711–723
Cut (Edit menu), 256, 656
CUTCLIP command, 256, 656
cutting
    objects to the Clipboard, 255
    OLE objects, 664
    text, 340
cutting edges
    objects as, 275, 276
    in paper space, 277
CYLINDER command, 550
Cylinder option (Solids, Draw menu), 550
cylinders (solid), creating, 550
cylindrical coordinates, specifying, 522

D

dashed lines, snapping to points on, 164
data. *See* external data
data integrity, 701–704
    causes of loss, 701
    checking, 701
    ensuring, 702–704
    restoring, 701
database objects
    changing, 701
    connecting to new, 672
    hierarchy, 677
    making current, 669
    See also database tables
database table keys, 676
database tables
    connecting to, 668–669
    defining key columns, 676
    exporting links associated with, 698
    keys, 676
    modifying, 673–675
    registering, 677–680
    setting link paths, 677–682
    See also rows (in database tables)
databases. *See* drawing database; external databases
DATE system variable, 79
datum (reference point), 376, 426
    determining coordinates, 376
datum axis, 427
datum dimensions. *See* ordinate dimensions
datum reference frames, 426
datum reference letters
    adding to feature control frames, 426
    illustrated, 424
dBASE III, connecting to, 668–669
DBLIST command, 197
DBMS drivers, and AutoCAD, 683
DCL (Dialog Control Language), 57
DDATTDEF command, 442
DDATTE command, 444
DDATTEXT command, 447
DDCOLOR command, 311
DDEDIT command, 337, 348, 363, 443
DDEMODES command, 332, 547
DDGRIPS command, 238
DDIM command, 369, 389, 407, 418, 419
DDINSERT command, 104, 438, 440, 441
DDMODIFY command, 192, 321, 337, 338, 348, 350, 351, 419, 548, 644, 646, 648, 651
DDPTYPE command, 145, 182, 183
DDRENAME command, 123, 308, 333
DDRMODES command, 37, 103, 161, 163, 224, 225, 226
DDSELECT command, 235
DDUCS command, 115, 121
DDUCSP command, 526
DDUNITS command, 99, 117, 265
DDVIEW command, 215, 494
DDVPOINT command, 528
decal effect, 613
decimal dimensions, suppressing zeros, 411
defaults, 746
    drawing names, 83
    initial environment, 749
    layers, 106
    measurement system default files, 86
    menu files, 68, 85
    templates, recovering, 111
Define New View dialog box, 215
definition points (of dimensions), 381, 746
    changing, 383
    illustrated, 382
    plotting, 382
DEFPOINTS layer, 308, 382
defpoints. *See* definition points (of dimensions)
degree sign (°), Unicode value, 707
DEL key, deleting characters, 74
Del option (UCS command), 124
Delete option (Tiled Viewports, View menu), 222
deleting
    characters, 74
    clipping boundaries (raster images), 651
    database table rows, 674
    groups, 242
    layers, 308
    lights, 601
    linetypes, 314
    named views, 216
    project names, 469
    tiled viewport configurations, 222
    title blocks, 105
    toolbars, 713
    tools from toolbars, 715
    UCSs, 124
    See also detaching; erasing; purging
demand loading xrefs, 452, 453–457, 465
dependent symbols, 464, 467, 747
    binding to drawings, 452, 463
    listing, 474
    names, 464, 467
    See also named objects
deselecting OLE objects, 666
destination applications, 654
Detach option (External Reference dialog box), 452
detaching
    raster images, 642
    xrefs, 452, 461
deviation tolerances, 413
Device and Default Selection dialog box, 509–511
diagonal lines, in contained images, 657

dialog boxes
    context-sensitive Help, 41
    creating, 57
    enabling/suppressing the display of, 63, 78
    making changes when opened transparently, 77
Dialog Control Language (DCL), 57
Diameter (Dimension menu), 374
diameter dimensions
    creating, 374
    definition points (illustrated), 382
    illustrated, 366
    styles, 400
diameter symbol (∅), Unicode value, 707
dictionaries, 354
    custom, 357
    switching, 355
DIESEL (Direct Interpretively Evaluated String Expression Language), 57, 747
diffuse color, 605, 607, 747
diffuse reflection, 596, 598
    setting, 573
digitizing drawings, 65
digitizing tablet, 65
DIM command, 366
DIMALIGNED command, 372
DIMALTD system variable, 410
DIMALTTD system variable, 410
DIMALTTZ system variable, 415
DIMALTU system variable, 410
DIMALTZ system variable, 411, 413
DIMANGULAR command, 375
DIMAPOST system variable, 410
DIMASO system variable, 368
DIMASZ system variable, 96, 393, 431
DIMAUNIT system variable, 408, 410
DIMBLK system variable, 378, 431
DIMBLK1 system variable, 378, 393, 431
DIMBLK2 system variable, 393, 431
DIMCEN system variable, 96, 374, 394
DIMCLRD system variable, 378, 391, 393
DIMCLRE system variable, 392, 418
DIMCLRT system variable, 378, 380, 416
DIMDEC system variable, 408
DIMDIAMETER command, 374, 394
DIMDLE system variable, 391, 393
DIMDLI system variable, 96, 391
DIMEDIT command, 385
dimension definition points. *See* definition points (of dimensions)
dimension format, 398–406
dimension geometry, 366, 389–398
    See also arrowheads; centerlines; center marks; dimension format; dimension lines; extension lines
dimension line arcs, 375, 747

dimension lines, 367
    coloring, 390
    editing, 390
    illustrated, 367
    order, 390
    placing dimension text in relation to, 402–406
    See also arrowheads; dimension text; leader lines
dimension properties
    copying, 250
    See also dimension styles
dimension scale, 394
    and the drawing scale, 395
    and the plot scale, 395
    setting, 389, 394–398
        in paper space, 395, 396
    See also scale factors
dimension style families, 366, 416
    creating family member styles, 416
    creating parent dimension styles, 388
dimension style names, 416
    displaying, 417
dimension style overrides, 366, 418
    applying, 419
    setting up, 418, 420
dimension styles, 366, 416, 420, 747
    applying, 420
    child, 416, 417
    comparing, 421
    creating, 388–416
    default, 369
    and the dimensioning system variables, 367, 388
    externally referenced, 423
    listing, 421–423
    named, 388
    parent, 388, 416
    restoring, 420
    selecting, 369
    See also dimension style families; dimension style overrides; named objects
Dimension Styles dialog box, 389
dimension text, 367, 747
    added text, 406–416
    aligning with dimension lines, 402–406
    coloring, 416
    editing, 386
    fitting within extension lines, 399–402
    formatting, 398–406, 414, 415
    geometric tolerances, 407, 424–429
    horizontal justification, 403
    illustrated, 367
    lateral tolerances, 413–415, 416
    moving, 387
    in ordinate dimensions, 376

dimension text (*continued*)
    orientation, 402–406
    prefixes and suffixes, 406–410
    replacing, 387
    resizing, 401
    returning to home position, 386
    rotating, 386
    suppressing zeros, 411
    text gap, 402, 416
    text height, 416
    text styles, 415
    text width, 402
    types, 367
    user text, 410
    vertical justification, 405
dimension units. *See* alternate units; primary units
dimension variables. *See* dimensioning system variables
dimensioning, 45, 365–420
    with alternate units, 409
    angles, 375
    arcs, 374, 375
    basic concepts, 366–368
    circles, 374, 375
    lines, 370–374
    in model/paper space, 396
    See also dimensions
dimensioning symbols, Unicode values, 707
dimensioning system variables, 367, 388, 747
    setup adjustments to, 96
dimensions, 365–420
    angular. *See* angular dimensions
    associative. *See* associative dimensions
    basic, 413
    components, 366, 389–398
    copying properties, 250
    creating, 369–381
        in paper space, 396, 488
    decimal, 411
    editing, 381–387
    elements, 366
    extending, 384
    formatting, 398–406
    geometry, 366, 389–398
    linear. *See* linear dimensions
    oblique, 385
    radial. *See* radial dimensions
    rounding off, 416
    scale factor, 99
    scaling, 389, 394–398
        in paper space, 395, 396
    selecting dimensioned objects, 381
    stretching, 383, 385
    trimming, 384
    types, 366, 381
        illustrated, 45, 366

dimensions (*continued*)
    See also arrowheads; centerlines; center marks; definition points (of dimensions); dimension lines; dimension scale; dimension styles; dimension text; dimensioning
    See also extension lines; leader lines
DIMEXE system variable, 96, 392
DIMEXO system variable, 96, 392
DIMFIT system variable, 400
DIMGAP system variable, 96, 379, 411, 414, 416
DIMJUST system variable, 405
DIMLFAC system variable, 396, 409
DIMLIM system variable, 414
DIMLINEAR command, 381, 411
DIMORDINATE command, 377
DIMOVERRIDE command, 419
DIMPOST system variable, 408
DIMRADIUS command, 374, 394
DIMRND system variable, 416
DIMSCALE system variable, 96, 378, 396
DIMSE1 system variable, 392
DIMSE2 system variable, 392
DIMSTYLE command, 369, 389
    command options, 419, 420
DIMTAD system variable, 406
DIMTDEC system variable, 409
DIMTEDIT command, 387
DIMTM system variable, 414
DIMTOFL system variable, 400
DIMTOL system variable, 414
DIMTOLJ system variable, 414, 415
DIMTP system variable, 414
DIMTSZ system variable, 393
DIMTVP system variable, 406
DIMTXSTY system variable, 378, 380, 416
DIMTXT system variable, 96, 378, 380, 416
DIMTZIN system variable, 415
DIMUNIT system variable, 408
DIMUPT system variable, 400, 405
DIMZIN system variable, 413
direct distance entry, 47, 747
    specifying points, 118
    using tracking with, 179
Direct Hatch option (HATCH command), 152
Direct Interpretively Evaluated String Expression Language (DIESEL), 57, 747
Direction Control dialog box, 98
directories, support directory search paths, 84, 745
disk space
    displaying free space, 197
    system requirements, 60
displacement point, for copying objects, 253
display. *See* screen

Display Image (Tools menu), 622, 623
    options, 621–624
Display option (Plot Configuration dialog box), 502
Display Order (Tools menu), options, 146
displayable attributes, 691–693
    creating, 692
    formatting, 692
    placing, 692
    updating, 691, 693
DIST command, 195
Distance option (Inquiry, Tools menu), 195
distance<angle display, 115, 117
distances
    calculating, 194
    chamfering objects by specifying, 285
    of faces from lights, 595
    setting camera distance, 533
    See also direct distance entry
distant light, 590
    defining paths, 602
    positioning, 603
    simulating sunlight with, 590, 604
dithering, 747
DIVIDE command, 182
Divide option (Point, Draw menu), 183
dividing objects, 182
    starting points, 181
documentation (AutoCAD), 33–37
    learning tools, 35
    online documentation, 34
    printed guides, 35
    user guidelines, 35
documents
    compound, 654, 656, 657
    server, 656
doglegs. See hook lines
dollar signs ($$), bound xref name characters, 463, 464
Donut (Draw menu), 144
DONUT command, 144
DONUTID system variable, 96, 144
DONUTOD system variable, 96, 144
donuts
    converting into arcs, 144
    drawing, 143
    editing, 144
    exploding, 144
double lines. See multilines
DOWN ARROW key, moving the cursor, 71
drafting standards, 92
drafting techniques, in 3D modeling, 577
drag and drop, inserting text files, 341
drag-and-drop cursor, illustrated, 659
dragging objects
    into AutoCAD, 659
    Dynamic Dragging mode, 274

dragging objects (*continued*)
    raster images, 636
    in tiled viewports, 221
drawing
    3D modeling, 55, 535–555, 567–569
    arcs, 139–141
        in polylines, 126
    circles, 73, 137–139
        tangent to objects, 138
    curves, 135–144
    donuts, 143
    ellipses, 141–143
    elliptical arcs, 142
    equilateral triangles, 132
    isometric circles, 143
    line objects, 126
    lines, 72, 126–135
        in tiled viewports, 220
    multilines, 131
    objects, 43–45, 125–157
    parallel lines, 126
    perpendicular lines, 163
    polygons, 132, 650
    polylines, 126–128
        freehand, 134
    with precision, 46–48, 159–198
    in 3D modeling, 579
    squares, 132
    surfaces, 575
    tutorials (online), 34, 36
    See also drawings
Drawing Aids (Tools menu), 160, 226, 263
Drawing Aids dialog box, 37, 102, 103, 161, 163, 263
drawing area. See drawing limits; graphics window (graphics area)
drawing boundaries. See drawing limits
drawing browser, 88
drawing database, 81
    binding, 452
    listing information, 196
    updating, 81
drawing environment, modifying, 81–87
Drawing Exchange Binary files. See DXB files (Drawing Exchange Binary files)
drawing extents, 747
    displaying, 197
    illustrated, 747
    zooming to, 208
drawing files
    browsing through, 88
    opening files containing database links, 702
    saving block definitions as, 438
    searching for, 88, 89
    See also drawings
Drawing Interchange Files. See DXF files (Drawing Interchange Files)

Index
769

drawing limits, 42, 747
    displaying, 100
    illustrated, 101, 747
    scaling views relative to, 205
    setting, 94, 100
    zooming to, 208
        in Aerial View, 213
    See also drawing extents
Drawing Limits (Format menu), 37, 101
drawing order (of objects)
    changing, 145
    regenerating, 146
    in Release 12 drawings, 146
drawing projects. *See* projects
drawing scale
    and the dimension scale, 395
    See also scale factors
drawing standards, 92
drawing status, displaying, 197
drawing time, tracking, 198
drawing units
    architectural, 118
    converting, 86
    measurement system default files, 86
    measurement systems, 86
    setting unit precision, 97
    setting unit type, 97, 118
    specifying, 42, 97–99, 118
    specifying feet and inches, 118
        in metric drawings, 409
    types, 98, 115
    See also angular units; English units; metric units
Drawing Web Format files. *See* DWF files (Drawing Web Format files)
drawings
    Aerial View updates from, 214
    archiving, 462
    ASEROWS operations affecting, 670
    attaching xrefs to, 457–461
    binding dependent symbols to, 452, 463
    binding xrefs to, 452, 462–464, 745
    creating new, 62, 86, 93–97, 110
    designing layouts, 54, 480–494
    dimensioning. *See* dimensioning
    embedded, editing, 658, 663
    embedding objects in, 662–663
    exiting, 90
    export file formats, 729–736
    extracting attribute information from, 441, 444–447
    import file formats, 736–741
    initial environment, 749
    inserting, 77, 438–440
        on the Web, 56
    isometric drawings, 162
    linked, editing, 657

drawings (*continued*)
    linking files to, 660
    linking objects to, 654, 659
    materials lists, 617, 697
    names, automatic save default, 83
    opening existing, 42, 87
        with the browser, 88
        dialog box display control, 78
        drawings containing database links, 702
        on the Web, 56
    panning. *See* panning
    plotting. *See* plotting
    previewing, 88
        before plotting, 497
    printing. *See* printing
    regenerating, 81, 146, 224, 225, 751
        changing views without, 203
        replacing shaded images, 572
    saving, 90
        automatically, 83, 90
        for batch plotting, 512, 514
        dialog box display control, 78
        export file formats, 729–736
        on the Web, 56
    scaling, 42, 92, 272
    setting up, 62, 91–111
    setup options, 42, 62, 94–105
    starting, 42
    tracking drawing time, 198
    viewing, 50, 199–226
        in 3D, 527–535
        with the browser, 88
        dynamic viewing (in 3D model space), 531–535
    working drawings, 753
    zooming. *See* zooming
    See also block references; drawing files; templates (prototype drawings); title blocks; views; xrefs (external references)
DRAWORDER command, 145
DSVIEWER command, 211
DTEXT command, 333, 335, 336, 342
duplicating. *See* copying
DVIEW command, 531–535
DWF files (Drawing Web Format files), 729
    creating, 729
    viewing, 56
DWFOUT command, 56
DWG files. *See* drawing files
DXB files (Drawing Exchange Binary files), importing, 737
DXBIN command, 737
DXF files (Drawing Interchange Files), 736
    creating, 730
    format, 447, 747

DXF files (*continued*)
    importing, 736
    unsupported font character sequences, 708
DXFIN command, 703, 736
DXFOUT command, 703
Dynamic Dragging mode, lengthening objects, 274
Dynamic option (ZOOM command), 203
dynamic scaling of raster images, 634
Dynamic Update (Options menu, Aerial View window), 214
dynamic updating, of Aerial View, 214
dynamic viewing (in 3D model space), 531–535
dynamic zooming, 203

E

Edge Surface option (Surfaces, Draw menu), 546
edge-defined surface meshes, creating, 545
edges, 747
    of faces, 578
EDGESURF command, 545
Edit Attribute Definition dialog box, 443
Edit Attributes dialog box, 444
Edit Row dialog box, 674, 675
Edit Text dialog box, 337
editing
    3D objects, 556–563
    attribute definitions, 443
    attributes, 444
    color depth, 588
    colors, 244, 247, 318
    database links, 687–689
    database table columns, 691
    database table rows, 673–674, 691
    dimension lines, 390
    dimension text, 386
    dimensions, 381–387
    donuts, 144
    embedded drawings, 658
    embedded objects, 663
    extension lines, 391
    feature control frames, 424
    in floating viewports, 476, 478, 488
    groups, 242
    hatches, 293–295
    layers, 244, 245, 317
    leader line annotations, 380
    leader lines, 380
    linetypes
        of layers, 107
        of objects, 244, 249, 319
    linked drawings, 657
    multiline styles, 282
    multilines, 281–283
    objects, 52–54, 227–233
        with grips, 237, 239
    OLE objects, 664–666

editing (*continued*)
    polygons, 133
    polylines, 128, 279–281
    project name paths, 471
    project names, 470
    solids, 561–563
    spline curves, 136, 283
    text. *See* editing text
    tool icons, 722
editing commands
    and OLE objects, 664
    selecting objects after choosing, 230–236
    selecting objects before choosing, 231, 237–243, 245
    using during slide viewing, 727
editing text
    on the command line, 74
    control keys, 340
    line text, 336
    multiline text, 348–351
        in a third-party text editor, 363
    multiline text objects, 363
ELEV command, 525, 547
elevation, 546, 747
    changing, 547, 548
    illustrated, 747
    setting, 547
    in UCSs, 525
Ellipse (Draw menu), options, 142
ELLIPSE command, 139, 142
ellipses
    axes, 141
    calculating areas/circumferences, 191
    drawing, 141–143
    as isometric circles, 143
    as rendered into PostScript, 735
    See also objects
ellipsis (enclosed) ([...]), wild-card character, 230, 307
elliptical arcs
    drawing, 142
    as rendered into PostScript, 735
embedded objects, editing, 658, 663
embedding, 654, 747
    commands for, 656, 658
    versus linking, 654
    objects, 655
        in drawings, 662–663
        in other application documents, 657
    URLs (Universal Resource Locators), 56, 729
Encapsulated PostScript (EPS) files. *See* PostScript files
END command, 90
END key, moving the cursor, 71, 74
End option (UNDO command), 80
ENDP command, 165
Endpoint (ENDP) object snap, 165

Index
771

endpoints, snapping to, 165
English units
    converting metric units to/from, 86
    default files, 86
    specifying feet and inches, 118
        in metric drawings, 409
ENTER key
    executing commands, 74
    repeating commands, 41, 75
environment maps, 612, 614
environments
    adding/removing, 669
    exporting links associated with, 698
    setting, 672
    See also AutoCAD environment
EPS (Encapsulated PostScript) files. *See* PostScript files
equal sign (=), block name symbol, 438
equilateral triangles, drawing, 132
Erase (Modify menu), 268
ERASE command, 268, 295
erasing
    freehand lines, 134
    hatch patterns, 295
    objects, 267
    raster images, 643
    undoing erasing, 268
error messages, xref, 472
errors
    correcting, 80
ESC key
    canceling commands, 41, 75
    removing objects/grips from selection sets, 238
evaluating expressions, 188
Exit (File menu), 90
EXIT command, 90
exiting
    AutoCAD, 90
    Grip modes, 239
Explode (Modify menu), 279, 440
EXPLODE command, 128, 144, 440
exploding
    blocks (block references), 49, 279, 440, 748
    donuts, 144
    groups, 243
    objects, 278, 748
    polygons, 133
    polylines, 128
Export (File menu), 729
Export Data dialog box, 729
Export Links dialog box, 698
exporting
    3D objects, views, lights, and materials, 731
    bitmap images, 733
    database link information to files, 697–699

exporting (*continued*)
    drawings, 729–731
    file formats for, 729–736
    materials, 617
    PostScript images, 733–735
    raster images, 732
    regions, 731
    rendered images, 624
    solids, 731
    surfaces, 731
    text files, 730
    vector graphics, 732
    to the Web, 56, 729
expressions (mathematical), evaluating, 188
EXTEDGE system variable, 558
Extend (Modify menu), 273, 384, 559
EXTEND command, 384
extended intersections, snapping to, 166
extending
    3D objects, 558
    dimensions, 384
    objects, 52, 273
        See also chamfering objects
    polylines, 274
    rays, 274
    See also stretching
extension lines, 367
    editing, 391
    fitting text within, 399–402
    forcing an internal line, 400
    illustrated, 367
    oblique, 385
    order, 390, 404
    origins, 369, 373
        illustrated, 370
    placing dimension text in relation to, 403
extension origin offset, changing, 391
extents
    See also drawing extents
Extents option (Plot Configuration dialog box), 502
Extents option (ZOOM command), 208
external data
    accessing, 669–675
        with SQL, 56, 699–701
    data integrity, 701–704
    modifying, 673–675, 683, 699–701
    structuring, 697
    viewing, 670–672, 691
External Database (Tools menu), 668, 670, 671, 673–675, 678, 684, 687, 692, 694, 698, 700, 701, 703
external database commands (ASE commands), 56, 683, 697, 699, 701
    checking loading of, 702
    loading, 703

external database commands (*continued*)
    reloading, 669
    unloading, 669, 702
external database configuration editor, 669
external databases, 667–704
    ASEROWS operations affecting, 670
    changing current database object selection, 669
    connecting to existing databases, 668–669
    connecting to new databases, 672
    cursor, 670
    cursor states, 670
    querying, 56, 699–701
    storing nongraphic attributes in, 667
    See also database objects; database tables; external data; external database commands; rows (in database tables)
External Reference (Insert menu), 458–463, 468
External Reference dialog box, 449–453, 463
external references. *See* xrefs
extract (attribute information) files
    formats, 446
    See also template files (for extracting attribute information)
extracting
    attribute information, 441, 444–447
    coordinates from selected points, 521
EXTRUDE command, 549, 552, 567
Extrude option (Solids, Draw menu), 552
extruded objects
    creating, 552
    removing/plotting hidden lines, 492, 501
    tapering, 553
    top and bottom surfaces, 567
    See also 3D objects
extruded text, as rendered into PostScript, 734
extrusion, 748
    See also thickness

F

F1 key, context-sensitive Help, 41
F2 key, toggling the graphics window and command window with the text window, 71
F3 key, turning running object snaps on/off, 174
F5 key, cycling through isometric planes, 163
F6 key, cycling through coordinate display types, 115
F7 key, toggling Grid mode, 102
F9 key, toggling Snap mode, 37, 103
faces (of 3D objects), 578, 748
    angles to lights, 594
    appearance, 579
    distances from lights, 595
    edges, 578

faces (*continued*)
    intersecting faces, 578
    limiting, 577
    overlapping faces, 578
    types, 578
    See also back faces (of 3D objects)
faceted surfaces. *See* meshes
FACETRES system variable, 549, 579, 736
falloff angle (of spotlights), 591, 592, 600
Fast Zoom mode, 203, 209
    and Aerial View, 210
    turning on/off, 210
feature control frames, 424, 748
    adding datum reference letters to, 426
    adding geometric tolerances to, 425–429
    appending to leader lines, 378, 379
    editing, 424
    illustrated, 424
Feature Legend dialog box, 500
features (of AutoCAD)
    advanced features, 55–56
    new features in Release 14, 35, 465
features (of objects)
    feature size symbols, 426
    material conditions, 426
    See also feature control frames
feet
    specifying, 118, 409
    suppressing zero values, 412
fences, 748
    selecting objects with, 233
file formats
    BMP format, 587, 620, 627
    CDF format, 446
    for exporting, 729–736
    for extract (attribute information) files, 446
    for importing, 736–741
    for raster files, 632
    SDF format, 446
    stereolithograph format, 735
    TGA format, 587, 620, 627
    TIFF format, 587, 620, 627
    See also files
file names
    long, 77
    special characters for, 107, 123, 222, 325
FILEDIA system variable, 78
files
    acad.mnu file, 68, 85
    acad.ps, 740
    acad.psf file, 735
    acad14.cfg file, 494, 508
    ACIS files, 731, 737
    Big Font files, 328
    BPL files, 512
    CDF files, 446
    CUS files, 357

files (*continued*)
   DXB files, 737
   exporting database link information to, 697–699
   FMP files, 352
   fontmap.ps file, 740
   installed files, 62
   linking files to drawings, 660
   log files, 473
   measurement system default files, 86
   PC2 files, 498, 508–510, 512
   PCP files, 498, 510, 512
   plotting to, 514
   PLT files, 514
   PostScript Support file, 735
   Readme file, 62
   saving rendered images to, 620
   script files, 751
   SDF files, 446
   SHX files, 353
   slide files, 751
   STL files, 735
   support files, 84, 745
   template files, 444–446, 447
   temporary files, 86, 752
   XLG files, 473
   See also BMP files; drawing files; DWF files; DXF files; extract (attribute information) files; file formats; file locking; file names; libraries; menu files; plot configuration files
   See also PostScript files; PostScript support file; text files; WMF files
Fill command, 224
fill lights, 589, 591
Fill mode, turning on/off, 224
Fillet (Modify menu), 289, 562
FILLET command, 560, 562
fillet radius, setting, 289
filleting
   3D objects, 560
   arcs, 290
   circles, 290
   lines, 289, 291
   objects, 53, 289–292
      without trimming, 290
   parallel lines, 292
   polylines, 291
   solids, 562
FILLETRAD system variable, 289
fillets, 289–292
FILLMODE system variable, 144, 147, 224
fills, 44, 748
   PostScript fills in 2D polylines, 740
   See also solid fills

FILTER command, 236
filtering
   aliasing (in rendering), 613
   layers, 306–308
      frozen, 486
   linetypes, 315
   selection sets, 235
filters. *See* point filters
finding and replacing multiline text, 351
Fit options (Format dialog box), 399–401
fit points (for spline curves), 283, 748
   approximation points, 744
   interpolation points, 749
   moving, 283
fitting dimension text within extension lines, 399–402
flat projections. *See* parallel projections (of 3D views); perspective views
floating objects
   guidelines, 436
   See also block objects
floating viewports, 55, 487, 748
   aligning views, 490
   changing views, 487
   configuration options, 481, 482
   controlling layer visibility, 298, 304
   controlling visibility, 484–487
   creating, 481–483
   dimensioning in, 397
   editing in, 476, 478, 488
   filtering frozen layers, 486
   freezing/thawing layers, 303, 484
   hiding borders, 487
   limiting active, 487
   listing frozen layers, 486
   in paper space, 476
   rearranging, 484
   resizing, 484
   rotating views, 492
   versus tiled viewports, 217
   turning on/off, 486
Floating Viewports (View menu), options, 482, 493
Flyout Properties dialog box, 721
flyouts (for tools), 719, 721
   creating, 721
   displaying, 67
FMP files, 352
font map file, 740
font mapping, 352
   in importing PostScript files, 740
   tables, 352–353
Font tab (Preferences dialog box), 84
FONTALT system variable, 353
FONTMAP system variable, 352, 353
fontmap.ps file, 740

fonts, 326, 748
    Asian fonts, 329, 708
    assigning to text styles, 326–330
    AutoCAD interface, 84
    changing, 326
    declaring, 740
    noncurrent font character display, 707
    non-Unicode encoded fonts, 706
    PostScript fonts, 333
    proxy fonts, 328
    SHX fonts, 328, 343, 352
    specifying, 328, 329, 343
    specifying an alternative default, 353
    substituting, 352–354
    and text styles, 326, 346
    TrueType fonts, 327, 344
    Unicode fonts, 328, 705–709
    unsupported font Unicode character conversion, 706
    See also Big Fonts; font mapping
form tolerances, 424
format codes, for multiline text, 359–362
Format dialog box, 399–406
formatting
    dimensions, 398–406
    displayable attributes, 692
    See also formatting text
formatting text, 337
    characters, 334, 342–344
    dimension text, 398–406, 414, 415
    lateral tolerances, 414, 416
    line text, 334–336
    multiline text, 342–348
        in a third-party text editor, 359–362
        in multiline text objects, 346–348
    stacked text, 345
    words, 334, 342–344
forward slash. *See* slash
fractions, stacked, 345
Frame option, Image option (Object, Modify menu), 644
freehand lines
    ensuring accuracy on slow computers, 135
    erasing, 134
    sketching, 133–135
freezing layers, 300, 301–303, 748
    in floating viewports, 303, 484
    versus turning off layers, 301
From object snap, 164, 173, 176
frozen layers
    filtering, 486
    listing, 486
Full Preview option (Plot Configuration dialog box), 497

G

Gap option (Annotation dialog box), 402
geometric characteristic symbols, 424
    illustrated, 424
geometric points. *See* points (geometric)
Geometric Tolerance dialog box, 425, 428
geometric tolerances, 407, 424–429
    adding, 425–429
    composite, 427
    form tolerances, 424
    positional tolerances, 424, 427
    projected tolerances, 427
Geometry dialog box, 390–396, 430
geometry, dimension geometry, 366, 389–398
Global (View menu, Aerial View window), 214
Gouraud renderings, 585
graphics cursor. *See* crosshairs
graphics window (graphics area), 40, 748
    colors, 83
    fonts, 84
    illustrated, 40
    restoring when minimized, 71
    toggling with the text window, 71
grid, 42, 47, 100, 748
    aligning, 160–163
    in floating viewports, 487
    illustrated, 47
    limits, 100
    setting spacing, 102
    turning on/off, 101
    UCS orientation and, 119
    See also snap
GRID button (status bar), 66
GRID command, 102
Grid mode
    toggling, 101
    See also grid
GRIDMODE system variable, 79
Grip modes, 748
    exiting, 239
    options, 239
    turning on/off, 238
GRIPBLOCK system variable, 238
grips, 53, 115, 237, 748
    base grips, 239, 240
    determining coordinates, 115
    editing dimensions, 381
    editing hatches, 295
    editing OLE objects, 664
    editing with, 237, 239
    and groups, 237
    illustrated, 237
    making multiple copies with, 239, 254

Index
775

grips (*continued*)
    marking objects with, 237
    mirroring objects, 260
    moving dimension text, 387
    removing from selection sets, 238
    rotating objects, 266
    scaling objects, 272
    and selection highlighting, 226
    stretching dimensions, 383
    stretching objects with, 270
    for text objects, 336, 348
    turning on/off, 238
    within blocks, 237, 238
Grips (Tools menu), 238
Grips dialog box, 238
GROUP command, 241, 243
Group option (UNDO command), 80
group selection, toggling, 242
groups, 240–243
    creating, 240, 317
    deleting, 242
    editing, 242
    and grips, 237
    highlighting members, 240
    listing membership groups, 240
    object selection cycling, 242
    reordering members, 240, 243
    selectability, 240
    selecting, 242

H

handles, 749
hard disk space, system requirements, 60
hardware linetypes. *See* plotter linetypes
hardware requirements, 60
hatch areas. *See* hatch boundaries; islands
hatch boundaries, 152
    boundary sets, 153–155
    copying, 293
    defining, 152–155
    detecting, 153
    editing, 293
    selecting, 293
    selecting objects within, 153
HATCH command, 151
    command line options, 152
Hatch (Draw menu), 151, 153, 154
Hatch option (Object, Modify menu), 293, 294
hatch patterns, 156
    AutoCAD-supplied, 156
    defining, 157
    duplicating, 154
    editing, 293, 294
    erasing, 295
    removing associativity, 151, 293
hatch properties, copying, 250
hatch styles, 155

HATCHEDIT command, 293, 294
Hatchedit dialog box, 293, 294
hatches, 44, 150
    associative. *See* associative hatches
    copying properties, 250
    creating, 150–157
    editing, 293–295
    styles, 155
    See also hatch boundaries; hatch patterns; hatching
hatching, 44, 148, 150–157
    associative, 744
    See also hatch boundaries; hatch patterns; hatches
Help, 34, 41
    additional resources, 36
    context-sensitive, 41
    learning tools, 35
HELP command, 63
Help menu, accessing information from, 63
Help topics, accessing, 63
hidden-line images, 566
    creating, 570–571
    smoothness, 549, 579
hidden lines (in 3D objects)
    plotting/not plotting, 492, 501
    removing. *See* hiding hidden lines
hidden surfaces, removing, 575
Hide (View menu), 570
HIDE command, 301, 492, 534, 570
Hide Lines option (Plot Configuration dialog box), 493, 501
Hide option (DVIEW command), 534, 571
Hideplot option (Floating Viewports, View menu), 493
Hideplot option (MVIEW command), 492, 501
hiding
    background objects, 570
    floating viewport borders, 487
    objects, 301
    OLE objects, 665
    raster image boundaries, 644
    raster images, 649
    toolbars, 716
    See also hiding hidden lines
hiding hidden lines, 492, 534, 570
    abutting objects and, 568
    of all objects, 570
    intersecting objects and, 568, 569
    objects on hidden layers and, 569
    of selected objects, 571
    surfaces defined for, 567–568
Highlight mode, turning on/off, 226
HIGHLIGHT system variable, 226, 230
highlighting
    group members, 240
    selected objects, 226

highlights. *See* specular reflection
HLS color system, 595, 749
HOME key, moving the cursor, 71, 74
Home option (Align Text, Dimension menu), 386
home position (dimension text), 386
home position (plot area), 504, 505, 506
hook lines, 377
    See also leader lines
horizontal dimensions
    creating, 370
    illustrated, 366, 370, 371
    See also dimensions; linear dimensions
Horizontal Justification options (Format dialog box), 403
hotspot angle (of spotlights), 591, 592, 600
How to... (online documentation), 34
HPSCALE system variable, 97
HPSPACE system variable, 97
hyphen (-)
    dialog box suppression character, 78
    wild-card character, 230, 308

I

ID command, 195
ID Point option (Inquiry, Tools menu), 195
IGES (International Graphics Exchange Specification), 749
Ignore hatch style, 156
Image Adjust dialog box, 648
Image Clip option (Object, Modify menu), 650–651
Image dialog box, 634–643
    attaching and scaling images, 634
    changing image file paths, 640
    detaching images, 642
    displaying, 636
    erasing images, 643
    naming images, 641
    previewing images, 639
    reloading images, 642
    unloading images, 642
    viewing image information, 636–639
Image File Details dialog box, 639
image mapping (in rendering), 611–616
    antialiasing in, 613
    coordinates, 612
    as cropping, 613
    process steps, 612
    projection effects, 613, 615
    projection types, 615–616
    scaling, 612
    as tiling, 613, 615
    See also rendering maps
IMAGEADJUST command, 648
IMAGEATTACH command, 636
IMAGECLIP command, 650–651

IMAGEQUALITY command, 648
importing
    3D Studio files, 737
    ACIS files, 737
    DXB files, 737
    DXF files, 736
    file formats for, 736–741
    materials, 611, 617
    multiline text files, 358
    PostScript files, 739–741
    RTF files, 341
    text files, 341, 358, 736
    WMF files, 738–739
inches
    specifying, 118, 409
    suppressing zero values, 412
INDEXCTL system variable, 456
indexing objects, 456, 465
infinite lines, 48
    drawing, 184–187
    extending, 274
Inherit Properties option (Boundary Hatch dialog box), 154
initial environment, 749
inquiry methods, 196–198
inscribed polygons, drawing, 132
INSERT command, 438, 440
Insert dialog box, inserting blocks, 440
INSERT key, turning insertion mode on/off, 74
Insert Object dialog box, 663
inserting
    blocks (block references), 49, 77, 434, 438–440
        at intervals, 180–183
    drawings, 77, 438–440
        on the Web, 56
    paper space objects, 438–440
    points, at intervals, 180–183
    raster images, 633
    special characters, 344
    text files, 341
    Unicode characters, 344
    xrefs, 463
Insertion (INS) object snap, 169
insertion base point, specifying, 437, 439
insertion mode, turning on/off, 74
insertion point (text), specifying, 348
insertion points
    insertion base point, 437, 439
    snapping to, 169
INSERTOBJ command, 658, 660, 662
Inside Horizontal option (Format dialog box), 406
Installation Guide, 34, 35
installed files, 62
installing AutoCAD, 60–62
interface. *See* AutoCAD interface

Index
777

INTERFERE command, 555
internal lines (between extension lines), forcing, 400
internal points, specifying, 150, 151
International Graphics Exchange Specification (IGES), 749
International Standards Organization (ISO), 749
Internet Utilities, 56, 729
interpolation points, 749
   See also fit points
INTERSECT command, 149, 555
Intersect option (Boolean, Modify menu), 555
Intersection (INT) object snap, 166
intersections
   editing, 282
   snapping to, 166
   of solids, 555
   trimming, 277
intervals, specifying, 180–183
inverse linear attenuation of light, 595
inverse square attenuation of light, 595
islands, 749
   hatch styles and, 155
   illustrated, 150
   removing, 152
ISO (International Standards Organization), 749
ISO 8859 Latin/1 character set, as rendered into PostScript, 734
isolation levels, choosing, 682
ISOLINES system variable, 549
isometric circles, drawing, 143
isometric drawings, 162
isometric planes, 162
isometric snap style, 749
Isometric Snap/Grid mode, setting, 162
isometric views, 162
ISOPLANE command, 163
italics, formatting text in, 343, 346

J

Join option (Tiled Viewports, View menu), 219
joining
   polylines, 280
   tiled viewports, 219
justification. *See* text justification

K

kanji text, 328
key columns (in database tables), defining, 676, 678–680
keys
   database table keys, 676
   navigation keys, 71, 74, 75

L

L, least material condition symbol, 426
languages
   checking spelling in other languages, 355
   converting Asian language character strings, 708
   programming language support, 57
   unsupported font Unicode character conversion, 706
Large Buttons option (Toolbars dialog box), 718
LASTPOINT system variable, 195
lateral tolerance symbol (±), 413
lateral tolerances
   adding, 413–415
   aligning, 414, 416
   deviation, 413
   specifying as limits, 413
   suppressing zeros, 415
   symmetrical, 413
Layer & Linetype Properties dialog box, 107, 109
   assigning layer colors, 305
   assigning layer linetypes, 306
   changing linetype descriptions, 314
   creating new layers, 299
   deleting layers, 309
   filtering linetypes, 315
   freezing/thawing layers, 302, 485
   locking/unlocking layers, 304
   renaming layers, 308
   setting linetype scale, 315–317
   setting the current layer, 300
   setting the current linetype, 313
Layer (Format menu), 107, 299–309, 485, 486
layer colors, 106
   assigning, 305
   assigning to pens, 309
   changing, 107
   default color, 298, 305, 310
   and line width, 106
LAYER command, 107, 299–309, 485
layer indexes, 456
layer linetypes
   assigning, 306
   changing, 107
   default linetype, 298
layer names, 106, 299
   special characters for, 107
layer properties
   assigning, 305–306
   copying, 250
   filtering layers based on, 306–308
   inheritance, 299
   retaining in xref-dependent layers, 309

layers, 48, 106–109, 298–309, 317, 749
    assigning to objects, 317
    associating one line width with more than one layer, 499
    of block objects, 435
    for chamfers, 285
    controlling visibility, 300–304
        in floating viewports, 304
    creating, 106, 298
    default, 106
    DEFPOINTS layer, 308, 382
    deleting, 308
    dependent xref layers, 467
    editing, 244, 245, 317
    for fillets, 289
    filtering, 306–308
    filtering frozen, 486
    freezing/thawing, 300, 301–303
        in floating viewports, 303
    illustrated, 435
    indexes, 456
    linetypes. *See* layer linetypes
    listing frozen, 486
    locked, 304
    locking/unlocking, 304
    making current, 246, 300
    naming, 106, 299
    organizing, 106, 298
    plotting, 300
    of raster images, 644
    renaming, 299, 308
    sorting, 298
    turning on/off, 48, 301
    See also layer colors; layer linetypes; layer properties; named objects
Layout option (Tiled Viewports, View menu), 218
layouts
    and plotting, 475
    designing, 475
layouts (in paper space), designing, 54, 480–494
Leader (Dimension menu), 378
LEADER command, 378
leader lines, 367, 368
    annotations, 368, 380
    appending feature control frames to, 379
    associativity, 368, 380
    automatic, 400
    creating, 377–381
    editing, 380
    editing annotations, 380
    illustrated, 367
    simple, 368
    spline, 378
    See also annotations; arrowheads; hook lines
Learning Assistance, 35

Learning Assistance (Help menu), 36
Learning AutoCAD (online tutorial), 34, 36
learning tools (Help menu), 35
LEFT ARROW key, moving the cursor, 71
left mouse button. *See* pick button (mouse)
Left option (Align Text, Dimension menu), 387
lemon-shaped solids, creating, 551
LENGTHEN command, 275
lengths
    chamfering objects by specifying, 287
    changing lengths of objects, 274
letters, selecting, 343
libraries
    search paths, 84, 745
    slide libraries, 751
library of materials, importing/exporting materials from/to, 617
license agreement, 61
light
    ambient light, 589, 598, 743
    attenuation, 590, 595, 744
    color systems, 595
    distant light, 590
    light colors, 605
    reflection types, 596–599
    See also lights (for rendering)
light blocks, 600
    updating of pre-Release 14 blocks, 628
light bulbs, simulating light from, 591
light colors, 605
LIGHT command, 601–604
Light option (Render, View menu), 601
lighting principles, 594
lights (for rendering), 588–592
    adding, 600
    ambient light, 589, 598
    angles of faces to, 594
    deleting, 601
    distances of faces from, 595
    distant light, 590
        defining paths, 602
    fill lights, 589, 591
    intensity, 600
    modifying, 601
    point lights, 590
    positioning, 600, 602–604
    removing from the current scene, 601
    settings, 600
    and shadows, 589
    spotlights, 591
    surface reflection, 596–599
    surface reflection colors, 605
    types, 589–592
    See also light
Lights dialog box, 600
Lights option (Render, View menu), 600

limits
  specifying tolerances as, 413
  See also drawing limits
LIMITS command, 37, 101
Limits option (Plot Configuration dialog box), 502
LIMMAX system variable, 37, 101
LIMMIN system variable, 37, 101
Line (Draw menu), 119, 126
LINE command, 119, 126, 127
line-hiding. *See* hiding hidden lines
line objects, drawing, 126
line segments, 126
  filleting, 289
line text, 333
  aligning, 335
  creating, 334
  editing, 336
  fitting between points, 335
  formatting, 334–336
  for leader lines, 378
  properties, 337
line text objects, 336
line widths
  associating one line width with more than one layer, 499
  specifying with colors, 106, 498
Linear (Dimension menu), 371, 410
linear dimensions
  creating, 370–374
  definition points (illustrated), 382
  illustrated, 366, 370
  rotated. *See* rotated dimensions
  types, 366, 370
  See also aligned dimensions; baseline dimensions; continued dimensions; dimensions; horizontal dimensions; ordinate dimensions; vertical dimensions
lines
  baselines, 745
  centerlines, 367, 393
  chamfering, 286
  chamfers, 285
  creating meshes between, 542
  dimensioning, 370–374
  drawing, 72, 126–135
    in tiled viewports, 220
  filleting, 289, 291
  infinite, 184–186
  joining to polylines, 280
  line segments, 126, 289
  mirror lines, 259
  offsetting, 126
  parallel lines, 126
  perpendicular lines, 163

lines (*continued*)
  removing overlapping lines from 3D drawings, 516
  rubber-band line, 163, 751
  tessellation lines, 549, 579, 752
  types, 126
  See also construction lines; dimension lines; extension lines; fillets; hidden lines; leader lines; linetypes; multilines; objects; polylines; rays
lines (of text)
  starting new, 340
  wordwrapping, 361
  See also line text; multiline text
Linetype (Format menu), 108, 315, 490
LINETYPE command, 109, 126, 312
linetype descriptions, changing, 314
linetype scale
  copying, 250
  and multiline scale, 132
  setting, 315–317, 490
linetypes, 48, 108–109, 126, 311–317, 749
  assigning to layers, 306
  assigning to objects, 108, 317
  AutoCAD versus plotter, 312
  of block objects, 435, 436
  copying, 250
  default, 126
  deleting, 314
  descriptions, 314
  editing
    layer linetypes, 107
    object linetypes, 244, 249, 319
  filtering, 315
  hardware versus software, 499
  illustrated, 311
  loading, 108, 312
  making current, 126, 249, 313
  objects associated with, 108
  plotter linetypes, 499, 500
  in polylines, 320
  of raster images, 644
  renaming, 313
  scale factor, 99, 316
  scaling, 316
    in paper space, 316, 490
  for short lines, 108
  sorting, 298
  in xref layers, 467
  See also linetype scale; named objects; plotter linetypes
link path names, 677–682
  defining, 678–682
  duplicate, 685, 686
  exporting links associated with, 698
  identical, 685
  primary, 681–682

link path names (*continued*)
    referencing in blocks and xrefs, 684–686
    secondary, 681–682, 701
    unique, 685
Link Path Names dialog box, 677, 679
link paths (of database objects)
    setting, 677–682
    in xrefs, 678
linked image paths, 633
linked OLE objects, editing, 657
linking, 56, 654
    database table rows to objects, 676, 683–684
    versus embedding, 654
    files to drawings, 660
    objects to drawings, 654, 659
    OLE commands, 656, 658
    views to other application documents, 256, 656
    See also attaching
links (OLE), 749
    breaking, 661
    changing, 661
    updating, 654, 660
links (to external databases), 683
    accessing link information stored in drawings, 702
    to blocks, 686, 689–690
    deleting, 688–689
    editing, 687–689
    exporting link information to files, 697–699
    locked layers and, 704
    opening drawings containing, 702
    synchronizing, 701
    to xrefs, 686, 689–690
Links dialog box (database links), accessing links in blocks and xrefs, 689–690
Links dialog box (OLE links), 660–662
LIST command, 197, 319
List option (Inquiry, Tools menu), 197
List View option (External Reference dialog box), 449
List View option (Image dialog box), 637
listing
    database information, 54, 196
    dimension styles, 421–423
    dimensioning system variables, 421–423
    drawing time, 198
    layers, frozen, 486
    properties, 196
    raster images, 637–638
    symbol tables, 474
    system variables, 80
    tiled viewport configurations, 222
    user coordinate systems, 123
    xrefs (xref definitions), 449, 473

LMC, least material condition symbol, 426
Load or Reload Linetypes dialog box, 312
loading
    demand loading xrefs, 453–457
    external database commands, 669, 703
    linetypes, 108, 312
    PC2 files, 498, 510
    PCP files, 498
    raster images, 642
    See also attaching
locating points, 46, 114, 119, 195
lock files. *See* file locking
locked layers
    editing links for objects on, 704
    editing objects on, 244, 304
locking
    files. *See* file locking
    layers, 304
log files, 473
long file names, 77
loops, creating regions from, 148
low-resolution monitors, displaying more on, 84
LTSCALE system variable, 97, 109, 490
LUNITS system variable, 99
LUPREC system variable, 99

M

\M+ character sequences, 708
M, maximum material condition symbol, 426
macros, associating with tools, 719
magnet (object snap lock), 175
magnifying glass (cursor), 495
magnifying views. *See* zooming
main window, 40, 66
    illustrated, 40, 66
Make Displayable Attribute dialog box, 692
Make option (Block, Draw menu), 437
manuals, viewing, 64
mapping. *See* color mapping; font mapping; image mapping (in rendering)
maps
    color maps, 746
    shadow maps, 593
    See also rendering maps
Mark option (UNDO command), 80
marker (object snap marker), 175
markers. *See* blips; center marks; point markers
marking actions, 80
MASSPROP command, 192
Match Properties (Modify menu), 251
MATCHPROP command, 250–252
material condition symbols, 426
    illustrated, 424
material conditions (of features), 426
materials (for rendering), 604–611
    attaching, 610–611
    coloring, 607

materials (*continued*)
    defining, 606–609
    detaching, 611
    duplicating, 609
    exporting, 617
    importing, 611, 617
    modifying, 609
    process steps, 606
    producing materials lists, 697
    properties, 604, 607–609
    refractive index, 606
    rendering, 611
    solid materials, 614
    surface color variations, 605
    transparency, 606
Materials dialog box, 607–609
    attaching materials, 610
Materials Library dialog box, 617
Materials Library option (Render, View menu), 617
materials lists (in drawings), 617, 697
Materials option (Render, View menu), 607, 609
mathematical expressions, evaluating, 188
mathematical operators, 188
MAXACTVP system variable, 487
MAXX title block attribute definition, 105
MAXY title block attribute definition, 105
MEASURE command, 180, 182
Measure option (Point, Draw menu), 181
MEASUREMENT system variable, 86
measurement systems
    default files, 86
    specifying, 86
    switching, 86
measurement units. *See* alternate units (for dimensions); angular units; drawing units; English units; metric units; primary units (for dimensions)
measuring objects in intervals, 180–182
    starting points, 181
memory (RAM)
    displaying free space, 197
    freeing up. *See* performance improvements
    system requirements, 60
menu bar, 66
    illustrated, 40
menu files
    acad.mnu file, 68, 85
    default, 68, 85
    specifying, 85
menu groups, in toolbar names, 713
menus, 68
    button menus, 745
    choosing options, 68
    context-sensitive Help, 41
    custom, 85
    customizing, 711

menus (*continued*)
    default, 85
    specifying, 68, 85
    starting commands from, 73
    See also cursor menu; menu files
merge rendering, 586–588
meshes (faceted surfaces), 535, 537
    closing, 539
    components, 578
    converting AutoSurf surfaces into, 579
    Coons surface patch meshes, 545
    creating, 537–548
        between objects, 542
        for smooth shading, 578–579
    density, 537, 578
    edge-defined surface meshes, 545
    irregular, 539
    polyface meshes, 541
    polygon meshes, 539
    predefined surface meshes, 538
    rectangular meshes, 539
    removing/plotting hidden lines, 492, 501
    ruled surface meshes, 542
    simulating with elevation/thickness, 546–548
    surface of revolution meshes, 544
    tabulated surface meshes, 544
    uses, 537
messages (command line), viewing, 70
metafiles. *See* WMF files
metric units
    converting English units to/from, 86
    default files, 86
Microsoft Windows. *See* Windows 95
Midpoint (MID) object snap, 165
midpoints, snapping to, 165
MIF (Multibyte Interchange Format), 708
MINSERT command, 440
minus sign (-)
    mathematical operator, 188
    zoom cursor, 201
MINX title block attribute definition, 105
MINY title block attribute definition, 105
Mirror (Modify menu), 260
Mirror 3D option (3D Operation, Modify menu), 558
MIRROR command, 260, 556
mirror lines, creating, 259
MIRROR3D command, 558
mirroring
    3D objects, 558
    objects, 253, 259–261, 749
    text, 260, 336, 348
MIRRTEXT system variable, 260, 336, 348
mistakes
    redoing actions, 80
    undoing actions, 45, 80

MLINE command, 126, 127, 128
MLSTYLE command, 283
MMC, maximum material condition symbol, 426
model space, 54, 476, 749
    dimensioning in, 396
    drawing limits, 101
    illustrated, 479
    plotting from, 476
    restoring named views, 493
    saving views, 493
    scaling dimensions, 396
    settings, 95
    setup wizard effects on, 95
    slide appearance in, 726
    switching to, 478
    TILEMODE system variable and, 477
    views in, 476, 527
Model Space button (status bar), 478, 479
model space UCS icons, 478
models, 749
    See also 3D Modeling; 3D objects; drawings; objects (AutoCAD)
modes, 749
Modify dialog box, 547
Modify Distant Light dialog box, 602
Modify Image dialog box, 644–646
Modify Light dialog box, 601
Modify Materials dialog box, 609
Modify MText dialog box, 350
Modify Point Light dialog box, 602
Modify Text dialog box, 338
modifying. *See* editing
monitor resolution, and slide appearance, 726
monitors
    low-resolution, 84
    monochrome, 309
    system requirements, 60
monochrome monitors, using color numbers, 309
mouse, 64
    buttons, 64
    practicing with, 64
Move (Modify menu), 235, 264
MOVE command, 235, 556
move cursor, 664
moving
    dimension text, 387
    multiline text objects, 350
    objects, 263–267
        by stretching, 269
    OLE objects, 664
    raster images, 645
    tools, 715
MSLIDE command, 727
MSPACE command, 479
Mtext. *See* multiline text

MTEXT command, 338–340, 344, 346, 348, 359, 362
MTEXTED system variable, 358, 363, 379
Multibyte Interchange Format (MIF), 708
Multibyte shape numbers, 708
Multiline (Draw menu), 128
Multiline Edit Tools dialog box, 282
multiline intersections, editing, 282
Multiline option (Object, Modify menu), 281
Multiline Properties dialog box, 130
multiline scale, 131
    and linetype scale, 132
Multiline Style (Format menu), 129, 130, 283
multiline styles
    creating, 129–131
    default file, 130
    editing, 282
    naming, 131
    saving, 131
    using existing, 131
Multiline Styles dialog box, 129, 283
multiline text, 338
    boundaries, 362
    creating, 339
        in a third-party text editor, 358
    editing, 348–351
        in a third-party text editor, 363
    finding and replacing, 351
    format codes, 359–362
    formatting, 342–348
        in a third-party text editor, 359–362
    importing files, 358
    for leader lines, 378, 379
    properties, 339, 346–348, 350
    See also multiline text objects; text styles
Multiline Text Editor dialog box, 339, 343
    Character tab, 343
    creating multiline text, 340
    finding and replacing multiline text, 351
    setting multiline text properties, 346–348
multiline text objects, 326, 348
    editing, 363
    formatting, 346–348
    height, 339
    moving, 350
    See also multiline text
Multiline Text option (Text, Draw menu), 339, 341, 343, 345, 348, 359, 362
multiline text properties, setting, 339, 346–348, 350
multilines, 128
    adding elements to, 129
    background fills, 131
    capping, 130
    coloring, 131
    drawing, 131
    editing, 281–283

Index
783

multilines (*continued*)
    end caps, 128, 130
    illustrated, 128
    joints, 128, 130
    properties, 130
    scale, 131
    See also multiline styles
multiple copies, making, 239, 253
Multiple Copy mode, 239
MVIEW command, 479, 481, 482, 487
    command options, 492, 501
MVSETUP command, 481, 482, 491, 492

N

named objects, 228–230
    dependent symbols as, 464
    purging, 228
    renaming, 229
        in groups, 229
Named UCS option (UCS, Tools menu), 123
Named UCS option, Plan View option (3D Viewpoint, View menu), 530
named viewport configurations. *See* viewport configurations
named views, 749
    deleting, 216
    naming, 214
    restoring, 216, 493
    saving, 214, 493
    See also views
Named Views (View menu), 215, 216, 494
naming
    dependent symbols, 464, 467
    layers, 106
    multiline styles, 131
    named views, 214
    raster images, 641
    text styles, 325
    tiled viewport configurations, 222
    user coordinate systems, 123
    xrefs, 463
    See also file names; renaming
navigation keys, 71, 74, 75
Nearest (NEA) object snap, 171
nested blocks, 435
nested xref paths, changing, 468
nested xrefs, 457
    clipped, 464
nesting, blocks, 435
networks, demand loading xrefs from, 456
NEW command, 87, 94, 95, 104, 110, 111
New Distant Light dialog box, 603
New Light dialog box, 600
New Style dialog box, 325
New Toolbar dialog box, 713
Node (NOD) object snap, 168, 181
nodes, 749

nonbreaking spaces, inserting, 340
None (NONE) object snap, 172
nongraphic attributes
    selecting objects with, 694–697
    storing, 667
Normal hatch style, 156
normals, of surfaces, 575, 749
noun/verb selection, 749
Noun/Verb Selection option (Object Selection Settings dialog box), 237
NURB surfaces, export file format, 731
NURBS curves. *See* spline curves

O

object colors, 309–311
    assigning, 317
    changing, 318
    color names, 310
    color numbers, 309
    default color, 310
    editing, 244, 247, 318
    making current, 247, 310
    specifying, 310
    See also colors
Object Group (Tools menu), 241, 243
Object Grouping dialog box, 241, 243
object layers
    assigning, 317
    editing, 244, 245, 317
    making current, 246, 300
object linetypes
    assigning, 108, 317
    editing, 244, 249, 319
object linking and embedding. *See* OLE
object properties, 48
    assigning to block objects, 436
    copying, 250–252
    editing with the Object Properties toolbar, 244–249
    listing, 196
    See also colors; elevation; layers; linetypes; thickness
Object Properties toolbar, 244–249, 312
    assigning colors to layers, 311
    character matching, 244
    editing object colors, 244, 247, 319
    editing object layers, 244, 245, 318
    editing object linetypes, 244, 249, 320
    freezing/thawing layers, 302
    illustrated, 244
    locking/unlocking layers, 304
    making a color current, 311
    making a layer current, 300
    making a linetype current, 313
    turning layers on/off, 301
object selection cycling, 242, 302
Object Selection Filters dialog box, 235

Object Selection Settings dialog box, 234
Object Snap mode
    See also object snaps; Snap mode
Object Snap Settings (Tools menu), 173, 176
object snap tools, illustrated, 164
object snaps, 47, 164–177
    AutoSnap, 174–176
    choosing from the cursor menu, 173
    cycling through, 174
    disabling, 172
    entering on the command line, 172
    magnet, 175
    marker, 175
    multiple, 172, 173
    and OLE objects, 664
    Quick snap option, 172
    running object snaps, 173, 751
    SnapTips, 174, 175
    specifying, 172–177
    specifying points with, 164–177
    target box, 172, 174
    tools (illustrated), 164
    turning on/off, 174
objects (AutoCAD), 750
    adding to selection sets, 245, 318
    aligning at intervals, 181
    arraying, 253, 261–263
    assigning colors to, 317
    assigning layers to, 317
    assigning linetypes to, 108, 317
    in blocks. *See* block objects
    breaking, 180, 278
    calculating areas/circumferences/perimeters, 191
    chamfering, 53, 285–288
    changing lengths, 274
    changing the drawing order, 145
    coloring, 48, 317
    complex, 276
    copying, 52, 253–263
        with grips, 239, 254
        to the Clipboard, 255
    counting objects linked to database rows, 697–699
    creating, 125–157
        and embedding, 662
        in paper space, 488
    creating meshes between, 542
    creating regions from overlapping objects, 148
    cutting to the Clipboard, 255
    cycling through group objects, 242
    deleting database links to, 688
    dividing into segments, 182
    dragging. *See* dragging objects
    drawing, 43–45, 125–157

objects (*continued*)
    drawing circles tangent to, 138
    duplicating. *See* copying
    editing, 52–54, 227–233
        with grips, 237, 239
    embedding in other documents, 657
    erasing, 267
    exploding, 278
    extending, 52, 273
    extruded, 492, 501, 552
    filleting, 53, 289–292
    floating, 436
    hatching, 151
    hiding, 301
    identifying with color numbers, 309
    indexing, 456
    linking to database table rows, 676, 683–684
    listing database information on, 196
    making an object layer current, 246, 300
    measuring in intervals, 180–182
    mirroring, 253, 259–261, 749
    moving, 263–267
        by stretching, 269
    named. *See* named objects
    offsetting, 52, 253, 258
    paper space objects, 438–440
    pasting into AutoCAD, 256
    positioning 2D objects in 3D space, 536
    proxy objects, 702
    removing, 53
        from selection sets, 236, 238
    removing parts of, 278
    as rendered into PostScript, 734
    resizing, 268–277
    rotating, 263, 264–266, 556
    scaling. *See* scaling objects
    selecting. *See* selecting objects
    sizing new objects, 94
    smoothness, 549
    snapping to points on, 164–177
    specifying intervals on, 180–183
    stretching, 52, 268–270
    symbols, 49, 752
    trimming, 52, 275–277
    visibility, 301
    See also 3D objects; blocks; database objects; drawing database; features (of objects); groups; named objects; object colors; object linetypes; object properties
    See also OLE objects; selection sets; shapes; *and specific objects*
objects, custom, 157
objects, proxy, 157
Oblique (Dimension menu), 385
oblique stroke arrowheads, 390

oblique strokes. *See* tick marks
obliquing angle (of text), setting, 331
ODBC database, accessing, 668
Offset (Modify menu), 258
OFFSET command, 126, 131, 258
offset snaps, 239, 254
offsetting
    lines, 126
    multiple copies, 239, 254
    objects, 52, 253, 258
    rendered images, 623
OLE (object linking and embedding), 50, 653–666, 750
    terminology, 654
OLE Links (Edit menu), 660–662
OLE Object (Insert menu), 662
OLE objects, 654, 662
    copying, 664
    cutting, 664
    deselecting, 666
    displaying, 665, 666
    editing, 664–666
    embedded, editing, 658, 663
    embedding, 655, 662–663
    hiding, 665
    limitations in AutoCAD, 666
    linked, editing, 657
    linking, 654, 659
    moving, 664
    pasting, 662, 664
    plotting, 666
    resizing, 664
    selecting, 665
OLELINKS command, 658, 660
online help. *See* help
online manuals, viewing, 64
online tutorials
    Learning AutoCAD, 34
    multimedia tutorials, 36
OOPS command, 80, 268
opacity maps, 612, 614, 750
Open (File menu), 87, 88, 89
OPEN command, 88
opening
    the Aerial View window, 211
    DXB files, 737
    DXF files, 736
    existing drawings, 42, 87
        with the browser, 88
        dialog box display control, 78
        drawings containing database links, 702
        on the Web, 56
operators, mathematical, 188
Optimizing Pen Motion dialog box, 516
options (command options), 41
ORACLE database, accessing, 668

order of precedence of mathematical operators, 188
Ordinate (Dimension menu), 376
ordinate dimensions, 376
    automatic, 376
    creating, 376
    definition points (illustrated), 382
    dimension text, 376
    illustrated, 366, 376
    See also dimensions
orientation (of text). *See* text orientation
origin, 750
    adjusting the plot origin, 504
    displaying the UCS icon at, 122
    indicating the UCS origin, 525
    locating a new UCS origin, 120
    WCS origin, 119
Origin option (UCS, Tools menu), 121, 122
ORTHO button (status bar), 66, 164
ORTHO command, 164
Ortho mode, 47, 164, 750
    and freehand sketching, 133, 134
    as ignored by AutoCAD, 163
    Isometric Snap/Grid mode and, 162
    toggling, 164
    UCS orientation and, 119
orthogonal, 750
orthographic projections. *See* parallel projections (of 3D views)
OSMODE system variable, 174
OSNAP button, 174
OSNAP command, 174
Osnap Settings dialog box, 174, 176
    displaying, 174
Outer hatch style, 156
Outside Horizontal option (Format dialog box), 406
overall dimension scale. *See* dimension scale
Overall Scale (Geometry dialog box), 394
overlapping lines, removing from 3D drawings, 516
overlaying xrefs, 459
overrides. *See* dimension style overrides

P

\P, dimension text separator symbol, 410
PAGE DOWN key, moving the cursor, 71
PAGE UP key, moving the cursor, 71
Pan (Mode menu, Aerial View window), 213
Pan (View menu), options, 202
pan box (Aerial View window), 213
PAN command, 200, 301
panning, 51, 750
    with Aerial View, 212
    freezing layers and, 301
    interactive (Realtime mode), 200, 202
paper, positioning the view on, 504–506

Paper Size dialog box, 504
paper size, setting, 503
paper space, 54, 476, 750
    creating objects, 488
    dimensioning in, 396
    drawing limits, 101
    illustrated, 478
    layer visibility, 298
    plotting from, 476
    restoring named views, 493
    saving views, 493
    scale factors, 489
    scaling dimensions, 395, 396
    scaling linetypes, 316, 490
    scaling objects, 270
    scaling views relative to, 100, 207, 208, 488
    setting the dimension scale, 395, 396
    settings, 95
    setup wizard effects on, 95
    slide appearance in, 726
    switching to, 477
    TILEMODE system variable and, 477
    UCS limitations, 525
    views, 476, 527
    See also floating viewports
Paper Space button (status bar), 478, 479
paper space objects, inserting, 438–440
paper space UCS icon, 477
paragraph text. *See* multiline text; paragraphs
paragraphs
    format codes, 359–362
    selecting, 343
parallel dimensions. *See* baseline dimensions
parallel lines
    drawing, 126
    filleting, 292
parallel projections (of 3D views), creating, 531
parent dimension styles, 416
    creating, 388
parentheses (()), mathematical operators, 188
partial plot configuration files. *See* PCP files
parts lists, extracting attribute information for, 441, 444–447
Paste (Edit menu), 257, 659, 662
Paste Special (Edit menu), 257, 659
Paste Special dialog box, 258, 659
PASTECLIP command, 659, 662
PASTESPEC command, 659
pasting
    objects, into AutoCAD, 256
    OLE objects, 662, 664
    text, 258, 340, 341
        to the command line, 74, 79
        to the text window, 71
    views, into other documents, 656

paths
    distant light paths, 602
    See also search paths
Pattern option (Boundary Hatch dialog box), 294
patterns. *See* hatch patterns
PC2 files, 498, 508, 509
    associating with drawings, 512
    creating, 508
    loading, 498, 510
PCP files, 498, 508, 511
    associating with drawings, 512
    creating, 510
    loading, 498
PDMODE system variable, 145, 182, 183
PDSIZE system variable, 145, 182, 183
PEDIT command, 133, 137, 280, 321, 539
PELLIPSE system variable, 142
Pen Assignments dialog box, 500
pen plotters
    assigning colors to pens, 106, 300, 309, 498, 499, 500
    single-pen, 300, 499
    See also pen widths; pens
pen speed, configuring, 499, 500
pen widths
    assigning colors to, 499
    configuring, 498, 500
pens
    adjusting inward, 501
    assigning colors to, 106, 300, 309, 498, 499, 500
    assignments, 498–501
    optimizing motion, 515
    pen speed, 499, 500
    See also pen widths
performance improvements
    calibrating plotters, 516
    demand loading xrefs, 453, 456
    freezing layers, 301
    indexing objects, 456
    limiting drawing resolution, 579
    optimizing pen motion, 515
    and precision, 579
    specifying support directories, 84
    speeding up plotting, 515
    speeding up raster image display, 642, 648
    turning off Aerial View window dynamic updating, 214
    turning off viewports, 486
    turning off visual elements display, 224
    unloading external database commands, 669, 702
    unloading raster images, 642
    unloading xrefs, 452, 462
    using SHX fonts, 352

perimeters, calculating, 191
period (.), wild-card character, 230, 307
Perpendicular (PER) object snap, 169
perpendicular lines, drawing, 163
perspective views, 507
    creating, 531, 532
PFACE command, 541
Phong shading, 585
Photo Raytrace renderer. *See* photorealistic renderers; raytraced renderer
Photo Real renderer. *See* photorealistic renderers
photorealistic renderers, 582
    antialiasing control levels, 581
    bitplane setting, 581
    and complex geometry, 577
    light reflection parameters, 598, 599
    mapping, 611–616
    shadow generation, 592–593
    smooth shading option, 578
pick button (mouse), 64, 750
    interactive zooming/panning, 201, 202
    object selection cycling, 233
    sketching freehand, 133, 134
    zooming, 201, 495
Pick Points option (Boundary Hatch dialog box), 151
PICKADD system variable, 245, 318
pickbox
    illustrated, 231
    selecting objects with, 231
PICKDRAG system variable, 232
PICKFIRST system variable, 231, 237, 245, 696
PICKSTYLE system variable, 240, 242, 293
pigment colors, 605
PLAN command, 530
plan view, 750
    displaying, 530
    illustrated, 750
    UCS icon in, 527
Plan View option (3D Viewpoint, View menu), options, 530
planar projection (in image mapping), 615, 750
planes
    clipping, 746
    construction, 115, 746
    isometric, 162
PLINE command, 126, 137, 139, 549
PLINEGEN system variable, 320
plines. *See* polylines
plot area, 504
    adjusting the plot origin, 504–506
    home position, 504, 505
    setting, 501–503
    setting plot rotation, 504–506
PLOT command, 497–511, 515

Plot Configuration dialog box, 496, 502–511, 514, 516
plot configuration files, 498, 508–511
    associating with drawings, 512
    See also PC2 files; PCP files; plotter configurations
plot configurations. *See* plotter configurations
plot files, 514
plot origin, adjusting, 504–506
Plot Preview, zooming limits, 201
Plot Rotation and Origin dialog box, 505
plot rotation, setting, 504–506
plot scale, 92, 100
    and the dimension scale, 395
    setting, 506–508
plot spooling, 512
PLOTROTMODE system variable, 506
plotter configurations, 494
    changing, 495, 498
    creating, 508
    reusing, 508
    saving, 498, 508
    setting up, 498–511
    See also plot configuration files
plotter linetypes
    configuring, 499, 500
    previewing, 500
plotters
    assigning colors to pens, 106, 309, 498, 499, 500
    calibrating, 516
    configuring, 498–511
    home position, 505
    preparatory checks, 495
    setting up, 497
    sharing with nonsystem driver users, 512
    single-pen, 300
    specifying, 496
plotting, 55, 476, 494–517
    basics, 495–497
    batch plotting, 512–514
    circuit diagrams, 502
    from the command line, 497
    definition points, 382
    to files, 514
    improving performance, 515–517
    layers, 300
    OLE objects, 666
    preparing for, 54–55, 495
    previewing output, 497
    to printers, 55, 515
    removing hidden lines, 492, 501
    scaling, 506–508
    solids, 498, 501
    speeding up, 515

plotting (*continued*)
    spooling, 512
    text height, 395
    trace fills, 498
    view plotting options, 501
    wide polylines, 498, 501
plotting units, specifying, 503, 506
PLT files, 514
plus sign (+)
    mathematical operator, 188
    UCS icon symbol, 121
    zoom cursor, 201
plus-or-minus sign (±)
    lateral tolerance symbol, 413
    Unicode value, 707
plus-or-minus tolerances. *See* lateral tolerances
Point (Draw menu), 145
point acquisition, defining hatch boundaries via, 155
point filters (coordinate filters), 746
    specifying points with, 177
point lights, 590
    attenuation rate options, 595
    positioning, 602
    spotlights, 591
point markers
    creating, 145
    inserting at intervals, 180–183
    styling, 182
point objects
    creating, 144
    snapping to, 168, 171
    styling, 144
Point Style (Format menu), 144
Point Style dialog box, 145
pointer, on-screen form, 64
pointing devices, 64–65
    tablet, 65
    See also mouse
points (geometric), 750
    approximation points, 744
    calculating, 188, 189
    camera point, 532, 533
    centering views on, 207
    control points, 746
    displacement point, 253
    extracting coordinates from selected points, 521
    fit points, 283, 744, 748, 749
    fitting line text between, 335
    inserting at intervals, 180–183
    internal points, 150, 151
    interpolation points, 749
    locating, 46, 114, 119, 195
    offsetting objects through, 259
    snap base point, 160
    snapping to points on objects, 164–177

points (*continued*)
    specifying, 64
        by calculation, 188, 189
        with coordinate systems, 114–118
        with direct distance entry, 118
        with object snaps, 164–177
        with point filters, 177
        from temporary reference points, 176
        with tracking, 178–180
    specifying boundaries with, 155
    See also base point; coordinates; definition points (of dimensions); insertion points; point markers; point objects
polar arrays, 750
    creating, 261, 557
polar coordinates, 46, 114, 116
    locating points with, 119
    specifying, 117, 118
Polar option (Array, Modify menu), 262
Polar option, 3D Array option (3D Operation, Modify menu), 557
polyface meshes
    creating, 541
    displaying invisible edges, 542
    export file format, 731
Polygon (Draw menu), 132, 133
POLYGON command, 132
polygon meshes
    creating, 539
    export file format, 731
    surfaces defined by, 568
polygon selection windows, 232, 751
    CPolygons, 232, 746
    WPolygons, 232, 753
polygon windows. *See* polygon selection windows
polygonal clipping boundaries, 465
polygons
    calculating areas/perimeters, 191
    circumscribed, 133
    clipping boundaries, 465
    crossing polygons. *See* CPolygons
    drawing, 132, 650
    editing, 133
    exploding, 133
    inscribed, 132
    rotating, 266
    window polygons. *See* WPolygons
Polyline (Draw menu), 127
polyline clipping boundaries, 465
Polyline option (Object, Modify menu), 280
polyline segments
    centering linetype patterns on, 320
    chamfering, 288
    extension line origins, 369
    tapered, 274
    tapering, 280

polylines, 44, 537, 751
   as boundaries, 148
   calculating areas/perimeters, 191
   chamfering, 288
   clipping boundaries, 465
   closed, 148, 568
   drawing, 126–128
      freehand, 134
   editing, 128, 279–281
   exploding, 128, 279
   extending, 274
   filleting, 291
   joining, 280, 552, 553
   linetypes, 320
   smoothed. *See* splined polylines
   smoothing, 136, 279
   See also objects; polyline segments; splined polylines; wide polylines
positional tolerances, 424
   and projected tolerances, 427
PostScript files
   AutoCAD PostScript interpreter, 740
   color mapping, 741
   configuring Windows for output to, 626
   creating, 733–735, 740
   customizing, 735
   display quality, 739
   font mapping, 740
   importing, 739–741
   objects as rendered in, 734
   PostScript Support file, 735
   saving rendered images to, 621, 626
   scaling, 734
PostScript fills, in 2D polylines, 740
PostScript fonts, in Release 14, 333
PostScript images
   color mapping for imported images, 741
   exporting, 733–735
   saving rendered images as, 621, 626
PostScript Support file, 735
pound sign (#), wild-card character, 230, 307
precedence of mathematical operators, 188
precision
   drawing with, 46–48, 159–198
      in 3D modeling, 579
   in DWF files, 729
   in DXF files, 730
   and performance, 579
   setting unit precision, 97
preferences (environment), setting, 81–87
Preferences (Tools menu), 82, 352, 357, 454, 470–471
PREFERENCES command, 72, 82, 353, 358
Preferences dialog box, 81–87
   Files tab, 352, 357, 469–471
   Performance tab, 454

Preferences dialog box (*continued*)
   Printer tab, 509
Preset UCS option (UCS, Tools menu), 526
PREVIEW command, 496
Preview Effective Plotting Area dialog box, 497
previewing
   drawings, 88, 497
   plotter linetypes, 500
Previous option (ZOOM command), 203
primary units (for dimensions), 407–409
   suppressing zeros, 411
Primary Units dialog box, 408
prime symbol ('), feet specifier, 118
Print (File menu), 496–511, 514–516, 625
Print dialog box, altering rendered images for printing, 625
print preview, zooming in, 495
printers
   plotting to, 515
   raster printers, 498, 499, 505
   See also plotters
printing, 55
   rendered images, 624–627
   speeding up, 515
   See also plotting; printers
procedural materials (for rendering), 614, 751
processors, system requirements, 60
programming language support, 57
project name paths
   adding/deleting, 470
   editing, 471
project names
   adding/deleting, 469
   editing, 470
   See also project name paths
projected tolerance symbol (Ⓟ), 427
projected tolerance zones
   adding, 426
   setting height, 427
projected tolerances, 427
projection lines. *See* extension lines
projections
   image mapping types, 615–616
   parallel projections (of 3D views), 531
   perspective views, 507, 531, 532
projects
   organizing, 91–111
   See also project name paths; project names
PROJMODE system variable, 558
prologue sections, PostScript Support file, 735
prompts (command line), 751
   command history, 70
   Command prompt, 73
   selecting command options, 73
   transparent command prompt indicator (>>), 76
   viewing, 70

properties
    materials properties, 604, 607
    multiline properties, 130
    toolbar properties, 713
    See also layer properties; text properties
Properties (Modify menu)
    modifying line text, 337
    modifying multiline text, 350, 351
    modifying raster images, 644–646
    setting thickness, 547
Property Settings dialog box, 252
proxy fonts, 328
Proxy Information dialog box, 158
proxy objects, 157
    handling, 702
PS files, font mapping order, 354
PSFILL command, 735, 740
PSIN command, 739, 740
PSLTSCALE system variable, 316, 490
PSOUT command, 733, 735, 740
PSPACE command, 478
PSPROLOG system variable, 735
PSQUALITY system variable, 739
PURGE command, 228
Purge option (Drawing Utilities, File menu),
    options, 228
purging
    named objects, 228
    raster images, 642
    text styles, 333
    See also deleting

Q

QTEXTMODE system variable, 225
Quadrant (QUA) object snap, 168
quadrants, snapping to, 168
quadrilateral solid fills, creating, 147
querying external databases, 699–701
question mark (?)
    noncurrent font display character, 707
    wild-card character, 230, 307
Quick (QUI) object snap, 172
Quick Reference Card, 35, 36
Quick Setup wizard, setting up new drawings,
    37, 94, 95, 96, 97, 99, 101
Quick Text mode, turning on/off, 224
Quick Tour, 35
QUIT command, 90
quotation marks
    long file name delimiters, 77
    reverse quote ('), 230, 308

R

radial dimensions, 374
    creating, 374
    definition points (illustrated), 382
    diameter dimension styles, 400
    illustrated, 366
    See also diameter dimensions; dimensions
rails (of ruled surface meshes), 542
RAM (Random Access Memory). *See* memory
raster file formats, 632
Raster Image (Insert menu), 634–643
raster image boundaries, 643, 649
    bitonal, 646
    clipping boundaries, 649–651
    properties, 643
    showing/hiding, 644
raster images, 56, 631–651
    accessing file details, 638
    attaching, 633
    bitonal, 643, 646, 648
    brightness, 647
    clipping, 648, 649–651
    clipping boundaries, 649–651
    contrast, 647
    detaching, 642
    displaying, 642, 648, 649–651
    dragging, 636
    erasing, 643
    fade, 647
    hiding, 649
    image paths, 633, 640
    inserting, 633
    layers, 644
    listing, 637–638
    modifying, 643–651
    moving, 645
    naming, 641
    pasting bitmaps into AutoCAD, 257
    previewing, 638
    purging, 642
    quality, 648
    redrawing speed, 642, 648
    reloading, 642
    resizing, 645
    rotating, 645
    scaling, 633, 635, 645
    selecting, 643, 644
    unloading, 642
    updating, 642
    viewing information, 636–639
    See also raster image boundaries

raster printers, 516
    assigning colors to pen widths, 498, 499
    home position, 505
RASTERPREVIEW system variable, 90
Ray (Draw menu), 187
ray casting. *See* point acquisition
RAY command, 187
rays, 48, 184
    creating, 187
    extending, 274
raytraced renderer, 582
    antialiasing adaptive sampling, 581
    refractive effects, 606
    See also photorealistic renderers
raytraced shadows, generating, 593
Readme file, 62
Realtime option (Pan, View menu), 202
real-time zooming and panning, 200–202
RECTANG command, 549
rectangles, breaking, 180
rectangular arrays
    creating, 261, 262
    rotating, 263
rectangular meshes, creating, 539
Rectangular option (Array, Modify menu), 262
Rectangular option, 3D Array option (3D Operation, Modify menu), 557
rectangular window clipping boundaries, 465
Redo (Edit menu), 80
REDO command, 80
redoing actions, 80
Redraw (View menu), 81
REDRAW command, 81, 146
redrawing the screen, 81, 751
    raster images and, 648
    turned off layers and, 301
reference angles, rotating objects by, 265
reference card (*Quick Reference card*), 35
reference points
    specifying points from, 176
    See also point markers; point objects; points (geometric)
references. *See* block references; xrefs (external references)
reflection (of light)
    color, 605, 608
    diffuse reflection, 573, 596, 598
    effects (illustrated), 598
    types, 596–599
    See also specular reflection (highlights)
reflection color, 605, 608, 751
reflection maps, 612, 614, 751
refractive index, of materials, 606
Regen (View menu), 81
REGEN command, 81, 146, 224

regenerating drawings, 81, 146, 224, 225, 751
    changing views without, 203
    replacing shaded images, 572
    thawing layers and, 301
Region (Draw menu), 148
REGION command, 148
regions, 44, 148
    calculating areas/perimeters, 191
    composite, 149
    creating, 148–150
    export file format, 731
    versus surfaces, 568
regular polygons. *See* polygons
relative angles, rotating objects by, 264
relative coordinates, 751
    2D (*X,Y*), 116
    cylindrical, 523
Reload option (External Reference dialog box), 452
Reload option (XREF command), 462, 467
reloading
    external database commands, 669
    xrefs, 452, 462, 467
Rename (Format menu), 229
RENAME command, 229, 308, 333
Rename dialog box, 229
Rename Style dialog box, 332
renaming
    layers, 299, 308
    linetypes, 313
    named objects, 229
        in groups, 229
    scenes, 619
    text styles, 332
    toolbars, 718
    user coordinate systems, 123
Render (View menu), options, 583, 585, 588, 600, 601, 609, 617–620
Render blocks, updating of pre-Release 14 blocks, 628
RENDER command, 301, 572, 585, 620
Render dialog box, 583–585
Render option (Render, View menu), 583, 585, 588, 620, 626
Render renderer (AutoCAD Render), 582
    configuring, 580–581
    related applications, 628–629
Render Window
    accessing, 585–586
    background color, 583
    features, 627
    illustrated, 586
    printing images from, 625
    saving images from, 621
        to PostScript files, 621, 626

rendered images, 566
    copying, 624
    cropping, 622
    displaying information on, 585
    exporting, 624
    Gouraud renderings, 585
    merging with background images, 586–588
    offsetting, 623
    poster-size, 625
    printing, 624–627
    redisplaying, 624
        in viewports, 622
    saving, 620–621
        to PostScript files, 621, 626
    smoothness, 549, 579
renderers. *See* photorealistic renderers; raytraced renderer; Render renderer (AutoCAD Render)
rendering, 566, 574–629
    against background images, 586–588
    all objects, 583–585
    antialiasing and, 580
    AutoSurf surfaces, 579
    back faces, 577
    background color, 583
    basic operations, 582–628
    basic option, 582
    bitplanes and, 581
    blocks, 611
    color depth, 581, 588
    configuring, 580–581
    cropping the screen in, 583
    materials, 611
    merge rendering, 586–588
    output options, 580
    preparing models for, 575–579
    process steps, 574
    Render Window/viewport features, 627
    screen resolution for, 580
    selected objects, 585
    speed of, 593
    stopping, 582
    types, 582
    See also image mapping (in rendering); lights (for rendering); materials (for rendering); rendered images; shadows
rendering maps
    blend value, 613
    combining, 613
    types, 612, 613
Rendering Preferences dialog box, setting Render Window background color, 583
renderings. *See* rendered images
repeating commands, 41, 75

replacing
    dimension text, 387
    multiline text, 351
REPLAY command, 587, 622
reports, producing, 697
resizing
    arrowheads, 401
    the command window, 69
    dimension text, 401
    floating viewports, 484
    objects, 268–277
        See also extending; scaling objects; stretching; trimming
    OLE objects, 664
    raster images, 645
    the target box (object snap), 174
    tools, 718, 719
resolution
    in 3D modeling, 579
    and aliasing, 580
    low-resolution monitors, 84
    for rendering, 580
    snap resolution, 752
    See also precision
Restore option (DIMSTYLE command), 420
Restore option (Tiled Viewports, View menu), 222
Restore option (UCS command), 123
restoring
    data integrity, 701
    dimension styles, 420
    named views, 216, 493
    previous views, 203
    tiled viewport configurations, 222
    tools from toolbars, 715
    the UCS to the WCS, 121
    user coordinate systems, 123
return button (mouse), 64, 751
    executing commands, 74
RETURN key, starting new paragraphs, 340
reverse quote ('), wild-card character, 230, 308
REVOLVE command, 551, 553
Revolve option (Solids, Draw menu), 553
revolved solids, creating, 553
Revolved Surface option (Surfaces, Draw menu), 544
REVSURF command, 544
RFS, feature size symbol, 426
RGB color system, 595, 751
RIGHT ARROW key, moving the cursor, 71
right mouse button. *See* return button (mouse)
right-hand rule, applying, 520
RMAT command, 609, 610, 629
Rotate (Modify menu), 265

Index
793

Rotate 3D option (3D Operation, Modify menu), 556
ROTATE command, 265, 556
Rotate option (3D Viewpoint, View menu), 528
ROTATE3D command, 556
rotated dimensions
    creating, 371, 372
    illustrated, 370, 372
rotated rectangular arrays, creating, 263
rotating
    3D objects, 556
    3D views, 528
    dimension text, 386
    floating viewport views, 492
    objects, 263, 264–266, 556
        with grips, 266
        See also mirroring
    the plot area, 504–506
    polygons, 266
    raster images, 645
    rectangular arrays, 263
    selection sets, 254
    user coordinate systems, 119
    the XY plane, 119
rotation angles, for text, 331, 348, 362
roughness (of surfaces), and specular reflection, 599, 608
rounding off dimensions, 416
rounds (fillets), 289–292
rows (in database tables)
    adding, 675, 699
    ASEROWS operations affecting, 670
    counting objects linked to, 697–699
    creating text objects from, 691–693
    cursor state options, 670
    deleting, 674
    deleting links to, 689
    editing, 673–674, 691
    linking to objects, 676, 683–684
    making current, 671
    selecting, 671
    selecting objects linked to, 694–695
    viewing, 671–672
Rows dialog box
    editing rows, 673–674
    linking rows to objects, 684
    viewing rows, 671–672
RPREF command, 585
RTF files
    importing, 341
    inserting, 341
rubber-band line, 119, 163, 751
ruled surface meshes, creating, 542
Ruled Surface option (Surfaces, Draw menu), 543
RULESURF command, 542
running object snaps, 751
    setting, 173

S

S, feature size symbol, 426
saturation, of colors, 595
Save (File menu), 90
Save option (Display Image, Tools menu), 621
Save option (Tiled Viewports, View menu), 222
Save option (UCS, Tools menu), 123
SAVEAS command, 90
SAVEIMG command, 620
SAVETIME system variable, 90
    setting, 90
saving
    blocks (block definitions), 49, 438
    buttons, 722
    drawings, 90
        automatically, 83, 90
        for batch plotting, 512, 514
        dialog box display control, 78
        export file formats, 729–736
        on the Web, 56
    multiline styles, 131
    named views, 214, 493
    plotter configurations, 498
    rendered images, 620–621
        to PostScript files, 621, 626
    tiled viewport configurations, 222
    user coordinate systems, 120, 123
Scale (Modify menu), 271
SCALE command, 271
scale factors
    alternate scale value, 409
    dimensions, 394–398
    English-metric/metric-English unit conversions, 86
    objects, 271
    paper space, 489
    raster images, 633, 635
    setting, 99, 205–207, 208, 271
    setup adjustments to, 93, 99
    views, 205–207, 208
    See also dimension scale; drawing scale; linetype scale; plot scale
Scale option (ZOOM command), 207, 508
Scaled to Fit option (Plot Configuration dialog box), 507
scaling
    block references, 434
    dimensions, 394–398
        in paper space, 395, 396
    drawings, 42, 92, 272
    image mapping, 612
    linetypes, in paper space, 316, 490
    objects. *See* scaling objects
    plotting, 506–508
    PostScript files, 734
    raster images, 633, 635, 645

scaling (*continued*)
    views, 205–207, 208, 507
        relative to paper space, 100, 207, 208, 488
    WMF files, 738
scaling objects, 270–272
    with grips, 272
    in paper space, 270
    by reference, 271
    by a scale factor, 271
SCENE command, 601, 620
Scene option (Render, View menu), 619
scenes, 618–620
    adding lights to, 619
    changing viewpoints, 619
    defining, 619
    deleting/modifying, 619
    removing lights from, 601, 619
    renaming, 619
schema
    adding/removing, 669
    exporting links associated with, 698
screen
    cropping for rendering, 583
    redrawing, 81, 751
    resolution. *See* resolution
screen previews
    browsing, 88
    determining the format, 90
script files, 751
scripts, 57, 78
    running commands in, 78
    running slide shows with, 78
SDF (Space-delimited File) format, 446
search paths
    AutoCAD library search paths, 84, 745
    raster image paths, 633, 640
    See also link paths (of database objects); project name paths; xref paths
searching for drawing files
    by browsing, 88
    by file specifications, 89
SECTION command, 562
Section option (Solids, Draw menu), 562
sectioning solids, 562
Select Color dialog box, 248, 305, 310
SELECT command, 231, 237, 644, 696
Select File dialog box, 87
Select Objects dialog box, creating selection sets, 695
Select Slide File dialog box, 728
selecting
    associative hatches, 293
    blocks, 181
    database table rows, 671
    objects. *See* selecting objects
    OLE objects, 665
    raster images, 643, 644

selecting objects, 230–243
    after choosing an editing command, 230–236, 381
    before choosing an editing command, 231, 237–243, 245
    close together, 233
    customizing object selection, 234
    cycling through objects, 233, 242
    dimensioned objects, 381
    with fences, 233
    in groups, 240–243
    within hatch boundaries, 153
    linked to database rows, 694–695
    with nongraphic search criteria, 694–697
    noun/verb selection, 237, 749
    with a pickbox, 231
    with a pointing device, 237
    with selection windows, 231
    in tiled viewports, 221
    within enclosed areas, 232
    within or crossing enclosed areas, 232
    See also selection sets; selections
Selection (Tools menu), 234
selection cycling, 242, 302
selection fences. *See* fences
selection highlighting, turning on/off, 226
selection sets, 230, 751
    adding objects to, 245, 318
    copying, 253
        with grips, 254
    creating, 230
        from graphic and nongraphic data, 695–697
        from objects linked to database rows, 694–695
    erasing, 268
    filtering, 235
    named. *See* groups
    removing grips from, 238
    removing objects from, 236, 238
    rotating, 254
selection windows, 231, 751
    crossing selections, 231, 746
    selecting objects with, 231
    window selections, 231
    See also polygon selection windows
selections
    crossing, 231, 746
    cutting/copying/pasting to/from the Clipboard, 255, 340
    toggling group selection, 242
    window, 231
Send to Bottom option (Display Order, Tools menu), 146
Send Under Object option (Display Order, Tools menu), 146
servers (source applications), 654
Set Layer Filters dialog box, 306

set time variables, displaying, 198
settings. *See* defaults; preferences (environment); system variables
setup options (for drawings), 62, 94–105
    See also Advanced Setup wizard; Quick Setup wizard; templates (prototype drawings)
setup program, running, 60–62
setup wizards
    creating new drawings with, 63, 86, 93, 94–97
    See also Advanced Setup wizard; Quick Setup wizard
SETVAR command, 80, 122
Shade (View menu), options, 572
SHADE command, 301, 572
shaded images, 566
    creating, 571–574
    replacing with the original wireframe images, 572
    smoothness, 549, 579
SHADEDGE system variable, 573
SHADEDIF system variable, 572, 573
shading, 148, 566
    diffuse reflection and, 573
    flat, 571
    methods, 573
    Phong shading, 585
    surface angle and, 572
    See also shaded images
shadow maps, generating, 593
shadows, 592–593
    generating, 592–593, 604
    lights and, 589
    object color effects on, 592
    raytraced shadows, 593
    and rendering speed, 593
    shadow mapped, 593
    volumetric shadows, 592
shape numbers
    Multibyte, 708
    Unicode, 706, 707
shapes
    3D shapes, 536, 538, 548
    and hatch lines, 156
    simple geometric shapes (illustrated), 43
SHIFT key
    adding objects to selection sets, 245, 318
    making multiple copies, 239
    removing objects from selection sets, 236, 238
SHIFT+END keys, moving the cursor, 75
SHIFT+HOME keys, moving the cursor, 75
SHIFT+LEFT ARROW keys, moving the cursor, 75
SHIFT+return button
    choosing object snaps, 173
    displaying the cursor menu, 64, 68

SHIFT+return button (*continued*)
    starting tracking, 179
    using point filters, 177
SHIFT+RIGHT ARROW keys, moving the cursor, 75
shot blocks (pre-Release 14), updating of, 628
shrinking views. *See* zooming
SHX files, 353
    font mapping order, 354
SHX fonts, 328, 343, 352
Single Line Text option (Text, Draw menu), 334, 335
Single option, Attribute option (Object, Modify menu), 444
single-pen plotters
    assigning colors to pens, 300, 499
    multipen plotting, 517
Single Point option (Point, Draw menu), 145
sizing
    arrowheads, 429
    new objects, 94
    text, 100
    See also resizing
SKETCH command, 134–135
sketching freehand, 133–135
    ensuring accuracy on slow computers, 135
SKETCHING system variable, 134
SKPOLY system variable, 134
SLA (Stereolithograph Apparatus), 735
slash (/)
    mathematical operator, 188
    stacked text indicator, 345
SLD files. *See* slide files
SLICE command, 563
Slice option (Solids, Draw menu), 563
slicing solids, 563
slide files, 751
    See also slides
slide libraries, 751
    viewing slides in, 728
slide shows, running with scripts, 78
slidelib utility, 728
slides, 726
    creating, 726
    displaying, 726
    removing from view, 728
    uses, 726
    viewing, 726, 727
        in slide libraries, 728
    See also slide libraries
smooth shading, 751
    creating meshes for, 578–579
smoothing angle, specifying, 578
smoothness (of 3D images), 549, 579
snap, 37, 42, 47, 102, 752
    aligning, 160–163
    in floating viewports, 487

snap (*continued*)
    setting spacing, 37, 102
    turning on/off, 37, 103
    UCS orientation and, 119
    See also grid; object snaps
snap angle, 751
    changing, 160
snap base point, changing, 160
SNAP button (status bar), 65, 66
SNAP command, 37, 103
snap grid. *See* snap
Snap mode, 752
    and freehand sketching, 134
    See also Object Snap mode; snap
snap resolution, 752
snap rotation angles (in rotated arrays), 263
SNAPANG system variable, 161, 263
SNAPBASE system variable, 161
snapping to points on objects, 164–177
    See also snap
snaps
    isometric snap style, 749
    offset, 239, 254
    See also object snaps
SnapTips, 174, 175
software license agreement, 61
software requirements, 60
solid-filled circles, creating, 143
solid fills
    creating, 147
    and hatch lines, 156
    hiding before importing WMF files, 738
    surfaces defined by added thickness, 567
solid modeler, 536
solid projection (in image mapping), 616
solids, 536, 548
    2D. *See* solid-fills
    AME solids, 577
    boxes, 549
    calculating areas/perimeters, 191
    chamfering, 561
    combining, 554
    complex, 149, 536
    composite, 554
    cones, 549
    creating, 536, 548–555
    cylinders, 550
    editing, 561–563
    export file formats, 731, 735
    extruded, 492, 501, 552
    filleting, 562
    intersections, 555
    lemon-shaped, 551
    plotting, 498, 501
    removing/plotting hidden lines, 492, 501
    as rendering materials, 614
    revolved, 553

solids (*continued*)
    sectioning, 562
    shapes, 536, 538, 548
    slicing, 563
    spheres, 551
    subtracting, 555
    surfaces defined by, 568
    torus/tori, 551
    wedges, 552
Solids (Draw menu), options, 549–554, 562, 563
SORTENTS system variable, 146
sorting
    layers/linetypes, 298
    xrefs, 450
source applications, 654
SPACEBAR
    executing commands, 74
    repeating commands, 75
Space-delimited File (SDF) format, 446
spaces
    in the command line, 76
    inserting nonbreaking, 340
spatial indexes, 456
special characters
    inserting, 344
    for names, 107, 123, 222, 325
    Unicode characters, 328, 344
    wild-card characters, 229, 307
    See also Special Characters section in this index
specular reflection (highlights), 596–597, 598, 752
    colors, 605, 608
    sizing (roughness), 599, 608
SPELL command, 355, 356, 357
Spelling (Tools menu), 354
spelling, checking, 354–357
    in other languages, 355
SPHERE command, 551
Sphere option (Solids, Draw menu), 551
spheres (solid), creating, 551
spherical coordinates, specifying, 524
spherical projection (in image mapping), 616
SPLFRAME system variable, 280, 542
Spline (Draw menu), 136
SPLINE command, 137
spline curves, 135, 537, 750
    Bezier curves, 745
    B-spline curves, 745
    calculating areas/circumferences/perimeters, 191
    converting splined polylines into, 136
    drawing, 135–137
    editing, 136, 283
    fit points, 283, 744, 748, 749
    leader lines, 378
    order of, 283

Index
797

spline curves (*continued*)
    snapping to tangent points on, 171
    versus splined polylines, 136, 280
    tolerances, 136, 283
    See also objects; splined polylines
spline leaders, creating, 378
Spline option (Object, Modify menu), 284
splined polylines
    converting into spline curves, 136
    creating, 136, 279
    joining, 280
    versus spline curves, 136, 280
SPLINEDIT command, 137, 284
splines. *See* spline curves
SPLINESEGS system variable, 280
SPLINETYPE system variable, 280
splitter bar (command window), 69
spooling plotting, 512
spotlights, 591
    attenuation rate options, 595
    positioning, 602
SQL (Structured Query Language), accessing external data with, 699–701
SQL Cursor dialog box, 700
SQL Editor dialog box, 700
square brackets ([]), alternate units delimiter, 409
squares, drawing, 132
stacked text
    creating, 345
    text styles and, 346
standard libraries. *See* libraries
STANDARD text style, settings, table, 324
Standard toolbar, 67
standards for drawing, 92
Start from Scratch option (Create New Drawing dialog box), 63, 93
start-up, system variable setup adjustments, 96
Start, Center, Length option (Arc, Draw menu), 140
starting
    AutoCAD, 42, 62
    drawings, 42
    tracking, 179
STATS command, 585
status bar, 41, 66
    illustrated, 40
    Model Space button, 478, 479
    Paper Space button, 478, 479
    SNAP button, 65
STATUS command, 197
Status option (Inquiry, Tools menu), 197
Stereolithograph Apparatus (SLA), 735
stereolithograph format, writing solids in, 735
STL files, creating, 735
Stretch (Modify menu), 269, 384
STRETCH command, 268, 384

stretching
    dimensions, 383, 385
    objects, 52, 268–270
    OLE objects, 664
    See also extending
Style (Dimension menu), 369, 388–419
STYLE command, 326, 330–333
style families. *See* dimension style families
styles, 92
    hatch styles, 155
    isometric snap style, 749
    See also dimension styles; multiline styles; text styles
SUBTRACT command, 149, 549, 551, 555
Subtract option (Boolean, Modify menu), 555
subtraction
    creating composite regions by, 149
    subtracting areas from combined areas, 192
    subtracting solids, 555
sunlight, simulating, 590, 604
support directories, specifying, 84, 745
support files
    AutoCAD library search paths, 84, 745
    PostScript Support file, 735
surface of revolution meshes, creating, 544
surfaces, 535
    in 3D modeling, 567–568
    AutoSurf, 579
    curved, 535
    drawing, 575
    export file formats, 731
    faceted. *See* meshes (faceted surfaces)
    light reflection, 596–599
    light reflection colors, 605
    normals, 575
    removing hidden, 575
    removing/plotting hidden lines, 492, 501
    roughness, 599
    with tops and bottoms, 567
    See also meshes
Surfaces (Draw menu), options, 147, 540–546
SURFTAB1 system variable, 543, 544, 545
SURFTAB2 system variable, 543, 544, 545
Symbol dialog box, 425, 428
symbol tables, 752
    listing, 474
    names, 453, 463, 708
symbols, 49, 752
    See also dependent symbols; special characters
symbols of termination. *See* arrowheads
Synchronize option (ASEADMIN command), 701
synchronizing database links, 701
SYSCODEPAGE system variable, 709
system, reconfiguring, 60

Index
798

system requirements, 60
system variables, 41, 79, 752
    as indicated in this manual, 37
    listing, 80
    resetting, 80
        transparently, 77, 79
    setup adjustments to, 96
    See also dimensioning system variables; *and names of specific system variables*
systems of measurement. *See* measurement systems

T

tables. *See* database tables; rows (in database tables)
tablet (digitizing tablet), 65
Tablet mode, 65
    commands working in, 65
    sketching in, 135
TABMODE system variable, 65
TABSURF command, 544
tabulated surface meshes, creating, 544
Tabulated Surface option (Surfaces, Draw menu), 544
Tangent (TAN) object snap, 171
tangent points, snapping to, 138, 171
tapered polyline segments, extending, 274
tapering
    extruded objects, 553
    polyline segments, 280
target box (object snap), 172
    resizing, 174
task methods as indicated in this manual, 37
template drawings. *See* templates (prototype drawings)
template files (for extracting attribute information)
    creating, 446
    sample, 447
    structure, 444–446
template materials (for rendering), 614
templates (prototype drawings), 42, 92, 110–111, 752
    creating, 110, 298
    creating new drawings with, 63, 86, 93, 110
    initial environment, 749
    recovering the default, 111
    saving, 111
    standard, 110
    starting AutoCAD with, 63
    See also template files
temporary files, 752
    restricting on networks, 456
    specifying location, 86
temporary reference points, specifying points from, 176

termination symbols. *See* arrowheads
tessellation lines, 549, 579, 752
    illustrated, 752
text, 45, 323–363
    aligning. *See* text alignment
    coloring, 83, 343, 347, 350, 359
    colors, 83
    copying, 340
        to the command line, 75
    cutting, 340
    editing. *See* editing text
    formatting. *See* formatting text
    mirroring, 260, 336, 348
    obliquing angle, 331
    pasting, 258, 340, 341
        to the command line, 74, 79
        to the text window, 71
    as rendered into PostScript, 734
    scale factor, 99
    sizing, 100
    stacked, 345, 346
    thickness, 548
        surfaces defined by, 568
    turning on/off, 224, 568
    types, 323
    underlining, 343, 346
    uses, 323
    See also annotations; attributes; characters; dimension text; line text; multiline text; special characters; text editors; text files; text objects; text properties; text styles; words
text alignment
    line text, 334
        options (illustrated), 335
        specifying, 335
    multiline text
        options (illustrated), 348
        specifying, 346, 347
    of ordinate dimensions, 376
text colors, in the main and text windows, 83
TEXT command, 333, 335, 336
text control codes. *See* control codes (text)
text display, turning on/off, 224, 568
text editors
    creating multiline text, 358
    default, 357
    editing multiline text, 363
    formatting multiline text, 359–362
    specifying for multiline text, 357
    See also Multiline Text Editor dialog box
text files
    accommodating non-ASCII characters, 328
    exporting, 730
    importing, 341, 736
    inserting, 341
text fonts. *See* fonts

Index
799

text gap (dimension text), 402, 416
text height
　plotting, 395
　setting, for dimension text, 416
　specifying, 326, 330, 362
　text styles and, 346
text insertion point, specifying, 348
text justification
　line text, 334, 335
　multiline text, 346, 347, 362
　See also text alignment
text objects, 336, 348
　creating from database rows, 691–693
　grips, 336
　and hatch lines, 156
　thickness, 548
　See also annotations; attributes; displayable attributes
Text option (Object, Modify menu), 337, 349, 363, 443
text orientation
　changing, 326
　for dimension text, 402–406
　setting, 331
text properties, 324
　copying, 250
　line text, 337
　multiline text, 339, 346–348, 350
　See also fonts; text alignment; text color; text height; text justification; text orientation; text styles; text width
Text Style (Format menu), 325, 326, 329–333
Text Style dialog box, 324, 325, 326, 329, 332
text styles, 323, 324–333, 334, 752
　assigning fonts to, 326–330
　and character formatting, 346
　creating, 324
　default settings, table, 324
　defaults, 324, 342
　and fonts, 326, 346
　making a text style current, 332
　modifying, 324, 326
　naming, 325
　overriding default settings, 342
　purging, 333
　renaming, 332
　specifying, 346, 362
　　for dimension text, 415
　　while creating line text, 335
text width, dimension text, 402
text window, 40, 70–72
　colors, 83
　displaying, 71
　fonts, 84
　illustrated, 70
　navigating in, 71
　restoring when minimized, 71

text window (continued)
　setting preferences, 71
　toggling with the graphics window and command window, 71
TEXTFILL system variable, 327
TEXTSIZE system variable, 97
TEXTSTYLE system variable, 332
texture maps, 612, 613, 752
TGA images
　displaying, 587, 620
　saving, 620, 627
thawing layers, 301–303, 752
　in floating viewports, 303, 484
thickness, 546, 752
　changing, 547, 548
　copying, 250
　setting, 547
　surfaces defined by added thickness, 567
THICKNESS system variable, 548
3 Point option (UCS, Tools menu), 120, 526
3 Points option (Arc, Draw menu), 139
"3D", index topics beginning with. See Numbers section in this index
tick marks, as arrowheads, 393
TIFF images
　displaying, 587, 620
　saving, 620, 627
tilde (~)
　dialog box display character, 78
　wild-card character, 230, 307
tilde-ellipsis (enclosed) ([~...]), wild-card character, 230, 308
tiled viewports, 51, 216–223, 476, 477, 752
　configuration options, 218
　displaying, 217
　dragging objects in, 221
　drawing lines in, 220
　versus floating viewports, 217
　joining, 219
　making current, 220
　selecting objects in, 221
　subdividing, 218
　uses, 216, 220–221
　See also viewport configurations; viewports
Tiled Viewports (View menu), options, 218, 219, 222
TILEMODE system variable, 477, 479, 752, 753
　turning on/off, 478
tiling, in image mapping, 613, 615
TIME command, 198
Time option (Inquiry, Tools menu), 198
time, tracking drawing time, 198
title blocks
　adding, 103, 105, 476, 480, 488
　adding borders to, 103, 480
　customizing, 104
　deleting, 105

title blocks (*continued*)
    specifying viewports for, 105
Tolerance (Dimension menu), 425, 428
TOLERANCE command, 426, 429
tolerances, 365
    for spline curves, 136, 283
    See also geometric tolerances; lateral tolerances
tool icons
    creating/editing, 722
    displaying, 719
toolbar buttons. *See* tool icons; tools
TOOLBAR command, 713–717, 721
toolbar properties, displaying, 713
toolbars, 67, 712, 752
    adding tools to, 714
    aliases, 713
    closing, 68
    creating, 712–713
    customizing, 711–723
    deleting, 713
    deleting tools from, 715
    displaying, 67, 713, 716
    displaying properties, 713
    docked, 40, 67, 717
    docking, 68, 717
    floating, 40, 717
    floating docked toolbars, 717
    hiding, 716
    modifying, 712, 718–719
    names, 713
    renaming, 718
    reshaping, 718
    restoring tools from, 715
    Standard, 67
    starting commands from, 72
    top level, 712
    undocking, 717
Toolbars (View menu), 712–716, 718–723
Toolbars dialog box, 713–716, 718–723
tools
    adding space between, 718
    adding to toolbars, 714
    associating commands with, 719–721
    copying between toolbars, 715
    creating, 719–720
    deleting from toolbars, 715
    displaying commands associated with, 718, 719
    icons, 719
    moving between toolbars, 715
    object snap tools, 164
    repositioning, 718

tools (*continued*)
    resizing, 718, 719
    restoring from toolbars, 715
    See also flyouts; tool icons; toolbars; tooltips
tooltips, 65, 67
    showing, 718, 719
TOOLTIPS system variable, 719
TORUS command, 551
Torus option (Solids, Draw menu), 551
torus/tori (solid)
    creating, 551
    self-intersecting, 551
trace fills, plotting, 498
traces
    hatching and, 156
    surfaces defined by added thickness, 567
TRACKING, 179
tracking (feature), 47, 178, 752
    specifying points with, 178–180
    starting, 179
tracking, drawing time, 198
TRANSPARENCY command, 647
Transparency option, Image option (Object, Modify menu), 646
transparency, of materials, 606
transparent command character ('), 77
transparent command prompt indicator (>>), 77
transparent commands, 76, 752
    entering, 77
Tree View option (External Reference dialog box), 451
Tree View option (Image dialog box), 638
Trim (Modify menu), 275, 559
TRIM command, 275
trimmed NURB surfaces, export file format, 731
trimming
    3D objects, 558
    dimensions, 384
    objects, 52, 275–277
        chamfered, 286
        See also chamfering objects
TRIMMODE system variable, 287, 290
tripod. *See* axis tripod
TrueType fonts, 327
    inserting Unicode characters for, 344
TTF files, font mapping order, 354
tutorials (online)
    Learning AutoCAD, 34
    multimedia tutorials, 36
two dimensions, drafting limitations, 519
"2D", index topics beginning with. *See* Numbers section in this index
TXT files. *See* text files
typefaces. *See* fonts

Index
801

U

U command, 80
\U+ character sequences, 706, 707
UCS (Tools menu), options, 120, 123
UCS command, 161, 526
    command line options, 120, 123
UCS Control dialog box, 121, 123
UCS icon, 46, 753
    displaying, 121, 122, 525
    illustrated, 46, 122
    in model space, 478
    in paper space, 477
UCS Icon option (Display, View menu), 122
UCS icons, illustrated, 520, 525, 527, 753
UCS Orientation dialog box, 526
UCSICON command, 122, 525
UCSICON system variable, 122
UCSNAME system variable, 123
UCSORG system variable, 122
UCSs. *See* user coordinate systems
UCSXDIR system variable, 120
UCSYDIR system variable, 120
underlining (of text), 343, 346
underscore (_), foreign language translation character, 719
Undo (Edit menu), 80
UNDO command, 80
undoing
    actions, 45, 80
    erasing, 268
Unicode Character Map, illustrated, 344
Unicode characters
    inserting characters for TrueType fonts, 344
        unsupported font character conversion, 706
Unicode fonts, 328, 705–709
    and Big Fonts, 707
Unicode shape numbers, 706, 707
UNION command, 149, 554
Union option (Boolean, Modify menu), 554
Unitless setting (Current AutoCAD Units list), 634
units
    plotting units, 503, 506
    See also alternate units (for dimensions); angular units; drawing units; English units; metric units; primary units (for dimensions)
Units (Format menu), 97
UNITS command, 99
Units Control dialog box, 98
Unload option (External Reference dialog box), 452
unloading
    external database commands, 669, 702
    raster images, 642
    xrefs, 452, 462

unnamed (anonymous) blocks, 437, 744
UP ARROW key, moving the cursor, 71
updating
    of Aerial View, 214
    of associative hatches, 293
    blocks (block references), 438, 440
    drawing databases, 81
    links, 654, 660
    of pre-Release 14 Render blocks, 628
    raster images, 642
    redrawing the screen, 81, 751
    regenerating drawings, 81, 146, 751
    xrefs, 448
URLs (Universal Resource Locators), embedding, 56, 729
user coordinate systems (UCSs), 46, 113, 119, 753
    defining, 524–527
        in 3D space, 525
    deleting, 124
    elevation in, 525
    indicating the orientation, 46, 122, 525
    listing, 123
    naming, 123
    paper space limitations, 525
    relocating, 119–124
    renaming, 123
    restoring, 123
        to the WCS, 121
    rotating, 119
    saving, 120, 123
    selecting preset, 526
    See also named objects; UCS icons
User Defined option (Format dialog box), 403
user dimension text, 410
User's Guide, 34, 35, 36
    conventions, 37
Using Help (online documentation), 34

V

variable attributes, 441
    specifying values, 441, 442
variables
    set time, 198
    See also dimensioning system variables; system variables
variances. *See* lateral tolerances
vectors, 753
vertex/vertices, 753
    multiline, 281
vertical bar (|)
    dependent symbol name character, 464
    dimension style xref name separator, 423
vertical dimensions
    creating, 370
    illustrated, 366, 370, 371
    stretching, 384

vertical dimensions (*continued*)
    text width, 402
    See also dimensions; linear dimensions
Vertical Justification options (Format dialog box), 403, 405
video displays, system requirements, 60
view box (Aerial View window), 211
View Control dialog box, 215, 494
View option (Display Image, Tools menu), 622–624
View option (Plot Configuration dialog box), 502
View Selections option (Boundary Hatch dialog box), 154
viewing
    drawings. *See* viewing drawings
    external data, 670–672, 691
    slides, 726, 727
        in slide libraries, 728
    See also views
viewing direction (in 3D model space), setting, 528–530
viewing drawings, 50, 199–226
    in 3D, 527–535
    with the browser, 88
    dynamic viewing (in 3D model space), 531–535
viewpoints (in 3D model space), 753
    in floating viewports, 487
    infinite lines and, 184
    setting a viewing direction, 528–530
viewport configurations
    floating viewports, 481, 482
    tiled viewports, 218, 753
        deleting, 222
        listing, 222
        naming, 222
        restoring, 222
        saving, 222
viewports, 753
    Aerial View updates from, 214
    borders as cutting edges, 277
    changing while sketching, 135
    cropping rendered images in, 622
    offsetting rendered images in, 623
    printing rendered images from, 627
    redisplaying rendered images in, 622
    rendering features, 627
    saving rendered images from, 620
    specifying for title blocks, 105
    See also floating viewports; named objects; tiled viewports; viewport configurations
VIEWRES command, 209, 579

views, 200, 753
    aligning floating viewport views, 490
    centering on points, 207
    changing without regenerating drawings, 203
    copying and linking, 256
    displaying multiple, 216–223
    isometric views, 162
    linked, editing, 657
    linking to other documents, 656
    in model space, 476, 527
    naming, 214
    in paper space, 476, 527
    plotting options, 501
    positioning lights with, 603
    positioning on paper, 504–506
    print preview, 495
    restoring previous, 203
    saving, 214, 493
    scaling, 205–207, 208, 507
        relative to paper space, 100, 207, 208, 488
    See also 3D views (in 3D model space); Aerial View; named views; panning; plan view; viewing; viewpoints (in 3D model space); viewports; zooming
virtual screen display, 753
visibility
    in floating viewports, 484–487
    turning visual elements on/off, 224–226
    in xref layers, 467
VISRETAIN system variable, 309, 451, 467, 468
visual elements, turning on/off, 224–226
volumetric shadows, 753
    generating, 592
VPLAYER command, 302, 303, 485, 486
VPOINT command, 301, 528, 531
VPORTS command, 223
    command line options, 222
VSLIDE command, 727, 728

W

W, UCS icon symbol, 122
warning beeps, turning on/off, 82
WBLOCK command, 437, 438, 687
WCS icon, illustrated, 122, 753
WCS. *See* World Coordinate System
Web. *See* World Wide Web
WEDGE command, 552
Wedge option (Solids, Draw menu), 552
wedges (solid), creating, 552
What's New (Help menu), 35, 36
WHIP! plug-in, 729
wide lines, hiding before importing WMF files, 738

wide polylines
    calculating areas/perimeters, 191
    exploding, 128
    extending, 274
    plotting, 498, 501
    surfaces defined by added thickness, 567
wild-card characters, identifying named object groups, 229, 307
Window option (Plot Configuration dialog box), 502
Window option (ZOOM command), 203
window polygons. *See* WPolygons
window selections, 231
windows
    CPolygon, 232, 746
    graphics screen, 748
    main window, 40, 66
    WPolygon, 232, 753
    zoom windows, 202
    See also Aerial View window; command window; graphics window (graphics area); main window; Render Window; selection windows; text window
Windows 95
    configuring for output to PostScript files, 626
    long file names, 77
Windows Clipboard. *See* Clipboard (Windows)
Windows File Manager, inserting text files, 341
Windows Metafile (Insert menu), 738
Windows metafiles. *See* WMF files
Windows NT, long file names, 77
Windows Render Options dialog box, 588
Windows system printer, 516
wireframes, 535, 536, 566, 753
witness lines. *See* extension lines
wizards. *See* Advanced Setup wizard; Quick Setup wizard; setup wizards
WMF files
    converting to AutoCAD format, 257
    creating, 732
    format, 257, 732
    hiding solid fills/wide lines before importing, 738
    importing, 738–739
    pasting into AutoCAD, 257
    scaling, 738
WMFOPTS command, 739
WMFOUT command, 732
word wrap, 361
words
    adding to custom dictionaries, 355, 357
    correcting, 355
    formatting, 334, 342–344
    removing from custom dictionaries, 357

words (*continued*)
    selecting, 343
    word wrap, 361
working drawings, 753
World Coordinate System (WCS), 46, 119, 753
    restoring the UCS to, 121
    See also world coordinates
world coordinates, 753
    specifying, 753
World option (UCS command), 121
world size, specifying, 94
World UCS option, Plan View option (3D Viewpoint, View menu), 530
World Wide Web
    browsing, 56
    exporting drawings to, 56, 729
WPolygons (window polygons), 232, 753

X

\X, dimension text separator symbol, 410
X-datum ordinate dimensions, 376
XATTACH command, 459
XBIND command, 452, 463
XCLIP command, 464
XCLIPFRAME system variable, 465
XDATA command, 447
XLG files, 473
XLINE command, 185
xlines. *See* construction lines
XLOADCTL system variable, 452, 455
XLOADPATH system variable, 456
XREF command, 104, 459, 461, 462, 468
    command line options, 452, 462, 463, 467, 686
xref definitions, 463, 467
    listing, 449, 473
xref log files, 473
xref paths
    changing, 467
    defining alternates, 469–471
    nested, 468
xrefs (external references), 49, 433, 448–474, 748
    attaching, 451, 457–461
    binding, 462–464, 686, 745
    versus blocks, 448
    circular references, 472, 746
    clipdepth, 466
    clipping, 464–466
    clipping boundaries, 464, 465
    creating, 77
    database links to, 686
        accessing, 689–690
    definitions, 463, 467
    demand loading, 452, 453–457
    detaching, 452, 461
    dimension styles, 423

xrefs (*continued*)
    error messages, 472
    exploding, 279
    inserting, 463
    interrelationship information, 451
    layer visibility, color, and linetype, 467
    link paths in, 678
    listing, 449, 473
    loading, 453–457
    log files, 473
    managing in the External Reference dialog box, 449–453
    missing reference files, 472
    names, 450, 463
    nested, 457, 464
    overlaying, 459
    reference trees, 473
    referencing link path names in, 684–686
    reloading, 452, 462, 467
    sorting, 450
    unloading, 452, 462
    updating, 448
    uses, 448
    See also xref paths
X,Y coordinates. *See* 2D Cartesian coordinates
XY plane
    rotating, 119
    shifting, 120
    See also construction plane
X,Y,Z coordinates. *See* 3D Cartesian coordinates
XYZ point filters, 521

Y

Y-datum ordinate dimensions, 376

Z

zeros (in dimension text)
    suppressing leading/trailing zeros, 411, 415
    suppressing zero feet/inches, 412
Zoom (Mode menu, Aerial View window), 212
Zoom (View menu), options, 200–210
ZOOM command, 201, 301, 489
    command line options, 200–210, 508
Zoom In (View menu, Aerial View window), options, 214
zoom windows
    defining, 202
    illustrated, 202
zooming, 50, 200–210, 753
    with Aerial View, 211, 213
    cursors, 201, 495
    to the drawing extents, 208
    to the drawing limits, 208, 213
    dynamic, 203
    exiting Realtime mode, 201
    in floating viewports, 487
    freezing layers and, 301
    infinite lines and, 184
    interactive (Realtime mode), 200
    Plot Preview limits, 201
    in print preview, 495
    restoring previous views, 203
    scaling methods, 205–207
    scaling views relative to paper space, 489
    by specifying boundaries, 202
    windowing method, 202